THE STATISTICAL ACCOUNT OF SCOTLAND

General Editors: Donald J. Withrington and Ian R. Grant

VOLUME III

THE EASTERN BORDERS

THE
STATISTICAL ACCOUNT OF SCOTLAND

GENERAL EDITORS' INTRODUCTION

The *Statistical Account of Scotland* has been used by generation after generation of social historians enquiring into the local or national affairs of Scotland in the later 18th century. It is an unrivalled source, and historians of other countries, as well as their sociologists, geographers and natural scientists, have long regretted having no similar body of evidence available to them. Sir John Sinclair, determinedly cajoling the parish ministers of the Established Church to respond to his long list of over 160 queries, intended his statistical enquiry to enable the country, and its government, not only to assess its current state but to prepare better for a better future—"ascertaining the quantum of happiness enjoyed by its inhabitants and the means of its future improvement", moral as well as economic or political. The quality of the returns he received was generally good and was often excellent, and the parochial reports provided the Scots of the 1790s with a uniquely valuable analysis of their own times: the same reports provide us today with an incomparable view of Scotland two centuries ago, through the sharp eyes and the often sharp words of men who knew their localities very well indeed.

However, the original *Account*, printed in twenty-one volumes in the course of the 1790s, is difficult and often exasperating to use. Sinclair published the parish returns just as they came in to him; therefore the reports for one county or for part of one county may be scattered throughout a dozen volumes or more. Readers of the original printing must have the index in volume xx in order to search out easily the particular returns they want, and even then they may overlook the supplementary replies eventually published in volume xxi. Furthermore, Sinclair's indexes of subjects and persons in volume xxi are woefully inadequate.

In this new edition we have brought together the parish returns in groupings by county and have printed them in alphabetical order, thus avoiding a major difficulty in using the earlier compilation. This new arrangement will not only

iii

assist those who wish to use the *Account* as a whole, it will also be especially useful to local historians and to others engaged in local or regional researches with an historical basis: and the new format makes much easier a direct comparison of the Sinclair *Account* with the *New Statistical Account*, published by counties in 1845. So large is the volume of material for Aberdeenshire and Perthshire, however, that these counties have required two volumes each in this reissue. And we have decided to gather together in one volume all the returns from western island parishes, in the Inner and Outer Hebrides and in Bute, rather than leave them scattered among the returns from mainland Ross-shire, Inverness-shire and Argyll: these have a coherence in themselves which would be lost if placed with their respective counties.

Each of the twenty volumes in this reissue is being edited by a scholar who contributes an introduction showing the significance of the *Statistical Account* reports for the region and assessing their importance for modern historical and other social studies. Each volume will also contain an index (of the more important topics discussed in the returns, but not of persons or places) which will make the *Account* more accessible to and more immediately useful to all students, not least to pupils in schools where Scottish local studies are being introduced or extended. We are grateful to James Hamilton for his help in preparing the indexes.

We believe that the significantly improved format of this reissue will make more widely useful, and more widely used, an already acknowledged vital work of standard reference.

Ian R. Grant   Donald J. Withrington

THE

STATISTICAL ACCOUNT

OF

SCOTLAND
1791 – 1799

EDITED BY SIR JOHN SINCLAIR

VOLUME III

THE EASTERN BORDERS

With a new introduction by
T.I. RAE

EP Publishing Limited
1979

This is volume III of a reissue in twenty volumes of *The Statistical Account of Scotland,* originally published between 1791 and 1799. In this reissue all the parish accounts for individual counties are printed together for the first time, with a new introduction and index in each volume.

Volume I of this reissue carries a general introduction by Donald J. Withrington.

ISBN 0 7158 1000 6 (set)
0 7158 1003 0 (vol. III)

British Library Cataloguing in Publication Data
The statistical account of Scotland, 1791—1799.
Vol. 3: The Eastern Borders. — (New ed.)
1. Scotland — History — 18th century
1. Sinclair, *Sir* John, *bart, b. 1754*
941.107'3   DA809
ISBN 0—7158—1003—0

Printed in Great Britain by
REDWOOD BURN LIMITED
Trowbridge & Esher

CONTENTS

vii

Contents

Contents

PEEBLESSHIRE

INTRODUCTION

In this region, the east and central borders, Sir John Sinclair's request for statistical information about each parish elicited a fine response. The writers almost without exception tackled their task with interest and enthusiasm, and the majority of their descriptions, despite the individual and idiosyncratic emphases some of them made, show a remarkably consistent approach to the problem. In writing the eighty-three parish accounts for this region, seventy-two ministers were involved. Only four accounts were definitely written by laymen (Christopher Douglas, a local physician, compiled the account of Kelso, perhaps because the minister, Cornelius Lundie, who was approaching his eightieth year, felt too old to do it); two more were anonymous and probably by laymen. Several ministers compiled more than one account: George Drummond, who moved from Cranshaws to Mordington in 1792, Robert Russell who moved from Ettrick to Yarrow in 1791, and Charles Findlater who moved from (West) Linton to Newlands in 1790, each wrote the accounts for both of their parishes. George Cupples, minister of Swinton, also wrote the account of Whitsome on behalf of his father-in-law, John Waugh, who was over eighty; Thomas Somerville (Jedburgh and Ancrum) and John Walker (Traquair and Innerleithen) compiled accounts for parishes bordering on their own for reasons which are no longer obvious.

The experience and knowledge of their parishes which these writers brought to the task obviously varied. Of the seventy-two ministers, twenty-eight had held the parishes they were describing for twenty years and more, some of them like Alexander Duncan of Smailholm and Robert Turnbull of Sprouston for almost fifty; they could obviously write with considerable authority. But most of the eighteen who had held their charges for fewer than five years seem to have taken great pains to acquire the requisite knowledge, and the quality of the information presented by them differs little from that provided by their more experienced seniors. It is interesting to note that three of the younger men, David Anderson (Kirkurd), Alexander Ker (Stobo) and Charles Findlater (Newlands), remained in their parishes long enough to write reports of them for the *New Statistical Account* published in 1845.[1]

For the majority of the writers, the accounts of the 1790s form their only published literary work. The average minister was probably content to prepare his sermons, carry out his other pastoral duties, raise his generally numerous family, organize the cultivation of his glebe,[2] and perhaps indulge himself in a little private study of theology and the classics. Several published a few sermons or other theological works, and were honoured by their universities with doctorates in divinity. A few were men of considerable intellectual ability and attainment. Samuel Charteris, who curiously did not write the basic description of his parish of Wilton but a corrective appendix to the anonymous original contribution, had declined to succeed Adam Smith in the chair of Moral Philosophy at Glasgow University, and, writing and thinking in his own parish study, preferred to publish numerous sermons and literary essays. Thomas

---

1 Information about the ministers has been compiled from Hew Scott, *Fasti Ecclesiae Scoticanae* (rev. edn., Edinburgh, 1915—1950), vols. i and ii.

2 For an interesting account of the problems faced by a minister in the economic cultivation of his glebe, see Newlands, 845—60.

Somerville, minister of Jedburgh under the patronage of Sir Gilbert Elliot of Minto, deliberately set out to supplement his parish stipend with the products of his pen; from 1780 a number of historical, political and philosophical works enhanced his scholarly reputation and brought him, in 1798, the offer of the chair of Church History in Edinburgh University (which he too refused), membership of the Royal Society of Edinburgh and the friendship of Sir Walter Scott. His autobiography can still be read with pleasure and profit. Walter Anderson, author of the lengthy, stylishly-written account of his parish of Chirnside, was also a historian with several published works to his credit; but perhaps he was not so highly regarded, for he appears to have paid for their publication himself. Robert Gillan was to retire in 1800 as minister of Hawick, and thereafter devoted himself to literary pursuits as the editor of *The Scottish Pulpit* and the author of textbooks on geography and astronomy. For two of the ministers, authorship of their parish accounts stimulated further activities in the same field: Robert Douglas of Galashiels and Charles Findlater of Newlands extended their local studies to write, respectively, *A General View of the Agriculture of the Counties of Roxburgh and Selkirk* (1798), and *A General View of the Agriculture of the County of Peebles* (1802).[1]

But the majority of ministers did not have the literary talents of men such as these, and probably looked on their contributions to Sinclair's volumes as an imposition. There was bound to be a certain unevenness of performance: some are deliberately vague about certain facts (for example, the numbers of seceders in their parishes); some seized the opportunity to grind a personal axe. But nevertheless the results, despite a few lapses, achieved a remarkable overall coverage and consistency of information which makes them as valuable and as interesting to-

---

1   For Somerville, Anderson, Gillan and Findlater, see *Dictionary of National Biography*.

day as when they were written. To some extent this was due to the careful instructions which Sinclair gave to his contributors; but even more it is due to the care, and perhaps enthusiam, that most of the individual writers brought to fulfilling Sinclair's plans.

The south-east borders of Scotland, the region covered by this volume, consists of the counties of Berwickshire, Roxburghshire, Selkirkshire and Peeblesshire. This area forms a distinct geographical unit, to a certain extent isolated from the rest of Scotland by the ring of moderately high hills enclosing the Tweed basin: to the north the Lammermuir, Moorfoot and Pentland Hills; to the west the heights of the southern uplands; to the south the Cheviot Hills and the narrow coastal plain at the extreme east of the frontier with England. Within the rim of this horseshoe of hills lies a plateau intersected by the deep-cut dales of many swift-flowing rivers; this plateau in turn encloses the wide valley of the lower Tweed and its major tributary, the Teviot. Most of the region is hilly country, above 500 feet, and provides a stark contrast with the fertile plains of the valleys.

In such difficult country, routes have always been of special importance — in the early period for military and administrative purposes, later for economic and social use; these old, traditional roads south from Edinburgh had served the region for centuries and still exist today — by the east coastal plain, through the gaps between the Pentland, Moorfoot and Lammermuir Hills. By 1776 these roads had all been clearly delineated for the traveller in Taylor and Skinner's road maps.[1] The coast road entered Berwickshire at Cockburnspath, and passed through Coldingham and Ayton on its way to Berwick-on-Tweed. The Soutra road made its way through Lauder and Greenlaw to enter England at Coldstream; at

---

1 George Taylor and Andrew Skinner, *Survey and maps of the roads of North Britain or Scotland* (London, 1776).

Lauder it branched into two important side roads, one leading through Smailholm to Kelso, the other through Lessudden (St Boswells) and Ancrum to Jedburgh. The Stow road led through Selkirk and Ashkirk to Hawick; while to the west the Peebles road continued through Stobo and Drumelzier to Moffat and Dumfries. To these north-south routes, Taylor and Skinner added detail of the one main east-west route; leaving Berwick on the English side of the frontier, it entered Scotland at Coldstream, and continued through Kelso up the valley of the Teviot to Hawick, where it joined the road from Edinburgh and continued westward to Langholm and Carlisle.[1]

Their depiction in Taylor and Skinner's atlas probably meant that these main roads were in reasonable condition. Except for parts of Selkirkshire and Peeblesshire where 'statute labour is exacted in kind and is found to be inadequate to the keeping of the roads in proper repair', commutation of the statute labour provisions had taken place throughout the region, and money was levied for road repairs by assessment on valued rents.[2] The heritors were anxious to improve communications, and they played an active part in establishing turnpikes and tolls for these main roads which, although opposed at first, came to be 'universally acknowledged to be of signal benefit to the country'; new road and bridges were actively planned.[3] And not only roads: in 1792 a proposal was made, commented on favourably by many of the ministers, to build a canal from Berwick to Kelso and Ancrum; and it is interesting to note that within twenty years, in 1810, Thomas Telford was asked to design a cast-iron railway through the centre of this region which was intended to improve communications

1 Ibid., plates 1—5, 37.
2 Skirling, 890; Oxnam, 628; Roberton, 702.
3 Ayton, 13—15; Cockburnspath, 90; Mordington, 273; for correspondence of Roxburghshire heritors and other papers relating to roads, see N(ational) L(ibrary of) S(cotland), MS. 13413.

from Berwick to Glasgow by means of horse-drawn trucks.[1]

Neither of these ambitious schemes came to anything; but they are symptomatic of the fact that the heritors and other gentlemen involved in the direction of affairs were more concerned with long-distance communications than with short-distance routes for the common people of the countryside. In the hillier parts of Peeblesshire, Selkirkshire and Roxburghshire many parishes had no made-up roads at all, and even in lowland areas the local roads were in a very bad state. The minister of Swinton took it for granted that 'of course the roads are deep, miry, and often almost impassable in winter; when new made, they seldom continue good for any time'. In some parishes it was believed that the commutation of statute labour provided insufficient funds for the upkeep of the roads; in others, the fact that commutation had not taken place was blamed for their badness; in Broughton there was neither uplifting of commutation money nor the imposing of statute labour.[2]

Short-distance travel was generally difficult and undertaken only when necessary. The major roads, maintained by tolls, provided the economic life-lines of the region; and along them travelled not only coaches and the mail but also numerous carts taking surplus produce to larger markets, returning laden with imported goods. Peeblesshire, Selkirkshire and the northern parts of Roxburghshire and Berwickshire traded with the Lothians, where the principal markets were at Dalkeith, Musselburgh, Haddington and the rapidly-growing city of Edinburgh. Sheep, cattle, grain and other produce were sold there, and from there in return were obtained

1 *Report to the Heritors of the County of Roxburgh respecting the Practicability and Expence of making a Navigable Canal from Berwick to Kelso and Ancrum-bridge* (printed by James Palmer, Kelso, 1792); Eckford, 436; Hounam, 490; for a plan of Telford's proposed railway, see N.L.S., MS. 13452.

2 Swinton, 285; Minto, 602; Sprouston, 667; Broughton, 740

some basic necessities — coal, lime, salt, wood for building, and iron — and more luxurious merchant goods.[1] The southern parts of Berwickshire and of Roxburghshire, even as far west as Castletown, traded with Northumberland; livestock was sold in Morpeth, Newcastle and Sunderland, grain in Berwick, and from Northumberland were obtained necessary supplies of lime and coal. A certain amount of coastal trade based on the harbours of Eyemouth and Berwick also took place.[1]

The importance of these lines of communication serves to emphasise the character of the country. It was primarily an agricultural region, but one within which were two contrasting forms of agriculture. Put in its simplest terms, the hilly land and plateaux forming the rim of the horseshoe round the Tweed valley were principally devoted to pastoral farming, the raising of sheep, while the lower-lying lands of the river valleys were ideal for exploitation by the plough; the approximate divide was the 500-foot contour line. Patches of arable land did of course exist in the hills, and sheep and cattle were raised in the valleys where 'the most considerable part of the farms...is ploughed, though a few cattle and sheep are also kept on them',[1] but overall there was this distinct contrast within the region.

By the early 1790s the land of the valley parishes was well on the way towards total enclosure. This, the basic and most important feature of agricultural development, had taken place, according to the writers of the accounts, within the previous twenty to thirty years; the old rigs had disappeared, to be replaced by fields enclosed by hedges and ditches or by dry-stone dykes. This move was initiated by the proprietors of the land: 'it is their province to show, what may, and should be done; but as the utmost reach of their labour is limited,...the exten-

1 See e.g. Gordon, 192.
2 See e.g. Bonkle, 19; Hutton, 211; Ladykirk, 219, 220.
3 Ancrum, 322.

sion of agriculture over any large district of a country, must be looked for, and can only come from the letting of farms to tenants'.[1] The real improvement was carried out by the tenants who now had greater continuity of tenancy; they were actively encouraged by their landlords to open up new land, to manure it with lime (often paid for by the proprietor), and to initiate new methods of husbandry. Associated with the enclosures were the plantations. The value of these was not only in the profitable use of land which would otherwise be waste, but in the shelter which the trees would afford not only the new fields and their crops but also the flocks of sheep in winter. Plantation was essentially a long-term policy and, as such, was not likely to be carried out by a tenant; many writers emphasise the importance of the proprietors in this mode of improvement. Some plantations, such as those on the Dunglass estate, had been planted at the beginning of the century and were well-established by the 1790s, but the majority were 'young plantations of fir and white wood' which would require some time to mature. Nevertheless, the minister of Mertown could vividly and enthusiastically describe his parish of 'excellent enclosures, beautiful hedge-rows, and thriving plantations'.[2]

The opening-up of formerly waste land and the new cultivation of land which had been tilled for centuries depended for success on the use of fertilizer and the establishment of appropriate rotations of crops to prevent the exhaustion of the soil. The most commonly used fertilizer was lime. Although the qualities of clay marl were known, the tenants found its use laborious and its beneficial effects too long in materialising; they preferred 'the prolific power and quick effect of lime', despite the fact that it had to be carted expensively from Lothian or

---

1 Chirnside, 51.
2 Cranshaws, 128; Cockburnspath, 91; Ancrum, 319; Mertoun, 253.

Northumberland. In the coastal parishes seaweed was used by many farmers who believed especially in its efficacy
for producing crops of barley.[1] Lime was used
throughout the region not only to improve the fertility
of the fine loams of the valleys but also the rougher soils
of those parts of the hilly country which came into
tillage. To this dependence on lime was added the rejection of the old Scotch plough and the almost universal
adoption of Small's plough drawn by two horses,
sometimes referred to as the 'English' plough.

The main crops of the valley parishes of the region
were barley, oats, some wheat, pease, turnips and
potatoes. The grain crops grew effectively, and the
hinterland of Eyemouth and Berwick could in good years
furnish 40,000 to 60,000 bolls for the export market.
But success here was certainly due to the adoption of effective and balanced rotations. The rotations used varied
from place to place, even within the same parish, according to the nature of the soil; in Cockburnspath two
totally different rotations existed side by side for heavy
and for light soils, and similar though not identical rotations were used in inland parishes.[2] In those areas where
wheat was grown it seems to have been confined to the
heavier soils; turnips thrived better on light soils. But
the key to the success of these various rotations lay in the
use of grass and clover, generally sown at the same time
as wheat or barley to provide in the following year a
season of hay and pasture. This procedure was extolled
by many of the ministers: 'the chief object...that the
skilful farmer has in view...(is in) meliorating the pasture
for his cattle and sheep, by sowing his fields with artificial grass seeds, particularly rye-grass and white
clover, which thrive well on all the dry grounds that
have been improved with lime'; 'because by means of it,

---

1   Chirnside, 43; Cockburnspath, 85—86.
2   Chirnside, 45; Cockburnspath, 84; Greenlaw, 202; Lilliesleaf, 559.

land would be rested from exhausting corn crops, and yet produce what was equal to the best value of them'.[1]

This deliberate cultivation of pasture, in conjunction with the growing of turnips, led inevitably to the development of mixed farming even in primarily grain-producing areas. Both pasture and turnips were essential features of the various rotation systems; but they had to be profitable in themselves, and their full benefit could be achieved only in conjunction with the feeding of sheep and cattle which grazed on the enclosed pasture in summer and ate in the turnip fields in winter. The turnips could be lifted and carted to other fields, perhaps on other farms in other parishes, to be devoured by the sheep; but farmers preferred the sheep to eat the turnips where they were grown, because the sheep not only provided additional natural fertilizer but also, trampling down the light turnip-growing soil as they fed, solidified the ground beneficially prior to the next ploughing. Within each turnip field, the sheep would be confined by nets to specific areas of turnips before being moved on to the next section. Farmers who did not wish to be involved in sheep-raising would either buy in sheep for fattening and immediate re-sale, or would rent out their fields to sheep-dealers.[2] Whatever method was used would bring profit to the turnip-grower.

The existence of ample and regular feeding for stock, especially in the south-east of Berwickshire, encouraged experiments to improve stock. 'Public spirited gentlemen and farmers, have of late purchased, at very high prices, some fine bulls and cows, from the best places, and best breeders in England', and also sheep of 'the English breed introduced by Mr Bakewell, and since carried on by the Messrs Culleys, and other eminent breeders, both in Northumberland, and this country.'

1 Abbey of St Bathans, 3; Chirnside, 46.
2 Mordington, 265; Crailing, 419; Cockburnspath, 85; Dunse, 147; Greenlaw, 201.

The new breeds of sheep fattened quickly and had a good fleece; they had a profitable sale to dealers from Morpeth and other English markets, and the wool could be sold to agents for manufacturing in Leeds and other Yorkshire towns or in Aberdeen. The success of this development in the lower-lying farmlands of the Merse is shown by the fact that these farmers could sell or hire out their finest improved rams for breeding purposes further inland, as far west as Liddesdale.[1] The emphasis of the writers of the accounts of this area is always on sheep-improvement, yet experimental breeding of cattle and horses was being carried on simultaneously, though with less immediately obvious effects.

The lower-lying lands of the Merse and Teviotdale were well advanced agriculturally by the 1790s. A map of Berwickshire, published in 1797 by John Blackadder[2] shows the wide valley of the lower Tweed as a patchwork of enclosed fields and plantations, and the contrast with the hillier areas is made clear. The accounts themselves emphasise this contrast, especially those of Peeblesshire, Selkirkshire and the higher parishes of Roxburghshire, for the ministers were very well aware of the advances which were taking place in agriculture and longed for them to become effective in their own parishes. Admittedly most of the land in these parishes was hilly and more adapted to pasture than tillage; but between the hills, in the valleys and haughs, was land which was suitable for some arable development. The minister of Selkirk petulantly complained that the farmers in his parish were failing to realize the potential of this land, difficult though it was to till, and implied that there were no enclosures, no rotation of crops, no turnip growing and no raising of artificial grasses and clover. This was an exaggeration even for his own parish, for he elsewhere admitted that there were some

1   Bonkle, 18—19; Ladykirk, 217—18; Castletown, 385; Cavers, 411.
2   For Blackadder's manuscript draft of this map, see N.L.S., MS. Acc. 7115.

enclosures where fine turnips were raised, and that 'the parish produces much more grain (wheat excepted), than is sufficient for the support of the inhabitants'.[1] 'Agriculture is here only in its infancy' wrote the minister of Innerleithen, and any improvements that had taken place were far from universal. There was some plantation and some enclosure, but it existed side by side with the old infield-outfield system; some lime was used as fertilizer, but its use was not widespread; in a few places modern rotation systems were used in the enclosures, but elsewhere the old traditional methods were general. Some farmers used modern ploughs, but many more retained the old Scotch plough because they believed it was 'best adapted to the nature of the ground'; those in Stobo who had revived the practice of ploughing with oxen did so because their horses became unmanageable pulling the plough through stony ground, and oxen were cheaper to maintain.[2] The farmers in these areas were perhaps right to resist the encouragements and blandishments of their ministers, full of the lore of modern agricultural methods; they knew their own land and its limitations, and they appear not to have been slow to improve where improvement was possible and profitable. Land was gradually being enclosed among the hills, and, as the minister of Eddleston reported, 'The culture of turnips and sown grass hay, becomes every year more extensive'.[3]

Nevertheless, in these hilly parts of the region, tillage formed a minor part of the agricultural economy; the main business was raising sheep on the rough hill pastures. This differed considerably from the pastoral side of farming in the lower-lying areas. There was no enclosing of the sheep 'in hirsels, nor in folds by night';

1 Selkirk, 712—13; 715, 719.
2 Innerleithen, 764, 774; Kirkurd, 783—4; Linton, 797, 804; Lyne, 813; Stobo, 891—2.
3 Edlestown, 746.

they were 'permitted to wander at large in their respective pastures'. There was no winter-feeding on turnips, no summer-feeding on pastures of clover and rye grass; 'every farmer provides a considerable quantity of hay against the storm' of winter, but generally the free-roaming sheep sought their nourishment from the mosses and natural grasses 'which rise in their respective seasons throughout the year'.[1] Experiments, naturally, were made to improve the breed, and rams were purchased from the eastern borders; but the general opinion was that many of the crosses, especially those with the Bakewell breed, were not successful in the hills. In some places it was found 'that the quality of the wool was thereby deteriorated'. In others it was found that, although the wool improved, the health of the sheep was affected and they were 'less able to bear the severity of the winter storms, and never thrive upon a wet pasture'. Lack of hardiness in these cross-bred sheep was a common complaint, but the writer of the Yarrow account believed this assertion was not proven and accused the farmers in that parish of 'a tenacious adherence to ancient maxims and customs' for their failure to experiment. In some instances this may very well have been true, but from the experience of other hill parishes where breeding experiments had taken place it is clear that expensive English rams were not the answer, and 'judicious farmers now study to improve the shape of the breed, by selecting the best lambs of both sexes for breeding, without introducing a foreign mixture; and to enlarge the size and render the wool finer, by increasing the shelter upon their farms, by affording their flocks plenty of food, and by rendering their pastures sweeter and better' by keeping less stock and draining boggy ground.[2]

Hill sheep were more liable to disease than their lowland counterparts, probably because, being free-

1 Castletown, 385—7.
2 Hawick, 449; Melrose, 564; Linton, 799; Tweedsmuir, 912—13; Yarrow, 725.

roaming, they were more subject to extremes of weather, and many ministers write learnedly of the problems of the shepherds. Throughout the hill parishes the practice of smearing sheep in the autumn with a mixture of butter and tar was universal. This had a dual purpose: 'to destroy the vermin that breed on sheep, and protect the animal against the inclemency of the weather'. The ratio of butter to tar varied from parish to parish, depending on the amount of weather-proofing necessary, more butter being used in lower-lying areas; 'but the total disuse of tar has never had a good effect'. By some it was believed that smearing improved not only the quality but also the quantity of wool; yet, although necessary, 'this operation, no doubt, lessens the value of the wool'.[1] Nevertheless, the selling price of laid wool (as the smeared fleece was termed) was beginning to rise at this time owing to war conditions and to the difficulty which manufacturers had in importing finer foreign wool. Sheep-raising, in fact, was becoming a highly profitable form of agriculture, and in the next two decades was to become even more so, as the prices that local manufacturers and agents from Yorkshire were prepared to pay for wool continued to rise.[2]

Despite the disparity between the upland and lowland parts of the region, for these had developed differently and reached different stages in the process of improvement, it is clear that, taking the region as a whole, agriculture was healthy and thriving. Enclosure of the old rigs and the development of new crop rotations in the lowland areas, improvement of stock in both lowland and upland areas, were all proving profitable to tenant farmers. How profitable is shown by the fact that they could easily afford to pay considerably increased

---

1   Selkirk, 713—15; Tweedsmuir, 912; Hawick, 449.
2   Robert A. Dodgshon, 'The economics of sheep farming in the southern uplands during the age of improvement, 1750—1833', *Economic History Review*, 2nd ser., xxix (1976), 552—4, 556.

rents, at least double those of twenty years before and often triple; as the minister of Bedrule commented, the tenants 'all manage their farms according to the modern practice of husbandry — both for the advantage of the tenants, and the patrimonial interest of the proprietor'.[1] The improved financial status of the tenant farmer in time affected his social status; 'with respect to depth of information', commented the doctor at Kelso, 'and liberality of sentiments, they ought to be esteemed what they really are, a society of independent country gentlemen'. But this favourable view was not shared by all; the minister of nearby Eccles thought 'it is very improper to elevate men too high above their station. As many of our farmers have got a very narrow education, riches have often the unhappy effect of making them proud, and leading them to treat their superiors with insolence and contempt'.[2]

Yet agricultural improvement was not all gain. If there was social elevation for some members of the tenant class, this was balanced by the social depression of other members of the same class. In the early years of the eighteenth century, multiple tenancy of an agricultural settlement was the norm, both in lowland and upland areas. One of the first effects of 'improvement' was the reduction of multiple tenancies to single tenancies in order to produce a more efficient farm unit. Later, as efficiency and economy came to be related to larger size, many of these small single-tenant units were amalgamated into larger farms. To this reorganization should be added the total abandonment of many settlements in marginal hill country.[3] Both processes meant that former tenant farmers had to accept a lower social status, often as farm servants, or move to another part of the parish or country. Many ministers commented on

1 Eccles, 158; Bedrule, 331.
2 Kelso, 516; Eccles, 158.
3 R.A. Dodgshon, 'The Economics of Sheep-farming' 557—8; Martin L. Parry, 'The abandonment of upland settlement in southern Scotland', *Scottish Geographical Magazine*, xcii (1976), 56—58.

this process: 'there are many empty houses in the parish, and many have of late been demolished' because of the amalgamation of farms; and in some places they regretted that small villages had entirely disappeared. But their concern is in no way for the dispossessed former tenants, but for the effect of farm amalgamation on the size of the population of the parish.[1]

Larger farm units meant that more of the work was done by farm servants than by the tenant farmer himself. There were three main categories of agricultural employee in the region. The hind was a married man, and it was generally expected that his wife and some of his children would also assist in farm work. He was furnished with a cottage, and was paid mainly in kind — an allowance of barley, oats and pease, land for grazing a cow, a patch of ground for growing potatoes, the monetary value of this payment was variously assessed at between £13 and £20 per year. Unmarried male and female farm servants, who lived with the farmer and received board from him, were hired by the year or half-year; their wages varied between £5 and £10 per year for men, and £2 to £5 for women. Day labourers received 1s. to 1s.2d. per day in summer, slightly less in winter, and there were special rates for harvest work rising to 1s.6d.; they were generally provided with meals at the farmers' expense, and preferred 'getting their victuals to an allowance in money'.[2] In the Merse, the hind was preferred to the boarded servant as being more reliable, but both types of labourer seem to have been required on the average farm. Day labourers probably led a more precarious existence, being employed only when extra tasks required to be done. The wages of all farm workers were regarded as high — 'servants' wages are doubled within these 40 years'; 'this being a border country, is

1 Hounam, 478; Fogo, 179; Mertoun, 255—6; for the writers' attitude to population see below, pages xxii—xxv.
2 Eccles, 153; Dunse, 137; Langton, 227; Yetholm, 669.

the cause of the high wages of the labourers', their level being affected by the even higher wages paid in Northumberland.[1]

Although agriculture was the main form of industry in the region it is probably true to say not much more than half of the working population was directly engaged in it. Fishing provided a living for families in the coastal parishes; cod, herring, haddock and whiting being provided for the markets of Duns, Kelso and Edinburgh; lobster too was profitable, being a special delicacy for the London market. Much of this fishing was done from natural harbours, as at this time only Eyemouth was developed with man-made piers.[2] River-fishing provided 'excellent sport to the angler', for trout abounded in all the rivers and burns; but this salmon and trout fishing in the lower reaches of the Tweed was regarded more as a commercial proposition, and much of the controlled catch — some of which was 'carried to London alive, in wells in the Berwick smacks' — was sold profitably. Ministers of the Tweedside parishes in the upper reaches of the river complained that, because of the methods employed for catching fish nearer the sea, the valuable salmon seldom reached their area and their parishioners were deprived of a share in that profit.[3]

But, throughout the region, the majority of those not employed in agricultural labour were the craftsmen whose occupations were essential to the existence of rural society — masons, carpenters and thatchers, wrights and blacksmiths, weavers, tailors and shoemakers; and, of course, the shop-keepers, bakers, butchers, brewers and carriers who provided extra food, drink and a few luxuries for the people of the countryside. These craftsmen and traders formed a significant proportion of a village population; for example the

1   Bowden, 375; Dunse, 138; Westruther, 302.
2   Cockburnspath, 89—90; Coldingham, 95; Eyemouth, 169—72.
3   Castletown, 384; Hutton, 210—11; Makerston, 554; Innerleithen, 765; Traquair, 902.

parish of Chirnside, with a total population of 961 of which 475 were female and 260 children below the age of 10, required for its support no fewer than 81 craftsmen and 16 tradesmen.[1] Except for some of the hill parishes, this proportion was maintained throughout the region; in the rural areas roughly one-tenth of the total population was engaged in craft or trade, although one cannot so easily assess what proportion these groups had in the working population.

The craftsman, despite his skills, was not necessarily much better off than the agricultural labourer. Masons received between 1s.2d. and 2s. per day, carpenters and joiners between 1s. and 1s.8d., the variation partially depending on whether or not they received meals on the job; tailors, who generally worked in the home of their client for the time being, invariably received their meals and were paid only between 6d. and 10d. per day.[2] This suggests that in the rural areas there was not much economic difference between various members of the working class but, although this is not noted by the ministers, it is probable that a craftsman regarded himself as socially superior to an agricultural labourer.

The majority of the villages in which these craftsmen and tradesmen congregated were small, seldom exceeding 600 in population. But despite evidence to suggest that several small villages in some areas were becoming extinct,[3] the general picture seems to be of the consolidation of the population into villages, often under the active encouragement of the local proprietor. The planned feuing of ground at places like West Gordon, Swinton and Morebattle had led to the development of active village communities, absorbing many of the families which had been dispossessed by the amalgamation of farms.[4] Existing villages and towns increased in size:

---

1 Chirnside, 57.
2 Dunse, 138; Langton, 227; Bowden, 375; Morbattle, 592—3.
3 Mertoun, 255—6.
4 Gordon, 190; Swinton, 258; Morbattle, 588.

Duns had doubled its numbers and now contained over 2000 people, and Hawick had roughly the same population; Kelso had over 3500 inhabitants. These places had developed into having the status of towns and were important centres for the surrounding areas.[1] The royal burghs, so important in former ages, still retained some of their importance, but they were not developing to the same extent. Jedburgh had 2000 inhabitants and Peebles 1500, but their populations were static or declining; Selkirk and Lauder had barely 1000 inhabitants each.[2] The royal burghs were losing their former significance.

Lauder, in fact, had little hope of development although it had a strategic geographical position on a main north-south route. What it did not have, in the Lauderdale foothills of the Lammermuirs, was the increasing improved agricultural prosperity in its hinterland which would have made it a viable centre. Other royal burghs, more satisfactorily sited in late eighteenth-century terms, did not have this disadvantage; yet, despite attempts to found manufactories at Peebles and Selkirk, development was slow in coming. The common explanation was made by the minister of Jedburgh: 'there is rather a want of industry in the town of Jedburgh, owing to the destructive influence of borough (*sic*) politics'; and this was amplified by the minister of Selkirk who, recognizing the possibilities of the town for development, commented: 'but it is a royal burgh, and as such, suffers in all its best interests, and social intercourse. To acquire political power, and not commercial property, is the great object of the principal citizens'. Hawick claimed to have 'all the privileges of a royal burgh, except that of sending a representative to Parliament, for which it need not repine; as it is thereby freed from many temptations to idleness and dissipation,

1 Dunse, 132; Hawick, 457; Kelso, 513.
2 Jedburgh, 490; Peebles, 873; Selkirk, 716; Lauder, 232.

to which the inhabitants of royal burghs, by their politics, are often subjected'.[1]

Whether or not one accepts this plausible reason for the failure of royal burghs to develop as effectively as they might have done, it remains true that it was the inhabitants of the other towns who seized the commercial and industrial initiative in the region. Hawick and Kelso, burghs of barony subject to the Duke of Buccleuch and the Duke of Roxburghe respectively, each had an efficient burghal organization which could boast of the paving and repair of its streets and the provision of a piped water supply. Kelso was primarily a commercial centre, a market town serving a wide hinterland with basic goods and luxuries — groceries, hardware, drapery, hosiery, wines and spirits, and tea; there was a thriving shoemaking industry and extensive weaving, although this was not developed on an industrial basis. Hawick was more industrialized with various branches of textile work — carpet-making, linen and woollen cloth-manufacture, and stocking-making.[2]

Industrial development in this primarily agricultural region was not easy, mainly owing to the necessity for importing coal from the Lothians or Northumberland. Optimistic proprietors had sought coal within the district without success, and the former coal-mining at Cockburnspath had been abandoned. Mineral deposits of copper were known, but were 'not sufficiently rich to defray the expense of working'.[3] There was no basis for the type of heavy industrial development taking place in central Scotland; what development there could be had to be related to the agricultural nature of the border area. A certain amount of agricultural machinery was made: a 'wheel-wright manufactory' at Edrom made the ploughs designed by James Small but, oddly enough, it was in

1 Jedburgh, 500; Selkirk, 711; Hawick, 452—3.
2 Hawick, 452—5; Kelso, 512, 516—17.
3 Cockburnspath, 87; Bedrule, 338; Lauder, 231; Bonkle, 18; Longformacus, 251—2.

decline; and in Hawick there was a factory constructing some 60 winnowing machines each year, supplying the entire area including Northumberland. But, apart from paper mills at Ayton and Edrom, respectively employing 80 and 55 highly-paid hands, the main industrial development lay in textiles.[1]

The border region was not one of the traditional areas of Scottish woollen manufacture, and, in the seventeenth and most of the eighteenth centuries, the clip of border sheep was exported to the Lothians and Aberdeen for processing, as well as to the woollen mills of Yorkshire. Although much of the wool was still sold there, the improvement in the quality of local wool provided one of the stimuli for the development of local manufactures. Local entrepreneurs, men with few capital resources beyond their meagre savings, banded together in groups to exploit the local wool, the local water-power and such surplus labour as existed. New spinning and carding techniques were imported to produce the yarn for the handloom weavers, and the cloth was milled, dyed and finished under the eye of the master clothier-manufacturer.[2]

It must be remembered that this industrial development was in its infancy at the time these accounts were written. Linen manufacture as a domestic industry was still important in places like Coldingham, Earlston and Melrose; but already the writing was on the wall, and the Melrose linen industry was in decline, unable to pay the local spinners the higher wages which the wool manufacturers in neighbouring Galashiels, with their new equipment, could offer.[3] Woollen manufactories had been established at Innerleithen, Ednam and

1 Edrom, 164—5; Hawick, 451; Ayton, 11.
2 For a more detailed exposition of the rise of border woollen manufactories, see Clifford Gulvin, *The Tweedmakers*, Newton Abbot, 1973, 38—68.
3 Coldingham, 104; Earlstoun, 146; Melrose, 564—5.

Hawick, and were proposed for Duns and Peebles;[1] but Galashiels was the place where cloth-making was in the most thriving condition. The minister, Dr Robert Douglas, described the processes in detail — the sorting of the wool by quality, spinning (generally in a domestic situation but with multiple-spindle machines), weaving (again domestic), and the milling, dyeing and finishing of the cloth, the entire process superintended by the master-clothiers who had purchased the wool in the first place and would sell the finished product at a profit. The profit, Douglas asserts, was not very great; because their capital was so slight 'they are obliged to purchase on credit, and at a high rate, every necessary article of manufacture, and to sell the produce instantly, at whatever ready money it will fetch'. What the modest Douglas does not tell here is how he personally encouraged the industry in 1791 by investing £1000 of his own money to provide a 'Cloth Hall', a marketing centre in the town whereby clothiers could improve their selling prices and profits.[2]

The industry provided employment for a large number of people — 50 journey-men in the processing stages, 241 spinners and an unspecified number of weavers. These could not all have resided in Galashiels, which at this time had a population of under 600, and they clearly came from the outlying parts of the parish or from neighbouring parishes such as Melrose. At Innerleithen up to 80 hands were employed in the factory itself, carding and spinning by water-powered machinery; weaving, the number employed again unspecified, was done outside the factory building. At Hawick cloth manufacture employed only 31 people. More significant for this town's industrial development had been the establishment in 1771 of frame-knitting for hosiery, the business on which its future prosperity was to depend; already 65

1   Innerleithen, 768; Ednam, 444—5; Hawick, 455; Dunse, 135; Peebles, 870.
2   Galashiels, 689—94, 696; Gulvin, *The Tweedmakers*, 62—63.

people were employed, and the Hawick industry was
beginning to rival the Aberdeen hand-knitted stocking
industry — offering reduced production costs by the use
of machinery. But at this time the main industry in
Hawick, employing some 360 people, was that of carpet-
making; established in 1752 its products included not only 'Scotch carpets' but also rugs and woollen
tablecloths.[1]

At the time of the writing of the accounts this
predominantly agricultural region already showed the
beginnings of the industrial development which was to
diversify its economy, and alter the population balance.
The classic interpretation, that this is caused by movement of people from outlying areas as a result of
agricultural improvements into the towns and villages
where crafts and manufactures were developing, over-
simplifies the situation. Population changes were taking
place, but they were considerably more complex and
defy detailed analysis within the scope of this introduction. The following points are based on the three population counts of the second half of the eighteenth century:
Alexander Webster's survey of 1755, the emunerations
made by the ministers for their accounts in the early
1790s; and the first government census of 1801. The
figures for each count are given in the Appendix to this
Introduction.

The most reliable survey was the 1801 census; the
other two were less accurate but are sufficiently reliable
to help indicate the basic trends. In the region as a whole
the population showed a steady increase between 1755
and 1801 but, from the ministers' figures, there was a
decrease in Selkirkshire and Peebleshire in the 1790s. The
effect of industrial development is by no means immediately apparent; the population of Hawick parish
shows a minimal increase, while that of Galashiels parish

---

1   Innerleithen, 768; Hawick, 454—5; Gulvin, *The Tweedmakers*, 41.

actually shows a decline in the 1790s. One has to
recollect that the town of Hawick was expanding in its
manufactures across the Teviot into Wilton parish, and
that it is the considerable increase in the population of
that parish which is more significant. For Galashiels it is
important to note that while the entrepreneurs of the
new textile industry lived in the town, the spinners and
weavers were drawn from the surrounding countryside,
particularly the parish of Melrose, and the expected 'industrial' population-increase seems to occur there. Other
towns with embryonic textile industries, Peebles and Innerleithen, show no significant population increases
either in their own or neighbouring parishes. The coming of industry to the border region had not yet produced any large population centres. The only town which
materially increased in size was Kelso, a centre of craft
and commerce rather than industry; and this is balanced
by the severe loss of population suffered by Jedburgh
which, in the opinion of Thomas Somerville, was caused
by 'the Union between the two kingdoms, by which the
trade of Jedburgh was, in a great measure, ruined',
especially the 'very advantageous contraband trade'.[1]

In the countryside, particularly in Berwickshire and
Roxburghshire, the surprizing fact is the increase in
population. This is especially noticeable for the parishes
in the lower Tweed valley (where Chirnside showed an
increase of 150 per cent on the Webster figures, rising to
200 per cent in 1801) and in the Teviot valley. Many of
the hill parishes on the slopes of the Cheviots and Lammermuirs also recorded not inconsiderable increases. Yet
most of the ministers write eloquently about the
evidence for depopulation in the countryside — the abandoned farms and cottages, and in some cases villages —
which they attribute to 'the too general practice of letting the lands in great farms' and 'converting the arable

---

1 Jedburgh, 490—1.

into pasture land'.[1] It is clear that these were potent factors in depopulating certain areas; yet the fact remains, based on figures supplied by the ministers themselves, that in most parishes the population had increased. Two factors may help to explain this dichotomy.

The clue to the first is provided by the writer of the account for Linton, Peebleshire. Charles Findlater had access to the report of a presbyterial visitation of his parish taken in 1777; this showed that the population in that year was 20.7 per cent greater than in Webster's 1755 survey. His own survey in 1791 showed a decrease of 7.5 per cent on the 1777 figures, yet, even with this decrease, the population was still 11.7 per cent higher than the Webster figures.[2] If this pattern is applicable to other parishes, particularly other hill parishes (and there is no reason to suspect it is not), it suggests that in these areas the real increase in eighteenth-century population came in the third quarter of the century and was then followed by the decline which the ministers bemoan. Although the statistics indicate for such parishes a higher population in the 1790s in comparison with Webster, the trend is in fact downwards because the peak had been reached some twenty years earlier. Unfortunately there is no general population survey between 1755 and 1790 to prove or disprove this hypothesis.

The second factor, more applicable to the fertile low-lying parishes, is that the new agriculture, despite the fact that it created some depopulation through farm amalgamation, could support — and in some respects required — a larger population. 'Advanced cultivation of the fields', wrote the minister of Chirnside, 'brings along with it an augmented population to every village, or township, in adjacency to it'. Arable farming in enclosures with Small's plough might require fewer

1   Hounam, 468—9.
2   Linton, 805—6.

ploughmen, but it did require more day labourers for
hedging, ditching, haymaking, harvesting and especially
for the labour-intensive turnip cultivation. 'Superfluous
hands betake themselves to other occupations. . .such as
making and repairing the public roads' and remain
within the parish; hence in these more prosperous
agricultural areas there is no population decline but a
positive increase.[1]

Yet, despite the overall increase in the population of
the region, there must have been some emigration to the
towns of midland Scotland and overseas. In general the
ministers are loath to admit loss of their parishioners in this
way. The minister of Swinton asserts that 'nothing that
can be called emigration had happened here for many
years', although some seek employment outside the
parish 'often from whim or caprice', a statement which
indicates some degree of mobility. The minister of
Hounam, on the other hand, is more open about it, and
admits that some of his parishioners 'disperse annually in
all directions. . .some to England, where servants wages
are rather higher than in Scotland, and some to America
and the Indies'. It is unlikely that his parish was unique
in this respect.[2]

The interest of the ministers in the numbers of people
in their parish, their agonies over the signs of depopulation, even their unwillingness to admit that anyone
would voluntarily leave, reflects a concern for their
parishioners, for whose moral and social welfare they accepted a profound responsibility. Yet their religious
responsibility by no means extended to all the inhabitants of their parish because of the numbers of
adherents of the various secession churches. Some
ministers were deliberately vague about their numbers,
in statements varying from 'very inconsiderable' to

1 Chirnside, 53; Mordington, 271.
2 Swinton, 289; Hounam, 476.

'seceders are numerous'. The minister of Galashiels, with the complacent tolerance of indifference, wrote: 'concerning the numbers, and the peculiar tenets, of these various separatists from the establishment, the present incumbent has never been led to make any particular inquiry, from an opinion, that. . .the speculative points, on which they may differ, are of very little importance'.[1] Yet overall the numbers of seceders were considerable, and in many parishes, where ministers were prepared to give the information, seem to have amounted to between one-sixth and one-third of the total population. In Jedburgh the combined rolls of the Relief, Burgher and Anti-burgher congregations amounted to almost 2000, while the Established Church could muster only 800; this, the minister is anxious to point out, was due to the fact 'that the sect called the Relief Congregation had its origin in Jedburgh'.[2]

Despite the widespread prevalence of adherence to seceding tenets, congregations were established only in certain centres.[3] This meant that seceders in many parishes had to travel, often considerable distances, to attend worship in their faith; or alternatively their ministers held services in outlying parts at more or less regular intervals. Their numbers, their religious zeal, and the eagerness with which they held themselves apart from the Established Church in matters such as the bap-

---

1 Foulden, 185; Wilton, 662; Galashiels, 697.
2 Bowden, 374; Earlstoun, 146; Jedburgh, 495.
3 Burgher congregations were established by the 1790s at Ayton, Cockburnspath (Stockbridge), Coldstream, Dunse, Hutton (Horndean — but no church building), Lauder (in 1796), Castletown, Hawick, Jedburgh, Kelso, Lessudden (Newtown), Stitchell, Yetholm, Selkirk, Linton, and Peebles (in 1794); Antiburgher congregations were at Ayton, Dunse, Earlstoun, Greenlaw, Lauder, Bowden (Midholm), Hawick, Jedburgh, Kelso, Morbattle and Peebles; Relief congregations were to be found at Coldingham (in 1794), Dunse, Earlstoun, Jedburgh, Kelso and Newlands (Robert Small, *History of the congregations of the United Presbyterian Church* (Edinburgh, 1904), vol. i, under 'Duns' and 'Edinburgh Southern' Presbyteries; vol. ii, under 'Kelso' and 'Melrose' Presbyteries). The writers of the accounts did not always admit the existence of these congregations in their parishes (e.g. Earlstoun, Greenlaw, Stitchell). The following information about other churches is, however, based on the accounts; there were Cameronian congregations at Chirnside (72), Cavers (412), Kelso (512) and Peebles (873); and there was also an Episcopal chapel, and meeting-places of Methodists and Quakers at Kelso (512).

tism and registration of their children, on the whole
roused antagonism in the parish ministers. A few ex-
pressed a tolerant attitude — 'the character of separatists
and adherents scarce admits of any shade of distinction,
unless it be, that the former have the appearance of
greater zeal in religious matters than the latter'; but in
general they preferred to minimize their importance —
'being composed of the inferior ranks of the people,
(hence) their defection has not diminished the contribution for the parochial poor'.[1]

The minister of Ayton was alluding to the fact that in
general throughout Scotland the poor of a parish were
supported by collections taken for the purpose at the
church doors; his point, however, is weakened by the
fact that throughout this region, including his own
parish, other arrangements existed for the supports of
the poor which were so extensively used as to make the
eastern border counties stand out from the rest of
Scotland in the quality of their poor relief. Church collections were still used for the relief of poverty, the
mortcloth was still hired out for the benefit of the poor,
and those parishes fortunate enough to have specific endowments for the purpose employed the interest in
relief; in some towns such as Hawick and Kelso, friendly
societies were springing up which supported their
members in time of sickness and old age. But the general
method of poor relief, which distinguishes this region
(apart from many parishes in Peeblesshire) from much of
the rest of Scotland, was the levying of a poor-rate by
assessment on the heritors and tenants of the parishes,
'the only legal mode, though not universally observed'.[2]

The heritors, on the initiative of the ministers and kirk
sessions, were summoned at regular intervals, in some
parishes half-yearly, in others quarterly, or 'as cir-

1   Roberton, 705; Ayton, 13.
2   Edrom, 165; Bedrule, 342; Linton, 808; Hawick, 457; Kelso, 524—5; Sprouston, 648.

cumstances require'; tenants were allowed to attend 'as they pay one half. . .and are best acquainted with the state of the poor, in their own neighbourhood'. At such meetings the poor roll and the general state of poverty in the parish was examined, and the heritors. . .cheerfully assess themselves to the full amount of what the minister and session deem necessary', half of the sum assessed to be paid by the heritors, the other half by the tenants, in proportion to the valued rent of their land. The money was collected and put in charge of a local official, who distributed it weekly to those who had been admitted to the poor roll. When a poor person was admitted to the roll, an inventory was taken of his effects and these were conveyed by a bond to the heritors 'to prevent persons, who may be possessed of concealed property, from alienating the public charity'; the goods could be sold by public roup after the death of the impoverished person. In many parishes the levying of poor-rates had been established as early as the 1740s, and many regarded it as the most effective way of providing some form of social welfare: 'charity is here reduced to a regular system of operation, which does not leave its objects to a precarious subsistence, but secures for them a certain well-regulated relief in the day of poverty and distress'.[1]

Effective though it was, assessment did not meet with unqualified approval; it was 'a method, however well intentioned, . . .often hurtful to the deserving poor, to humanity, and the interest of those on whom the burden is laid' because it was alleged to 'weaken parental and filial affection' and prevent people 'from laying up against the time of need'. In Newlands, where rates were not levied, this was 'to the end that no certain dependence may be created, destructive of industry and exertion'.[2] The fear was that a regular system of welfare

---

1   Wilton, 660—1; Mertoun, 258; Hounam, 473—4; Jedburgh, 496—8; Melrose, 572.
2   Bedrule, 342; Wilton, 663—5; Coldstream, 119; Newlands, 834.

encouraged shamelessness and laziness, and discouraged family loyalty and thrift. Others denied these effects emphatically: 'the people in general. . .cannot bear the idea of being put on the poor's roll, even when they are in distress', wrote the minister of Ayton; while Samuel Charteris, in his supplement to the anonymous account of his parish of Wilton, provided a point-by-point refutation of this attitude, believing that poor relief by assessment 'tends to strengthen pastoral, and parental, and filial love', and that 'the law which gives a maintenance to the poor, is one of the bulwarks of the British government, by which it is defended from the rage of want and despair', a counter to any revolutionary tendencies among the common people.[1]

The widespread use of assessment for poor relief in this region may be due to a greater incidence of poverty, especially the migrating poor. The main roads to England passed through the area, and the minister of Coldstream, on the actual frontier, specifically comments on the 'sick and distressed persons returning to Scotland, a great number of which pass this way' and who required relief.[2] It is clear from his account that in his parish at least such relief did not come from the assessment money but from other funds, yet it is possible that the necessity for providing this extraordinary relief had some influence on local decisions to adopt the method of assessment for the native poor. It is difficult, in fact, to estimate with any degree of accuracy the incidence of poverty. Many of the writers of the accounts give the numbers of the people on the poor roll, and this suggests that on average throughout the region they amounted to between 2.5 per cent and 3 per cent of the population. But there were wide variations: Lessudden and Mordington were as low as 0.6 per cent, while

1 Ayton, 12; Wilton, 663—5.
2 Coldstream, 119.

Melrose was as high as 6 per cent. Without a precise knowledge of the standards which were applied to assess qualification for admission to the poor roll, standards which undoubtedly varied from parish to parish, such figures can be no more than an approximation.

To the parish minister's responsibility for the spiritual welfare of his flock and for their social welfare when they were distressed, was added some responsibility for their education in the parish school. In general the ministers were proud of their parish schools and of the quality of education given in them, and they emphasise its social value: 'the children of the hinds are carefully sent to the parish-school, to learn reading, writing, arithmetic, and the first principles of religion;. . .(and) the farmers are enabled to give their children all the real advantages of what is usually called a *liberal education*'. Even in some country parishes additions were made to this basic curriculum, practical subjects like book-keeping, mathematics and mensuration (surveying) being popular; and Latin was often available for those who wished to study it.[1] Many parishes supported more than one school, especially those geographically extensive where many children were 'too remote from the parish school' easily to attend it. Tenants in these remoter areas would band together to contribute the salary for a schoolmaster in their locality, as, for example, at Lempetlaw in Sprouston parish; or a master might be maintained on the interest of a charitable mortification as at Hadden in the same parish, or at Mellerstain in Earlston parish.[2]

In the towns it seems to have been normal for there to be more than one school. In Duns, in addition to the parish school which was held 'in very great repute' and accepted boarders, there was also a girls' boarding school where not only reading and writing were taught but also

---

1 Legerwood, 248—9; Hutton, 214; Bowden, 376; Lessudden, 536; Traquair, 908.
2 Sprouston, 653; Earlstoun, 148.

the more feminine arts of sewing, embroidery, music and dancing. Kelso possessed a Latin or grammar school as well as the parish English school; but in addition there were four other English schools, several schools for girls for teaching sewing, and a School of Industry where poor girls were instructed in reading, writing, sewing and 'moral duties'. Peebles, too, had both a grammar and an English school, and many scholars from other parts of the kingdom were boarded there and at various private schools in the town.[1] But a complete picture of education in the towns cannot be obtained from these accounts; for reasons best known to themselves, the ministers of Lauder, Jedburgh, Hawick and Selkirk failed to mention the educational facilities available in these towns.

It is difficult to assess how many children were able to take advantage of the education available. At Cockburnspath, where the minister calculated the number of children of school-age (between 3 and 10) at 180, some fifty to sixty generally attended school.[2] Similar figures for other parishes suggest that less than one third of children of school age received any regular education, though more received some. Attendance at school was irregular: domestic and agricultural tasks kept children at home at certain times of the year; and many probably never attended at all through the inability of their parents to pay the quarterly fees, although some parishes allocated money from their poor funds to pay for the education of poor children. The fees, small though they were, formed an important part of the schoolmasters' income. The heritors, who were responsible for providing the school-houses and paying the masters, often paid no more than the 100 merks Scots basic annual salary required by law, although in many parishes this had been

1 Dunse, 136; Kelso, 519—20; Peebles, 875.
2 Cockburnspath, 88—89.

augmented to £100 Scots (£8.6s.8d. sterling). The master could often supplement this by small fees from carrying out the offices of session clerk, precentor or collector of the poor-rates; but even so, unless he had a large number of pupils paying fees, his total annual income would average no more than between £16 and £20, little more than 'the value of a labouring servant's wages and board'. In general, ministers denounced the poverty forced on young men taking up teaching as a profession; 'every well-educated and virtuous man shrink(s) back from it as a place of hopeless penury, or follow(s) some other employment besides his school, in order to gain a decent livelihood for his family', a fact derogatory to 'that singular system of education from whence the Scottish people have derived such consequence, and on the proper management of which the welfare of society so greatly depends'.[1]

The welfare of society in matters of health was in general regarded as good by the ministers, a fact they attributed to the quality of the climate and the drainage of bogs and swamps, which as a by-product of agricultural improvement had eliminated the causes of some ailments. The most common complaint, they asserted, was rheumatism which, 'caused by bad and damp houses, and low living, in general afflicts the lower class as they advance in life'. Periodically the region was visited by smallpox epidemics, which had not yet been controlled by the use of inoculation; religious prejudices, especially among seceder congregations, were preventing its adoption, although in some areas 'the prejudices against inoculation are fast wearing out'.[2] Medical care of the inhabitants of the region was not extensive. Few parishes had a resident doctor, and those who did practice in the area settled in the larger villages and the towns

1 Newlands, 861; Glenholm, 758; Roxburgh, 624.
2 Bonkle, 17; Innerleithen, 764; Bowden, 376; Greenlaw, 196.

— Coldstream, Swinton, Smailholm, Lauder, Jedburgh and Kelso. Only Kelso is reported as having a hospital, supported by public subscriptions and some contributions from neighbouring parishes, with a ward accommodating twelve patients and an out-patient service.[1] But in medicine, as in education, one must be wary of drawing conclusions too precisely from these accounts; it is clear that in some parishes the writers have ignored the existence of a resident physician or surgeon.

This border region, then, was primarily an agricultural society which, with the widespread adoption of modern improved farming methods, could support a larger local population and was beginning to become more affluent. The diet, even of relatively poor people, was beginning to improve, with more frequent use of 'animal food' to supplement the normal sustenance of oatmeal and potatoes; moreover, 'every house almost without exception has its clock, and not a few of the owners have watches besides'. But this was countered by other evidence of an 'affluent' society, the pernicious habits of drinking tea and whisky, both regarded as extravagant, superfluous and debilitating commodities.[2] The development of the textile industries, and of towns such as Hawick and Galashiels which later were to dominate the region by their size, was as yet in its infancy. The centres of commerce and culture at this time were relatively small towns like Duns, Peebles, Jedburgh and Kelso, which were not to be subjected to extensive industrial development in the future. These were the places where the market economy thrived, where physicians and lawyers practised, the centres to which the surrounding countryside looked. Public libraries at Duns and Kelso brought 'the best modern authors', the writers of the Scottish Enlightenment, to the people

---

1 Kelso, 522, 525; Sprouston, 654.
2 Coldingham, 105; Swinton, 295.

there and in neighbouring parishes, 'by which (the farmers) are enabled to acquire an extent of knowledge and information' and satisfy 'their laudable literary curiosity and taste for the belles lettres'.[1]

The writers of the accounts do not hide the difficulties and disadvantages of life in the region, especially those ministers in Selkirkshire and Peeblesshire where improved agricultural technology had not yet fully penetrated. But, optimistically, they share with their fellows in Roxburghshire and Berwickshire where improvement had already proved a successful bringer of relative affluence a belief in beneficent progress, a belief not yet scarred by knowledge of the horrors of industrialization in central and western Scotland. In a sense their optimism was justified: the border region has remained predominantly agricultural, unspoilt by later industrial development, and industry and agriculture together have brought to it a measure of quiet prosperity.

T.I. RAE

Department of Manuscripts
National Library of Scotland

1 Dunse, 142; Kelso, 524; Gordon, 194; Swinton. 296.

APPENDIX

BERWICKSHIRE

† OSA date	Parish	Population in 1755	1790s	1801	Percentage 1755/1790s	Change 1755/1801
1791—3	Abbay of St. Bathans	80	164	138	+ 105	+ 72
1790	Ayton	797	1245	1453	+ 56	+ 82
1790	Bonkle and Preston	691	622	674	− 10	− 2
1791—3	Channelkirk	531	600	640	+ 13	+ 21
1791	Chirnside	383	961	1147	+ 151	+ 199
1793	Cockburnspath	919	883	930	− 4	+ 1
1791	Coldingham	2313	2391	2391	+ 3	+ 3
1785—6	Coldstream	1493	2521[1]	2269	+ 69	+ 52
1791—2	Cranshaws	214	164	166	− 23	− 22
1788	Dunse	2593	3324	3163	+ 28	+ 22
1791	Earlston	1197	1351	1478	+ 13	+ 23
1791—3	Eccles	1489	1780	1682	+ 20	+ 13
1790	Edrom	898	1336	1355	+ 49	+ 51
1790—1	Eyemouth	792	'1000'	899	+ 26	+ 13
1797	Fogo	566	450	507	− 20	− 10
1793	Foulden	465	344	393	− 26	− 15
1791	Gordon	737	912	802	+ 24	+ 9
1785	Greenlaw	895	1210	1270	+ 35	+ 42
1790—1	Hutton	751	920	955	+ 23	+ 27
1792—3	Ladykirk	386	'590'	516	+ 53	+ 34
1793	Langton	290	435	428	+ 50	+ 47
1791	Lauder	1714	'2000'	1760	+ 17	+ 3
1794—5	Legerwood	398	422	495	+ 6	+ 24
1791	Longformacus	399	452	406	+ 13	+ 1
1791	Mertoun	502	557	535	+ 11	+ 6
1792—4	Mordington	181	335	330	+ 85	+ 82
1792	Nenthorn	497	'400'[2]	395	− 20	− 20
1793	Polwarth	251	288	291	+ 15	+ 16
1791	Swinton and Simprin	494	898	875	+ 82	+ 77
1791	Westruther	591	730	779	+ 24	+ 32
1794—5	Whitsom and Hilton	399	590	560	+ 48	+ 40
	All parishes	23906	29875	29682	+ 25	+ 24

ROXBURGHSHIRE

1792—3	Ancrum	1066	1146	1222	+ 8	+ 15
1790—1	Ashkirk	629	539	511	− 14	− 19
1793	Bedrule	297	259	260	− 13	− 12
1794	Bowden	672	860	829	+ 28	+ 23
1793	Castletown	1507	1418	1781	− 7	+ 18
1794	Cavers	993	'1300'	1382	+ 31	+ 39
1790—1	Crailing	387	672	669	+ 74	+ 73
1791	Eckford	1083	952	973	− 12	− 10

1791—3	Edenham	387	'600'	598	+ 55	+ 55
1792—3	Hawick	2713	2928	2798	+ 8	+ 3
1790—1	Hobkirk	530	'700'	760	+ 32	+ 43
1791	Hounam	632	365	372	– 42	– 41
1799	Jedburgh	5816	3288	3834	– 43	– 34
1792	Kelso	2781	4324	4196	+ 55	+ 50
1792	Kirktoun	330	342	320	+ 4	– 3
1792—3	Lessudden	309	'500'	497	+ 62	+ 60
1793	Lilliesleaf	521	630	673	+ 21	+ 29
1790—1	Linton	413	383	403	– 7	– 2
1790—1	Makerston	165	255	248	+ 55	+ 50
1782	Maxton	397	326	368	– 18	– 7
1791—3	Melrose	2322	2446	2625	+ 5	+ 13
1796—7	Minto	396	513	477	+ 30	+ 20
1794—5	Morbattle	789	'789'[3]	785	0	0
1793	Oxnam	760	690	688	– 9	– 9
1796—7	Roxburgh	784	840	949	+ 7	+ 21
1790	Smailholm	551	421[4]	446	– 24	– 19
1791—3	Southdean	480	714	697	+ 49	+ 45
1791	Sprouston	1089	'1000'	1105	– 8	+ 2
1790—1	Stitchel and Hume	959	'1000'	921	+ 4	– 4
1795	Wilton	936	1215	1307	+ 30	+ 40
1797	Yetholm	699	976	1011	+ 40	+ 45
	All Parishes	31392	32391	33705	+ 3	+ 7

SELKIRKSHIRE

1790—1	Etterick	397	470	445	+ 18	+ 12
1791	Galashiels	998	914	1018	– 8	+ 2
1791-2	Roberton	651	629	618	– 3	– 5
1790—1	Selkirk	1793	'1700'	2098	– 5	+ 17
1793	Yarrow	1180	1230	1216	+ 4	+ 3
	All Parishes	5019	4943	5395	– 2	+ 7

PEEBLESSHIRE

1791—2	Broughton	367	264	214	– 28	– 42
1790	Drummelzier	305	270	278	– 11	– 9
1793	Edlestown	679	710	677	+ 5	0
1790—1	Glenholm	392	300	242	– 23	– 38
1796—7	Innerleithen	559	560	609	0	+ 9
1790—1	Kilbucho	279	362	342	+ 30	+ 23
1792	Kirkurd	310	288	327	– 8	+ 5
1791	Linton	831	928	1064	+ 12	+ 28
1792	Lyne and Megget	265	152	167	– 43	– 37

1790—1	Manor	320	229	308	− 28	− 4
1790	Newlands	1009	891	950	− 12	− 6
1791	Peebles	1896	1920	2088	+ 1	+ 10
1790—1	Skirling	335	234	308	− 30	− 8
1790—1	Stobo	313	318	338	+ 1	+ 7
1791—3	Traquair	651	446	491	− 31	− 24
1792—3	Tweedsmuir	397	227	252	− 43	− 36
	All Parishes	8908	8099	8655	− 9	− 3

SUMMARY TABLE

Berwickshire	23906	29875	29682	+ 25	+ 24
Roxburghshire	31392	32391	33705	+ 3	+ 7
Selkirkshire	5019	4943	5395	− 2	+ 7
Peeblesshire	8908	8099	8655	− 9	− 3
Total	69225	75308	77437	+ 9	+ 12

† The dates given in this first column indicate, as nearly as possible, the actual year in which the count of population was made. The parish account itself often gives this information: failing that, the date is either that indicated by Sinclair at the start of each volume of the published *Account* or is the date of publication of the appropriate volume in the 1790s.

1. A quarter was here added to the report of 1785—6 which included only ex- aminables.
2. The account actually states 'between 300 and 400' but the latter figure is used elsewhere.
3. The account says 'the number of inhabitants is supposed to be nearly the same as in the return made to Dr. Webster...'
4. The number given in the account is 335 of examinable age to which a quarter is added to give a better estimate of the total population.

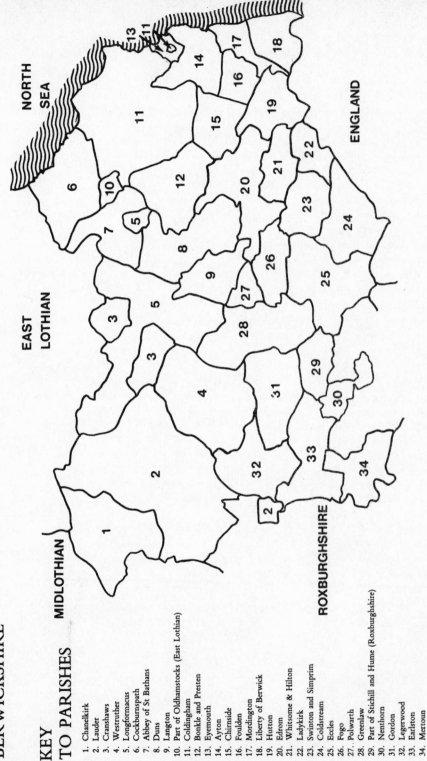

BERWICKSHIRE

KEY
TO PARISHES

1. Chanelkirk
2. Lauder
3. Cranshaws
4. Westruther
5. Longformacus
6. Cockburnspath
7. Abbey of St Bathans
8. Duns
9. Langton
10. Part of Oldhamstocks (East Lothian)
11. Coldingham
12. Bonkle and Presten
13. Eyemouth
14. Ayton
15. Chirnside
16. Foulden
17. Mordington
18. Liberty of Berwick
19. Hutton
20. Edrom
21. Whitsome & Hilton
22. Ladykirk
23. Swinton and Simprim
24. Coldstream
25. Eccles
26. Fogo
27. Polwarth
28. Greenlaw
29. Part of Stichill and Hume (Roxburghshire)
30. Nenthorn
31. Gordon
32. Legerwood
33. Earlston
34. Mertoun

NORTH
SEA

EAST
LOTHIAN

MIDLOTHIAN

ENGLAND

ROXBURGHSHIRE

PARISH of ABBAY of St. BATHANS.

(COUNTY OF BERWICK, SYNOD OF MERSE AND TIVIOTDALE, PRESBYTERY OF DUNSE.)

By the Rev. Mr. JOHN SKED.

Situation, Extent, Soil, Climate, &c.

THE fmallnefs of this parifh, and its retired fituation, afford but little fcope for ftatiftical inveftigation; being fituated in that mountainous part of Berwickfhire which ftretches into the middle of the Lammermoor hills, where the foil in general is barren, and the country but thinly inhabited. Its form is irregular; its greateft extent from E. to W. is about 6 or 7 miles in length, and in fome places its breadth from S. to N. about 3 miles. The parifh in general is hilly, greater part of which is covered with heath. On the fide of the water of Whitadder, and the fmall rivulets which run into it, there are, in many places, confiderable tracks of low lying grounds which are naturally fertile, and which, when properly cultivated, are capable of producing all kinds of grain,

grain, wheat not excepted. Beſides the haugh lands, there are, in many of the higher parts of the pariſh, conſiderable quantities of the land in tillage, the greater part of which has been improved by lime brought from Eaſt Lothian ; and, in favourable ſeaſons, the farmer commonly finds a very good return. The ſoil is light and dry. Though, from the elevated ſituation of the pariſh, the climate is cold, yet it is in general healthy, and few diſeaſes prevail among the inhabitants.

River.—The only river in the pariſh is Whitadder, which is here a conſiderable ſtream, being about 15 miles from its ſource, and having received, in its courſe, the river Dye, the rivulet Monnynuk, and numberleſs other ſmaller ones. It abounds with plenty of trouts, and affords excellent ſport to the angler. Salmon and ſea-trout are ſometimes found in it in ſummer, though ſeldom in great quantities. Prodigious numbers of them come up during the prohibited months for fiſhing, and lodge their ſpawn in the channel of the river. There is but too much reaſon to regret, that the inhabitants deſtroy them at that time, as it tends both to injure their own health, by making uſe of the fiſh in the weak and unhealthy ſtate in which they then are, and is a great prejudice to the ſalmon-fiſhing in the river Tweed.

Population.—According to Dr. Webſter's report, the number of ſouls then, was 80. There are at preſent 164 inhabitants in the pariſh, of whom 85 are males, and 79 females ; all of whom, except a few mechanics, are employed in purpoſes of huſbandry, either as day-labourers, hired ſervants to farmers, or ſhepherds. They are in general ſober, frugal, and induſtrious, and are contented with their ſituation. When

the

the prefent incumbent was fettled here in 1775, the number of inhabitants was 145.

Agriculture.—Though, like other parts of Lammermoor, the lands are in general more adapted to the breeding of cattle and fheep than the raifing of corn, yet, on all the different farms there are confiderable parts of the ground under cultivation ; and on fome of them different kinds of grain, particularly early oats are produced, little inferior in quality to thofe that are raifed in the lower parts of Berwickfhire. The chief object, however, that the fkilful farmer has in view in making ufe of the plough in this part of the country, is not fo much the immediate return from the corn he raifes, as the meliorating the pafture for his cattle and fheep, by fowing his fields with artificial grafs feeds, particularly rye-grafs and white clover, which thrive well on all the dry grounds that have been improved with lime. Thofe who have followed this method, have not only been able to keep a much greater quantity, but have alfo, by this means, an opportunity of greatly improving the breed both of their cattle and fheep. Turnips are alfo raifed on moft of the farms in this neighbourhood, though in much fmaller quantities than might be expected, as the foil is peculiarly adapted to the cultivation of that ufeful plant *.

Heritors, Stipend, &c.—There are 6 heritors in this parifh, none of whom, excepting one of fmall property, are refident. The

---

* *Price of Labour.*—The wages of male fervants who get their board in the houfe, are from 7 l. to 8 l. a-year ; of female fervants, from 3 l. to 4 l. Servants who have families and keep a houfe, are paid in grain, have a cow grazed, and other perquifites, which may altogether amount to between 14 l. and 15 l. The wages of day-labourers are about 1 s. in winter, and above it in fummer ; but in hay time and harveft, they have confiderably more.

The rental of the parish is about 600 l. a-year. The Crown is patron of the church. The value of the living, exclusive of the manse and glebe of 14 acres, is about 52 l. a-year. The church is a very ancient building; it was formerly large, measuring 58 feet by 26, but a part of the wall was lately taken down by the desire of the heritors, and the size of the church greatly contracted; it is still sufficiently large to accommodate the inhabitants of the parish.

Antiquities.—Between the church and the water of Whit-adder, are the remains of an ancient nunnery; it is almost totally demolished, the stones having been carried away for other purposes; from the vestiges, however, which are still to be seen, the building seems to have been of considerable extent. From any materials that I have been able to collect, this nunnery, of Abbay of St. Bathan's, seems to have been founded by one of the Countesses of March, during the reign of King William the Lyon, who succeeded to the Crown of Scotland in 1165, and reigned 49 years; so that it must have happened between 1165 and 1214. In 1296, Ada, Countess of March, swore fidelity for this nunnery to Edward I. King of England, who had then subdued great part of Scotland; and in return, directed a writ to the sheriff of Berwick to restore to the nunnery all its lands and tenements. It was a cell of South Berwick, and the nuns were of the order of Bernardines or Cistertians. This religious order had been begun by Robert, Abbot of Milesme, in the diocese of Longres in France, in 1098—were called Monachi Abbi, White Monks, from their wearing white robes, except a black coul or scopular—were called Bernardines from Bernard, the great propagator of the order, who founded 160 monasteries, divided into 36 provinces, whereof Scotland was 26th, and had 13 monasteries—were called Cistertians from their chief house

and

and monasteries in Cistertium in France. There is in the wall, near the altar-place in the church, a font stone with a lead pipe in the bottom, and from springs in the braes to the south, the church and buildings adjoining had been supplied with water by means of lead pipes, part of which have been seen by people thereabout, after being dug up about 40 years ago. To the south, and round the church and nunnery, were gardens, now arable land, and on that account were called the Precinct Yards, and round the whole had been a walk of 3 tire of stones, which have also been seen by those who raised part of them. After observing that the nunnery lies upon the south side of the water of Whitadder, it may be added, that there are pleasant haughs adjoining, sheltered from the north, by Shannabank wood of natural oak, on a steep brae, rising to a great height, and forming at top a semicircle, and from the east, by Blackerstone braes and natural wood there. On the south of these haughs, and at a small distance from the nunnery, issues a spring called St. Bathan's well, that neither fogs nor freezes, and prevents a dam-lead from Whitadder serving a corn-mill below, being locked up with ice in winter. About a quarter of a mile from the nunnery, on the same side of the water, lie the foundations of a small chapel and yard holding that name; but there are no marks of people having buried in it: about a mile from the nunnery, on the other side of the Whitadder, is situated Trois Fontaines (3 springs or wells) on the side of Manegnut water which empties into the Whitadder here, where the remains of a chapel and burying-ground are yet extant. It has always been handed down, that a subterraneous passage went from the nunnery of St. Bathan's, below the water of Whitadder, to this chapel, where the nuns passed along to be confessed by the clergy from Coldingham, who had a house at God's croft in this parish, and at a little distance from the
chapel.

chapel. Trois Fontaines was alfo a cell of South Berwick ; but I have not been able to find any writings relating to it, and fo can give no further account of it.

Trees, Game, &c.—On the lands of Abbay and farms adjoining, grow naturally the oak, the mountain-afh, the hazel, the birch tree, befides other trees ; the honey-fuckle, the anife, the rafp, the juniper, the brier, and bramble, &c. On the lands are plenty of moorfowl, partridge, gray plover, hares, rabbits, &c.

Country Seat.—I beg leave to add, that about a mile eaft from the village of Abbay, is a country feat of the Earl of Wemyfs, called the Retreat. It was built by his Lordfhip about 12 years ago, upon his eftate of Blackerftone, and though not within the bounds of this parifh, deferves to be taken notice of in the ftatiftical account of it, as it tends very much to beautify this part of the country. The houfe is of a circular form, and built after a new and fingular plan : as the elegant fimplicity of the architecture, the neatnefs and convenience of the different apartments, and the manner in which the grounds around it are laid out, do great credit to the tafte of the proprietor ; fo its retired fituation on the banks of the Whitadder, in the heart of a mountainous country, together with natural wood, and the extenfive plantations with which it is furrounded, render it a truly delightful and romantic retreat.

PARISH OF AYTON.

*By the Rev. M*r GEORGE HOME.

Name, Situation, &c.

THE parifh of Ayton feems to take its name from the water of Eye. It lies in the county of Berwick, prefbytery of Chirnfide, and fynod of Merfe and Tiviotdale. The parifhes by which it is bounded are Eyemouth and Coldingham on the north, Chirnfide on the weft, Foulden and Mordington on the fouth, and by the fea en the eaft. The parifh is about 4½ miles long, and 4 broad : It was once of larger extent, when Lammerton, Rofs, and Shiels belonged to it. The foil is in general fertile, and particularly adapted for the turnip hufbandry. There is about 2 miles extent of fea coaft. The fhore is high and rocky. The hills in this parifh lie chiefly in the fouthern extremity. The foil of fome of them, efpecially of a ridge of no very confiderable height, is in general well adapted for producing corn or grafs.

Cultivation and Produce.—Agriculture has undergone a great change in the courfe of a very few years. Inftead of five or fix fucceffive white crops, the farmers will feldom allow two to follow each other ; for they derive confiderable advantage from introducing a green one, and occafionally fallow, between

tween the white crops. The experience of this neighbourhood has rather a tendency to prove, that money expended
in the cultivation of moor lands has ſeldom turned to a good
account, and that planting is the beſt mode of improvement;
the effects of water, however, has not been tried. Lime o-
perates at firſt, but loſes its effect as a ſtimulus upon a ſecond
trial. Though the appearance of moor lands may be changed by culture and artificial graſſes, they will not feed well;
and, when wet or cold, are believed to lay the foundation of
the *rot* in ſheep, a diſtemper which proves extremely fatal.

Two horſes only, are at preſent uſed in the plough here,
inſtead of four oxen and two horſes, which was formerly the
practice. They will perform the ſame quantity of labour
equally well, and in much ſhorter time. The Engliſh plough
is chiefly uſed in this pariſh. The lands produce moſt of the
common vegetables, plants, and trees. Artificial graſſes are
much uſed Of late the farmers here directed their attention, and with great ſuccefs, to ſtock. They find that the
lands in graſs make a profitable return. By feeding, too, the
ground is enriched for future crops. The advantage of feeding ſheep on the lands, in the proper ſeaſon, with turnip, is
ſenſibly felt; and this practice is ſuppoſed to be preferable to
a ſummer fallowing; and is, at the ſame time, no loſs to the
farmer.

Plantations of all kinds of trees are much encouraged by
the preſent proprietor of the eſtate of Ayton, which contributes greatly to enrich and beautify the country. His lands
ſome years ago were all *run-rig* *, as was very much the caſe,
particularly

---

* A common field, in which the different farmers had different ridges alloted them in different years, according to the nature of their crops.

particularly upon the boarders, with a view to engage the people to a mutual defence and protection of their property, in times of turbulence and hostility. They are now divided, have convenient farm-houses, and are highly improved. Harvests are rather early here than late. The greatest part of the lands in this parish is inclosed with hedges. Fences of this kind are recommended both by their beauty and utility. The rise of rent seems to have operated here as a spur to exertion and improvement in agriculture. The farms have rather decreased in number. Some of them, though but few, extend to 500 or 600 acres.

Air and Distempers.—The air is dry and salubrious. The fogs arising from the sea seldom penetrate above a mile from the shore. The ague was very common prior to the improvements and inclosing of lands; but since that time this disorder has scarcely been known here, except during the last very open winter.

Horses, Sheep, &c.—The horses bred and used here are slender; but they are very active, and able to undergo much fatigue: They have advanced much in value. The breed of sheep is both good and large; their weight, at an average, is about 18 or 20 lbs. *per* quarter. Four of their fleeces yield a stone of wool. Five sheep may be maintained upon an acre of some of the best lands. The number of sheep in this parish, till within these ten or twelve years past, was small. Great advantage arises from the large breed lately introduced: Besides yielding more wool, they are fit for the market in two years time; while sheep of the smaller size require to be kept three years before they are ready for the market. The wool of the large sheep is, without doubt, of a coarser quality; but this disadvantage is

more

more than compenfated by the quantity. On rich lands even the fmall kind of fheep would increafe in fize, and their wool become more plentiful, though of an inferior quality. The wool fells from 12 s. to 15 s. *per* ftone. Oxen here are commonly fed till they weigh from 60 to 100 ftone.

Fifh.—The water of Eye contains good trouts, but not in any quantity. Cod, ling, haddocks, whitings, flounders, hollyback, mackrell, and other kinds of fifh, are caught here in their feafons. Lobfters yield confiderable profit; they are chiefly bought up for the London market. Herrings have been got in great quantities; but they, as well as the other kinds of white fifh, have failed much for thefe two years paft. The fifhermen have lately difcovered the method of catching turbot, which brings a good price.

Population.—In 1741 the village of Ayton feems to have contained about 320 fouls, and the country part of the parifh about the fame number. In 1773 the village contained about 360 fouls: The numbers in the country part were alfo increafed. In 1780 the number of the inhabitants amounted to 1146, of which 420 were in the village, and 726 in the country part of the parifh. In the prefent year, 1790, the number amounted to 1245. The village contains 147 families; there are 202 males and 229 females above ten years of age, and 51 males and 47 females below 10 years of age. The country part of the parifh contains 136 families, which confift of 263 males and 310 females above 10, and 53 males and 90 females below 10. From this ftatement it may be remarked, that during the laft ten years the population of the village has received an addition of 109, while the country part of the parifh has fuffered the decreafe of 10 in its numbers. On the whole,

whole, the increafe of inhabitants within the laft 50 years, may be ftated at above 600.

Village of Ayton.—The village of Ayton is fituated on the banks of the Eye. About 30 new houfes have been feued in it within thefe 15 years; they confift of two or three ftories, and are covered with tyles. The village has been improved by ranging thefe new buildings upon a pleafant floping bank fronting the fouth.

Manufactures.—A paper-mill was lately erected here at confiderable expence. It employs about 70 or 80 work people, and circulates about L. 25 *per* week. The wages earned by the paper-makers are high. This manufacture gives employment to a number of young perfons, who are taken in at eight years of age. There is a wind-mill here, which was a pretty extenfive work. It manufactured a good deal of flour during the American war, but has done little or no bufinefs fince. There are four water-mills in this parifh; one brewery, which does not carry on an extenfive trade; a bleachfield, which was eftablifhed many years ago, and fucceeds: It employs about 7 or 8 hands.

Church and Stipend.—The parifh church appears to be an old edifice, and has lately received feveral improvements, which its former ftate rendered extremely neceffary. The ftipend, including a late augmentation, and the value of the glebe, is about L. 135 *per annum*. The Crown is patron.

Poor.—The number of the poor belonging to this parifh is variable. The heritors and tenants are affeffed to the extent of L. 30 or L. 40 *per annum* for their fupport. To this fund is added one half of the contributions at the church, which,

at

at an average, is about 1 s. 2 d. weekly. The other half is diſtributed under the inſpection of the kirk-ſeſſion in occaſional charities. Part of it, together with the money ariſing from marriages and the uſe of the pall (mort-cloth) is applied to educate poor children and pay church officers. The expence incurred for the maintenance of the parochial poor has increaſed near two thirds during the incumbency of the preſent miniſter The people in general, however, cannot bear the idea of being put on the poor's roll, even when they are in diſtreſs. During a late period of ſcarcity meal was purchaſed for the uſe of poor houſeholders, and ſold at a very moderate price ; but few applied for the benefit of this aid, except thoſe who were accuſtomed to receive charity.

Price of Proviſions.—The price of butcher meat is from $3\frac{1}{4}$ d. to 4 d. *per* lb. Engliſh weight ; it has advanced about 1 d. *per* lb. within theſe 6 or 8 years. The price of pork is variable. Haddocks, which ſold formerly at 4 d. or 6 d. *per* ſcore, now often bring as much a piece. A gooſe is ſold here for 2 s. ; a pair of ducks for 1 s. 3 d. ; a pair of hens for 1 s. 6 d. ; a turkey for 2 s. 6 d. ; butter ſells for 7 d. and cheeſe for 4 d *per* lb. The prices of grain may be aſcertained from the fiars of the county.

Wages.—The wages of a labourer are 1 s. a day ; a carpenter's and maſon's, 1 s. 4 d. ; a taylor's, 1 s. Threſhing of corn is uſually paid by what is termed *lot*, *i. e.* 1 boll is allowed for every 25 bolls that are threſhed. The wages of a maſon and his labourer, &c. are generally ſettled at ſo much a rood. A hind receives 2 bolls of barley, 1 boll of peaſe, and 10 bolls of oats ; he has a cow's graſs, a houſe and yard, and as much ground as will ſerve to plant a firlot of potatoes. He is likewiſe allowed what coals he may have occaſion for in his family,

mily, paying only the prime coft, which is about 2 s. 8 d. *per* cart load, including the tolls; the carriage is equal to 4 s. *per* load. The hind's wife reaps in harveft for the houfe. He has alfo L. 1 allowed for fheep's grafs. A man fervant receives from L. 5 to L. 7 *per annum,* with bed and board; a maid fervant from L. 2 to L. 4 *per annum.*

Sectaries.—There are feveral fectaries in this parifh. The firft was a fociety of Antiburghers. Their number is very fmall. Their minifter is provided with a very good houfe, and receives from them, perhaps, about L. 40 *per annum.* There is alfo a Burgher meeting-houfe in the village, rather of a better appearance than the other; the fect of Seceders who attend it are more numerous than the former, and of principles more accommodating to the times. They alfo provide a houfe for their minifter, and allow him, probably, L. 60 or L. 70 *per annum.* Both thefe houfes have been built fince the 1773. Though a confiderable number have attached themfelves to the different fectaries, yet, being compofed of the inferior ranks of the people, their defection has not diminifhed the contribution for the parochial poor. Little is allotted by them to the maintenance of their own poor; yet they contribute with zeal, many of them with liberality ill fuited to their circumftances, for the fupport of their ecclefiaftical eftablifhment.

Roads.—The roads in the parifh are getting into good repair. The poft road is now made, and fupported by two turnpikes, which were lately erected; one at the extremity of the county towards Eaft Lothian, and the other at Berwick bounds. When they were firft propofed, they met with keen oppofition; but they have fince been univerfally acknowledged to be of fignal benefit to the country. The ftatute

labour

labour is commuted. Putting up the roads to auction, has been the mean of getting them made much cheaper than formerly.

Improvements suggested.—It would be an advantage to this parish, as well as to Eyemouth, if the mail-coach would drop a bag, containing such letters as are addressed to the inhabitants of each, which would relieve them from the expence of sending to Berwick or Press. If the woollen or cotton manufacture were introduced and encouraged here, the condition of the people might be greatly improved. To take the duty off coals carried coast-ways to Eyemouth, as is done at Dunbar (to which port Eyemouth belongs) would greatly promote the establishment of manufactures. This duty yields but a mere trifle to government, and subjects the people here to a state of entire dependence on Northumberland for fuel. As the coal hills adjoining to this part of the country are almost entirely engrossed by one person, it would be rather surprising if he did not avail himself of this advantage, by keeping up the price of so important an article.

Miscellaneous Observations.—The kelp made here is supposed to be about 15 or 20 tons annually. There are some quarries in this parish, the stones of which answer for building; and are supposed to be impregnated with an iron ore. Freestone is confined to a small part of the shore. The free-stone must be transported to the harbour of Eyemouth, and then carried by land. Corn is carried to market in carts, which have been used here for the space of 40 or 50 years. On the hills on the south side of the parish are the remains of two camps, supposed to be Roman or Saxon. Several urns, and broken pieces of armour, have been found here. In the low grounds towards the north-west, are the vestiges of three encampments,

campments, thought to have been Danish or Pictish. History mentions the castle of Ayton, but scarcely any vestiges of it now remain. The names of places seem to be derived chiefly from the Saxon. There is one public, and two private schools in the parish. The established schoolmaster, as is too generally the case, has not a provision adequate to the importance of such a charge. There are two white thread-makers in the parish. There are two or three bridges; one of them was built by aid from government: They are of great utility. Two boats crews only belong to Ayton.

In 1673, there appears to have been 24 heritors, including portioners and feuers, in this parish: In 1790, there are about 14. At the former period, they were more distinguished by family and rank. There were 6 of the name of Home, each of some distinction; now there is only one of that name; their lands having been disposed of by the great heritors. There are, however, several descendants of portioners who still retain their possessions.

The people, in general, are disposed to industry. Since the induction of the present minister there is a very visible change in their mode of living and dress. Though the farms are much higher rented than formerly, yet the tenants are, in every respect, much more expensive than they were 15 years ago. Tradesmen and labourers in the village are addicted to the pernicious habit of using tea. Of late, also, from the low price of whisky, the execrable custom of *dram-drinking* is gaining ground, even among the women of the lower class. Habits so inimical to health, industry, and morals, ought to be checked if possible. Two persons belonging to this parish have been banished from Scotland since the incumbent was settled. He knows only of one person who

has

has been guilty of ſuicide. There is no want of employment
for the people. They ſeem contented with their ſituation
and circumſtances, and are not ſtrangers to the comforts of
life.

This pariſh has ſeveral advantages. It is near markets,
for diſpoſing of grain, cattle, or ſtock on the farms, being
7 miles from Berwick and 2 from Eyemouth. It is at no
great diſtance from coal: The price, however, conſidering
that diſtance, is certainly high. The poſt road to London
goes through the pariſh: And the vicinity of the ſea affords
a good ſupply of moſt kinds of fiſh. The pariſh of Ayton
does much more than ſupply itſelf with proviſions.

UNITED PARISHES OF BONKLE AND PRESTON.

(*County of Berwick.*)

By the Rev. Mr ROBERT DOUGLAS.

Name, Situation, Extent.

THE parifhes of Bonkle and Prefton, were originally two feparate parifhes, but are now united. *Bonkle* is fuppofed to be derived from *bona cella*. It lies in the county of Berwick, prefbytery of Dunfe, and fynod of Kelfo. It is nearly a fquare of fix miles, and contains 8,900 acres.

Soil.—In the high lands towards the Lammermoor hills, the foil is thin, dry, heathy, and poor; but it has of late been much improved by lime. The reft of the parifh, and particularly on the banks of the Whittater, confifts of a fine fertile loam.

Air and Difeafes.—As in moft parts of the eaft of Scotland, the air is very healthy. Formerly the people were very fubject to agues in the fpring; but fince improvements have commenced, and been carried to a very confiderable ftate of perfection, this difeafe has almoft totally difappeared. This effect is attributed to the bogs and fwamps being drained, and to the improvement of the furface.

Quarries.

Quarries—There is whin ſtone in different parts, and good free ſtone quarries upon the banks of Whittater, both very fit for building houſes, and incloſing ground.

Minerals.—A copper mine was diſcovered in Lord Douglas's eſtate, at a ſmall farm called Hoardweel. It was wrought about twelve years ago, by an Engliſh company, and had a very promiſing appearance, the ore being very rich ; but, although the vein continued, it ceaſed to bear metal, and was abandoned. It is thought the trials made to recover it were not ſufficient.

Land Floods.—The river Whittater runs with great rapidity, and at ſome places riſes 15 feet perpendicular above its ordinary channel, overflowing the haughs and carrying off great part of the ſoil. Attempts have been made by ſeveral heritors to make barricadoes, but few of them have been ſucceſsful. A very great flood happened in October 1775, which carried down every bridge, excepting the bridge at Preſton, in this pariſh. They have ſince been rebuilt at very conſiderable expence.

Cattle and Sheep.—The cattle bred in this and the neighbouring pariſhes, particularly in the diſtrict between this and Tweed, are conſiderable in point of number, and as large as any bred in Scotland. But people of ſkill are of opinion, that they are not ſo good as our land can rear, nor of a kind that fatten ſpeedily. Some public ſpirited gentlemen and farmers, have of late purchaſed, at very high prices, ſome fine bulls and cows, from the beſt places, and beſt breeders in England. They have not yet, however, become general. The bulls are let out to the country at two guineas. Sheep is the great ſtaple of the low parts of this pariſh, and of this
county

county in general. They are the English breed introduced
by Mr Bakewell, and since carried on by the Messrs Culleys,
and other eminent breeders, both in Northumberland, and
this county. The criterion of their goodness and sort, is
getting sooner and more easily fat, than any other animal,
bearing a valuable fleece, and enriching the land upon which
they are fed. There are two different ages at which they
are sold; the first when they are about 18 months old, after
the first fleece is taken off, when they are called *dunmotts*, at
which time they usually sell from 24 s. to 34 s. The second
time is after their second fleece is taken off, when they are
called *wedders of the first head*, and are 28 months old, when
they sell from 32 s. to 38 s. each. The fleece weighs from
seven to eight pounds each, and sells from 4 s. 6 d. to 5 s.
The ewes are kept for breeders, and are sold, after having
three lambs, from 24 s. to 34 s. These sheep are bought by
dealers, and driven to Morpeth market, where they are again
sold, and killed at Newcastle, Shields, and Sunderland, for
the use of the coallieries and shipping; and many are driven
to Yorkshire, and farther south. The wool is sold to agents
from Leeds, and other manufacturing towns in Yorkshire;
some is shipped at Berwick for Aberdeenshire, and a small
quantity sent to Edinburgh and Stirling. The best pastures are appropriated for feeding sheep in summer, and
they are mostly fed for five months in winter, upon turnip,
of which very large quantities are raised. An acre of good
pasture, value a guinea, will fatten three; and the average
expence of turnip is 3 d. *per* week, each sheep, when fed to
the highest extent, which for the winter five months is 5 s.
each. It is computed that two ewes rear three lambs. High
prices are paid for the hire of rams of good breeds, viz.
from 10 to 30 guineas is common *per* season. Some have
paid double or more for the season of the best bred rams.
Each

Each ram will impregnate from five to fix ſcore of ewes. It is a certain fact, that no animal follows the properties of the male ſo much as ſheep ; and therefore, the breeder is ſeldom diſappointed. The higheſt breed alſo bear the fineſt wool, though not always the greateſt quantity. Our farmers pay as much attention to the breed of their ſheep, as is paid to the higheſt breed of galloping horſes in England ; and I believe they bring much greater profit.

Agriculture.—As ſoon as the crop is off the ground, and ſometimes before the ſhocks are removed, they begin to plough. They ſow peaſe as early as the ſeaſon will permit ; after that oats, and then barley ; and laſtly turnip, which commonly begins in the laſt week of May, and finiſhes by the firſt of July. They begin to reap in the laſt week of Auguſt, and generally finiſh in the firſt week of October.

Marle and Lime.—There is a great quantity of clay marle along the banks of the Whittater. It was formerly uſed as a manure to great advantage, and poſſeſſed at an average, two-fifths of calcareous matter ; but its operations are very ſlow, though laſting. The obligations in the tenants leaſes, in regard to the rotation of crops, and the obligation of having ſo great a quantity in graſs, at leaſt for the laſt 10 years of a 21 year's leaſe, have induced the farmers to prefer lime as a quick manure, though they are obliged to drive it 15 miles. Marle for raiſing crops of corn will laſt ſix times longer than lime.

Poor.—The poor in this pariſh, as well as every other in this county, are maintained by an aſſeſſment laid on by the heritors themſelves, according to their ſeveral valued rents, one half of which is paid by the heritors, and the

other

other half by the tenants. There are no legacies, and the collections are inconfiderable. There are no begging poor allowed in this county. Two conftables are appointed with falaries, whofe bufinefs is to go through the county, to attend fairs, markets, and public meetings, and take up all gypfies, tinkers, beggars, and diforderly perfons, who cannot give a proper account of themfelves. They are carried before the neareft juftice of peace, who commits them to the county jail for fome days; they are then conducted to the extremity of the county, neareft their own refpective parifhes; and befides the falary, the conftables have 9d. *per* mile, for carrying them to jail, which expence is paid out of the rogue money. By this inftitution the county is kept free from beggars; and very few petty thefts are committed, as people of that defcription have connections together, and know they can fcarcely efcape.

Fuel.—Before the introduction of improvements, the farmers, &c. burned turf, which were principally taken from the Lammermoor hills. But, fince improvements commenced, and the people knew the value of their labour, nothing but coal is ufed. It is all brought from Northumberland, at a diftance of 15 miles, through very bad roads; and confequently driven in fummer, when the Tweed is fordable.

Ploughs.—There are about 50 ploughs in the parifh. They are all chain ploughs, and are drawn by two horfes, without a driver.

Roads.—The roads and bridges in this parifh are better than in moft parts of this county, owing to its not being a great thoroughfare, to the vicinity of materials, and to the attention to having the ftatute labour properly applied. The
roads

roads, in the greateſt and beſt parts of the county, are bad beyond expreſſion, and are a reproach to this rich and thriving diſtrict.

Farms, &c.—The farms in this pariſh are from L. 200 to L. 600 a year. There are but few ſmall farms. The whole pariſh under the Lammermoor hills, as well as the whole low parts of the county, are incloſed, principally with hedge and ditch.

Population.—There has never been any record kept of the population of this pariſh. Since the practice of letting large farms, this pariſh has decreaſed conſiderably in point of numbers of the people. From an exact ſtate of the population, taken November 1790, it ſtands thus :

Number of families -	131
of perſons -	622
of males -	280
of females -	342
below 10 years -	160
from 10 to 20 -	146
from 20 to 50 -	231
from 50 to 70 -	74
from 70 to 100 -	11
Seceders of all denominations - -	130

In Dr Webſter's report the number of ſouls is 691.

Stipend.—The miniſter's ſtipend is 35 bolls of meal, 17 bolls 2 firlots of barley, and L. 485 : 15 Scots; the glebe would rent at L. 20 Sterling; ſo that the value of the ſtipend may amount to L. 90 Sterling, yearly.

School.

School.—The schoolmaster's salary, school-fees, and his emoluments as precentor and session-clerk, amount to L. 12 : 16. The heritors employ him for collecting the poor's money, and the statute road money; and for these he has L. 3 : 15. In this parish there are no Roman Catholics or Episcopalians; no lawyers, writers, physicians, surgeons, or apothecaries.

PARISH of CHANNELKIRK,

(COUNTY OF BERWICK, SYNOD OF MERSE AND TIVIOT-
DALE, PRESBYTERY OF LAUDER.)

By the Rev. Mr THOMAS MURRAY.

Name, Extent, Surface, Climate, &c.

THIS pariſh does not furniſh much room for ſtatiſtical inveſtigation, and the obſervations which occur reſpecting it, may be comprehended within narrow bounds. The preſent name of the pariſh is evidently modern, and is happily deſcriptive of the nature of the ſoil, which is in general a light thin earth, on a deep bed of ſandy gravel. In our records, which are preſerved as far back as 1650, the name of the pariſh is ſpelled *Chingelkirk*. *Chingle*, I preſume, is the old Scotch word, ſynonimous to the modern term Channel *. The extent of this pariſh is conſiderable,

---

* Dr FORD, in his account of the pariſh of Lauder, has given an etymology different from this. He ſays, that the ancient name of the pariſh
was *Children's kirk*, becauſe dedicated to the children of Bethlehem, or the
Holy Innocents. As the Doctor, however, has given us no authority in
ſupport

derable, being full 6 miles in length, and nearly 5¼ in breadth. Its figure is nearly circular. The furface of the country is in general hilly, particularly to the W. and N. where the parifh is bounded by a high ridge of hills, which divides the counties of Eaft and Mid Lothian from Berwickfhire. The hills are covered with heath, and all paftured with the old Scotch breed of black-faced fheep. The parifh is well watered by a variety of ftreamlets, which fall from our mountains, the union of which forms the river *Leader*, or *Lauder*. From the height of the fituation, and the light dry nature of the foil, the climate is remarkably healthy. Epidemic and chronic difeafes are unknown. As a proof of the falubrity of the climate, the laft incumbent held the benefice 42 years, and his predeceffor for no lefs a period than 52. The climate, for 6 months of the year, is however extremely cold, fubject to fevere frofts, and great falls of fnow.

Soil, Cultivation, Produce, &c.—There are in the parifh from 1500 to 2000 acres of land in tillage. The foil, as I have already faid, is in general a light dry earth, on a deep bed of fandy gravel. It is well adapted to the culture of turnip, potatoes and clover. The following is the ufual rotation of crops on the beft land : 1. oats ; 2. turnips ; 3. barley or oats ; 4. clover, &c. Agriculture has made a wonderful progrefs within thefe laft 20 years in this parifh. This, like moft other improvements in fociety, has been chiefly owing to the fkill and attention of an individual. The gentleman to whom I allude, is Mr Robert Hogarth, tenant

---

fupport of this opinion, and as I find no fuch thing is mentioned in Spottifwood's appendix to Hope's Minor Practicks, I am difpofed to confider it as a mere conjecture, and am of opinion that the obvious etymology firft mentioned is the beft.

tenant in Carfrae *. It is about 25 years since he came to this part of the country, from the eastern boundary of Berwickshire. At that period, our farmers were total strangers to the culture of turnip, and very little acquainted with the modern and new approved method of meliorating land by lime and sown grasses, &c. He introduced the culture of turnip and clover; and by the success which attended his exertions, the neighbouring farmers were soon convinced of the superiority of this new method of managing land, to the old fashioned practice of exhausting and ruining the soil, by a multiplicity of white crops in succession. The culture of turnip and clover is now accordingly become very general, and in no place of Berwickshire is that useful plant produced in greater quantity, or of better quality, on the same extent of land. Mr Hogarth has also lately introduced the white faced long woolled sheep, from Northumberland; and notwithstanding the coldness of the climate, they promise, from the trials already made, to answer extremely well. It must, however, be observed, that they are not pastured on the heath covered hills, where, from experiments in similar latitudes, they are not found to thrive. In summer, they are fed within enclosures, where the soil has been highly improved; and in winter, are prepared by turnip, for the market. The introduction of the potatoes was still later than that of turnips. I am assured, it it not above 14 years since they were planted in the fields. They are found to suit the nature of our soil remarkably well; no where are they produced of better quality, and in seasons, when the corn is high priced, constitute fully the half of the food of our cottagers. There are about 30 farmers in the parish. The farms are in general small, excepting those

---

* This belongs to the Marquis of Tweeddale.

thofe belonging to the Marquis of Tweeddale, which are pretty extenfive. This Nobleman is by much the greateft proprietor in the parifh; his property being equal to one-fourth of the whole. The number of ploughs in the parifh is about 50. They are all of the Englifh conftruction, or what are known by the name of *Small's* ploughs *.

Number of Black Cattle, Sheep, &c.—The number of young cattle annually reared, I have not been able to afcertain, but I am well informed, that not fewer than 100 bullocks and cows are yearly fed on turnip for the butcher. Of the black-faced fheep, which pafture on heath, there may be from 6000 to 7000. The number of black cattle is from 400 to 500.

Population.

* With refpect to the agriculture of the parifh, it may be in general obferved, that the quantity of grain produced, in good years, is confiderably more than fufficient to fupport the inhabitants; but in cold and wet feafons, our oats and barley do not ripen properly, and are often very ill got. In harvefts 1782 and 1783, the fituation of the farmers, and inhabitants in general, was truly deplorable. It was the end of December before the harveft was finifhed, after the greateft part of the crop had been deftroyed by froft and fnow. Without a fupply from other quarters, a real famine would have taken place; our farmers were obliged to buy the whole of their feed-corn for crop 1783, from the eaft parts of the county, and from the Lothians. Some Dutch oats were alfo brought from Leith, at an exorbitant price. The *red oats*, fo called, I prefume, from their colour, prevail very much in the parifh at prefent. They are found to fuit the foil and climate, better than any early fpecies that has hitherto been tried. They ripen as foon as the Dutch and Polifh; are more luxuriant on the ground; and not fo apt to fall by the wind. The principal crops in this parifh are oats and rough bear; peafe grow very readily on our light foil, but from the coldnefs of the climate, very feldom attain complete maturity; oats are fown as early in March as the froft will allow; bear from the middle of April to the end of May. The time of harveft is very uncertain; it is very feldom general, however, before the end of September.

Population.—According to Dr Webſter's report, the number of ſouls, in 1755, was 531. The population, as appears from the records of the pariſh, is much the ſame that it has been for 100 years paſt, and amounts to about 600 ſouls. The annual number of births, for 50 years paſt, is 18 ; of deaths, 13 ; of marriages, 6. We have no inſtances on record of remarkable longevity. Many, however, have reached their 90th year, and there are ſome perſons now living, of that age.

The tradeſmen and mechanicks are,

Weaver,	-	1	Wright,	- -	1
Tailors,	- -	6	Maſons,	- -	3
Shoemakers,	-	2	Millers,	- -	3
Smiths,	- -	2	Gardener,	- -	1

Rent, Heritors, &c.—The land-rent of the pariſh is at preſent about L. 2000 a-year ; but as the moſt extenſive farms are at preſent low rented, it might eaſily riſe to L. 3000 a-year. There are 12 heritors, 3 of whom only are reſident ; George Somerville, Eſq; of Airhouſe, Henry Torrans of Kirktonhill, James Juſtice of Juſticehall.

Miſcellaneous Obſervations.—Peat and turf, of which there is plenty in the pariſh, was formerly the only fuel uſed by the inhabitants. But ſince the public roads were made, and kept in good repair, coal, although brought from a diſtance of 12 miles, is found by our proprietors and farmers, to be on the whole the cheapeſt fuel. This change is to be attributed to the advanced price of labour, which makes the expenſe of procuring peat and turf, when every thing is conſidered, greater than that of coal *.

Stipend,

---

* The wages of houſehold ſervants, employed in huſbandry, are from L. 7 to L. 8 Sterling annually, beſides victuals; female ſervants receive from

Stipend, Poor, &c.—The Earl of Marchmont is patron of the parifh. The living confifts of L. 600 Scots, and 3 chalders of victual, half oats, half barley. The glebe confifts of nearly 9 Englifh acres of land, but the one half lying detached almoft a mile from the other, and the whole being unenclofed, it is of very inconfiderable value to the minifter. The living, glebe included, is not worth more than L. 84 Sterling a-year; as the incumbent intends to raife a procefs for an augmentation of ftipend, he wifhes thefe facts to be generally known. The church is built in the old Popifh form of a crofs. When it was erected is uncertain. It underwent a thorough repair in the year 1702. The manfe and offices were rebuilt 7 years ago, and are at prefent in good repair.—The number of poor on the parifh roll is at prefent 12. The annual expenfe of fupporting them amounts to L. 30 a-year, which fum is raifed by collections in the church, and by affeffments on the heritors.

Manners

from L. 3, 10s. to L. 4 yearly. Day-labourers get from 9 d. to 10 d. a-day, with victuals; carpenters, 1 s.; mafons, 1 s. 2 d.; tailors, 8 d. Dalkeith is the market-town to which our farmers carry their grain; it is diftant about 14 miles. Their carts return loaded with coal or lime. We have butcher meat of all kinds from Dalkeith; and in fome feafons of the year, are tolerably well ferved from Lauder, which is not above 6 miles diftant from us. The prices vary at different feafons, according as the markets are fupplied. Beef, was laft Chriftmas as high as 6 d. the lb. Mutton, 4½ d. Lamb has not been below 4 d. the lb. all this feafon. The want of fea and river fifh is much felt in this part of the country. The ftreamlets which fall from our mountains, indeed, abound with very fine trout; but the infamous practices of taking them with nets, and deftroying them with lime, which have for fome years paft been very prevalent, have greatly diminifhed the different fpecies of this excellent fifh.

Manners and Morals of the People.—The preſent incumbent having been but a few months reſident in the
pariſh, has not yet had time to be individually acquainted
with all his hearers; but from the general acquaintance
he has obtained of them, he has no heſitation to pronounce
them a frugal, induſtrious, and happy ſet of people. They
live harmoniouſly with each other, and ſupport their families decently on the fruits of honeſt induſtry. One feature
in their character, which, in an age of levity and irreligion
like the preſent, deſerves to be particularly remarked, is the
regular attendance of all ranks on public worſhip, and their
decent behaviour when thus employed. Will the writer
of this paper be ſuſpected of enthuſiaſm, when he aſſigns
this as one cauſe of the induſtry and comfort which prevail
among the people at large?

Antiquities.—It is probable that Channelkirk, when
Popery was the Eſtabliſhed Religion of the country, was a
place of conſiderable note. The memorials, however, are
few; a perennial ſpring of excellent ſoft water, about a
quarter of a mile W. from the kirk, is called the well of
the Holy Water Cleugh, a name which ancient ſuperſti-
tion had conferred. The Girthgate, that is, the road which
the monks kept in their way from Melroſe Abbey to Edinburgh, paſſes through the weſtern boundary of the pariſh.
It is a broad green path, on which the ſurrounding heath
never grows. On this road, a few miles due W. of the
church, are to be ſeen the ruins of an old building, commonly known by the name of the Reſh Law, or Reſtlaw
Haw. Tradition tells us, that this was the place where
the monks and pilgrims ſtopped, or reſted for refreſhment,
it being about halfway between Melroſe and Edinburgh.
A great many Pictiſh and Scottiſh encampments are to be
ſeen in this pariſh and the neighbourhood; they are all of

a round or oval figure, and are called rings by the common people. The Roman encampments were fquare or rectangular, but there is none of them in this part of the country.

Advantages and Difadvantages.—The chief advantage of this fituation is a contiguity to the public road, which leads from Edinburgh to London. It is kept in excellent repair by the money collected at the toll bars, and by the ftatute-labour commuted into money, according to the number of fervants and horfes kept by the farmers; without this, improvement of every kind would have been impracticable. The difadvantages of our fituation are, the coldnefs of our climate, and confequently our frequent cold and wet harvefts. Were the practice of enclofing land and planting more general, the climate would be confiderably improved. Clumps of fir and white wood, judicioufly difpofed on the heights, would fhelter our flocks from the ftorms of winter, and defend our habitations from the N. and N. W. winds, to which they are at prefent much expofed. Our landed gentlemen are beginning to fee the advantages of enclofing and planting; about 500 acres are already enclofed, and I doubt not but this improvement will advance with confiderable rapidity. This part of the county of Berwick, from the number of fheep which it fupports, and its vicinity to the public road, feems well calculated for the eftablifhment of an woollen manufacture; and from the prefent flourifhing ftate of that which was eftablifhed many years ago at Galafhiels, the Noblemen and gentlemen of Lauderdale might promife themfelves the higheft advantages from a fimilar erection in the neighbourhood of Lauder.

THE
STATISTICAL ACCOUNT
OF
SCOTLAND.

PARISH of CHIRNSIDE.

(COUNTY OF BERWICK, SYNOD OF MERSE AND TIVIOT-
DALE, PRESBYTERY OF CHIRNSIDE.)

By the Rev. WALTER ANDERSON, *D. D.*

Situation, Extent, Estates, &c.

CHIRNSIDE is the name of a considerable village
and parish, in the shire of *Berwick*, vulgarly called the *Merse*, but, more properly, the *March*, upon the
E. border of Scotland. It is also the seat of a presbytery;
and, as such, it is stated in the list of the presbyteries *,
instituted in the reign of James VI. 1581; when the Dio-
cesan Court, or Synod of Jedburgh, now called that of
Merse

* Vide Calderwood's Church History, fol. edit. p. 100.

Merse and Tiviotdale, confisted of only four presbyteries; viz. that of Kelso, Dunse, Chirnside and Jedburgh.

It has no natural and well marked boundaries. The large stream of Whittadder, or Whitewater, terminates it upon the S., and a deep morass, called Bellymire, is its confine, in the opposite quarter. The elevated and expanded hill of Chirnside, and the contiguous one of Idington, when taken together with their wide skirts, may be reckoned as comprehensive of the whole parish. The figure is oval, and its longest line, extending eastward from Whittadder bridge to the extremities of Foulden and Ayton parishes, is computed to measure $3\frac{1}{2}$ English miles, or under 4. Its greatest breadth will hardly reach to 3. Upon a calculation, the number of acres in the parish, will amount to about 6523. The whole land, if we except 5 or 6 small portions, consists now of 5 estates; two of which, Chirnside and Idington, are separate baronies, and both of considerable antiquity *.

The lands of Ninewells are next in valuation after Idington. The 4th estate, called East Mains, and holding of the barony, is the property of John Molle, Esq., a lineal descendant of an old family of that name in Tiviotdale, and parish of Morbattle. The 5th is that of Blackburn in the Mire, the property of Mrs. Bruce, the relict

---

* The former, to which the largest territory belongs, had, probably, become an appendage of the lordship of Home, when the chief of that family, Lord Warden of the East March, after being engaged in the revolt of Francis, Earl of Bothwel, had returned to his duty, and obtained, as his share in that forfeited chieftain's spoils, a grant of the Abbey of Coldingham, anno 1596. The donation would involve claims to, or, at least, facilitate the acquisition of lands in the nighbourhood of that well endowed priory. Hence, the lands of Ninewells appear, from the charters, not to hold of the barony of Chirnside, but of the lordship of Home.

relict of David Bruce, Esq., who resided in Fife. Of these heritors, 3 have present residence, William Hall, Esq. of Whitehall, the principal proprietor, and patron of the parish, Joseph Home, Esq. of Ninewells, and the above named heritor of East Mains. The barony of Idington, in the beginning of this century, possessed by a Sir Andrew Lauder, of the Valleyfield family, has been, for above 50 years back, the property of the Hays of Drummelzier, whose present representative is Robert Hay, Esq., resident at Dunse Castle, the usual seat of his family.

Name, &c.—The etymology of the name *Chirnside*, is of somewhat difficult explication ; yet if we take its first syllable to be Gaelic, as the other is Saxon, or English, its import and propriety may be understood. The word *cairn*, well known to denote in Erse, the rude sepulchral monument of stones, raised by the Saxons and Danes, in honour of their warriors who fell in battle, is written, in some specimens we have of that language, with a *ch* ; and, at large, *charne*, or *chern* *.

The

* In this orthography, if the proper one, in Erse, the change of the open vowel *a* or *e*, into an i, which is more mute, may be easily accounted for, from the abbreviated sound being most affected in common discourse. Chernside would be readily pronounced Chirnside. But there is a difficulty in understanding how the harsh and uncouth pronunciation of the *ch* could be admitted in that word, when it is generally avoided in the dialect of the country. The fact is, that, although the book-learned, and better sort, do adopt it, the common people almost universally agree in its rejection. They pronounce *Shirnside*, as (turning the *ch* into an *sh*) they do in shance, shoice, shair, shopin, sheese, &c. &c. And even although they often hear the English pronunciation of church, they can make no more of it than *surch*. The name of *Shirnside*, or *Chernside*, therefore applied to the village, may be presumed to signify a town, or place hard by the *chern*, or kern ; the *ch* in the Saxon alphabet being founded often like a *k*.

The veſtige of a cairn, although not now in accumulation, but the raiſed ground, rather hollowed out in the middle, is obſervable on the eaſtern, and higheſt ſummit of the hill ; near to which the row of the village, on that ſide, begins. Idington Hill, which, with a ſmall interval, is a continuation of the ſame ridge, ſhows yet more apparently, the place and remains of two cairns. The heaped ſtones of one of them, were but lately carried off ; and, it is known, that, in their firſt demolition, about 40 years ago, a ſtone coffin, its figure ſaid to be an oblong ſquare, was taken up entire, and conveyed to a gentleman's place in the neighbourhood. In the track of Lammermuir, between Chirnſide and Dunglaſs, ſeveral of theſe cairns were, of late years, very conſpicuous, as they are found moſt numerous upon the E. coaſt of Scotland, adjacent to that of Northumberland, and of Yorkſhire, often invaded and occupied by the Danes and Saxons.

Chirnſide Hill, and Proſpects from it, &c.——Among the ſeveral eminences which disjoined from the edge of Lammermuir, on the N., project into the Low Country of Berwickſhire, Chirnſide Hill is a moſt remarkable one. It is diſtinguiſhed from others of them, by its elevation and ſemicircular aſpect to the S. joined with the great expanſion of its ſummit, and its gradual declination to Whittadder water. It commands, as moſt of them do, the view of a country, the richeſt in ſoil (with the exception of the Carſes) of any in Scotland ; and, we may add, in its preſent ſtate of culture and fertility, not inferior to the beſt improved lands of England ; unleſs we take into the account the forced gardens and nurſeries around the metropolis, and ſome meadows, glutted with manure, or formed out of ſwamps in the fenny counties,

ties. The landfcape beheld, is that of a plain, waved
with long ridges, running chiefly in one direction, and
of more than 25 miles extent from the Bay of Berwick
to the Tiviotdale Hills, on the W.; while directly S.,
and at almoft the fame diftance, the famed hills and
chaces of Cheviot form a boundary truly grand. About
60 or 70 years ago, this profpect, although ftriking and
noble over the country, was a naked one, and had little
or nothing of the beauty arifing from extenfive agriculture, enclofed fields or plantations. If fome groves or
ftrips of trees marked, here and there, the feats of the
gentry or nobles, befides thefe, and a few enclofures,
joined with them, hardly any thing but wafte land, or
the pooreft culture, was difcoverable. Nature, indeed,
wore a robe that indicated a deep foil. The uncultivated grounds produced immenfe tracks of heath, over-
fpread with thick furze, or tall whins, and, in fome drier
places, with broom; which, in the fpring and through
the fummer, fhed the golden gleam of their flowers, and
their fragrance, all around.

The eye of a fpectator, on Chirnfide Hill, now has in
profpect a country, of the extent defcribed, all of it in
remarkable cultivation; the corn fields and pafture lands,
almoft every where, enclofed and divided by hedges and
ditches. Large plantations not only appear around the
gentlemens feats, but reach, in feveral places, to the
extremities of their lands; fo that they feem to be con-
joined to each other. Of fuch a pleafant fcene, we have
here an immediate exhibition. The plantations of Whitehall, forming a quadrangle, with fome contraction on its
E. and W. fides, and running on in lines of half a mile,
advance up the hill, from near the banks of Whittadder to the croft lands of the village, now turned, in

                                                    part,

part, to a rich and beautiful ſheep-park. Between the W. ſide of that plantation, and where the hedge-row of Ninewells approaches to it, there is ſeen, in the open-ing, a ſection of Whittadder, to which Blackadder-water, there near its confluence, comes forward as a tangent. A little above both theſe plantations, and where a grove of trees intercepts to a ſpectator, at the manſe and other houſes in the ſame declivity of the hill, the diſtinct view of Whittadder, that clear ſtream is caſt into curious and picture ſque appearances. In one ſtation, it glitters be-tween the ſtems of the trees, reflecting intermiſſive and tremulous beams of light. In another, it ſhows, like a bright edging or half coronet, to their green tops. In a third, where the trees do not interpoſe, it is thrown into a ſhining curve. The high banks are ſeen, in con-tiguity to thoſe of Blackadder-water. The plantation and encloſures around Allanbank houſe conſpire with thoſe of Blackadder to complete the viſta, and ſhut the ſcene *.

Village,

---

* The hill of Chirnſide, beſides the views and plantations, poſſeſſes, in almoſt the whole of the extent, a natural fertility of ſoil, although with very conſiderable difference and variation; and it contains alſo great and valuable ſtores of free ſtone and marl. The former lies, in many places, not more than 2 or 3 feet under the ſurface. Its colour is between red and white, and the grain ſuch as renders it not too hard to be wrought by the chiſel, yet very durable. Its chief bed appears in the middle of the ſouth ſide of the hill, where the old path-way aſcending it, is, in a manner, turned, the moſt part of its length, into a rugged pavement. As quarries of ſtone riſe towards the hill, the marl banks are formed, moſtly, in the declivities and dips it takes towards Whittadder; the ſloping grounds on the ſides of which are entire accummulations of its ſtrata; being all either of the clayey kind, or the more lumpiſh and ſtony. Of ſhell marl, no traces appear; nor is it found in the neigh-bourhood, nor any where in the ſhire, but in very ſmall quantities. The

former

Village, Agriculture, &c.—The line of the village
runs, as it has done for various generations, in two
rows of houses, E. and W., over the broad summit of
the hill, to the length of more than half a mile. Another row of them, not so compact, descends the hill in
a S. direction. Departing from the former, at an opening near the middle, called the *corss*, and properly the
cross, it has the church for its termination. A little
aside from the other houses in this line, called the Kirk-
gate, stands the manse, with the glebe-ground on three
sides of it, at the distance of about 100 yards, or more,
from the church, in a lower situation. Before the division of the lands of the barony, into the separate
shares of its proprietors in the 1740, and for many
years after that period, the village houses made that
mean appearance common to all others in the country.
Reared at the expense of the landholders, and furnished
gratis to the farmers, or, at a very small rent, to other
tenants, they were of such construction, in their materials and dimensions, as, in comparison with those now
built, we would call the best of them hovels, or huddles
of stone, clay and wood. Until the late Mr. Hall,
clerk of Session, erected his two pavilions as office-houses
to a future mansion, and the deceased Mr. Home of
Ninewells, in the year 1745, built the present dwelling-
house of his family, and some repairs were made on
that

former is of several colours; light, grey, pale, blue, and dark; and
some whitish and red. It proves equally good in each of these colours,
when soft; at least, with the exception of the last one, which rather
participates of sand. As the stony sort is often found very hard, it has
been taken, even by gentlemen acquainted with its ordinary appearance,
for common stone, and built into fences. The total ruin of them, in 2
or 3 years, discovered, to their surprise, the mistake they had made.
Its application as a manure, will be afterward considered.

that of Eaſt Mains, no edifice of a modern ſtructure was
to be ſeen in the whole pariſh *.

We

* The church, indeed, had its low walls and its ſteeple of a tower-
like form, built with free ſtone, bedded with lime; and its 2 ailes compoſed of rough aſhlar. The caſtle, or ſtrong houſe of Idington, now
quite demoliſhed, was of the compilement of all the old towers, partly
of free and whin ſtones, and ſome lime joined with clay mortar. The
houſes of the inferior heritors and portioners of land differed little from
thoſe of the farmers, into the compoſition of which free ſtone or lime
hardly entered. The manſe, as it ſtood at the deceaſe of the late miniſter in the 1755, humbly reſembled them in its form, covered with
thatch, and with a deep *cume-ceil;* in the ſecond floor, it had no more
than 36 feet of wall for all its length, unleſs what was called an outer-
houſe, or kitchen, made up of *cat and clay,* was reckoned a good part
of it. Before the barony of Chirnſide was divided among the heritors,
in conſequence of a decree pronounced by the Court of Seſſion in the
1740, it is to be obſerved, that there were no outfield farms, excepting
thoſe belonging to the three mills in the pariſh. The village, like others
in the country, comprehended all the houſes and cottages appertaining to
the ſeveral proprietors, great and ſmall. Adjacent to the manſion-houſe of
ſome of the former, there was what was called the mains farm, or that of
his domain or houſehold. Hence, as the land was in time parcelled out
into ſeveral farms, ſo many of them diſtinguiſhed only by their poſition in
different quarters, are known here, and in other pariſhes, by the common
deſignation of mainſes. In the barony, at the period mentioned, there
were only three of thoſe farms, and another in that of Idington. During the continuance of the blended property of the ſeveral heritors, the
further extenſion of farms and ſteadings was prevented by the common
property they had in the outfields. Of theſe, the only uſe which could
be made was that of a paſturage for all the cattle and ſheep of the village. Upon the remembrance of ſome old people ſtill living, the particular account of them is ſaid to have been, 63 ſcore of ſheep, and 13
of black cattle; and the whole number of horſes is reckoned, not ſo
exactly, at 60. The value of one ſheep's paſture was 8d.; of an ox
or cow 20d.; and of a horſe 2s. 6d. Beſides the common moor adjacent
to the village, a commonalty, running in a certain track ſeveral miles
into Lammermuir, appertained to the barony of Chirnſide. The privilege of it is known to have been uſed in the late miniſter's time, who
claimed upon it the paſturage of ſome lambs or ſheep.

We may further judge of the general poor condition of
the arable land (except the S. croft, which was let in acres)
that, in the sworn valuation of it, the best, or infield
part, was rated in the decree of division at 5s.   The
estimate was so minutely exact, as to include various
rates, from that highest one to the lowest, at 1½d. the
acre.   This last, indeed, respected the most barren and
scalpy point of the hill, so incumbered with large whin
stones, as to be thought incapable of culture.   For the
old arable, or S. croft, which was, as in other places of
the village, tilled land, the tenants of acres, or portioners of an acre, paid from 6s. and 7s. to 10s. ; a rent as
high in those times, as when now they pay 30s   This is
not to be considered as occasioned altogether by the lower value of money, and its greater circulation among the
inferior ranks of people.   An acre of land could not
then, by any known art or industry, be made to produce what it now does ; not so much from the increased
fertility of the soil, as from the more advantageous uses
to which its fertility can now be turned; by a crop of
potatoes, or of red clover, or turnip, being joined to
one of corn, even in the same little field *.

From

* Instead of those late and signal improvements in agriculture, it appears, that one stated method of ploughing, and the same succession of
corn crops, being here, and all over the country, invariably observed ;
every attempt to a better practice was restrained, when the use of marl
or lime, as a manure, was unknown, and that of dung was the sole one ;
a certain quantity of it arising from the confinement of the cattle during
winter, could only be obtained.   Scantily it served to keep the acres of
the S. croft, and the infield of the N. in any tolerable heart.   The outfield had no other benefit, but that of being fallowed ; which, in those
days, amounted to no more than giving the ground a ploughing or two ;
and then, after an exhausting crop, resigning it to its natural produce,
which was only a more abundant one of weeds.   In consequence of the
old

From what has been ſaid of the village and barony of Chirnſide, previous to the diviſion of the lands, according to

old run-ridge, the arable, and the intermixed property in the outfield, inconveniencies, even in the ordinary courſe of the land tillage, were neceſſarily incurred. Adapted to the ſtate of the country, under the policy of the feus, and calculated for common defence, eſpecially in the conſtant predatory wars carried on in the borders of the two kingdoms, it embarraſſed rather than promoted the culture of the fields. The acres, and ſmaller lots of the arable, were laid out in ſuch a manner, that balks, or ſtrips of untilled ground, being interpoſed between eve-ry 5 or 6 ridges, a waſte of the beſt land was thus made for the ſake of marches, not only between the grounds of the different proprietors, but amidſt the lots and ſubdiviſions of acres, into which they were caſt. In the ſhape of the ridges, no alteration, howſoever proper, could be at-tempted; and all the difference of the operations of the plough, con-ſiſted in taking either a deeper or ſhallower furrow, or a wider or cloſer one. The unalterable curvature of the ridges had a tendency to collect moiſture in all flats or dips of the ground. Within the compaſs of the acres, and their diviſions, no uſeful drains could be formed. In the out-fields, they were often impracticable, from interjections of ſeparate pro-perty, or the boundaries of it being indiſtinctly aſcertained. In ſuch circumſtances, it was no wonder that the huſbandmen of thoſe days, whom we are now too ready to accuſe, not only of want of ſkill, but of an in-dolent and obſtinate adherence to their old cuſtoms, would find it very difficult to make new or uncommon exertions. That they were tar-dy, in general, may be underſtood, from their having certain days, or weeks at leaſt, marked out, eſpecially in the ſpring ſeaſon, for com-mencing their labours. Their ploughs drawn by more oxen than horſes, both but poorly fed through the winter, could not accelerate their work. It is to be obſerved, that the tradeſmen in the village, who had por-tions of acres, either hired their ploughings of the farmers, or elſe con-joining not only the horſes, but the cows they had among them, made ſhift, with a common or borrowed plough, to perform more thriftily, if not ſo properly, the tillage required. An old ſaying, retailed about the time of making the bear ſeed, is an evidence that the ſeaſon of it was more apt to be poſtponed than anticipated. " It is not too late," it was ſaid, " when the leaves of the aſh cover the *pyet's* (*i. e.* magpie's neſt." The ſcreaming of this noiſome bird, at the building her neſt on her favourite tree, is ſeldom heard ſooner than about or after the middle of June.

to the shares of the greater and smaller proprietors, it is evident, that impediments were laid in the way of any improvements in agriculture, or increase of population. The decree of division was the first step that led to views of the former, as it put it in every heritor's power to cast his estate into the best shape he could for melioration. The many banks of clay marl had, indeed, attracted the attention of one or two of the gentlemen proprietors, and some feeble trials of it, as manure, had been made by them; but from want of proper knowledge of its qualities, or of sufficient perseverance in the labour it required, nothing of consequence was effectuated. What was done by the late Mr. Hall, within his enclosures, served, however, as a pattern and encouragement to other heritors, to engage in the experimental work; and it happened, fortunately, not only for the better agriculture in the parish, but of the neighbourhood, that two gentlemen, the late Mr. Home of Ninewells, and Mr. Molle of East Mains, found it convenient, to take their whole lands into their own management; a circumstance requisite, when new methods of culture, or new manures, are to be tried in any part of the country, before the tenants can be supposed to assume them into practice. These proprietors became real farmers of their estates; and residing constantly in the country, not only improved their own knowledge in agriculture, but soon taught the tenants, near them, to correct various defects and errors attending its ordinary course. This was done with the more effect, as the enterprises of these gentlemen were gradually carried on; and, in point of expense, little exceeded what the farmers, who had any considerable stock, could afford. From them, lessons were taken of more assiduous, and earlier ploughing; of straight, and closer ridges;

of

of water furrowing; of feed well winnowed, or changed, and the more effectual working of the lands in fallow.

The beds of marl, fo precious in eftimation by the gentlemen, did not correfpond to what the tenants expected from the ufe of it, as a manure. 300 loads of it required to an acre of ground, was found an infuperable labour : however great its ultimate benefit was underftood to be, its lumpy and hard fubftance did not diffolve, fo as to incorporate thoroughly with the foil, in lefs than 4 or 5 years ; a return too tardy to be waited for, by thofe who had their annual rents to pay. Only 2 or 3 of the ableft farmers in the country, who had long, and eafy tacks, ventured to continue, in a certain extent, the ufage of it ; others, who had come under engagements to marl 2 or 3 acres, in the courfe of a year, either failed in the performance, or importuned their landlord for a relaxation from it *.

If

* The difcovery and proof of the prolific power and quick effect of lime, efpecially upon new lands, gave hopes of its being adopted in place of marl, to the equal contentment of the proprietors and tenants. Although the lime was not to be got nearer than from the Berwick kilns, or thofe on the other fide of the Tweed, both of them at the diftance of 10 or 11 miles, yet the quantity of it neceffary to an acre being only 10 or 12 cart loads, taken up in fhells, which, if well burnt, produced the double in flack lime, the difadvantage of the carriage appeared to be compenfated. But, ftill, the purchafe-money being added to the carriage of the lime, rendered the expenfe of both too heavy for the tenants; who, not yet affured of all the benefit of the lime *manure*, were not difpofed to engage in it, but upon certain terms, with their mafters. When leafes were entered into between them, a compromife commonly took place about the lime to be laid upon the lands; a fixed quantity of which being carried home by the former, was to be paid for by the latter. Much to the advantage of the tenants, who lived at no greater diftance from the lime kilns than Chirnfide, as this agreement was, the benefit of it was not taken to the extent it might have

been :

If the more abundant crops of corn, confequent to the melioration of the foil, had not been followed with a rife of the value of that commodity, the tenants in the county of Berwick, would hardly have been in any better circumftances than thofe in the pooreft Lowlands of Scotland. It has been obferved, what fhifts they were often put to, even when agriculture was in the loweft ftate, about difpofing of their ground to any advantage. The average price of every kind of it, was confiderably below that of the Lothians. The cuftom had long obtained of having a larger firlot, than the ftandard one ; and, as the quantity of corn was increafed by better cultivation, and manure, they found it neceffary to allow the gratuity of a boll

to

been : fo common and natural is the fear and doubt about the fuccefs of any new fcheme to thofe who, by the failure, may incur irreparable lofs. Some tenants would run no hazards until they faw fuller proofs of the fertilizing quality of the lime. Others, blundering in their manner of applying it, threw it upon wet ground, or buried the fubftance under deep furrows. But thefe miftakes being corrected, and the fructifying power of the lime becoming more and more vifible, the tenants were fatisfied with fmaller allowances of it in gratuity ; and the more enterterprifing of them hefitated not to purchafe it. The change made by it upon unopened lands, excited a demand for large outfield farms, in preference to the confined infield. The beft of the former, and what included fome of the latter, generally rofe from 3s. to 5s. The S. croft of Chirnfide, appropriated to the acre-men, gave from 12 to 15s. If fome tenants, who, before the efficacy of lime was known or fufficiently proved, had leafes of 19 years, and at a low rate, granted them, and yet, for want of ftock, or of a fpirit of enterprife, did not become fo wealthy as they might have been, we need not admire, if we reflect again upon what has been faid of the low prices of corn and cattle, thofe difcouraging circumftances to the hufbandman, and which could not be remedied, but by the gradual advancement of commerce. It may be added, that it is fit, and *providentially* well ordered, that no new difcovery or improvement, even in the moft neceffary arts, fhould be carried rapidly to its perfection, but that, by a progreffive knowledge and fkill in it, not 1, but 2 or 3 generations may have fome fhare in the benefit.

to the ſcore, for the encouragement of merchants ; which has been but lately laid aſide. It has been ſince thought, that the gentlemen farmers, and the tenants; were too liberal in this conceſſion, ſince that country, which had the 2 ſea-ports of Berwick and Eyemouth, could, and did, in ſome years, furniſh from 40,000 to 60,000 bolls of corn to the market, would have been conſtantly applied to, without ſuch inducement by the corn-merchants at Edinburgh, and other towns. It had, however, a good effect ; as, inſtead of commiſſions being only given to cor-reſpondents at the ſea-ports, to purchaſe certain quanti-ties of grain, the agents of the merchants came, and, re-ſiding in Berwick for ſome time, dealt themſelves with the farmers upon the ſpot. This market, before but par-tially opened, gave freſh vigour to the operations of the plough, and prompted, eſpecially, the preparing and ma-nuring of more land, for wheat crops, that brought round ſums into the hands of the huſbandmen. Their gains were, as yet, no more than what their great expenſe, in the purchaſe of lime, and their other labour, required : But the honeſt ground of that wealth, to which they af-terward attained, was now laid on that perſevering in-duſtry, joined with much economy in their manner of living, which they continued to practiſe and exemplify.

Chirnſide Hill was as much, and rather more, adapted, to paſturage, than to agriculture ; and it has been men-tioned, what ſcores of ſheep, and black cattle, traverſed the common field. Confined within the bounds of each he-ritors poſſeſſion, after the diviſion of the lands, it requir-ed ſome time, on the part of the gentlemen farmers, be-fore either their paſture, or their breed, could be amend-ed. Purpoſes of this, particularly with reſpect to the ſheep, were entertained ; but, as yet, the encloſures, ex-

cept

cept those of Whitehall, were few, and not properly prepared to receive them. The few wedders and ewes, kept by the gentlemen for domestic use, had instructed them in the profits to be made of this useful animal; than which, if duly fed, and attended to, no other can be turned to more account. The laying down of lands, manured, and in good condition, for pasture, was one of the greatest objects in husbandry; because, by means of it, land could be rested from exhausting corn crops, and yet produce what was equal to the best value of them. This could not be doubted, when experience showed what fields, of a more early, and sweeter grass, than the natural kind, could be obtained, by the sowing of white clover-seed. The use and advantage of the red clover, mixed with rye-grass seed, had also been proved in the luxuriancy of its crops, that might be cut for the labouring cattle, or made into hay. The neighbourhood of Northumberland, where much attention had been paid to the breed of horses, afforded the opportunity of improving that of the country, when now the ploughing with oxen began to be disused, and, in the lighter lands, the more expeditious and tractable two-horse draught, to be adopted. In general, it appeared, by the improvements in husbandry made by the gentlemen farmers, that its progress was such, as to combine the proper and advantageous breed of all the live stock upon farms, and especially that of sheep, with the growth of corn. Whence might be added, the profits of the diary, to those of the barn-floor; and, in particular seasons, the defects of the latter be, in some measure, compensated by the benefits of the former

In

* While, yet, the enclosed and meliorated lands were retained in the possession of the proprietors, the culture of potatoes in the fields had been tried

In consequence of all those improvements, agriculture and husbandry, in the two baronies of the parish, were fast advancing to that signal stage at which they are now arrived. Not only all the infield, but almost the whole outfield and moor-land, was, from the year 1770 to the 1780,

tried with much success. A vegetable that could be easily reared, and at little expense, which, desirable at the tables of the rich, afforded a wholesome and cheap food to the poor, and might be used in place of bread, appeared to deserve the attention and labour of the husbandman in a great degree. But the production of it in large quantities, was soon found to reduce the value to little or nothing. As it could not answer all the purposes of corn-meal, it could never be made such an object to the cultivation of land, or the public in general, as the latter. Crops of potatoes came, therefore, to be regarded as subsidiary only to those of grain; so useful, indeed, that they could not be wanted in the most plentiful years; and, in those of scarcity, would keep lower the price of meal, when poor families, having the resource of potatoes, would require smaller quantities of it. The fine light mould of Chirnside crofts, was well adapted to their production; and accordingly, all the common kinds, were advantageously cultivated by the acre-men; while the farmers found it of equal benefit to themselves and their cottagers, to have a proper supply of them, in every season. In this stage of agriculture, and from about the year 1760, or 1765, the S. croft land had risen from 12 and 15, to 16 and 20 shillings. The price of a summer's grass for a cow, in an enclosure, was a guinea; open, but improved fields, laid down in grass, were rated at 16 shillings: Still the value of land was advanced, not only in fields of 10, 20, or 30 acres, but in extensive farms. A great encouragement to it arose from the cultivation and growth of field turnips; by means of which a food, cheaper, and more nourishing than hay, could be procured for the winter maintenance of sheep and black cattle. Besides this important use, no plant was found to meliorate the land so much, by delivering it from all weeds. It might be cultivated to advantage, either in broad cast or in drills. The repeated hoeings requisite to reduce the immense vegetation of the plants, so that those allowed to remain might grow to a useful size, might be reckoned the only considerable expense attending the culture of the turnips, fed on which, more milk could be got from the cows in winter; the sheep and black cattle, kept in good condition, or some of the latter being taken up and stall-fed, might be fattened and well sold to the butcher market in the spring.

1780, either enclofed, or put into an improved condition. Knowledge and fkill, in the two great departments of farming, were gradually fo promoted, that in any offered farm, whether by a firft entry to it, or by a renewal of his former leafe, every farmer of ordinary underftanding could judge of the reafonablenefs of the rent, and conditions propofed to him.. What ftocking was required, what expenfe for lime, what fhare might be taken by him in the coft of enclofures, and to what account his proper management of the lands in culture, by the plough or in pafture, might be turned, were matters not of vague, but nearly of a juft and certain computation. By all the principal farmers, as well as the gentlemen, the powers of the feveral forts of ploughs, the Scotch, the Englifh, the feathered-fock, and the plain, the drill, and others of later invention, were known, and fuch of them ufed as fuited the different grounds to be laboured *.

The chief difficulty in the letting, and taking of land, at the rates, to be immediately mentioned, appeared to be
relative

* In the courfe of the period mentioned, when numbers of new farms were taken upon the outfield and moorlands, through the country, live ftock of every kind rofe to a high value, on account of the vaft demand for them. The yoke of oxen advanced from 10l. and 11l. to 15l. and 16l.; and the fcore of fheep, of the beft Lammermuir breed, to about the fame fum. The price of horfes came to furpafs all conception. Thofe fufficient for the plough and cart could not be bought lower than 15l. or 16l.; and the faddle ones of fize, bore much the fame price. This phenomenon continued, and, in late years, grew more wonderful, by the ftill greater rife of the horfe-market. It is afcribed to many of the ableft farmers difcontinuing their ufual breed of horfes; while they beftowed fo much attenion to the increafe of their fheep and black cattle. The weft country and Irifh horfes, thus becoming almoft the only fupply of the market, the price put upon them might be faid to be whatever the dealers in them pleafed.

relative to thoſe farms, in which large tracks of new
ground were to be opened, and manured with lime. Experience had proved, that the ſoil, eſpecially if light,
might be ſo ſtimulated, as in 2 or 3 years, to loſe its fertility altogether, and could not admit of repair, but by
being laid down in graſs paſture, for a conſiderable time;
reſtrictions, therefore, were to be preſcribed to the tenants,
with reſpect to this, by ſpecial articles in their leaſes.
The limiting the quantity of ſuch hurtful culture, and
how long the land was to be reſted, in caſe the leaſe was
to be extended to a number of years, afforded ſome ground
of diſcord. The keeping up of the fences, either already
made by the landlord, or to be afterward reared by compact with the tenants, at a mutual expenſe, likewiſe occaſioned heſitation on the part of the latter. But where
theſe points did not impede agreements, large farms
were let in the pariſh at ſeveral prices, from the loweſt at 12s. to the higheſt at 20s. the acre; the intermediate rates, and theſe not reckoned the deareſt, being
about 16s. The ſouth croft land roſe from above 20s. to
30s., and that of the north to 25s.

Having thus traced the progreſs, both of the value
and improvements of the whole lands in the pariſh, during a courſe of 45 years, and ſhown how they kept
pace with each other, the reſult of the inveſtigation pre-
ſents the comparative and ſtatiſtical eſtimate of land
property. The farms which, in the beginning of that
period, gave, at an average, 3s. the acre, now give 12s.;
and thoſe at the medium of 5s. now afford 20s.; whence
the increaſe of the real rent appears to be quadruple.
That this advancement, apparently vaſt, was no greater
than the produce of the lands in their cultivated ſtate,
and the raiſed value of their various productions could
admit,

admit, we have this inconteſtible proof, and which does
much credit both to the landlords and the tenants :—In
all the large farms, taken in the pariſh, for 20 years
back and more, there are only 2 or 3 inſtances in which
a change of the tenants (12 in number, when thoſe of
the mills are reckoned), has taken place ; and in one
of theſe inſtances, there was a ſurceaſe of the family of the tenant. With this ſmall exception, the preſent tenants are either thoſe who have ſucceeded to
former leaſes of their fathers, or, being in poſſeſſion of
their own for many years, have renewed them again.
If it be aſked, What are their circumſtances ? The anſwer is, They are not only thoſe of credit and wealth,
but that ſome of the farmers are in ſuch a degree of
both, as will probably raiſe the rank of their families.

But a miſtake is here to be taken notice of, too readily entertained, either by the invidious or the ſuperfi-
cial ſpeculators, on what has been ſtated above, of the
quadrupled value of land property ; who, notwithſtanding what has been proved, that the tenants have profited
highly by this event, raſhly conclude, that the proprietors are the only, or greateſt gainers in conſequence of
it. So far is this opinion from being juſt, that it may
be affirmed, on the contrary, that had the landlords, either here or in moſt other parts of the S. of Scotland,
forborn their exertions, and ſpared their expenſes of
improvement, their rents, in the progreſſive courſe of
trade and population in the Britiſh dominions, would
have been, by this time, more than doubled to them.
But it is to be preſumed, that ſome of them, when they
reckon the coſt of their agricultural improvements,
will, for the ſake of the good done to their country,
                                                    adopt

adopt the fentiment of Old Hefiod, and fay, *that the half profit is better than the whole*.

Wherever the lands, in any country, are cultivated in the manner, and to the extent, that has been reprefented, there an increafed population muft take place. For, whether the proprietors retain and improve their own lands, or let them to tenants, the greater the extent of the culture is, the more hands are required to carry it forward. To this affertion, it will be objected, that the heritor may caft around his manfion-houfe pleafure-grounds, or extenfive fheep-fields, which employ few labouring people; but, befides that the inftances of the firft cafe are rare, and confined to the greateft proprietors, it is to be confidered, that unlefs mere wildernefes be created by them, in place of fine lawns, or walks of pleafure, fuch works, as the latter, cannot be accomplifhed without a vaft deal of previous cultivation, and calling in labourers of feveral kinds. As to their fheep-fields, if t .e flock much exceed one convenient for domeftic fervices, they muft have the knowledge, and exert all the attention, of real hufbandmen, to find this fole ufe of their lands always profitable; for even the beft fubftitution of the management will prove defective. Thus, in the ordinary courfe of things, it muft come to pafs, as it ought to do, that the proprietors of lands, to whom it belongs to begin all new improvements, and to verify in practice their good effects, will not find it for their intereft, or their pleafure, to act the part of real farmers, for a length of time, and beyond a moderate extent. It is their province to fhow, what may, and fhould be done; but as the utmoft reach of their labour is limited, and muft be flow in the progrefs, the extenfion of agriculture over any large diftrict of a country, muft be looked for, and can

only

only come from the letting of farms to tenants ; that clafs of people, who, accuftomed to all the care, induftry, and labour required in hufbandry, will be able to produce more from their fields, and make more of what is produced, than any landlord can do.

It has been faid, and often repeated and believed, that the letting farms of large extent to tenants, as well as the retention of them in the hands of the proprietors, was a great and public grievance, and the caufe of the depopulation of many of the old villages in Scotland. But that, furely, cannot be called a grievance, which, in its aim and iffue, was productive of the greateft public good. The queftion was, How the outfield lands were to be brought to a ftate of culture ? Thofe lands that lay without the reach of dung, and to which none could be afforded, and that for fucceffive generations, had yielded only fuch miferable crops, as were not worth the labour. Without a migration of tenants to them, or the proprietors becoming the farmers, there was not a poffibility of their being meliorated. But what tenants could, or would go forth to an enterprife new, and juftly accounted hazardous to them ? None, certainly, but thofe who had fome more ftock, and either fuperior fkill or more boldnefs, than others. Even to fuch, the removal from the known infield culture to the bare outfield, would appear a fort of exile, and a rifking of their fubftance. They had, therefore, many allowances made to them by the landlords ;— leafes as long as they defired ; and when the manure of marl and lime was introduced, other advantageous conceffions that have been mentioned. Yet, upon the divifion of the barony lands, there were only three of fuch farms fet off by the late Mr. Hall. In confequence of 2 or 3 of the tenants in the village removing to thefe

farms

farms, and the lands they left being caft into allotments, not agreeable, or not accommodated, to fome of the remaining hufbandmen, 4 or 5 of them are reported to have quitted their places; a diminution of the village people fo inconfiderable, as hardly deferves to be mentioned; efpecially when it is confidered, that their room would be fupplied either by other tenants, or the account of their families equalled by the addition made to the numbers of Mr. Hall's day-labourers, called *groat men;* of which a confiderable number was retained throughout the year, for the purpofes of ditching, hedging, and fence-building, and other works carried on in the extenfive plantations of Whitehall. The 2 other heritors, who farmed their own eftates, found it neceffary, for fimilar reafions, to keep their people about them; fo that, for a courfe of years, the village continued to have nearly the fame number of houfes and inhabitants. Nor were thefe diminifhed by the prefent proprietor; who, engaging in operations of hufbandry, extended over almoft the whole of his lands, required fo many ploughmen, or hinds, and work people of feveral forts, that they and their families were not reckoned, at a grofs compenfation, to be fewer than 90 or a 100, kept up during a currency of 10 or 12 years. This circumftance merits fpecial attention, when we come now to give an account of the population of Chirnfide, increafed much beyond what could be expeded from any particular advantage in its local fituation (excepting its falubrity, and its free ftone quarries), and furpaffing that of any other fuch village in the fhire *.

The

* Advanced cultivation of the fields brings along with it an augmented population to every village, or townfhip, in adjacency to it, unlefs there be,

The ftatement now to be given of the prefent population of the village and parifh of Chirnfide, will fufficiently verify what has been afferted of the unqueftion-
able effect of the land culture, to advance it in a fignal
degree, in any other fuch country place, which has the
advantage of a natural good foil, and where the landlords are not referved in granting feus, or many years
leafes of grounds for houfes; although that village were
but indifferently favoured, by the fituation, for the introduction of any very confiderable manufacture. This
confideration deferves more regard than what now appears

be, what obtained too long in many places of Scotland, an averfion on the
part of the heritors, to grant grounds for houfes and areas neceffary to
them, either in the mode of FEU tenures, or of long leafes, reckoned equivalent to them. The objections to thefe tenures, as either difadvantage-
ous, or inconvenient alienations of their property, were not foon overcome
among the landlords in general. But offers and folicitations for them becoming more frequent, it appears, that, in the year 1767, 9 of them had
been admitted by Mr. Hall, and his predeceffor, in the form of long leafes;
yet it was not till the year 1770, that a progreffive addition, both to the
rented houfes of the village, and thofe in leafes, was gradually carried on,
to the 1790, which may be reckoned that of the prefent eftablifhment of
the village as to the number, and condition of its houfes; although, in the
two following years, fome new ones were built. In this manner, while
the principal heritor added to his houfes in property, a certain number at
intervals of time, and granted fuch leafes of grounds, as have been mentioned, to purchafers, a new town may be faid to have been built between
the two, in the courfe of 21 or 22 years; the former being reckoned to
have erected 20 houfes, and the latter 26. Thofe of the proprietors building are, feveral of them, accommodated to the reception of 2 or 3 families,
and 1 or 2 capable of containing as many more; fo that there cannot be now,
as formerly, any computation made of the number of families from that
of the houfes. All the new ones are neatly conftructed of free ftone, fome
of them having 2, and others 3 ftories; 31, or more of them, are covered
with red tiles, and 5 with blue flates; and a few, for which other heritors have afforded ground, have the lately approved covering of the corded
thatch.

pears to be paid to it; when our fpeculations of advancement in opulence and population are turned, almoft wholly, upon the multiplication and encouragement of cotton-mills, and other fuch manufactures, as
correfpond not only to the domeftic ufe and confumption
of their articles, but fuppofe the greateft imaginable
foreign demand for them, the benefit of which cannot
be long affured to any particular nation, from the rival-
fhip of it in other countries, the change of fafhion in
clothes and drefs, and the variable, and often unaccountable fluctuation of commerce from one feat of it to another. The only commodities that have a never-failing
confumption, and a perpetual requifition for them, are
the firft gifts of Providence to man, the fruits of the
earth, improved and extended by his labour, and the
cattle multiplied over a thoufand hills. In the poffeffion
of thefe, the natural ftrength of any nation is placed,
and the riches derived from them are fure. The Britifh ifles, peculiarly fuited to the attainment of this internal and permanent opulence, require only to join to
it, and their home manufactures, the fifheries of their
feas, to have a population unimpaired by long unhealth-
ful foreign voyages, and unconfumed by the difperfion
of their inhabitants, in colonies, over every climate of
the earth, which, not thriving, are the burials of them;
and when profpering, either draw more benefit than they
give to the parent countries, or throw altogether off their
connexion with them. But if, in the world of Europe,
as it has gone for fome centuries, and may proceed,
there be fome political neceffity, that fuch commercial
and colonial enterprifes fhould be promoted, yet, furely, the ardour for them, whether it arifes from a fuppofed augmentation of public credit, and branches of
revenue,

revenue, or party gains, ought not to be pufhed fo far as to be injurious to the internal welfare of the people at large. It will be endangered, and fuffer feveral ways, if a proper balance between agriculture and commerce be not attended to, and, as much as poffible, maintained. If, for the fake of working up a multiplicity of materials for the purpofes of the latter, the bulk of our common people be drawn into the cities and manufacturing towns, fo that the country villages, whence muft come food and provifions for the whole community, are left with a fcarcity of labourers in hufbandry, the farmers muft then either pay fuch extravagant wages as the defective number of them will infift upon, and confequently raife the prices of their corn and cattle, or elfe be induced to diminifh the land culture, and look for their profit to their live ftock, which can be managed with the feweft hands. In years unfavourable to the growth of corn, this abatement of its fowing will be fenfibly felt. A loud cry, for its dearth, foon comes from the manufacturing towns. The journeymen threaten to leave their work, or to have higher wages. Perhaps, too, a manufacture unfuccefsful, or not anfwering the expectations of its mafters, breaks up. The difbanded workmen crowd into cities, already in tumult, and increafe the unhappy commotions.

But, here, dropping this difagreeable part of the fubject, we only fubjoin, that every landlord, who, by his encouragement of agriculture, and affording room for the eftablifhment of houfes, cherifhes the village induftry and population, is worthy of much praife. He promotes that labour abfolutely neceffary to the life of man, and which, while it multiplies the fpecies, tends

to

to preſerve them, in a ſtate the leaſt liable to be corrupted ; and proves a counter check to the employment
of the great body of the common people in thoſe arts,
which the prevalence of luxury, and the unbounded extenſion of foreign commerce require, but that are not
carried on in any nation, without the morality of the
lower claſſes being vitiated to ſuch a degree, as may
ſoon become deſtructive of its welfare.

Population.—According to Dr. Webſter's report, the
number of ſouls in 1755, was 383 *. The ſtate of the
population in the year 1791, is exhibited in the following table.

Souls in the village,	-	609	16 ditto, -	3 -	48
—— in the country,	-	352	2 ditto, -	2 -	4
			9 ditto, -	1 -	9
Total, -	-	961	Maſons, -	-	15
			Carpenters, -	-	12
Families in the village,	-	150	Spinning-wheel wrights,		2
—— in the country,		64	Coopers, -	-	4
Males, -	-	485	Thatchers, -	-	7
Females, -	-	476	Weavers, -	-	12
Below 10,	-	260	Dyer, -	-	1
Between 10 and 20,	-	175	Tailors, -	-	10
20 and 30,	-	141	Shoemakers, -	-	10
30 and 40,	-	115	Smiths, -	-	8
40 and 50,	-	103	Gardeners, -	-	7
50 and 60,	-	73	Corn-merchant,	-	1
60 and 70,	-	63	Shop-keepers,	-	6
70 and 80,	-	27	Brewer, &c. -	-	1
80 and 90,	-	4	Publicans, -	-	5
5 families, of 8	-	40	Butcher, -	-	1
10 ditto, - 7	-	70	Carriers, between Berwick, Chirn-		
4 ditto, - 6	-	24	ſide and Edinburgh, once a-		
94 ditto, - 5	-	470	week, -	-	2
74 families, of 4	-	296			

Sheep,

* From a calculation made by Dr. Anderſon, he computes the population of the village of Chirnſide, and of the country part of the pariſh, to
have been 595 at or about the year 1740; and thinks Dr. Webſter's
report reſpects examinable perſons only.

Sheep, Black Cattle, &c.—It is almoſt unneceſſary to ſtate the number of ſheep, black cattle and horſes, either in the barony, or whole pariſh of Chirnſide, comparatively, with what it was 30 or 40 years ago; for it is not in the ſuperior number, but in the better breed and condition of thoſe animals, that the great difference appears. It is ſuch, indeed, in both theſe reſpects, throughout the pariſh, as to be in proportion to the preſent general meliorated ſtate of the land, compared with its former ſterility. Beſides the improvement of the breed of the ſheep by commixture with the larger kinds of Cheviot, and the North Riding of Yorkſhire, which the gentlemen farmers, and the tenants of the richeſt lands have procured, even the original Lammermuir ſort has grown much in ſize, and in the value of their fleeces, by their better paſture. Of the firſt, none are ſold lower than 30 s., and the ſecond give a guinea, and above it. Neither of them are expoſed, as formerly, to be ſtarved, for want of fodder in the winter ſtorms; but both have, beſides ſome quantity of hay, the more ample proviſion of the field-turnips made for them. Of the two, ſo bred and nouriſhed, we can reckon in the barony about 80 ſcore; while the flocks in the extenſive farms of the two Idingtons and of Blackburn, may be computed at near a half of that number. The black cattle in the barony, including in it, as before, the farms of Ninewells, are not fewer than 14 ſcore. The oxen are either of the Fife breed, or thoſe got at the tryſts of Falkirk and Crieff. Some of them, when put into good condition, are ſold, at the Dunſe and Berwick fairs, to Engliſh drovers; others are diſpoſed of at home, either for working cattle, or for the butcher. The ſtall and tur-
nip-

nip-fed are, ſome of them, of the large Engliſh breed.
The cows are of various kinds ; but moſtly (excepting
a few Highlanders) of the Dutch or large ſize. The
number of horſes taken up, in the 1792, as liable to the
ſtatute labour, and comprehending in it 16 mares with
foals, amounts to 173 ; and to it, notwithſtanding the
preſent enormous price of horſes, we may, at a gueſs,
add 15 or 20 more for the ſaddle.

Upon the whole of the agricultural improvements,
and the population of the pariſh, it is to be remarked,
not only that the latter is founded upon, and grows
from the former ; whether in any country village or
townſhip, or in the other parochial diſtricts, but that
the increaſe of the population of both will be more or
leſs, according as the improved land about the village is
either readily let in ſmall portions, feued, or in leaſes of
many years, by the proprietors, or with reſerve, or a
reſtriction to yearly tenants. Wherever the artificers
and tradeſmen thrive, they will naturally deſire to make
purchaſes upon the moſt liberal footing ; and they will
prefer having them, and give the moſt for them in the
places of their habitation, and where they have already
acquired houſes and yards. They, by this means, are
fixed upon the ſpot, and their poſterity will not migrate
from it. In the admiſſion of yearly tenants of acres, or
portions of them, a preference is always due to the
married, before the unmarried. The former, indeed,
are moſtly thoſe who require to be accommodated with
pieces of land ; and it deſerves particular notice, how
much the meliorated ſtate of it enables the meaneſt of
them, who are induſtrious, to ſubſiſt their families. Out
of an acre, although rented at 30s., a day-labourer,

without

without any other expenfe but that of the ploughing, and without abftracting above 2 or 3 days of his earnings throughout the year, can raife, in crops of corn, potatoes, turnips or clover, what is, at leaft, of 5l. value to him, and what he could not obtain with that money. The maintenance of his cow, through the winter, that moft neceffary article attained by him, is done equal to 25s. or 30s. of that fum. All the other labour his little field requires, is performed by him, and his wife or family, at fpare hours. The difference between him and the artificer is, that he does no daily work at home, and yet is confined, within a certain diftance, for his employment; and therefore he engages himfelf, at a low daily wage, for the whole year, unlefs he can depend upon having jobbs of weekly work in continuance. Excepting the fmiths and weavers, the other artificers and trades people can eafily change their abodes, where they have not made purchafes of houfes; as they have, fo generally, done in Chirnside, from the encouragement given them, joined to the facility and cheapnefs of the quarries *.

Antiquities.

---

* If to this fixed population of the village be added, that of dividing the large farms into fmaller ones, with leafes only of a moderate extent the population in the parochial diftricts will emulate that of the village; and in the refpects that have been mentioned, its increafe will be preferable to it. That the proprietors fee this public advantage to be confiftent with their particular intereft, appears by the fubdivifions already made in fome of the greater farms of the parifh. Like all other matters that have a natural courfe, this meafure cannot fail, gradually, to be followed; fo that, as it was found neceffary, in the firft improvement of land, that either the heritors themfelves fhould take large quantities of it into their own hands for melioration, or elfe let it extenfively, in leafes of many years

Antiquities.—When monuments of antiquity are looked for and found, in any part of our iſland, they are
either Britiſh and Druidical, or Roman, or Daniſh and
Anglo-Saxon, or Norman, or thoſe introduced in the
feudal times ; and, perhaps, ſome peculiar to the borders of Scotland and England. Of the 1ſt, there are,
apparently, none in this pariſh. The ſame might have
been ſaid of the 2d claſs, had not the accidental diſco-
very, made about 6 or 7 years ago, of 2 ſmall urns or
vaſes, of the ſepulchral form, generally acknowledged
to be Roman, led to a different opinion. In digging into a bank of gravel, rarely found in this country, but
a ridge of which riſes upon the ſouth edge of Billy-
mire, the picks of the workmen ſtruck upon 2 cavities,
about 18 inches below the ſurface of the ground ; from
each of which fell one of theſe urns, together with the
fragments of human ſkeletons, ſkulls and bones. Both
the urns were taken up entire, and remain ſo in the
poſſeſſion of Mr. Hall of Whitehall *.

That

years to capable tenants, ſo, in order to make tho moſt of improved
ground, and to advance its cultivated ſtate, it becomes equally requiſite to
contract the extent of the farms, and by the admiſſion of more tenants upon ſhortened, but reaſonable leaſes, to promote a more ſpecial and effectual melioration of the lands, in proportion to the greater number of
people collected upon them; and who, as knowledge, in the various
branches of agriculture increaſes, will always find ſufficient employment,
and prove, that wherever the moſt abundant food and proviſion for man
and the ſerviceable animals is produced, there the moſt, or very remarkable
increaſe of the numbers of the people, will certainly take place.

* They are compoſed of common red clay, about the height of a human
ſpan, and have, on their outſide, ſome downward ſtrokes of coarſe mould-
ing. The cavities, from which they were diſlodged, were about 6 feet in
length, and their breadth nearly equal to that of an ordinary grave. Their

ſides

That the ancient Caledonians did not confume with fire, but fimply inter their dead, and that the monuments of their graves were only the heaped clod, or the grey ftone ; whence fubfequently came the accumulated cairns, in conformity to the traditional ordinance of the Norwegian, or Danifh god of war, Woden, has been commonly admitted among antiquaries. But it is contended by fome of them, that the South Britons had adopted the cuftom of burning the bodies of their dead, from their continental neighbours in Armorica (the inhabitants of Bretagne) in ancient Gaul ; who are faid to have practifed it, even before the Romans invaded Britain : yet, although this be a very difputable point, it is not doubted, that the ufage of the conquerors had been partly followed, not only by the natives of the fubjugated countries in the S., but alfo by thofe who dwelt between the 2 Roman walls ; fome of whom being frequently in leagues, and profeffed amity with that civilized people, learned, as their hiftorians affirm, many of their cuftoms and arts. Hence, it is alleged, that fuch numbers of their fort of fepulchral urns have been dug up, in places where the Romans are not known to have

---

fides, rudely conftructed of ftones, with mortar of lime, had a few unfhaped flags extended over them ; upon which the plough-fhare appeared to have fometimes grazed. May we not, therefore, juftly conclude, that at or near the place where fuch fepulchral remains, as thofe defcribed, were found, fome Roman troops, if not an army, had taken, not only their paffage, but a temporary ftation ; efpecially, as it would require fome fpace of time for burning, in their manner, and collecting the bones of their dead, or flain ; who, when of rank, were diftinguifhed, by having fome more honoured part of their afhes put into urns; and for the depofiting and prefervation of which, the gravelly or drieft ground was always looked for, and chofen.

have ever carried their arms ; so that unless they be
found near their colonial towns, or to their military
roads, or acknowledged vestiges of their encampments
and stations, they are more likely to be the funeral deposits of the Britons than of the Romans *.

Having

* But, independent of the vestige of a Roman highway, which is not
discoverable in any part of the county, but very apparent in the neighbouring, and more inland one of Tiviotdale, about Jedburgh or Caerton
Common, we have the best authority, (that of Tacitus, in his life of Agricola), to assert, that this famous commander of the Roman legions marched
in this tract of the east coast, when, after having invaded Scotland in one
campaign, he entered it again with more powerful forces. His land army, says that historian, was conducted by him so near the sea, as to keep
sight, as much as possible, of his fleet, that sailed along the coast. This could
not possibly be done by him in this pass of the country, to any advantage, if
he marched his army northward, at a greater distance from the sea, than
that of Chirnside Hill. In a mile or two beyond it, the hills of Lammermuir arise, and are so cast, as to allow only of some peeps of the sea. Within its distance, almost every eminence shows it in more extended views ;
besides this passage into East Lothian being shorter, and less mountainous.
But, we shall suppose, that he kept still closer to the sea, which is most
probable, and directed his march on this side of the Tweed, so near as the
towns of Ayton and Coldingham now stand, yet it is hardly to be thought,
that he would have no detached party of his troops, to cover the flank of
his army on that side, when he was entering into a pass of the country,
unavoidable and difficult. If such a necessary detachment was made only
at 2 or 3 miles distance, to observe the enemy, their route, a little westward from the main body, would either bring them to Chirnside Hill, or
very near its border. Accordingly, in favour of this supposition, what do
we meet with, hardly so far as the throw of a javelin from its south extremity, but, on the other side of Whittadder that bounds this parish, and on
the ground of the Allanbank estate——a place called Chester-knows, a
name of auspicious import to the antiquary, when he investigates the
progression of the Roman arms in Britain. In that place, he might have
beheld (as the writer of this account did 30 years ago), the conspicuous remains of an ancient, or very old military entrenchment. Mounds of
earth, in signal elevation, and evidently artificial, appeared to the eye, at a
considerable

Having here no remains of the Danifh, or Anglo-Saxon antiquities, but thofe of the cairns above mentioned, we come to obferve what appearances there are of the feudal kind, efpecially as found in the eaft border of the two kingdoms. In every barony fo fituated, and of the nobler and more extenfive fiefs, there was generally, *firft*, the baron's caftle, placed either on the advantageous ground of a hill or precipice, or in the environs of a running water or fwamp. In fome advanced

considerable diftance. On a nearer view, the ground occupied by them, rifing towards Whittadder-bank, facing the north, and almoft perpendicular, difcovered it to be well chofen for defence, on that quarter; while a double, or triple line of ramparts, fecured it upon its declivity, and where it was accefsible. They run E. and W., and in a ftraight direction. There appeared to be veftiges of two other lines, although much funk, and then partly invaded by the plough, which run from the extremities of the former towards the bank of the water. The whole entrenchment forming a fquare, but here properly made oblong, on account of its contiguity to Whittadder, might have induced any antiquary to pronounce it, upon a furvey, a Roman one. Its ramparts are now very much demolifhed, yet not quite overthrown, by the repeated attacks of the hufbandman. It is no ftretch of fancy, but very natural to fuppofe, that a detachment of troops, moving from Chefter-knows north and eaftward, in order to rejoin their main army, and having to pafs Belly-mire, in the direct and proper line of their march, would be attacked by their enemies in the defiles to be made, at that deep bog, and fuffer confiderably in the encounter, although they might gain the victory. This (upon the fuppofition made), appears to have been the cafe with the Romans; who, having repulfed their enemies, with the lofs of fome of their captains, had time to find out the ridge of gravel upon the bank of the mire, and there formally depofit their urns. Before the firft mentioned expedition of Julius Agricola into Scotland, committed to him by Titus Vefpafian, about the 80th year of the Chriftian æra, this country was but very imperfectly known to the Romans, and any intercourfe with the natives, either in war or peace, hardly began, until he led his army as far as the Frith of the Taus, or Tay, and afterward exploring the coafts with his fleet, afcertained Britain, (viz. England and Scotland), to be one ifland.

ced angle of the latter, or where the bridge or caufeway over either of them led to the caftle, there was
often a fort (fuch as that known at Dunfe, immediately
below the town, connected with the caftle), called the
Bar-nay, or Barnekin. Still more advanced, and, as
the rife of the ground favoured the pofition, ftood the
tower of watch, overlooking the country around it, but
facing the quarter of the enemy. It either ftood fingle,
and was of a conftruction fit for fome defence, or being
built commodioufly clofe by or in adherence to the
ftrong-houfe of fome of the vaffals, which therefore was
called, corruptly, the Peel, and properly, the Pile-houfe,
could be more eafily guarded from a furprife. In feveral places, the church fteeples, or bellfries, were fo fa-
bricated as to ferve for the *fpeculatoria*, or alarm towers. On this account, although they were otherwife
refpected, they were frequently fet on fire by the fuperior enemy. Of a ftructure no lefs firm, and often with
thicker and ftronger walls, but lower, was erected the
baftile, or prifon of the barony, or parochial diftrict ;
and, upon fome eminence not far from it, was fixed the
grim and terrific fpectacle of the gallows, or gibbet.

In this parifh, there is a place called Old Caftles, having Belly-mire clofe on the north fide, with much broken ground, and fome difcoveries of the foundations of
buildings about it, which point it out as the fite of the
baron's caftle in fome early days. But as to any particulars relative to it, tradition is entirely filent *.

* Yet a probable reafon may be affigned for this. The Earls of Dunbar, who joined to their title that of March, and were early, and often appointed wardens of the eaft border, had not their refidence here, but in Eaft
Lothian ; although the barony of Chirnfide, moft probably appertained
to

The laſt mentioned veſtige of feudal antiquity was that of the baſtiles. Thoſe priſons, having a Norman name, denote their introduction, or their more frequent erection by the conqueror. They were more numerous in the marches of the borders than any where elſe, for obvious reaſons, and they were alſo made much ſtronger. Fully, and generally occupied, they could not fail to be, in

---

to them, and came afterward to be acquired by the family of Home. Both theſe lords had, beſides it, various fortreſſes of far more importance to them. Between the two great proprietors, it is likely the baron's caſtle here had been neglected, and allowed to fall to ruins. This is the more preſumable, as its ſituation, on the ſouth ſide of the bog, expoſed it to be aſſaulted more eaſily by the Engliſh invaders. The erecting another fort, on the oppoſite ſide of the mire, now called Ferny Caſtle, appears to have been no way neceſſary, unleſs it was to ſupply the defect of the other. A tower, however, reported to have been built by an Earl of Dunbar, and conveniently ſituated for obſervation, hard by the church-yard, kept its place : its demolition was not ſo long ago, nor ſo entire, but that the late beadle of Chirnſide, and other old people, had ſeen its ruins, and its grooved ſtones carried off, by the maſons. Whether the Earl of Dunbar and March, who, along with Lord Douglas, met the Engliſh warden of the marches, Lord Neville, at Belly-mire, in the year 1586, for the purpoſe of concluding a truce, as mentioned in the border hiſtory, may be reckoned to have been that earl, who, according to tradition, built or repaired the tower of Chirnſide, is uncertain; but the fact recorded gives occaſion to obſerve, why the place of a bog was appointed for ſuch a meeting. It is accounted for, by conſidering the violent and particular animoſity, with which the parties, at war in the borders, were inflamed againſt each other. Their conſtant and mutual defiances, and incurſions, kept up reſentment; ſo that when the wardens were to meet for negotiating a truce, the infractions of it among their armed trains, were always to be apprehended. To prevent their coming to blows or ſcuffles, they were kept at ſome diſtance from each other, by a ſlough, or interſection of the ground, choſen for their meeting, until, at leaſt, all the preliminaries were ſettled between the wardens. Hence, Hauden ſtank, and the Bounden-road, are often mentioned as the places of their conventions, for treaties; and yet, even thoſe precautions did not always prevail for their peaceable termination.

in the parts of the 2 kingdoms, liable to reciprocal and continual ravages. Towards their being tenanted, not only the prisoners of war, who were kept for mutual exchange, or until they gave pledges for their ransom, but the many marauders and banditti, in time of peace, when taken, also much contributed. Although hanging was the common and ordained fate of the latter, there were parties of them protected by some chiefs of the hords in the recesses of Cheviot Hills, whom it was found proper to spare, from the dread of the most attrocious and bloody revenge of their deaths. On account of these circumstances, the bastiles, on the east border of Scotland, and especially those in the Merse, were built in the strongest manner, and so placed, as to secure them from any open assault, or concealed surprise, by an enemy so near at hand, and ready to attempt the rescue of the prisoners. Of all the grounds in the parish, that now called the Bastel-dikes, where shaped stones, and such as are used for cornices and lintels of doors, have been often turned up by the plough, is naturally the most fenced and inaccessible. It runs out in the west end, like a promontory, upon the broad stream of Whittadder, which there makes a turn upon its north banks, that are, at least, 150 feet high, and have little more declivity than an upright wall. Much broken land, interfected with rivulets, secures it on the north side ; and it is only open on the east, where there is, first, a sloping descent, and then a steep path-way down to Idington Mill upon the water. The castle, or strong house, of that village and barony, was also a close guard to it. This description of our old parochial bastile, leads to a remark, which, I know not whether it has been made before, that these edifices not only served the pur-

pofes

pofes of prifons, but that, taken together with the caftles or tower-houfes of the chieftains, near which they
always ftood, they conftituted a chain of fortreffes, running, partly on Whittadder and on Blackadder banks,
from almoft the one end of the county to the other.
Thus, we can reckon a line of them, at fhort diftances,
in this neighbourhood, viz. Kello-baftel, in Edrom parifh ; the Bafteldikes-here ; Foulden-baftel ; and the
Baftel-riggs, in Ayton parifh ; befides others weftward
of Kello, the names of which I do not now exactly recollect *.

Mifcellaneous Obfervations.—Chirnfide, as a barony,
had, and ftill holds the privilege of an annual fair, at a
late feafon of the year, but accommodated to the demand for its old ftaple commodity ; which was that of
facking, or bags for corn. It draws together a good
many

* To conclude the antiquities, there are only two names of places in the
parifh, befides Chirnfide, which require etymology, or explication. The
firft is that of Pepperlaw, a fteading, or place of farm-houfes, fituated on
an eminence, making part of the bank of Belly-mire. The name, although
odd, is intelligible, when written, or pronounced, as it ought to be. The
Pepperlaw, which denotes the hill upon the fide of a muddy rivulet, fuch
as iffues from a bog, or mire; the word Pepper, being German, or Saxon,
fignifies black pepper; and therefore, is applied to a ftream of a black colour. It has indeed, its interpretation, in the name of Blackburn, given
to the village, on the eaft fide of the mire, near which runs a brook of the
fame fource, and complexion. An eafy fwamp, is, in fome places, called the
Pepper, and there is one well known by that name near Newbeath, in
Eaft Lothian. The other name wanting derivation, is Idington, about
which I can only offer a flight conjecture, not having had opportunity of
feeing its orthography in any old papers; which, yet, I fufpect may be
Eddington, denoting a place where there are eddies, or deepening of the
fhallow water into pools; a circumftance that is apparent and remarkable,
all along the entry to it from the W. to the N.

many people ; but few to purchase its former merchandise, which is found in too small and trifling quantities to be an object to the farmers, and much less to the corn-merchants ; the former now buying their corn-sacks by dozens ; and the latter, by several hundreds together, from the large sales of them opened in Berwick, Dunse, and other places ; which are supplied from the manufactures of Dunbar and Haddington, and also from London. It would appear, from the little attention paid here, and all over this country, to the growth of hemp, that there is naturally more solicitude about the filling, than the fabricating corn-sacks ; yet this is not a sufficient reason for having no manufacture of them at all. Our old band of 12 weavers, however, is exactly kept up ; if we add to the 10 present masters, 2 apprentices belonging to some of them. Their looms, indeed, are not near so much employed in the fabric of woollen cloth as formerly, when the wealthiest farmers, as well as the common people, were generally clothed from the webs made of the yarn spun by their wives and female servants. In the decline of this thrift, many years ago, the manufacture of linens, coarse and fine, in various degrees, has chiefly occupied the trade ; and 1 or 2 of them wove linen equal to the best Holland. They still have reputation in this branch, to which that of the lint-spinners, in the village, also contributes. Several of them are both expert and diligent, and, using the 2 hand-wheel, will often accomplish 2 slips of more than middling yarn in a day. The sale for it is ready, if not to the weavers at home, to the agents for the factories at Edinburgh, appointed at Dunse and other places. For 4 slips, or a spindle, they get 14d. or 15d. When the spinning, which lasts them through the winter and

the

the spring, is over, and a suspense of employment enfues, there is always a call for such of them as are not engaged for summer-service, to assist in the planting of potatoes, and performing the work of hoeing them, and the repeated weedings of the turnip fields.

To what has been said of the improved knowledge of the farmers in all the operations of the plough, we have to add, the advantage and convenience they find in the number of hinds, or bred ploughmen, expert and able to perform any agricultural work required of them, who appear, in the hiring market-days, at Dunse and Berwick. Even when a half-year servant is only wanted for carting, and other common work upon a farm, there are few lads here at the age of 18 or 20, used to country service, who cannot occasionally supply the place of a hind; and, in lighter land, at least, manage the plough with propriety and neatness. It is owing to this early usefulness of the young men bred in the country to the farmers, that their wages, several years past, were much raised, and generally complained of, especially by those who could not employ them with equal advantage. When, at first, the farmers were averse to grant their demands, the spirited and stoutest betook themselves to Northumberland, where the tenants, possessing long leases, and having coal and lime at hand, were able to afford the greatest encouragement to labourers of every kind. It must be acknowledged, that many of them learned there to do their work more completely; and such of them as returned here, deserved the wages they asked. It is near 30 years since no good labouring servant could be got for less than 6l. or above it, and now they are not hired below 8l. or 9l.; which is just about the triple of their wages 40 years ago.

ago, and wanting but a fourth of the improved value of the land, proves, that, in a free country, ſuch as Britain, the labouring people can never ſuffer long by ſmall wages, unleſs induſtry generally ceaſes, or is relaxed; and that they will always, as they are well entitled, have their hire advanced, in proportion to exertions made in the ever-profitable labours of the fields.

It is not to be foreſeen, or eaſily imagined, what acceſſions a country village may receive, in conſequence of the grants of long leaſes, or feus, to purchaſers. Beſides thrice the number of maſons and ſmiths, four times that of wrights and ſhoemakers, and more than double that of tailors, without reckoning their apprentices, ſtated in the preceding table, together with their maſters, we have of 4 gardeners, 2 that keep nurſery grounds; and among the merchants, 1 that is a dealer in corn, for himſelf, and alſo an agent, reſident: and what there was yet leſs reaſon to expect, in the number of publicans, 1 who has ſucceeded ſo well in that occupation, as to have erected, at a very conſiderable expenſe, large buildings, for a brewery and malting, joined with a bakery. This encouragement, in the vending great quantities of ale and wheat bread through the country, appears to be the recompenſe due to his undertaking and induſtry. Here we cannot help again recollecting, what was the caſe in the old village, where every ſixpence worth of wheat bread was brought from Dunſe or Berwick; when a houſe for a baker, and a ſeller of ale, built by the late Mr. Hall, was ſoon deſerted by the tenants, and allowed to fall down, and the preſbytery's entertainment could only be found at the bellman's habitation. Yet, in thoſe days, the people were not inactive in ſuch branches of trade, as

were then known, or accounted, in the leaſt degree, profitable *.

Religion and Morals of the People.—The people, in general, are in religion ſincere, and as little addicted to ſu-
perſtition, or enthuſiaſm, as in any country pariſh. Even
ſo far as the nominal religious diviſions obtain among
them, they operate not to rancour, or any obſervable de-
pravation of the Chriſtian temper and ſpirit. Although
Antiburghers and Burghers, to a certain number, have
been known among them, almoſt even ſince the origin of
Seceſſion, and a Cameronian meeting-houſe has been lately erected in the middle of the village, the bulk of the
people continue attached to the Eſtabliſhed Church. The
individuals of families, that follow theſe ſectaries, are conſiderable in number; but whole families of them are very
few. Among the former, eſpecially of the Burgher, or of the
Relief claſſes, there are ſeveral who frequent thoſe congregations,

* Of this, the eggman of the village afforded a remarkable example.
Not contented with being, what ſome of his fraternity were, in other
places, the firſt merchant in ſmall wares, he formed the ſcheme of carrying on his particular trade in a ſuperior manner. Well known in the country, and having credit at Berwick and Dunſe, he took from Mr. Hall 2 or
3 acres of land. He purchaſed 2 of the ſtouteſt horſes he could find; and
taking his travels 20 miles up the country into Lauderdale and Gala
Water, and paying for his eggs as he went along, he engaged ſuch a number of cuſtomers in the line of his march, as furniſhed a complete load of
them in his four large creels. Piled up nicely, they generally amounted
from 1600 to 1800, and frequently exceeded that number. His market
was Berwick, where the ſtaple commodity for export to London, being
eggs and ſalmon, his payment was ſure and ready, for an article reckoned
to make the annual return of above 6000 l. to the merchants; while that
of the other was eſtimated at 8000 l. or 9000 l. To the benefit of this
place, and that of his many cuſtomers, who kept by him, he preſided in
the trade for more than 20 years, and got to himſelf conſiderable gain.

gations, as hearers, but choose not, or are not admitted to communicate sacramentally with them. Hence the frequent applications made here, and in other parishes, for baptism, and admittance to the communion table, by a good many, who seldom appear in the churches, but upon these occasions. With whom are those people to be numbered? Are they to be reckoned of our church, or among the dissenters? These questions are material, when we estimate the increase or decrease of the one, or the other. The children baptized in the church, although, for the reason given, not entered into the register, to within a fourth of their number, are not only no fewer than they were in any former period, but not much short of being, in proportion to the augmentation of the parishioners. We have constantly had, for above 30 years, from 8 tables of communicants to 9, or a few more; each service comprehending 35 or 40. The tables of this year were filled up to 8, and a few over: We may therefore reckon, that we stand nearly at an equal balance, and in the best token of adherence, which is that of sacramental communion, that the scale is rather more in favour of the church, than of the dissenters.

In the discharge of Christian duties, and in the morality of their lives and actions, the common people, comparatively with others, are laudable. The virtues of honesty and charity are in esteem and practice among them. The sympathy which they express, and the meanest of them testify, by affording all the help in their power to their neighbours in distress, is very remarkable. In all their occupations and trades that have been mentioned, they are industrious, and many of them thriving. None of them complain of poverty, till they are really in want. The frugality of
the

the married women, who have children (and moſt of them have many), and their care and conſtant employment, under the burden of them, are ſuch as to require only ſobriety and induſtry, on the part of the men, to bring up their families in a creditable way. When theſe virtues are wanting, or fail in the huſbands, and the attraction of the ale and dram-houſes prevails with them, their mates, unable to do more than their accuſtomed labour, become depreſſed; and the more ſo, becauſe the viſible want or diſorder in the houſe is generally, and often moſt unjuſtly, imputed to them ; to which ſentence many of their own ſex too readily aſſent. From ſenſibility and dread of this reproach, their ſpirits ſubſide. Languor of body and mind ſeize them. Various affections unhinge their frame. They behold their children around them, in want of bread, which they cannot ſupply. Their eyes are ſet dead with the ſight. They agonize, until they can ſee no more. Their offspring cry to a helpleſs father ; they embrace his knees, when it is a chance, if he is in a condition to take one of them into his arms. Irreclaimable in his vicious habit, if he lives with them a year or two, they are half ſtarved, and ſome of them are ſure to drop ; and if he die, which may be better for them, they fall to be maintained upon the pariſh charity.—So woful are the effects which the intemperate uſe of ſpiritous liquors may be obſerved to produce in all pariſhes !

The ſalubrious air, from the elevation of Chirnſide Hill, joined with the dry and comfortable houſes of the inhabitants, exempts them from the epidemical diſeaſes of agues, or intermitting fevers, that formerly prevailed. Of the putrid kind, there are few. The moſt common complaint is of rheumatiſm, or pains in the joints

and

and limbs. In the ſawing of wood, and the working of quarry ſtones, the men generally ſtrip themſelves to a thinner ſhirt or waiſtcoat than was uſed in the days of their fathers ; and, from the changeability of a day, in the months of winter and ſpring, expoſe themſelves to catch rheumatic obſtructions. But the diſeaſe with many, is the incurable one, of approaching old age. There were ſeveral inſtances, in the laſt generation, of longevity, to the extent of 85 and 90 years, and 1 or 2 to near 100. The apparent health and meaſure of ſtrength, which ſome above 70 now poſſeſs, promiſe their arriving at a remarkable length of years. Fatal here, was the viſitation of the ſmall pox in the end of the year 1791, and through the winter months and ſpring of the year 1792 ; when, by a contagion in the natural way, between 30 and 40 children were carried off. The preſervative means of inoculation might have been, at no expenſe, obtained ; but, from the prejudices of a ſuperſtitious kind, ſtill remaining with ſome female parents, there was no application made for the remedy, until it could not be ſafely uſed. The ſubſcriptions now entered into at Dunſe, and conſiderably advanced, for a diſpenſary of medicines and phyſical advice, *gratis*, to the poor, propoſed to have extenſion over a large diſtrict of the country, may, along with other phyſical benefits, produce that of preventing like calamities by the ſmall pox ; when the means of preſervation will be ſo eaſily obtained, and the ſalutary practice of inoculation being extended, will afford conviction of its happy effects to the moſt ſcrupulous parents.

Curioſities.—In the ſmall number of them in this pariſh, it has happened, that about 2 or 3 weeks ago, mere

accident

accident brought a curious ſtone into view. It had
dropped from the top of a quarry, worked immediately
under the deſcribed Cheſter-knows. Captain Home's
attention to it, was occaſioned by the maſon's bruſh being ſtuck into it, and the ſingularity of its having a hole,
and its heavy weight, induced him to have it brought
home. It is moſtly of an orbicular form ; and although
of a ſubſtance as hard as marble, it is perforated exactly
in the middle ; it is convex on all ſides but one, which is
flat ; while its other ſurface is not only rough, but fret-
ted, as if it had been artificially raiſed into ſmall notches.
Its weight, yet untried, may be between 2 and 3 ſtone.
Upon conſidering theſe particulars, it was ſuggeſted, that
being evidently worked upon, and fitted to ſome purpoſe
of art and utility, it might be the upper part of a *moletrina* or hand-mill, for corn, ſuch as was uſed by the Romans in their campaigns. That it correſponded to this
conjecture, is evinced from the aptitude of the perfora-
tion, to admit an iron axis or ſpindle, of near an inch
thick, which, terminating in the ſocket of an under ſtone,
excavated for holding corn, and wide enough to receive
into it this upper part ; and being moveable by a handle
fixed to its top, could make the found ſtone act as a grinder of the grain, with all its power of attraction. Since
paſſing this judgment upon the ſtone, Captain Home has
been informed, by the tenant of the ground, where the
Cheſter-knows are, that, in the courſe of his agriculture, he had met there with a large hollowed round
ſtone, which, being ſunk 3 or 4 feet deep into the earth,
was allowed to remain in its place. Whether this ſtone upon its being inſpected, or dug up, may be the wanted tally to that in Mr. Home's poſſeſſion, we know not ; but if
the latter be itſelf judged, by the intelligent in ſuch antiquities,

quities, to be the grinder of a Roman ſtone-mill, the trenches upon the Cheſter-knows can hardly be doubted to be the remains of an encampment, or temporary ſtation of Roman troops ; and from this being aſcertained, a probability ariſes of their having marched through this part of the country, in the lines, and with the military conduct above ſuppoſed *.

Church,

* There are three ſprings or wells of water, which have curioſity ; one of them upon the S. extremity of the Eaſt Mains eſtate, has its copious iſſue in a bed of marl. Its taſte, and the ochre colour of its ſlime, prove it to be a pretty ſtrong chalybeate, or mineral water ; but being impregnated with marly particles, it is glutinous upon the palate, and therefore not ſo light upon the ſtomach. It has been formerly, and is ſtill reſorted to, by ſome of the common people, affected with ſcorbutic eruptions ; but with what benefit is not, to my knowledge, well aſcertained. Some old book is ſaid to report its medicinal virtues and vogue. The other two ſprings that riſe in the place called Spence's Mains, a little weſt of the church-yard, deſerve notice, not from any ſingular quality in either, but from the one being ſoft water, and the other hard, when their diſtance from each other is not above 6 or 7 ſteps. —The old plane tree at Ninewells, which, in the grove a little E. of the houſe, rears its ſtraight ſtem, and lofty top, is an object that attracts the eye, to ſuch a production in the vegetable ſyſtem. It meaſures, by the girth, 17 feet of ſolid wood, below the boughs ; which, although generally ſtrong, and ſpreading, have at their top a fading, which marks their ſuffering by the endurance of the blaſts of many winters, which cannot be reckoned fewer than 150, in revolution : For the oldeſt people of the laſt generation, when aſked about its appearance, in their memory, ſaid, that they never remembered it but in full growth, and with ſome marks of its being at the age of declining.——A ſpecies of the gypſum, if not the beſt kind, but of which ſome plaſter has been made for ceilings of rooms, little inferior to that of Paris, or very good ſtucco, ſhows itſelf on the ſide of Whittadder banks, oppoſite to this, where yet there is the ſame appearance of that ſubſtance. Its quantities, ſuch as it is, here, and in the neighbourhood, are vaſt ; and if tried in powder, to fertilize land, to the degree alleged of the gypſum, large ſupplies of it can be furniſhed.

Church, Manse, Stipend, School, Poor, &c.—That the church here may be 2 or 3 centuries old, appears from the architrave, or coarse fluting of its principal door, and also from a stone, of about a foot square, taken down at the rebuilding of the east aile, or old choir, having a few rude and faded characters upon it, which, just legible, are these: Help the pvr (poor); and the figures 1573, joined with them. That the church might be older than this signature upon the choir aile, is not improbable, from the appearance its walls have of being much pieced up in the inward side. Its vaulted roof has been, many years since, taken down, and converted into the present one of cupples, and blue slate, with serking of deals. It was, probably, among the first in this country so covered; the advantage of which, in point of interest as well as propriety, when compared with the continual repairs of the thatched roofs, was long and late of being apprehended or admitted by many heritors. It is now in ordinary and tolerable condition, but has not yet received such decent reparations within, as are exemplified in several neighbouring churches *.

The

* The tomb-stones of the church-yard cannot be passed over, as they exhibit that of the Reverend Mr. Henry Erskine, first minister of the parish after the Revolution 1688; whose sons, Ebenezer and Ralph, were the principal and famous leaders of an open and well known secession from the Established Church. The first was reckoned the pillar of the party; while Ralph was allowed to be the best scholar, with a vein for Latin and English poetry, but particularly fertile of riddles, in both of which the elegiac distichs upon the tomb-stone of his father sufficiently bear record. Mr. Henry died in the year 1696, and was interred, not in burial-ground of the Episcopal ministers, and as such, resigned to their successors in office, but in considerable separation from it; and what is rather remarkable, there was no fraternity of coffins and bones between the clergy of the two churches, by those of Mr. Millar, his immediate

successor,

The manfe, rebuilt in the year 1757, is well conftructed in its walls and roof, but its dimenfions are rather narrow for a large family. The office-houfes have
been, fome years fince, alfo rebuilt. The glebe, confifting of 8 Englifh acres and a rood (the ftations of
houfes being included), is fenced with hedge and ditch,
and has a fubdivifion in the fame fafhion. The ftipend
amounts to nearly 39l. in money, and 4 chalders of victual, three parts of which are oats, and a third bear.
The communion elements are comprehended.   William
                                                  Hall,

fucceffor, who was foon called to Leith, nor by thofe of the late Mr.
Home, who was buried in the vault of the Ninewell's family in the E.
aile. The late bellman, who lived to above 80, and remembered Mr.
Lattie, the Epifcopal clergyman, who retired to Eymouth, faw, (reckoning
that gentleman, and the prefent incumbent), the fucceffion of five minifters in the parifh church.

Yet, another infcribed ftone, with a carved fcutcheon over the epitaph,
deferves attention. It is that of Mr. William Aitkenfon (Aitchifon), whofe
natural genius, prompted by an able fchool-mafter here, rendered him
early fuch a proficient in writing, arithmetic, geometry, and other parts of
mathematics, as carried him out of the line of an operative mafon, under
his father, and marked his ability to proceed in that of the liberal fcien-
ces. He went to London; where, obferving the advertifed want of a writing and arithmetical mafter, in one of the academies, he prefented himfelf
as a candidate for the place. The produced fpecimen of his penmanfhip
was fo much fuperior to that of the other candidates, that the judges fufpected it to be a borrowed piece of copperplate, until it was authenticated by his writing, in their prefence. By accefs to books of fcience, and
other opportunities of acquiring knowledge, during his continuance in the
academy, for feveral years, he became well qualified to be himfelf head
mafter of one. It was, accordingly, opened in a large houfe, clofe by
Hammerfmith, and kept up with reputation and fucçefs, for a few years,
until his health declined. Being advifed by his phyficians to try his native air, for a recovery, he returned here. His aged parents faw him
in the habit of a gentleman, and received, as fuch, in feveral refpectable
families. But although he lived, with fome hopes of a reftoration of
health, for about 2 years, the diftemper of his conftitution proving invin-
cible, deprived him of life, at the age of 35.

Hall, Efq. of Whitehall, is patron of the parifh.—The
falary of the fchoolmafter is 100 merks Scots, or, which
is near the fame, 1 month's cefs of the parifh. His
houfe is prefently in good repair, and of fuch length, as
affords a large room for the fchool. To his falary, are
added, the emoluments of feffion-clerk and precentor,
and that of an allowance for being collector and diftri-
butor of the affeffments for the poor upon the parifh
roll.—Thefe are levied, not at fixed meetings of the heritors, but occafional ones ; when intimation is made
from the defk, that the former affeffment being expended, a meeting of the heritors is defired, on a day mentioned, to make a farther provifion for the poor. At
their meeting, the account of the expenditure is prefented by the collector ; and then the ftate of the roll being
confidered, and what alterations have enfued, or may
be, from obferved circumftances, made in it ; fuch an
affeffment is appointed, as correfponds to the fupply required, until another meeting of the heritors be called.
The one half of the collections made in the church is
regularly taken up by the collector, and go in aid of
the affeffments. The other remains with the feffion,
to be diftributed in cafes of cafual diftrefs, to indigent
people not admitted upon the poor's roll.

Notwithftanding the birth of Mr. David Hume happened not at Ninewells, but at Edinburgh, this parifh
may claim him as a native. He was bred up here from
his infancy, and he never confidered himfelf as an alien,
from the accidental locality of his birth. His monument, erected upon the Calton-hill, at Edinburgh, where
he died, is only infcribed with his name, and the year
of his death. It is enough ; for (as this fimple figna-
ture

ture implies) to the literary world the reſt is well known.

P. S. There can be now no doubt entertained, that the ſtone taken up by Captain Home, is, what it was conjectured to be, the grinder of a Roman moletrina. The ſtone, ſunk into the ground, has been inſpected, and found hollowed out, and of the capacity and ſhape, proper to its being the under part of a corn hand-mill, of a large ſize. The grinder weighs 5 one-half ſtone Engliſh; ſo that its weight, compared with its bulk, is little inferior to that of lead. The ſpar, from which it fell, was cloſe by the excavated ſtone.

PARISH of COCKBURNSPATH,

(County of Berwick, Presbytery of Dunbar, Synod of Lothian and Tweeddale.)

By the Rev. Mr Andrew Spence.

Name, Surface, Sea-coaſt, &c.

THIS pariſh, formerly called *Colbrandſpath*, is ſituated upon the ſea-coaſt, in the ſhire of Berwick, and contiguous to Eaſt Lothian. It was but a ſmall pariſh till the annexation of Auldcambus; but at what time this happened is uncertain. The pariſh conſiſts of two parts; one high and mountainous, the other comparatively low and even. The upper diviſion makes part of the great ridge of Lammermuir, which, at the weſtern extremity of the pariſh, approaches to within about three miles of the ſhore, and which runs into the ſea in the rocky promontory of Faſt-caſtle, a little beyond its eaſtern limit. The ſame diviſion is nearly followed by the minerals, the upper part conſiſt-ing of ſchiſtus rock, the lower, of ſtrata of ſandſtone, coal, &c.; their line of junction paſſes through the middle of

the

the parish, nearly in a direction from N. E. to S. W. Their
actual meeting may be seen at the bottom of some of the
glens, but still better in a rock washed by the sea at a place
called *Sickar Point*, where the strata of sandstone lie hori-
zontally on the broken edges of the schistus, whose beds
are at that particular spot nearly in a vertical position; a
scene highly interesting to those who attend to the minera-
logical history of the globe. Several thick beds of gravel
lie upon the sandstone of the lower division, composed of
rounded pieces of schistus, whinstone, porphyry, granite, and
sometimes limestone; all of which it is probable have been
carried into their present position by some great revolution
of the globe, since none of them, except the schistus, occur
in this parish, in their native place. On the upper side,
towards the hills, these beds consist of small stones intermixed with sand, and are loose and detached; upon the shore
the stones are large, and bedded in clay. It is probably
owing to this circumstance that the soil near the sea is a
strong clay, and that farther up is light, and sometimes
gravelly.—The shore is high, consisting of a set of cliffs
about 100 feet above the level of the sea; they are formed
either of sandstone, or of the beds of clay, mixed with large
stones mentioned above; they are in some places rocky
and perpendicular, in others sloping rapidly, but covered
with grass, affording sweet pasture for sheep. Behind the
cliffs the country rises gently towards the hills in a waving
form, and is intersected by many deep ravines, whose sides
are sometimes sloping and covered with grass, but are in
general rocky, and finely wooded; in each a little brook
flows. This mixture of rocks, woods, pasture, and cultivation, produces much picturesque scenery, both lively and
romantic. Owing, however, to the want of hedge-rows, or
old enclosures, and to the low situation of the woods, the
country,

country, as seen by a traveller merely passing along the
great post-road, has somewhat of a bare appearance.

Agriculture.—In this parish we meet with every variety
both of soil and of climate, and a general spirit of industry
and emulation prevails among the tenants, which leads
them to make the most of every situation. The soil of the
lower division is partly strong and partly light, each good
of its kind; but they answer best when combined together
in one farm, as by this means a farmer can employ his
strength at all seasons, and in all weathers. The rotation
for the strong land, which lies chiefly along the shore, is
fallow, wheat or barley, with broad clover and rye-grafs;
after the clover, oats; then peafe or beans; and again barley or wheat. The best farmers frequently sow barley
after fallow, instead of wheat; for it is difficult upon strong
land, except after fallow, to hit the proper season for barley, and then the ground is in fine preparation for grafs-
feeds; whereas wheat upon fallow is often too strong, and
consequently false, and the grafs-feeds sown with it frequently fail; on the other hand, wheat after beans or peafe,
if the ground is clean, seldom fails to yield a good increase.
The rotation upon the light land of the lower division of
the parish, which lies principally upon its upper side, is
turnip, barley, clover, oats. The upper division of the parish, making part of Lammermuir, partakes somewhat of
its soil and climate; but by the industry of the farmers
and proprietors, in the cultivation of turnip and grafs, and
the proper use of lime, the face of the country has been
greatly changed for the better.

Great tracts of land, which formerly were covered with
heath, or over-run with furze, being brought to a set
of excellent breeding farms, great part of which is kept in
pasture. In these farms the sheep have been much improved

proved by the introduction, to a certain adequate degree, of the Northumberland breed. The full Northumberland breed has been lately tried with great succefs by a proprietor on fome of the rich land of the parifh. The farmers of the lower divifion in general keep no ftock, but eat off their turnips with fheep and cattle bought in for the purpofe, and fold when fit for the butcher. Sometimes the turnips are eaten upon the fpot by fheep, fometimes they are led off to grafs-fields for fheep and cattle ; in the laft cafe the good farmer thinks it neceffary to lay fome manure upon the fpot, which, even with this help, is found rather to fall fhort of the land upon which the turnip has been eaten as it grew : by this management the ground is kept in fuch heart, that an excellent crop of turnips is fometimes raifed after the oats, without dung being laid upon that crop. The upland farmers feldom feed for the butcher, but give all their turnips to the keeping ftock ; they likewife frequently buy turnips from the lower farmers, and bring down their ftock to eat them. In the lower divifion of this parifh the harveft is in general very favourable, and the farmers fhow great activity on that occafion ; fo that when a bad feafon does occur, they fuffer lefs than in many other places ; they employ great numbers of Highlanders at that time, who come into the country for the purpofe, and no wages are fpared when the feafon requires a ftrefs of hands. In the upper divifion the harveft is often late, and of courfe fubjected to more fevere weather.—No limeftone has been found in this parifh ; but lime is got from the kills at Thornton-loch, at the diftance of three or four miles along the great poft-road. The lands of the lower divifion of the parifh are very much benefited by the ufe of fea-ware as a manure. It confifts chiefly of the kind known by the name of tangle (*fucus palmatus*), having a very long ftalk, and a broad fpreading leaf ; it feems to

grow

grow upon all the rocks which are never left bare by the
tide, and whofe depth, below the furface of low-water, does
not exceed twenty fathoms; it thus occupies a fpace along
the fhore, of about half a mile in breadth, in which it grows
like a foreft, rifing eight or ten feet from the bottom; the
flat blade of the plant being vifible when the fea is at its
loweft ebb. This belt of fea-ware may be diftinguifhed in
a boat by the colour of the water, and is well known to the
fifhermen, from whofe report the above account is chiefly
taken. In violent ftorms, the fea tears the plant from the
rocks, and drives it on fhore; it is then eagerly carried off
by the farmers, who fpread it directly upon the ground
where it is to be ufed, and plough it in as faft as poffible.
It is the opinion of many good farmers, that a cart-load of
good ware is at any feafon of the year equivalent to an
equal load of dung; but at the time of fowing barley, it
is confidered as at leaft of double value; partly owing to
its being, as they fay, ripe at that feafon, having the
ftrongeft manuring quality, and partly to its efficacy in
producing fine crops of barley, both in quantity and quality. When the ground is very dry, the ware is often
fpread upon the ground after the corn is fown, or even
fprung; and when applied in this manner, it is fuppofed to
produce the beft and the fureft effects. Ware-barley is
much efteemed by the brewers, and is in great requeft for
feed; particularly by the upland farmers, as it is faid to
ripen at leaft a week earlier than any other; fo that it fells
for a fhilling the boll higher than the current price.—The
parifh contains between 7000 and 8000 acres: There are
nearly 200 acres in wheat fown yearly in the parifh, and
about 400 in turnip.—The rent for the ftrong land upon
the coaft is L. 2 the acre Scots; from 10 s. to L. 1, 10 s.
for the light land of the lower divifion: The upland farms
are not confidered as let by the acre.—There are 57 ploughs,
126 horfes, about 500 cattle, and between 4000 and 5000
fheep.

ſheep. The farms are from L. 60 to L. 450 yearly rent. Of late years many ſmall farms have been thrown into a few large ones, and ſeveral new farm-houſes, with complete office houſes, have been built; on the other hand, as by this diſtribution fewer hands are employed than formerly, many houſes of an inferior ſort have gone to ruins. A threſhing-mill has been erected about three years ago by a tenant at his own expenſe, and anſwers well.

Coal.—About the cloſe of the laſt century, coal was worked in this pariſh by a regular ſet of colliers, and ſalt-works were carried on; ſince that time the works have been given up, though the late Sir John Hall of Dunglaſs made many attempts at coal, but without ſucceſs. No fire-engine has ever been uſed.

Population.—According to Dr Webſter's report, the population in 1755 was 919. The ſtoppage of the collieries, and the loſs of the various advantages connected with them, ſeems to account for a ſtriking diminution of population which took place early in this century, as appears by the regiſters both of this pariſh, and that of Oldhamſtocks. Of late years, the number of inhabitants has undergone a ſecond diminution, by the alterations which have been made in the diſtribution of land into large farms inſtead of ſmall ones, one containing now what was formerly three or four.—The poſt-office, which was formerly at Auldcambus in this pariſh, is now removed to the Preſs, in the pariſh of Coldingham; about 40 years ago, there were five brewers in Cockburnſpath, and for many years there has not been one in the pariſh till Whitſunday 1791.—The preſent number of ſouls, by an exact account taken in April 1793, is 883; of theſe 406 are males and 477 females. At an average, the births for 10 years, from 1721 to to 1731, amounted to 35 yearly; from 1781 to 1791 they are only 24. There are at present 197 householders. The number of married persons is 287. There are 5 widowers, and 35 widows.

	Males.	Females.	Total.
Children under 3 years of age,	41	39	80
From 3 to 10, - -	91	89	180
From 10 to 20, - -	92	104	196
From 20 to 30, - -	38	59	97
From 30 to 40, - -	48	55	103
From 40 to 50, - -	34	50	84
From 50 to 60, - -	22	32	54
From 60 to 70, - -	26	36	62
From 70 to 80, - -	13	7	20
From 80 to 90, - -	1	6	7

There are 16 farmers, 16 fishermen, 12 weavers, 12 day-labourers, 9 tailors, 7 wrights, 6 smiths, 5 grocers, *i. e.* trifling merchants, 3 masons, 2 coopers, 1 wheelwright, 1 baker, 1 brewer, 1 gardener, and 1 shoemaker [*].

Heritors, Rent, Stipend, School, Poor.—There are 6 heritors of this parish, but none reside in it. The valued rent is L. 6561 : 3 : 11 Scots money. The real rent is between L. 4000

* *Diseases.*—There are no diseases peculiar to this parish; agues or intermitting fevers were formerly frequent, but are scarcely now found to occur, unless the person infected has brought the disease from another quarter. This may in some measure be owing to the greater attention that is now paid to diet, air, and cleanliness, and the more general use of animal food. Inoculation, though frequently practised, and always with success, has not yet become general. The prejudices of many have been so strong, as not to yield either to the apparent certainty of success, nor to the offer of having the attendance of a surgeon, employed by the family at Dunglass.

L. 4000 and L. 5000 Sterling. The church is ancient, and very uncomfortable, but is soon to be repaired. There are Seceders, both of the Burgher and Antiburgher perfuasions. The living, which is in gift of the Crown, confifts of 2 bolls of wheat, 38 of barley, 50 of oats; with L. 40 : 16 : 8 Sterling, including L. 40 Scots for communion elements, and a glebe of about 6 acres of arable land. The manfe was repaired in 1791, and has a garden contiguous.—There is an eftablished fchoolmafter in Cockburnfpath, his falary is L. 100 Scots. He has a dwelling-houfe, fchool-houfe, and garden. Perquifites as feffion-clerk, may be about L. 1, 15 s. Sterling. From 40 to 60 children generally attend the fchool. The wages the quarter are, for reading Englifh, 1 s. 6 d.; writing, 2 s.; arithmetic, 2 s. 6 d.; and Latin, 3 s. There has always been a fchool alfo at Auldcambus, for the benefit of that part of the parifh; but as there is no fettled falary, and there is a vacancy at prefent, it is not probable it will be again filled up.—The poor at prefent on the roll are 6, all females but one, and feveral others receive a fupply occafionally. There are no poors rates. The funds from which they are fupplied, are, the intereft of 500 merks, the collections at the churchdoor, and dues from private baptifms, and irregular marriages. Their allowance is therefore but fmall. None, however, beg; and as they are generally induftrious, they make a tolerable fhift. The lady of a gentleman, who refides in a neighbouring parifh, and is principal heritor of this, affifts and relieves many; and when they are in diftrefs, fupplies them with wine, bark, and other remedies. Were it not for her attention and liberality, the want of refiding heritors, and of poors rates, would be feverely felt.

Fifhing.—There are 16 fifhermen in the parifh, who are employed in catching in their proper feafon, cod, ling, fkate,

fkate, whitings, flounders, lobfters, and crabs, &c. Haddocks, which for fome years had difappeared, have this fpring been again found in confiderable quantities, but the price is greatly advanced. For many years, the beft haddocks were fold at 6 d. the fcore, and now they fell at from 2 s. to 5 s. The herring-fifhing is fometimes very advantageous; in fome feafons, above 100 boats have been collected at the Cove, and been very fuccefsful. The white fifh is in general fold to carriers, who take them to Muffelburgh, from whence they are carried on women's backs to the Edinburgh market. The lobfters have, for thefe many years, been fold by contract, at a fixed price for certain fizes, to Mr Fall of Dunbar, who fhipped them off to London. About 40 years ago, an attempt was made by Sir John Hall of Dunglafs, to clear a bafon, and make a harbour at the Cove. The wall was confiderably advanced, when a ftrong wind from the N. E. raifed fuch a heavy fea, as almoft entirely deftroyed the work, and it was not again renewed. A road had been cut through a rock, for an eafy accefs to the fhore, by which carts ftill pafs under ground, about 60 yards. Cellars were alfo cut out of the folid rock, and would have been very ufeful and commodious.

Roads.—This parifh has the peculiar advantage of being interfected by public roads, which afford eafy and convenient communications to all quarters. The great eaftern road from Edinburgh to London by Berwick, paffes through the parifh, cutting it nearly from S. E. to N. W.; the road from Dunbar to Dunfe cuts it from north to fouth; and a new road is lately begun, but not yet opened, by which it is propofed to form an eafy and fhort communication between Eaft Lothian and Berwickfhire, along a valley, which paffes near Renton, in the parifh of Coldingham.

Coldingham. Befides thefe, there is a number of roads cut along the fteep banks, in order to procure fea-ware for manure, which is driven in at 6 different places on the fhore of this parifh. The poft-road croffes three of the ravines already mentioned, as interfecting this parifh; firft, the Dunglafs burn, at its entry on the weft fide, over an old bridge, which is very inconvenient; next, at the Tower; and laftly over the Peas. It croffes the two laft by bridges, built in the year 1786, when the road was al-tered, in order to avoid the very dangerous pafs which it croffed near the fea. The Peas bridge is 123 feet from the bottom of the water of the burn to the top of the rail; it is 300 feet long, with the parapet walls, 15 feet wide, and 6 feet from the level of the road to the top of the rail; in paffing by the Peas bridge, the road is lengthened between ¼ and ⅓ of a mile; but a great faving is obtained in point of level, as the level of the prefent bridge is 100 feet in perpendicular height, above the fpot at which the old road croffed the Peas burn, near the fea; and the old road upon the eaft fide rofe through a perpendicular height of 150 feet, at a declivity of nearly one in five.

Woods, &c.—About Dunglafs, there is a great deal of fine wood and valuable trees, fome of which are in this parifh; a fmall part of thefe woods is natural, or has fprung as ftock fhoots from natural wood cut over, but by far the greateft part was planted about the beginning of this century. There are about 100 acres of natural oaks, called Penmifhiel wood, about half of which have been cut fince the year 1750. None have been cut for the laft 10 years, the remainder are about as old as the century. There is alfo a good deal of wood on the fides of many of the deep ravines, with which the parifh is interfected. Fuel is fcarce and expenfive. Some peat and turf are ufed,

but

but in general coals. They are moftly brought from Dunbar, where they coft from 5 s. to 11 s. the boll, which is
11½ cwt. with the addition of carriage. They this winter
coft fometimes 14 s. the boll, and were often not to be had
at any rate. Wages are much the fame here as in the
neighbouring parifhes, and are ftated in their accounts.

Antiquities.—Part of the church ftill remains at Auldcambus, called St Helen's Kirk. From the nature of the
building, and other circumftances, it is fuppofed to have
been erected fome time in the feventh century. About a
quarter of a mile from the Peas bridge, the remains of an
ancient caftle are ftill ftanding, called the Old Tower. It
appears to have been a place of confiderable ftrength, but
nothing certain is known concerning it. This parifh, lying near the boundary of the kingdoms, and containing
many very ftrong military paffes, has been frequently the
fcene of war; and this appears, by the camps of various
kinds ftill vifible on many of the rifing grounds, and by
the traces of military entrenchments in the glens.

PARISH of COLDINGHAM.

(COUNTY OF BERWICK, SYNOD OF MERSE AND TIVIOTDALE, PRESBYTERY OF CHIRNSIDE).

By JOHN RENTON, *Efq. of Chefterbank*.*

Extent, Surface, &c,

THIS parifh is the largeft of any in this country, but not of the greateft value, as it includes a common moor, which contains above 600 Englifh acres, of a very poor qua- lity. There is no map of this parifh. In fome parts, it is between 6 and 7 miles in length, and as much in breadth, and is of a very irregular figure. The appearance of this pa- rifh is rather flat, there being no high hills in it, but a great proportion of rifing grounds, of eafy afcent, and gentle declivi- ty, which are, with a few exceptions, all acceffible by the plough, and which, as well as the valleys and plain ground, are of a fertile foil, excepting the heights about St. Abb's Head,

---

* The parifh of Coldingham being at prefent vacant, the Statiftical Account of that diftrict was very obligingly undertaken by Mr. Renton.

Head, and other lesser parcels, which are bare and rocky, and part of the farms upon the edges of the common moor, which are of a coarse and cold soil, and excepting also the far greatest part of that moor itself, which, in its natural state, produces nothing but heath on the dry parts, and bent, and the coarsest sort of grass on the swampy wettish parts. This great common was, about 20 years ago, divided by the Court of Session among the heritors having interest therein, after much litigation, and at the expense of 1500 l. and upwards; considerable improvements, by enclosing, draining, and liming, have been made thereon, by several of the heritors. But it is believed few of them will find those improvements turn out to their advantage, as the soil is, in most parts, thin, marshy, and of the mossy kind, and the bottom of a tough, cold bluish clay. The general opinion seems to be, that the best use that it can be turned to, is by planting it. There are several peat mosses in this extensive moor; but few of the peats are of the black hard kind: they are generally of a brownish colour, soft and porous, and burn away in a blaze, are fitter for kindling than lasting fires, and as such they are now commonly used. The mosses themselves being much worn out, the digging and drying the peats has become more difficult and expensive, and they are now, from different causes, in a good measure, deserted, although peats and turfs were the principal fuel used in this parish from the earliest times; and this accounts for the barrenness and sterility of the moor, as the surface must have been repeatedly paired and carried off by the inhabitants, in the course of many ages.

River, Fish, Sea-Coast, &c.—The water of Eye, is the only water worth mentioning in this parish, it rises in the parish of Cockburnspath, very near the west boundary of this parish, and has its course through this and the parish of Ayton,

ton, and runs into the sea at Eyemouth. In this water there are plenty of trouts of excellent quality, generally small : there are indeed some pretty large, from 16 to 24 inches in length, but none of the true salmon kind. There is also a beautiful lake of water, about a mile west of St. Abb's Head, called Coldingham Loch. It is of a triangular figure, about a mile in circumference, and said to be several fathoms deep in some parts : the water is clear, and must be produced from springs, as there are no burns that run into it, and although it has no visible outlet, the depth always appears to be the same. The only fish in it, are the perch from 5 to 8 inches long, compact and firm in appearance, but dry eating. This lake appears to be well suited for a pleasure-boat, but there is none on it at present. It is situated many fathoms above the level of the sea. The extent of the sea-coast, in this parish, is about 6 miles from Eyemouth parish to that of Cockburnspath, and upon this part of the coast, the promontory of St. Abb's Head is situated, about which, and on the westward of it, the shore is dangerous and inaccessible, except at Lumsden shore, at which there are several fishing boats, and, on the eastward of St. Abb's Head, a considerable part of the shore is smooth and of easy access, particularly at Coldingham sands, and the farm of Northfield, where there are also several fishing boats : but there is no harbour for ships in this parish ; the only harbour in Berwickshire being at Eyemouth, the best and most accessible of any between Holy Island and Leith. There is a fine bay between St. Abb's Head and the fort of Eyemouth, in which ships bound for Eyemouth cast anchor and wait the time of tide for going into the harbour. Great plenty of fish are caught in the sea, on this part of the coast, such as haddocks, whitings, cod, and ling ; lobsters, crabs, and other shell fish ; turbot, skate, and herrings, all of excellent qualities, which, after supply-

ing

ing the people in this neighbourhood, are carried to Dunfe, Kelfo, &c., and a great part are carried to Edinburgh. The haddocks have almost deserted this coast for these 2 or 3 years, but the cod and ling are more plentiful, and of better quality than formerly. The difference between the highest and lowest tides, on this shore, is about 20 feet; and there are great quantities of sea-weed, commonly called sea-ware, thrown ashore here, the coarser part of which is carried off with avidity, and applied as manure to the land near the shore. The finer parts are manufactured into kelp, and produce from 30 to 40 tons yearly. The greatest part of this finer sort, grows upon the rocks situated between the high and low water-marks, and is cut and manufactured into kelp only once in 3 years.

Town of Coldingham.—The town of Coldingham appears to have been of very high antiquity; for the monastery was one of the most ancient and flourishing on the east of Scotland, and previous to the confecration of the famous St. Cuthbert, the bishop of Lindisferne, *i. e.* Holy Island, which was performed in the Cathedral of York, in the year 685. This monastery, then a famous and stately edifice, was consumed and burnt *. The town of Coldingham stands in a snug dry valley,

---

* It is said (Sir D. Dalrymple's Annals, vol. I. p. 48.) to have been rebuilt by King Edgar, in the year 1098, and that at its confecration to the Virgin, he affifted in person, when it was conftituted into a priory of Benedictines, to which a colony of Monks from Durham were introduced; and that for feveral fucceeding generations, it continued to depend upon the convent of Durham; that K. Edgar ordered a house to be built for himself, at a fmall diftance from the church (part of the walls of which houfe are ftill to be feen, and are called Edgar's walls at this day); and befides this manfion-houfe, he beftowed on the priory, the lands of Auld Cambus, Lumfden, Renton, Swinewood, Fairneyfide, the 2 Aytons, Prenderguest, and Grainfmouth, all places in the neighbourhood, and

valley, having a fmall rivulet of excellent water running upon each fide of it, and is about a mile diftant from the fea. It is furrounded with rifing fields of gentle afcent, all of ex-cellent quality ; but there are no profpects from the town be-yond half a mile's diftance. It appears from old writings, and by parts of the foundations of old buildings, that feveral of the crofts about the town, now arable, had been anciently the fites of houfes and gardens. It muft, therefore, have been much more populous than it is at prefent *. Before the com-mon moor was divided, this town was dull and unpleafant, in appearance, as all the houfes were covered with turfs and divots from that moor. All the inhabitants were averfe to the divifion, becaufe they forefaw, that this fervitude, and that of the peats and turfs for fuel, would be much con-fined.

and at prefent known by the fame names; as alfo, the lands of Swinton, and 24 beafts for tilling them ; and likewife the lands of Paxton, Fifhwick, and all the lands adjoining to the latter, lying between Harnden and Knabton, places of great extent and value on the banks of the river Tweed, and ftill called by the fame names ; and that he alfo gave to this church, the fame privileges which were at that time poffeffed by Holy Ifland and Norham, viz. 37 days to all who fled thither, and half a merk of filver to the Monks of Coldingham from every plough in Coldingham fhore, for which the poffeffors of thefe lands voluntarily fubmitted and engaged for its punctual payment.

* The prior refided here with all his train and dependents; and the church and other buildings about it were extenfive and magnificent, but are all now in complete ruins, except the prefent kirk, which is dark within, and fhabby with-out. The revenue of this priory muft have been very confiderable ; for, befides the temporal lands which belonged to it, they had right to the drawn teinds of 13 parifhes. After the general annexation, this priory was erected into a tem-poral lordfhip in favour of John Stuart, a natural fon or grandfon of K. James the 5th. It feems he had fold a great part of the lands and teinds, and the remainder were carried off by the Earls of Home, by decreets of apprifing and other legal diligences. They have been long in poffeffion, and partly by voluntary, and partly in confequence of decreets of valuation and fale, have fold the fubjects adjudged, at leaft the far greateft part of them, but have ftill right to the feu-duties of a great number of feuars and heritors.

fined. But in place of their being sufferers by the division, it has turned out much to their advantage, for great numbers of them were employed all the summer time in digging and preparing peats and turfs; but after they were, in a great measure, restricted from that servitude, they found more profitable employment, from the spirit of improvements which had become general, and were soon able to get coals for their fuel: and they are now in a more thriving condition in every respect, than they enjoyed before the division; for, since that period, they have not only built a good many new houses, which they have covered with tiles, and some with blue slates, but they have rebuilt several of the old houses and covered them with this sort of covering; and the town has now a more lively and cheerful appearance, and their wealth and population are visibly increasing. The number of souls in this town, at present, is 718, whereof 317 are males, and 401 females.

Population.—According to Dr. Webster's report, the number of souls then, was 2313. By an accurate list made out in the year 1791, the heads of families in this parish are 529; the number of souls 2391, of whom 1136 are males, and 1255 females. There were 643 under 10 years; 502 between 10 and 20; 938 between 20 and 50; 213 between 50 and 70; and 95 between 70 and 100. By the session-clerk's attestation, it appears, that from the 1st of January 1790 to 1st January 1793, there have been 113 baptisms, 70 deaths, and 31 marriages: That the assessments laid on by the heritors, for the paupers, have been at the rate of 4 months land-tax, *communibus annis*, for these last 3 years, or 69l. 7s. 4d. Sterling yearly, exclusive of the collections at the church doors; and the numbers of the poor are increasing, which may be ascribed to the too common use of tea, and the immoderate use

use of whisky. There is not a single surgeon in this parish.
The people in general are moderate and healthy ; few agues
of late years ; fevers and confumptions are the ordinary fatal
diseases here, especially to young women. Few of the common people will allow inoculation; they say it is an encroach-
ment upon the prerogative of providence; and it is in vain to
tell them, that prudence is the gift of providence, and that it
is their indispensible duty to use every prudential and approved means to save the lives of their children.

Stipend, Heritors, &c.—The Crown is patron. The manfe
and offices are in good repair, and the kirk was divided a-
mong the heritors, new feated and repaired about 20 years
ago. The glebe and the garden are among the beft in this
presbytery. The stipend, which, by a procefs of augmentation in 1739, was converted into money, is 88 l. 13 s.; and
the minifter has right to the teinds of the 7 fifhing boats in
this parish, for which the laft incumbent accepted of 20 s.
yearly for each of thofe boats. By the converfion of the
victual stipend in 1739, into money, the minifter thought
himfelf a confiderable fufferer. By the land-tax or cefs-roll
of this county, it appears there are 67 heritors, great and
fmall, in this parish, and that our monthly cefs is 208 l. 2 s.
Scots ; that 1 l. 12 s. Scots, or 2 s. 8 d. Sterling of monthly
cefs, is equal to 100 l. Scots of valued rent, being the qualification of a commiffioner of fupply ; and that there are only
19 of thefe 67 heritors, whofe valued rent amounts to that qualification. None of the heritors whofe real rent exceeds 400 l.
Sterling, refide within the parish ; and almoft all the fmaller
heritors poffefs their own lands. Some of them are in eafy circumftances, others not. Within thefe 40 years, the full half
of the lands in this parish have been fold by their former
proprietors, and have always met with ready purchafers; and
the

the rents, as well as the price of land here, are ftill advancing.

Agriculture.—Before the fpirit of improving land began to appear here, there were 3 confiderable villages befides the town of Coldingham, viz. Renton, Auchencraw, and the 2 Preftons; but fince that, the heritors have built good farm-fteadings upon the moft centrical parts of their outfields. Hence, the villages of Renton and Eaft Prefton, have difappeared, and Auchencraw and Weft Prefton have dwindled to lefs than the half of what they were before that period. There are above 60 farms in this parifh, befides the acres that lie around the town of Coldingham. The rents of the farms are from 20 l. to 500 l. and upwards. Several of the heritors who poffefs their own properties, as well as our principal farmers, are inferior to none in induftry and fkill for the improvement and management of land to the beft advantage *.

Some

* Previous to the year 1760, almoft the whole farms in this and the neighbouring parifhes were laboured and cropt in the following manner, viz. about one-fourth of the arable land as infield, and the other three-fourths as outfield; but for the better underftanding that mode of cropping and management, fuppofe a farm confifting of 400 acres of arable land (befides meadow and marfhy ground unfit for tillage) to have been let, the tenant became bound by the leafe to fallow and dung one-fifth part of the infield yearly, and not to take above 4 crops thereof between fallowings, one of which to be barley, and another a peafe crop, and fo on through the courfe of the tack: and with refpect to the outfield, he was allowed to have only one-third part of it in corn, in any one year, which third he was obliged to fallow, and to give it 3 or more ploughings between Whitfunday and the enfuing feed time; and after taking 3 crops of oats off it fucceffively, he was obliged to allow it to lie in ley for 6 years before it was again riven out and fallowed, and fo on with the other two-thirds of the outfield, until the expiration of his tack. By that mode of management, the land was fo much wafted and worn out, that the fourth crop of the infield, and the third from the outfield, frequently did not produce the double of the feed; and the only pafture fuch a farmer had for fupporting his ftocking of

horfes,

Some years prior to 1760, a few individuals, of more than ordinary penetration and difcernment, having difcovered the mighty effects of lime in Northumberland, they ventured to make experiments of its effects upon the lands in Berwickfhire; and from their exertions and fuccefs, a fpirit of improvement became general : and in confequence of the great demand for lime, additional lime-kilns were erected, both upon this, and on the other fide of Berwick, and the great quantities pro-duced from them, as well as what was brought in fhips from Sunderland, and landed at Eyemouth, have been truly amaz-ing. Our farming heritors and freeholders above alluded to, in this parifh, foon began and carried on the improvements of their feveral poffeffions, with equal fpirit and fuccefs. They foon difcovered the inefficacy and impropriety of their former mode of cropping, and relinquifhed it unanimoufly; and, in place thereof, adopted a quite new and different fyftem. They began it by fallowing and cleaning all their old infield, and then fowing upon it barley or oats, and red and white clover, with a fmall mixture of rye-grafs ; fome of them did, and o-thers did not lay their muck upon that fallow : becaufe old infield, even when it appears to be worn out and wafted by corn crops, will produce luxuriant crops of clover and rye-grafs, without manure ; and fo it happened with thofe im-provers. They did not even beftow any. lime upon that old infield fallow, as lime has been found to have little effect up-on old infield ; and it only difcovers its powers upon frefh land. And having thus difpofed of their infield, by laying

it

horfes, black cattle, and fheep, was the poor grafs upon the two-thirds of out-field ley, and the meadow and marfhy fpots in the farm in the fummer and au-tumn, and dry ftraw in winter and fpring. The poor condition in which thefe animals appeared, in the months of March and April every year, demonftrated the fcarcity and poor quality of their food. They were fmall, lean, and very weak.

it off in graſs, partly for hay, and partly for paſturage, which
afforded them plenty of meat for their horſes employed in driving lime, and carrying on their improvements in the next, and
other years, they then applied their whole ſtrength for manuring their outfield, at the rate of 40 to 50 bolls of lime-
ſhells * to the Engliſh acre, which, after being fallowed, and
ſo limed, produced three good crops, viz. oats, barley, oats ;
or, oats, peaſe, barley. They then fallowed, and, laying all
their muck upon the fallow well pulverized, they formed it
into drills, and ſowed turnips on the drills, which were eaten
by their ſheep in the winter, and then ploughed and ſowed it
up with graſs-ſeeds, in the ſame manner as the infield ; and
ſo they went on with the reſt of the outfield, and by the end
of 10 or 12 years, their farms were all thus improved, and
were all managed and cropt thereafter as infield, and in the
following manner, viz. They commonly allowed their ſown
up graſs ground to remain in graſs for at leaſt 3 years, ſome
4 or 5, and haying and paſturing it alternately; and after ſowing it out for corn-crops, they took only three crops from the
richeſt and beſt parts of the farms ; theſe were oats, barley,
oats ; or, oats, peaſe, wheat, if the land had any tolerable mixture of good clay in it ; and they then fallowed it, ſowed up
the turnip-land with barley, oats, and graſs-ſeeds, as before.
In their middling ſoil, they took only two crops of corn, oats
and barley, and thereafter fallow, turnip, barley and graſs-
ſeeds ; and in the weakeſt and lighteſt of their ſoil, they only
took one crop of oats, and then fallow, turnip, barley, and
graſs-ſeeds ; and in this ſecond courſe they alſo gave it another liming of 25 to 30 bolls lime-ſhells the acre, and commonly with the ſecond crop of the ſtrongeſt and middling ſoils ;

and

---

* Our boll of lime is 4 buſhels or half a quarter. The price of what is imported at Eyemouth, is 1 s. 2 d. the boll ; and that brought from beyond Berwick is 8 d., beſides the carriage.

and their whole dung and fulzie was always beſtowed on the turnip fallow.

Their chief objeᴄt is to have the lands laid down into graſs in good heart, and it will improve every year, if paſtured with ſheep; and after a farm is improved, in manner above written, our farmers have never leſs than half of it in graſs, and ſome of them two-thirds; becauſe they find that ſuch rich graſs fields bring them as much profit as their corn fields do. If ſo, the lands muſt be in the higheſt condition, and may be kept ſo by prudent management, at no conſiderable expenſe. It is by too many corn crops, and too frequent crops of hay, that lands are deteriorated, to prevent which ſhould be the chief attention of landlords and their managers. No ſenſible honeſt farmer will ever attempt to injure or run out his farm by ſcourging crops, towards the end of his tack; and no capricious fool will ever find ſuch diſhoneſt means profitable. By departing from the old, and adopting this new ſyſtem of management, our farmers have reaped profits equal to their expeᴄtations; their corn fields have been far more produᴄtive, and their ſtocking of all kinds bring them more than triple the prices they were ſold at, before their farms were ſo improved. Of late years, they have ſold their hogs at or above 20 s. a-head; their two-years old from 25 s. to 30 s.; and their older ſheep between 30 s. and 40 s., and ſome at higher prices. No pains nor expenſes have been ſpared to procure the breed both of black cattle and ſheep fitteſt for their ſeveral paſtures. In ſmall farms, where there are no ſheep, the tenants let their turnip crops from 2 l. to 4 l. the acre. The turnip belonging to the greater farmers are eaten by their own ſheep. Our beſt landlords have no ſcruple to let their farms to good farmers for 25 to 31 years, where the farms are not improved; and indeed no tenant will take a leaſe of any ſhorter duration, where he has the farm to improve at his

own

own expenfe. Many of the landlords allow the incoming te‑
nants a confiderable deduction from the yearly rent, for buy‑
ing lime for affifting them in their improvement *.

Manufactures.—We have few manufactures in this parifh,
owing to our diftance from collieries. But although our coals
are dearer, our grain is cheaper by 18 d. or 2 s. a boll, than
it is about Glafgow and Paifley. Our fupernumerary young
men go partly to England, and partly to Edinburgh, and o‑
ther populous towns in Scotland, in queft of employment.
Very few of them relifh either the failor or foldier's way of
life. Our young women are, for the moft part, employed in
fpinning, of which they make very fmall wages, not exceed‑
ing 2 s. a-week. It is faid that fundry manufacturers in E‑
dinburgh, and other places, have of late years fent them quan‑
tities of lint to fpin here, which they return in yarn; and that
this employment increafes every year. Our handicraftfmen
and

* The yearly gains or wages of a fingle hind in this parifh, are 10 bells oats,
2 bolls barley, 1 boll peafe, a houfe and a fmall kail yard, a cow's meat, land
for fowing a firlot of potatoes, the carriage of 3 or 4 carts coals, from 20s. to
30s. for fheep-money, their victuals while working at hay, or in harveft; his
wife reaps in harveft for the houfe, and fhe and her bairns, that can work, get
from 3d. to 6d. a-day, for weeding turnips and potatoes, and for gathering and
carrying off ftones from the fown grafs grounds. The lotmen or threfhers of corn,
get the 25th boll in name of wages; fome farmers give them a bottle of fmall-
beer at a certain hour of the day, which is very neceffary, and it enlivens them
much. A ploughman or carter who lives in the farmer's houfe, gets from 6l.
to 7l. yearly: a day-labourer gets 10d. in winter, and 1s. the reft of the year,
winter being reckoned at 4 months: mafons and wrights from 16d. to 20d. a-
day: the other tradefmen are commonly paid for piece work: a maid fervant
gets from 3l. to 4l. a-year. All thefe wages, except the hinds and herds, who
are paid in kind, have been raifed one-third part, at leaft, within thefe laft 40
years. Even the hind's and herd's are increafed, by the difference of their cow's
meat and the fowing of potatoes; fome of them are allowed to fow a peck or a
half of lintfeed, and every faithful fervant commonly gets fome additional gra‑
tifications from their mafters and miftreffes.

and labourers feem to depend upon the farmers for their fubfiftence, as they are principally employed by them. There
are, however, about 36 mafter weavers in the parifh, who,
befides what they weave for the inhabitants, manufacture a
good deal of linen and woollen cloths for fale. They are generally in eafy circumftances, and fome of them are becoming
rich in that line of life.

Profeffions, Manners, &c.—There are feveral fhopkeepers
in the town of Coldingham, but none of them deal extenfively. No writers or attorneys of influence; nor is there
one fingle juftice of peace refident in this large parifh. No
Papifts, Epifcopals, or Unitarians. The eftablifhed Prefbyterian religion is the only manner of worfhip attended to and
profeffed here; there are, however, a few feceders, who attend the Burgher and Antiburgher meetings at Ayton. They
tax themfelves with a proportion of the expenfe of building
the meeting-houfes, and the preacher's ftipend. Thus they
facrifice their money, as toll-dues, for the fafeft or fureft paffage to the regions of complete happinefs in a future ftate.
The generality of the people in this parifh are fober, frugal,
and induftrious, plain and decent in their drefs and deport-
ment, and very few of them difcover any defire for fineries,
or expenfive amufements. The only extravagance they are
guilty of is their breakfafting upon tea, in place of pottage,
the conftant morning diet of their more athletic anceftors,
which debilitates them; (here I do not include the principal families) and the immoderate ufe of whifky, which too
many of the lower clafs are guilty of, which deftroys them.
This is owing to the cheapnefs of thefe two fuperfluous and
pernicious articles, which appear to be objects more fit for
taxaticn than coals, candles, leather and foap, which are as
neceffary in the pooreft families, as their meal and milk.

Exports,

Exports, &c.—The quantities of grain, particularly oats, and barley, for we do not grow much wheat or pease, as well as the numbers of black cattle and sheep, sold from this parish, at Eyemouth, Berwick, and to mealmakers, *communibus annis*, are very considerable, but cannot be ascertained with any degree of exactness; and it is impossible to know the number of quadrupeds, without a special survey. All roots and vegetables necessary for the kitchen are raised in great plenty in this parish; and we sell a great share of our potatoes: but there is neither hemp nor lint raised here, except by some individuals, who raise a little of the latter for their family purposes, and their servants for theirs; and all our grain is commonly got into the barn-yards by Michaelmas O. S. except in cold, wet seasons, such as the last, and also excepting the farms adjoining the common moor: there the corns are three or four weeks later in ripening than those in the warmer and more fertile fields.

Disadvantages.—The greatest disadvantage peculiar in this parish, is the distance and dearth of fuel. Since the division of the common moor, our chief fuel is coals, which we bring in carts from the collieries in Northumberland, at the distance of 14 miles from the centre of this parish. The Author of Nature, who always acts for good and wise purposes, for the general good of the whole creation, hath denied the benefit of coal-mines to every part of the county of Berwick; at least none such have as yet been discovered. The legislature, in supplement and addition to our want of that necessary article, did, in Queen Anne's days, saddle all water-borne coals that should be landed at Eyemouth, our only sea-port, with a duty of 3 s. 8 d. the ton, and at same time exempted Dunbar, North Berwick, and all the other ports in the Frith of Forth from payment of any duty for coals. How far that law can

be

be reconciled with equity and juftice, which are, or ought to be the foundation of all laws, cannot be eafily conceived.

Birds of Paffage, Sea-Fowl, &c.—There are only two birds of paffage, the woodcock and the dotterel, ever feen here ; the firft frequents the woods, and are few in number ; the fecond appear in vaft numbers on the heights. They both arrive in the fpring, and are feldom feen here after the month of June. There is alfo a prodigious number of fea-fowls, known by the names of fcouts and kittywakes, with a mixture of fea-gulls, that arrive in the fpring yearly, upon the high and inacceffible rocks on the fouth fide of St. Abb's Head. They breed incredible numbers of young ; and about the end of May, when the young are faid to be ripe, but before they can fly, the gentlemen in the neighbourhood find excellent fport by going out in boats, and fhooting great numbers of them ; when they are killed or wounded, they fall from the rocks into the fea, and the rowers haul them into their boats. Their eggs are pretty good, but their flefh is very bad ; yet the poor people eat them. They leave the rocks about harveft ; and none of them are ever feen here before the next fpring. Where they go to in winter, nobody knows.

Antiquities.—There are the remains of a church, or chapel of eafe, on the heights of St. Abb's Head. Part of the fide-walls are ftill ftanding upright *.

Faft

* It is faid that this promontory got its name from Lady Ebba, who was daughter of one of the kings of Northumberland, in the time of the heptarchy ; that a violent war having happened in her father's dominions, in which he was defeated, fhe found it advifable to take refuge in Scotland ; and that accordingly fhe, accompanied by fome friends and domeftics, went to fea in a fmall veffel, bound for fome port in the Frith of Forth ; but a contrary wind having fprung

Fast Castle is situated on the banks of the sea, on the N. W. corner of this parish. It is now in complete ruins. It must, from the steepness of the rocks on which it stood, have been inaccessible on all parts, except by a narrow neck, or entry from the land, of a few feet in breadth. At the date of Gowry's conspiracy, it belonged to Logan of Restalrigg. Every body knows his fate, or rather that of his family. Several years after he was in his grave, he was tried and condemned, and his whole estates were forfeited, and bestowed upon the then Earl of Dunbar, for his being engaged in that conspiracy: A silly body of the name of Sprot, a notary in Eyemouth, produced some treasonable letters that passed between Gowry and Logan; and he was rewarded by being hanged at Edinburgh cross. There was a fortalice, or family castle at Renton, another at Houndwood, one at West Preston, and one at East Preston, in which the proprietors of these estates resided. They have been all demolished, since the commencement of this century, and the stones and materials applied to other purposes.

The

sprung, they could not weather the Head, but landed in some part near it, probably at Coldingham sands; and being hospitably received by the bishop or prior of Coldingham, she was soon appointed Abbess, or some such dignified rank in that church, and, from a principle of gratitude, built that chapel at her own expense, after which the promontory was known by the name of St. Abb's head. There is also a tradition, and it even appears in some part of the history of these times, (which by the by the writer hereof never read), that upon an invasion of the Danes, this Lady Ebba, or some of the succeeding Abbesses, and her or their nuns of Coldingham, cut off their noses, for preventing their being violated by these terrible foes. And by way of contrast to that very singular mode of preserving their chastity, it is said that the Pope, in some of his charters to this Convent, indulged the Monks with the use of some females at certain periods, *ob purganda renis*; and that some of these charters are preserved in the cathedral of Durham to this day. And it has been always currently reported and believed here, that all the principal writings and archives of this priory were carried off and deposited at Durham, some time before the Reformation, and also some of their largest bells.

The only camp that now appears to have been in this parifh, is that upon the height called Warlaw, on the weftward
of Auchencraw. It is of an oval form, and contains 5 or 6
acres of very poor moor land; but hiftory and tradition are filent about it.

Roads, &c.—Previous to the year 1772, the roads in this
county were repaired by the ftatute-work in kind, but which
was much neglected; and what part thereof that was performed,
as always done in the moft flovenly and injudicious manner.
By that time feveral inclofures were made by our improvers,
upon the fides of the highways. Neceffity is the ftrongeft
prompter; and the gentlemen being fenfible of the continual
trefpaffes that muft happen to their fences, unlefs the roads
were made paffable, they applied for, and obtained an act of
parliament for making turnpike roads, and for converting the
ftatute-labour into money. No turnpikes were ever erected
in confequence of that law, in this parifh; but the ftatute-
work, fo converted, was rigoroufly exacted, and applied under the direction of the diftrict meetings. The amount of
thefe converfions in this parifh, fince 1772, may be about
3000 l. Sterling. The great poft-road leading acrofs the common moor, naturally rough, wet, and deep, fwallowed up a
great part of thefe converfions for many years, and a new feparate turnpike act was thought neceffary, for completing
and upholding the repairs of that great road from Dunglafs-
bridge to Berwick bounds, which was accordingly obtained;
and at fame time a fine new bridge was built over the Peafe
water, and that whole great poft-road is now completely repaired. Hence this part of the poft-road, through Berwickfhire, which was formerly the worft and moft dangerous part
of it, between Edinburgh and London, is now in perfect
good repair; and the increafe of travellers, efpecially in carriages.

riages, far exceeds all expectation ; and our ſtatute conver-
ſions, which exceed 140 l. Sterling yearly, will, it is believed,
be ſufficient for forming and ſupporting all the other roads in
good condition, under proper management, which hitherto
ſeems to have been exceptionable.

The greateſt part of the lands in this pariſh have been encloſed within theſe laſt thirty years, (if we except the common moor), generally by ditch and hedge, and ſome with
ſtone-fences ; and there is little doubt of the whole being encloſed in a few years hence, (with the above exception).
Thorn hedges thrive well here, ſo do trees of all ſorts ; but
our artificial plantations are few. There are a good many natural woods, near the head of the water of Eye. They conſiſt chiefly of oak, hazel, and birch. Some parts of theſe woods
are let to tanners, who peel and carry off the bark of the oak
trees, and ſell the timber to farmers. The bruſhwood and
loppings are bought for fuel.

PARISH of COLDSTREAM,

(COUNTY OF BERWICK).

By JAMES BELL, D. D.

Name, Situation, Soil, Air, &c.

THE ancient name of the pariſh was Lennel, and the ruins of Lennel church, diſtant from Coldſtream about a mile and a half nearly, ſtill remain. Eaſtward from this church there was formerly a little town or village called Lennel, which was ſo entirely deſtroyed in the Border wars, that the ſite of it is not known to me. Coldſtream was the ſeat of a priory or abbacy which belonged to the Ciſtertian order, and was ſituated near the Tweed, where a ſmall water, called Leet, falls into it. Of this ancient ſtructure a vault only remains. It is probable that a village was formed near it, which, from the pleaſantneſs of the ſituation, and the protection afforded by the abbacy to the inhabitants, increaſed to the ſize of a ſmall town. Before General Monk marched into England to reſtore the Royal Family, he made Coldſtream his head quarters, and raiſed that body of men, which, being in ſucceſſion recruited, has been called ever ſince the Coldſtream Regiment of Guards.—

Coldſtream

Coldstream is situated in the county of Berwick, presbytery of Chirnside, and Synod of Merse and Tiviotdale. Placing the foot of a compass at Lennel church, taking 4 miles for a radius, and the river Tweed as a diameter, a semicircle described on the north of that river will give a general idea of the extent and form of the parish. The length from E. to W. is from 7 to 8 miles; the breadth 4 miles at an average. Coldstream is bounded by Ladykirk on the E. by Simprin (now united to Swinton) on the N. by Eccles on the W. The river Tweed is the southern boundary. The general appearance of the country is flat. The rising grounds in the parish do not deserve the name of hills.—The soil for the most part is rich and fertile; near the Tweed light; inclined to clay backwards. A broad slip of barren land runs through the parish from E. to W. called the Moorland.—The air is in general dry and healthy. Coldstream is situated at a considerable, and nearly equal distance from the Chiviot and Lammermoor hills. When the weather is showery, especially if the wind be westerly, the clouds (from the west) take the direction of one or other of these hills, pour down their contents upon them, and leave this parish untouched. There is much more rain at Dunse and Wooller than here. According as the summer is wet or dry, Coldstream is benefited or hurt by the locality of its situation. Agues prevail in some seasons, but not regularly. Headaches, toothaches, and nervous complaints in general, are more frequent here than in other places with which I have been acquainted. Perhaps the easterly fogs and rains, together with the frequent blowing of the wind from that quarter, may be the causes of these complaints. In the village, the children of the poorer inhabitants are liable to the scrophula.

Tweed.

Tweed.—Tweed produces bull-trouts, whittings, gilfes, falmon, and all other kinds of fifh common to the rivers in the fouth of Scotland. Bull-trouts make their appearance in Tweed during the fpring months, and foon after go a-way. When they come in numbers, they are thought to prognofticate a plenteous feafon for gilfes and falmon.—The intercourfe carried on between Berwick and London, by means of the Berwick fmacks, and the recent difcovery of carrying frefh fifh to a diftant market, preferved in ice, render the price of gilfes and falmon as dear at Coldftream as in the metropolis. Tweed is open to fifhing from the 10th of January to the 10th of October. In the rivers to the north, which abound in fuch fifh, the *clofe* feafon, as it is called, which comprehends the reft of the months, varies, and is earlier, I believe, for the moft part in proportion to the latitude of thefe rivers northwards in Scotland, to the Tay, Don, and Dee. The fifheries in the Tweed are of fmall value here, but not fo near Berwick. The gentlemen concerned in them have of late been at great pains to protect and extend them. They reckon nothing more beneficial than the taking care that the protection afforded to the fifh, be obferved, during the clofe feafon, with the utmoft ftrictnefs. Meetings have been held by the gentlemen of Merfe and Tiviotdale, lately, to deliberate concerning the practicability and expediency of rendering Tweed navigable, or of cutting a canal through thofe two counties to the fea.

Minerals, &c.—Befides good freeftone, pebbles, feemingly of a good quality, are found among the ftones and fand on the banks of Tweed, as well as in the fields nigh that river. Whether there is coal, is not yet certain. Some trials have been made without fuccefs. A company near Newcaftle,

Newcaftle, employed in that bufinefs, engaged lately to
make the experiment on a great fcale, and for that end entered into terms with Lord Binning. The writs were extended, an agent from his Lordſhip came to Coldftream to
finiſh and fettle the affair ; but thefe colliers of the fouth
broke their faith with him, and difappointed our hopes.—
Shell-marl was found in one marſh, and there is plenty of
rock-marl in many parts.

Population.—According to Dr Webfter's return, about 40
years ago, the numbers were 1493. From the roll of examinable perfons in 1785 and 1786, the numbers were
2017. In the country part of the pariſh, were 292 males,
387 females, 176 children. In the town and a few houfes
adjacent to it, the numbers were 1162. Number of families in the town, 305 ; in the country, 189. I muſt remark,
however, that the examination-roll is by no means a ſtandard by which the number of the inhabitants of a pariſh is
to be eſtimated. This roll is ufually made up by the officer
of the feffion, called the kirk-officer, who is feldom a perfon in whom any truſt in a matter of this inveſtigation can
be repofed. The age at which children are to be inrolled
is not afcertained. Parents, according as they have been
anxious to forward, or have been negligent in their education, are defirous to have the names of their children early
inferted in or withheld from this parochial record. Still,
however, it gives a general profpectus of the population of
a pariſh. I muſt add, that the feffion-officer in this pariſh
is one of the few to be depended upon for accuracy.

Annual

Annual births,	from 1740 to 1749 inclusive,		38.6
	from 1750 to 1759,	-	47.4
	from 1760 to 1769,	-	53.1
	from 1770 to 1779,	-	51.2
	from 1780 to 1789,	-	43.8
	Average,		46.82

Annual deaths,	from 1740 to 1749,	-	18.7
	from 1750 to 1759,	-	19.3
	from 1760 to 1769,	-	16.1
	from 1770 to 1779,	-	22.1
	from 1780 to 1789,	-	28.5
	Average,		20.94

Previous to the year 1786, the number of burials could only be ascertained from the register of mortcloth money interspersed among the records of the kirk-session. The poor who were buried at the public expence were not taken notice of except occasionally, so that there must be some small degree of inaccuracy in the above average account of burials. In the town of Coldstream there are about 34 day-labourers, 20 carters, several of whom farm 3 or 4 acres of land, 17 weavers, 11 shoemakers, 15 wrights, 9 masons, 6 bakers, 4 butchers, 4 smiths, 5 gardeners, 3 sadlers, 5 tailors, 11 merchants, 13 innkeepers and ale-sellers, 1 physician and 2 surgeons. There is a Seceder Meeting-house in Coldstream.

Agriculture, &c.—The parish produces the ordinary vegetables, plants and trees, to be found on the south eastern border of Scotland. At Kersfield, which belongs to Mr Morison of Morison, the trees are of a large size. At Hirsel, the seat of the Earl of Home, a few trees near the house excepted,

cepted, the plantations along the small water Leet are not as yet of age. There are no natural woods, forests, waste or common grounds. Near Tweed on this side, and still more remarkably on the opposite bank, as far as the Chiviot, and the ranges of hills contiguous to it, the want of trees attests the border desolations. Plants in far greater variety are to be found in the lower parts of Clydesdale and Renfrewshire than in this parish and its neighbourhood. This part of the Merse and downwards along Tweed, is not a rich field for a botanical journey. Husbandry is well understood in the Merse. By the Merse I do not mean the shire of Berwick. That shire consists of three parts: 1. Lauderdale; 2. that range of hills which, under different names, extends westward from the head of Leader water, to the sea below the town of Berwick; and, 3. that track of country which is situated between those hills and Tweed. That charming and fertile track is properly the Merse, Lauderdale excepted. The parish supplies itself in provisions, and sends cattle and corn to other markets. We have an early harvest, and the sowing of the crops is adjusted to this. The gross rent of the parish may be about L. 6000 Sterling a-year or more. The rent of fishings is L. 93.

Wages and Prices.—A mason's wages in summer are 1 s. 6 d.; a day-labourer's 1 s.; a man reaper's 1 s.; a woman reaper's 8 d.; a mower's 1 s. 4 d.; men servants wages are from L. 7 to L. 10, yearly; women servants are L. 3. The hinds roll, as it is called, or wages of a hind the year, at an average, are 8 bolls oats, $2\frac{1}{2}$ peas and barley, coals led, a cow's grass, a pig and poultry allowed to be fed at the direction of the master. Hinds form the principal class of servants belonging to the great farmers in this neighbourhood. Good beef, mutton, veal and lamb, sell at 4 d. the lb;

pork

pork at 3 d.; butter at 6 d; cheeſe at 5 d.; hens from 8 d to 10 d.; ducks from 6 d. to 8 d.; geeſe 2 s.; turkeys, 2 s. 6 d.; ſalmon and gilſes at the Billingſgate price.

Manufactures.—There is no town in the ſouth of Scotland ſo well ſituated for manufactures, in my humble opinion, as Coldſtream. The country in its neighbourhood, on both banks of the Tweed is rich in corn and cattle. The price of coals is moderate. We are diſtant from Berwick about 15 miles. The great road between London and Berwick, the road between Berwick and Kelſo, and between Dunſe and Northumberland, all paſs through the town of Cold-ſtream. Goods manufactured here might be thus carried in various directions into England and Scotland, by ways of communication already opened up. Should the projected plan of a canal be executed and carried near this place, the price of coals would be reduced, and all the advantages would be reaped, which ariſe from an inland navigation. From the excellent nature of the ſoil, flax might be raiſed to ſerve the purpoſe of a linen manufacture. The good quality of our barley would favour a diſtillery or a brewery; neither of which we at preſent have. Our ale, beer, and porter, come from Ednam. But the woollen manufacture is that for which Coldſtream is particularly well ſituated. The breed of ſheep is excellent, and is ſtill improving. I am not ſure if the wool, by which the trade and manufactures of Leeds have riſen to ſuch vaſt importance, be in general equal to what is produced in the Merſe, Tiviotdale and Northumberland. Yetham, Galaſhiels, Hawick, places far diſtant from coals, and not enjoying our advantages of communication, are puſhing the woollen manufacture with ſuc-ceſs. Were a proper plan ſet on foot here for carrying on
that

that manufacture, it is hard to say to what extent it might in time arrive.

Stipend, School, Poor, &c.—The church was built in 1716; the manse in 1782. The stipend is L. 80 in money, 2 chalders in meal, and 1 chalder of barley. The glebe is 12 acres of very good land. The patron is Lord Binning. There are 16 heritors, 4 of whom reside.—The salary of the schoolmaster is L. 16 Sterling. Previous to the year 1735, the poor seem to have been entirely supported by the Sunday collections and the contributions of charitable persons. It appears, that in that year, the session admitted on their roll as constant pensioners, 3 persons at 4 d. and 3 at 2 d. a-week. At that time the affairs of the poor were entirely in the hands of the kirk-session, and continued so till about 1740. It appears, that in 1737, the first demand was made upon the heritors to give a regular assistance to support the poor. It was not, however, in general, punctually obeyed on their part. In 1741 the session requested that the Justices of the Peace would call for the poor's list, and appoint overseers, &c. conform to an act of session 1. of parl 1. of Charles II. This remonstrance seems to have had the desired effect; for in 1742, it appears, that half the collection was ordered to be given to the overseers for the poor. The weekly pay of the poor in 1743 was about 10 s. Sterling. From the year 1765, the heritors kept a regular minute-book and a cash-book; their accounts after this being altogether unconnected with the kirk-session records. In May 1765, the number on the poor's roll was 22, in aid of whom 19 s. 1 d. Sterling was the weekly assessment. The highest allowance was one shilling. The quarterly assessment was L. 13 Sterling. In 1770 the quarterly assessment was L. 18, and in 1774, it amounted to L. 25, besides L. 4 levied

from

from the town of Coldstream. The weekly payment being
L. 2 : 6 : 11. The number on the poor's roll 34. In the
year of scarcity, 1783, meal was sold at reduced prices to the
poor, at the expence of the heritors and tenants, to the a-
mount of L. 112 Sterling. For the inrolled poor the quarterly assessment was L. 40, 14 s. the weekly pay L. 3, 4 s.
The number on the list 46. No demand has been made on
the session since 1773. Half of a quarterly assessment was
paid by the session in 1780 or 1781. The collection money
goes to relieve tradesmen laid off work by sickness, persons
overlooked or not sufficiently provided in the poor's list,
poor whose claims upon the parish being dubious, are not
entered on the list of the heritors, genteeler families decayed
not on the roll, sick and distressed persons returning to Scotland, a great number of which pass this way, and the like.
Owing to the high assessment of the parish, the collection is
small. From 1785 to 1790, the yearly amount of poor's
rates has exceeded L. 220, the weekly pay above L. 4. Two
evils have arisen from the rapid increase of the poor's rates.
The one is, that trusting to these rates, the common people
do not endeavour to provide any thing for a time of sickness
or scarcity, or for the approach of old age. The other is,
that these rates have, in a great measure, deprived them of
the natural feelings of giving aid to their relations in distress.
The nearest ties of consanguinity are disregarded, and the
holiest affections of humanity are thus extinguished. No
person almost is ashamed of having his father, mother, brother, or any other relation, on the pauper's list.

Miscellaneous Observations.—The only part of the parish
subject to inundations is the Lees haugh, which is situated
between the house of Mr Marjoribanks of Lees and Cornhill, and which is bounded by Tweed on the S. and E.
and

and by Leet on the N. The greateſt land-flood remembered by the oldeſt people then alive, happened in May
1783.—A very remarkable thunder-ſtorm happened in
this pariſh on the 19th day of July 1785; a very accurate
and ſcientific account of which, by Captain Brydone, is to
be found in the Philoſophical Tranſactions of London.—
There are two obeliſks in the pariſh, which were both e-
rected by Alexander the late Earl of Home. The one
ſmall, built on the centre pier of a Chineſe bridge, conſiſting of two arches, over the water Leet. The other larger, which exhibits in miniature the elegant and beautiful
proportions of the Obeliſcus Matthei at Rome. This is
erected at the foot of a wooded bank nigh the Leet, and
was intended by Lord Home as a monument, in memory
of his eldeſt ſon Lord Dunglaſs, who died in America of
the wounds he received in the battle of Cambden.—There
are two ſmall tumuli in the Kersfield eſtate on the top of
a ſteep bank of the Tweed. The tradition is, that the
bodies of thoſe who fell in one of the border battles are
buried in them.—The ſize and ſtature of the people on
this ſide of Tweed being the ſame with thoſe on the other
bank, the following notanda of the Northumberland
militia, which were communicated to me by Mr John
Hall, ſurgeon, who officiated in that corps in the laſt war,
will illuſtrate the ſubject. The height of the men was
from 5 feet 8¼ inches to 5 feet 10½ inches; ſome of the
grenadier company were 6 feet, 6 feet 1 inch, and 6 feet
2 inches; the loweſt ſize 5 feet 7 inches. They were in
general very ſtrong made, particularly the claſs firſt mentioned. It was remarked by judges, that this battalion,
though conſiſting of fewer men than other battalions from
the ſouthern counties, yet occupied as much ſpace in the
line of brigade. The perſon who furniſhed the cloathing,

found

found that a greater quantity of cloth was neceſſary for them, than for thoſe of the ſouthern counties, numbers being equal.—The people are much diſpoſed to induſtry in the line of huſbandry. We have no manufactures. Thoſe who are fond of a military life, have a predilection to the Coldſtream Regiment of Guards.—The number of ale-houſes have the worſt effect upon the people, encouraging almoſt every ſpecies of vice.—The language is diſtinguiſhable from that ſpoken on the other ſide of Tweed, by the ſoft ſound of the letter R. From that river ſouthward, as far I believe as Yorkſhire, the people univerſally annex a guttural ſound to the letter R, which in ſome places goes by the name of the Berwick *burrh*.—The names of one or two places in the pariſh are derived from the Latin, as Darn-*cheſter* and *Lares*-croft, the grounds of which lie contiguous. Bil-cheſter and Row-cheſter, in the neighbouring pariſh of Eccles, are of the ſame derivation. The word " Law" annexed to the name of ſo many places in the pariſh, atteſts, that it had belonged to the kingdom of Northumberland during the Heptarchy; as Hirſel-law, Caſtle-law, Spy-law, Carter-law, &c.

PARISH OF CRANSHAWS.

(PRESBYTERY OF DUNSE, SYNOD OF MERSE AND
TIVIOTDALE, COUNTY OF BERWICK.)

By the Rev. MR. GEORGE DRUMMOND.

———————

Name, and Situation.

THERE is no certain account, nor even any conjecture which has the least appearance of probability, with regard to the origin of the name of this parish.———Part of the parish of Longformacus intersects it in the middle; so that one half, and indeed the largest half of this district, lies at the distance of 4 or 5 miles from the church. An inconvenience which attends many parishes in this part of the country.

Population.—There are only 164 inhabitants in the parish, of whom 84 are males and 80 females. The population of this, and many of the neighbouring parishes, has of late considerably diminished. The only reason that can be assigned for this diminution is the monopoly of farms. About 50 or 60 years ago there were above 16 farmers in the parish; the whole is now in the possession of 3 only. The return to Dr. Webster in 1754 was 214 souls.

Climate,

Climate, Rivers, &c.—The elevated ſituation of the pariſh, being in the middle of Lammermuir hills, renders the air ſharp and cold ; it is however pure and healthy ; and during the ſummer months the climate is tolerably mild and tempe-rate. Though in all the different ſeaſons there are frequent fogs, yet as they are generally confined to the tops of the hills, the health of the inhabitants is ſeldom injured by them *.

The Whiteadder or Whitewater runs along the N. and E. ſides of the pariſh.—The river Dye alſo runs through part of this diſtrict. They are inconſiderable ſtreams, but abound with trout of an excellent quality. The banks of both were formerly covered with natural wood, which rendered the ap-pearance of the country in ſummer moſt delightfully romantic ; but now there is not a tree or even a ſhrub to be found on them.

There are no manufacturers of any kind in the pariſh. Its inland ſituation and great diſtance from proper fuel, are un-favourable to their eſtabliſhment. The generality of the in-habitants are therefore employed in agriculture. There are 2 maſons, 4 joiners, 2 weavers, 1 blackſmith, and 1 taylor, chiefly employed in working to the people of the pariſh and neighbourhood, ſeldom manufacturing any articles for ſale. The inhabitants in general are frugal, ſober and induſtrious, free from diſſipation, and not addicted to drinking, or any o-ther ſpecies of intemperance. As a proof of their induſtry and ſobriety, it deſerves to be mentioned that for more than 20 years

---

* There are few epidemical diſtempers in this part of the country. The moſt prevalent diſorder is the rheumatiſm, probably owing to the changeable-neſs of the weather, and the coldneſs and dampneſs of the houſes. Fevers are not frequent. And the ague, which prevails ſo much among the common people in the lower parts of Berwickſhire, is almoſt unknown here. The peo-ple in general live to a conſiderable age. Among the ſmall number of in-habitants this pariſh contains, there are at preſent 6 perſons above 70 year of age, two of whom are above 80.

years preceding 1788, there was only one perfon upon the poor's roll, and fince that time there have been only two on that lift.

Agriculture.—As the greateft part of the parifh confifts of high hills, covered with heath or bent, the lands in general are more adapted to the breeding of cattle and fheep than the raifing of grain. There are, however, on all the different farms, a confiderable quantity of arable ground, which is very ferviceable to the tenants, as it fupplies their families with corn, and provides fodder for their cattle in winter. The foil, being light and dry, is fuitable for raifing of turnips and fown grafs. Of late the farmers have availed themfelves of the advantages arifing from this kind of foil, and have already carried this fpecies of improvement to a confiderable height. Their principal dependance being on cattle and fheep, renders the culture of turnips and fown grafs an object of great importance ; not only as being the beft food for thefe animals, but fometimes the only food that can be got for the fheep, for in fevere winters the fnow is commonly fo deep as to prevent their getting any nourifhment either from the grafs or heath. Before the introduction of the turnip hufbandry, and the raifing of clover and rye-grafs, the farmers were frequently obliged in the winter feafon to drive their fheep into the low country, and purchafe hay for them. This was not only attended with great inconvenience and expence, but fometimes alfo with the lofs of a confiderable part of their flocks, owing to the difficulty of driving them through the deep fnow, and the weak and reduced condition in which the animals generally were before their owners had recourfe to this expedient.

The introduction of the ufe of lime as a manure has been of great benefit to the arable grounds in the neighbourhood. Very confiderable crops of oats, barley and peafe have by means

thereof

thereof been raiſed from land which in its natural ſtate was of little or no value. And it has not only the effect of occaſioning a more luxuriant and plentiful, but alſo a much earlier crop; a circumſtance of great importance in a hilly country like this, where the harveſt is commonly late, and the grain in danger of being injured by the froſt before it comes to maturity. Another advantage reſulting from it is, that it is peculiarly favourable to the growth of clover. Nay, in this cold climate, it is abſolutely eſſential to its vegetation. For it has been found by various trials, that even on the beſt and moſt fertile ſpots in this part of the country, it is impoſſible to raiſe this uſeful plant without the aid of lime; whereas, by employing this manure, the worſt of the arable land may be made to produce it. And it is a circumſtance worthy of obſervation, that ſo great is the efficacy of lime for promoting its vegetation, that, by laying a quantity of it on the ſurface of the moſt uncultivated ground, it cauſes white clover to ſpring ſpontaneouſly. This circumſtance is the more remarkable, as there have been many accidental inſtances of this effect of lime in the midſt of the wildeſt moors, by the breaking down or overturning of the carts employed in carrying it: And that too, at ſo great diſtance from any other lands where this plant uſually grows, as renders it difficult to account how the ſeed could have been conveyed; and yet repeated experience has ſhewn that lime laid on ſuch land, whether by deſign or accident, has uniformly had the effect of deſtroying the heath or bent, and occaſioning the vegetation of white clover, in great abundance.

It is proper, however, to obſerve, that notwithſtanding the tendency which lime has to meliorate the ſoil, yet a conſiderable part of the arable ground in this and the neighbouring pariſhes has been much injured by the improper uſe of it, or rather

ther

ther by the injudicious management of the land after laying
that uſeful manure upon it. For although, of all the calcareous
manures, lime is unqueſtionably the beſt, yet as it acts rather
as a ſtimulus than a ſubſtantial manure, and cauſes the land to
make its greateſt exertions in the way of vegetation, it has a
tendency to exhauſt the ſoil, if not cropped with caution.
When it was firſt employed in the cultivation of the lands of
this pariſh, little attention was paid to this circumſtance. The
difficulty of driving lime at the diſtance of 16 or 17 miles
through very bad roads, induced the farmers to take as many
crops as the land would yield, to refund them for their expence
and trouble. And by theſe means after taking eight or nine crops
of oats ſucceſſively, it was commonly left in a ſtate of total
ſterility, incapable of producing either graſs or corn. This
pernicious practice is now in a great meaſure laid aſide; and
the generality of the farmers diſcover equal ſkill and caution both
in the mode of managing and cropping the lands which they
improve with lime, and alſo in the means which they uſe for
recovering what had formerly been impoveriſhed by over-cropping.

Horſes, Cattle, and Sheep.—There are about 30 horſes, 200
black cattle, and 3500 ſheep in the pariſh. The horſes are all
kept for the purpoſes of huſbandry. There are few bred in the
pariſh, and none at all for ſale. The cattle are but of a ſmall
kind; are bred for ſale, and bring from L. 4 : 10 to L. 5 : 5
a head when three years old. The ſheep, which are of the
ſmall black faced kind, are ſold lean after they are three years
old. The average price for ſome years paſt is from 9 to 10
guineas the ſcore. The farmers ſeem to think that this kind of
ſheep is moſt ſuitable to the paſture, and have on that account
made no attempts to improve the breed. They carry a coarſe
kind

kind of wool ; it is all laid with tar, and has for ſome years paſt ſold from 9s. to 10s. 6d. per ſtone *.

Miſcellaneous Obſervations.—The value of the living, including the glebe, is ſcarcely L. 50 a year. The ſtipend is only L. 36 : 19 : 5 The glebe conſiſts of about fifteen Engliſh acres, moſt of it tolerably good land. It has of late been much injured by the inundations of the Whitewater, which has conſiderably diminiſhed its value. The church was built in 1739. The manſe ſome years earlier. They have both been lately repaired. The patron is Charles Watſon Eſqr. of Saughton †.

As

* The wages of male ſervants, who get their board in the houſe, are from L. 6 to L. 7 a year, and female ſervants from L. 3 to L. 4. Servants who have families, and keep houſes of their own, receive a certain quantity of meal or grain, have ſo many ſheep grazed, are allowed to keep a cow, have their fuel brought home, and ſeveral other perquiſites ; the value of which may amount to about L. 13 or L. 14. The wages of a labourer by the day is 1s. in ſummer, and 10d. in winter ; except in hay time and harveſt, when they receive conſiderably more. The wages of women, for weeding turnips, pota‧ toes, &c. is 5d. per day.

† In different parts of the pariſh are traces of ſeveral antient encampments, though none of them appear to have been of any conſiderable extent. They are ſo much effaced, as to render it difficult to diſtinguiſh of what kind they have been.—Cranſhaws caſtle, the property of Mr. Watſon of Saughton, is an oblong ſquare of 40 feet by 24. The walls are 45 feet high, and it has a battlement on the top. It is a very antient building, and before the union of the two kingdoms, had been uſed as a place of defence, to which the inhabitants of this part of the country were accuſtomed to retreat, upon ſudden incurſions of the Engliſh borderers. There are in many of the neighbouring pariſhes the remains and ruins of ſimilar edifices, but this is the only one in this part of the country that is ſtill entire. It has been lately repaired by its preſent proprietor, and is occupied by him as a dwelling houſe, when he viſits this part of his eſtate.

On a hill, on the weſt ſide of the pariſh, are two heaps of ſtones of an immenſe ſize, each containing, as is ſuppoſed, many thouſand carts-load. A tradition

As the planting and raiſing of wood is of the greateſt importance to the country in general, ſo it would in this and the
neighbouring pariſhes be particularly beneficial to landholders
and tenants, not only as being the beſt mode of employing
waſte land, but likewiſe from the ſhelter it could afford, if
judiciouſly laid out, in ſurrounding the valuable fields that are
already, or may yet be, improved for raiſing corn and hay. But
the greateſt advantage ariſing from it would be the ſhelter it
would afford to the flocks of ſheep in winter. Many farmers
in this part of the country have in one night loſt a third, and
ſometimes near the half, of their ſheep by a heavy fall of ſnow.
The efficacy of planting for preventing loſſes of this kind is
well known to all ſtore farmers. The ſhortneſs, however, of
leaſes in general gives little encouragement to the tenant to
raiſe wood for this purpoſe at his own expence, becauſe before
he could derive much benefit from it, his leaſe would expire.
It may therefore be ſuggeſted as an object worthy the attention
of proprietors in this part of the country, as they muſt ultimately be the gainers by an improvement of this kind, not only on
account of its greatly inhancing the value of their farms, from
the ſecurity which it would afford to the tenant for the ſafety
of his ſheep in winter, but likewiſe from the value of the wood
itſelf; the ſoil, as appears from experiments that have already
been made, being very favourable to the raiſing of different kinds
of timber.

tradition has long prevailed, that they had been collected together to com-
memorate the death of two twin brothers who fell in battle, when they were
commanding oppoſite armies, and from thence the hill on which theſe piles
are erected, obtained the name of Twinlaw. Upon a tradition of this kind,
unſupported by accounts from hiſtory little dependence can be put, eſpecially
as it is entirely ſilent with regard to the quality of the perſons, and the time
when the tranſaction happened. It is probable, however, that ſomething
memorable had happened at that place; as it was cuſtomary for the antients
to adopt this mode of tranſmitting to poſterity the remembrance of events they
conſidered important or remarkable.

PARISH of DUNSE,

(COUNTY OF BERWICK.)

By the Rev. Dr ROBERT BOWMAKER.

Name, Situation, Soil and Air.

BERWICKSHIRE is nominally divided into three diſtricts, the Merſe, Lammermoor and Lauderdale. The Merſe is that flat part of the county, which is bounded by the river Tweed on the S. and S. E.; by part of Tiviotdale and Lauderdale on the S. W. and W. and by the Lammermoor hills on the N. W. and N. with the town of Berwick at the eaſt point. It is a plain of at leaſt 25 miles from E. to W. and 15 from N. to S. and takes the name of Merſe from being a border county. At the head of this plain, and in the very centre of the county, ſtands the town of Dunſe, encompaſſed on the W. N. and E. by the Lammermoor hills. Its name is derived from the old Celtic word *Dun,* 'a hill,' its original ſite having been on the top of a moſt beautiful little hill, which is called Dunſe Law. This hill ſtands upon a baſe of between 2 and 3 miles in circumference, and riſes in a gradual aſcent on all ſides, till it terminates in a plain of nearly 30 acres; the whole hill may contain about 250 acres. It is 630 feet above the level of the

the fea. Afterwards the town was built at the foot of the hill, on the S. where it now ftands. Dunfe is the prefbytery-feat of that name, and belongs to the Synod of Merfe and Tiviotdale.—The parifh is an oblong fquare of 8 miles from N. to S. and 5 from E. to W. It is bounded on the N. by the parifh of Abbey St Bathan's, on the N. W. by Longformachus, on the W. and S. by Langtoun, on the S. E. by Edrom, and on the E. and N. E. by Prefton and Bunkle. That part of the parifh which runs up into Lammermoor is hilly, and very much covered with heath; and thofe tracks of it which are cultivated are, in general, a fharp, gravelly, dry foil, on which the tenants grow very good barley, oats, turnip and clover. In the fouth part of it, the foil is a rich, light, deep loam, fome of it a ftrong clay, and very fertile.—The air is dry and healthy. The ague was a very prevalent diftemper about 40 years ago, and alfo the putrid fever, which laft, in fome particular years, cut off a great number of the inhabitants; but in confequence of the rapid improvements in agriculture, begun at firft by the gentlemen, and followed up with great fpirit by the tenants, the country has been much drained, and the climate greatly changed. The cleaning of the ftreets of the town, and of ditches in parks adjoining to it on the fouth, has alfo greatly contributed to the health of the inhabitants. It may be remarked alfo, that 40 years ago, when the ague was very prevalent in the Merfe, it was not known in Lammermoor, nor is yet.

Dunfe Spaw.—There are no mineral fprings in the parifh. But there is one within a very few yards of the boundary, on the fouth, in the eftate of Mrs Carr of Nifbet, in the parifh of Edrom. It is called Dunfe Spaw, from its vicinity to the town, being only a mile diftant. It was difcovered in 1747, and was very much reforted to for feveral

veral years. Some years ago, it was repaired at the expence of a gentleman, who was cured of a ſtomach diſorder, by the Spaw water. This mineral water is nearly of the ſame kind with that of Tunbridge, the moſt celebrated chalybeate water in England. Dunſe Spaw, according to the analyſis of it, publiſhed by Profeſſor Home at Edinburgh, 1761, contains iron, ſea-ſalt, a marley earth, and fixed air, or what is called aerial acid. Like moſt other chalybeate waters, it does not carry well, unleſs the uſual methods are practiſed, in tranſporting the foreign chalybeate waters. Although the water may be thus carried to a great diſtance, without loſing its properties in a conſiderable degree, yet it muſt unqueſtionably be drunk with greater advantage on the ſpot. This water is found very ſalutary in complaints of the ſtomach, weakneſs of the inteſtines, diabetes, and a great variety of other diſorders. The beſt months for drinking Dunſe Spaw, are June, July, Auguſt, and September, when the valitudinarian, and perſons ſubject to chronic diſorders, may, by a courſe of theſe waters, reap every advantage to be procured by any chalybeate water whatever.

River.—The water of Whitadder abounds in trout, but of no high flavour, nor rich in quality. There is alſo in this river a larger ſort of fiſh, called a whitling; it is a large fine trout, from 16 inches to 2 feet long, and well grown; its fleſh is red, and high coloured, like ſalmon, and of full as fine a flavour; it is a moſt delicate fiſh, and affords moſt excellent ſport to the angler. It goes to the ſea in its ſeaſon, and returns ſtrong, vigorous, and healthy; but if, from the ſmallneſs of the river in a dry ſeaſon, it is prevented from getting to the ſea, it becomes lank, ſmall, and ſpiritleſs, and loſes its red colour and flavour. The Whitadder falls into the Tweed, about 12 miles E. from Dunſe,

and

and 3 miles above Berwick. From the Tweed, which a-
bounds in fine ſalmon, a great many of theſe fiſh get into
the Whitadder, and in the months of September and October are found 30 miles up that river, paſſing into the ſmall
brooks among the hills in Lammermoor, till their backs
are not covered, and there lodge their ſpawn among the
gravel. No part of the Whitadder is rented, and the fiſhes
are killed with the rod or liſter.

Population.—According to Dr Webſter's report, about
40 years ago, the numbers were 2593. Within theſe 60
years laſt paſt, the number of inhabitants in the town of
Dunſe has been doubled; and though the town has not in
that time extended itſelf much to any of its wings, yet many empty ſpaces have been built upon, and many old houſes,
which contained only 1 or 2 families, have been rebuilt upon larger plans, and now contain from 4 to 8, and ſome of
them 10 families. There are ſcarce any veſtiges of old
houſes. Many new ones have been built of late years, and
ſeveral are now building. By a very exact liſt, taken 3
years ago, the number of ſouls in the town was 2324; in
the country part of the pariſh, 1000. In all, 3324.

Abſtract of Baptiſms, Marriages, and Burials, for ten years.

Years.	Baptiſms.	Marriages.	Deaths.
1780	93	63	61
1781	84	59	85
1782	58	42	95
1783	114	47	59
1784	97	39	70
1785	89	44	30
1786	91	53	61
1787	86	32	64
1788	95	39	43
1789	98	37	51

In

In the 1782, the ſmall-pox raging, accounts for the number of deaths that year. In 1733, there were 130 children, who died of the ſmall-pox in the ſpace of 3 months. In 1783, one man died at the age of 99, whoſe baptiſm is recorded in the regiſter now before me, in 1684. Another, a pauper, died this year, aged 93. There are now living iu the town 12 perſons, between 80 and 90. One 90, who ſupports his family by his own labour, and enjoys as good health, and has as fine a flow of ſpirits as any perſon at the age of 25. Another, in my own family, (my father), who was born the 4th of July 1694, and is at preſent (April 1791) in perfect health, and going about. There is 1 phyſician, 3 ſurgeons, and 8 gentlemen of the law in the town. There is an Antiburgher, a Burgher, and a Relief miniſter, whoſe congregations are made up of a mixed multitude from all quarters. Three weekly carriers to Edinburgh, 1 to Kelſo, 1 to Dunbar, 1 to Eyemouth, 2 to Berwick, twice a week.

Agriculture, &c.—There are 14 tenants in the pariſh, who rent from L. 100 to L. 300 a-year; and about the ſame number, who rent from L. 30 to L. 100. The pariſh is in general incloſed. The bondages to which the tenants were formerly ſubjected are now entirely done away; there is nothing but rent to be paid. Wheat, barley, and oats, are the principal crops of grain; turnips are raiſed in great quantities, and turn to good account, in feeding ſheep and black cattle, and let from L. 4, 4 s. to L. 5, 5 s. an acre; and in the immediate neighbourhood of Dunſe, are let from L. 5, 5 s. to L. 7, 7 s. and are uſed in the town chiefly for milch cows. Cabbages are alſo planted in conſiderable quantities, and are more ſuitable for cows than turnips are, as they do not ſcour the cattle ſo much; and if the ſpoiled leaves of the cabbages are taken off, the milk, cream, and
butter

butter will be as good as from graſs; beſides, the ſpoiled
leaves may be given to young cattle, and nothing is loſt.
Potatoes too are raiſed in great quantities, and the land for
them is let from L. 4 to L. 6 an acre; the proprietor or tenant only ploughs it, and the renter cleans them, digs them
up, and carries them home. A great deal of graſs-ſeeds
are ſown annually, but little flax is raiſed, and no hemp.
Very great improvements are making in the breed of
ſheep and black cattle. In the S. part of the pariſh, the
lands are let from 15 s. to L. 1 an acre; in the N. part,
which is high ground, the land is not let by the acre, but
a cumulus rent is paid for the whole farm. Such has been
the ſpirit of improvement within theſe laſt 5c years, that
farms in the pariſh, which were let at L. 35 and L. 40, pay
now L. 210, and the tenants doing well. In no county of
Great Britain is there a more reſpectable tenantry, than
there is at preſent in the county of Berwick; many of
them rent from L. 500 to L. 1200 a-year; men well informed in ſcience, and moſt intelligent and induſtrious in
their profeſſion; and in every 10 or 15 years, ſome of them
are purchaſing property of L. 200, and even L. 500 a-year;
on which they enjoy, *otium cum dignitate*, the juſt reward
of their attention, labour, diligence, and good ſenſe; and
all this under the great diſadvantages, of being diſtant from
10 to 20 miles from lime and markets, and in a county
where victual is cheaper than in any county in Scotland.
There is plenty of marl, but lime, though diſtant, is conſidered as a cheaper manure. The county of Berwick exports from the ports of Berwick and Eyemouth, above
80,000 bolls of victual, and fully the ſame quantity is carried annually to the weekly markets of Edinburgh, Dalkeith, Haddington, and Dunbar. Land is ſold from L. 30
to L. 80 an acre. Houſes are rented from 10 s. to L. 20.
Property does not often change, either in lands or houſes.

Manufactures.

Manufactures.—There are no manufactures carried on here to any great extent; an woollen manufacture is to be fet on foot at Whitfunday firft, the houfes are building, and the fpinning machines are already brought from England. There is a very fmall tannery; but it is in contemplation to have one foon upon a large fcale by a fubfcription, in fhares of at leaft L. 25 the fhare, by the inhabitants. Hides to the extent of L. 400 a-year have been bought here by commiffion, and fent to Haddington, where they are tanned, the expence of carriage, L. 33. We have here a very large bleachfield.

Proprietors, &c.—The number of heritors is above 40, 12 of whom poffefs property from L. 100 to L. 2000 a-year in the parifh; the reft are fmall portioners, from 1 to 30 or 40 acres; only a few of the principal heritors refide. Robert Hay, Efq; of Drumelzier is proprietor of one half of the parifh; he refides at Dunfe caftle, a large ftately venerable old building, fituated about half a mile above the town, and commanding an extenfive view to the fouth, as far as the Cheviot hills. It is furrounded with rifing grounds on the weft and north, and the beautiful hill of Dunfe Law on the north eaft. On the north and weft too, are feveral hundred acres of thriving planting, much of it very old. In the bofom of this plantation is a fine bafon of water called the hen-pond; it is above a mile in circumference, and in fummer vaft numbers of wild ducks refort to it.

Stipend, School and Poor.—The ftipend is 66 bolls 1 firlot barley, 66 bolls 1 firlot oats, 64 bolls meal, and L. 40 in money, with $91\frac{1}{2}$ acres glebe. Mr Hay of Drumelzier is patron. A moft complete and excellent manfe was built in 1783. A new church is now building on a large fcale, ſcale, and moſt elegant plan.—The ſchool of Dunſe has long been in very great repute. The number of ſcholars is from 90 to 100, 60 or 70 of whom are learning the languages, the others are learning writing, arithmetic, mathematics, &c. The fees for the languages are 5 s. the quarter; 3 s. 6 d. for writing and arithmetic, and 2 s. 6 d. for Engliſh; book-keeping, and the higher parts of mathematics and navigation, are taught by the piece at a certain agreed ſum. The ſalary is L. 12, and a houſe well calculated for accommodating boarders. The board is only L. 16 a-year. There is alſo a female boarding ſchool, where every branch of female education can be got on the following terms: Reading and plain white ſeam together, at 5 s. the quarter; tambour and coloured work, and embroidery at 7 s. 6 d.; muſic at 10 s. 6 d. the month, or L. 5, 5 s. a-year; writing 5 s. and dancing 6 s. the month; board L. 16 a-year. The preſent directrix has a ſalary of L. 18 from the heritors, and other inhabitants, for a certain number of years.—The number of poor upon the roll is at preſent 90, the annual amount of the contributions for their relief is L. 230. There are no legacies, nor mortified money. The funds for their ſupport ariſe, 1ſt, from an aſſeſſment upon the lands, according to the valued rent, the one half paid by the landlords, and the other by the tenants; at preſent it is 12 month ceſs upon the lands. 2dly, The ſeveral incorporations pay quarterly into the fund, L. 3 : 9 : 6 Sterling. 3dly, The unincorporated, viz. the ſurgeons, lawyers, merchants, publicans, &c. are aſſeſſed annually by themſelves; that aſſeſſment at preſent is L. 3, 19 s. the quarter. The ſeſſion alſo pay a proportion of their collections weekly into the general fund. Theſe ſeveral funds are collected by an overſeer of the poor, appointed by the heritors. When at any time the fund is unequal to the expenditure, a meeting

ing of the heritors is called, and an additional affeffment is laid on, (but only upon the heritors and tenants), proportioned to the demand. Every pauper who comes upon the roll muft give in an affignation to all the effects belonging to them. The poor too are buried at the expence of the fund, amounting to 17 s. each, if adults.

Prices, Wages, &c.—About 50 years ago, the prices of provifions were greatly below what they are at this time ; butcher meat was not then fold by weight, but when weighed after having been bought, was found not to exceed 1½ d. the lb. Dutch weight for beef, mutton, and pork ; lamb was bought at 6 d. and 7 d. the quarter. At prefent beef and mutton are 4 d. pork 3¼ d. veal from 3 d. to 5 d. and lamb, even in July, is never below 3 d. the lb. ; at prefent (the beginning of April) it is 1 s. the lb. Wheat is from L. 1, 5 s. to L. 1, 12 s. ; barley from 12 s. to 16 s. and oats from 10 s. to 14 s. the boll upon an average; but the Berwickfhire boll is a 24th part, or ¼ peck in the boll, larger than the Linlithgow meafure ufed in the Lothians. The farmers fervants who have families, and engage by the year, are called hinds, and receive 10 bolls oats, 2 bolls barley, and 1 boll peas, which two laft articles are called hummel corn, a cow grazed in the fummer, and ftraw through the winter, ¼ boll potatoes planted, fome lintfeed fown, with fome other fmall confiderations, the whole amounting to about L. 13. A fingle man fervant receives from L. 6 to L. 8 a-year, with victuals, but few fingle fervants are now employed. Labourers, by the day, are paid 1 s. in fummer, and 9 d. and 10 d. in the winter quarter ; in hay-time, 1 s. 6 d. without victuals, except a bottle of ale at noon, and another in the afternoon, with ½ d. worth of bread to each. In harveft, the wages of a man are from 1 s. to 1 s. 6 d. with victuals,

victuals, thoſe of a woman, 10 d. and 1 s.. The wages of
a maſon are from 1 s. 4 d. to 2 s. the day, a carpenter
from 1 s. to 1 s. 8 d. The wages received by the different
claſſes are fully ſufficient for the ſupport of their families ;
and ſuch as are ſober, and have been fortunate in getting
induſtrious wives, ſometimes ſave conſiderably. When
any fall into want from bad health or misfortune, they
receive an interim aliment from the poor's funds ; they
are often relieved and ſupported by the voluntary contributions of the inhabitants at large. Upon the diſtreſs of
any family, two of their neighbours, by going through
the town with a ſubſcription paper, will, in a few hours,
collect ſeveral pounds. Women ſervants have from L. 3
to L. 4 a-year. This being a border county, is the cauſe
of the high wages of the labourers, &c.

Ale-houſes.—There are no fewer than 27 ale-houſes in
the town of Dunſe, many of which are kept by low people,
who do not depend upon their retail altogether, but who
carry on, at the ſame time, ſome other profeſſion, or rather from a ſpirit of indolence, they keep an ale-houſe, to
help the emoluments of the profeſſion they followed ;
which profeſſion, in conſequence of the habit of idleneſs
and drunkenneſs which they have contracted, is ſoon in a
great meaſure laid aſide, and the family reduced to beg-
gary. It is, in conſequence of people of this deſcription
keeping ale-houſes, that others of the ſame ſtation are induced, from old acquaintance with them, to frequent their
houſes, and which frequently grows into ſuch a habit, as
greatly to hurt the circumſtances, and diſturb the peace of
their families. Beſides, 'tis in houſes of this ſort, that the
profligate of both ſexes find lodging, where they get in-
toxicated, and from whence they ſally forth, in the dark
hours of the night, to commit depredations on the inno-
cent,

čent, virtuous and unſuſpecting members of the community. 'Tis in theſe houſes alſo that they depoſit the fruits
of their depredations, and are furniſhed with means of future intoxication. It is a laudable practice (authoriſed by
law) which ſeveral counties have of late adopted, not to
allow any perſon to take out a licence to keep an ale-
houſe, without that perſon ſhall produce, from the miniſter, a certificate of his moral character. At the ſame
time, we have publicans here, in high repute, who have
the beſt accommodations, and where as good entertainment can be got as in any place in Great Britain.

Poſt-office.—Formerly the Dunſe bag came by Oldcambus to Dunſe, afterwards the office was removed from
Oldcambus to the Preſs, and, of late years, has been removed to Berwick, by which circuitous conveyance, our
Edinburgh letters are charged 4 d. inſtead of 3 d. in conſequence of the diſtance round by Berwick, being more
than 50 miles. But though the bag for the convenience
of the poſt-office is now ſent on to Berwick, and the diſtance by that means increaſed, there is no reaſon that we
ſhould pay more for our letters now, than we would have
done, had they continued to be ſent from the Preſs. Beſides, the letters to Kelſo go alſo by Berwick, which is
farther from Berwick than Dunſe; the inhabitants of that
town, upon an application to the General Poſt-office at E-
dinburgh, got a deduction of a fourth upon their Edinburgh letters, but the memorial from the town of Dunſe
upon the ſame ſubject was treated with ſullen ſilence.
The letters alſo have been accuſtomed to be delivered,
time immemorial, to the inhabitants to whom they were
addreſſed, at their houſes; but of late years the man who
holds the office here, has made a demand of 1 d. more
than the poſtage, for the letters delivered by him. We
have

have preſented a memorial upon this alſo, to the Poſt-maſter General at Edinburgh, in which we ſhewed how the law ſtood, and the ſeveral inſtances in which it had been decided in the Courts of England againſt the poſt-maſters, but no redreſs has been obtained. We have at laſt ſent a copy of the ſame memorial to the Poſt-maſter General at London, with the different caſes referred to ; and the only anſwer which we have got, which was in the middle of March, was, that the memorial was under con-ſideration : As that is likely to be all the anſwer which we are to get, we have reſolved to demand that juſtice from the laws of the land, which our fellow ſubjects have received, and which theſe offices have refuſed us.

Hills.—Cockburn Law riſes from a baſe of at leaſt 6 miles in circumference to a conical top, which, on the north and ſouth ſides, is a mile from the baſe, and is ſur-rounded by the river Whitadder on 3 ſides. On the north ſide, and a little below the middle of the hill, are the ruins of a very old building, by ſome called Wooden's hall, but commonly called Edin's or Edwin's hall. It conſiſts of 3 concentric circles, the diameter of the inner-moſt 40 feet, the thickneſs of the wall 7 feet, the ſpace between the innermoſt and the ſecond wall 7 feet, be-tween that and the third or outer wall 10 feet; the ſpaces between theſe walls have been arched over, and divided into cells of 12, 16 and 20 feet long ; they ſeem to have been of conſiderable height, but as all the roofs have long ſince fallen in, the height cannot be preciſely aſcertained. The ſpace within the inner circle ſeems never to have had any roof, as there are no fragments nor ruins there. The building is not cemented with any ſort of mortar ; the ſtones, which are whin, and many of them very large, are all grooved into one another, that is, the concavity of

the

the one receiving the convexity of the other, ſo that they are locked together, and yet all theſe locks are different : it is ſuppoſed to have been a Pictiſh building, and afterwards uſed as a military ſtation. What the original name was, we have no tradition of ; but in after times, it has gone by the name of Edin or Edwin's hall, from a Prince of that name, who was King of Northumberland, and whoſe dominions extended as far north as the frith of Forth. From this Prince the city of Edinburgh took its name. It would appear that Edwin had taken poſſeſſion of this ſtrong poſt, for a military ſtation, for an army of obſervation, as the Danes were frequently invading Scotland, both by ſea and land. There are ſeveral of theſe military ſtations in this neighbourhood, both to the eaſt and weſt of Cockburn Law. This hill, being 900 feet above the level of the ſea, is a fine land-mark for mariners on the German Ocean, and is ſeen at a great diſtance from that ſea, conſequently any fleet from the north would be eaſily and readily deſcried from that ſtation.

Learned Men.—The celebrated metaphyſician and theologiſt, John Duns Scotus, was born in Dunſe in 1274. Camden, in his Britannia, and the authors of the Biographia Britannica contend that he was born at Dunſtone in Northumberland, but bring no argument, but their bare aſſertion to ſupport it. Nothing is more certain, than that the family, of which this extraordinary man was a branch, were heritors of the pariſh of Dunſe, and continued to be proprietors of that eſtate which now belongs to Mr Chriſtie, till after the beginning of the preſent century, called from them in all ancient writings Duns's half of Grueldykes. Theſe lands are adjoining to the town of Dunſe. The father of John Duns Scotus had been a younger brother of the family of Grueldykes, and reſided in the

town

town of Dunfe. The fite of the houfe where he was born is ftill well known, and has been in ufe, generation after generation, to be pointed out to the young people by their parents, as the birth place of fo great and learned a man.

Mifcellaneous Obfervations.——In 1782-3, when victual was at a very high price, the heritors, and other inhabitants in good circumftances, contributed very largely for the fupport of the poor and indigent, and fold at leaft 20 bolls weekly, from the 3d of December 1782, to the middle of Auguft 1783, at one-third below the market-price. The inhabitants are humane and generous to all real objects. They are alfo induftrious and œconomical, and contented with their fituation and circumftances.—There is a public library in Dunfe; which was eftablifhed in 1768, confifting of about 60 fhares, at L. 2 a fhare, and 6 s. a-year; the fhares are transferable, like any other property. From the original L. 2 for each fhare, and the 6 s. alfo advanced for the year's reading, we were enabled to buy at once near L. 150 worth of books, and from L. 12 to L. 15 has been expended annually upon books ever fince that period.— There are 3 great fairs in Dunfe. At thefe is a very great fhew of fine cattle and horfes. At leaft L. 20,000 Sterling is received for cattle at thefe fairs, which are chiefly purchafed by Englifh dealers. There is alfo a good deal of fheep.—The roads were originally made and kept up by the ftatute-labour, except the two great roads from Edinburgh to London, the one by Greenlaw and Coldftream, the other by the Prefs and Berwick, which were made by fums borrowed by the gentlemen of the county upon the turnpikes. The ftatute-labour is now commuted at 7 s. 6 d. each horfe, and 3 s. on houfeholders. The queftion refpecting turnpikes on the great roads to coal and lime, and

the

the two ports of Berwick and Eyemouth, is now agitating among the proprietors, but not yet ſettled.—There was a conſiderable common in the environs of Dunſe, conſiſting of ſeveral hundred acres, a few years ago, that has been divided; by which a large piece of land, which had been for ages paſt an eye-ſore to every traveller, and of no value to any, is now an ornament to the neighbourhood, and profitable to many.—We have abundance of freeſtone quarries in the pariſh, and alſo in the neighbourhood, the rock lying from 3 feet to 10 below the ſurface. There is alſo an inexhauſtible fund of whinſtone within a mile of the town, all above ground, lying in immenſe large ſlabs, one upon another, and may be broken into the ſhape of flags, with the leaſt trouble, and of any ſize. We are 15 miles diſtant from coal, and bring them all from Northumberland, as alſo our lime.—On the 18th September 1790, was found, 3 miles S. E. from Dunſe, a bird very rare in Scotland. It was killed by a cat, and diſcovered to be the bird called Hoopoe by the Engliſh, Wedhop by the Germans, the Upupa of the ancients, deſcribed by Pliny, Ariſtotle, Pauſanias, Ælian, &c. The bird is common in Germany, and ſometimes even in England. A few days after, another Upupa, of a greener colour, was ſeen flying about the garden at Kimmergham, but ſoon diſappeared.—There is a very remarkable wall in the pariſh, incloſing near 100 acres of ground, called Borthwick Park, belonging to the family of Langton; it is of moorſtone, without any ſort of mortar, and never had any covering, either of ſod or any thing elſe; it has ſtood 179 years, and never was known to need any repair till within theſe 4 years; and though it is but low, yet, in conſequence of the unevenneſs of its texture, and the ruggedneſs of its top, neither horſes nor cattle ever ventured to leap it.

PARISH of EARLSTOUN,

(COUNTY OF BERWICK.)

By the Rev. Mr LAURENCE JOHNSTON.

Name, Situation, Soil, Air, &c.

THE parish probably derives its name from being originally the residence of the Earls of March, one of whom lived here about the middle of the 13th century. It is by some called Arsehilltoun, because the village is in a low situation, and almost surrounded with rising grounds. However, I take the other to be its true name, and this to be only a corruption of it; for there is no doubt that the family of March lived here at the period above mentioned. The parish is about 6 miles in length, from E. to W. and from 3 to 4 in breadth. It is bounded by the parishes of Lauder and Melrose on the W. and S. W.; by Mertoun on the S.; by Smalholm and Nenthorn on the S. E. and E.; and by Gordon and Legertwood on the N. E. N. and N. W. It is situated in the west end of the county of Merse or Berwick, in the presbytery of Lauder, and Synod of Merse and Tiviotdale. The soil is not all the same; some parts of it are clay, others a light dry soil, and other parts are a desirable mixture of both. And as the

foil,

foil, fo the climate is alfo different. It is more mild in the weftermoft parts of the parifh, where the foil is generally light and dry, than in the eaftermoft parts of it, where the foil is ftronger and wetter. But, notwithftanding the difference of both foil and climate, the people are in general healthy; many of them arrive at old age. The moft common difeafes are agues, rheumatifms, and fcrophula. The frequency of the laft is probably owing to intermarriages. The ague has not been fo frequent thefe 2 years paft as formerly; but confumptive complaints are more common, probably owing to the fcrophula; as it is moftly thofe who are of that habit that become confumptive. About 14 or 15 years ago, the Honourable Mr and Mrs Baillie, both very humane and benevolent, caufed inoculate, at their expence, above 70 children in this parifh and neighbourhood; all of whom did well, except 2, who were of a fcrophulous habit. Ever, fince inoculation has been rather more generally practifed, and has been the happy means of preferving many lives.

Rivers.—The river Leader runs along the W. end, and the river Eden along the E. end of the parifh. Both have their fource in Lammar Muir, and run into Tweed. They formerly abounded with very fine trout, the firft alfo with falmon. But fince the farmers have fet about improving their farms, neither falmon nor trout are near fo plenty in either. This is thought to be owing to the liming of the grounds on each fide of the rivers, which, by heavy rains, is often wafhed down into the rivers, and is fuppofed either to fcare or kill the fifh.

Plantations—There are large plantations of wood in the E. end of the parifh, which are a great ornament to that part of the country, as well as a benefit to the adjacent
fields,

fields, to which they afford great ſhelter. There are alſo ſtrips and clumps of planting lately made in other parts of it, which, when grown, will add greatly to the beauty of the place, and be a conſiderable benefit to the proprietors.

Population.—At the time of Dr Webſter's report, the numbers were 1197. There are at preſent (1791) 670 males, and 681 females. In all, 1351 ſouls. 653 are of the Eſtabliſhed Church, the reſt are Sectaries. I do not think it has increaſed in numbers of late years. The farms are now much larger than formerly. What uſed to ſerve 12 or 13 farmers, is now occupied by 4, which muſt rather diminiſh than increaſe the number of inhabitants.

Manufactures, Agriculture, &c.—Although the pariſh conſiſts chiefly of villages, yet very few manufactures are carried on in it. The principal one is linen cloth. There are between 40 and 50 weavers looms, moſtly employed weaving linen, and the greateſt part of that cloth is for ſale. We have only one woollen manufacturer, though no place can be better ſituated for carrying on that branch of trade, than the village of Earlſtoun is. Leader runs along the weſt end of it, where there is an extenſive beautiful haugh, and there is plenty of wool, if not in the pariſh, yet in the neighbourhood, to ſupply 20 manufacturers, though they manufactured to a conſiderable extent. Nor can any part of the country be better accommodated with roads. The turnpike between Edinburgh and Jedburgh, goes cloſe by the weſt end of the village, and the great road from Edinburgh to London, by Kelſo, goes within $1\frac{1}{2}$ mile of the eaſt end of it. There are 4 mills in the pariſh, which manufacture a conſiderable quantity of all kinds of grain. Beſides what the inhabitants of the pariſh conſume, they make into meal and barley above 7000 bolls,

bolls, Linlithgow meaſure, every year; all which is carried to Dalkeith and Edinburgh markets. Coal and lime
are brought home in return.—There are about 2000 ſheep
kept in the pariſh. The farmers alſo rear a conſiderable
number of black cattle every year. Beſides theſe, they
buy many in the autumn; which, with theſe of their own
that are of proper age, they fatten on turnips. They are
now beginning to breed horſes. This will probably be the
means of lowering the price of that uſeful animal, which,
for ſome years paſt, has been very high. Horſes are abſolutely neceſſary in this part of the country, for it is by them
the farmers labour their farms, and drive their corn to
market. They never work with oxen now, as they uſed
to do formerly.—The moſt common crops in this pariſh
are oats, barley, and peas. There is alſo ſome wheat every
year; but the quantity of it is ſmall, in proportion to the
other kinds of grain. Turnips and potatoes are very general, and commonly very good. There is now a great
quantity of clover and rye-graſs ſown, and ſome flax for
private uſe. The oats that grow on the grounds about
Fans, are much eſteemed for ſeed. In ſeed-time, they generally ſell for 3 s. or 4 s. a boll more than other oats, and
there is uſually a conſiderable demand for them at that
ſeaſon. Of late years the quality, both of ſheep, black
cattle, and horſes, has been greatly improved, and their
numbers increaſed, owing to the improvements that have
been made in huſbandry; and if the farmers continue
in the ſame ſpirit of improving their farms, which I hope
they will, there is not the leaſt doubt but their black cattle,
horſes, and ſheep, will ſtill improve, both in quality and
number.—The valued rent of the pariſh is L. 5948 : 13 : 11$\frac{6}{12}$
Scots. There are about 40 proprietors in it, 3 of whom
are freeholders; the others are all feuers or portioners.

Stipend,

Stipend, School, and Poor.—The ſtipend is 112 bolls, half oats, half barley, about L. 34 in money, and a glebe, about 8 Engliſh acres. The manſe was built in 1724, and the church in 1736. The King is patron.—There are 2 ſchools. The parochial ſchool is in the village of Earlſtoun ; the ſalary L. 7 : 19 : 5 Sterling ; the maſter has alſo the intereſt of 500 merks Scots, mortified for teaching the children of inrolled poor. The other ſchool is in the village of Mellerſtain ; the maſter of it has L. 5 yearly ſalary, which is the intereſt of L. 100 Sterling, mortified by the family of Mellerſtain, for teaching a certain number of poor children. There is alſo a Sunday's ſchool in each of theſe villages, patroniſed and ſupported by the Honourable Mrs Baillie.—There are many poor people in this pariſh. About 30 are inrolled, who receive a weekly allowance, according to their neceſſities. For this purpoſe, a ſum is raiſed twice a-year, by aſſeſſment on the heritors and tenants. The ſum levied theſe 2 years paſt has been about L. 70 a-year.

Miſcellaneous Obſervations.—The famous Thomas the Rhymer, (whoſe real name and title was Sir Thomas Lermont), was a native of this pariſh. He lived at the weſt end of Earlſtoun, where part of his houſe is ſtill ſtanding, called Rhymer's Tower. And there is a ſtone built in the fore wall of the church, with this inſcription on it, ' Auld ' Rhymer's race, lies in this place.' He lived in the 13th century, and was co-temporary with one of the Earls of March, who reſided here then.

There are 2 fairs held at Earlſtoun. One on the 29th of June, for ſheep, black cattle, and horſes. It is reckoned the ſecond beſt fair in the ſouth of Scotland, both for ſheep and black cattle.—The other fair is held on the third Thurſday of October. It is only for black cattle and horſes.
There

There is often a good ſhow of black cattle in it, but no-thing like what is in the June fair. There are 4 public houſes in the pariſh. But on the fairs, almoſt every low houſe is a public one.

One great diſadvantage under which this pariſh labours, is the want of fuel. The common people burn turf and peat. Thoſe in the neighbourhood of Mellerſtain are con-veniently ſituated for fire-wood, which they get at a very moderate rate. The better ſort of feuers and farmers burn coal, which is uſually from the neighbourhood of Dalkeith, a carriage of about 24 or 25 miles, which neceſſarily makes the price of coals ſo high, that the poor cannot purchaſe them. Lime is alſo carried about 22 miles, from which it is likewiſe very high priced.

PARISH OF ECCLES.

(County of Berwick—Presbytery of Dunse—Synod of Merse and Tiviotdale.

By the Rev. Mr. ADAM MURRAY, *Minister.*

Origin of the Name.

ECCLES is evidently derived from the word *Ecclesia*, which, in the Greek, signifies a congregation, assembly, or meeting of people. Sometimes it signifies the place where the meeting is held; and, in modern times, it is confined to an assembly of Christians meeting together for devotion and worship, and agrees with the Latin phrase, *Cætus sanctus Christianorum, aut ædes sacra.*—From an appendix to HOPE's *Minor Practics*, by the late JOHN SPOTTISWOOD, Esq. of Spottiswood, advocate, (which takes notice of all the religious houses in Scotland, at the time of the Reformation), it appears, that ECCLES, in the county of Berwick, was anciently the seat of the nunnery of the *Benardine*, or *Cistertian Nuns*. It was founded in the year 1154, according to HARDEN; but

COWPAR

COWPAR fays, in his book, *anno dom.* 1155, *conventus moncalium fecundo, venit ad Eccles**.

Extent and Situation.—The extent of this parifh is very confiderable, being no lefs than 8 miles from E. to W., and nearly 6 from N. to S. It lies adjacent to the county of Roxburgh, on the W ; and contains above 11,000 acres of ground, fcarcely one acre of which is wafte or ufelefs.

Soil and Improvement.—The foil is in general good, and confifts of various kinds ; loam, gravel, and deep clay. The clay foil is môft prevalent ; and as there is a confiderable mixture of fand in it, when it is properly cultivated, and proper manure applied, it bears very luxuriant crops of every kind. It is the opinion of fome writers, that lime is not fitted to improve a clay foil. The reverfe of this, however, has been found in this parifh. Without lime, we can neither have wheat nor grafs ; but with it, the moft abundant crops of both. Indeed it requires a greater proportion of lime than foils of a lighter texture †. Towards the S. it is more inclined to gravel ; and in feveral farms there is found a very rich loam, capable of producing almoft any crop. Our crops, in general, when not hurt by a wet fpring, or exceffive drought,

---

* It was founded by Corfpatrick Earl of March, father to Earl Waldave, and confecrated to the Virgin Mary. Ada de Frazer was priorefs of Eccles, in the year 1296. There is in the public records, lib. 21. No. 537, a charter, whereby Marieta Hamilton, priorefs of Eccles, difpones to Alexander Hamilton of Innerwick, the village and lands of Eccles, in the year 1569 ; which charter was confirmed by Queen Mary, at Edinburgh, the 11th of May the fame year. This place was enacted into a temporal lordfhip, in favour of George Hume, afterwards Earl of Dunbar.

† The late Mr. Trotter of Belchefter laid on no lefs than 90 bolls of fhells to the Englifh acre ; and though the foil was a deep clay, it produced as rich grafs as any in Berwickfhire.

drought, or rains in ſummer, are very prolific ; and perhaps there is no place in Scotland more diſtinguiſhed for luxuriant crops of wheat, graſs and peaſe, than Eccles. The ſurface, being, in general, low and flat, is apt to be injured in ſpring and autumn by exceſſive rains ; and conſequently the riſing grounds are the beſt, becauſe not expoſed to the pernicious influence of ſtagnant water. The whole of the pariſh is arable. The farms are all encloſed in the very beſt modern manner ; and on many eſtates, the hedge rows, which are all in a thriv-ing ſtate, when ſeen at a diſtance by the traveller, exhibit the appearance of a highly cultivated garden. Of late years, great improvements have been made in agriculture, through the whole county of Berwick ; but in no pariſh have they been carried on with greater rapidity, and to greater advan-tage, than in this. Notwithſtanding the diſtance from lime, which is above 14 Engliſh miles, the carts and horſes of al-moſt every farmer in the pariſh drive 6 days in the week, during the ſummer months ; firſt for lime to the turnips, and afterwards for the fallow. In conſequence of this induſtry, the farmers in general are wealthy and opulent, and live in a ſtile and manner very different from their fathers †.

Agriculture.

†The writer of this article is old enough to remember, that butcher meat was ſeldom ſeen on a farmer's table, except on a Sunday. But how is the ſcene changed! No perſon now entertains better than the farmer, nor is there more neatneſs or elegance any where to be found, than in their houſes; and as all this is the effect of induſtry, they have an unqueſtionable title to enjoy the fruits of their honeſt labour. Formerly, in this county, eſtates were made only by gentlemen in the *law* department. But the caſe is now entirely altered. There are, in the county of Berwick, above a dozen farmers, who, by their in-genuity and induſtry, have acquired very conſiderable eſtates; and there is every reaſon to believe, that many more will ſoon be in the ſame independent ſituation. The price of labour has kept pace with the progreſs of improvement. Twenty years ago, domeſtic men ſervants could have been had for 4l. and 5l.

a year,

Agriculture and Produce.—If not prevented by rain in the
spring, *oats* are sown in the month of March and beginning
of April; and if the summer is favourable, they are commonly reaped from the end of August to the middle of September.
Barley is generally sown in April and the beginning of May,
and is reaped as soon as the oats. Pease, cold seed, if the
weather admits, are sown in February and the beginning of
March. When sown later, they seldom come to perfection.
Wheat (a great quantity of which is produced in the parish),
is generally sown upon fallow in the end of September.
A number of farmers sow wheat after pease; and, if the
land is clean, and the pease a good crop, it generally succeeds;
though some are of opinion, that it is a species of husbandry
not to be imitated. Wheat is also sometimes sown in the
spring, after turnips; but the crop is seldom good, as it is
generally very late, and neither gives much wheat nor flour.
Although there are no lands in Berwickshire, that will produce
turnips of greater size and quantity, than some farms in this
parish, yet the most judicious farmers are of opinion, that
they can turn their lands to greater account. The inconveniences attending turnips, on a clay soil, are the following:
1*st*, They cannot be taken off without injuring the land materially, as the water stands the whole winter in the tracks of
the wheels, and the ground cannot be properly prepared for
the next crop. 2*dly*, It is absolutely impracticable to *feed*
sheep

a year, they cannot now be got for less than 9l. and 10l. per annum. Female
servants are in the same proportion. Formerly, they could have been got for 2l.
a year; they have now got up to 4l. and 5l. The wages of men labourers at
hedge and ditch, are from 1s. to 1s. 3d. a day, from the 1st of March to the
1st of November; and from 8d. to 10d. the rest of the year, except that, in
time of harvest, they are from 1s. 6d. to 2s. a-day. Work, however, such as
enclosing, and weeding turnip, &c. is generally done by the piece.

sheep upon such land, as the animals never have a dry bed, and are often up to the belly in mud and water. In these places of the parish where the soil is light, great profits are made by feeding sheep on turnips. They are generally let at from 4l. to 5l. the English acre; and the writer hereof has once and again sold them for 5 guineas.

Climate and Diseases.—The climate of Eccles, from its low and flat situation, is by no means the most healthy; and from the marsh *miasma*, (arising from rain water stagnating on the surface of a soil, chiefly clay), the people are peculiarly obnoxious to diseases of debility, such as agues, nervous fevers, chronic rheumatisms, &c. Within these last 20 years, these diseases were almost epidemic, among the lower classes of the people. Of late, however, they are much less frequent, and greatly milder. This may be attributed to two causes: 1*st*, To the advanced state of agricultural improvement, and especially draining of land; which, by drawing off the rain water that formerly stagnated on the surface, has rendered the soil dryer, and consequently more wholesome: 2*dly*, To the lower classes being more comfortably clothed and lodged, and living more on animal food than formerly. That the influence of a damp climate is corrected by a generous mode of living, is abundantly evident from this circumstance, that while the poorer sort are often visited by the abovementioned diseases, the gentry and opulent farmers almost always escape. Among the causes, which have contributed to lessen the influence of the diseases peculiar to this climate, there is one, which the incumbent's personal knowledge of its happy effects will not allow him to omit; the *wearing of* FLANNEL *next the skin.* Nor is it difficult to account for this effect. Rheumatism proceeds evidently from the perspiration being obstructed on the surface of the body; and nothing but flannel will preserve

this

this difcharge uniform and equable, in a climate which is fubjected to fogs, and to the vapours which arife from water ftag-
nating on the furface of the ground. Could people be prevailed on univerfally to adopt this practice, it would do more
to alleviate, if not extirpate nervous difeafes, than the united
powers of the whole *materia medica.*—The ravages made by
the fmall pox were formerly very great; not lefs than a third
part of all thofe infected being carried off by this malignant
difeafe : But fince the introduction of inoculation, which of
late has become very general, the baneful influence of this
difeafe has been greatly mitigated *.

River and Fifh.—This parifh has no river that runs through
it, but the Tweed; which feparates Scotland and England,
wafhes the fouthern boundary, and affords a very lucrative
falmon fifhing, though at the diftance of near 20 miles from
the fea. The property belongs to the Earl of HOME.

Population.—In a furvey made by Dr. Webfter, about 40
years ago, the number of examinable perfons in the parifh of
Eccles, was - - - - - - - 1240
And the number of fouls, - - - - - 1489
From a very accurate furvey of the prefent inhabitants,
taken by the writer hereof, the number is not lefs
than - - - - - - - - - 1780

Confequently, in the fpace of 40 years, there has been an increafe of 291.

As

* It is rare to hear of one dying out of many hundreds who fubmit to this
falutary practice, while thofe families, who, from ignorance, obftinacy or prejudice, could not be prevailed upon to try the falutary experiment, have been
punifhed by the lofs of more than half their children. It is much to the honour
of the gentlemen in this parifh, that they have-done every thing in their power
to

As agriculture is the principal buſineſs carried on in the pariſh, the inhabitants are moſtly employed in that particular branch. There is a conſiderable number of tradeſmen, ſuch as ſmiths, carpenters, and plough-wrights, who are all employed by the farmers, and are generally in eaſy circumſtances. No man in this pariſh is unemployed ; and there is rather a want of hands for labour, than a ſuper-fluity.

Abſtract of Marriages †, Baptiſms, and Burials, for 3 Years, viz. from the 1ſt of October 1789, to the 1ſt of October 1792.

	Baptiſ.	Marr.	Bur.
From 1. Oct. 1789 to ditto 1790,	80	10	23
From 1. Oct. 1790 to ditto 1791,	72	13	20
From 1. Apr. 1791 to 1. Apr. 1792,	86	16	22

Cattle, &c.—The number of cattle and ploughs in the pariſh is as follows :

Number

to reconcile the minds of the common people to this uſeful practice, by paying the expence of inoculating the children of the poor around them. In this way, they have done more to promote the practice, than either reaſon or eloquence could have effected.

† To account for the ſmall number of regiſtered marriages, it is to be obſerved, that the practice of marrying in a clandeſtine and irregular manner ſtill ſubſiſts upon the Borders; and though the ſynod of Merſe and Tiviotdale have done every thing in their power to repreſs it, yet it is ſtill kept up by ſome members of the Church of England, who ſacrifice the dignity of their profeſſion to a little tranſient emolument.—There are alſo many more baptiſms than theſe which are regiſtered; but of late years, ſince the *tax* of *threepence* was paid to the King, over and above the uſual fees of regiſtration, many cannot be prevailed on to enrol their childrens names. The miniſter has done every thing in his power, to convince them of the propriety of the meaſure; but many individuals ſtill continue obſtinate and refractory.

Number of labouring horses, solely employed in the plough,	266	Number of calves reared annually by ditto and labourers,	1000
—— ditto from 2 to 3 years old,	70		
—— riding and carriage ditto,	50	Ditto of black cattle,	2838
—— foals reared by the farmers,	200	—— ploughs *,	133
	586		

Sheep and Wool.—Our farmers do not breed many sheep. This is owing to the nature of the soil, which often produces that baneful disease, well known by the name of the *rot*. The greatest proportion is consequently bought in, and fed off. The lambs are generally sold in the months of June, July, and August, and the ewes about Michaelmas and Martinmas. The wool of these sheep is not very valuable, as they are generally bought in from mountainous counties, such as Tweeddale and Lammermuir. Such wool sells from 10s. to 12s. per stone. As for the sheep purchased from Northumberland and *Bishoprick*, they are of a very superior kind. The wool of that staple generally sells from 18s. to one guinea per stone, and the carcase weighs from 70 lb. to 80 lb. There are only 2 farmers in the parish who are breeders of sheep ; which turn out to great account. The sheep which they breed, are equal to any bred in Northumberland, both for weight and fineness of fleece ; and, as a proof of this, 100 lambs, with the wool of the ewes, were sold for 100 guineas ; and a considerable profit was made of them, both by the butcher and manufacturer.

Union of Farms.—About 25 or 30 years ago, the farms in the parish of Eccles were very small, and several gentlemen
of

---

* There would be many more ploughs, if there was not a considerable quantity of land laid off in the best order, both for breeding and feeding.

of ſmall eſtates farmed their own lands. At this period, little profit aroſe from agriculture; and it is only ſince farms were united, that great profits have been made. It is now to be feared, however, that farming is going to the oppoſite extreme; and the writer hereof cannot help thinking, that too great property, and too extenſive farming, is a very great loſs to any country. In the pariſh of Eccles, ſome farms are far too extenſive, conſidering the good quality of the land. Some tenants poſſeſs above 900 acres, ſeveral 800, and ſcarcely can a farm of 50 or 60 acres be got for any rent. In land ſuch as that of Eccles, there ought not to be a farm exceeding 300 acres. This quantity of land would ſupport a family very decently, and beſides afford an ample proviſion for their children; and, in the opinion of ſome, it is very improper to elevate men too high above their ſtation. As many of our farmers have got a very narrow education, riches have often the unhappy effect of making them proud, and leading them to treat their ſuperiors with inſolence and contempt.

Rent and Proprietors, &c.—The rent of this pariſh, at preſent, is nearly 11,000l.; and it will advance conſiderably in a very ſhort time, as ſome old leaſes, upon extenſive eſtates, muſt ſoon expire. There is no farm, ſince the author has been miniſter of the pariſh, but what has been doubled in rent, and ſome of them have been tripled; and if grain and ſtock continue to hold the value they do at preſent, it would not be ſurpriſing, if, in the courſe of a few years, the rental of this pariſh ſhould exceed 18,000l. or even 20,000l. per annum. There is a farm, near Eccles, that expires in a year or two, rented at 180l., and it is credibly reported, that 480l. has been offered, and refuſed.—There are above 30 gentlemen, proprietors of eſtates; ſome of whom poſſeſs 1,400l., many 800l. and 900l. per annum, many conſiderably leſs, and ſome ſmall heritors,

heritors, who do not exceed 100l. per annum. Our tenants are in number 56; and many of our gentlemen retain as much land in their own hand, as accommodates their families with the neceffaries of life.

Ecclefiaftical State.—The incumbent has had great difficulty to afcertain the extent of the ancient *Nunnery*. It appears to have been nearly a fquare of 6 acres; extending rather farther to the S. and W. than to the E. and N. The only veftige remaining of it is two vaulted cells †, which the late Sir John Paterfon converted into two cellars, for holding wine, ale, *&c.*—The old church was a Gothic building, in the form of a crofs, vaulted and covered with large flag ftones, dedicated to St. Andrew, the tutelar faint of Scotland, and ornamented with a crofs, and a very elegant fteeple. The building might have ftood for many centuries, and it was with the greateft difficulty it was taken down. But as it was too fmall to accommodate the inhabitants, the proprietors of the parifh took it down about 20 years ago, and built a very handfome modern church on the fame ground, 75 feet long,

by

† The burial ground contiguous to thefe vaults is all flagged with fine ftone, 4 feet beneath the furface; which is a clear proof that there have been many more cells, of a fimilar kind to the former; and as the ground, when turned up, exhibits only a mixture of fand, lime, and earth, it appears to be nothing but the rubbifh of the fallen vaults. It is faid, that the principal entrance to the nunnery was from the W., where there was a very fpacious gate, beautifully fculptured, and adorned with a variety of figures. Before the front door of the manfion houfe of Eccles, a ftone coffin was dug out, above fix feet long, and covered above with flag ftones. As it had been buried above 200 years, every part of the body was reduced to afhes. As the infide of the ftone was pretty fmooth, and the whole portrait of the perfon vifible (though in afhes), Sir John Paterfon had the curiofity to collect the whole, and (wonderful to tell!) it did not exceed in weight one ounce and a half!

by 35 broad; where 1000 people are very conveniently seated.
It was built after the model of the Chapel of Eafe in Edinburgh, is in every refpect well finifhed, and is, without difpute, the beft and handfomeft country church in Berwickfhire.
The prefent incumbent was the firft minifter who preached in
it. The manfe and offices were built at the fame time. They
were removed from the place where they formerly ftood,
which was a little to the S. W. of the manfion-houfe of
Eccles; and as the heritors would not confent to the removal,
unlefs Sir John was at the whole expence of the new buildings, he acceded to the conditions. The glebe was exchanged
at the fame time, and placed very conveniently in the front
of the manfe. It confifts of rather more than 20 acres of
good arable ground, and is well worth as many pounds Sterling. As the ftipend, when the prefent minifter entered to
the charge, did not exceed 72l., every thing included, he was
obliged to purfue for an augmentation. The Lords of Seffion
granted one to the extent of 30l.: But, what is extremely
hard on him, although it is above 18 years fince it was obtained, the allocation is not yet finally fettled. Several of the
heritors, indeed, paid by the firft allocation, but many more
have refufed payment; and there are arrears, at this moment
due, to the extent of feveral hundred pounds.

Poor.—The poor, that are rated in the books, amount to
the number of 30 perfons; and the parifh is affeffed in 120l.
per annum for their fupport. As for the induftrious poor,
when families may want occafional fupport, they are relieved,
either from the money collected on the Sabbath-day, or by
the generofity of the gentlemen in the parifh. The author
mentions it to their honour, that on a proper reprefentation
of diftrefs, he has always found them liberal and beneficent.

Antiquities.

Antiquities.—From our vicinity to England, it might have been expected, that we should have had many memorials of those bloody contests, which formerly subsisted between the neighbouring kingdoms. We have only, however, one of this kind. It is a monument erected to one of the PERCIES, who fell in a bloody engagement with one of the rival family of Douglas. It consists of a large square stone, full 9 feet above the surface. On one side of the square appears the greyhound, which is the Percie's crest; on another, the figure of a naked man, in rude sculpture; and, on the other two sides, the ancient sword and battle-ax are pourtrayed †. It stands nearly a mile to the N. E. of the village of Eccles.

Disadvantages.—Among the natural defects in the situation of Eccles, must first be mentioned the want of *running water.* In times of severe drought, our brooks and rivulets are often entirely dried up; and our farmers are sometimes obliged to drive their cattle to the Tweed, a distance of between 2 and 3 miles. Another disadvantage under which we labour, is our distance from coals and lime. We are obliged to bring both these articles from Northumberland, which is not less remote than from 14 to 18 miles. Hence fuel becomes a most expensive article in housekeeping; and the distress of the lower ranks, in severe winters, is unspeakably great. Our distance from markets is also another inconvenience. Our

farmers

---

† There is no inscription whatever to be traced on this stone; so that it is impossible to ascertain its antiquity. It must, however, have been considerably prior to the Union. The late Sir John Paterson wished to have it removed near the mansion of Eccles, but found the thing impracticable. The monument is fixed in a large stone basis, which it penetrates; and the workmen followed it some feet into the earth, without being able to get to the foundation. The place where it stands is called *Dead Riggs,* from the great number of the slain; and so dreadful was the slaughter, that tradition reports, that a little streamlet, in its neighbourhood, *ran with blood for* 24 *hours !*

farmers cannot depend on a ready fale, and quick return of money, in any market nearer than Berwick, which is diftant almoft 20 miles ; and it is to that place, accordingly, that they commonly fend all their wheat and barley. Kelfo, indeed, is within 6 miles of Eccles ; but as no corn merchants attend there, to buy grain for exportation, the only purchafers are country millers, who buy it for internal confumption, and with whom it is generally difagreeable, and often unfafe to deal. The circumftance, which enables us to ftruggle under thefe inconveniences, is the goodnefs of our public roads ; and the gentlemen of the county deferve high praife for the attention they have paid to this important particular, and the regulations they have made for keeping the roads in a ftate of good repair.

PARISH OF EDROM.

By the Rev. Mr WILLIAM REDPATH.

Name, Situation, Surface, and Air.

THE antient name of this parish was Etherham, derived from *Ether*, the original name of Whitewater, and *Ham*, a village on its banks. Edrom is situated in Berwickshire, presbytery of Chirnside, and synod of Merse and Tiviotdale. It is about 10 English miles long and 6 broad. It is bounded by the parishes of Dunse, Langton, Polworth, Fogo, Swinton, Whitsome, Hilton, Chirnside, Preston, and Bunkle. The appearance of the country is flat, except towards the Lammermuir or Cheviot Hills. A great part of the soil is fertile, and produces good corn when well cultivated ; part moorish and barren ; and part clay or shallow. Formerly the air was moist, but is now considerably drier, on account of the inclosing and draining every part of the country. Lakes and pools of water are drained, and corn made to grow where the water stood. The air is salubrious. The best proof of this is the longevity of the inhabitants. Several in the parish have attained to 70, 80, and 90 years of age. The fevers, consumptions, and agues, which formerly prevailed here, were thought to have been owing to the moisture of the country. Since it was drained and inclosed,

closed, fevers and agues have ceased very much, and instead of appearing every year, only come once in four or five years.

Population.—The population of this parish is believed to have been much less 50 years ago than it is at present. Agriculture was not then in that flourishing state in which it now is ; and manufactures have only begun within these 15 or 20 years. From the decreet of locality for stipend in the year 1733, it appears that the number of catechisable persons was near 800 ; and the whole, at that time, might amount to more than 900, or near 1000. About 13 years ago, they amounted to 1200 souls. The following table will give some idea of the population of this parish in 1790 :

Souls - - -	1336
Males - - -	613
Females - - -	723
Annual average of births -	40
Annual average of deaths -	10
Annual average of marriages -	12
Heritors - -	9
Farmers - - -	38
Mechanics - -	34
Inhabited houses - -	211
Persons in a family at an average -	6

The number of horses in the parish is about 280, of sheep 3000, and of black cattle 600.

Manufactures.—There is a paper-mill, a lint-mill, and a wheel-wright manufacture. Fifty-five persons are employed in the paper-mill, 5 in the lint-mill, and about 5 or 6 in the wheel-wright manufactory. The wages paid per day in the

first

first is L. 2 : 15 : 0. The value of the paper made yearly amounts to L. 5000 Sterling. When the wheel manufacture was carried on by James Small, 15 journeymen were employed. He introduced one of the best ploughs made in Scotland. A variety of useful manufactures, especially linen and woollen, a cotton-mill, stocking manufacture, and bleachfield, might be established. There is abundance of fine sheep for wool, and a lint-mill is an encouragement to grow flax. There is plenty of fine water and corn to support manufactures. Four hundred persons might be employed by a linen and cotton mill.

Wages, Prices, and Poor.—A labourer's wages is 10d. or 1s. per day ; masons and carpenters 1s. 6d. ; tailors 6d. and their meat. The usual wages of male servants employed in husbandry is 50s. or L. 3 per half year, with their board ; of female servants 30 or 40 shillings. All butcher's meat, through the greatest part of the year, is 3¼d. and 4d. per pound ; butter 8d. ; cheese 3¼d. if Scotch ; English is 5d. and 6d. ; wheat generally 30 shillings per boll ; oats are 12, 14, 15, and 16 shillings per boll, Berwickshire measure ; barley is 16, 18, and often 20 shillings per boll. The number of poor in this parish receiving alms is 12. The annual assessment laid on the heritors, tenants, and mechanics, for their maintenance, is L. 10. Several of the poor are likewise assisted by the weekly collections, kirk-session fund, hearse and mortcloth money.

Rent of Land.—The best arable ground is 15 and 20 shillings, and the best pasture 25 and 30 shillings per acre. The rent of several farms is L. 300, L. 400, L. 500, and L. 600 *per annum ;* but there are more at L. 100, L. 50, L. 30, and L. 20. The rent of the whole lands of the parish is about
L. 6493

L. 6493 Sterling *per annum.* From a decreet of locality obtained in 1733, it appears that the rent amounted then only
to L. 2000 Sterling yearly. One of the heritors marled and
inclosed his whole estate, and the rent rose from L. 500 to
L. 1500 a year. Another marled the whole of his land,
inclosed it with stone dikes, and the rent rose from L. 500
to L. 1200 or L. 1300 *per annum.* Every estate, within
these 20 years, has risen in proportion. Almost the whole
of the parish is inclosed.

Church and Stipend.—The church was built in 1732, and
has been well repaired since the present incumbent was settled. The spirit of making churches neat and decent has
spread to the neighbouring parishes. The stipend, including the glebe, is about L. 110 Sterling *per annum.* The
crown is patron.

Mineral Springs and Rivers.—There is one remarkable
mineral spring, called *Dunse Well*, in the estate of Nisbet.
It appears that a number of gentry and nobility formerly resorted to this water ; but it is fallen into disrepute.
There are two rivers in the parish, viz. Whitewater and
Blackwater, commonly pronounced *Whitadder* and *Blakad-
der*. Whitewater rises in the Lammermuir Hills, near the
confines of Lothian, runs near 30 or 40 miles, and discharges itself into the Tweed about 2 miles from Berwick. It
abounds with small trout. A great number of salmon come
up and spawn in it. Blackwater rises likewise in Lammermuir, above Greenlaw, and after a course of about 16 or 18
miles, falls into the Whitewater, at a village called Allan-
town, in this parish. It is celebrated for as fine trout as any
in Scotland.

Roads.—The roads are tolerably good. They have been
greatly

greatly improved within thefe 30 years. The money raifed in the parifh for repairing them is about L. 115 Sterling yearly, by taxing every horfe at 7 s. 6 d. and every cottager at 1 s. 6 d. There are few or no turnpikes, except on the poft roads. The country is divided in opinion about the advantages or difadvantages of them.

Manners, Cuftoms, &c.—There is a very great alteration in the manners, cuftoms, drefs, and ftile of living, of the inhabitants of this parifh, within thefe 30 years. All ranks have more elegant or commodious houfes, finer cothes, and better food.

PARISH OF EYEMOUTH.

(*County of Berwick.*)

By the Rev. Mr GEORGE TOD.

―――――――

Extent, Soil, Surface, &c.

THIS parish is of small extent, not exceeding 800 acres English measure. It was part of the priory of Coldingham; and before the Reformation, it is said, that the prior of Coldingham had a chapel of ease here, and that it was erected into a parish, no sooner than in the reign of King James VI. This parish is about a mile square, including the farm of Highlaws, but its marches with those of Coldingham, are indented, and very irregular. About one half of the lands are let in two farms, viz. Linthill, and Beanrigg. The rest are possessed by the inhabitants of Eyemouth, in small parks and acre-dale. The feuers, small heritors, who are also mechanics, possess their own lands. Eyemouth is a borough of barony. Mr Home of Wedderburn, our present representative in Parliament, is the superior, and is also proprietor of more than nine tenths of the land in the parish. The yearly rent is from 25 s. to 40 s. *per* acre English. There is not one foot of bad or waste ground. The lands were all open twenty years ago; but they are now almost all inclosed, and the rents are near double of what they were then. The soil, in general, is good, and produces every sort of grain, of

a

a good quality ; as well as fow:: grafs. turnips, and potatoes. The climate is dry, and perhaps as little rain falls here, as in any other part of Scotland.

Antiquities.—Here are the remains of a regular fortification upon a fmall promontory ftretching out to the fea, which is faid to have been erected by the Earl of Hertford, afterwards Duke of Somerfet, when going to invade Scotland, while he held the regency, in the minority of Edward VI. It was demolifhed by treaty in Queen Mary's reign, foon after the battle of Pinkie. Though all the rocks along the coaft are of the common hard whinftone, yet the promontory, upon which this fortification has been built, confifts of what is called *pudding ftone*. It is remarkably hard, and will cut like marble, and even ftands the fire. The two piers were built of it, which ftand both weather and water without the leaft appearance of wafte.

Harbour and Trade.—At the beginning of this century, Eyemouth was a mere fifhing town; but, after the Union, it gradually increafed; and, owing to its vicinity to England, it became remarkable for fmuggling ; but that pernicious trade being much quafhed, the gentlemen of this county, amongft their firft improvements, erected a pier on the weft fide of the harbour, about the year 1750, that coft about L. 2000, which was raifed by fubfcription ; and, about the year 1770, another pier was built upon the eaft fide of the harbour, which coft above L. 2500 ; which laft pier was planned and executed by Mr Smeaton.

" The harbour of Eyemouth," Mr Smeaton remarks, " lies at the corner of a bay, in which fhips can work in and out at all times of tide, or lie at an anchor fecure from all winds, except

except the northerly and north easterly. From this circumstance, its situation seems very advantageous : But, as the
mouth of the river or harbour lies open to the northerly
winds, ships cannot lie in safety therein, without going up
beyond the elbow of the present quay, where the water being
shallower by several feet, and the breadth much contracted,
the harbour is not only defective in point of capacity, but in
safety also ; for, at a full sea, (the mouth being wide), the
sea tumbles in with so much impetuosity, that great seas find
their way round the elbow, and make the vessels, even there,
lie not so quiet as is to be wished. In order, therefore, not
only to enlarge the harbour, but very greatly to increase
the safety of vessels lying therein, it is proposed to build a
north pier to defend the harbour's mouth ; and, to this end,
nature has furnished a ledge of rocks, not only capable of
making the most excellent of all foundations for such a pier,
but in as advantageous a direction as could be wished ; upon
which a pier is proposed to be built according to the plans
accompanying this Report ; For, according to the direction
therein specified, the harbour will be defended from all such
seas as annoy the bay ; and the only points from whence the
harbour could be affected by seas coming in through the
mouth, is land locked by the points of the bay ; so that the
harbour will, in its whole extent, be perfectly safe in all winds.
It is also to be noted, that the same circumstances which concur to make the harbour safe in all winds, afford the means
of vessels getting in and out in all winds ; and this proceeds
from the entry into the harbour lying nearly at a right angle
with the direction into and out of the bay. It also is a great
advantage that there is a good flow of tide, which at spring
tides is said to be twenty feet ; and there is at the lowest ebb
several feet of water, at low water, between the proposed
pier heads; so that there will be seldom less at neip tides than

sixteen

fixteen or feventeen feet of water in the harbour; which is capable of receiving veffels from three to four hundred tons, according as they are more flat, or more fharp built, and which afterwards can, upon a greater flow of tide, be got into a more advantageous birth. Another advantage to the executing the propofed defign arifes from a great quantity of rough rocks that lie at the north wefterly point of the bay, very proper for building the outfides of the body of the pier, the infides of which may be done with rough ftones, won or blafted from the rocks, neighbouring to that upon which the pier is propofed to be built. By this means, the pier may be executed at a trifle of expence, in proportion to the extent and utility of the defign; for the rocks, that are reprefented within the intended pier, will be removed and made fmooth, fo as to procure an addition of harbour-room at little or no charge, as they will be ufed within the pier. When this is done, there will be an addition of harbour-room in the fpace between the elbow before mentioned and the pier-heads, capable of holding thirty fhips of middling fize, with fufficient paffage; and which, in time of war, will be very ufeful on this coaft, not only for the refuge of coafters from the enemy, but, in bad weather, for privateers, and the fmaller fized veffels acting offenfively."

Previous to the erection of the firft pier, there was very little fair trade carried on; but, ever fince it was built, much corn and meal have been brought into the county, and fhipped here, for Leith and other markets, to the extent of 20,000 bolls annually, and, in fome years, more than double that quantity. For feveral years paft, there has not been a fingle fmuggler refiding in this parifh. The former dealers in that illicit trade are now all dead, or removed to diftant parts. Not one of them died rich, and the far greateft part of them

became

became bankrupt. For twenty years and upwards, we have had at leaſt two wholeſale merchants, who import wood, iron, flax, tar, and other foreign goods. There is one good inn, and too many alehouſes.

Manufactures.—We have no manufactory here; nor is there any in the whole county, except two paper-mills, one near Dunſe, and the other near Ayton.

Fiſhing.—There are only ſix fiſhing crews in this place, who take abundance of fiſhes, the greater part of which are carried to Edinburgh. But, in place of ſix, there is room for ſixty boats, as our coaſt abounds with fiſhes of all kinds, and of a good quality. We have alſo a herring fiſhery; and, in ſome years, millions are caught; and, after ſerving the country demand, the reſt are partly ſalted, and made into what are called *white herrings,* and partly manufactured into red herrings, and both are ſent to London, and foreign parts, where they generally bring a good profit. Formerly they caught the herrings at what they called the *Ground Drove,* which laſts only a few days; but now they alſo fiſh for them by a *Float Drove,* which laſts for ſome months; ſo that they now get ten times the number they got formerly, and the herrings are of a far better quality, becauſe they never come to the ground till they are about to ſpawn.

Fuel.—There is no other fuel than coal. If we were not almoſt prohibited from ſupplying ourſelves with Scottiſh coals, with one of the moſt unreaſonable duties that ever was impoſed, viz. 3 s. 4 d. a ton, no other coals would be uſed. We complain of another grievance. This port is a branch of the Cuſtomhouſe of Dunbar, and our merchants are obliged to go there, which is a diſtance of 20 miles, to report e-

very

very cargo, and get fufferances to load or unload, and thereafter to go back again for cockets and clearances, which is at
tended with much dangerous delay, and no fmall expence.

Difeafes.—The air here is reckoned healthy. We are not
afflicted with any infectious or epidemical difeafes, except the
fmall-pox, the bad effects of which have of late been prevented by inoculation. The only complaints that prove mortal in this place, are different kinds of fevers and confumptions;
and thefe are moftly confined to the pooreft clafs of people,
and afcribed to their fcanty diet.

Population.—At prefent, there are about 1000 fouls in the
parifh. In Dr Webfter's Report, the number is 792.

Births in the parifh,		Deaths,	
in 1788	20	in 1788	17
in 1789	35	in 1789	10
in 1790	19	in 1790	7

Church.—The ftipend is partly victual and money, and arifes
partly from teinds of fifhes, which being fo variable, cannot
well be eftimated. The glebe confifts of about ten acres of good
land, and may be eftimated at fifteen guineas yearly. The
manfe and church are in bad repair. There are no Papifts
nor Epifcopals in the parifh, and only ten or twelve Seceders.

Prices of labour.—The wages of wrights and mafons are
from 1 s. 4 d. to 1 s. 8 d. a day; of labourers, from 10 d. to
1 s.; labouring fervants within the houfe from L. 6 to L. 7.
per annum; a maid-fervant receives about 30 s. the half-
year.

Mifcellaneous

Miscellaneous observations.—There is great plenty of sea-ware thrown in here, the coarsest part of which is applied for manuring the lands, and the finest part is manufactured into kelp. There are very few law-pleas or disputes in this parish, because we have only *one writer*.

PARISH OF FOGO.

(COUNTY OF BERWICK, SYNOD OF MERSE AND TEVIOT-DALE, PRESBYTERY OF DUNSE.)

By the Rev. JOHN TOD *

Name, Situation, and Extent.

THE origin of the name of this parish cannot now, perhaps, be fully ascertained. There are no places nor
appearances in the neighbourhood from which the name
seems to have been derived. The parish is situated in the
county of Berwick, within the bounds of the presbytery of
Dunse, and synod of Merse and Teviotdale; and is bounded by the parish of Greenlaw, on the west; Polwarth, on
the north; Swinton, on the east; Eccles, on the south and
south-west. The extent is not very great, being about six
miles

---

* Some additional observations, by a friend to Statistical Inquiries, are interspersed.

miles in length, from eaft to weft, and between three and four miles in breadth, from fouth to north. The figure of it is regular, being very little interfeded by other parifhes. It lies about 8 miles north of Coldftream; 4 fouth weft of Dunfe; 10 north-eaft of Kelfo; and about 15 from the fea-ports of Berwick and Eyemouth.

Rivers.—The river Blackadder, which runs through this parifh, takes its rife out of fome moffy grounds in the parifh of Longformacus, (hence its proper name *Blackwater*, vulgarly pronounced Blackadder, or Blackatter). Soon after its rife, it is joined by a fmall rivulet from the parifh of Weftruther, about fix miles north-weft of Fogo. It enters the parifh on the weft end, and, running eaft, divides it nearly into two parts; from thence continuing its courfe about fix miles, falls into the Whitadder, which difcharges itfelf into the Tweed three miles above the town of Berwick. It abounds with a particular fpecies of trout, much larger than the common burn trout, of an excellent flavour, and remarkably fat.

One peculiarity is obferved of the Blackadder, that no falmon can live in it; and if any happen to enter, which they feldom do, even in the fpawning feafon, they are always found dead, a little way up from the mouth of the river, although the Whitadder, from whence they come into it, abounds with them from the Tweed, and carries them many miles above the place where it meets with the Blackadder. Every other ftream in this country, communicating with the Tweed, has the falmon in great plenty during the feafon. The above-mentioned fource, (the moffy grounds of Longformacus), is commonly afcribed as the reafon why that fifh cannot frequent the river.

Soil.

Soil.—This is of two kinds; the first, a deep rich loam, comprehending all the lands near the river, and for a considerable tract of the parish; the other, a light or moorish loam, upon a tilly bed; this last is naturally wet, but produces good corn and grass in ordinary seasons. The whole parish is arable, excepting a few acres on some of the banks of Blackadder, and some marshy or swampy grounds. But those places that will not admit the operations of the plough, are not unproductive of good pasture. The soil, in general, seems equally adapted for grass or tillage. A great part of the parish is inclosed, although a considerable quantity still lies open. Since the year 1780, above 150 acres of land, nearly waste, or approaching to it, have been brought into cultivation. About 1200 acres yet remain waste and uninclosed. Some of these are allowed thus to remain, chiefly on account of their bad quality, as being supposed incapable of repaying any expence that might be laid out on their improvement; but others are left in a state of nature, owing more to the negligence of the possessors than to any other cause.

Produce.—The produce of this parish is very valuable. The principal crops are oats and barley; some wheat and pease, and a considerable quantity of clover and rye-grass are sown, and succeed well. Large quantities of potatoes are raised, and constitute no small part of the food of the inhabitants. Turnips are a valuable crop here, as they answer the soil, and are extremely serviceable in feeding cattle during winter: they are likewise much used for the keeping stock. The course of cropping on a loam, incumbent on a retentive sub-soil, is usually the following : 1. Oats or barley. 2. Fallow. 3. Wheat. 4. Grass-seeds. 5. Pasture, commonly four years. The rotation on the moor-soil,

or

or gravel is generally turnip, barley, or oats; grafs from one to three years; oats.

A confiderable number of horfes are bred in the parifh, both for private ufe and fale. The black-cattle are of a large kind, and many are raifed as well for the market as for private ufe. The number of fheep now bred in the parifh is confiderable. Some of them are of the large Englifh kind, but in general they are of a middling fize; they produce a great quantity of wool, and of a good quality. It is a cuf-tom to buy in a number of ewes about the month of October, from Northumberland, and fome from the weftern parts of the county and Teviotdale, in the fpring, about March. Thefe, leaving the wool and lamb in fummer, are fed and fold off towards the autumn. Upon the whole, the produce is many times greater than what is neceffary for the con-fumption of the inhabitants. The largeft of the black-cattle fed in the parifh, and the heavieft of the fheep, are fent into England; the fmaller and lighter kinds are fold in the markets at home. Moft of the corn is difpofed of in the neighbouring markets, and what remains for fale is fent to Berwick and Eyemouth.

State of Property.—The heritors of the parifh, poffeffing properties above 20 acres, are Mortonhall, Harcarfe, March-mont, and Caldra: none of whom are refident except the laft. The quantity of land occupied by thefe heritors can-not be exactly afcertained, as a great part of it has never been meafured; but, from the beft calculation that can at prefent be formed, it appears to be 4127 acres; of which, about 57 acres are under planting.—Number of tenants oc-cupying above 20 acres is 15, of whom three are non-refi-dent; but their farms are fuperintended by grieves or over-feers.

Rents.

Rents.—The proven rental of the pariſh, in the late proceſs of augmentation, was L. 2180.

Conſiderable improvements have of late been made on
the property in the pariſh, as incloſing, liming, draining,
&c. One of the heritors, and one or two of the principal
farmers, have made not a few improvements, but by far
the greateſt part of them have been done by the tenants at
large.

Roads.—In general, the parochial roads are not in the
beſt repair ; there are at leaſt ſix miles of them quite in diſrepair, and probably muſt continue in that ſtate, as the
funds at preſent are not ſufficient to keep in repair the
roads that have already been made.

Population.—The population of this pariſh has of late
been greatly diminiſhed. The veſtiges of old houſes are to
be ſeen in every part of it. Several villages almoſt totally demoliſhed, oecaſioned by the monopoly of farms, now
ſo cuſtomary in this country. There are inſtances in this,
and the neighbouring pariſhes, of one perſon poſſeſſing
three, four, or ſix, very conſiderable farms, every one of
which was formerly conſidered as ſufficiently large for one
perſon to occupy. The population, in 1755, according to
Dr Webſter's account, was 566 ſouls. It may be now ſtated at 450.

All the inhabitants are farmers and cottagers, with a few
tradeſmen, employed for the purpoſes of huſbandry ; as three
ſmiths, and two joiners or wrights, with 45 labourers.
There are no manufactures in the pariſh. But it is ſupplied
with three corn-mills. Thraſhing-machines are beginning
to make their appearance, being introduced by one or two
of the farmers. Since the year 1780, there have been rebuilt

built three farm or manſion-houſes, and three farm-ſtead-ings, with manſion and cow-houſes.

Church.—The walls and roof of the church were repair-ed in 1775. The miniſters of this pariſh were, Meſſrs Meth-ven, Methven, Pringle, Moodie, Home, and Home ; which laſt was, in 1785, ſucceeded by Mr John Todd the preſent incumbent. The manſe and offices were rebuilt in 1787. All the inhabitants are of the Eſtabliſhed church, except a few Diſſenters, moſtly of the Relief ; and theſe attend the pariſh church occaſionally.

School.—The ſchool-houſe is in good repair. The ſchool-maſter's ſalary is L. 7 : 1 : 1 Sterling.

Poor.—There are only four perſons at preſent on the poor roll ; ſome others, from accidental circumſtances, often receive a temporary ſupply. The heritors and kirk-ſeſſion generally meet three times in the year to make proviſion for the poor for the enſuing four months, when they ad-mit on the roll, or increaſe the allowance of thoſe whoſe neceſſities may ſeem to require it. The number of paupers, upon a ten years average, preceding the year 1784, is five : and upon a ten years average, preceding 1794, is ſeven. The funds for the maintenance of the poor ariſe from the weekly collections in the church, the intereſt of ſome mor-tified monies belonging to the poor of the pariſh ; and, for what more is neceſſary, the heritors have recourſe to the legal method, and aſſeſs themſelves according to the pro-portion of their valued rent. The yearly aſſeſſments, upon the average of ten years, preceding 1784, were L. 11, 17 s. 1¾ d. Sterling : and the average of ten years, preceding 1794, were L. 23, 2 s. Sterling.

All

All the teinds in the pariſh are valued, from whence are paid the ſtipend, which was lately augmented, the ſchool ſalary, and the ſums neceſſary for repairing the church, manſe, offices, and ſchool-houſe. The ſtipend is now fixed at L. 100 *per annum*; the old ſtipend was L. 77, 10 s.; conſequently there has been an augmentation of L. 22, 10 s.

Antiquities.—The only mark of antiquity found in this pariſh is at a village called Cheſters, which has all the appearance of an old Roman encampment; but now very much defaced.

There is an ancient bridge over the Blackadder, at Fogo, of great advantage to the neighbourhood, as in the winter ſeaſon the water frequently cannot be forded. This bridge is kept in repair by the county, and is the only one in the pariſh.

Diſadvantages.—This place and neighbourhood labour under the diſadvantage of being at a diſtance from coal, the only fuel uſed in the pariſh. It is brought from Northumberland, at the diſtance of about 12 miles. Lime is very ſcarce and dear. To theſe circumſtances, unfavourable for agriculture, and the comfort of the people, may be added the thirlage to mills.

PARISH OF FOULDEN.

*(County of Berwick—Presbytery of Chirnside—Synod of Merse
and Tiviotdale.)*

By the Rev. Doctor DAVID YOUNG.

———————

Extent and Soil.

THE parish of Foulden, in its form, approaches nearer to
that of a square than any other; and, in breadth, is about 2
miles, and in length 2¼. The soil, on the S. side, is a strong
clay; towards the middle of the parish it becomes more loamy,
and on the N. it turns considerably light.

Cultivation and Produce.—The whole lands in this parish lay
formerly *run-rigg;* which, however unfavourable to improvement, was indispensably necessary, as a bond of defence in
those days, when the inhabitants of the Borders were in the
practice of committing depredations upon one another. Although these acts of plunder were relinquished, after the revolution in 1688, it was not till within these 40 years, that a full division

fion of property took place ; but fince the lands were divided, they have been in general well inclofed, and brought to a confiderable degree of cultivation. They yield plentiful crops of wheat, barley, oats, peafe, turnips, potatoes, and grafs.

Rents, Cattle, &c.—Although thefe lands fully bear the above defcription of foil and good quality, the beft of them, excepting fome crofts, were let no higher than 10s. per acre ; but fince the old leafes expired, they are now advanced from 10s., to 20s., 30s., and even 40s., which is not too high, confidering the fhort diftance from market and lime. Formerly, a large tract of land, on the north fide of the parifh, called *Foulden Muir*, was occupied by the refidenters in the village, by way of ftents, or pafture for cows and horfes, and, in that ftate, paid very little rent. The grafs of thefe grounds being always in great plenty, and of good quality, fuggefted the advantage of bringing them into a ftate of cultivation. About 30 years ago, when improvements in agriculture were introduced into this part of the country, this piece of land was accordingly plowed up, and yeilded a profufe crop, from a good foil. It was foon after let out into different farms, which now pay about 300l. of yearly rent. Some part of this land has been found unfit for hufbandry, and is lately planted with firs, which promife a good return in due time. Lime is very much ufed in this part of the country. There is fhell marl in the parifh, but it has never been properly tried ; and, for a number of years paft, it has been entirely neglected. There is nothing remarkable in the mode of hufbandry, nor in the inftruments employed in it. The breeding or feeding of fheep has not been tried here, although great part of the lands are very fit for both purpofes. The late proprietor had a fine tafte for the breeding and feeding of cattle. His horfes were the beft in the country, and it is but 3 years fince the laft

of

of his breed of oxen were fold.   One ox weighed 128 ftone,
ᷓnd was of a very fine fhape and make.

Climate, River, &c.—This parifh, and fome other lands ad‑
joining, ftand upon a confiderable elevation, which continues
to rife, towards the N., for 2 miles; and then flopes gradually,
until it reaches the fea banks, which are very high and rocky.
There is a river, called *Whittadder*, which runs on the S.
fide, and empties itfelf into the Tweed, near Berwick.   The
bed of the river is very deep, being in no place under 40
yards, and in many places 50 yards, from the top of the bank.
Thefe banks are cut, upon the N. fide, into very deep dens
by nature, through which rivulets of water run, from the
whole lands in the neighbourhood, throughout the year.   Thefe
circumftances, added to an almoft unbounded profpect to the
S. and W., muft contribute to render the air pure and dry,
and confequently lefs fufceptible of noxious or infectious
taints.   It has been frequently remarked here, that the dif‑
eafes, which are peculiar to our climate, fuch as intermittent
and common continued fevers, putrid fever, and fore throat,
are fcarce known amongft us, whilft they are fometimes very
frequent and mortal, in the parifhes immediately adjoining.
Thefe difeafes have indeed made their appearance here at fuch
times, but unaccompanied with that malignity, which rendered
them fo fatal to thofe attacked with them, in lefs elevated
and more moift fituations.   For thefe 7 years and upwards,
only one young perfon has died, a female of 16 years of age,
and one child.   Good health is enjoyed through life, with
very little interruption; and, except thefe two, none have
died (refiding in this parifh), during the above mentioned
period, who had not reached at leaft 60 years; and it is not
unfrequent to attain the age of 80, and even 90 years, in the
full poffeffion of every faculty.

Population.

Population.—As the records have not been regularly kept, the ancient ftate of the population cannot be precifely afcertained. A confiderable village, containing about 60 families, being now reduced to 16 only, is fuppofed to have diminifhed the population; and it is the opinion of old refidenters, that the number of fouls is not fo great now, as it was 40 years ago; although, upon comparing the average of baptifms for the laft 7 years, with that of the fame number of years half a century ago, there appears to be very little difference. Hence fome incline to think, that although a number of old people have died, and feveral others have left the bounds to refide elfewhere, the permanent population is ftill nearly the fame; and the reafon they give, is, that feveral new farms have been erected, with a number of houfes, containing many families, which bear a near proportion to the reduction, which has taken place in the village. The former opinion, however, feems neareft the truth, the return to Dr. Webfter, in 1755, having been - - - - - - - - 465

And the number of perfons at prefent (1793), being only 344

Decreafe, - 121

Annual average of births, - 6	Perfons under 10 years of age,	100
—————— marriages, - 1	—— between 10 and 20, -	40
—————— deaths, - 1	—————— 20 and 50, -	170
Number of males, - - 170	—————— 50 and 70, -	30
—————— females, - 174	—————— 70 and 90, -	4

Ecclefiaftical State.—The number of Seceders is very inconfiderable; fo that the people, in general, attend the ordinances of religion in the parifh church; which was rebuilt in 1786. The manfe was built about 14 years before. The ftipend, by a late decreet of augmentation, is 56l. 10s. in money, and three chalders and a half of barley and oatmeal, equal parts. There is an allowance of 2l. 10s. for the expences of

the

the facrament; and the glebe and garden is worth 20l. Sterling. JAMES WILKIE of FOULDEN, Efq. is patron*.

Antiquities.—There is an old ruin, called *Foulden*, which appears to have been a place of fecurity and ftrength, in the times of the Border contefts. There is alfo a property, called *Nunlands*, where there was an eftablifhment of nuns in former times; but no record or tradition has been met with, that gives any hiftory of either †.

Markets and Roads.—There are 2 fairs held annually in the village; but little or no bufinefs is done at them. A very few cattle appear fometimes for fale, and a fmall quantity of wool. Formerly, great quantities of fhoes were fold at the fairs here, and were bought by the people in Northumberland.—The roads in this neighbourhood have lately undergone a great repair, in confequence of feveral turnpikes having been erected.

* The prefent incumbent fucceeded Mr JOHN BUCHANAN, whofe predeceffor, Mr ROBERT PARK, was the firft Prefbyterian minifter of this parifh after the Revolution in 1688; the Epifcopal clergyman having continued in the charge about eleven years after Prefbyterian church-government was eftablifhe in Scotland.

† There was alfo a fortified wall on the eaft end of the village of Foulden, the remains of which were taken down fome years ago. The chief defign of it feems to have been, for a defence to the refidence of LORD ROSS, who took an active part in the wars between England and Scotland, and who was proprietor of the eftate of Foulden in thofe days.

PARISH OF GORDON.

(COUNTY OF BERWICK.)

By the Rev. Mr ALEXANDER DUNCAN.

Name, Situation, and Extent.

IT is ſaid that ſeveral perſons of the name of Gordon
came to Britain with William the Conqueror, one of
whom, having viſited Scotland during the reign of Malcolm
Canmore, and having fortunately killed a wild boar, that
had greatly infeſted this neighbourhood, received, as a reward, a grant of certain lands in Merſe or Berwickſhire, to
which he gave his own name of Gordon. From him the Dukes
of Gordon are deſcended, and in memory of this gallant action, the white boar makes a part of the family arms. The
Duke of Gordon is ſtill ſuperior of ſome lands in the pariſh.
Thoſe of Eaſt and Weſt Gordon, Huntly, and Huntly-wood,
belonged in property to his anceſtors; one of whom, however, having obtained very conſiderable poſſeſſions in the
north, was thence induced to change his place of reſidence,
and to live in that part of Scotland.

The pariſh was formerly of very large extent; but has
ſince been diſmembered, and part of it called Durrington-
laws, annexed to Longformacus, 12 miles diſtant. Out of it,
about the year 1647, was alſo erected the pariſh of Weſtruther, or Woolſtruther, comprehending Baſſendean, a
church

church and parifh, formerly in the prefbytery of Melrofe. Gordon is fituated in the county of Berwick, in the prefbytery of Lauder, and in the fynod of Merfe and Teviotdale. The church ftands at Weft Gordon, 33 miles diftant from Edinburgh, and 23 from Berwick. The great road from Edinburgh to London, by Greenlaw and Cornhill, runs through the northern part of it, for about two miles. Gordon is ftill a parifh of great extent, being 7 miles long from W. to E. but unequal in its breadth, one half being about 2 miles, the other half 4 miles broad ; the figure is confequently irregular.

Soil, Climate, Rivers, &c.—The furface is uneven. There are three or four rifing grounds, or hills, one of which is of fome height, and is not yet entirely cultivated, though two fides of it are plowed ; the others are all cultivated to the top. There are many pieces of good arable land, fome of it clayey, but more light and fandy. There are alfo great tracts of moor, of mofs, and bog. The air is not unwholefome, though, from the quantity of mofs and bog, damps muft arife. Some years ago agues were prevalent. Of late confumptions have been more common than formerly. The river Eden runs through this parifh from N. to S. and Blackadder runs on the north fide for a mile or two, both fmall rivers, in which there are fome trouts and eels. There are whinftones in great abundance, and fome white and red freeftone. The former are on the furface, the latter dug out of the ground ; both are ufed for building.

Cattle.—Improvements in the breed of fheep and cattle have made rapid progrefs, fince the turnip hufbandry commenced 15 or 16 years ago. At that time fheep were fold, at a year old, for fix or eight fhillings. By raifing for them
better

better food, and mending the breed by croſſing with Mr Culley's rams, they have, this year, been ſold at the ſame age,
for fifteen and ſixteen ſhillings. Black cattle alſo are greatly
improved in number and value. In winter 1775-6, there
were only 11 beaſts fed with turnips for the butcher, and in
winter 1781-2, at the diſtance of only ſix years, there were
200 fattened in the pariſh, beſides ſome ſcores of ſheep.
This buſineſs is ſtill continued and increaſed, though not ſo
much in the numbers of cattle fed, as in feeding them to
greater value. L. 10 was, at that time, reckoned a great
price; now they are fed to L. 15, L. 18, and even L. 20
value.

Population.—Since the erection of the pariſh of Weſtruther, the pariſh of Gordon has been conſidered as conſiſting
of about 600 examinable perſons. The returns to Dr Webſter, in 1755, was 737 ſouls. In 1771, when the firſt liſt of
examinable perſons was taken by the preſent incumbent,
they conſiſted of 630, in 1778, of 530. In 1790, they roſe
to 676, and, in 1791, a particular liſt of all deſcriptions and
ages having been made, the number of ſouls was found to be
912. Of theſe 472 are females, and 440 males. The number
of inhabited houſes is 217, ſo that there are more than four
to each family. Although a regiſter is kept, as appointed
by act of Parliament, of marriages, chriſtenings, and burials, it is ſo inaccurate, that no confidence can be placed in
it. The ſeſſion-clerks, in place of taking 3 d. for each marriage, take it for each proclamation of banns; ſo that a couple, proclaimed in the pariſhes where each reſided, and
married in a third pariſh, have paid three times inſtead of
once.

The

The following, however, is the amount, fuch as our re-
gifters afford, for the laft three years, of

	Marriages,	Births,	& Deaths.
In 1788, there were -	2	27	14
In 1789, - -	7	16	11
In 1790, - -	4	21	17
	13	64	42

The average therefore appears to be 4   21   14

Though there are no remarkable inftances of longevity,
many perfons have died, aged from 70 to 90. One or two
are now alive aged 92 years. The number of Seceders
amount to 130. There are neither Epifcopals nor Roman
Catholics in the parifh. The diminution of the number of inhabitants, from 1771 to 1778, was owing to two or three
fmall farms, in different places in the parifh, having been let
to one tenant. The increafe of population from 1778 to 1790,
was vifibly owing to feuing ground by a plan for a village
at Weft Gordon, where, though purchafers have built good
houfes for themfelves, and fome for tradefmen and day-labourers, the farms being better cultivated, yet the tenants
have been obliged to build houfes to accommodate their fervants and labourers. Many of the tenants and their fervants
have 6 or 7, and fome 8 and 10 children by one wife. A
farmer died this year, who had 15 children by one wife, 9
of whom furvived him. A mealmaker died lately, who had
been twice married, and was the father of 18 legitimate
children, 9 of whom furvived him. A labouring man died
a few years ago, aged 80, who had been the father of 20 legitimate children, of thefe only 3 furvived him. He had
been thrice married.

Agriculture,

Agriculture.—Since the turnip huſbandry commenced, much greater quantities of corn have been raiſed in the pariſh. In the year 1775, one farm produced no more rough bear, than what was neceſſary to ſow the ground again, pay the ſervants their proportion of wages, and maintain the family. The ſame farm, within theſe three years, produced barley for theſe neceſſary purpoſes (which is ſuperior to bear 2 s. 6 d. or 3 s. the boll,) and from it were ſold 240 bolls, in the Lothian markets, at 18 s. the boll and upwards. The proprietors, ſenſible of the induſtry and activity of their tenants, have adopted a wiſe plan to promote further improvements, by giving them a renewal for 21 years, ſeveral years previous to the expiration of the old leaſes.

Church.—The king is undoubted patron of this pariſh. In 1767 the Earl of Home claimed the patronage, and raiſed an action of declarator, when, after a litigation of 18 months, his claim was diſmiſſed for want of evidence. The incumbent, in conſequence of that deciſion, was ſettled in 1770. The number of heritors is 8. None of them reſide in the pariſh.

Poor.—The poor are regularly ſupplied by a meeting of the heritors, miniſter and elders, who aſſeſs the pariſh half yearly for that purpoſe. Their numbers have been from 12 to 24, young and old, yearly. In 1783 oat-meal was at 2 s. 6 d. and upwards, the ſtone, bear and peaſe-meal were ſcarcely to be had. The heritors of the pariſh gave money to the kirk-ſeſſion, to enable them to ſell oat-meal to poor houſeholders at a diſcount of 8 d. and 6 d. the ſtone, which was of great uſe to preſerve them from want. White peaſe were imported at Leith and Fiſherrow in ſpring and ſummer. The farmers and miniſter brought white peaſe from Leith,

&c

&c. carriage free, and then fold the meal at the prime coft of the peafe at Leith, to all in the parifh who had no horfes of their own; this was continued for five months.

Wages, Fuel.—Men fervants wages are L. 6 and L. 7 a-year; women's L. 3 and L. 4.; day-labourers get 1 s. a-day, more or lefs according to ability; mafons 1 s. 8 d. carpenters 1 s. 6 d. tailors 1 s. Peat and turf is the common fuel, but from the expence of labour to obtain them, coals are more ufed than formerly, though purchafed at 1s. the hundred weight, or brought 24 miles from the Lothians.

Antiquities.—There are two farms in the parifh, called Rumbleton and Rumbletonlaw, which, tradition fays, is a corruption of Romantown and Romantownlaw. At the latter farm, there were lately appearances of extenfive fortifications on a law or hill, which is now all plowed over, and inclofures made with the ftones. At Huntly there are remains of walls, like fome caftle or fortified place. Near the manfe, appearances of fortifications ftill remain, and the place ftill retains the name of *the Caftles.* There it would appear the anceftors of the Duke of Gordon's family had formerly refided.

Manufactures and Commerce.—There have been, for many years, three corn mills driven by water, employed in grinding corn for the Lothian markets; which have manufactured more than ten or twelve thoufand bolls in one year. The mill mafters, and many other people called meal-makers, drive the meal to Edinburgh, Dalkeith, Muffelburgh, Preftonpans, &c. Formerly they ufed to carry it on horfes backs; but, for upwards of 25 years paft, fince the turnpike roads were made through Berwickfhire, they have carried it in

carts,

carts, drawn by two horses, and, in return, they bring salt, coals, merchant goods, oysters, iron, wood for building, and great quantities of burnt limestone, which greatly forwards the improvements in husbandry.

Miscellaneous facts and Observations.—During more than 30 years, only one estate has been bought or sold. The rest have all gone by succession. By the sale of that estate and successions since, the property has been in five different hands during the course of 24 years. Some families have been, for many generations, in the same farms. One of them had been proprietors of the land they now rent: Another of these families say, that their forefathers have been in the farm for 200 years, and the other two, that their ancestors have been 300 years in the farms *.

The roads are repaired by converting the statute labour, according to an act of Parliament passed 16 or 18 years ago. But there is still little amendment made, consequently they are in very bad order. The best land is let at 20 s. a guinea, and L. 1, 3 s. the acre. The inferior at all prices, according to comparative value: 110 acres of moor lands were feued 3 or 4 years ago, the best quality at L. 5 the acre, the second best at L. 3, and the worst at L. 1 16 s. with 1 s. the acre of feu annually. The people are sensible of the great benefit of inclosing land.

A rage for raising tobacco prevailed in 1782, and many acres of the best land were occupied with it, which diminished the crops of corn. But a bill, passed in parliament in 1783, cured

---

* A great grandmother of one of the present tenants, in one of these farms, told his neighbour, who died not many years ago, that she stood in her own door, and saw the walls of Home Castle beat down by Oliver Cromwell's cannon.

cured the frenzy. That bill allowed only 4 d. the pound for the tobacco, though it was no illicit trade; whereas, to many, 1 s. the pound would fcarcely have paid the price of land rent, the expence of labour, &c.

The manner of living, drefs, and manners of the people are greatly improved, within thefe laft 20 years. Learning, in particular, is more generally diffufed than formerly, in proof of which it may be remarked, that feveral of the farmers here, have become fubfcribers to the public libraries in the neighbouring town of Kelfo, by which they are enabled to acquire an extent of knowledge and information, to which, otherwife, they could not have had accefs.

PARISH OF GREENLAW.

(COUNTY OF BERWICK, SYNOD OF MERSE AND TIVIOT-
DALE, PRESBYTERY OF DUNSE.)

By the Rev. Mr. WILLIAM SIMSON.

Extent, Name, Soil, Surface, &c.

THE parifh of Greenlaw is between 7 and 8 miles in
length, from N. to S. ; and, on an average, about
2 miles in breadth. In this parifh, there are feveral of
thofe round hills, or detached eminences, which, from
their conical figure, are well known in Scotland by the
name of Laws. It is from one of thefe, which, in the
original uncultivated ftate of the country, being greener
than the reft, that the parifh evidently derives its name.—
The foil is extremely various. In the S. part of the parifh, it confifts of a deep, ftrong clay, and produces excellent wheat, barley, oats, hay, and fine pafture. In proceeding northward, it becomes worfe. In many places,
it is wet and fpongy ; and both the grain and grafs are of
an inferior quality ; but fuch parts as are dry, bear good
oats, excellent turnips, and heavy crops of clover and rye
grafs.

grafs. The N. part of the parifh is moftly a mountainous tract. Some of the hills are dry and improved towards the bottom; others are wet, and covered with fhort heath, and fit only for fheep-walks, and the raifing of young cattle. On the W. fide of this tract, there is a mofs of confiderable extent, from which the inhabitants of the town of Greenlaw, and all who live in the N. part of the parifh, are fupplied with peats of a tolerably good quality. There is no map of the parifh. About one half of it is enclofed, and two thirds of it arable.

Climate, Difeafes, &c.—The climate is as various as the foil. At Greenlaw, which is well fheltered by hills, the air is rather mild; in the S. of the parifh, it is more fo; but on the high grounds, and efpecially towards the N., it is keen and penetrating. It may be faid to be a healthy diftrict, few or no epidemical difeafes being peculiar to it. In the fpring, however, agues, rheumatifms, and intermittent fevers, are frequent: but it is remarked, that thefe difeafes are neither fo violent, nor of fuch duration in this parifh, as in thofe to the S.; which is owing, perhaps, to this part of the country being more hilly; the waters, confequently, being lefs apt to run into a putrid ftate. Formerly, the fmall pox carried off great numbers; but the prejudices againft inoculation are faft wearing out. The people, in general, are become reconciled to this practice, by feeing the remarkable fuccefs with which it is attended. Mr. Alexander, furgeon in this place, has, in the courfe of the laft 10 years, inoculated upwards of 500, of which number only 1 died.

Rivers.—Blackater, or Blackwater, is the only river which runs through this parifh. Its waters are of a dark
blackifh

blackifh colour ; and it is from this circumftance it derives its name. It abounds in excellent trout. In fummer, and even in winter, it is commonly but a fmall
ftream ; but being fed by a number of rills and fmall torrents, which iflue from the neighbouring hills, it fwells
fometimes unexpectedly to a great fize, and overflows, to
a confiderable extent, the valley grounds through which
it paffes.

Rent, &c.—The valued rent of the parifh is 6836l.
3 s. 11 $\frac{6}{12}$d. Scots. The real rent about 3550l. Sterling.
The rent of land varies according to its quality and fituation. Near the town of Greenlaw, where it is let in
fmall portions, the rent is from 1 l. to 1 l. 10s. an acre *;
enclofed arable farms from 10s. to 20s. 6d. an acre : unenclofed farms, which are partly in tillage, and partly
ftocked with fheep, are not let by the acre, but in the
lump. The farms are, in general, from 70l. to 350l. a-
year ; but there are fome from 70l. down to 50l. ; and a
few fmall poffeffions below 20l. It ought to be obferved
alfo, that feveral farmers, fome of whom refide in the
parifh, and fome out of it, but all having farms in it, poffefs lands to the value of 500l., and even 700l. a-year.
About 50 years ago, the real rent of the parifh did not
much exceed the third part of what it is at prefent. Some
of the beft lands were, about that time, let at 5 s. the
acre.

This great rife of rent is not owing to any confiderable
rife in the price of grain : For even fo far back as towards the end of the laft century, grain fold, *communibus
annis* †, nearly as high as it is now. But the caufes,
which

* When mention is made of acres, in this account, the Englifh acre
is always meant.

† See the tables of fiars of the county of Berwick.

which have chiefly contributed to raise the rent so greatly,
are the great rise in the price of sheep and cattle, and
the vast improvements which have been made in agriculture, by which more grain is raised than formerly; and
much artificial food, such as turnips, clover, and rye grass,
&c., has been introduced, which has contributed, in no
small degree, both to improve the cattle, and to augment
their numbers.

Formerly, the parish was almost totally unenclosed, and
let out in small farms. From scarcity of manure, an inconsiderable portion only of these farms could be kept in
good condition for tillage. This, which was called croft
land, lay in the immediate neighbourhood of the farm-
stead; and all the manure, which was made upon the
farm, was laid upon it. The rest, which was termed
outfield, was partly cropped with oats, without any kind
of manure whatever, except what was sometimes folded,
which was generally but a few acres; and partly allowed
to lie waste, pastured by some stunted half-starved sheep
or cattle. When that which was cropped was quite exhausted, it was allowed to rest, and a portion of the other
waste ground taken up in its place. A few crops of oats
exhausted it also; it was then allowed again to lie waste,
and another portion was ploughed and cropped with oats;
and so with the rest. The tenants then were very different from what they now are: They wrought as hard, and
fared as meanly as their servants: their houses were small
and inconvenient; and the whole face of the country exhibited nothing but marks of extreme indigence. This
wretched system of husbandry, and the poverty which was
the consequence of it, were not peculiar to this parish,
nor even to this corner of the kingdom, but prevailed almost all over Scotland; and arose no less from the state

in

in which commerce then was, than from ignorance in agriculture. Before the Union, Scotland had no foreign market for her fheep and black cattle ; and, confequently, had no motive to raife more of thefe than her own do-meftick confumption demanded ; which, at that time, was extremely fmall, as little butcher meat was then ufed. But no fooner had the Union opened a market for thefe valuable articles of commerce, than an influx of wealth, unknown in former times, began to pour into the northern part of the ifland. This influx of wealth increafing, as the price of cattle rofe, gradually produced a happy change in the fyftem of agriculture ; and was, doubtlefs, one of the principal caufes of the improvement of the country : For landlords of difcernment foon perceived, that it would be as profitable to cultivate land for rearing and feeding cattle, as for raifing grain. They, therefore, enclofed their grounds, and united feveral of their fmall farms. Thefe, they either improved themfelves, or let to opulent and enterprifing farmers, who had money fuffi-cient, not only to ftock their farms, but alfo to improve them ; and who had the good fenfe to perceive the ab-furdity of the manner in which agriculture had been car-ried on, and the fagacity to forefee the advantages which would refult from introducing a more improved fyftem. In this parifh, thefe farmers laboured under many local difadvantages : They were at a great diftance from lime, which was the only fpecies of manure they could com-mand : They were ftill farther from markets, where they could difpofe of their grain : The roads to both, when they began their improvements, were bad ; but, by their perfeverance and fpirited exertions, they furmounted eve-ry obftacle ; and (which is much to their honour), have converted a great part of the parifh from a bleak and ne-

glected,

glected, into a beautiful and well cultivated diſtrict. They now reap the fruits of their induſtry : Moſt of them are in eaſy circumſtances, and live in a comfortable manner.

Roads.—When a ſpirit for improvement in agriculture firſt appeared in this part of the country, the roads were in bad repair. The only way of tranſporting grain or meal to the Lothian markets, was on horſes backs. It is obvious how expenſive this mode of carriage muſt have been. But beſides being expenſive, it was attended with another, and even greater inconvenience : In winter, when there was moſt grain to diſpoſe of, and the farmers ſtood moſt in need of money for paying their rents, the roads, or rather tracts, were often impaſſable. But ſince that branch of the great road from London to Edinburgh, which runs through this pariſh, was made (which is near-ly 30 years ago), there has been conſtant acceſs with carts to the Dalkeith market. A cart with 2 horſes, carrying 5 load of meal, can perform 2 journeys in the week, and returns home laden with coal or lime. The roads to Ber-wick and Eyemouth were, till lately, in a bad ſtate ; but now they are in good repair. The principal croſs roads in the pariſh are alſo much improved. All theſe roads do great honour to the publick ſpirit of the gentlemen who planned and promoted them ; for they have put, as far as human art can, this diſtant inland tract of the country on a level with thoſe places that are more favourably ſituated with reſpect to markets.

Mode of Cultivation and Price of Labour.—The ploughs generally uſed, are the Engliſh kind, drawn by 2 horſes ; but when ſtrong ſtiff land is broken up, the Scotch plough is uſed, which is drawn by 4 horſes, or 2 horſes and 2

oxen.

oxen. Since the late improvements were introduced into
agriculture, the price of labour has greatly encreafed. A-
bout 40 years ago, farmers men fervants, who had their
victuals in their mafters houfes, received from 3l. to 4l.
a-year; the women from 2l. to 2l. 10s.: At prefent, the
men receive from 7l. to 9l. a-year; the women from 3l.
to 4l. But moft of the men fervants, employed in hufbandry, are married, and eat in their own houfes: They
receive, for meat and wages, a certain quantity of grain,
fome money, and food for a cow for the whole year; a-
mounting in all to between 15l. and 16l*.

Crops.—The principal crops in this parifh are, wheat,
barley, and oats. Some peafe alfo are fown, but in fmall
quantities, as the foil is found not to be very fuitable for
the growth of that kind of grain. Heavy crops of clover
and rye-grafs are raifed on almoft all the improved lands.
Turnips have been much cultivated of late, and are found
to fucceed well in the dry grounds. The farmers either
feed cattle with them in the houfe, or fell them to dealers
in fheep, to be eaten on the ground. When eaten in the
fields, they generally fell at about 3l. an acre; but fome
years, they are much higher: This year (1793) fome
fields

---

* Formerly, men day-labourers, when they furnifhed their own victuals, had only 6d. a day; now they have from 1s. to 1s. 2d., except in
the time of mowing, when the wages are 1s. 6d.; in harveft, the men
get 1s. 2d. a-day, with their meat; women, 8d. or 9d.: but reapers
are generally hired for the harveft. The wages of the men are about
1l. 6s.; thofe of the women about 1l. 1s. Women receive for working at hay, and weeding turnips, 8d. a-day, without meat: the day-
wages of a mafon are from 1s. 8d. to 2s.; of a carpenter from 1s.
6d. to 1s. 8d.; of a cabinetmaker the fame. Work, however, of all
thofe kinds, is generally done by the piece. A tailor receives 8d. a-day,
with his meat.

fields fold fo high as 6l. 1os. the acre. Potatoes are a general crop, and are of vaſt ſervice to the poor people. About Martinmas, the price of them is ſeldom above 1od. or 1s. the firlot.

Mode of Cropping.—The ſame mode of cropping does not prevail through the whole pariſh, but is varied according to the ſoil and climate. On lands fit for bearing wheat, the mode of cropping followed by the principal farmers is this : When a field is taken up that has been paſtured for ſome years, they take 2 crops of oats ſucceſſively ; but if it has not been paſtured, and been only 1 year in hay, they take only 1 crop of oats ; then fallow it, and after the fallow, ſow wheat in the autumn, with graſs ſeeds in the ſpring : If they do not ſow graſs ſeeds, which is ſome-times the caſe, with the wheat crop, they then take a crop of peaſe after the wheat ; and after the peaſe a crop of barley, along with which they ſow the graſs ſeeds. On light dry land, fit for turnips, when taken up after it has been paſtured, they take 2 crops of oats ſucceſſively ; but if it has been only 1 year in hay, only 1 crop of oats, then turnips, and after the turnips, barley with graſs ſeeds. Till of late, it was the general practice to take 2 crops of hay before they laid their fields in paſture ; but ſeveral farmers have found, by repeated trials which they have made, that it is more profitable not to cut their fields, which they intend for paſture, but to put their ſheep or cattle upon them the year immediately after they are ſown. And they are of opinion, that the firſt 2 years thus paſtured, are fully as valuable as the 3 next following.

Number of Horſes, &c.—There are about 280 horſes, of all ages, in the pariſh, and 850 black cattle : the number
of

of fheep amounts to about 2500. The attention which has been paid, for fome years paft, to the improvement of the breed of fheep, has greatly increafed the value of the wool. In 1791 and 1792, laid wool fold from 14s. to 18s. 6d. a-ftone; and white wool confiderably higher. This year it has fallen about 2s. the ftone.

Population.—According to Dr. Webfter's report, the number of fouls in 1755 was 895. An accurate enumeration of the inhabitants of the parifh was made in fummer 1785. They amounted then to 1210, of whom 223 were below 8 years of age. Of the 987 who were above 8 years, 832 were of the Eftablifhed Church; 62 were Burghers; 82 Antiburghers; 7 Cameronians; and 4 of the Relief perfuafion. There are 7 heritors, 3 of whom refide in the parifh. About one half of the inhabitants live in the town of Greenlaw; the reft live in farmfteads and detached houfes, and in a fmall village, in the N. part of the parifh, which contains about 60 people. Almoft the whole of the town of Greenlaw is feued *. The feuars are about 80 in number. There are feveral inftances of longevity in the parifh. Some years ago, 2 perfons died upwards of 90. There is 1 alive at prefent aged 93, another 87, and feveral fomewhat above 80.

ABSTRACT

---

* Feuing is a mode of holding landed property very common in Scotland. The purchafer holds of a fubject fuperior, to whom, befides the money given when the lands are bought, he pays a perpetual yearly acknowledgment, which is termed feu-duty. The purchafe money paid for the grounds feued in Greenlaw is 80l. the Englifh acre, and the feu-duty 16s. 10d. The Earl of Marchmont is fuperior.

ABSTRACT *of the* BAPTISMS, MARRIAGES, *and* BURIALS, *from the* 1ſt *of* October 1785 *to the* 1ſt *of* October 1793.

YEARS.	MARRIAGES.	BAPTISMS.	BURIALS.
1786,	9	21	7
1787,	9	13	9
1788,	10	11	12
1789,	3	9	9
1790,	8	10	13
1791,	14	5	12
1792,	6	12	10
1793,	8	11	16

Stipend.—The ſtipend is 100l., with a manſe, and a glebe of about 10 acres. The church was lately repaired and new ſeated ; and although it is too narrow, conſidering the length of it (which is the caſe with almoſt all old churches), and rather too ſmall for the congregation ; yet it is, upon the whole, a comfortable place of publick worſhip. The manſe ſtands in need of being repaired. The Earl of Marchmont is patron.

State of the Poor.—The heritors and kirk-ſeſſion meet twice a-year, about the terms of Whitſunday and Martinmas, for the purpoſe of making proviſion for the poor. At each of theſe meetings, an aſſeſſment is made, ſufficient for maintaining thoſe that are admitted upon the roll for the enſuing half year. The one half of the aſſeſſment is paid by the heritors, and the other by the tenants. There are 41 perſons at preſent upon the roll ; and the ſum aſſeſſed to maintain them, for the current half year, is 62l. 11s. 6d. About 5 years ago, the ſums levied for

the

the fupport of the poor, were not much above one-third of what they now are.

Manufactures.—Manufactures have not yet been introduced into this parifh. The only branch that has been attempted, is one of woollen cloth; but how it will fucceed, it is impoffible to fay, as it is yet in its infancy. Cabinetmakers work is extremely well executed here : 8 or 10 tradefmen are conftantly employed in making houfehold furniture for gentlemen in the neighbourhood; but none is made but what is commiffioned.

Character.—The inhabitants of this parifh are, in general, a fober and induftrious people. There are fome, indeed, of a different character : Thefe, however, are but few. No inhabitant of the parifh has either fuffered capital punifhment, or been banifhed for many years paft; and only one inftance of fuicide has occurred in the memory of the oldeft perfon living.

Difadvantages.—Perhaps few parts of the country, labouring under equal difadvantages, have made as great progrefs in improvement as this parifh has done. Its diftance from markets neceffarily diminifhes the price of grain; and its diftance from coal and lime as neceffarily increafes the price of fuel and manure. The town of Greenlaw, which is nearly the centre of the parifh, is 30 miles from Dalkeith, 20 from Berwick, and about the fame diftance from Eyemouth; and almoft all the meal, and even part of the grain, that is carried to thefe different markets, is bought up to be tranfported to more diftant parts of the country : What is carried to Dalkeith, is thence conveyed by land carriage to Glafgow, which is

near

near 80 miles from Greenlaw. The neareſt coal and lime are in Northumberland, about 20 miles diſtant. Yet, notwithſtanding all theſe diſadvantages, not only the S. part of the pariſh, where the ſoil is good, but alſo many other parts, where it is of inferior quality, are, by being well encloſed and well limed, made as fertile as it is poſſible to render places ſo unfavourably ſituated for improvement.

Antiquities.—The ruins of two ancient religious houſes are ſtill to be ſeen in this pariſh. They belonged to the priory of Kelſo, when popery was eſtabliſhed in this country [*].

Hints for Improvements.—1. It has been already obſerved, that ſeveral of the hills, in the N. part of the pariſh, are improved towards the bottom. No part of them, however, is encloſed. This is a great loſs to the farmers, as they cannot, with all their care and attention, keep their ſheep from the turnips in winter, nor ſown graſs in the ſpring. A few encloſures, therefore, would be of great benefit ; and would amply compenſate for ſuch ſums of money as would be neceſſary for making them.

2. Several

* About a mile N. from the town of Greenlaw, an old wall, or earthen mound, with a ditch on one ſide, known by the name of Harrit's, or Herrit's Dike, runs acroſs the pariſh. It cannot now be aſcertained, either what the height of the wall, or depth of the ditch originally was ; but neither of them ſeems to have been conſiderable. By the encloſures, which have been lately made in the country, the greateſt part of this wall has been deſtroyed. About 60 years ago, it could have been traced 14 miles eaſtward ; and tradition ſays, it proceeded, in the ſame direction, as far as Berwick. It is ſuppoſed to have extended weſtward to a place in the pariſh of Legerwood, called Boon ; a word, in the Celtic language, ſignifying boundary or termination. It is not known by whom, or at what time this wall was built, nor for what purpoſe it was intended.

2. Several parts of the fame farms are dry and arable, but have not been in tillage for at leaft 100 years paft. Thefe, in their prefent ftate, are worth very little : Were they taken up and well limed, and, after a crop or two of oats, fown with white clover feed, their value would be confiderably increafed. They would become moft excel‑ lent pafture grounds either for fheep or cattle.

3. The greateft improvement that could be made in this parifh, would be to plant fome of the high grounds with fuch trees as beft fuited the foil. Plantations, when judicioufly made, are ornaments to the richeft and beft cultivated diftricts : but on high and expofed places, they are not only ornamental, but greatly beneficial. They break the violence of the winds, and render the air more mild and temperate. In few parts of the country do the winds rage with greater fury than on fome of the high grounds in this parifh : yet thefe are almoft all quite bare, and deftitute of trees. It is unneceffary to point out all the various places where plantations might be made to advantage ; it may be proper, however, to mention the following : Were a ftripe of plantation drawn acrofs the parifh, about half a mile to the S. of the town of Green‑ law, it would be both a great ornament to the country in general, and a vaft benefit to the lands through which it paffed. Another ftripe, about the fame diftance N. from the town, drawn likewife acrofs the parifh, would be no lefs ornamental and advantageous. Befides. thefe, feveral clumps of trees ought to be raifed in places far‑ ther N. In fevere winters, when the frofts are intenfe and of long continuance, and the ground covered with fnow, all thefe various plantations would be of fingular benefit. They would afford a conftant fhelter to the fheep ;

ſheep ; and thereby prove the means of improving and preſerving thoſe valuable creatures, on which the wealth and proſperity of the country ſo much depend.

A TABLE

PARISH OF ROBERTON.

(Counties of Selkirk and Roxburgh——Presbytery of Selkirk——Synod of Merse and Teviotdale.)

By the Rev. Mr. JAMES HAY, Minister.

Situation, Extent, Rivers, Lakes, and Fish.

THE parish of Roberton, in the presbytery of Selkirk, lies in the western extremities of the shires of Roxburgh and Selkirk, where they march with the county of Dumfries. It is estimated about thirteen miles in length, and six in breadth.——The water of *Borthwick*, running to the E. from the high grounds, where the shires of Selkirk and Dumfries meet, divides the parish into two parts, nearly equal. The water, *Ale*, flowing from a beautiful circular lake, of nearly 2 miles in circumference, in the N. W. quarter of the parish, holds, while in it, a course nearly parallel to the Borthwick, from which it is about 2 miles distant.——Besides Alemuir Loch, there are several smaller lakes, in which there is abundance of fine perch and pike ; and in one there is to be found an excellent red trout, much resembling
ling

ling that of Lochleven. The waters, Borthwick and Ale, augmented in their course by a great number of rivulets, abound with trouts of the best quality ; but it is only in the spawning season that they are visited by salmon.

Game, Woods, and Mosses. The diversion of shooting may here be as much enjoyed as that of angling, as there is plenty of all the common kinds of game.—That the part of this parish lying in the shire of Selkirk, was within the bounds of the royal forest, appears from the valuation of the land. The valuations, in proportion to present rents, are uniformly higher in Selkirk-shire than in Roxburgh-shire. At present, there is but little wood in the parish: In a few years the banks of the Borthwick will be more covered, as some proprietors are at present rearing considerable plantations.—Mosses are numerous ; almost every farm has its particular moss. The minister has the privilege of casting peats, by a yearly rotation, in no less than 5 of them. The marl, found in some of these mosses already drained, is of the best shell kind ; and has, for many years, been profitably used. Peats vary much in quality in the different mosses.

Surface and Soil.—The parish is hilly ; but there is no hill of extraordinary magnitude or height in it. From the Borthwick and the Ale, the land rises by a gentle ascent. The lower grounds are in a state of cultivation, and there are some spots of planting along the Borthwick ; the higher grounds are employed in pasturage ; the summits between the Ale on the N., and the Teviot on the S., are, in part, mossy, but generally covered with grass or heath ; and those spots, only, where mosses are wrought, appear black. Grass is predominant ; and the general appearance of the parish, to the eye, is that of grassy hills.—The soil, locally varying, is, in

general,

general, of good quality. The greateſt part, even of the higher grounds, is of a hard gravelly, or rocky bottom. In the higheſt and weſtern part of the pariſh, there is a conſiderable proportion of wet and boggy land. From land, which has a ſouthern expoſure, has been drained, or is naturally dry, crops have been raiſed as early, and as good, as from lands many miles lower down the country. The peculiar fitneſs of the ſoil, for the paſturage of ſheep, is evinced by their reputation in the country for ſoundneſs, for carcaſe, and for wool.

Climate and Diſeaſes, &c.—The ſituation of the pariſh, nearly centrical between the E. and W. ſeas, ſufficiently indicates the nature of the climate*—Though this pariſh appears level, when viewed from heights, greatly inferior to the Ettrick hills on the N., and thoſe of Liddiſdale on the S ; yet it is ſo high, as always to intercept ſome portion of the moiſture of thoſe heavy clouds, which are ſo often ſeen attracted to either or to both of theſe quarters. The autumnal rains are particularly violent, and ſometimes of long duration. In the months of November and December, they are accompanied with ſuch boiſterous winds, that only a few houſes can perfectly exclude the waters of the weſtern tempeſt. There are inſtances of houſes, built with lime, and judged ſufficient, through which theſe rains force their way every winter. The noxious effects of a damp atmoſphere were formerly prevented by the copious uſe of ſpirits, and now by better houſes and clothing ; but flannel is little, if ever, uſed by the labouring people, among whom rheumatiſm is a general complaint,
almoſt

---

* At BRANXHOLM, in the immediate vicinity, ⅓ more rain falls than at Dalkeith ; and ½ more at Langholm, 18 miles W. of Branxholm, than at it. *Vid. Edin. Phil. Tranſ. Vol. I.*

almoſt invariably accompanying the decline of life. Unleſs the weather be tempeſtuous, the labours of the field are never interrupted, on account of a caſual, though heavy rain. Notwithſtanding the great moiſture of the climate, to which the labouring inhabitants are expoſed, they are healthy, robuſt, and generally reach a good old age. No inſtances of rare longevity occur; but there were recent, and there are exiſting examples of great vigour and activity, in perſons who have ſeen fourſcore years.

Produce and Cultivation.——All the ordinary kinds of grain, and ſometimes wheat, are raiſed in the pariſh, but it is thought not in proportion to the conſumption. The mode of culture has, of late, been greatly reformed by the introduction of green crops, graſs ſeeds, and eſpecially the judicious uſe of marl. There is, perhaps, too great a proportion of the arable land ſtill kept in tillage; but this is a miſtake, which is becoming every year more obvious, and will ſoon be corrected. Much of the land is fit for the growth of flax; but its culture muſt be neglected, as unproductive, till a flax mill be erected ſomewhere in the neighbourhood. It is for the breeding and feeding of ſheep, that the ſoil and climate are beſt adapted, and to which, accordingly, the chief attention of the inhabitants is directed. The ſheep paſture has been greatly meliorated, by the burning of heath, draining of wet lands, and uſe of marl *.

Proprietors and Rent.——There are 11 heritors; 4 of whom have houſes, and generally reſide in the pariſh. One manſion-houſe,

---

* For breed, management, &c. of ſheep, crops, rates of wages, prices of proviſions, &c. ſee Statiſtical Account of the pariſh of Hawick, *Vol.* VIII. *Num.* 32. Hawick is the market town of this diſtrict.

houfe, formerly the feat of an ancient family, is falling into ruins. The valued rent is 10,950l. Scotch ; the prefent actual rent exceeds 3000l. Sterling.

Cattle.—The number of cattle is computed to be, as under:

18,000 fheep,   358 black cattle,   127 horfes.

Produce.—There are 358 bolls of grain yearly fown, and 95 packs of wool annually fold.

Fuel.—Peats are the principal fuel, and are reckoned as dear as coals from Lothian or Northumberland, a diftance of 30 miles. The convenience of this fpecies of fuel, its being near at hand, and procured at a feafon, when fervants upon farms could not be otherwife fo profitably employed, give it the preference ; and cottagers, living near moffes, make it a bufinefs, through the year, to carry peats from the diftance of 8, and even fometimes 14 miles, to Hawick ; where they are fold, at the rate of from 3s. to 4s. the fingle cart load, and from 1s. 3d. to 1s. 6d. the back load.

Roads.—The expence of fuel is heightened by the badnefs of the roads. The principal road in the parifh, and the moft direct one from Dumfries, &c. to the towns of Hawick, Selkirk, &c. is along the Borthwick, but is made only half way up this parifh, and not even formed where it enters that of Wilton. The gentlemen of Dumfries-fhire have carried this line of road nearly to the confines of their own county ; and it is to be regretted, that they have not been feconded by proprietors of land in the counties on the E., in a meafure of fuch obvious importance. The heritors of Roberton are at prefent improving, at a great expence, their part of this road,

and

and forming fome others. The road money, for the Rox-
burgh-fhire part of this parifh, is levied by an affeffment of
from 7s. to 10s. on the 100l. Scotch of valued rent: For that
in Selkirk-fhire, by the ftatute labour.

Ecclefiaftical State.—Roberton is a modern parifh. *Haffendean*, the old one, about 9 miles lower down the country,
was annexed to Minto and Wilton. This was erected from
parts of the parifhes of Hawick, Selkirk, Wilton, and Haffendean. The fuppreffion of Haffendean, and erection of Roberton, took place about the year 1682. The decreet is fuppofed
to be loft. The kirk bears the infcription 1695 *. In 1789,
it received a complete repair. About the fame time the
manfe was alfo repaired; and in 1791, new offices were built.
The King is patron. The ftipend, (including communion
elements), confifts of 77l. money, 14 bolls meal, and 12
bolls barley, Teviotdale meafure. The grain, and part of the
money, is paid from lands, in what was the old parifh of Haffendean; and, before an augmentation was obtained in 1788,
by the prefent incumbent, there was no more than 9l. paid
to him, and 3l. to the minifter of Wilton, from lands within
the prefent cure, upon the fuppofition, that the remaining
part of the old ftipend, paid in money, by the Duke of Buccleugh, was for his lands in Haffendean; and this is the probable fuppofition.

School.

---

* There are to be traced the remains of 2 chapels; in one of which, on the other
fide of the Borthwick, and oppofite to the prefent kirk, curates from Haffendean
were wont to officiate. The church-yard of the other, (which is faid to have
belonged to the diocefe of Galloway), at Borthwick Brae, about 2 miles farther up the fame water, is ftill ufed as the principal burying ground in this
neighbourhood. GRIEVE and POTT are the names moft frequent on the tomb
ftones.

School.—A new school-house was built in 1790. The schoolmaster has the ordinary legal salary, some perquisites as session-clerk and precentor, and a small fee from the heritors, for uplifting and distributing the poor's money. Till something be done by the public to render country schoolmasters more comfortable and independent, the important office which they bear, cannot be filled by men of education, or talents, and consequence enough to benefit society, as they, with some encouragement, might do.

Poor.—The average number of poor on the roll, young and old, may be about 32. They are supplied by collections made in the kirk and quarterly assessments. A sum is always kept in hand for occasional supplies ; and, if such fund should fail, the minister has hitherto had the approbation of the heritors for taking credit, till such fund be replaced by the collections, or by a new assessment. The expence of their maintainance for the current year is 124l.

Population.—The return to Dr. Webster, in 1755, was - - - - - - - 651

The number of inhabitants, of all ages, in 1791, and 1792, was - - - - - - 629

Decrease *, - - - - 22

Of

* Formerly there were several hamlets, of which no vestiges now remain. The greatest collection of families, in one place, does not exceed 5 or 6. There is no village, and no licensed retailer of spirits in the parish. The expence of rearing houses is the great obstacle to population, and appears to be one cause also of the advanced price of labour. Cottages that fall down are seldom rebuilt.

Of thefe there are,

Males.	Females.	Married Pairs.	Families.
309	320	85	136

Employments.—Of thefe families 28 are tenantry; the reft confift of fhepherds, hinds, day labourers, and fome tradefmen. The number of the latter, owing to the neighbourhood of Hawick, is fmall. There is not a fhoemaker in the parifh. The nature of the foil and climate has fuggefted to herds and labourers the ufe of a kind of a ftrong leather fhoe, with a wooden fole, fhod with iron. This is purchafed in the market town, mended at home, and known by the name of *clogs*.

Condition and Character.—The inhabitants, in their feveral ftations, are comfortable and independent; nor are there wanting inftances of confiderable wealth. They are equally induftrious and frugal. There are a good many feparatifts from the Eftablifhed Church; Burghers, Antiburghers, and Cameronians; but no Epifcopalians or Roman Catholics. The character of feparatifts and adherents fcarce admits of any fhade of diftinction, unlefs it be, that the former have the appearance of greater zeal in religious matters than the latter. In other refpects, they are much alike. If the Seceders think themfelves more religious, thofe belonging to the Eftablifhment fancy themfelves better moral men, and more heartily attached to Government. Happily no party rancour is known, and no religious or political controverfies interrupt the exercife of that fympathy to one another in diftrefs, and of that neighbourly and obliging difpofition, which are the more ftriking and diftinguifhing features of the Chriftian character.

Antiquities,

Antiquities, Cascade, &c.—There are several remains of encampments and fortifications. One large square encampment,
flanked by a rivulet, whose banks are steep, having the
Borthwick in front, and artificial ramparts towards the hill,
bears to this day the name of *Africa.* Between this, and
others of a circular or semicircular form, the *Cat-rail* (of
which some vestiges, though with breaks, may still be traced),
is supposed to have run *. One of these semicircular encampments, above 2 miles from the square one, and of which it
has a distinct view, has, for its diameter, the steep and craggy
bank of a rivulet, where there is a beautiful cascade; the fall
of water being about 20, and the breadth 6 feet, when the
rivulet is in flood.

* *See* GORDON's *Itin.*

PARISH OF SELKIRK.

(COUNTIES OF SELKIRK AND TEVIOTDALE.)

By the Rev. MR. THOMAS ROBERTSON.

Minister of that Parish.

Name, Antient State, &c.

THE antient name of this parish is derived from the Celtic. *Scheleckgrech* *, (since corrupted into Selkirk,) signifies, in that language, the kirk in the wood, or forest; expressing thus, in one word, the situation of the place itself, and the state of the surrounding country.—It is probable, that all the neighbouring districts were formerly one continued forest. It is certain, that the banks of the rivers, by which the country is so happily intersected, were once adorned with woods; amidst which, those plaintive airs were produced, the natural simplicity of which, are the pride of Scotland, and the admiration of strangers.—The forest is now reduced to a state of nakedness. But exertions are now making to remedy this evil, and the muses, it is probable, will be again induced to

revisit

* See Sir James Dalrymple's antiquities, p. 403.

revifit their native groves, which are preparing for their reception *.

To reftore this country, however, to its former ftate of refpectability, as well as beauty, it muft be indebted to the proprietors of the foil, for replacing not only the woods, but the inhabitants, which the impolitic practice of adding farm to farm, and the fatal operation of poors-rates, have compelled to leave their native home †. It is painful to fee (as in this parifh) one perfon rent a property, on which one hundred inhabitants were reared to the ftate, and found a comfortable fubfiftance. It adds to the bleaknefs of the fcene, to fee a few fhepherds ftrolling over the face of a country, which formerly, was the nurfe of heroes, who were juftly accounted the bulwark of their native foil, being ever ready to brave danger and death in its defence. Of this we have a memorable proof, in the pathetic lamentations of their wives and daughters, for the difafter of the field of Flowden, " where their brave for-
" refters were a' wed away."

Here too, the inhabitants of the town of Selkirk who breathed the manly fpirit of real freemen, juftly merit particular
cular

---

* The Landholders, ʃin general, are making confiderable plantations ; and, it is faid, the Duke of Buccleugh, in particular, means to referve, in all his future leafes, the banks of the rivers, for planting. If planted with the Swedifh maple, the leaves would furnifh food in confiderable quantities, for their fheep, during the winter feafon.

† The only additional circumftance tending to the depopulation of this part of the country, is, the diffipation of the lower ranks, which makes them afraid of marriage, and defirous of enjoying the pleafures, without the burdens of matrimony.

cular attention. Of 100 citizens, who followed the fortune of James IV. on the plains of Flowden, a few returned, loaded with the ſpoils taken from the enemy. Some of theſe trophies ſtill ſurvive the ruſt of time, and the effects of negligence *. The deſperate valour of the citizens of Selkirk, which, on that fatal day, was eminently conſpicuous to both armies, produced very oppoſite effects. The implacable reſentment of the Engliſh reduce their defenceleſs town to aſhes, whilſt their grateful ſovereign (James V.) ſhewed his ſenſe of their valour, by a grant of an extenſive portion of his foreſt, the trees for rebuilding their houſes†, and the property, as the reward of their heroiſm ‡.

Rivers.

* A ſtandard, the appearance of which beſpeaks its antiquity, is ſtill carried annually, (on the day of riding their Common), before the Corporation of weavers, by a member of which, it was taken from the Engliſh, in the field of Flowden.—It may be added, that the ſword of William Brydon, the town clerk, who led the citizens to the battle, (and who is ſaid to have been knighted for his valour), is ſtill in the poſſeſſion of John Brydon, a citizen of Selkirk, his lineal diſcendant.

† Some have very falſely attributed to this event, that ſong,
" Up with the ſouters of Selkirk, and down with the Earl
of Hume."
There was no Earl of Hume at that time, nor was this ſong compoſed till long after. It aroſe from a bett betwixt the Philiphaugh and Hume families; the ſouters (or ſhoemakers) of Selkirk againſt the men of Hume, at a match of football, in which the ſouters of Selkirk completely gained, and afterwards perpetuated, their victory in that ſong.

‡ The original grant was of 1000 acres, but of this the ſurrounding

Rivers. ——The rivers, Etterick and Yarrow, unite a little above, and terminate in the Tweed, about a mile and a half below, Selkirk. For 5 miles above its junction with the Etterick, the Tweed is still adorned with woods, and leads the pleased imagination to contemplate, what this country must have been, in former times. The Yarrow, for about 5 miles above its junction with Etterick, exhibits nature in a bold and striking aspect. Its native woods still remain, through which, the stream has cut its turbid course, deeply ingulphed amidst rugged rocks. Here, certainly in a flood, stood the descriptive Thomson when he saw it,

" Work and boil, and foam and thunder thro'."

Newark-Castle. ——Upon a peninsula, cut out by the surrounding stream, in the middle of this fantastically wild scene of grandeur and beauty, stands the castle of Newark, whose only inhabitants now are the mopping owl, and chattering daw. ——This is supposed by many, to be the birth place of Mary Scot, the flower of Yarrow; but, she was descended from the Dryhope, and married into the Harden family. Her daughter was married to a predecessor of the present Sir Francis Elliot, of Stobbs, and of the late Lord Heathfield *.

Pown.

ing heritors have wrested from the town of Selkirk, much more than the half, by a claim founded upon the right of pasturage. The town still draws a revenue of about L. 250 *per annum*, from the remainder.

* There is a circumstance, in their contract of marriage, that merits attention, as it strongly marks the predatory spirit of the times. The father-in-law agrees to keep his daughter, for some time after the marriage

Town.——The town of Selkirk is pleasantly situated on a rising ground, and enjoys an extensive prospect, in all directions, especially up and down the river Etterick. The soil around it, is dry, and the harvest early. From its open situation, and almost equal distance from both seas, it is less rainy than any other part of this country. By a measure of rain kept accurately for ten years, and compared with one kept at Hawkhill, in the neighbourhood of Leith, for the same time, Selkirk was found to exceed only one half inch yearly *.—— There is no place in this country so free from epidemical diseases; and were the citizens equally supplied with the other comforts of life, as with wholesome air, no town in Scotland would produce a greater number of aged inhabitants. There a good many from 70 to 80, 3 at and above 90, and one died lately at 106.

That Selkirk, though distant from coal, is happily situated for carrying on the woolen trade, Hawick on the one hand, and Gallashiels on the other, clearly demonstrate. But it is a royal burgh, and as such, suffers in all its best interests, and social intercourse. To acquire political power, and not commercial property, is the great object of the principal citizens. There is, however, one exception, a considerable incle manufactory being very successfully caried on, by Baillie William
Roger,

marriage, for which the son-in-law binds himself to give him the profits of the first Michaelmas moon.

---

* By a regular attention to the pluviameter, barometer and Fahrenheit's thermometer, for ten years, the mean quantity of rain yearly is $31\frac{1}{4}$ inches. The medium heighth of the barometer $29\frac{2}{10}$. The medium of heat 43 degrees. Nor did the medium of heat differ one degree during these ten years.

Roger, (which regularly employs 50 hands,) and by whofe in-fluence, a ftocking manufactory is attempted on a fmall fcale. A tannage, too, in the neighbourhood, is the property of one of the inhabitants.

The burgh lands of Selkirk are worth more than L. 1000 *per annum,* and are divided into a great number of fmall pro-perties. This circumftance, alfo, tends to damp that fpirit for manufactures and commerce, by which the inhabitants of towns are in general diftinguifhed. Such is the rage of the citizens to become lairds, that all their wealth is laid out in purchafing acres or half acres, on which many of them, and the wretched beafts that till them, are half ftarved. As all the burgh lands, are, in the occupancy of the proprietors, there is none to be rented. A few fpots have been got for nurferies, at L. 3. per acre.——The burgh lands fell from L. 40 to L. 70 per acre, Englifh meafure.

State of Agriculture, and of Sheep Farming.—The lands in this parifh are generally hilly, and more adapted to pafture than tillage; but moft of the farms have a large portion of low ground, lying towards, and along the fides of the rivers. They have not hitherto been managed to that advantage of which they are very capable. If you afk the farmers, why they plough the faces of their hills, by which they hurt their fheep walk, and derive not from their miferable returns, an equivalent for feed and labour? If you afk them why they cut their ben-ty paftures, the beft fupport of their fheep in the winter frofts? they anfwer, Becaufe they cannot fupport their black cattle in winter without thefe aids, as they can neither raife hay nor turnips. How eafily might this evil be remedied, and the value of their farms encreafed, by drawing a ftone dyke a-long their low grounds, and confining the farmer to a proper management

management of theſe, as the only arable part of his farm. For example, one-fourth oats, one-fourth turnips, potatoes, &c. one-fourth barley, and one-fourth hay. This rotation will afford every farmer in this pariſh, abundant ſupport for his family, his flocks, and his cattle, however ſevere the winter may be. From what calamities would not this preſerve them; we ſhould not then ſee them when ſtorms ariſe, driving their ſtarved flocks to the leſs ſnowy hills of Annandale; nor purchaſing hay at an extravagant price, and carrying it through almoſt impaſſable roads to their flocks, when their ſtomachs are too weak to receive or digeſt it. The management of flocks begins to be better underſtood, and the farmers, by putting fewer upon the ſame ground, have encreaſed the ſize of their ſheep, leſſened the diſeaſes to which they are liable, and improved the quantity and quality of the wool, more than by all the other means, hitherto diſcovered.

To two diſeaſes, of a very ſerious nature, the flocks here are ſtill expoſed. The one, a fever, to which the hogs or ſheep of the firſt year are ſo liable in winter, and eſpecially in variable weather, with intermitting froſts, that the farmer reckons himſelf fortunate, if he loſes only three of each ſcore in his hirſle. This diſeaſe, (the braxy, as ſome call it), has been examined, and is found to ariſe from the withered graſs on which the animal then feeds, and the want either of liquid, or muſcular motion in the ſtomach to diſſolve it. The conſequence is, that the dry and unconcocted food enters the inteſtines in an impervious ſtate; the obſtructions excite an inflammation, a fever and mortification, of which the animal dies. A remedy, has, with ſucceſs, been attempted. Turnips, from their purgative nature, have been found capable, not only of preventing, but of curing the diſeaſe. The tops of

firs

firs, however, from their refinous nature, (if fuch plantations are weeding) will be found ftill more effectual*.

The other difeafe, known only within thefe 50 years, is of a much more alarming nature, as it affects not only our whole flocks, but the fhepherds and their dogs. It is a fpecies of tick, with which our paftures fwarm. They begin to appear about the end of March, and retire about the middle of Auguft. Unlike to the other animals of the blood-fucking tribe, which fall off when full, thefe feldom let go the hold, till, if their number is fufficient, they drain the whole blood in the body of their fuffering victim. Numbers of fheep, of all ages, but efpecially the young, die of this difeafe. The fheep too, that furvive it, peftered with thefe vermin, feed not to the condition or value they otherwife would. Burning the benty paftures where they breed in the fpring, is found to leffen the evil ; but no means are yet difcovered by which it can be eradicated. An experiment was tried, laft year, by a farmer in this parifh, who anointed the bare part of the thigh of fix of the moft difeafed lambs in his flock with mercurial ointment ; and the fhepherd, who was to obferve the confequence, declared, that the following day he carefully examined them, and found not a fingle tick upon one of them : and being further defired to watch if they remained clean, declared they did.— Should this remedy prove effectual, it will coft only a halfpenny per fheep *.

It is an univerfal practice in this place, to falve, or fmear
the

---

* It is probable that falt would anfwer the fame purpofe.

† A mercurial preparation, or one made up with arfenic, or even any decoction made from tobacco, or, the common broom, will kill thefe vermin when on the fkin. In the pafture, liming, or watering, will anfwer the purpofe effectually.

the sheep with a composition of butter or tar, which, though it spoils the colour, yet is said to improve the quality, and to increase the quantity of the wool. It saves the flocks also, from the influence of the winter rains, from scab and vermin of every kind, except the tick.

The quantity of tar, used in smearing the sheep, varies according to the height of the sheep walk, and the want of shelter. In the low parts of the country, they do not use one half of the quantity, that is necessary in the high lands; which is from $1\frac{1}{2}$ to 3 lb. of butter to each Scots pint of tar.

The farms here are never valued according to the quantity of acres, but the quantity of sheep they will maintain; and the pasture of these, according to their size, and the soundness of the ground, is valued at from 1s 6d. to 3s. per head.———— The grounds on the east side of the Etterick are all green, and may be called downs, rather than hills; those betwixt Etterick and Tweed are heathy and high; the Peat-law, and Three Brethren, in particular, two of these hills, are, the first 1964, and the last 1978 feet above the level of the sea, and from 1604 to 1618 above the bed of the river at Selkirk.

Markets—This place is well supplied with excellent lamb after the 20th of May, and high-flavoured mutton, from the 20th of June to Martinmas; and, if the winter is mild, to Christmas. The veal is not good, but the farmers, who are in the habit of buying Highland cattle, and feeding them for a year, supply the market with very fine small beeves, and make a very good rent, as they buy from L. 3 : 10, to L. 4, and sell from L. 6 : 10 to L. 7.——A few of the farms that are inclosed, have raised as fine turnips, and exhibit as good a breed of cattle, as are to be met with any where. One farmer, this season, fed his 3 year olds, from 50 to 60 stone,

and

and from 3 to 6 ftone of tallow, and fold them from L. 16 to L. 17.

General State.—The number of fheep in this parifh are computed to be 22000 : horfes, 265, of which two thirds are farm horfes ; black cattle, 735. Valued rent, L. 15826 Scots. Real rental, L. 4223 fterling. Country heritors, 17 ; burgage heritors, 91 ; farmers, 26. The ftipend 100 guineas, *per annum*, with a manfe and a glebe. The Duke of Roxburgh is patron.———The parifh, exclufive of the lands of Todridge, which are detached, and at a confiderable diftance, may be about 10 miles fquare.

Population.—The number of examinable perfons, about 50 years ago, is faid to have been 1700. The number of fouls, as reported to Dr Webfter, for the year 1755, was 1793. By an exact furvey, lately made, the number of all ages, now exifting, amounts to nearly 700, in the country, and 1000 in the burgh *. There is in Selkirk, a meeting of Burgher Seceders, the only one in the country. What their number may be in Selkirk parifh is not accurately known ; but it cannot be confiderable. There are no Roman catholics. The medium number of births, deaths, and marriages, for the laft 3 years, were calculated, and found to be, births, 43 ; deaths, 35 ; marriages, 19, annually.

The Poor.——Poors-rates have long been eftablifhed here, to the great prejudice of induftry and virtue, among the lower clafs of citizens. " The parifh is bound to fupport us," is
their

* Any decreafe of population is entirely in the country part of the parifh, as the numbers in the burgh, have, for more than a century, been nearly the fame.

their apology for diffipation, through every period of life.——
The young men receive, *per annum*, from L. 6 to L. 8 of wages, and the young women, from L. 3 . 10 to L. 4 : 10, with
their maintenance. Labourers, 1s in fummer, 1s 2d. in harveft, and 10d in winter, per day. Women from 6d. to 8d. in
fummer, and 1s in harveft. This, however, is inadequate to
their expences, when they are in health, and makes them
a conftant burden upon the public, whenever any misfortune
happens to them. Such a mode of living is but a miferable
preparation for the cares of matrimony, and the burden of a
family. In that ftate, the ruftic beau finks into a peevifh and
complaining churl. The gaily attired fhepherdefs becomes a
prey to ftupid infenfibility and floth, equally indifferent about
her perfon and her houfehold affairs; and the virtue of
both, if it hath withftood the attacks of youthful diffipation, is
again fubjected to the dangers, which arife from the reftlefs
calls of pinching poverty, and the cries of ftarving infants.——
The extinction of fmall farms, which has barred their ambition, and damped any fpirit of oeconomy, is here attended
with fatal effects; whilft their unfortunate dependance upon
the poors funds, makes them lefs difpofed to induftrious exertion. This, too, diffolves the ties of natural affection, while
it multiplies the number, and increafes the neceffities of the
poor. If the children fuffer from the want of economy and
virtue in their parents, the parents are abundantly repaid by
the neglect of their children, when bending under the double
load of infirmity and indigence. They will tell you, without
a blufh, that the parifh is better able to fupport their aged parents, than they are; while you will fee them, at the fame
time, in the prime of life, unclogged with families, in-
dulging themfelves in every fpecies of debauchery common to
that rank of life. But the mifchief ends not with them; many who fill higher ftations, and whofe circumftances are not
only

only eafy but affluent, make their contributing to the poors funds an excufe for throwing their near relations a burden upon the public. While the feelings of nature are thus ftifled, and its laws are thus tranfgreffed, it were devoutly to be wifhed, that the laws refpecting the poor, productive of fo many baneful confequences, would provide this equitable antidote : " that all who are in circumftances, and who, by law, would fucceed to the property of any one, were they rich, fhould be obliged to maintain them when poor." The public, as it is only the laft heir, ought to be only the laft refort, of thofe who have none elfe to fupport them. From thefe obfervations, it would appear, that poors-rates, without a fyftem of management not yet practifed in the country parifhes, is urtfriendly to the caufe of virtue in general, and to the beft interefts of thofe they are intended to ferve.——It is an undoubted fact, that, when people are taught to depend upon any means of fupport, which flow not from their own laudable induftry and economy, the meannefs of the thought degrades every virtue, and opens the door to every vice, that can debafe the foul. Their only dependance ought to be upon their own labour and exertions, which, when joined to economy, will always furnifh them with the means of a decent maintainance. Promoting their induftry is the beft provifion that can be made for them. Premiums are chearfully given for the encouragement of commerce : Might not the fame means be employed, for promoting virtue and induftry in humble life ? A very fmall fum, properly laid out for that purpofe, would do more good, than all that is beftowed on the prefent fyftem. With what honourable pride would not the poor man's heart fwell, and with what renewed vigour and alacrity, would he not difcharge the duties of his ftation, when he felt his virtues publicly regarded, and rewarded by his fellow citizens? With what fhame and remorfe, would not the profligate wretch endeavour to

conceal

conceal his mifery, defpifed and condemned by thofe among whom he lived, and without any juft claim to their affiftance? Even during the infirmities of age, their fupport fhould be a voluntary gift, and not compulfatory; and fhould depend upon the character they maintained, in their early days, for their honefty and virtue.

The number of the poor, though gradually increafing, conftantly varies. There were, upon the roll of laft year, in the country part of the parifh, 20; and the annual fum provided for their relief, was L. 54 : 12. In the burgh, the number was 22, the fum provided was L. 60.

The collections, at the church-door, are dedicated to the relief of incidental misfortunes, among thofe who have no fhare in the fund above mentioned, or who happen to fall into circumftances of peculiar diftrefs, between the meetings of the managers. By thefe means, many are prevented from coming upon the funds, to which, on every occafion, they difcover a ftrong propenfity, and which it is not always eafy to hinder.

All the money mortified to the poor of this parifh, is 200 merks, the donation of William Ogilvie, Efq. of Hartwoodmires; of which, the kirk-feffion are managers.

Scarcity in 1782.——The parifh produces much more grain, (wheat excepted) than is fufficient for the fupport of the inhabitants.——In 1782, however, the crop was very deficient, and the poor were reduced to very great diftrefs To encreafe the poors funds proportionally was a dangerous experiment, and could only extend to fuch as were upon the roll. To relieve the neceffities of all the indigent, by donation sin meal or money, was impoffible. A fcheme, much more effectual than either, was adopted by the town of Selkirk :—They put L. 50 into the hands of a citizen well acquainted with the ftate of

the

the country, and the victual trade, with power to purchase meal, wherever he found it of the best quality, and most reasonable, and to retail it at prime cost, among the parishioners. By these means all were regularly supplied, below the retail price, till that was reduced from 2s 10d. to 2s 2d. per stone. By this plan, the town lost only the interest of the L. 50, and 1s per day to their agent, while they did a more, essential service to the whole inhabitants of the parish, than if 100 guineas had been distributed amongst them. Even the poor of other parishes, when meal was not elsewhere to be had, were permitted to share in the advantages of this plan.

Miscellaneous Observations.—The rivers, fields, and woods, in the neighbourhood, abound with all the fish, game, birds of song, of prey, and of the migratory species, common in the southern parts of Scotland. Among the multitude of sparrows, bred in the thatched roofs of the houses in Selkirk, one appeared, some years ago, perfectly white. It was more slender and more beautiful in its appearance, than the common sparrows, and, in some respects, resembled a canary bird; but was of a purer and more glossy white.————There is at Haining-Lin, in the neighbourhood of Selkirk, a spring of steel water; from which, though it is but weak, the poor of a scorbutic or schrophulous habit, derive advantage.———— The only fossil, that merits attention in this place, is, an inexhaustible fund of shell marle. It produces wonderful effects upon light and dry soils; but its utility to the country in general, must depend upon the discretion with which it used, and the terms at which it can be purchased.——In this parish there remain no monuments of antiquity, but some military stations, and a fossee perfectly visible on both sides of the Yarrow, which was the western defence of Montrose's camp, before the battle of Philiphaugh. It was probably thrown up,

to

to prevent any ſurprize from the Harehead wood, to which it is very near, and runs almoſt parallel.————Some ſkulls of the urus*, and a Roman ſpear, with which theſe animals were deſtroyed, were found lately, in a moſs, near to Selkirk, and preſented to the ſociety of antiquaries.————
One of the moſt diſtinguiſhed characters, which this, or any pariſh in Scotland, has given birth to, in modern times, was Andrew Pringle, Lord Alemoor, whoſe amiable manners, learning, and eloquence, rendered him equally the object of admiration, as the friend, the ſcholar, and the judge. Deſtined by nature, to fill the higheſt departments in the ſtate, with honour to himſelf, and advantage to his country ; although his bodily infirmities damped theſe proſpects when full in view, and with-held from the public the great ſervices for which his abilities were formed, yet they robbed him not of gaiety of mind, ſuavity of manners, philanthropy, and public ſpirit, till they laid him, (much lamented by his friends and country), in an untimely grave.

---

* For the deſcription of this animal, and the honorary rewards conferred on thoſe who diſtinguiſhed themſelves in deſtroying them, ſee Cæſar's Commentaries, lib. vi. chap. 5.

PARISH OF YARROW.

(County of Selkirk.—Presbytery of Selkirk.—Synod of Merse and Teviotdale.)

By the Reverend Mr ROBERT RUSSELL.

Extent.

YARROW, though inferior in extent to some parishes in the north, yet exceeds in magnitude any in the south of Scotland. Its greatest length cannot be estimated at less than 18, nor its breadth than 16 miles.

Surface and Soil.—The general appearance of the country is mountainous. On all sides the hills erect their towering heads, and soon terminate the prospect. The soil is various. In the haughs, in some places, it is deep and fertile; in others, it is light and unproductive. Upon the hills it partakes also of considerable variety. In some parts, the sides are dry and arable; in others, they are spongy and susceptible of no cultivation. The tops are generally mossy, and fit for nothing but pasturage and fuel. The crops are frequently indifferent. Some years they scarce repay the labour and expence incurred in raising them. This is occasioned by the general dampness of the atmosphere, which produces, especially in the upper parts of the parish, a luxuriancy of straw,

but

but hinders the grain from coming to great maturity. In dry and hot feafons, which occur rarely, the cafe is otherwife : Then the grain is fufficiently ripened, and abundantly productive.

Climate.—The air for the moft part is moift and raw. This is owing to the mifts that fo frequently float upon the fummits of the hills, and the vapour that is continually exhaled by the fun from the marfhy grounds. It does not appear, however, to be unfavourable to health, as the people here attain to as great longevity as thofe of drier climates.

Lochs and Rivers.—There are two lochs adjoining to each other, partly in this parifh, and partly in Etterick. The one is called the Loch of the Lows, and the other St Mary's Loch. Thefe are noticed in the account of the parifh of Etterick.—The only rivers in this parifh are the Etterick and Yarrow. The courfe of the former has been already defcribed, vol. 3. page 295. The latter takes its rife from St Mary's Loch, and after an eafterly courfe of 15 miles is abforbed in the Etterick, a little above Selkirk. Both rivers run with great rapidity, and fwell to a prodigious height. Small falmon occafionally afcend their ftreams ; but the fifh with which they chiefly abound are trout of a moft delicious flavour.

Mountains and Hills.—The hills are, in general, fteep and towering. The moft remarkable are thofe called *Blackhoufe Heights.* The higheft point of elevation, above the level of the fea, meafures 2370 feet. For the moft part, the mountains exhibit a green appearance. Upon fome few, there is a confiderable quantity of heath. No rocks are vifible.

Sheep,

Sheep, Horses, and Black Cattle.—The sheep constitute the chief part of the animal productions of this parish, and are of a superior quality, in point of good carcase and delicate taste. The horses and black cattle do not rise above mediocrity. Their respective numbers, as nearly as can be ascertained, are as follows; sheep, 55,000; horses, 149; black cattle, 545.

Wool.—The wool is of various qualities. In the lower part of the parish, it is of a considerably fine texture, and sells at the rate of 18 s. the stone. In the upper part, it is of a very coarse pile, and does not bring more than 6 s. or 7 s. For a great series of years, the sheep farmers paid no attention to this valuable article. Their chief study was to produce a good carcase, rather than a fine fleece. Hence the coarse black faced kind of sheep constituted their principal store. Of late years, however, their system of rearing sheep hath undergone a considerable alteration, particularly in the lower district of the parish. Induced by the high price of fine wool, the farmers in this quarter are gradually quitting the old species, and introducing the Cheviot breed. For this purpose, they are at great pains every season to procure tups of a fine quality. Nor have their laudable efforts to improve their stock of sheep been unrewarded. Some, who began early their career of improvement, have trebled the price of their wool. Others again, who were later in their commencement, have doubled it. But these improvements are solely confined to the farms about and below the church. All above remain in their former unimproved state. Still the old breed of sheep are reared, whose wool is of the coarsest kind, and little adapted for manufacture. Although convinced of the great advantage resulting from rearing the Cheviot species, yet the farmers there are afraid to try the experiment,

experiment, from an idea that their lambs could not fuſtain the ſpring colds and ſtorms to which their farms are ſubjeſt. That their farms are in a high elevation, and greatly expoſed to the winter ſtorms, and the ſpring blaſts, is beyond all controverſy : But, whether their fears and apprehenſions upon this head are well grounded, remains yet to be proved. No experiments have been made, and conſequently no certain concluſions can be drawn. Some, who have had a good deal of experience in rearing the fine woolled ſheep, alledge that they are not ſo delicate as many repreſent them, and that they would thrive very well in many places where a tenacious adherence to ancient maxims and cuſtoms have as yet prevented their introduſtion. This being the caſe, it is to be hoped that thoſe ſtoremaſters who have hitherto been prevented from rearing the Cheviot breed, by long eſtabliſhed habits or groundleſs fears, will ſoon ſurmount theſe, and concur with ſpirit and vigour in forwarding the improvement of the ſtaple commodity of the country, which tends both to promote the proſperity of the nation, and to advance the intereſt of individuals.

Birds.—The tame are geeſe, turkeys, hens, and ducks. The wild conſiſt of the partridge, moorfowl, hawk, crow, wood-pigeon, thruſh, blackbird, bullfinch, lark, linnet, and the ſparrow. The migratory may be reduced to the lapwing, cuckoo, plover, woodcock, and ſwallow. In ſevere winters, ſwans have alſo made their appearance in the lochs already mentioned.

Population.—In Dr Webſter's liſt in 1755, the numbers are rated at 1180. In this there was probably ſome miſtake. From a ſurvey of the pariſh taken this year, the inhabitants amount to 1230. Of theſe, 584 are males, and 646 are females.

males. What the ancient population was, cannot now be well afcertained, as all the old records were burnt about 30 years ago along with the manfe. The aged people all agree in afferting, that it confiderably exceeded the prefent; and their teftimony is corroborated from the numerous remains of old houfes. Various caufes may be affigned for this depopulation. One, undoubtedly, may be imputed to the monopoly of farms, which diminifhes the number of farmers families. Another may be attributed to the averfion of the farmers to rebuild cot-houfes, which decreafes the clafs of cottagers. A third may be afcribed to the manufactures carried on in other parts of the country, which draw off the inhabitants from fuch parifhes as this, where they have not as yet found their way.

Abftract of Births, Burials, and Marriages, for the laft fix years.

Years.	Births.	Burials.	Marriages.
1787,	28	12	12
1788,	23	10	6
1789,	19	9	9
1790,	17	10	8
1791,	20	15	8
1792,	24	21	8
	131	77	51

Longevity.—In this parifh, fcarcely any perfon ever attains to 100 years. There is, however, one inftance of this remembered. A woman died here feveral years ago at the great age of 106. At prefent, there are feveral perfons bordering upon 90, but none exceed it.

Eminent

Eminent Perfons.—This parifh has given birth to a famous military character, Colonel William Ruffell of Afhyfteel, whofe heroic exploits in India reflect honour upon himfelf, and do credit to his country. One, in particular, deferves to be recorded, as it difplays the moft undaunted fpirit, and the moft intrepid valour. When Manilla, the capital of the Phillippine Ifles, was ftormed by the naval and military forces under the command of Admiral Cornifh and General Draper, he, at the head of a felect party, was the firft man that entered the breach, and took poffeffion of the city. Never was courage put to a feverer teft, and never was heroifm more difplayed. When the arduous and dangerous nature of the enterprife is duly confidered, it may well be compared to the moft celebrated martial atchievements either of ancient or modern times.

Mary Scott, " the flower of Yarrow," fo highly celebrated in fong, was alfo a native of this parifh. According to tradition, fhe was the daughter of Walter Scott, Efquire, of Dryhope, and was reckoned the faireft and moft handfome woman in the foreft. Hence fhe had a number of fuitors, who folicited the honour of a matrimonial alliance with her. In preference to all other candidates, fhe gave her hand to Scott of Harden. From this marriage there fprung a daughter, who was wedded to the eldeft fon of the Baronet of Stobbs, commonly called " Gibby with the golden garters." From them are defcended the prefent Sir William Elliot of Stobbs and Lord Heathfield. A circumftance relating to their marriage-contract merits a place in hiftoric records, as it ftrongly marks the predatory fpirit of the times. Finding it inconvenient to take home his wife, Gibby befought his father-in-law to lodge her for fome time. With this requeft he complied, upon condition that he was to receive, for her board, the plunder of the firft harveft moon. A moft fin-

gul r

gular paction, and highly characteristic of the licentiousness and barbarity of the age in which it was made.

Farmers.—In former times, the farmers were much more numerous than at present. Several farms, which were occupied by 2 or 3 persons, are now possessed by one man, which has occasioned a great diminution of the farmers. Their present number amount to 40, who rent farms from 60 l. to 360 l. *per annum.*

Agriculture.—This parish is not remarkable for agriculture. Wheat is never attempted, as both the soil and climate are unfriendly to its growth. Sown grass and flax are but rarely raised. Barley, oats, pease, potatoes, and turnips, are the chief crops produced, and these but in small quantities. The number of acres annually employed in raising these may be estimated at 1000. The remainder of the parish consists wholly of sheep pasture. But what may be the quantity of acres it contains in whole, cannot be accurately defined, as a complete measurement has never taken place. Calculating upon the number of sheep, horses, and cattle, maintained by it, they cannot be less than 60,000.

Seed-time and Harvest.—In favourable seasons, the farmers begin to sow about the middle of March, and to reap about the middle of September. Both seed-time and harvest are often, however, by reason of the prevalency of rains and colds in this country, much later. April is sometimes considerably advanced before sowing commences, and November is frequently far gone before the crops are all cut down and lodged in the barn-yard.

Imports and Exports.—Owing to the little arable land in the

the parish, it is unable to supply itself with provisions. Hence considerable quantities of meal of all kinds are annually imported. But, on the other hand, to counterbalance this disadvantage under which the parish labours, it exports yearly an immense number of sheep, a few horses and black cattle, and a considerable quantity of wool and cheese.

Wood.—This parish formerly abounded with wood, insomuch that it received the designation still belonging to it, of *Etterick Forest.* But the name is now egregiously misapplied, as every remnant of the old wood hath entirely disappeared. From the great quantities of oak still found in the mosses, it seems to have constituted the principal species. The new plantations are but rare and small. At Hangingshaw, the once beautiful, but now ruinous seat of the Murrays of Philiphaugh, there is a considerable quantity of thriving wood. Small clumps of planting are also found upon most of the farms belonging to the Duke of Buccleugh, and which, in a few years, will be of great service to the parish. At present, it labours under a great disadvantage, from the scarcity of this necessary article.

Church, School, and Poor.—In former times the parochial church stood in a situation, and went by a name, very different from its present position and denomination. It was situated upon the side of St Mary's loch, and was stiled St Mary's kirk. As this is the very western extremity of the parish, it was found extremely inconvenient for the generality of the parishioners. Consequently, about the year 1640, it was judged necessary to alter the place of worship, and to erect the present church, which is about 8 miles to the eastward of the old one, and much more centrical for the parish. But although the situation of the church was changed, that

of

of the glebe was continued and ſtill is, which conſiſts wholly
of ſheep paſture, and contains at leaſt 200 acres of ground.
The old burial ground alſo remains, and is ſtill employed as
ſuch. In it ſeveral families, both of this and the adjacent pariſhes, inter their dead. The ſtipend, including the rent paid
for the above mentioned glebe, may be valued at 120 l. Sterling. There has been no augmentation ſince the year 1731.
At that time it was conſidered as a good living. The funds
for augmentation are ſtill very great. The right of patronage is veſted in the Crown.—The parochial ſchool is at preſent in a very flouriſhing ſtate. Engliſh, writing, arithmetic,
book-keeping, land-ſurveying, and mathematics, are taught
after the neweſt and moſt improved methods. The ſalary is
only 100 merks Scots, which is a ſum by no means adequate
to the extent and land rent of the pariſh, and totally inſufficient either to ſupport the dignity of a ſchoolmaſter, or to
reward him for his uſeful labours. The ſchool-houſe is in
excellent repair, and accommodated for lodging ſeveral boarders. Laſt winter, the ſchoolmaſter had 8 ſcholars boarded
with him. Beſides the parochial ſchool, there is another ſituated upon the Etterick river, where the branches of education already mentioned are alſo taught. For this ſchool
there is no ſalary allotted. The ſchoolmaſter has nothing to
depend upon for his ſubſiſtence, but the emoluments ariſing
from the ſchool fees, and a guinea gratuitouſly given annually
by that benevolent nobleman the Duke of Buccleugh. Were
the other heritors to imitate his laudable example, and thus
countenance a ſeminary of learning highly neceſſary for the
place, it would ſurely be highly for their honour. As they
are noblemen and gentlemen of the moſt reſpectable characters, and generous diſpoſitions, it is to be hoped, this will be
brought about upon a proper application to them. The
ſchool houſe is in good order, being built lately, partly by
ſubſcription,

subscription, and partly by the surplus of poor's rates.—
There are 57 persons upon the poor's roll at this time. None
of them are permitted to stroll and molest other parishes.
They are liberally supported at their own homes. Every
person's case is duly considered twice in the year, and a sum
is allotted to them suitable to their exigency. Besides the
weekly collections on Sunday, the funds appropriated for
their maintenance are the assessments upon the heritors and
tenants. Since their first institution these have increased
considerably. At their commencement they were moderate,
owing to the small number of pensioners. Now these are
greatly multiplied, and the poor's rates are egregiously swel-
led. Last year they amounted to 120 l. Sterling. Though
established upon generous principles, and destined to relieve
virtuous poverty and distress, yet their benevolent design is
in some measure counteracted, by the temptation they hold
out to sloth and dissipation. There is reason to suspect, that
many taking advantage of this provision for indigence and
trouble, squander away what they earn, and are at no pains
to secure for themselves a subsistence, either when laid upon
a bed of sickness, or subjected to the infirmities of old age.
But notwithstanding its abuse in some instances, it is surely a
noble institution, and reflects the highest honour upon this
country, which is attentive to every class of citizens, and de-
sirous that every individual should enjoy, if not the comforts,
at least the necessaries of life.

Fuel.—The fuel generally made use of is peat. In the upper part of the parish it is of an excellent quality, and found
in great abundance ;—in the lower it is both very scarce and
bad. Upon which account the farmers in this district commonly make use of several cart load of coal, which they drive

all

all the way from Lothian. But thefe as they coft 3 d. the ftone by the time they are laid down here, are far beyond the purchafe of the poor people. Their fole dependence is upon the peat and the heather.

Land Rent.—On account of the rifing prices of fheep and wool, the rent of the parifh has increafed very much of late years. At prefent it amounts to 7000 l. Sterling The valued rent is 31,377 l. 9 s. 8 d. Scotch. An immenfe valuation for a fingle parifh.

Wages.—The wages ufually paid to fervants employed in hufbandry are from 6 to 7 l. Sterling to males, and from 3 l. 10 s. to 4 l. to females. Day-labourers receive 8 d. together with victuals, without them 14 d. Taylors, fhoemakers, weavers, mafons, and wrights, earn from 15 to 20 d. *per* day. Wages of all kinds have rapidly increafed of late years, and are ftill upon the rifing hand.

Antiquities.—Throughout all the parifh, there are numerous remains of old caftles, formerly the feats of the feudal barons. Their conftruction and fituation highly mark the rufticity and ferocity of the times in which they were built. They are for the moft part conftructed upon the fides of the hills, in the rudeft and ftrongeft manner; and have been evidently defigned to protect the poffeffors of them from the affaults ot neighbouring chieftains and Englifh invaders, with whom they lived in a ftate of perpetual warfare.

Difadvantages.—This parifh labours under feveral difadvantages, one of which is the diftance of coal and lime, together with free-ftone; the former of which are diftant 30,

the

the latter 18 miles. Another originates from the distance of market towns. Selkirk is the nearest, and even it is distant 8 miles from the manse. The bad state of the roads constitutes a third. It is only of late years that any attention hath been paid to them. Now a communication for carriages is opened up the Yarrow river, from Selkirk to Moffat and the west country. Another road is carried up the Etterick river, as far as Etterick church; but both these, especially that of Etterick, require great amendments. The cross roads are all in a state of nature, and in some places are excessively deep. The snow also at times is productive of great inconveniency and hardship to the storemasters in the upper district of the parish. Frequently they have been obliged to fly to the low countries for provision for their flocks, and after all their toil and expence many of them have been cut off. In the years 1772 and 1774, they sustained immense losses. Some whole farms were almost desolated by the mortality among the sheep, occasioned by the severity of the winters. The scarcity of bridges is likewise a great drawback upon this parish. Frequently is the traveller, by the swelling of the rivers, either obstructed altogether upon his route, or obliged to go many miles about, in order to pursue his journey.

Miscellaneous Observations.—No particular manufactures are carried on in the parish. Household expences are greatly increased of late years. Landed property seldom changes. The best arable land is not worth more than a guinea *per* acre. Very little of the parish is inclosed. The dress of the inhabitants is much altered from what it was 20 or 30 years ago. A spirit for feuing at present prevails among the people. One whole farm belonging to the Duke of Buccleugh

was

was this year feued out into fmall parcels, upon which the feuers are building very neat houfes.

The people are in general fober, devout, and induftrious. None have been banifhed the country in the memory of any perfon now living. They enjoy in a confiderable degree the comforts of life, and appear to be contented with their circumftances and fituation.

PEEBLESSHIRE

PEEBLESSHIRE

KEY TO PARISHES

1. Linton
2. Newlands
3. Eddleston
4. Innerleithen
5. Traquair
6. Peebles
7. Lyne & Megget
8. Stobo

9. Kirkurd
10. Skirling
11. Broughton
12. Kilbucho
13. Glenholm
14. Drumelzier
15. Manor
16. Tweedsmuir

17. Part of Selkirkshire
18. Part of Culter (Lanarkshire)

MIDLOTHIAN

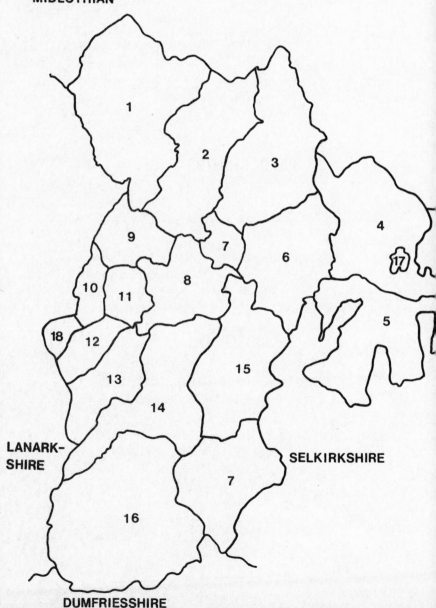

**LANARK-
SHIRE**

SELKIRKSHIRE

DUMFRIESSHIRE

PARISH OF BROUGHTON.

(County of Tweedale.—Presbytery of Biggar.—Synod of Lothian and Tweedale).

By the Reverend Mr THOMAS GRAY.

Estate of Broughton.

THE estate of Broughton has been, for a great number of years, in the possession of the Murrays of Stenhope, who resided in the parish, and was sold by the late Sir John Murray commonly called Secretary Murray (having acted in that capacity to the Pretender), to James Dickson of Edrum, member of Parliament for this district of burrows in the year 1762, and above eight years afterwards, it was sold by his heirs to the present Lord Justice Clerk, now proprietor of the whole parish. The mansion-house on this estate was burnt about 18 years ago, and is not yet rebuilt. The village of Broughton was rebuilt by the late James Dickson, Esq; after the English fashion, and remarked by passengers for its neatness.

The form of this parish is two ridges of hills, with a valley between them, and the village of Broughton at the lower end of the valley, 4 miles in length and 3 in breadth.

Soil and Air.—The soil is generally of a deep wet clay, and produces good crops in dry seasons.—The air is dry and healthy,

healthy, and no diftempers are prevalent here, but fuch as are every where common.

Population.—The antient ftate of population in this parifh was 400 fouls. In 1755, it was 367. The prefent ftate of population is 264. There are 142 males, and 122 females.

In the village of Broughton there are 20 dwelling houfes, which contain 36 people, and 61 children.

In the country part of the parifh 167 refide, which, with the 97 that live in the village, make up 264 fouls, the a-mount of the prefent population.

The annual average of births, - -	7
————————— of deaths, - - -	5
————————— of marriages, - -	3
Souls under 10 years of age, - - -	75
—— from 10 to 20, - - - -	57
—— from 20 to 50, - - -	96
—— from 50 to 70, - - -	31
—— from 70 to 100, - . - -	5

There are twelve farmers in the parifh, and they employ in hufbandry 28 male fervants, and 23 females.—There are 4 weavers in the parifh, 4 wrights, 1 taylor, 1 fmith, 1 mil-ler, 2 fhoemakers, and 3 fhopkeepers.

The people in this parifh are well affected to the prefent eftablifhment; at the ordination of the incumbent, there was not one feceder in the whole parifh; there are now 8 who were Seceders from the Church before they came into this parifh.

Productions.—There is no natural wood, nor fruit trees in the parifh; but feveral plantations of fir and hard timber, in a thriving condition. There are 200 black cattle, and up-wards of 2000 fheep, and 80 horfes, young and old.—There are

are 400 acres in tillage, 300 in corn, 60 in bear, 30 in peas, and 10 in potatoes.—The parish supplies itself with provisions, and exports corn, cattle, and wool, to a considerable extent.—There is no hemp, and very little flax raised in the parish, being found, from experience, not to agree with the soil and climate.—The soil answers sown grass extremely well, and there are about 30 acres, at an average, laid down with grass seeds every year, which produce very plentiful crops All the other lands are in pasture.

They in general sow their corn and pease in the month of March, and reap in September; their bear in April, and reap in August.

Miscellaneous Observations.—This parish labours under a great disadvantage in regard to fewel, having none but coal, and that at the distance of 16 miles; lime is at the distance of 12 miles.—Another disadvantage this parish labours under, is the want of residing heritors, which is a great loss to the poor, especially in these parishes where there are no poor rates, as in this case, the poor are supported by the poor.

The language spoken here is English, with the Scotch accent; but from what language the names of places in the parish are derived, is impossible to say.

The land rent of the parish is about 700 l. a year.—The cot-houses, in the parish, at an average, 1 l. yearly.

Church and Poor.—The value of the living varies somewhat, in proportion to the price of meal, the stipend being 35 l. in money, and 3 chalders of oat meal, at an average 80 l. including the glebe. Patron, Duke of Queensberry.

The number of the poor receiving alms, at an average, are 8; and there being no poor rates in the parish, they are supported by the Sunday's collections, and the benefits arising

from

from the mort cloth and proclamation of banns. It would be a good fund towards the maintenance of the poor, and a good mean for the preventing of the crimes of unchastity and child murder, if the stool of repentance, which is, no doubt, a relic of Popery, was legally abolished, and a fine in money established in its place, in proportion to circumstances and situations, wherever the scandal was not removed by marriage.

The wages of a day-labourer in husbandry, 1 s. *per* day; of wrights, 1 s. 2 d.; of taylors, 1 s.; and of masons, 1 s. 8 d. without victuals.—The common wages of male servants, 6 l. of female, 3 l. *per* year, with victuals.—There are 14 ploughs in the parish, of the Scotch kind, and upwards of 50 carts.

Ancient Buildings.—There are the remains of ten castles, commonly called towers, which appear to have been houses of great strength. In the under storey they had a wooden door of uncommon thickness, full of iron-spikes with broad heads, and a strong iron-gate that opened in the inside. One of these doors and gates was preserved in the parish for a long time as a piece of antiquity, and has been seen by several now living. In one of these castles the great Macbeth is said to have lived; and it is called Macbeth's Castle to this day. Mr James Dickson, late proprietor of this parish, employed workmen to dig up the foundation of part of Macbeth's Castle, in search of treasure and antiquities; but nothing was found but some pieces of old armour, and coins of no great consequence.

Roads.—The public road which runs through the parish, and leads to Moffat, is kept in good repair; but the bye-roads are very bad, and many of them impassable, no statute

labour

labour having been performed, nor commutation money up-lifted, for the laſt ten years.—There is only one bridge in the pariſh over Biggar water, about a quarter of a mile from the village ; and, being upon the public road, and of great advan-tage to travellers, the water in the winter ſeaſon being often impaſſable, is kept in tolerably good repair.

School.—There is only one ſchool in the pariſh, ſalary 5 l. 16 s. 8 d. which, with ſchool wages and other perquiſites, may amount to the ſmall living of 11 l. or 12 l. yearly ; and, for that ſum, from 20 to 30 ſcholars are regularly inſtructed in the different branches of education.

There is one inn and two alehouſes in the village.

Cottages.—There are no new houſes built in the pariſh of late, nor cottages, but a great many cottages pulled down, the farmers finding more loſs than profit ariſing from the keeping up of cot-houſes : The throwing down of cottages muſt be one principal reaſon of the decreaſe of popula-tion in country pariſhes, and of the increaſe of population in towns and villages, and a principal reaſon of the ſcarcity of ſervants, and the increaſe of their wages ; the poor people being baniſhed from the country, take up their reſidence in towns, and breed their children to manufactures, who would otherwiſe have all been bred to the plough ; and, if manu-factures continue to flouriſh, and this growing evil, of throw-ing down cottages, and baniſhing the poor from the country parts of pariſhes, is not ſpeedily corrected, it is more than probable that ſervants for carrying on the purpoſes of agri-culture will not be obtained.

There is one fair in the year in the village, held upon the 4th of October, originally for black cattle, but now chiefly for the hiring of ſervants, and the ſtoremaſters ſelling their cheeſe.

PARISH OF DRUMMELZIER.

(County of Tweedale.—Presbytery of Peebles.—Synod of
Lothian and Tweedale.)

By the Reverend Mr WILLIAM WELSH.

Name, Soil, and Climate.

THE antient and modern name of this parish is the
fame, and is said to signify, in the Gaelic, " Here is
a plain," which accords very well with the situation of the
village that is built on a rivulet called Pow Sail, at the head
of a haugh of about 300 acres of inclosed land, divided into
sixteen parks, in grafs, rented about 20 s. *per* acre ; 30 years
ago, uninclosed, they set at 7 s. *per* acre.   The parish is 12
miles long, and, at an average, about 3 broad.   The face of
the country is beautifully varied with hill and rock, rivulets
and small plains, lying on the Tweed.   The soil is light, but
fertile.   The air is healthy.   The most frequent diseases are,
slow fevers, confumptions, and rheumatisms.   There are no
fish but trout and salmon.

Population in 1755,	-	-	-	- 305
—— —— in 1790, males,	-	-	123	
———————— females,	-	-	147	
				—— 270
				Sum

Sum of births, from 1744 to 1790,	-	=	403
—— of burials for that term,	-	-	- 255

Difference, - 148

This, and most of the neighbouring parishes, are greatly decreased in number. A third of the inhabitants live in the
village, the rest in farm and cot-houses. We have only 6
farmers, 7 weavers, 4 taylors and apprentices, 2 masons, 2
smiths, and 6 day-labourers; the rest are shepherds, cow-
herds, and ploughmen. There are only one Seceder, and
one Episcopalian. The people are industrious. Only four
old persons, and a dumb man, receive charity.

Productions.—There is little natural wood here, only at
Polmood, a small one which formerly has been pretty large;
but has been destroyed by bad management, and particularly
by sheep. The soil is very fit for trees of every kind, and
the late Sir James Nasmyth planted a great deal of fruit
trees, as well as fir, which have thriven very well. There is
no wheat. The grain is barley, pease, and oats. The farmers also sow turnip, and plant a considerable quantity of
potatoes, of which the people are fond, and think that a sta-
tue ought to be erected to the memory of Sir Walter Raleigh, who first brought them to Britain. Few grass seeds
are sown on account of the sheep, which are great enemies
to them.—Servants wages are high. A man, 6 l. *per annum;*
a maid servant, 2 l. for the summer half year, and about
25 s. for the winter. The wages they receive enable families
generally to live in a very different manner indeed from the
poor in England, as they buy no articles of luxury.—Provisions are double the price they were 40 years ago, which
bears hard upon schoolmasters, and others, whose salaries
have not been augmented. A lamb costs 5 s. or 6 s.; a
sheep,

fheep, if fat, 11 s. or 12 s.; a fowl, 1 s.; butter, 10 d. *per* lib.; cheefe, 6 s *per* ftone. The ploughs ufed are of the Scotch kind.—Few Englifh, except by gentlemen or improvers, the land being full of ftones.—The celebrated Merlin is buried here; but no other perfon of great diftinction.

PARISH OF EDLESTOWN.

(COUNTY AND PRESBYTERY OF PEEBLES.—SYNOD OF
LOTHIAN AND TWEEDALE).

By the Rev. Mr PATRICK ROBINSON, *Minister.*

Name, Situation, and Extent.

THE village of EDLESTOWN, from which this parish
takes its name, is situated 17 miles south from Edinburgh, and 4 miles N. from Peebles, on the post road from
Edinburgh.—The length of the parish, from N. to S. is 10
miles, and its greatest breadth, from E. to W. 7 miles.

Hill, Prospect, Lake, River, &c.—DUNDROIGH, or *Druid's
Hill*, which is situated two miles east from the church, is
2100 feet above the level of the sea, from which, in a clear
day, can be seen the Cheviot Hills, with part of Tiviotdale,
Annandale, Clydesdale, Perthshire, Fifeshire, the Frith of
Forth, the city of Edinburgh, and the counties of East, West,
and Mid Lothians.—There is a lake about 2 miles to the N.
E. of the village of Edlestown, nearly of a circular form, and
about 2 miles in circumference. The only species of fish
which it contains, are pikes and eels. This lake gives rise to
the water of South Esk, which empties itself into the sea at
Musselburgh. Edlestown Water, which passes this village,
and runs into the river Tweed at Peebles, takes its rise from
various

various ſprings on the north and north-weſt boundaries of the pariſh, and at Cowey's Linn has a fall of 35 feet. There are no diſeaſes peculiar to this pariſh. The ague is not known in it. In the year 1783, the poor were liberally ſupplied; and the inhabitants of the pariſh, during that year, were more free from ſickneſs than uſual.

Surface, Cultivation, Produce, Exports, &c.—Though the greateſt part of the pariſh conſiſts of hill ground, and is devoted to the paſturage of ſheep and black cattle, yet every ſtore farm, one excepted, and on which a ſhepherd only reſides, contains as much arable land as occupies from one to three ploughs.—The crops conſiſt of beans, ſown graſs, oats, peaſe, potatoes, and turnips. The culture of turnips and ſown graſs hay, becomes every year more extenſive; and as it is found profitable to the farmer, as well as ornamental to the country, there is little doubt that it will ſoon be general. —The produce, after ſupplying the demands of the pariſh, enables the farmer to export annually from 1100 to 1200 bolls of bear; and their exports of oats and peaſe, taken together, may amount nearly to the ſame number of bolls. The groſs rent of the pariſh is doubled within the laſt 20 years. All the tenants are in a thriving ſtate, and many of them are opulent.

Prices of Proviſions and Labour.—The neareſt market for proviſions is Peebles, which is well ſupplied with meat of all kinds, the prices of which are nearly the ſame as at Edinburgh. The wages of ſervants and labourers have increaſed lately, and have been nearly doubled within the laſt 20 years, which is owing, in a great meaſure, to the decreaſed population, not only of this pariſh, but generally throughout the county of Tweeddale. A good ploughman receives 8 guineas

neas *per annum*, with victuals. If married, he has alſo a houſe and garden, with as much land as is ſufficient for ſowing two pecks of bear, two pecks of potatoes, and a lippy of lintſeed. The wages of maid ſervants are, in ſummer, from 1 l. 15 s. to 2 l. 10 s. Sterling, and, in winter, from 1 l. 5 s. to 1 l. 15 s. Sterling. Day-labourers receive from 1 s. 2 d. to 1 s. 6 d. without victuals ; and carpenters, maſons, tailors, and weavers, have lately increaſed their wages about one third.

Population.—The number of inhabitants in this pariſh has varied at different times, but has greatly decreaſed of late, as will appear from inſpecting the following table ; although there is a ſmall increaſe upon the whole, within theſe 40 years.

STATISTICAL TABLE OF THE PARISH OF EDLESTOWN.

Number of ſouls, in 1755, as returned to Dr

Webſter	-	-	-	679	
Ditto in 1775	-	-	-	810	Increaſe 131
Ditto in 1793	-	-	-	710	Decreaſe 100

Total Increaſe in 38 years   31

AGES AND SEXES	Males.	Females.	Total.
Perſons under 10 years of age	57	74	131
———— between 10 and 20	84	62	146
———— ——— 20 and 30	54	69	123
———— ——— 30 and 40	46	39	85
———— ——— 40 and 50	36	28	64
———— ——— 50 and 60	35	26	61
———— ——— 60 and 70	32	27	59
———— ——— 70 and 80	25	12	37
———— ——— 80 and 90	2	2	4
In all	371	339	710

RELI-

RELIGION, HERITORS, &c.

Number of Seceders, of all denominations	90
———— Members of the Eftablished Church	620
———— Proprietors - - -	13
———— Tenants - - - -	23
———— Inhabitants in the village -	180
———— Penfioners on the roll, from	8 to 10
———— Public house - - -	1

STOCK.

Number of fheep - - -	8400
———— Black cattle - - -	620
———— Horfes - - - -	193
———— Ploughs, Scotch and Englifh -	48

LANDS AND RENTS.

Number of acres in the parifh - -		21,250	
———— ditto annually under crops -		1,400	
Valued rent in Scotch money	L. 3928	13	0
Real ditto in Sterling - -	2550	0	0
Of this fum, 12 farmers pay -	1300	0	0
———— Two pay about - -	250	0	0
———— Other two ———— -	200	0	0
———— Other two ———— -	150	0	0
And five who have families pay -	650	0	0
Loweft yearly rent of any farm -	20	0	0
Higheft ditto - - -	250	0	0

Extract from the Register of Marriages, Baptisms, and Burials, of the Parish of Edhestown, from 1st Jan. 1742, to 1st Jan. 1792.

Entries made	Mar.	Baptisms.		Burials.		Total of		
		Males	Fem.	Males	Fem.	Mar.	Bapt.	Bur.
within the year 1742	11	5	8	14	11			
———— 1743	9	10	11	9	8			
———— 1744	5	6	13	11	6			
———— 1745	8	8	5	15	11			
———— 1746	9	5	8	14	16			
———— 1747	13	7	13	11	12			
———— 1748	6	14	7	12	7			
———— 1749	7	11	10	4	4			
———— 1750	7	12	18	1	13			
———— 1751	10	8	10	10	12			
Total from 1st Jan. 1742, to 1st Jan. 1752	85	86	103	101	100	85	189	201
within the year 1752	7	12	7	12	5			
———— 1753	8	14	10	6	11			
———— 1754	10	10	9	14	10			
———— 1755	11	13	11	21	15			
———— 1756	4	10	11	13	24			
———— 1757	12	8	6	9	13			
———— 1758	9	13	10	4	5			
———— 1759	9	11	8	13	15			
———— 1760	6	13	13	11	11			
———— 1761	4	9	3	8	3			
Total from 1st Jan. 1752, to 1st Jan. 1762	80	113	88	111	112	80	201	223
within the year 1762	3	11	14	6	5			
———— 1763	5	9	9	13	15			
———— 1764	8	9	7	13	9			
———— 1765	8	0	14	6	15			
———— 1766	7	14	4	8	6			
———— 1767	8	9	4	7	13			
———— 1768	10	4	10	10	9			
———— 1769	4	14	8	10	9			
———— 1770	6	4	8	6	10			
———— 1771	9	10	9	13	8			
Total from 1st Jan 1762, to 1st Jan. 1772	68	94	87	92	99	68	181	191
Carried over						233	571	615

Extract from the Register of Marriages, Baptisms, and Burials, of the Parish of Edlestown, from 1st Jan. 1742, to 1st Jan. 1792.

Entries made	Mar.	Baptisms.		Burials.		Total of		
		Males	Fem.	Males	Fem	Mar.	Bapt.	Bur.
Brought forward						233	571	615
within the year 1772	11	4	11	5	4			
—— 1773	4	9	12	11	12			
—— 1774	7	10	9	10	19			
—— 1775	3	8	8	7	10			
—— 1776	7	9	4	4	7			
—— 1777	5	10	6	13	3			
—— 1778	9	11	8	8	3			
—— 1779	6	6	5	10	9			
—— 1780	7	7	7	11	9			
—— 1781	7	10	8	10	8			
Total from 1st Jan. 1772, to 1st Jan. 1782	66	84	78	89	84	66	162	173
within the year 1782	7	11	10	10	11			
—— 1783	5	11	12	11	5			
—— 1784	4	7	8	9	8			
—— 1785	5	8	8	8	6			
—— 1786	3	10	7	8	6			
—— 1787	6	10	4	5	2			
—— 1788	7	9	5	6	8			
—— 1789	3	11	5	13	9			
—— 1790	3	6	5	4	4			
—— 1791	8	3	9	4	7			
Total from 1st Jan. 1782, to 1st Jan. 1792	51	86	73	78	65	51	159	143
Total number of entries for 50 years	-		-		-	350	892	931

The number of those buried here, who were not inhabitants of the parish, from 1st Jan. 1772, to 1st Jan. 1782, is 57 ⎫
And from 1st Jan. 1782, to ditto 1792 - - - - 46 ⎭ 103

Which make in all, during the last 20 years - - 1034

Cauſes of Depopulation.—The above extract cannot aſcertain the number of marriages which have actually taken place within the pariſh, as proclamation of banns is made when only one of the parties reſides in it; but the regiſter of baptiſms applies ſtrictly to the ſtate of the pariſh, from which it appears, that its population has decreaſed gradually ſince the year 1762, which may be accounted for from the following cauſes: Firſt, 14 cottages, formerly occupied by married ſervants, have been allowed to fall into diſrepair. 2*dly*, Twelve of the farmers are batchelors. 3*dly*, Two of thoſe who are married have no children. 4*thly*, Other two do not reſide. 5*thly*, Two are widowers. 6*thly*, Of the 13 heritors, 8 are non-reſident, in which number are included all the great landholders; and, laſtly, of the remaining 5 who are reſidents, only one is married, whoſe landed property does not exceed 17 l. Sterling *per annum.* It is therefore preſumable, that ſome of the above cauſes of the depopulation of this pariſh may not be permanent; and that at ſome future period, it may be reſtored nearly to the population of the year 1775.

Horſes and Black Cattle.—All the above mentioned ſtock of horſes, black cattle, and ſheep, are reared within the pariſh. The horſes are of the ſame breed with thoſe uſed for draught all over the ſouth of Scotland. A few horſes are occaſionally bred for ſale, and bring from 10 to 20 guineas, according to their age or figure. Many black cattle are ſold annually, ſome in milk, and ſome lean to graziers and feeders; but more generally, ſince the introduction of turnip huſbandry, they are ſold fat to the butcher in February and March. Many of them are ſold at the fair, which is held annually for that purpoſe, on the 25th of September. The average weight of cows bred here, is 30 ſtone, and of full aged bullocks,

locks, 40 ſtone; but ſome of both kinds conſiderably exceed theſe weights.

Sheep and Wool.—The ſheep are all of the Tweeddale breed. The ſtore-maſters ſell their draught ewes with lamb in April, at from 10 l. to 11 l. Sterling per ſcore. Fat lambs are ſold from the rſt of July to the 25th of September, and bring, at an average, 6 l. the ſcore. Wedder and ewe hogs are ſold in June, the former from 8 l. to 10 l. the ſcore, and the latter from 6 l. to 8 l. per ditto; but the beſt of the ewe hogs are reſerved as ſtock. Ewes, which have not had lambs, are ſold to the butcher in July and Auguſt, at from 11 s. to 13 s. each; and old ewes, which have nurſed lambs, bring from 9 l. to 10 l. the ſcore, in November and December. The *yeld* ewes weigh, at an average, 10 lib. Dutch, per quarter, and the old ewes 8 lib. per ditto, and carry from 3 lib. to 5 lib. tron of tallow. The ſheep are all ſmeared with tar and butter, in November. They are ſhorn in June and July; and the wool is ſold from 5 s. to 7 s. per ſtone tron, according to its quality and cleanneſs.

Church, School, and Poor.—The church is ſuppoſed to be above 200 years old. Some of the ſeats in it bear date 1600. The money ſtipend, including 100 merks for communion elements, is 66 l. 13 s. 4 d. Sterling, with 53 bolls 1 firlot 1 peck 2 lippies of meal, and 21 bolls 1 firlot 1 peck and 2 lippies of bear. Lord Elibank is patron.—The ſchoolmaſter's ſalary is 8 l. 6 s. 8 d. Sterling, beſides 16 s. 8 d. as ſeſſion-clerk, and 1 l. 6 s. 8 d. Sterling, as collector of the poor's rate, which was eſtabliſhed here in 1752.—The annual aſſeſſment on the heritors and tenants, by equal proportions, for 20 years paſt, has been only 5 l. Sterling. The heritors and the miniſter have a meeting on the firſt Monday of May, and

and another on the firſt Monday of November annually, for fixing the quantum of the poor's rates, admitting penſioners, and granting them annuities, according to their neceſſities. There have been no beggars in the pariſh ſince the eſtabliſh-ment of a poor's rate. The penſioners on the heritor's liſt are all houſe-holders, and receive from 2 l. to 3 l. Sterling *per annum.* They have a fund of 325 l. Sterling at intereſt, which is annually increaſing; and it is probable, that, a few years hence, it will not be neceſſary to continue the parochial aſſeſſment. The one half of the weekly collections in the church, after paying the ſalaries of the ſeſſion-clerk and kirk officer, is appropriated to the ſupply of the poor who are not inrolled.

Character and Antiquities.—The inhabitants of this pariſh are generally oeconomical, induſtrious, and regular in their attendance on the ordinances of religion.—There are no re-mains of antiquity in the pariſh, excepting the veſtiges of two circular encampments, vulgarly called *rings.*

PARISH of GLENHOLM,

(COUNTY OF PEEBLES.)

By the Rev. Mr BERNARD HALDAN.

Name, Situation, Surface, Soil, &c.

THIS parish seems to derive its name from the nature and form of the spot; the most considerable part of it being a glen or strath, through which a small river runs, having some flat grounds along the river side, which grounds are commonly called holms.—It is situated in an inland country, distant from Peebles, the county town, about 12 miles S. W.; in the presbytery of Biggar, and Synod of Lothian and Tweeddale. It was anciently a curacy, pertaining to the parsonage of Stobo; when presbytery was established, it was comprehended in the presbytery of Peebles, and afterwards was joined to that of Biggar. The post road to Dumfries runs through the lower part of this parish. On the road here, at the distance of 28 miles from Edinburgh, in the opening of a strath, about a mile in breadth, is a small river, called Holm's water, crossing the road, which comes down between two ridges of hilly ground. The ascent of the hilly ground on both sides the water is easy and gradual, for a mile above the church; on the sides

of

of the braes and flats along the water, there is arable ground, which produces very good grain; the higher parts are a mixture of green and heath; but the tops of the hills are generally heath. The ftrath becomes narrower, and terminates in a high hill, which feparates this parifh from that of Cultar. In the lower end of the parifh, where the river croffes the high road, the country opens to the north eaft on both fides. This parifh hath alfo a confiderable extent from north to fouth; it begins about ¾ of a mile north from Holm's water, and runs fouth along the Dumfries road upwards of 4 miles, 3 of which are upon the banks of Tweed. By far the greateft part is fheep pafture; the arable ground is generally of a loofe and fharp foil, of a moderate depth, and in the fpots that are beft cultivated, the crops are ftrong and very productive. As this country is high and hilly, the air is damp, impregnated with vapour; mifts frequently hover about the tops of the hills; the clouds are often intercepted in their courfe, by the hills at the head of this ftrath, and brought down, fo that we have more frequent rains than in the low country: hence it is often a wet day at the head of this water, when it is dry weather in the lower end of the parifh; but notwithftanding dampnefs is the general quality of the air in this place, there have been feafons when it has fuffered feverely through drought. Colds and rheumatifms feem to be the prevailing diftempers. There is a flate quarry, which continued for many years to be wrought, but was fome time ago given up. There is alfo a limeftone quarry, which provides the farmers in this neighbourhood with lime for improving their land.

Population.—The numbers, according to Dr Webfter's report, 40 or 50 years ago, were 392. The population appears to have been greater formerly than now, as the

grounds

grounds were then parcelled out in fmaller poffeffions; and this is generally the cafe throughout this country, efpecially with refpect to the fheep farms, as the management of a fheep farm does not require fuch a conftant fuperintendance as renders the refidence of the poffeffor to be neceffary; hence there are many inftances of one farmer holding feveral farms, and fome of them at a confiderable diftance from the place of his refidence. One confequence of this practice is, that in this way, a fheep farm will let at a higher rate than otherwife, as the fupport of this family is not to depend wholly on the profits of that one farm. At prefent there are 300 fouls : was the account to be taken in the fummer feafon, it would amount to fome more, by the additional number of maid fervants, hired for the purpofe of milking ewes, and an addition of herds. Of the above 300, 135 are males, 165 are females, 76 are under the age of 10, 72 are from 10 to 20. The annual average of births is 9. So far as can be collected from obfervation, the annual average of deaths is 3 or 4 at moft. The annual average of marriages is 2. There are 10 handicraftfmen, 42 male fervants, 24 female, 3 ftudents at the Univerfity of Edinburgh, 14 Seceders, 2 perfons who were born in Jamaica, 158 who were born in other parifhes in Scotland, 44 married men, including widowers, and 18 bachelors, reckoning them from 20 years and upwards. Marriages have produced 4 children at an average : none have been obliged to leave the parifh for want of employment. There are 55 inhabited houfes.

Agriculture, &c.—The land rent is at leaft L. 1000. There are about 5000 fheep, 150 black cattle, 60 horfes, 340 bolls of grain fown, 50 acres in fown grafs, 28 acres in turnip, a part of which are allotted for fheep to pafture on, and part to fatten cattle for the butcher, with 14 acres of potatoes. The parifh is able to fupply itfelf with provifions.

There

There is ſome grain yearly exported, but leſs than formerly, the grounds being more in paſture. About 50 ſcore of
ſheep are yearly exported for the butcher. The time of
ſowing is in the firſt good weather in March, and the ordinary time of reaping is in September. There was anciently a conſiderable extent of ſheep ground at the head of the
pariſh, which was common to moſt of the heritors, but was
ſome years ago divided. There are 12 ploughs, generally
of the Scotch kind; 36 carts. Beſides the reſiding heritors, who farm moſt of their lands, there are 6 tenants, and
3 or 4 very ſmall ones. There are 2 diſadvantages this
place labours under. From its ſituation, the crops are often
hurt by the early froſts in autumn. Sometimes the froſt
will touch the crop in the month of Auguſt. In that ſeaſon, the hoar froſt will ſometimes hover as a miſt over the
low damp grounds, and the crops in thoſe tracks are more
or leſs hurt. It has been obſerved, that in a field of potatoes, growing in a declivity, that on the ſame ridge of potatoes, in the lower end, the leaves would be blackened
with the froſt, while in the upper end, they have remained
in their proper verdure. The loſſes to which the crops
are liable through froſts, as well as the advanced price of
labour, are inducing ſome to turn their grounds more into
paſture. Another diſadvantage, is the great diſtance from
coal, which is no leſs than 14 or 15 miles, and the labour
of driving home fuel gives a great interruption to the operations of huſbandry.

Stipend, School, Poor.—The value of the living is about L. 70
a-year, including 2 chalders of meal, and 1 chalder of bear. The
glebe is about 6 acres, very good in quality; the inconvenience
ariſing from the ſmallneſs of the glebe, is in ſome meaſure
remedied, by the incumbent's renting a ſmall farm of arable
ground.

ground. The patron is the Duke of Queenſberry. There are 8 heritors, of whom 3 reſide.—The ſalary of the ſchoolmaſter is 100 merks Scots, which is the *minimum* appointed by law. Fees for teaching, are 1s. the quarter for reading, and 2s. 6d. for writing and arithmetic. The number of ſcholars has been between 20 and 30. The ſalary and emoluments do not amount to the value of a labouring ſervant's wages and board; and hence the preſent ſchoolmaſter, finding his income quite inſufficient for the ſupport of his family, has had recourſe to ſhopkeeping, and this has created a prejudice againſt the ſchool, and made ſeveral averſe from ſending their children to it, apprehending that the courſe of teaching will be much interrupted by the buſineſs of the ſhop, which has greatly reduced the number of ſcholars, whereby the education of the youth in this place ſuſtains a loſs that is to be regretted.—The number of the poor has been ſometimes 4, ſometimes 3, or 2, at preſent there is only one who is ſupplied regularly once a-week, and other two who receive occaſionally. The annual average of the collections is about L. 6, 10s. It is a loſs to the poor funds here, that the moſt opulent of the heritors do not reſide. And though indeed the law makes a proviſion by aſſeſſments, in the caſe of the collections becoming deficient; yet the reſidenters in the pariſh would reckon it a hardſhip to be equally involved in an aſſeſſment with the non-reſiding heritors, notwithſtanding they contribute by their weekly collections. At the ſame time it muſt be owned, to the honour of both reſiding and non-reſiding heritors, that in winter 1782 and 1783, when there was extraordinary occaſion of attending to the poor, they very generouſly contributed a ſum to purchaſe meal.

Prices, Wages, and Fuel.—The price of proviſions is nearly the ſame with that of Edinburgh market.—The wages of labourers in huſbandry are generally 8 d. a-day

and

and their meat, and 1 s. without their meat. The wages
of a male servant are L. 6 a-year. The wages of a female
servant are L. 1, 5 s. in the winter half year, and L. 2 in the
summer half year. The reason why the summer wages do
so much exceed the winter, is the labour of the ewes milking, which is reckoned a severe task, which nothing but
high wages can induce them to engage in; and part of that
wage having been by long use paid in wool, the rise in the
price of that commodity has contributed to raise their
wages.—With respect to fuel, about 40 years ago peat was
almost the only kind of fuel that was used in this parish,
of which there is to be got very good in kind, but at a
great distance, on the top of steep hills, and difficult of access; and hence the principal inhabitants have entirely
quitted the use of that species of fuel for many years past,
and find they can more easily provide themselves with
coals, and only such as are thirled to certain mills, (of
which there are 2 in the parish), do cast a few on those
heights for the purpose of drying their grain at the kiln,
which they are obliged to furnish by their thirlage. The
cottagers are provided with a kind of peat, of an inferior
quality, which are to be found in low damp grounds, near
their dwellings, and are such as require a part of coal to be
used along with them. The coals are brought from a great
distance; some from Douglas, which is reckoned best in
quality, and is about 14 or 15 miles distant; and some are
brought from Carlop, which is somewhat nearer. The
price is 1 s. 6 d. a load, the load being 12 stone Dutch
weight.

Antiquities.—There are in the parish remains or vestiges
of 6 old castles or towers, which were inhabited by the ancient proprietors of the grounds, and seem to have been
built

built in a ftrong manner, for defence againft the borderers, who made frequent incurfions in thofe days. There are veftiges of what appear like camps, in 3 feveral places; but there is no tradition concerning them, to fhow whether they have been encampments in time of actual war, or have belonged to a chain of watching pofts, to convey an alarm from one part of the country to another; for they are in lofty fituations.—There is a plain by the fide of Tweed, on which there are feveral mounts, apparently artificial; on one of them there was an appearance of feveral rifing fpots of ground. The proprietor had the curiofity to caufe one of them be digged, and there found the fkeleton of a man, with bracelets on his arms; the body was inclofed in a ftone building, with a ftone cover; and nigh him was an urn. Another was alfo opened in the fame fpot, where they found the remains of a body, greatly confumed.

Poft-office.—The conveyance of letters to this parifh, is by the poft-office at Bield, which is 7 miles diftance. It is reckoned that this poft-office is not placed in the moft favourable fituation for accommodating the greater part of thofe in this diftrict, who have frequent correfpondence by poft; and that there is a public houfe in this parifh, on the poft-road, to which the opening of the bag might be transferred with advantage, viz. Rachane Mill. At Bield there is only one gentleman's family, and the minifter; whereas there are 9 or 10 in this parifh and neighbourhood, whom a poft-office in the above mentioned place would accommodate. If it be not thought proper to remove the poft-office from Bield, there fhould be allowed a bag to open at Rachane Mill. The gentlemen in this parifh, and others in the neighbourhood, lately joined in a
                                                            petition

petition to the poſt-office for that purpoſe, repreſenting that the having this commodious conveyance, would encourage ſuch an additional number of letters ſent by poſt, as would more than defray the expence that would be incurred ; and that, if it ſhould not, they would bind themſelves to pay the extra expence. But their application was refuſed.

PARISH OF INNERLEITHEN,

(County of Tweeddale or Peebles, Synod of Lothian and Tweeddale, Presbytery of Peebles.)

By the Rev. John Walker, *Minister of Traquair.*

Name.

THE water of Leithen, which falls into Tweed near the middle of the parish, gives name to the whole, and pours nearly all the water of its extensive surface into this noble river. This is the last great accession Tweed receives before it leaves the district to which it gives name. The old parish of Innerleithen received, as an addition, all that part of the suppressed parish of Kailzie which lay north of the Tweed.

The parish bears a nearer resemblance to an equilateral triangle than any other regular figure; each side of which amounts to about 9¼ miles. The course of the Tweed, from the boundary of the parish of Peebles on the west, to

the

the boundary of Stow on the east, forming the southern side ; and from Tweed-bank at Spittlehope Burn-foot to Blakehope Scarr, the north-west ; and thence to Tweed-bank, below Thornylee, the north-east. It contains, according to Armstrong, who made a map of the county about 20 years ago, 22,270 acres, Scots measure. What proportion the arable land may bear to the whole surface is not easily determined. The land in tillage, *communibus annis*, is considerably under 1000 acres, of all kinds of crops. The general appearance of the parish is broken, rugged, and precipitous, rising from the brink of Tweed, and the course of the Leithen, to near 1000 feet, without, in some places, leaving space sufficient for the breadth of a road, unless assisted by art, which has been but sparingly bestowed to that purpose. Though, to a stranger passing along the highway from Peebles to Kelso, nothing seems to strike his eye but stones or rock, yet there the indefatigable sheep find a variety of succulent plants, of which the apparent more abundant pasture of the northern exposure seems to be deprived. The parish gradually rises from Tweed to its northern point, where it meets with the contiguous parishes of Eddleston and Temple, which bound it on the north ; Eddleston and Peebles on the west ; Heriot and Stow on the north-east. Tweed forms the southern boundary, and separates Innerleithen from Traquair. Windle-straw Law is the highest ground in the parish, and is in the direction of the north-east side. Near this mountain, the counties of Edinburgh, Peebles, and Selkirk meet. The whole exposure of the parish being chiefly southward, is productive of fine grass. The sheep-walks, though high and elevated, are, from this circumstance, much valued by the farmer as sure spring ground ; at which season, from the inconstancy and severity of the weather, the animal, already reduced

by

by the winter ftorms, fuffers moft. From the fame caufe, an early vegetation arifes, which is denied to the northern expofure, and, from its fucculence, furnifhes fuftenance to the dam to fupport her tender brood.

Soil, &c.—In the courfe of ages, the decompofing power of the atmofphere, and the decay of vegetable fubftances, have formed the greater part of the foil. The common whinftone, and other fchiftic rocks, have formed the bafis of the greater part of the fuperftratum, which contains a confiderable proportion of clay, as may be fuppofed, becaufe formed from that clafs of rocks. The fubfidence from the Tweed and Leithen has formed the leaft, but moft fertile foil. This being fubject to inundation, is not fo fully under the power of the farmer as the hanging plains above either. In thefe, fprings burfting through the fiffures of the rocks, known by the name of *blind fprings*, and large ftones fixed in the earth, were unfurmountable difficulties to the inexperienced farmer of former times: now, though agriculture is here only in its infancy, the active and intelligent know how to overcome both, with prodigious advantage to themfelves.

Climate, Difeafes, &c.—The climate, in fuch an extenfive hilly diftrict, muft be various; the air, however, is dry and healthy. The banks of the Tweed have an early harveft, both from the fharpnefs of the foil, and the genial expofure. The loweft part of the parifh was fubject to an annual vifit of the ague about 20 years ago; but whether from the drainage of the land, or from the better agriculture of that particular part of the parifh, it has for fome time paft entirely difappeared. No epidemical difeafe afflicts the inhabitants at prefent. Rheumatifm, caufed by bad and damp houfes, and low living, in general afflicts

the

the lower claſs as they advance in life. A houſe for the
accommodation of this uſeful order of men is, for the moſt
part, conſtructed of ſtone and feal, is reared on a ſudden,
and the occupant inhabits it as ſoon as conſtructed. Ill ſecured from the effects of the weather, and ſcantily provided
with fuel, which is both dear and ſcaree, the ſeeds of this
diſeaſe are rooted into the conſtitution, which the vigour of
youth may for a while brave; but, as old age advances, ſeldom fail to manifeſt themſelves in great virulence, and im-
pair the ſtrength of manhood by immature old age. Innoculation for the ſmall-pox gains ground, from experience of
its uſefulneſs, though contrary to the theory of religious
prejudice.

Fiſh, &c.—Aſſociations have been formed to preſerve
the ſalmon in Tweed during cloſe-time, which can produce
no good, ſo long as ſalmon are not permitted to come up
beyond a certain length before this ſeaſon commences. The
intereſt of no claſs of men here is concerned in their preſervation. To make it ſo, the proprietors below muſt yield
up a few of their good fiſh, to give the people above them
an experimental proof of the difference betwixt good and
bad ſalmon. The want of this makes them unable to diſtinguiſh the good from the bad; and all is fiſh that comes
in the net. The firſt ſtreams in Tweed in which the ſalmon depoſit their ſpawn are within a few miles of the
bounds of this pariſh. The people here can judge, by the
appearance of the fiſh, whether it will depoſit its ſpawn in
Tweed or its feeders. Tweed formerly produced a great
quantity of ſalmon; now they are ſeldom to be caught, except after cloſe-time. Trout are to be met with in great
quantity both in Tweed and Leithen. Pike are found in
the old run of the Leithen. Birds are of the ſame kinds
all over the county. Quadrupeds the ſame alſo.

Mineral

Mineral Spring.—The water which issues out of this spring is of the same nature with that of Harrowgate. In many disorders it has been productive of much relief to the afflicted. To fill this account of cures performed, or to lengthen it by giving an imperfect analysis of its water, would be improper. Two strong facts, which have come to hand, and are well attested, of its sanative effects, ought not to be passed over. They both relate to cases of inflamation in the eyes. The first is of a girl of 10 years of age, almost blind, from the neighbourhood of Hawick, who, by continuing to use the mineral for about a month, for two seasons, returned home the last season perfectly recovered. The other is of a young woman from Galashiels, with a similar complaint, who, by staying five weeks, returned home with the full use of her eyes. The first could discern nothing distinctly when she came the first season. The last could not distinguish any object at the distance of 50 yards. These cures, with many others, can be very well attested. In all disorders of the blood, its effects are highly beneficial, particularly in cutaneous eruptions. The want of accommodation prevents a greater concourse of people from being benefited by this salutary spring. So far as that is afforded, it is at one season of the year fully occupied. The short distance from Edinburgh should make it a desirable watering place.

Population.—The number of souls in the parish amounts to 560. The males, 289; the females, 271. Average of marriages for the last six years, 4½. Baptisms, 16.

			Males.	Females.
Under 10 years of age,	-		72	66
Under 20,	-	-	63	44
Under 30,	-		42	53
Under 40,	-	-	29	31
Under 50,	-	-	29	25
Under 60,	-	-	25	21
Under 70,	-	-	19	24
Under 80,	-	-	8	7
Under 90,	-	-	2	0
			289	271

Making in whole, 560.

Of thefe, 388 inhabit the village of Innerleithen, and 222 the reft of the parifh. Population in 1755, by Dr Webfter's account, was 559.

It may not be improper to remark, that the whole of this extenfive parifh is in the hands of fourteen occupants; and that of thefe, two only are fulfilling the firft commandment with promife. Such are the hopes of the rifing generation, amid the wafte of men by the ravages of lawlefs ambition. Where the cottager meets with a mafter who gives him a cow's grafs, he finds himfelf able to raife comfortably a family for the ufe of his country. Their wants are few, and eafily fatisfied with milk and potatoes. To the credit of many of the farmers here, they affift in rearing, by thefe accommodations, a race of ufeful labourers for the fucceeding generation. Though the farmers in general feem to have an averfion at matrimony, it muft be mentioned to their credit, that they liberally affift thofe under them who do fo. The greateft number of the inhabitants are employed in agriculture, and the care of their numerous flocks; a few mechanics and tradefmen are all

that

that can be excepted ; and theſe no more than what the ſupply of articles of the firſt neceſſity require.

The village of Innerleithen, from its ſituation, boaſts of
many advantages. Pleaſantly ſituated on Leithen-water,
near its junction with Tweed, in the heart of a country
whoſe ſtaple is wool, in which proviſions of all kinds are
plentiful, it ſeemed formed by nature for a ſite of woollen
manufacture. What muſt have occurred to every one
ſince the value of manufactures were known in this country, was left to be accompliſhed by Alexander Brodie, Eſq;
of Carey-ſtreet, London. Some few years ago he erected
a large workhouſe, at conſiderable expence, from the patriotic purpoſe of promoting a ſpirit of induſtry in the vicinity
of the place which gave him birth. Upwards of L. 3000
Sterling were expended on the works and machinery,
which is of the beſt conſtruction ; but from cauſes which the
author does not chooſe to dwell on, the manufacture has
not gone on with that ſucceſs, to the advantage of the gentleman who erected it, that its firſt beginning promiſed.
The fault neither lay with him nor the conductor of the
work. Such as it is, it returns, on the whole, very well.
An infant manufacture, in a country *truly* paſtoral, has many
diſadvantages. The whole operations of teazing and carding are performed by water. The houſe conſiſts of five
floors ; the firſt and ſecond of which are occupied by the
operations performed by water, and which, had circumſtances been favourable, would have by this time been farther extended; ſpinning jeanies, looms, &c. of various con-
ſtructions, occupy the two next. The higheſt is a ſtore-
room for the raw material. From 27 to 80 hands are employed within doors, and as many at leaſt without the manufactory. Children from ſeven years of age are employed
in the operations of teazing and carding, and earn 2 s. 6 s. *per*
week. The beſt ſpinners can make 18 s. *per* week. The
                                                    beſt

beſt weavers as much. Theſe two laſt, in general, work by the piece. The dyers have a fixed weekly rate, which differs according to their qualifications. In the courſe of the firſt year after the work was begun, cloth was manufactured to the amount of L. 1200 Sterling, and has gradually increaſed.

The whole of Mr Brodie's attention as a uſeful member of ſociety is by no means direc̈ted to this one object. His extenſive operations in Shropſhire and London are too generally known to need particular mention. To promote a ſpirit of induſtry in this diſtrict, he engaged in this manufacture, and gave the direction of it to his nephew, who, though not at firſt acquainted with the trade in wool, by application, ſoon made himſelf maſter of the buſineſs.

Sheep, Horſes, and Cattle.—Upwards of 15,000 ſheep are kept, in general of the black-faced kind, as a breeding ſtock. There are 90 horſes, and about 200 head of black cattle. Few of the ſtoremaſters have thought of changing their ſtock of ewes and rams entirely, but they have of late purchaſed ſome of each, particularly the rams, ſince the price of wool has increaſed ſo conſiderably.

The ſheep paſtures and arable grounds are occupied by the ſame perſon, as is the caſe over all this diſtrict. It is not how many acres of arable, but how many ſcore of ſheep does the farm hold, which fixes the rent.

Stipend, Church.—The ſtipend is, *communibus annis,* about L. 110. The Duke of Queenſberry is patron. The glebe contains, for the ſite of manſe and garden ground, and crop and paſture, about 10 acres and a half. It has been aſked, What proportion of ground ought a miniſter to poſſeſs as glebe, that the occupancy may become profitable ? The anſwer muſt depend on ſuch a variety of circumſtances, that it cannot be of general application. If it is aſked, Will the
miniſter

minifter of Innerleithen have a profitable occupancy? No.
The land he poffeffes will not enable him to employ his
man and horfes half the time they ought to be employed.
Ground cannot be laboured without two horfes. Two he
muft keep, for the hiring of his ploughing he cannot obtain.
One horfe he ought to keep for parifh duty; and when this
requires one horfe, the other is thrown idle as to the tilling
the ground, and many other farming purpofes. Should he,
Apoftle like, abjure the ufe of horfes for his own accommodation, he may then drive in his fuel, and have his
little farm cultivated in proper feafon; but every year he
muft go to market for fodder to maintain his horfes; and
this the late incumbent confidered as an average expence
of L. 5 *per annum*; which, added to the wages and maintenance of a ploughman, renders the glebe a lofs rather than
profit to any incumbent. Without a cow, no family can
be comfortable in the country; the glebe, as yielding this
benefit, is, with all its pecuniary difadvantages, highly ufeful. Could the minifter of Innerleithen find people to hire,
for driving his coals and tilling his land, and be, by thefe
means, under no neceffity of keeping a man-fervant and a
pair of horfes, he might then not be under any difficulty of
providing fodder for two cows, and a horfe for parifh duty,
and by that means his glebe would turn out profitable.
As circumftances ftand, this cannot be obtained. Accommodation, therefore, and not profit, is all that can be looked
for. Twenty acres of farm, at a reafonable rent, would
render the clergyman's fituation comfortable, and the poffeffion of the glebe profitable. Such is the outline of an
anfwer to the queftion, as it relates to this parifh. The
writer of this report fpeaks not from theoretical fpeculation,
but from dear bought experience; and what is true in the
one cafe is fully applicable in the other. Both manfe and
church are in a good ftate of repair. The manfe was built

for

for the laſt incumbent; the church a few years ago, and, for
its ſize, is one of the neateſt country churches in the county.

The poor are ſupported by a poors-rate, one half paid
by the heritors, the other by the tenants. The rate has an
additional increaſe every year, which is a general obſervation made from every pariſh where this mode of proviſion
has been recurred unto. The ſeſſion have ſome funds in
their hands, which they diſtribute to the moſt indigent of
thoſe who receive the legal proviſion, in caſes of particular
diſtreſs. The late incumbent obtained from the Earl of
Traquair, when he fitted up the mineral well, the right of
diſpoſing of it, ſeaſon by ſeaſon, to ſome pauper, who, by
opening and ſhutting it to thoſe who reſorted to it, might
be entitled to any pecuniary gratuity they pleaſed to confer.
By the regulations, it was to be open two hours every
morning, and two every evening, Sunday evening excepted.
Mr Brodie, whoſe generoſity is only equalled by his im-
partiality, gives L. 5, 5 s. every year, to be diſtributed by
the clergyman to poor houſeholders. As ſoon as this gentleman had a permanent intereſt in the pariſh, he began to
feel for the wants of the indigent, and though not obliged
by law to provide for the poor, he made a law for himſelf,
by which he has contributed more to the needy, than the
moſt extenſive proprietor is bound to by law. This with
the circulation of money produced by thoſe employed in
the manufactory, many of whom are old people and children, who could have earned little or nothing, has benefited
the poor of the village very much.

Morals.—Whether the eaſier acquiſition of money has
had a tendency to improve the morals of the lower claſs,
may be eaſily determined by the experience of every body.
They are ſtill ſound in their religious principles, and pique
themſelves on being ſo. Religion and morality, or rather
that

that branch of it, fobriety, have long been at odds in this
diſtrict. Example goes beyond precept. The lower claſs
will, if poſſible, imitate their betters. What proportion
the Diſſenters may bear to thoſe who are of the Eſtabliſhed
Church is beyond the power of man to determine. The
various denominations among us uſe times of vacancy, if
poſſible, to carry off as many as they can ; and diſguſt, or
diſappointment, or any thing, in ſhort, may, with a little
ſophiſtry, become the pretext. Theſe cauſes have already
begun to operate, and what effects they ſhall produce time
alone can unfold.

School.—The average number of ſcholars may be betwixt
30 and 35. The greateſt number are in ſpring. The
ſchoolmaſter teaches Latin, Engliſh, writing, and arithmetic.
His emoluments of office are L. 100 Scots.

Mr Brodie, who equally regards, in his extenſive philanthropy, the ſuſtenance of the body and the improvement of
the mind, gives him L. 5, 5 s. for educating poor children.
His office of ſeſſion-clerk may yield L. 1. He has likewiſe
a free houſe and garden. His whole emoluments can hardly exceed L. 20 *per annum*. He has contrived to rear a
family upon this ſlender income. If emolument of office is
neceſſary to promote its uſefulneſs, this moſt important of
all employments for the good of ſociety, a country ſchoolmaſter, will ſoon be no more, unleſs ſome means are fallen
upon to render it more lucrative and reſpectable.

Antiquities.—Tower houſes are met with in a ruinous
condition at the mouth of every defile through this extenſive pariſh. Tradition is ſilent, except in two or three inſtances at moſt, by whom they were occupied. If the ſame
ſcenes of iniquity were practiſed in them all that the records
of the preſbytery of Peebles attaches to one of them, they
have

have defervedly become the habitation of owls. A ftrong fortification was erected, in times of hoftility, on a rifing ground immediately adjoining to the village of Innerleithen. Veftiges of the foffum are ftill difcernible on the outfide of the third line of circumvallation. Within the third of thefe lines there is a fpace of rather more than an Englifh acre, An immenfe quantity of ftones have been collected to form thefe lines. No cement feems to have been employed. The loofe ftones were, however, built with confiderable care. By whom conftructed, at what time, againft whom, are queries to be anfwered by conjecture only.

Names of Places.—Thefe are, in general, borrowed from the dialect of the language at prefent fpoken; fome from their prefent or former proprietors. Horfbrugh Caftle, Tower, and lands, derived their name from the anceftors of Horfbrugh of that ilk, a confiderable proprietor at prefent in the parifh. The origin of the name the writer learned, in the courfe of this inveftigation, to have arifen from the following circumftance :—During the time that Peebles was a hunting refidence to the Kings of Scotland, the King and his nobles were engaged in the fport of hawking. The hawk flew acrofs the Tweed after his prey. The river happened to be in flood; the King and the nobles could not follow. The anceftor of the family, of the name of either Hunter or Hamilton, was, at the time, ploughing on the lands, which afterwards, by royal grant, became his own ; acquainted with the river, whofe banks he cultivated, he loofed his plough, and with one of his horfes came acrofs the ftream, and reftored the hawk and his prey to the royal hunter ; for which meritorious fervice the King endowed him with all the lands within view of his plough north of Tweed. As he was croffing the river, either the King, or one of his attendants, cried out, *Horfe bruik weel*, and thence

the

the lands, and their owner, were called Horsebruik; which, in the course of time, have been changed into Horsburgh. *Valeat quod valere possit.*—The present proprietor has, independent of royal grant, a very just title to the lands on which he resides. They came into the family by an intermarriage with the name of Tait; but the present occupant, by judicious improvement, has raised their value, from scarcely L. 50 of annual income, to be worth L. 300 *per annum.* The only substantial improvement in planting and inclosing, in the whole parish, has been effected by him; and whilst he has given beauty to his vicinity, he has added considerably to his annual income. In a country like ours, where so much still remains to be done, every attempt to improve the face of the country merits its due praise, and ought not to be withheld.

Road up Leithen.—In summer 1794, this road, formed by subscription, and at present kept in repair by the same means, with the addition of the money for the commutation for statute labour, was begun to be used for the purposes of driving lime and coal. During the course of that summer upwards of 3000 bolls of lime, Linlithgow measure, and a considerable quantity of coal, were drove on it. This line of communications shortens the distance from coal and lime, from 12 to 14 miles. Both coal and lime are of better quality, and a considerable saving in toll-bar duty is obtained. The effects of opening this communication have already appeared highly beneficial to those who at first subscribed, and they are, as far as they are individually concerned, ready to enter into a second subscription, to carry the measure, as far as their ability allows, into complete effect. The narrow policy of others, who have not subscribed, and who have taken advantage of this communication, prevents them from subscribing at all. A public good

may

may by thefe means fall to nought, and the improvement of
this highly improvable diftrict be retarded. The accom-
plifhing this purpofe is worthy the patriotic fpirit of the
Honourable Prefident of the Board of Agriculture. In his
extenfive communications with the members of that Honourable Board, he may open the eyes of fome of them to
their own advantage, and may point out to the nation in
general the propriety of adopting this line of intercourfe
betwixt Carlifle and Edinburgh.

Advantages and Difadvantages.—In the account already
given, the advantages of this parifh have already been
pretty fully detailed. A pure air, a fertile foil, abundant
paftures, the means of inftruction afforded to all, even the
indigent, plenty of labour for the induftrious, a legal provifion provided for the needy, are a fhort recapitulation of
thefe. The difadvantages are, in fome refpects, likewife
hinted at. The greateft of thefe is, the diftance from fuel.
Peats are not to be obtained for general ufe. Furze was
formerly the dependence of the lower clafs for their winter fire ; but the induftry of a farmer, who began his occupancy at Whitfunday laft, has already gone far to remove
this fupply, and will foon make an abfolute fcarcity. The
lands he poffeffes were formerly rented at L. 84 Sterling
yearly ; now they are let in leafe for 19 years at L. 350
Sterling *per ann*. During the currency of the former leafe,
the lands might be fuffered to bear furze, and yet the rent
might have been paid. As things now ftand, he muft try
fome more productive mode of occupancy, elfe the price of
labour and rent cannot be paid ; the laft of which is quadruple what it was, and the firft double, in the courfe of
thefe laft fix years. The completing the road up Leithen
would bring the village of Innerleithen into a certainty of
having coals at all feafons of the year. An attention to
fobriety

sobriety would furnish them with the means of providing themselves with fuel of the best and cheapest kind. Comfortable at home, they would not need to seek enjoyment abroad. Contented with their condition, they would not follow those given to change. These reflections by no means are intended for general application. Under all the disadvantages already enumerated, the generality enjoy, in a confiderable degree, the advantages of civilised society. They love their country, are attached to its conftitution, and rejoice in the fecurity the laws afford. If any thing is awanting to meliorate their condition, it is reducing their religious knowledge to practice.

Real and Valued Rent.—As far as can be conjectured, the real rent is upwards of L. 3000 Sterling : The valued rent is L. 6639 : 1 : 2.

PARISH of KILBUCHO,

(COUNTY OF PEEBLES.)

By the Rev. Mr WILLIAM PORTEOUS.

Name, Situation, Soil, &c.

KILBUCHO is said to be derived from the Gaelic, and to signify the Cell of Bucho, but of whom nothing is known. The supposition of Bucho, being a corruption of Bede, would correspond with a variety of traditionary reports, concerning that saint; as it is said that a number of monks, of his order, settled here, and gave name to the church, &c. There is likewise an excellent well of water, called St Bede's. There are some beautiful banks said to have been raised by the monks. The parish is about 4½ miles from E. to W. and 3 from S. to N. Although, on the west, it is scarcely more than 1 mile from Clyde, and about thrice that distance, on the east, from Tweed, yet it belongs to Tweeddale. It is bounded by Culter on the W.; by Biggar and Skirling, on the N.; Broughton, on the E.; and Glenholm, on the S. Kilbucho is somewhat remarkable for 2 parallel ridges of hills, covered with heath and grass, stretching from W. to E.; and for 2 vallies, on the N. of each chain of hills.

The

The heath on the hills is preferved by frequently burning it; a tender growth fucceeds, which is delicious and excellent pafture for fheep. Carden, part of which is in the S. W. of this parifh, is about 1400 feet above the level of the Tweed. The parifh contains between 4000 and 5000 acres. The land is partly arable, and partly pafture ground. The foil is neither very good nor bad. There are 19 ploughs of land, and pafture for 200 fcore of fheep. The rental is little above L. 1000 Sterling a-year.

Population, &c.—According to Dr Webfter's returns, the numbers were 279. At prefent, the whole amount is 362. Of whom 187 are males, and 175 females. There are under 10, 105; from 10 to 20, 75; from 20 to 30, 50; from 30 to 40, 48; from 40 to 50, 37; from 50 to 60, 24; from 60 to 70, 13; from 70 to 80, 6; from 80 to 90, 4; from 90 to 100, 1 vigorous old man. For 2 years paft, the births have been 21, and the burials 4. At an average, there are 62 houfes, and 5 perfons to a family. There are about 8 or 10 day-labourers. The tenants generally prefer fervants hired for a year or half year. Day-labourers receive about 8 d. in fummer and 6 d. in winter. Men fervants, when married, get about L. 5 a-year, with their victuals, and a houfe; and L. 6, if unmarried. Thofe who are unmarried are ufually preferred.

Stipend, School, &c.—The ftipend is L. 43 : 7 : 4, and 48 bolls of victual, 2 parts oat-meal, and 1 part bear, with the ufual fervitude of mofs, &c. Captain William Dickfon is patron. There are 3 heritors.—The fchoolmafter's falary is L. 100 Scots, including the intereft of fome mortified money. The fees for teaching Englifh are 1 s. the quarter; for Englifh and writing, 1 s. 3 d.; and for arithmetic,

metic, 1 s. 6 d. As ſeſſion-clerk, he gets 6 s.; and 1 s. for every proclamation of banns.

Miſcellaneous Obſervations.—This diſtrict is at a great diſtance from coal. A good deal of peat is uſed for fuel. Attempts have been made to find coal in the pariſh, but have not as yet been ſucceſsful, it is thought, for want of perſeverance.—There are ſeveral incloſures, and leſs ground in tillage than in former times. The farmers rear and ſell a conſiderable number of ſheep. A conſiderable quantity of potatoes and turnip is raiſed here. Several good farm-houſes have been lately erected.—There is a tumulus in the N. E. ſide of the pariſh, another in the pariſh of Coulter, and a third in the pariſh of Lamington, all in a line weſtward, and about the diſtance of 3 miles from one another. They might ſerve as ſignals, by means of torches, along an extended plain, when hoſtilities ſubſiſted between England and Scotland. The Engliſh lay encamped on the hill of Corſcrine, in this pariſh, before the battle of Biggar.

PARISH OF KIRKURD.

(County and Presbytery of Peebles.—Synod of Lothian and Tweeddale.)

By the Reverend Mr DAVID ANDERSON.

———————

Name, Extent, &c.

THE termination *urd* is from the Celtic language, and
signifies a quarter or fourth part; hence the following
description of places at each extremity of the parish, Kirkurd,
Ladyurd, Netherurd, and Lochurd. The length of the parish, from E. to W. is $5\frac{1}{4}$ English miles; and its breadth,
from N. to S. from 3 to 4. The parish, in general, presents
a surface finely diversified; and, what is remarkable in a hilly
country, such as Tweeddale generally is, the low or arable
land bears almost an equal proportion, in point of extent, to
the high or sheep grounds. The parish, from actual survey,
contains 6620 acres. English measure. The soil is of different kinds. Towards the small river Tarth, it is mostly
loam; in one large farm we meet with clay; but the prevailing soil is gravelish. The light soil is preferable for
crops, as the parish lies in general high, being upwards of
600 feet above the level of the sea. Though the air is sharp,
it is pure and healthful. Distempers are far from being frequent. Rheumatism is the most prevalent. This is, in a
great measure, owing to the little attention that is paid to

warm

warm and dry clothing, and to the cold and uncomfortable houses of the poorer classes. Though there are no remarkable instances of longevity, except one man who died about 10 years ago, whose age was 92, (he was born in the parish, and resided in it all his life), yet the inhabitants arrive, in general, to a good age.

Rivers and Hills.—The Tarth runs along the north end of the parish, and divides it from Linton and Newlands. It abounds with a trout of a superior size and flavour from what is caught in the neighbouring rivers, owing perhaps to the stillness with which the river flows, and the abundant provision to be met with in its numerous pools. A few large trout or small salmon come up this stream from the Tweed after a flood ; but, as they only appear in spawning time, they are unwholesome food.

The highest hill is Hell's Cleugh, on the summit of which is a small cairn, called the *Pyked stane*, the boundary of three parishes, viz. Stobo, Broughton, and Kirkurd. From this cairn is a view of the country beyond the Forth, and a chain of mountains, from the east part of Fife, as far as Dunbartonshire. South of the Forth, the view extends as far east as North Berwick ; likewise to the Eildon Hills near Melrose, and Cheviot Hills in Northumberland. The height of this hill above the level of the sea was found by Captain Armstrong, who made a survey of the county, to be 2100 feet.

Proprietors.—There are four heritors, of whom only one resides at present in the parish. Mr Carmichael of Skirling, and Mr Lawson of Cairnmuir, have their principal seats here. The mansion-house of Kirkurd is a modern building, with an extensive policy. In the gardens are a green-house, an ice-house, and 3 small hot-houses. This place was vastly
beautified

beautified and improved by the late worthy proprietor, John Earl of Hyndford, who left Kirkurd, and other valuable eſtates, to his grandnephew John Carmichael of Skirling. Mr Lawſon has lately built at New Cairnmuir, or Netherurd, a large and elegant houſe. Around it are ſeveral incloſures and plantations of value.

Statiſtical Table.

Ploughs	- -	22	Old houſes pulled down,	
Carts	- - -	50	ditto - -	11
Horſes young and old		70	Married perſons -	86
Cows and young cattle		200	Unmarried men above 20	28
Sheep	- -	2000	———— women ditto	48
Valued rent, Scotch			Widowers - -	5
	L. 1108 : 15 : 4		Widows - -	10
Real rent, Sterling, about	- - L. 850		Of the eſtabliſhed Church - -	250
Farms above 50 l. each		3	Burgher Seceders -	23
——— under 50 l.	-	10	Antiburgher ditto -	11
Population in 1755	-	310	Relief ditto -	3
———— in 1792	-	288	Epiſcopalians -	1
Males	- -	131	Clergyman -	1
Females	- -	157	Merchant -	1
Under 10	- -	55	Schoolmaſter -	1
Between 10 and 20	-	56	Innkeeper -	1
———— 20 and 50	-	113	Smiths - -	3
———— 50 and 70	-	58	Carpenters - -	3
———— 70 and 80	-	6	Weavers and apprentices	4
Families	-	65	Shoemakers and ditto -	2
Houſes uninhabited	-	6	Taylors and ditto -	4
Houſes built within 10 years preceding 1792		12	Gardeners and ditto -	3
			Millers - -	2

Overſeer

Overseer	-	-	1	Marriages, ditto - 33
Male servants	-	44		Buried, ditto, in the pa-
Female ditto	-	-	38	rish - - - 34
Day-labourers	-	-	9	Buried, ditto, from other
Student	-	-	1	parishes - - 32

Baptisms for 10 years,
    from 1783 to 1792   51

Agriculture, &c.—About 480 acres are kept in tillage.
The common mode of farming in the croft land, (which receives all the house-dung of the farms), is to have a third
part under pease, potatoes, and turnips, as cleaning and meliorating crops; which third, the succeeding year (if not dúng-
ed with the cleaning crops) is dunged for bear, and next
year is sown with oats. Clover, and, in a great measure,
turnips, are excluded from the rotation, from the want of
inclosures, and the difficulty of defending them from the
sheep in winter. There may be about 240 acres of croft
managed in this way, viz. 80 in pease, potatoes, turnips, and
lint, 80 in bear, and 80 in oats, in a year. The remaining
240 acres under tillage are outfield, and are manured by the
cattle folded at night in summer, to keep them from the
growing corns The folds are inclosures made of sod, at
the expence of about 1½ d. or 2 d the running rood of 6
yards, at 4½ feet in height. The leys intended to be brought
into tillage are inclosed in this manner early in the spring;
the sheep and black cattle are kept in distinct folds; and 10
score of sheep may dung in this way about 3 acres in a season. When the corns are got off the fields in harvest, the
folds are levelled, and the ground ploughed. Three crops of
oats are, in general, taken successively after folding; but,
when the folded land is also limed on the sward, 5 crops are
sometimes taken. The land is then left to collect sward as
                                                         it

it may. This is the general defcription of the treatment of the land in tillage; but there are feveral exceptions, where a better fyftem is introduced; and the Norfolk fyftem of a rotation of four, feems to be approved of, where there is opportunity to carry it into practice. In a few inftances, the dairy farming has been introduced as the chief article of profit.

The Scotch plough is generally ufed, with two ftrong horfes, except in 4 inftances with four. Small's plough has likewife been introduced. The horfes, young and old, in this parifh, will amount to about 70. A few are reared for the market, and fold when young; but the generality is for private ufe, and to fupply the wafte of the old. Thirty head of black cattle, at an average of 4 l. each, may be fold yearly. The milch cows are, at an average, from 16 to 28 ftones weight. They produce from 4 to 10 Scotch pints of milk *per* day, a few 16 or 18. The fheep are of the common Scotch breed. The number that can be fpared is fold at different periods. In April, when big with young, at 10 l. or 11 l. *per* fcore; in September, to the butcher, or for further feeding, about 7 l. *per* fcore. The lambs are fold in July from 2 l. 10 s. to 4 l. *per* fcore. What remains after thefe different *drawings*, (as they are termed), are kept for ftock; they are all laid with butter or oil, and tar, about Martinmas. The wool of late years has been rapidly rifing in value. It was fold laft year, after being wafhed, at 6 s. 4 d. and 6 s. 6 d. *per* ftone; 7 or 8 fleeces of the wafhed wool generally go to the ftone.

Between 500 and 600 acres of land are inclofed, a confiderable part of which is well fheltered with trees, and fufficiently watered. This land, on an average, may be worth 16 s. *per* acre. About 150 of thefe acres, divided into parks of different fizes, command, by grazing, 160 l. *per annum.*

The

The lands are inclosed by hedge and ditch. The hedges and ditches are frequently in double rows, at the distance of a few feet from each other.

There are many valuable plantations both of the different kinds of hard wood, and the various species of fir. Some of these are arrived at their full growth, and young trees are gradually coming up to supply the waste of the old. The number of acres planted will amount to upwards of 200. There are no natural woods in the parish *.

Services, &c.—A few services are still performed by the tenants, such as driving of coals, casting, winnowing, and driving peats home. There are a considerable number, too, of kain hens paid. There is a public-house in the parish for the accommodation of travellers. It has no bad effect on the morals of the people, who are, in general, a set of sober and industrious men. Two great roads pass through this parish, the one from Edinburgh to Moffat, the other, lately made, from Peebles to Glasgow. They are upheld by road-makers, and are kept in tolerable repair. The statute labour

was

* In consequence of manufactures established in this, and particularly in the neighbouring county, there is a great demand for work people. Servants have of course become rather scarce in this part of the country. The wages are rising every year. A good ploughman earns 6 guineas, or upwards, and female servants from 3 l. to 4 l. *per annum*, with their victuals. There is no market here for provisions. The butcher meat is brought from Peebles, Biggar, or Edinburgh. Butter is sold, in general, at 8 d. *per* lib. ; ewe milk cheese at 6 s. 6 d. cow milk at 4 s. *per* stone ; eggs in summer, 4 d. in winter, 6 d. *per* dozen ; chickens 8 d. a pair ; hens 1 s. ducks 10 d. a piece. Day labourers earn *per* day, in winter, 6 d. in summer 8 d. with their victuals. Ditches, casting, and operations of that kind, are generally done by the piece, from 9 d. to 1 s. the running rood of 6 yards. Piece work is preferred by labourers. Carpenters wages are 1 s. a day, masons 1 s. 4 d. taylors 8 d.

was converted fome years ago by act of Parliament. The bridges are kept in excellent order.

Ecclefiaftical State.—The church was rebuilt in 1766, when it was removed about half a mile weftward from its former fituation in Kirkurd policy. Around it there is a piece of ground appropriated for burying; but, though this burial-ground has been now opened for upwards of 20 years, the old church-yard, for various reafons, is ftill very much ufed. The ftipend, with the addition of a manfe, and a glebe of 19 acres, will amount to upwards of 80 l. Sterling. The manfe, offices, and glebe, which were formerly at a confiderable diftance from both kirks, are now in the neighbourhood of the new. The manfe and offices were all new built in 1788. The greateft part of the new glebe (which was excambed for the old) has been inclofed by the minifter, at his own expence, with hedge and ditch. John Carmichael, Efq; of Skirling is patron.

Poor.—As there are no rates, the poor are fupported from the weekly collections in the church, by dues at proclamations for marriage, by dues for mort-cloths, and the intereft of a capital of 140 l. at 5 *per cent.*

Average of the annual expences of fupporting the Poor.

	No. of Poor.	Expence.
For 5 years preceding 1758,	$6\frac{2}{3}$	L. 5 4 $0\frac{4}{3}$
—————————— 1778,	$10\frac{1}{3}$	10 9 $6\frac{1}{3}$
For 10 years preceding 1792,	$6\frac{6}{10}$	9 7 $8\frac{7}{10}$

In 1782, the whole crop of oats in the parifh was froft bitten. It was not got in before the month of December. The meal was exceedingly bad, and fold at 2 l. 5 s. *per* load.

The

The farmers sustained great losses, after all the deductions that was made of their rents by the lairds. They bought the whole of their seed-oats next spring from Lothian and Roxburghshire. One heritor commissioned a considerable quantity of oats from Essex, sowed part of them himself, and distributed part among his tenants. The kirk-session bought several loads of oat-meal, and sold it to cottars and house-holders at 1 s. the peck. This, with the white beans brought from Leith, gave great relief. They have resolved this year (1792) to lay up a few loads of oat and bear meal, and sell it out at a reduced price, in case these articles should rise to an extravagant rate.

A society was established in this parish 6 years ago, named *the Kirkurd Friendly Society*, in order to raise a fund for the relief of distressed members. Each member pays 2 s. at entry, and 4 s. 4 d. a year, and continues 3 years before he receives any benefit; at the end of which time, if he is unable to work, is entitled to 2 s. *per* week. The capital is now 80 l. As the fund increases, they intend to make a small provision for their widows. For the two last years, the clergy have countenanced this society, by giving a sermon at the annual meeting. The collection at that time is for behoof of the Society.

School.—The schoolmaster's salary is 8 l. 6 s. 8 d. with a house and garden. The school and schoolmaster's house were all new built, with slated roofs, in 1773. The number of scholars, at an average, is about 20. The school wages are, for reading, 1 s. *per* quarter; for writing, 1 s. 6 d; for arithmetic, 2 s. The schoolmaster is also session-clerk and precentor, whose salary is 1 l. *per annum*, besides perquisites, for proclamations of marriages, recording of baptisms, and writing

ting testimonials, amounting to about 10 s. yearly at an average.

Miscellaneous Observations.—There is a copious sulphureous spring near Kirkurd-house. A chemical analysis was made of it some years ago by Dr Black of Edinburgh, by which it was found to be stronger than the sulphureous water at Moffat, but weaker than that at Harrogate. It has been used of late with success in several distempers. Coal, peat, and turf, are all used here for fuel. In gentlemens families, coals are always burnt; they are situated at 8 or 9 miles distance. Peats, to a great extent and depth, and of a very superior quality, are found in one farm in this parish; they are not cast. The tenants have a privilege of casting peats in different mosses in the parish of Linton, and consequently avail themselves of that privilege.

Until 1752, the large estate of Kirkurd was the resident property of Geddes of Rachan for 1100 years, while Rachan, from whence the title was taken, is reported to have been in the possession of the Geddes's for 1300 years. James Geddes of Rachan was born in this parish in 1710, was educated for, and practised several years at, the bar, but died of a consumption before he arrived at the age of 40. He published an Essay on the Composition and Manner of Writing of the Ancients, and left behind him several other tracts *.

Among

---

* In the parks of Kirkurd are two small mounts, called the *Castle* and *Law*. They are surrounded with a dike of an irregular form. Mr Gordon, in his Itinerary, thinks them artificial, but does not form any conjecture as to their use. There is to the east of these, a circular fortification on an eminence near Ladyurd, called the *Rings*, and another to the west, on the farm of Lochurd, called the *Chesters*; hence they are supposed to have been a military erection; and a place called *Camorigend*, a mile south to the last of these, farther confirms this idea.

More

Among the advantages formerly mentioned which this parish enjoys, may be added its vicinity to lime; but, notwithstanding of the acknowledged advantages arising from lime to land, the farmers here have not generally (as yet) availed themselves of it. One disadvantage which this place labours under, (and which was specified above), is the exaction of services; but there is another grievance under which the farmers groan, and which calls loudly for redress, and that is the payment of multure. The tenants are thirled to the mills, and pay a high multure, which is a great bar to improvement. By thirlage a forced employment is given to mills, for which there would be no demand, if things were left to their natural course. Though the generality of the country around is fitter for sheep pasture than tillage, yet no less than four corn-mills are found on the Water of Tarth, all in the space of about a mile and a half, two of which are situated within this parish.

More than 30 years ago, there was found in the Mount-hill a clay urn full of bones, which was surrounded with four broad stones, and covered with a stone on the top. There was lately found at the bottom of the same hill, a stone coffin, about $4\frac{1}{2}$ feet long, $2\frac{1}{2}$ feet wide, and $2\frac{1}{2}$ feet deep. Its bottom was gravel, the sides built of several stones, and the cover one entire stone. The body was not lying at full length, as, by the size of the bones, it appeared to have been about 6 feet long. The bones appeared entire when first discovered; but, upon being exposed to the air, and lifted up by the hand, they crumbled to dust. There was found among the bones three flint stones, one resembling a halbert, another of a circular form, and the third cylindrical. The first is supposed to be the antient weapon called the *stone celt*, the other were two kinds of warlike instruments. There was also discovered a small ring. This is a Druidical amulet; and it was an indication that a person of rank was here interred.

Hairstanes, so named, perhaps, from a few erect stones arranged circularly, is said to have been a place for religious worship. In the immediate neighbourhood is the Kirkdean and Temple lands.

PARISH OF LINTON.

By the Rev. Mr FINDLATER, *Minister of Newlands, former-ly of Linton.*

Name, Situation, and Extent.

THE origin of the name is uncertain. The river of Lyne, which rifes at the Cauldſtane Slaup, (a paſs over the Pentlands from Tweeddale to Weſt Lothian) runs through this pariſh, and probably Linton is ſo called from being the town on the Lyne. Linton is ſituated in the county of Tweeddale, and preſbytery of Peebles. Its contents may be about 25 ſquare miles. It is bounded on the north by the pariſhes of Mid-Calder and Kirknewton; on the eaſt by the pariſh of Pennycook; on the weſt by the pariſh of Dunſyre; and the remaining part by Dolphington, Kirkcurd, and New-lands.

Soil.—The ſoil of the hills is clayey, and they are covered with graſs, which feeds ſheep for the butcher; the ſheep, however, are ſubject to the rot. The low ground near the North Eſk is a clay ſoil on a lime-ſtone, but the land being high, is unfavourable to cropping. The remaining part of the hill ground is all covered with heath, with a ſmall mixture of graſs, and is fitter for breeding than feeding, which, in ge-neral,

neral, is the cafe with almoft all the pafture land in the parifh. Except on the North Efk, the cultivated land is either
a mofſy foil, or a fandy loam upon a gravelly bottom, and
remarkably adapted for the culture of turnip and potatoe.
There are fome lochs in the lands of Slipperfield, belonging
to Mr John Carmichael of Skirling, the largeft about a
mile and an half Englifh in circumference. They have
no outlet; the fprings feeming to equipoife the evapora-
tion. The water is mofs water. They abound in pike and
perch, but contain no eels. In a loch in Eddleftone parifh,
in the county of Tweeddale, called the *Water Loch*, there is
an outlet with a ftream which drives a mill; at certain feafons eels are caught in abundance, in creels, at the outlet.
The ftream falls into one of the Efk waters. Quere, Do eels
migrate for fpawning to running water only, or do they go to
the fea?

Climate.—Though the climate is rainy, and the air moift,
from the number of mofſes, yet, being well ventilated, the
exhalations never ftagnate or grow putrid, fo as to produce difeafes. The high lands of Tweeddale and Lanarkſhire, are all
fubject to harveft frofts, which often damage the crop. Thefe
frofts are generally dreaded about the latter end of Auguft and
during the month of September. Rainy weather about this
time generally terminates in this kind of froft, which, in the
year 1784, deftroyed the whole barley crop in the month of
Auguft. The higheft land is always the laft in fuffering by
this kind of froft; the loweft is in greateft danger. In a
calm evening after rain this froft is always apprehended;
when it fets in, a low white thick creeping vapour is obferved to arife, after fun-fet, from the running waters and low
lying mofſes, which gradually fpreads to a certain diftance,
and to a certain heighth, on the lands in the neighbourhood.
Thefe

These frost mifts are observed to attract each other; and, wherever they rest, they destroy vegetation when in a certain state, or where their baleful influence is not counteracted by particular circumstances. The half of a field contiguous to the running water or mofs is often destroyed, while the more remote half, on the same level, or part equally near, but more elevated, remains safe. In part of a field of potatoes in the line of the attraction of two mifts, the stems became black and soft like soap, while the neighbouring drill remained green and vigorous. These frost mifts manifest their noxious quality first on the potatoe stems, second crop of clover, and pease. It requires a greater degree of intensity in the frost to hurt other crops: It scarcely affects turnips. The stems of the potatoes and clover grow black and soft, and fall down; the leaves, and the pods of the pea, are spotted with white spots. The potatoe is supposed to grow no more, though the roots are safe; the pease, in proportion to their greenness, are soft, wrinkled, and watery, become of the colour of a pickled olive, and acquire a disagreeable sweetish taste: When threshed, the frost bitten are distinguished from the sound by throwing them into water; the sound sink, the others swim. A field of oats, when frost bitten, acquires in a few days a blueish cast; and barley, if early frosted, as in 1784, remains erect in the head, which acquires a redish brown colour, or, if later, a deadish whiteness. The kernels, when unhusked immediately after the frost, are wrinkled, soft, and watery, and, after a while, grow shriveled and dry. The kernel of frosted oats, even if threshed in spring, when examined between the eye and the light, appears cloudy, and not of that uniform transparency which sound grain possesses.

In the morning after the frost the vegetables are stiffened;
bu

but its effects are not obfervable till after fun-rife. If wind
arifes through the night to prevent the mift from fettling, or
if the next day is cloudy, and efpecially if it rains before fun-
rife, or if the field be fo fhaded by hills from the rifing fun
that the crop may be gently thawed by the increafing heat of
the atmofphere before the fun's rays fhine directly on it, no
danger is to be apprehended. In conformity to this experience, a fmall field of potatoes has been known to be faved
by fprinkling them with well water before fun-rifing. But
this can never be executed on a large fcale. Attempts have
alfo been made, though without fuccefs, to fave oats and barley, by dragging fomething over them, before fun-rife, to
fhake off the hoar froft, or *ryme* or *cranreuch*, as it is called,
which is depofited wherever the mift fettles. This froft affects the vegetation of corn only at a certain period of its progrefs. Peafe are frofted however green in the gràin, and the
greener the more readily; they are not killed by it when
hard ripe; but to this ftate they feldom arrive at Linton.
Barley and oats are not hurt by this froft when hard ripe,
and fit for the hook; and it is probable that they are not
hurt by it even though they are fhot, and the ear beginning
to fill, as long as the juices are watery, and have not yet
come to the confiftency of thickifh milk. It is certainly the
cafe with oats. In the year 1784, the froft was on the 17th
and 18th Auguft. The uppermoft grains of the oats, which
always fill fooneft, had thick milk in them, and were frofted
4 or 5 grains down the head. The grains below thefe all
ripened well. The barley, which might be about equally forward with the top grains of the oats, was totally deftroyed.
Probably the upper grains had fheltered the under ones from
the froft, the crop being very thick and ftrong; and this
might have been the reafon why the undermoft grains ripened: But as a proof, above all exception, *that the froft does not*

greatly

greatly hurt oats while the juices in the ear are watery, there were several contiguous fields sown with late seed oats, whose best ripened grains were no further advanced than the undermost grains in the field above mentioned, and they all ripened very well, though equally exposed to the frost.

Dr Roebuck's experiments on oats in 1782 corresponds with this observation ; for, even the last parcel he cut *was not ripe when cut ;* of course, it may be probably conjectured, that, in the time of the frost, none of the oats in question had thick milk in the ear.

Crops cut and stacked before the frost are safe, except pease, the upper surface of which will frost till they be thoroughly ripe. To save them, it is usual to turn the exposed side downwards, to thaw gradually before sun-rise.

This frost affects only low grounds, and only hardens a very thin crust on the surface of the earth. In 1782, the frost penetrated several inches into the ground, so as to destroy the roots of the potatoes.

Diseases.—A man called William Badie, or Beatie, a shoemaker, died a few weeks ago in Linton. About 16 or 17 years since, being afflicted with stomach complaints, contracted by drinking cold water when overheated in harvest, he was advised to swallow stones to help digestion, after the manner of birds with muscular stomachs. He was ever after afflicted with violent stomach complaints, and frequent vomitings, with a long train of nervous symptoms. He never suspected that the stones had lodged in his stomach, till happening to be seized with a vomiting, lying across a bed, with his head and body reclined downwards, and supporting himself

felf with his hands on the floor, feveral ftones came up. The man was of decent character; and from his own, and his neighbours reports, there is no doubt of the fact. The largeft ftone was the fize of a finger end. He threw up 13, which, being the Devil's dozen, might probably be the number fwallowed. Latterly, his furgeon made him vomit in an inclined pofition, and he threw up fand, which probably had fallen from his victuals into fome fack formed in the fto-mach by the weight of the ftones. The ftones muft have been lodged in his ftomach for about 16 years.

Mines, Minerals, Springs, &c.—There is white free-ftone at Deepfyke-head and at Spittlehaugh. The former quarry fupplies all Tweeddale. There is red free ftone in the ridge of Broomieleas, fupplying all Tweeddale with pavement flags.

There is limeftone at Carlops, and Whitefield, and Spittle-haugh, afforded in proportion to their relative fituation to the market, at 10 d. 1 s. and 1 s. 1 d. per boll of fhells, at the hill. Two bolls of fhells is a good loading for a one horfe cart. A boll of fhells, when flacked, yields from two to three bolls of lime.

There is coal at Carlops and Coalyburn, fold, accord-ing to fituation, at 6 d. and 7 d. per 200 weight at the pit. The feams are about 4½ feet thick, including a divifion ftone of 18 inches.

Fullers earth is found in a fmall feam below Bridgehoufe bridge over the Lyne, on the eaft fide of the water.

Marle is found in beds, formed feemingly by oozing fprings from lime-ftone, which encruft or petrify mofs by depofitions

of

of lime-ſtone. In theſe beds the ſhells of the common ſnail are obſerved rotten and friable. A blue marle, of a mixed conſiſtency between ſtone and clay, is found in a ſtratum about two feet thick, above the lime rocks of Carlops and Spittlehaugh. No whin-ſtone has been diſcovered, except detached ſtones in the bed of the river.

There is a ſpring lying north of Linton village about a mile, in Mr Chatto's land, called *Heaven-aqua Well*, ſome-what reſembling Tunbridge.

Animals, &c.—Beſides the domeſtic animals, and thoſe common to the country, the earn eagle is ſometimes, but rare-ly, ſeen on the heights. The golden creſted wren and the bullfinch are but lately come. The woodpecker has very lately appeared at Newhall on the North Eſk, where, pro-bably, we ſhall ſoon have the brown ſquirrel, which has ar-rived already at Pennycook, from the Duke of Buccleugh's *menagerie*. In winter, the huppoe, and ſome unknown birds, ſometimes viſit us. Our migrating birds are the ſwallows, green plover, curlew, ſand lark, a ſmall wader frequenting running water, and the red-ſhank, and other two larger wa-ders frequenting lochs; alſo the corn-craik and cuckoo; theſe appear in ſpring and leave us after midſummer. The felt-fare and wild gooſe appear in winter; the woodcock comes in September or October, and ſoon leaves us.

Plantations and Woods, &c.—Any large plantations of trees in the pariſh are as yet only in their infancy. The larix ſeems to thrive in the pooreſt ſoils and moſt expoſed ſitua-tions. Their durability in paling poſts, even when cut young, is well known. The natural wood is hazel, birch, mountain-aſh, and willows. Birch is generally found in the moſſes.

No

No oak has occurred, except once a large one in a moſs near the top of Mendic Hill. The ſheep prevent the growth of natural wood. The young ſhoots of heath, the year after it is burnt, is the great food of the ſheep. If burnt in winter it dies. The time allotted by the game laws for burning in ſpring is too ſhort, as heath is often too wet to burn in the limited time; but ſheriffs who know country affairs fine treſpaſſing farmers in moderation. There is a moſs plant with a white cottony head growing in moſſes, which is the firſt ſpring food of the ſheep. It ſprings in February, if the weather is freſh. It is commonly called *pull ling.* The ſheep take what is above the ground tenderly in their mouths, and without biting it draw up a long white ſtalk.

Grazing—There may, by a rough computation, be about 10,000 ſheep grazed in the pariſh, 130 horſes, and 460 cows. Swine are coming more and more into faſhion, both among farmers and houſeholders, for family uſe. Cows are from 20 to 26 ſtone weight, yielding from 6 to 8 Scots pints of milk per day. They are kept moſtly for family uſe, no attention being paid to dairy farming. The breed of horſes is much improved of late, particularly ſince the introduction of two-horſe ploughs, which are generally adopted. Engliſh ploughs, with the curved moldbroad and correſponding ſock, are coming into more general uſe, except for breaking up moor and bent. Small's plough is alſo coming into uſe. A few young horſes are reared from the plough mares for ſale. Of late, year olds are ſold from L. 6 to L. 10. The demand is greateſt for the males, which, *caeteris paribus*, draw from 30 to 40 ſhillings more than the females. A good ſtallion in the neighbourhood will be bought in at L. 40 or L. 50, and yield to his maſter a profit of from L. 15 to L. 20 annually.

The

The staple animal kept by the farmers is the sheep, excepting a very few farms where the hills are green, and where lambs are fed for the butcher. The sheep for sale are hogs, *i. e.* sheep of one year old, sold off in June or July before they are shorn. They are disposed of to the Highlands, or Oichil Hills in Fifeshire, at the Linton markets. The principal of these markets are two; the one held invariably on the third Wednesday of June old stile, the other that day week. Between twenty and thirty thousand sheep are generally sold at these markets annually, many being brought from other parishes. Some of the Tweeddale sheep are sold at Stagshaw, on the English side, and bought in by farmers to the Yorkshire fells, whence, when older, they are sold to grazing farms farther south. The Highlanders keep what they buy for two or three years, then sell them fat to Perth, Glasgow, and Edinburgh, about Martinmas; a considerable number, too, are sent up to England. Till of late, the great demand to the Highlands was for wedder hogs; lately, the demand was greatest for ewe hogs for breeding. The average price for these year old sheep at Linton markets, of late years, has been 9 s. a head. The superannuated breeding ewes are either sold fat at Martinmas to the butcher, at about 9 s. a head, or else sold with lamb, in the month of March, to the Lothian parks at 11 s.

The duration of a breeding ewe varies, in different farms, from 4 to 7 years. The farmer, when smearing them at Martinmas, examines their teeth and their eyes, and from thence judges whether he ought to keep them on his farm another year. When a farmer quits his farm, the new incomer knows that it is highly dangerous to bring in a breeding stock which has not been bred on the farm, and generally takes the breeding stock on the farm at from 14 s. to 16 s. a head. Rams

being

being unprofitable, the leaſt poſſible number of them is kept. From 40 to 50 ewes are generally allotted to one ram through Tweeddale, according to the poorneſs or richneſs of the paſture. An old fat breeding ewe from the hill grounds weighs from 6 to 8 pounds avoirdupoiſe per quarter, yielding from 4 to 8 pounds of Tallow.

The Tweeddale wool is in general coarſe, and ſells at preſent, if the ſheep are waſhed, at an average of 6 s. per ſtone Tron. It uſed formerly to go all to Stirling for carpets, ſhalloons, &c.; but of late it is bought much by Hawick people; part is ſent to Hawick, part to Leith, where it is ſhipped for England. Attempts have been made in Tweeddale, and in ſimilar grounds in Annandale, to improve the wool, by the introduction of Bakewell rams; but it is univerſally given up; the breed produced being, as is reported, a ſoft dull animal, always loitering in low grounds, unwilling to climb heights, and too ſpiritleſs to remove the ſnow with its feet to obtain food in winter. The chief food of the ſheep in winter is the graſs which in ſummer they reject, and allow to grow to its proper height. The common breed here is a ſhort tailed compact bodied ſheep, with black faces and legs. The ſheep are all ſmeared at Martinmas with a mixture of tar and train oil, or Orkney butter. Butter is preferred to train oil.

A ſtone and an half of butter, and 12 Scots pints of Norway tar, is reckoned, in general, the doſe for 80 old ſheep; 1¼ ſtones of butter, and 12 pints of tar, is the doſe for 50 year olds, or 60 two year olds. John Murray farmer in Buccam, in the pariſh of Galaſhiels, ſays, that when in Elibank, in Selkirkſhire, he was unſucceſsful in his competition for the premium granted for wool; he next ſeaſon ſmeared entirely with butter without tar, and eaſily gained the premium. The
Highlanders

Highlanders and Yorkſhire people prefer hogs in proportion to their blackneſs, thinking they are hardy bred in high or moſſy land. This may be a reaſon of ſmearing hogs heavily. There is no getting a very ſatisfactory account of ſmearing from the farmers: Some ſay it forms the wool into a wax-cloth, keeping the ſheep warm and dry; ſome ſay the tar is neceſſary for this purpoſe; John Murray, before mentioned, apprehends the butter ſufficient for this purpoſe, and that the tar is only neceſſary to kill vermin. Some farmers keep a few ſheep perfectly unſmeared, for pettycoats and ſtockings; they ſay they have perhaps more wool; but they think the wool degenerates in quality and quantity the ſucceeding year; and even the firſt year the experiment is not fair, as they always ſelect for the purpoſe the ſtrongeſt and fatteſt ſheep of the flock. They apprehend, too, that they fail ſooner.

The greateſt improvement that has been lately introduced in ſheep farming is light ſtocking. The ſheep are better, and the riſk of death is alſo by that means diminiſhed. It is not practicable by any other means than light ſtocking, to in-creaſe the winter food of the ſheep through Tweeddale; the arable land bearing ſo very inconſiderable a proportion to the hill ground. Plantations, in different parts of the ſheep farms, would be of great uſe for protecting the ſheep from ſtorms; but on a 19 years leaſe, which is the uſual term, no farmer will plant. On the 57 years leaſes lately granted by the Duke of Queenſberry, farmers are planting trees for this purpoſe at their own expence. In ſome of the breeding farms in Lin-ton, the farmer keeps a ſtock of breeding ewes; of their lambs he keeps a part, to replace the ſuperannuated ewes and rams which he annually ſells off. He ſelects the beſt for that pur-poſe: He alſo keeps a portion of the next beſt lambs for ſell-ing as hogs next year to the Highlands. The worſt portion

of

of the lambs he sells to a second class of farmers, who annually buy in lambs, and sell them all again next year as hogs to the Highlanders. A third class of farmers have a breeding stock of ewes; of their lambs they keep just as many as are sufficient to replace the breeding stock; the rest they sell to the second class of farmers. A few farmers keep a stock of breeding ewes; they sell all their lambs fat to the butcher, except what is necessary to keep up the breeding stock. One or two farmers who have low and improved land keep no sheep through winter, but buy in ewes with lambs in March, sell off the fat lambs in summer, and fatten the mothers on grass, selling them at Martinmas, or feeding them still farther on turnips.

This last mode of farming is in its infancy at Linton. It was introduced by James M'Dougal in Linton, a very intelligent man, who was 14 years with Mr Dawson at Frogden, about the time he commenced his improvements, first as a servant and then as an overseer. He has been about 12 years in a L. 50 farm at Linton. Mr Laurence Tweedie, lately come to the farm of Slipperfield near Linton, is adopting his mode of culture. He has an extensive sheep farm of the first description, but brings down his superannuated breeding stock to be fed off on turnips on his low lands. James M'Dougal buys in his ewes in March with lamb; feeds off the lambs on hill ground which has been laid down with white clover. The ewes which have missed lamb, and those whose lambs were first sold off, as they grow fat on the grass, are sold at Martinmas; the rest are brought down to the turnip, and sold about the middle of January. Before he practised feeding on the turnip, he sold all off at Martinmas, and reckoned himself well paid if he cleared 5 s. a-head for the lambs, and lost nothing by the ewes. The turnip im-

proves

proves the ewes about 2 s. 6 d. or 3 s. a-head, which is a profit of L. 2 : 10 : 0, or L. 3, from the acre of turnip, an acre feeding a fcore, befides the advantage of the dung and paddling on a light fandy foil. The fheep are inclofed in a web of net ftretched on a paling, their horns are fawn off, in frefh weather, without injury to the animal ; in wet weather they are allowed to go at large. They thrive fafter when at large ; but the turnip are fooner confumed, as they run to the frefh ones, and leave thofe that are half eaten. Turnip fucceeds beft at Linton when fown in the latter end of May.

The principal difeafes of fheep are, 1ft, Iliac paffion or ficknefs. It attacks the fatteft, when firft let down to the ftubbles, and ground allotted for their winter provifion : It is cured, when taken in time, by bleeding and purging. Turnips, or clover ftubble, are faid to cure it ; probably by occafioning a loofenefs. 2d, A diarrhoea, which attacks them in fpring, when the new grafs fprings quickly, after previous ftarving in a hard winter. 3d, Palfy, called *trembling*, or *thorter ill*, to which thofe fed on certain lands are peculiarly fubject. 4th, The rot, indifcriminately applied to confumption of lungs or liver : To this they are moft fubject in moift foft land. Rotten ewes have in fpring a goiter like the inhabitants of the Alps under the lower jaw, and are called *poked*, *i. e.* pouched ewes 5th, The fturdy, or water in the head : The fcull grows foft above where the water is lodged ; and they are fometimes cured by a trepan, performed by a herd's knife. 6th, Tup lambs are apt to die of caftration, particularly if it is performed in hot clofe weather, and efpecially if it thunders within two or three days. The operation is delayed as long as can be rifked for the fummer heat, to give them a better creft.

When

When the lambs are weaned, the ewes are milked for a longer or ſhorter time, according to the richneſs of the paſture; and the milk, mixed with the cow milk of the farm, is made into cheeſe, which ſells at about 6 s. per ſtone Tron. Milking, however, is much difuſed.

The names of ſheep are as follow:
1ſt, Ewe, wedder, tup, lambs, until they are ſmeared.
2d, Ewe, wedder, tup, hogs, until they are ſhorn.
3d, Gimmers, dummons, tups, until they are ſhorn.
4th, Old ewes, wedders, tups.

An intelligent herd knows all his ſheep from perſonal acquaintance, called *head mark*, and can ſwear to the identity of a ſheep as he could to that of a fellow ſervant. The artificial mark made with a hot iron on the noſe, or with a knife on the ears, he conſiders as a very equivocal mark of identity, like the cut or colour of a cot in the human ſpecies.

Corn Farming.—The different ſpecies of oats ſown at Linton are ranked as follows, according to their different degrees of earlineſs: 1ſt, Magbiehill oats, or barley oats, introduced by Mr William Montgomery of Magbiehill. 2d, Carnwath oats from the moors of Carnwath: They are 14 days latter than the Magbiehill. 3d, Late ſeed oats from Tweedſide, 10 or 14 days latter than the Carnwath oats. They will grow on worſe ſoil than the Magbiehill, but require ſtronger ſoil than the Carnwath. A prejudice long prevailed, but is now given up, that the meal of theſe was better than that of the Magbiehill.

The Lothian pea does not ripen in any year at Linton. The Peebles grey pea ripens ſometimes if ſown in March.
There

There is a Magbiehill pea, procured by the Lord Chief Baron's father. The peafe crop is always precarious at Linton.

The land under the plough in Linton parifh may amount to 700 or 800 acres, of which two-thirds may be outfield *.

The outfield is teathed by folding the black cattle in fummer over night, to keep them from the corns, and by folding the ewes when they are milked. The folds are fometimes limed in October, after the cattle are houfed: The land is then ploughed; the lime falls to the bottom of the furrow, but is brought up again by ploughing deeper next feafon. Three crops of oats is reckoned moderate cropping after a fold. On new limed folds fome farmers take four oat crops, then a crop of peafe, which will grow on outfield after lime, though not otherwife, then another crop of oats: The land is then left to gather fod as nature fhall direct. Twenty bolls of fhells, or at moft twenty-four, is the dofe for an acre.

The croft land † is varioufly treated. The approved rotation introduced by James M'Dougal is a rotation of four, viz. turnips with dung; then barley or Magbiehill oats fown with graffes; then a crop of hay; then Magbiehill oats. If the turnips are eaten on the field by fheep, this ftill farther enriches the land; fo that, in all probability, at the next going over, half the dung might be fufficient to raife a good turnip crop, and fet the rotation agoing. The fpare dung might be employed in converting fome of the outfield into croft. Under this rotation of four, potatoes are raifed in ftripes through the turnip field; fo that the land is dunged and paddled by the fheep which eat the turnip.

Lint

* That is, the open or uninclofed field.
† That is inclofed fields.

int is feldom fown, and only for family ufe. It is worth 10 or 11 fhillings per ftone when fit for the heckler. Four ftone from the peck is reckoned a good crop. Nobody will rifk the fowing it extenfively, except with the view of gambling for the Truftees premium.

Population.—The population of Linton, taken at a vifitation in 1777.

Inhabited houfes by feparate families in the village	102
Ditto in the country	134
Total	236
Souls in the village	353
Ditto in the country	650
Total	1003
Males	490
Females	513

The ftate of their ages.

Above 70	23
Between 70 and 50	146
———— 50 and 20	408
———— 20 and 10	224
Under 10	202
Number of marriages	162
The whole of the feceders (all Burgers) including young children of feceding parents	400

There is no regifter of burials or marriages. The regifter of baptifms is not very accurate: A fhilling is paid for regiftering, and poor people have an intereft in the omiffion.

Annual

Annual average of baptisms from 1736 till 1759, both inclusive, - - - - - $21\frac{9}{12}$
From 1759 till 1766 is very irregular.
From 1766 till 1789, both inclusive, is - $26\frac{2}{3}$

Population in 1791.

Inhabited houses in the village of Linton	-	59
———————— of Blyth	- -	12
———————— country part	- -	107
Total inhabited houses in the parish	- -	178

	Males.	Females.	Persons.
Inhabitants in Linton -	149	202	351
——— in Blyth -	26	28	54
——— in the country -	274	249	523
Total inhabitants in the parish			928
Above 70 years old			29
Between 50 and 70			146
Between 20 and 50			349
Between 10 and 20			186
Under 10 years old			218

The depopulation seems to be owing to sheep farms being rented to people who live at a distance; the houses of these farms being inhabited only by the herds instead of the farmer's family. Another circumstance must be attended to, viz. that, in 1777, Sir William Montgomery was making large improvements on his estate; but at present there are fewer labourers in the neighbourhood; and it is observable, that the greatest number of empty houses are near Sir William Montgomery's estate. Lord Hyndford also carried on many improvements, but at his death these improvements ceased.

The

The people are either farmers, or mechanics and shop-keepers; generally one, and sometimes two surgeons; formerly an exciseman; lead carters and carriers; no lawyers. Two or three looms work cotton cloth independently, or linen for the manufacturers in Edinburgh, or even Glasgow. There are about two dozen of looms in the village.

In the memory of old people, the mode of living is much altered. The great expence formerly was in drinking two-penny. The farmers ate no flesh but what died of itself; onions was a common relish to their bread. Their clothes were homespun and coarse. More flesh is now consumed even by cottagers, than formerly by farmers.

The situation of every class of people is much improved. Even within these few years labourers wages are considerably raised. A good ploughman gets L. 6, and meat in the house; or 6½ bolls of meal, and L. 1 : 6 : 0 annually, instead of meat. If he marries he gets a house, for which his wife shears all harvest with his master, who drives in her fuel, and gives her land for lint or potatoes. She generally gets offalls of milk and whey, &c. if she is liked. A good servant maid has L. 3 *per annum.*

Day labourers have 8 d. in summer and 6 d. in winter, with victuals; women at out-work 3 d. but oftner 4 d. with victuals. In harvest, men get 10 d. women 8 d. with victuals. Taylors 6 d. and victuals. Masons and joiners are over-proportioned to other labourers, from the demand to Edinburgh, and get 1 s. with victuals. Few enlist, as they have plenty of employment at home. Some six or eight may have emigrated to America; they write flattering accounts to their friends, but complain of their distance from religious ordinances.

ordinances. Except in cafes of occafional diftrefs, from dearth, ficknefs, or old age, a ftout labourer or ploughman, with an economical wife, can bring up a family of fix children without aid from the public.

Rent, Church, &c.—The heritors of the parifh, excepting trifling feuers, are 12 in number, of which only one has a domicile, where he occafionally refides.

The land rent may be - - - L. 2350
The rent from coal and lime - - - 150
The glebe and ftipend may be worth - - 85

The prefent minifter is Alexander Forrefter, a batchelor, who fucceeded in 1790. The manfe was rebuilt in 1779, the church in 1782.

The feceders are Burgers - - - 339
——————— Antiburgers - - 2
——————— Relief - - - 35
                                        ————
                              In all 376

There are no other religious fectaries in the parifh.

Poor.—There are no poors rates in the parifh. They are fupported by collections at the church doors, by dues at proclamations, and dues for mort-cloths kept by the kirk-feffion. In 1773, a legacy of L. 100 was left to the poor; before that they had one of L. 25. This ftock is at intereft at 5 *per cent.* In 1783, the treafurer had above the annual income a balance, which was then expended, with fome charitable collections and private donations, amounting to near L. 30. In that year the feffion did not buy meal and retail it at an under rate, but gave their contributions in money. In other parifhes, where the kirk-feffion bought and retailed meal

meal at an under rate, the retail trade was knocked up, and tradefmen who were not on their lift had to travel to Linton for meal. The feffion never admitted any poor to regular penfions ; but the treafurer, who was the minifter, gave occafional fupply, by the advice of difcreet people in the parifh.

Average of the annual expences of fupporting the poor in Linton.

For 4 years previous to 1773, when L. 100 was left them,
was   -   -   -   -   L. 10 18 8
From 1773, for 8 years, annual expence   16 19 3
From Martinmas 1782 till Martinmas 1785,
the expence is nearly the fame each year   31 0 0$\frac{1}{3}$
From June 1785 till June 1790   -   -   18 17 10

From the above may be deduced about L. 1 : 4 : 0, which is annually expended in fees to the feffion-clerk, beadle, and prefbytery and fynod clerks, and officers.

In 1782—3, people were fometimes difcovered living on nettles, or potatoes, without meal, and were relieved ; particularly one poor houfeholder, a day labourer, who was reported to the minifter as fick and ftarving. He was found exhaufted with hunger ; and faid, that he felt an *o'ercafting at his heart, and his lights were ay ready to lofe the ftaff.* Some Port wine, and a fupply of meal, put him in heart, and made him fit for work. The people lived then moftly on very wholefome white peafe, brought from Leith.

Parochial School.—The fchoolmafter's falary is L. 10, with a houfe and garden valued at L. 2 *per annum*. The fcholars feldom exceed 40 fummer and winter. The prices for teaching

ing are 1 s. 2 d. per quarter for English; 1 s. 6 d. for arithmetic, writing, and Latin. On account of the vacation in harveſt, the ſchoolmaſter's year is only 3 quarters. L. 20 *per annum* may be the value of his office.

Price of Proviſions.—Lamb 2½ d. per pound; mutton 3 d. to 3½ d.; beef 3 d. to 3½.; pork 3½ d. to 4 d.; ducklings 7 d. or 8 d. a-piece; chickens 3 d a-piece; hens for the ſpit 11 d.; butter 8 d.; ſkimmed cow milk cheeſe 2½ d.; ewe milk cheeſe 5 d. per Tron pound; ſweet milk per Scots pint 2 d.; ſkimmed milk ½ d.

Roads.—An act was got for the Linton and Noblehouſe roads from Edinburgh to Moffat, about 1756. They are made, and now upheld, at 50 ſhillings per mile, which is all the money that can be allowed above paying the intereſt of borrowed money, and without any ſinking fund to extinguiſh the principal. Statute labour is commuted, with advantage, at 4 d. for a day's work of a man.

Antiquities.—When the old church was taken down in 1781 or 1782, it appeared to have been built of the ſtones of an older one. Carved free ſtones were found in the middle of the wall, repreſenting in baſſo relievo a crucifix erect, ſupported by a pair of wool ſhears lying acroſs beneath, but no motto.

In a deep ſequeſtered glen in the lands of Carlops, at the junction of two deep glens which communicate with the firſt one, ſtands a projecting rock of free-ſtone, forming a natural nich, with a projecting canopy. It is called Harbour Craig. This, it is ſaid. was a retreat of conventiclers under Charles II. A great number of initials are carved rudely in the rock, and

dates

dates corresponding to the tradition. Near it is the moor called Harlaimuir, probably from some skirmish, of which there is no tradition. Near Spittlehaugh is a park called Chapelhill; there are no remains nor tradition of a building; but stone coffins have been found in the park, and in several parts of the parish. A Roman urn was found in a cairn at Garwaldfoot, by the late General John Douglas.

Miscellaneous Observations.—The village of Linton seems adapted for a woollen manufacture of coarse goods. The Lyne would drive considerable weighty machinery. Lime is abundant; coal is not dear; and every house in the village has a privilege of cutting peat *ad libitum* from the common mosses, which, all expences included, may be put into the winter stack at 8 d. the single horse cart.

Parish of Linton.
Rev. Cha. Findlater.

I beg leave to correct some mistakes in my report of Linton parish.

The average price of superannuated breeding ewes from

the hill farms should have been stated at 8s. a head; that of holding stock, purchased by an incoming tenant from the one who leaves the farm, at from 13s. to 15s. a head.

A decision too, in regard to the game laws, said in the first report to have been pronounced by the sheriff, is found to have been only pronounced by the justices.

UNITED PARISHES * OF LYNE AND MEGGET.

(COUNTY AND PRESBYTERY OF PEEBLES, SYNOD OF LOTHIAN AND TWEEDDALE.)

By the Rev. Mr. ANDREW HANDYSIDE.

Extent, Name, Soil, Culture, &c. *of Lyne.*

THE parish of Lyne is between 3 and 4 miles long, and near 3 broad. The origin of the name is uncertain, prehaps from the Gaelic word Linn, " a pool or water." The river, which runs from one extremity of the parish to the other,

---

* It appears from the Scots Acts of Parliament, (vol. i. p. 960.) that the parish of Rodonno, or Megget, was annexed to that of Lyne, about the year 1621; and that this took place in consequence of a joint petition from the proprietor and inhabitants of the former parish, to the Lords Commissioners for Plantation of Kirks, desiring that they might henceforth be considered as a part of the latter. It is singular that Megget should not have been united to one of the neighbouring

ther, is fo called, and being one of the largeft that falls into
Tweed in this county, might obtain the name of Linn, or the
Water, by way of eminence; and the name might afterward
be transferred to the parifh. The lower part of the parifh is,
in general, of a fharp gravelly foil, requiring frequent fhowers
in fummer. The upper part is hilly, and affords good pafture
for fheep, confifting of a proper mixture of heath and grafs.
In the year 1782, the crop in this parifh did not fuffer fo
much from the froft, as in feveral of the neighbouring ones.
The fharp nature of the foil, and the fouthern expofure of the
corn-lands, may account for this. The whole parifh is, at
prefent, divided into two farms; but about 60 years ago, it
was poffeffed by no fewer than 7 fmall tenants. The quantity of grain raifed in it is not great, as the number of acres
under tillage does not, at an average, exceed 160. The rotation of crops obferved, is the old one of bear with dung, then
oats, then peafe. Potatoes are alfo raifed for family ufe. No
grafs has hitherto been fown, nor turnips cultivated by the
farmers. This is to be afcribed chiefly to the want of enclofures, without which, thefe crops cannot be eafily protected
from the fheep and cattle, during the winter and fpring.

Extent, Surface, &c. of Megget.—The parifh of Megget is
fituated in the fouthern extremity of the county. It is between 6 and 7 miles in length, and near 6 in breadth. The
furface is very hilly. The tops of the hills are, in general,
covered with heath, and coarfe grafs, but the lower parts produce excellent pafture both for fheep and cattle. The climate
is not, upon the whole unhealthy, though from the high fituation of the country, it is damp and cold. On this account
the

bouring parifhes, rather than to Lyne, which is fo diftant from it. Perhaps the
fmallnefs both of the ftipends and cures might be the chief reafon; befides, both
parifhes at that period belonged wholly to one proprietor, Lord Hay of Yefter,
and it is more than probable that he had confiderable influence in procuring the
annexation.

the inhabitants are more subject to rheumatisms, than to any other complaint. The water of Megget rises at the head of the parish, and, after running the whole length of it, falls into St. Mary's Loch, a beautiful expanse of fresh water. This loch, with the loch of the Lows, from which it is separated by a narrow neck of land, may be near 5 miles long, and, in some places, 2¼ broad. Trout, pike, and eel, are found in both ; they are frequented by water-fowl of different kinds, particularly by wild-ducks. The quantity of grain raised in Megget is very inconsiderable, and insufficient, even in the best seasons, to maintain its inhabitants. But the quantity that Lyne can annually spare, would, upon an average, fully answer all the demands of Megget.

Population, &c.—According to Dr. Webster's report, the number of souls in Lyne and Megget in 1755, was 265. The population of Lyne parish in the 1792, was 72.

Under the age of 10,	16	Females, - - - -	38
From 10 to 20, - -	25	Number of horses, -	18
From 20 to 50, - -	22	———— black cattle,	64
From 50 to 70, - -	5	———— ploughs, -	4
From 70 to 100, - -	4	———— carts, - -	9
Males, - - - - -	34		

The population of Megget in 1792, was 80.

Under 10 years, - -	10	Number of inhabited hou-	
From 10 to 20, - -	16	ses, - - - - -	12
From 20 to 50, - -	42	——of acres under tillage,	40
From 50 to 70, - -	10	——of horses, - - -	15
From 70 to 100, - -	2	——of black cattle, -	54
Males, - - - - -	37	——of ploughs, - -	3
Females, - - - -	43		

The

The number of fheep in both parifhes is between 10,000 and 11,000.

As during the fummer there are 12 or 13 fervants more in Megget, and 3 or 4 more in Lyne parifh, moftly females, employed in milking ewes, making hay, &c. the population of both parifhes will amount, at a medium, to about 160 *.

There are no artificers nor mechanicks in either parifh, except 1 carpenter at Lyne, who has commonly 2 or 3 apprentices. The reft of the inhabitants are wholly compofed of farmers, fhepherds, and labourers, with their families. Their mode of living and drefs is much improved of late, and they enjoy, in moderation, the comforts and conveniences of life. They are far from being illiberal in their religious fentiments, and are truly exemplary for decency and hofpitality. All the parifhioners join in communion with the Eftablifhed Church, except 4 or 5 Cameronians, and fometimes 2 or 3 Seceders.

Church, Stipend, Heritors, &c.—The church is an old edifice, and appears to have been originally a Roman Catholic chapel. It was, till lately, in a ftate almoft ruinous, but is now undergoing a thorough repair. It will afterward be a commodious place for divine fervice. In Megget, their is neither church nor chapel of any kind. Public worfhip is therefore performed in the different farm-houfes by rotation, which is far from being either decent or convenient. The value of the ftipend, including the glebe, is about 83 l., befides the manfe. His Grace of Queenfberry is patron. He is alfo proprietor of both parifhes, except the farm of Henderland, and a fmall heritage, called Lyn-townhead. Lord Henderland,

---

* No parochial regifter, either of births, marriages, or deaths, is to be found; but it is highly probable that the population of both parifhes has decreafed confiderably, during the laft 40 years.

land, one of the senators of the College of Justice, is proprietor of the former, and takes his title from that farm. It is not easy to ascertain the real rent of the parish, as fines or grassums are taken at the beginning of leases, instead of advanced rent.

Instance of Longevity, &c.—The only remarkable instance of longevity that can be remembered, is that of the late minister, the Rev. Mr. Johnston. Though his age cannot be fully authenticated, as the register of the parish where he was born is lost, yet there is good reason to believe, that he died at the advanced age of about 102. In his dress and diet he was very homely and simple. Regarding the manners and customs to which he had been so long habituated, as a model for succeeding ages, in the decline of life he considered every deviation from them as a corruption. He had a strong antipathy to medicine of every kind, and it is doubtful if ever he made use of any in his life, except once. He enjoyed a state of health almost uninterrupted, officiated in public the Sabbath before his death, and was getting out of bed, in order to prepare for the duties of the next Sabbath, when he expired suddenly, in a fainting fit, without a groan.

Poor.—There are no poor in this parish, nor have there been any upon the poor's roll for many years past. This is owing not only to the frugality and industry of the inhabitants, but also to their sense of honour, and independent spirit. In establishing poor's rates, the design is certainly laudable, but experience teaches us that they are attended with many bad consequences. Wherever men can depend on suitable provision being made for them, when reduced to indigence, they are divested of the proper stimulus to exertion; they soon lose the sense of shame, and are tempted to squander away in dissipation,

what

what would otherwife have been laid up for the evil day. Some of the neighbouring parifhes are ftriking inftances of the truth of this obfervation. In our fifter kingdom, the evil is ftill growing worfe and worfe. If not fpeedily correbted, the burden of poor's rates will, in a fhort time, become altogether grievous and oppreffive.

Sheep.—Both in Megget and Lyne, the fheep are all of the black-faced, common Seotch kind, and they are not inferior in quality to any of that kind in this part of Scotland. Af- ter repeated experiments, the farmers in this diftrict, are con- vinced that their own breed is more hardy, of a better fhape, and more eafily fed than any other breed with which they are acquainted. Befides, they maintain, that there is a greater demand from England for Scotch fheep, than for thofe of any other kind. For thefe reafons, they apprehend that it would be very dangerous for them, whofe dependence is folely upon their fheep, to attempt any innovation, in this refpect, unlefs it were done on a very fmall fcale. Upon the banks of Yar- row water, a crofs breed, with finer wool, has been gaining ground for fome time paft, but they are found not to thrive fo well when carried to the higher grounds in Tweeddale. It is true, that an attempt has been lately made, with confider- able fuccefs, to change the breed upon a farm near the head of Moffat water ; but it ought to be confidered, that though fome of the land in that farm be among the higheft in the S. of Scotland, yet a confiderable part of it is not only low, but fheltered in fuch a manner, that when the farms in Meg- get are completely ftormed with fnow, the fheep on that farm are at no lofs for pafture. It is admitted, that the wool of the black-faced fheep, is, in general, very coarfe, but per- haps confiderable improvement might be made on it, by pay- ing more attention than is ufually done, to the fleece of the

rams

rams and ewes, which are kept as a breeding ſtock. After all, if it can be aſcertained, from experiment and undoubted facts, that any change whatever, either in the kind or management of ſheep, will, upon the whole, be more advantageous to the farmers, than the mode at preſent adopted, it is not to be doubted, that the ſagacity of that claſs of men, in this county, will ſoon induce them to purſue that plan.

Cauſes of Depopulation.—The cauſes commonly aſſigned for the decreaſe of population in this diſtrict, are the demoliſhing of cottages, and the junction of ſheep-farms. With reſpect to the firſt, farmers are now generally convinced of the neceſſity of encouraging cottagers, by building houſes for them, though the reverſe was too much the practice a few years ago. Cottagers, by living at a diſtance from towns, are commonly ſtrangers to diſſipation and vice, their children are often numerous and healthy, and almoſt always make the beſt country ſervants. But, with regard to the ſecond cauſe, men of obſervation are not ſo unanimous. For it has been warmly diſputed, whether extenſive farms be, upon the whole, favourable or unfavourable to the population and proſperity of a country. Before we can determine this point, it is neceſſary that we attend to the ſituation and circumſtances of the country where the farms lie. In the vicinity of a large town, where plenty of manure can be procured, or, in a rich ſoil, where, by means of lime and marl, cultivation may be carried to a high pitch, farms of a moderate extent are certainly proper, becauſe the culture of them requires many hands, and much attention. But in proportion as farms are more diſtant from the means of improvement, and the ſoil of them leſs rich, in the ſame proportion, it would appear, may they increaſe in ſize, becauſe the quantity of land under tillage being neceſſarily ſmall, leſs attention and induſtry are requiſite.

If

If this reasoning be well founded, it is evident that small farms may sometimes be united, and larger farms, in some cases, divided to advantage. But it may be said, does not the junction of small farms tend, in every instance, to diminish the population of a country, and is not the publick a sufferer by it? We must admit, that where the industry of the small farmer and his family cannot be turned into another channel equally beneficial to themselves and the community, this will be the case. On the other hand, at a period when the demand for manufacturers is great, and their wages high, it may be advantageous both to the individuals and the publick, that some of the small farmers become manufacturers. The case of this useful class of men, is indeed much to be pitied, when they are turned out of their small possessions, where there is no demand for their labour in any other line; they must then either emigrate or starve, and the country will, in a short time, severely feel the loss. It appears, then, that the state of trade and manufactures must have considerable influence in regulating the size of farms; so that what would be sound policy in this respect, at one period, would be the reverse at another. If it be said, that after all, the interest of the proprietor will naturally induce him to prefer the highest offer for his lands; and that as the extensive farmer can afford to give more rent than small tenants, the former will obtain the preference, and farms will continually increase in size; in answer to this, it may be observed, that neither the proprietor nor the farmer, even in a sheep country, will find it his advantage that the farm be more extensive than what one person can properly manage. The proper check, then, when farms become overgrown, appears to be at hand; and the wisdom of providence is equally conspicuous in this, as in many other instances, which often escape our observation.

On

On the whole, it will perhaps be found to be the foundest policy, that no restraint whatever be imposed either upon farming, commerce, or manufactures. When left to themselves, they will have a strong mutual influence on each other, and though one of them may appear to gain too great an ascendancy at a time, yet it will soon be checked by the others, and descend to its own proper level. When Government is so wise as not to interfere in these matters, it will find its advantage in the increasing prosperity of the whole state.

Antiquities.—About - of a mile W. of Lyne church, there is a famous Roman camp of about 6 acres in extent. The situation of it appears to have been chosen with great judgment. The road leading to it is still visible, and runs through the present glebe. The ground within the encampment has been frequently ploughed, and it is said, that Roman coins, &c. were frequently found in it. But as this camp has been often described, it is judged unnecessary to insist more on it. In Megget there are the remains of 2 old towers, which appear to have been built, partly for defence, partly for accommodating the Kings of Scotland when on their hunting parties in the forest. The traces of 3 or 4 roads in different directions across the hills are still visible, at what period, or with what design they were formed, is uncertain. Perhaps when the country was covered with wood, they were cut out for the King and his suite when they went a-hunting. At Henderland, there are the remains of an old chapel and burying-ground. The inscription on the tomb-stone of the famous freebooter, Cockburn of Henderland, is still legible. Boetius, Buchanan, and other historians, inform us, that gold was formerly found in Glengaber water, and some small traces still remain of the ground which had been dug in search of that precious metal.

Miscellaneous

Miscellaneous Observations.—Though a great part of the land in Lyne and Megget has been formerly covered with wood, yet, at present, there are only a few trees around the church and some of the farm-houses. The old trees natural-ly decay through time, and the growth of young ones is ef-fectually prevented by the sheep and cattle. In Megget, there is plenty of moorfowl in good seasons. The earn, a species of eagle that builds its nest in a small island in Lochskene, sometimes carries off a young lamb, even in view of the shep-herd. Besides the necessary attention which the flocks of sheep require, the inhabitants of Megget are mostly employed dur-ing the summer and autumn in making and carrying home their peats, in cutting and leading in their hay, and in laying up provision for the winter.

Advantages and Disadvantages.—At Lyne, the distance from coals and lime is not great, the roads are good, and there are 2 convenient bridges over the water. Thirlage is a griev-ance justly complained of. The want of a salary for a school-master, is hard on the lower class of people. Megget labours under particular disadvantages. There is no school of any kind nearer to it, than that of Yarrow, which is 8 or 9 miles distant. This want is severely felt, especially by servants who have large families, who must either send their children to a great distance for education, or be at the expense of teaching them at home. Yet, much to their credit, they are not inferior in religious knowledge to any of their neigh-bours. This must be ascribed chiefly to the diligence and at-tention of their parents, who are at considerable pains to in-still into the tender minds of their offspring, the principles of piety and virtue. There was indeed the sum of 50 l. Ster-ling mortified by a former minister of Lyne, and the interest of it was intended as a salary for a teacher ; but, though that

sum

fum be now increafed to 80 l. Sterling, yet the intereft of it
is far from being iufficient to fupport an eftablifhed fchoolmafter. Among the difadvantages peculiar to Megget, its
great diftance from Lyne church, which is about 14 miles,
ought not to be omitted. The river Tweed runs between
them, and the road is remarkably bad and fteep.

Means of Melioration.—As Megget is fometimes almoft
inacceffible during 2 or 3 months in winter, on account of
the fteep hills and rough roads, nothing would tend more to
promote the comfort and convenience of its inhabitants, than
a paffable road up Manor water. If it were carried up the
narrow glen oppofite to Manor-head, which is practicable,
and afterward down Glengaber water, great part of the prefent fteep pull would be faved, and the traveller would derive effential benefit from it. It is true, that the expenfe
would be confiderable, but the fum which was lately expended in obtaining an act of parliament for making roads in the
county, would have been fufficient for making that road.
It is certainly very hard, efpecially on poor counties, when
they are obliged to fpend about 400 l. Sterling, in order to
obtain leave to lay out their own money in the way they
think beft. The writer of this has no object in view, but
the good of his country ; and it will be admitted, that few
things are more conducive to its improvement, than good
roads upon a liberal plan, and in a proper direction. As this
is a national concern, and not confined to any particular diftrict, it is to be hoped, that at fome future period it may meet
with all the attention it deferves.

That confiderable improvement has been lately made on
the roads, cannot be denied ; but it will alfo be admitted,
that they are far from having attained that perfection, either
in the direction or execution of them, to which they may be
carried.

carried. It is certainly the intereft of every member of the community, that the communication from one place to another be rendered as eafy as poffible ; but gentlemen of landed property appear to be more concerned in this than others : For, if their tenants are obliged, on account of the fteepnefs and roughnefs of the road, to employ 4 carts in carrying what would otherwife have been an eafy load for 3, it is evident that the expenfe muft ultimately fall upon the proprietor. Though the management of the money arifing from turnpikes is, with great propriety, committed to the truftees of the different counties, yet it may be doubted if the planning and original direction of the roads be fafeft in the fame hands. Wherever men are interefted, there they are not competent judges ; this is perhaps the reafon, that, in making roads, the publick intereft is fometimes facrificed to the pretended intereft of individuals. Were the gentlemen of the different counties to agree, that the planning of the roads in their own county fhould be left to a deputation of gentlemen from a neighbouring one, the objection would, in a great meafure, be obviated ; for, in that cafe, private or political intereft would have fmall influence. With regard to the great roads through the kingdom, would it not be of advantage to the nation, were commiffioners appointed by parliament, under proper reftrictions, to fuperintend this branch of publick police ; and if 2 or 3 engineers were added to the commiffion, we might reafonably expect, that beauty and utility would foon be united, and their joint labours tend, in a confiderable degree, to promote the publick good.

PARISH OF MANOR.

(*County of Peebles.*)

By the Rev. Mr WILLIAM MARSHALL.

Name, Situation, Extent, &c.

FROM the old feffion records, the name of the parifh appears to have been commonly written *Manor*, and fometimes *Mannor*, but never *Manner*, as has been fuppofed by fome. It probably received the name of Manor, as being, during the time of Epifcopacy, the occafional refidence of the rector of Peebles, from which circumftance, he was called the Parfon of the Manor. Manor is fituated within the county of Tweeddale, and the prefbytery of Peebles, and belongs to the fynod of Lothian and Tweeddale. The extent of the parifh, from the fouth-weft to the north-eaft, is about 9 miles in length, and 3 miles in breadth. The number of acres is faid to be 18,110.

Soil, Climate, and Difeafes.—This part of the country, like the other parifhes in Tweeddale, is mountainous; but towards the bottom, where it is more open, there is excellent arable ground, which produces grain inferior to none in the county. The hills in the upper part of the parifh, on both fides of the Water of Manor, are very high, and fo clofely adjoining to each other, as to occafion very fudden inundations,

tions, when the rainy feafon fets in, on the approach of winter. The winds moft prevalent here, are the fouth and
fouth-weft, which are chiefly owing to the narrow ftrath;
there being a continued chain of hills, on both fides the water, for 6 miles. The air, though in fome of the higher
grounds intenfe, is both pure and wholefome, and fewer epidemical difeafes prevail here, than in moft parts of Scotland.
The arable land bears but a very fmall proportion to the pafture ground, and lies moftly at the bottom of the hills, along
the river Manor, and partly on the banks of the Tweed. It is
naturally fertile, and of a fharp foil; and the harveft is fully
earlier than in the neighbouring parifhes. There is indeed
part of the arable ground of a wet, tilly fubftance; but it
has lately undergone a material change, by means of drains
and ditches carried on by the proprietors.

Produce, &c.—Peafe, oats, bear, and potatoes, are the
common produce of the arable farms. A few years ago turnips were introduced into this parifh, for fattening cattle,
and have fucceeded as well as could be wifhed. There is,
however, one great hindrance towards carrying on this fpecies of improvement, which is, the want of inclofures;
otherwife the raifing of this moft ufeful vegetable, would be
ftill more general among the farmers. It is not eafy to afcertain the real value of the arable ground, as it is commonly
laid out in fheep pafture: At an average it may be worth
10 s. the acre. The mode of cultivation, obferved here, in
the rotation of crops, is the fame as in other places of
Tweeddale. It may likewife be obferved, that the wages of
fervants vary almoft nothing throughout the whole county;
the men getting about 6 l. and the women 3 l. *per annum.*
Provifions are the fame as at Peebles.

Cattle.

Cattle.—The number of horfes cannot well be afcertained, as the farmers very feldom keep more than what is neceffary for labouring their land. The number may be betwixt 80 and 90. A few black cattle are bred for fale, efpecially year olds; but, in general, they content themfelves with as many milk cows as they can conveniently keep, finding this equally profitable. The number of black cattle may be about 190. Sheep being the ftaple commodity of this country, the ftore-mafters appropriate moft of their time to that employment: And as other parts of Scotland, fimilar to this, have improved their breed of fheep, they are not behind their neighbours in this refpect. Accordingly, within thefe 10 years, the fheep farms have greatly increafed in value, at the fame time that the tenants appear to be doing well. The breed of fheep is the fame with thofe in other parts of Tweeddale, which are too well known to need defcription. Their number may amount to 8700. The wool, for feveral years paft, has fold from 7 s. to 9 s. the ftone.

Rent of the Parifh.—The valued rent is 3301 l. 18 s. 2 d. Scots; the prefent rent may be about 1685 l. Sterling. There are five heritors, two of whom occafionally refide, and are improving their lands with much fpirit and fuccefs. There is one tenant who pays about 100 guineas *per annum*, but does not refide in the parifh; there is another who pays 220 l.; two others pay 150 l. and five 100 l. a year each. The other feven pay from 20 l. to 60 l. of yearly rent.

Population.—The number of inhabitants appears to have greatly decreafed fince the beginning of this century. About 50 years ago, there were 35 tenants, whereas at prefent there are only 16, as above enumerated. The population, in 1755, amounted to 320; at prefent, it is only 229. This diminution is difficult to be accounted for, as it can hardly be afcribed to the

the junction of many small farms, like that of some other parishes; and it appears the more surprising, when it is considered, that upon the most exact average, taken from the
session records, for these last 30 years. the number of births
has been more than double the number of deaths. This will
be evident from inspecting the following table:

Population Table for the Parish of Manor.

	Males.	Females.	Total.
Number of souls in 1755,			320
———— ———— in 1791,	123	106	229
Decrease, - - - -			91
Number of births, from 1760 to			
1790, inclusive, -	140	136	276
———— deaths, from do. to do.	56	67	123
———— marriages, from do. to do.	47	47	94
Average of births during that period,	-	-	9
———— of deaths, ditto, -	-	-	4
———— of marriages, -	-	-	3
Number of persons under 10 years of age, in 1791,			49
———— ———— from 10 to 20,	-	-	52
———— ———— from 20 to 30,	-	-	54
———— ———— from 30 to 40,	-	-	28
———— ———— from 40 to 60,	-	-	28
———— ———— from 60 to 80,	-	-	17
———— ———— from 80 to 90,	-	-	1

Number of families,	42	Number of schoolmasters,	1
———— married couples,	17	———— wrights, -	4
———— widows, -	8	———— masons, -	2
———— widowers, -	3	———— millers, -	1
———— heritors, -	5	———— weavers, -	1
———— tenants, -	16	———— smiths, - -	1
———— servants, -	76	———— poor, -	3
———— clergymen,	-		

Poor.—There are only 3 penfioners upon the parifh lift, 2 of whom are partly fupported by the refiding heritors, and principal farmers. When thefe two heritors are mentioned, it is but doing them juftice to fay, that they are uncommonly attentive to the poor, and extend their charity to thofe, who, though once comfortably fituated, are now reduced in their circumftances. There is no parochial fund, but what arifes from the Sunday collections, which, at an average, do not exceed 2 s. weekly; and the intereft of 40 l. Sterling, which, together with occafional charities, anfwer every reafonable demand.

General Character.—The people are, in general, fober, induftrious, and well difpofed; attentive to their feveral fituations in life, and uncommonly charitable and humane. They are all of the Eftablifhed Church, except one family, and a few fervants, who are partly Burghers, and partly Antiburghers; the whole not exceeding 16.

School.—The parifh fchool has not been well attended for many years paft. This was greatly owing to the want of a proper fchool houfe; but, though the heritors have lately built a commodious one, it is fet down in fuch a part of the parifh, that there never will be a numerous fchool in it. At prefent there are not above 12 at the day fchool, and about 8 at the night fchool. The fchoolmafter's falary is 100 merks, and 12 s. as feffion clerk.

State of the Church.—During the time of Epifcopacy, the church was fituated 4 miles diftant from the prefent one, where it was perhaps more centrical. It bore the name of St. Gordian's Kirk. It was removed, about the middle of the laft century, to the bottom of the parifh, where it now ftands.

ſtands. For many years it remained in a ruinous ſtate, till, upon an application to the heritors, both it and the manſe were repaired. The preſent incumbent was admitted mini-ſter in 1788, upon the tranſlation of Mr Welſh to Drum-. melzier. His Grace the Duke of Queenſberry is patron. The ſtipend is paid in money, and amounts to about 70 l. 18 s. The glebe meaſures 23¼ Scottiſh acres.

Miſcellaneous Obſervations.—There are two very high hills in the pariſh, called Scrape and Dollarburn, from whence there is an extenſive view of the Lothians, Berwickſhire, and the Engliſh Borders. The latter of theſe is ſuppoſed to be 2840 feet above the level of the ſea. No antiquities are to be found in this pariſh, but a Roman camp, which is pretty entire; in the neighbourhood of which were found, ſome years ago, a Roman urn, and ſome antient coins, upon digging up a piece of ground, with a view to till it. At a ſmall diſtance from this camp, there is a tower raiſed upon an eminence. and commanding the beſt view in the pariſh. It appears to have been built ſeveral hundred years ago, and to have ſerved as a watch tower, to give ſignals of alarm, when the enemy made inroads upon the country, and com-mitted depredations. This pariſh, like others in the neigh-bourhood, labours under great diſadvantages, by being about 18 miles diſtant from coals. They are generally bought in ſummer, and coſt about 1½ d. the ſtone. The greater part of the inhabitants, however, uſe peats.

APPENDIX.

MANOR,

From a careful infpection of the feffion records, as far back as 1760, the number of births, marriages, and deaths, from the beginning of that year, to January 1791, are as follows:

	Births.	*Marriages.*	*Deaths.*
Males,	140	94	56
Females,	136	94	67
Total,	276		123
Annual average, about	9	3	4

PARISH OF NEWLANDS

By the Rev. Mr FINDLATER.

———————————

Situation, Soil, &c.

NEWLANDS is situated in the shire of Tweeddale and presbytery of Peebles. It is bounded by the parishes of Linton, Lyne, Kirkhurd, Stobo, Eddlestone, and Penicuik. The face of the parish is diversified with hills and valleys. The hills are in general clayey, more or less mixed with stones. The arable land is in general a clay loam, upon a close impervious tilly bottom. It is liable to poach in winter, and therefore not fit for turnip sheep feeding.

There is scarcely any heath in the parish. The pastures are all green; and white clover abounds where the land has been limed. Trees thrive every where, and thorn hedges grow very well. In high exposed situations on spouty clay soil, the oak seems to thrive better than any other white wood usually planted among evergreens, as on a hill top above Romanno. From the Wheam to Moothill bridge, the land is all enclosed and well wooded. Larix and other firs of a large size are to be seen at Lamancha and Wheam: At the latter, silver fir was lately cut which afforded planks of 27 inches.

Springs,

Springs, Mines, and Minerals.—Chalybeate springs abound every where. There is red free-stone in Broomyleas; and from Romanno down the Lyne whin-stone abounds. From Noblehouse to Wheam the hills abound in iron-ore and iron-stone, on which trials have been made, but hitherto without success. At Wheam, Lamancha, and Magbiehill, there is lime and coal. About that end of the parish there are also ochres, red and yellow, veins of manganese, and Stourbridge clay. A manufactory for converting ochre into paints is carried on by the Honourable Captain Cochrane at Lamancha.

Farming.—The whole land in tillage may be 1300 Scots acres, of which the outfield may probably be only one-half or three-fifths. Ploughing is mostly performed by four horses; in the lighter soil by two. At Scotstown, two stout oxen are trained to plough, yoked like horses, and seem to answer very well.

There may be 230 horses, young and old, in the parish; 600 cows, consisting of dairy cows, and young ones coming up to replace the old; besides about 100 more fed on fattening grass, or reared on coarse breeding ground: and 3000 sheep. Young horses are bred for sale from the plough mares.

Almost the first dairy farming in Tweeddale was begun in Wester Deanshouses, by Thomas Stevenson, the present tenant. The farm lies on the opposite side of the hill from Wheam. The farmer had the advantage of a house fitted up for himself by the Lord Chief Baron, when Sheriff of Peebles, with more conveniencies than usual for farm houses. Tempted by these advantages, and the vicinity to Edinburgh, the farmer turned his attention to cows, and found the

scheme

scheme profitable. His example was soon followed; and except in the sheep farms, all the farmers pay either the whole, or a considerable part of their rent, by their milch cows. The produce of a cow may be, at a medium, L. 3, 10s. 0d., or, where very particular attention is paid, L. 4, 10s. 0d. The cows are, at an average, from 26 to 30 stones weight. The cows being generally housed, their dung is carried to crofts in the vicinity, which occasions the proportion of outfield to croftland to be less here than in the neighbouring parish of Linton.

The sheep are all sold fat; lambs at about 6s. a-piece; old breeding ewes, at Martinmas, about 11s.; the wool about 1s. per stone dearer than at Linton. Scarcely any ewe milk cheese is made for sale in the parish.

Population.—From a visitation of the parish, begun 13th July, and finished 2d September 1790, it appears that the number of inhabited houses possessed by separate families,

is	182
The number of males are	448
——————— females	443
Total	891

State of their ages.

Under 100 and above 70	39
Under 70 and above 50	103
Under 50 and above 20	333
Under 20 and above 10	195
Under 10	220
Besides one man who says he is 101	1
Proportion of children to a marriage	$2\frac{14}{17}$
Bachelors above 20	70

The

The annual average of births from 1719 till 1749, both included - - - - - 26 9/10
From 1770 till 1790, both included - - 24
The inhabitants are composed of farmers, quarriers, other labourers, and a few of the most indispensible mechanics. There are 13 heritors, of whom 5 reside.

Wages, and Prices of Provisions.—Nearly the same as was mentioned in the foregoing parish of Linton.

Rent.—The gross rent of the parish is - L. 2500
From lime and coal about - - 100

Church, &c.—The value of the glebe and stipend is L. 115. The present minister, Charles Findlater batchellor, succeeded Dr James Moffat in June 1790. The manse was built 30 or 40 years ago, and the church was then repaired. The manse has received several additions and repairs within the last ten years.

Poor.—The poor are supported from a stock of L. 80, secured on a bond of the trustees for the roads at 5 *per cent.* and from voluntary contributions, and dues for proclamation and funerals, without poors rates. The annual average expence of the poor, from July 1773 till July 1782, L. 12 2 4¼
From July 1782 till July 1790, - - 21 1 11½
The difference from year to year in the last period is inconsiderable : The L. 80 stock having been got within that period, the poor were probably more liberally treated. In 1782 —3, meal was bought in by the session, and sold at an under rate. Some heritors maintained all the poor on their own lands The roads in Newlands are under the same act as in Linton, and statute labour commuted at the same rates.

Miscellaneous

Miscellaneous Observations.—Drochil Castle, at the confluence of the Terth with the Lyne, was built by Morton, Regent of Scotland. He was beheaded before it was finished.

In some parts of this parish the lands are thirled to mills, to the extent of the sixteenth of all the oats raised; horse-corn, and the seed sown on the farm, only excepted. So heavy a thirlage leads the farmer sometimes to sow other grain, when, if it were not for the thirlage, oats would be the more profitable crop.

Parish of Newlands.
Rev. Cha. Findlater.

The schoolhouse, as well as the manse and church, are now become very uncentrical, owing to the eastern extremity of the parish, which originally had no inhabitants, having become very populous; of consequence the number attending the established school is smaller than might otherwise be expected; the number may be 30 at an average.

The whole emoluments of the schoolmaster, arising from his salary (of L. 100 Scots), and dues for testimonials, 6d. each, extracts from the register, 6d. each, insertion of births in the register, 8d. each; fee as session-clerk, 10s. yearly; dues for teaching, viz. English at 1s. 2d. per quarter; reading and writing 1s. 6d. per do.; arithmetic 2s. per do.;—may amount to L. 13 or L. 14 annually; he has besides, a free house, and a trifling garden.

In the more remote parts of the parish, farmers families join and hire a lad to teach, at a very cheap rate.

The tax imposed on registrations of births, burials, and marriages, might be of use to gain political information. It has however (as to the mode of collecting it) been exacted without paying proper attention to the state in which registers were kept; and it also proves oppressive to the school-

masters

masters who collect it. 1*mo.* The act contains no clause obliging registers to be kept; and of consequence, where the schoolmaster has no dues for registration himself, in all such cases
he keeps no register at all; this is the case as to burials
and marriages. The schoolmaster has a fee for registering
births and baptisms; he therefore keeps that register. He
has a fee also for granting an extract of proclamation of
banns; he therefore keeps a register of proclamations: but
a proclamation is not a marriage, and the act extends only to
registers of marriages. The schoolmaster is indeed authoris-
ed by the act to compel the parishioners to registrate births,
burials and marriages, under penalty of a heavy fine; but as
he has no interest to volunteer himself in collecting taxes
where he has no fee for registrating, he does not use his
power. For, 2*do*, the allowance from government to schoolmasters for collecting is so trifling, that in the bulk of country parishes, it will not indemnify the collector. He is obliged to take out a licence from the stamp-office, authorising
him to keep a register, which costs him a crown. He is also
obliged, so often as required by the collector of the stamp-
duties, to post away to the county town where the office is
kept, at the distance sometimes of 20 miles, to account to
the collector for the duties he has raised, while his whole
emoluments are only an allowance of 2s. in the pound upon
what he has collected.

Supposing the act peremptorily enforced the keeping of
registers, so that the poor schoolmaster could demand all the
duties, without subjecting himself to the odium of volunteer-
ing himself in the business, the average of threepences collected on all, would not perhaps exceed 10s. or 12s. yearly
in the generality of country parishes; of course the whole allowance to the schoolmaster for his original advance for his
licence,

licence, and the expence of travelling to the office to account to the collector once or twice a year, would only be 1s. yearly.

The poor schoolmasters are meantime perpetually harrassed with letters from the stamp-collectors threatening them with prosecutions; if they omit keeping all registers, they have allowance from the act to do so; but as they have all a fee of 8d. or 1s. for every birth and baptism, which is a considerable addition to their small income, for fear of losing that, they in general subject themselves to the inconveniences before specified, and keep a register of births and baptisms, and no other.——This is a grievance which certainly requires parliamentary redress.

Noblehouse is the only inn in the parish; there are besides two alehouses, and two grocery shops, which sell drams.

There is a quarry of white freestone in Lamancha grounds. Excepting in the contiguous parishes of Linton and Newlands, there is no freestone in the county of Tweeddale, the stone being all mostly whin or slate.

In the lands of Lamancha there is an endless variety of clays; there is in particular a very thick bed of fire clay like the Stourbridge clay; also various beds of marle; there is likewise great abundance of alum slate.

In these lands there is also a vein of stone in a hill, supposed to be a native loadstone.

In these lands of Lamancha there are also in the hills nine different veins of iron ore, of considerable thickness, the same as the Lancashire ores; one of these veins is entirely grain ore; the rest are mixed with grain ore. Manganese is also found by itself and mixed with the iron ores. These ores are of easy access; the entry from the side of the hill; plenty of level, and no need of pits. These veins of ore extend through the hills belonging to the lands of Magbiehill.

No

No fair trial has yet been made of them. Ironstone is also found in the lands of Lamancha.

There is coal in the lands of Whim, Lamancha, and Magbiehill. The only vein wrought is the one nearest the surface; and no attempts have been made to find any other lying deeper.

There is also on these lands plenty of turf and peat.

The surface-soil of the hills, where the veins of ore are found, is mostly limestone gravel. The Countess Dowager of Dundonald has had the fine wooled Lincolnshire sheep pasturing on these hills and the low grounds for 20 years by-past, and she imagines they might suit the Shetland breed.

There is at Lamancha a chalybeate spring, vulgarly called the *Verture* (i. e. the Virtue) *Well*; seemingly containing a great quantity of fixed air, which holds the iron in solution.

The ochre work at Lamancha is now manufacturing paint for sale; it is to be had either in powder, or mixed with boiled lintseed oil, in quantities not less than ¼ cwt. The ochre is by different processes calcined, ground, and levigated by trituration with water.

The powder thus produced is the paint, known by country wrights under the name of *Spanish brown*; it is a remarkably subtile impalpable powder, of a deep dark red colour. What is sold mixed with oil is said to dry very quickly.

The paint in powder is almost entirely attracted by the magnet, which it seems is the test of excellence.

PARISH OF NEWLANDS.

Additional Information.

BY THE REV. MR FINDLATER.

Population.—It hath not been found convenient to make an actual enumeration of the population since the original Report was given in; few general causes have, however, occurred, to afford ground for conjecturing that it hath been any way materially affected.

The manufacturing of paint from iron ore at Lamancha (mentioned in the Report) has been discontinued; but the cessation of employment from this circumstance, would appear to have been more than compensated by the increased demand for labour at the lime quarries, and consequently at the coal mines.

No considerable difference hath taken place as to the mode of occupying the lands, to affect perceptibly the state of population. In two instances lands, occupied by the proprietors in grazing, have been let to farmers; in one of these instances, for the purpose of tillage, which rather speaks to increase of hands. In another instance, a farm, managed by the farmer upon the old unproductive system, has been taken into the proprietor's own hands for improvement; which no doubt bespeaks additional demand for labour. One considerable tillage farm has been let for grazing. No other instances worth mentioning, in point of magnitude, have occurred either as to union or disjunction of farms, or variation in their mode of occupancy.

There were few weavers in the parish dependent upon the weaving of cotton: of course the population was hardly at all affected by the shock given to manufacturing credit in 1793.

Balancing the different causes that have occurred, tending

ing to diminifh or augment the population, I fhould be led to fuppofe it increafed, fince the date of the report, by five or fix families.

The before-mentioned caufes relate rather to the local transference, than the real ftate of population upon the whole. It may be obferved, therefore, in general, that wages of all kinds have increafed fince the time of the report, by nearly one half of the then rate, in addition : Nor would this appear to be a mere *nominal rife* proportioned to the depreciation of money ; but a *real bettering of the labourers fituation :* For though butcher meat, till very lately, hath been generally dearer in nearly the fame proportion ; yet (excepting the dearth arifing from the Parliamentary hue and cry in 1795-6,) the prices of grain feem not to have increafed above the rate of one third or lefs of their then rate. In fo far then as greater facility of rearing families, affords greater incouragement to marriage and propagation, population upon the whole may be prefumed to be progreffive : unlefs we were to fuppofe an unfavourable difpofition in the elements, which indeed, within thefe 18 months, has manifefted itfelf to be peculiarly noxious to the feline fpecies ; cats, in this county, as in others, having died within that period, by cart-loads, of the yellow fever, as was fometimes imagined ;—the wrath of Apollo fell firft upon the dogs in the Grecian camp before Troy ; and in thefe days of gloom and of prophecy, the death of the cats was apt to be viewed with apprehenfion as the prelude of fome dreadful calamity.

For the reafons affigned in my original reports of this, or the adjoining parifh of Linton, no exact returns can be had of births, deaths, marriages, or their refpective proportions.

To lay open the infide of this parifh, and to afford a fketch of the *quicquid agunt homines*, it may be proper to fubjoin, (which I believe was omitted in the report,) An Arrangement

rangement of the Population in regard to Professions, which, though not founded upon actual and exact enumeration, but upon the rough computation of recollection, will be found very near the truth.

Handicrafts, who may occasionally have apprentices, or keep one or two journeymen :

Wrights, - -	7
Masons, - -	7
Weavers, - -	4
Blacksmiths, - -	4
Shoemakers, - -	3
Tailors, - -	3

Other professions,

Lime Quarriers, - -	20
Coal Hewers, - -	4

Inn keeper, having a considerable farm and keeping post chaises, — 1

Alehouse, keeping also provender for horses, — 1

Retail shops, selling also drink, - - 3

Retailers chiefly selling meal and barley, - 2

Established weekly carriers betwixt the parish and Edinburgh ; generally also retailers of small articles, as tobacco, soap, candles, wheaten bread, &c. 3

Cadgers, occasionally trafficking in eggs, poultry, skins, &c. for the Edinburgh market, - 2

Carters, professionally so, and possessing land for conveniency, at from 12l. to probably 25l. of rent, 8

Dairy and corn farmers, not occupied entirely by their farms, but occasionally performing carriages, &c. for hire, and renting farms from 30l. to 50l. or 60l. of yearly rent, - - 9

Dairy and corn farmers, entirely occupied by their farms, (one of them a considerable corn mer-

chant

chant) and renting at from 60l. or 70l. to a-
bout 130l.   -   -   -   13

Grazier and cattle dealer renting grafs parks at perhaps 200l. yearly,   -   -   1

N.B. Other grafs parks at about 150l. yearly, are
rented by a grazier not refident.

Sheep farmers, renting at from about 120l. to 250l.
yearly,   -   -   -   2

N.B. Perhaps about 40l. yearly is paid for fheep
lands, by a farmer who does not refide.

Proprietor, refiding and farming the whole of his
own lands, profeffionally,   -   1

Proprietor, refiding and farming the whole of his
lands, for improvement, with a view to letting
them,   -   -   -   -   1

Proprietors refiding conftantly, or for great part of
the year, and farming for conveniency, or to a
much greater extent lands, which might let to
farmers at from 60l. or 70l. to perhaps 200l. of
yearly rent,   -   -   -   4

Minifter, eftablifhed,   -   -   -   1

Minifter, of the Relief,   -   -   1

Excepting the menial fervants in the houfes or gardens of
the above refiding heritors, the remainder of the population
is made up of hired fervants or day labourers, employed in
agriculture and other improvement of the lands.

Moft of the handycraftfmen and day labourers, rent land
for the maintenance of one or two cows; fome of the
handycrafts, occafionally keeping a horfe: Several of the
day labourers (without renting land) have each a cow maintained through fummer and winter, by the proprietors of land
with whom they are engaged, and from whom they have
houfes: Farm fervants, heads of families, hired by the year,
have

have frequently a cow maintained summer and winter by the farmer, also whatever ground their dung can go over properly, for bear, potatoes or lint. Maid servants frequently have land for a 1-fourth peck sowing of lint: Cottars, of which there are not many, get from the farmers, land for lint; also what their dung will go over, for potatoes or bear: Shepherds have sheep grazed, and if heads of families, a cow also.

The above statements show the whole connection of the inhabitants with the lands.

There are no bakers nearer than the village of Linton, nor brewer than the burgh of Peebles; nor butcher except occasionally. Though there is a flesh market at Peebles, the conveniency of weekly carriers to Edinburgh makes it cheaper to get flesh, bread, &c. from thence, than to send on purpose elsewhere. There are no law practitioners nearer than Peebles; no midwife nearer than Linton; nor surgeons nearer than Linton or Peebles.

Inoculation is in use, though prejudices are still entertained against it, chiefly among the poorer classes. It seems uncertain whether or not inoculation for the small pox has *now* any perceptible effect upon population. The ravages of the disease upon its *first introduction* into any country has always been greater, than what could be compensated by propagation under the most favourable circumstances: Upon its *familiarization with the climate or constitution of the inhabitants,* its annual waste would appear easily reparable by the annual propagation. In this state of the matter, though inoculation may *preserve the individual,* it seems not *necessary to the preservation of the species.* It would be idle to suppose that, by any contrivance for the preservation of the individual, the species may be accumulated beyond *the demand for labour,* or, in almost nearly the same words, *the means of subsistence;* and to this extent population will of course ever be speedily carried,

where

where the *vis-genetrix* is not overbalanced in effect by causes of rapid and extensive destruction, such as war, famine, pestilence, earthquake, or inundation, or Sans-cullottes massacres.

Valued Rent——already stated in the original report.

Real Rent.——This may have increased by an addition of from 150l. to 200l. per annum; exclusive of coal and lime: which two last articles may have risen in rent about as much; and that not merely from the increased demand for lime, as an improvement of the lands; but from the increasing demand for coal as fuel; the farmers engaged in their agriculture, finding it more inconvenient than formerly, to spare the time and labour of their servants and horses in preparing fuel from the peat mosses.

Few farms have fallen out of lease since the date of the Report: Such as have, are raised by the addition of probably two-thirds of the former rent. The leases were formerly of nineteen years endurance; the rents all in money, excepting in some instances, a few poultry or carriages of fuel. The above statement applies generally through the county.

Those skilled in political arithmetic can best judge how far these rises in rent are merely *nominal*, being proportioned merely to the depreciation of money; and how far they are *real* and attributable to the increase both of agricultural capital and skill, by which the lands are rendered *really* more productive.

Taxation——(speaking merely of permanent taxation, and not of the war taxes) though increased, may, to a certain proportion of its extent, prove thus to be merely *nominal:* In so far as it is *real*, does it equal or exceed, or come short of the *real increase of wealth*, and the consequent ability to bear it?

Stipend, Glebe, &c.——The stipend has received no augmentation
tation

tation under the new views, of late adopted by our Law Courts upon this subject; although it has not been augmented since the year 1775. There was a delicacy preventing any application for a time; in consideration of liberal and expensive outlay by the heritors upon the dwelling houses at my accession to the benefice: The present season of high, though we trust, but temporary taxation, is unfavourable. It consists of 74l. in money, including communion elements; twenty-four bolls of bigg, or rough bear, and twenty-four bolls of oatmeal.

The Glebe consists of about sixteen acres, Scots measure; without including the privilege (belonging to every clergyman in a country parish) of cutting the grass of the church yard, which may contain about a rood of land clear of the church.

	Acres.
Of this quantity there may be occupied, -	
No. 1. By the site of the manse and offices and garden,	¾
—— 2. By a small grass inclosure before the dwelling house, - - -	¾
—— 3. By an inclosure round the houses and church yard; kept constantly in tillage, under a rotation of, 1st, Potatoes; 2d, Bear sown down with grass; 3d, Hay, mostly cut green for house feeding; 4th, Oats; and in four separate breaks or divisions, for convenience of having potatoe and green house feeding near at hand,	2½
—— 4. By an extent of flat land, lying rather discontiguous, upon the banks of Lyne water, subject to be flooded by that water, and which for that cause I have resigned entirely to pasture,	12
Total,	16

Manage-

Management.—Upon No. 4th and 2d, with the help of plentiful green house feeding from No. 3d, I pasture thro' summer two working horses and a riding poney, together with generally five small milk cows, (one of which I intend to calve about the end of January for winter and spring milk,) weighing, when moderately fatted, from 20 to 30 stones, Dutch weight. Such are my conveniences and sources of profit; the land remaining in tillage being however unfit to afford winter fodder for the cattle, this deficiency is in part made up by a small farm.

This farm, of about ten acres in extent, of middling quality, rather wet and spungy, I keep constantly in tillage in four breaks or divisions, and under rotation of four crops.

Acres.

Viz. In turnip, or one-fourth of it under potatoe, and
three-fourths turnip, - - $2\frac{1}{2}$
In bear, with grass seeds, - - $2\frac{1}{2}$
In hay, - - - $2\frac{1}{2}$
In oats, - - - $2\frac{1}{2}$

10

I find however, that the farm, with the part of the glebe in tillage, are insufficient to afford $6\frac{1}{2}$ or 7 months fodder, (the ordinary duration of our winters from grass to grass) to my three horses and five cows, with incidentally a young quay, reared to keep up the stock of cows, and now come home from hired summer grazing. To supply which deficiency, I rather chuse, in point of œconomy, to buy in annually 4l. worth of fodder, than take the other alternative of buying in cattle in summer, and selling at Martinmas; being conscious (as I suppose most of my brethren in office are) that we are but ill calculated to make a figure in the horse or cattle market.

Such

Such are the accommodations I have aimed at, and the way I take to fecure them.

Profit and Lofs are not eafily calculated in fuch a mixed concern.——In regard to my particular management the ftate would be fomewhat of the nature as below.

STOCK ADVANCED	L.	s.	d.	CURRENT CHARGES YEARLY.	L.	s.	d.
To 5 milk cows at 8l. each,	40						
To 3 horfes at 14l. each,	42			To annual intereft of ftock,	6	9	7
To 2 carts at 5l. each,	10			To wages in money to a dairy maid, herd and ploughman,	20		
To ploughs, harrows, and tackle,	5			To wages of occafional labour in hay feafon, turnip, and in harveft, - -	3		
To feed oats for 3½ acres of land in tillage,	2	3	9	To, fuppofe, half maintenance in victuals for 3 fervants as above charged at 1s. 3d. per week for each; the other half of their maintenance being derived from articles from the glebe and farm not charged to profit,	9	5	
To feed barley for fame quantity of land, with grafs feeds for ditto, -	4	8					
To feed potatoes or turnip for fame quantity,	2						
To winters maintenance for 2 working horfes, before a crop is obtained,	16						
To advance of fervants wages kept purpofely for the glebe and farm (above what would be neceffary for mere houfe work) before a return is obtained,	8			To hired grazing for a young quay once in two years,		10	
				To winter fodder yearly bought in, - -	4		
				To tear and wear of ftock charged at half the intereft,	3	4	9¼
Total ftock, L.129 11 9				To rent of the farm, of about 10 acres of land,	8	8	
				N.B. No rent is charged for the glebe.			
				Total yearly expence, L.54 17 4½			

The

The annual return of *profit* as under; the difposal of the crop, &c. being marked in the ftatement.

	Bolls.	L.	s.	d.
To $3\frac{1}{8}$ acres of oats (which from the number of cattle kept in proportion to the tillage, and the fodder bought in, is or ought to be in the beft order the foil will admit of) at 7 bolls per acre, produce,	$21\frac{7}{8}$			
Deduct for feed, - -	$3\frac{1}{8}$			
Remains,	$18\frac{6}{8}$			
Deduct oats for the horfes (of which the lefs fuffices, as in winter they are much fed upon potatoes,) - -	6			
There remains for maintenance to the fervants, but not for fale, -	$12\frac{6}{8}$			
To 3 and 1-8th acres of bigg, at 8 bolls per acre, produce, - -	$24\frac{1}{4}$			
Deduct feed, - - -	$1\frac{3}{4}$			
Remains,	$22\frac{3}{4}$			
Of this remainder fuppofe 9 bolls go for meal and pot barley for fervants maintenance, hence - -	9			
Remains for fale at 15s. per boll,	$13\frac{3}{4}$	9	16	6
To produce of five cows, in frefh butter, and calves, fold to Edinburgh, and in cream, milk, butter and cheefe for the family (over and above what goes to the maintenance of fervants and day labourers kept purpofely for the glebe and farm) at 5l. per cow, - - -		25	0	0
Carried over,	L,	34	16	8

Brought over,	L.34	16	3
To a fatted cow fold once in two years, at 9l. 9s. in renewing the ftock, *inde*, -	4	14	6
To eggs and poultry for family ufe, -	3	0	0
The hay and turnip and potatoes are all con- fumed in the family and by the cattle, and none fold, - - -			
Total,	L.42	10	9
Balance paid for conveniency of riding, and of work horfes for carriage of fuel, or for paying vifits in a cart in the family way,	12	6	7½
Thus equal to annual expence,	L.54	17	4½

If to this balance paid for conveniency, viz.	L.12	6	7½
be added, tax on the riding horfe, L.4 12 0			
Do. on 2 working horfes, 1 16 0			
	6	8	0

The faid conveniencies will coft me annually, L.18 14 7½ An expence at much under which they might all eafily be purchafed, if they could poffibly be obtained for hire.

From the above ftatement it would appear, that (exclud- ing the prefent high taxes) the profit or the lofs upon the glebe and farm in conjunction, muft be very trifling. If, however, I were confined to the poffeffion of the glebe by itfelf, (as I muft keep the fame fervants and cattle to ma- nage the glebe, as I do to manage both it and the farm, and as with nearly equal expence of management, the profitable return muft be greatly curtailed,) the lofs would be confide- rable.

General

General Obſervations on Glebes.——I. The original idea of aſ-ſigning glebes to the Clergy, ſeems to have been " to ſup-" ply them, through this means, with conveniencies ſuited " to their ſituation; that they might be enabled, without " unneceſſary diſtraction, to attend to ſuch miniſterial oc-" cupations and literary purſuits as correſpond with their " character and profeſſion."

The legal deſignation of the glebes of the Scots Clergy, viz. *four and an half Scots acres (including the ſite of his houſes and garden) of arable land; with contiguous paſture land, ſuf-ficient for the ſummer's grazing of two cows and one horſe,* did certainly, however, refer to cuſtoms exiſting at the time of the enactment, and which now no longer exiſt. The pa-riſhioners had been in uſe to plough the glebe and to carry the clergyman's fuel; ſo as to leave him the uſe of his *one horſe* entirely for the purpoſe of riding upon miniſterial duty; a cuſtom of which there are ſtill ſome traces remaining in various parts of the country.

Unleſs the enactment referred to ſuch exiſting cuſtom, it is not eaſy to conceive what could have induced the Legiſ-lature to fix upon an aſſignation of lands which is ſo pre-poſterous and ſo inhabile to any purpoſe of accommodation, as to ſeem rather deſignedly to have been contrived to create embarraſſment.

It cannot ſurely be ſuppoſed to have been the intention of the Legiſlature, that the clergyman, with his *one* horſe and cart, ſhould perſonally employ himſelf in the carriage of his fuel; or, that he ſhould guide his own plough; or, that his *one horſe* ſhould, ſingly, draw the plough. If, however, he hires a man-ſervant, who can dig, plough, ſow, mow graſs, build ſtacks, and in ſhort do every thing that may occur in the farming of the glebe; this ſervant, ſo complete in his kind, muſt be kept at an enormous expence in pro-

portion

portion to any return of profit or convenience to be obtained from his labour. The servant can make, comparatively, but slow proficiency in carriage of fuel with *one horse* and one cart; when, with equal eafe, he could, in half the time, perform the fame carriage with *two horfes* in two carts. Befides, with regard to ploughing, the clergyman muft either hire it, where fuch labour can be procured for hire, and keep his fervant looking on idle: Or, he muft commence horfe jockey (a profeffion in which he will make but a forry figure) and buy in annually another horfe to plough along with his *one horfe*, felling him again after his ploughing is finifhed, for want of fodder to maintain him: or, if it chance, that there is in his neighbourhood, fome fmall occupant of land, keeping, like himfelf, only one horfe, they muft co-operate in management by clubbing ftrengths—though it is evident that all fchemes of mutual co-operation, requiring confent of wills, are troublefome in the extreme; the adjuftment of the moft petty interefts occafioning ofttimes, upon fuch a fcheme, the fame expenfive wafte of time in difcuffion, as that of the moft weighty national concerns among allied powers. The *one horfe* too, muft neceffarily find little fpare time for the clergyman's riding, amidft fuch variety of occupation; and it muft coft his mafter no fmall degree of previous contrivance, to prevent his riding from interfering with his working, or his working with his riding, as alfo to carve out work for his fervant when his coadjutor the *one horfe* is taken from him. No fmall degree of fkill in horfe flefh is requifite alfo in the clergyman to enable him to felect fuch a paragon of an horfe as he requires, who muft neceffarily contain within the compafs of his own individual perfon the whole perfections proper to his fpecies, to fit him for that univerfality of employment to which he is deftined; his horfe muft be as fingularly univerfal

verfal *qua* horfe, as was the famous Garrick as an actor upon the ftage.

It is not now the cuftom of the parifhioners to plough the clergyman's glebe, or to carry his fuel; nor is it perhaps fit that fuch cuftoms fhould fubfift; being, fo far as they go, deftructive of that independence which it is certainly the great intention of an eftablifhment to fupport. As matters ftand, however, it is evident that a *mere legal glebe*, fo far from preventing embarraffment by fupplying conveniency, muft neceffarily occafion infinitely more diftraction to the clergyman in its management, than a large farm under direction of a confidential fervant; and alfo much more unprofitable wafte of labour.

The original intention of the Legiflature is not now, therefore, anfwered by the enactment; which is inapplicable to the exifting circumftances.

To anfwer that intention, it would be neceffary that glebes fhould be augmented to fuch proper fize of a farm, as would fully occupy (including carriage of fuel) a man-fervant and a couple of working horfes; affording alfo keeping for a horfe or poney ufed folely for riding: As alfo to fupport fuch a complement of cows as fhould confume the fodder raifed by the labour of the horfes, to yield dung for the land, and to produce milk and butter, &c. yielding profit adequate to the expence of an herdfman and dairy maid, in addition to the fervants neceffary for houfe fervice. Perhaps five or fix cows (according to the fize adapted to the pafture) might be a fufficient complement. And, according to the quality of the foil, from 30 to 50 or 60 acres, might fuffice for the extent of land.

The glebe might be augmented from the land moft convenient; recourfe being vefted in the proprietor whofe lands were allocated againft the other heritors, and a propor-

tional reduction of the ftipend being allowed to each, according to the proportion of what he pays for the augmentation of the glebe. It may be objected to this fcheme, that an inconvenience might be felt by the intrant clergy, in procuring ftock fufficient to occupy fo large a farm; moft clergymen having no funds, or very flender ones, when admitted to a benefice : When it is, however, confidered, that every clergyman upon his admiffion muft. in general, at all events, hire a man fervant and purchafe a couple of horfes, befides one or two cows ; the additional expence of this fcheme (confifting merely in the purchafe of perhaps four cows more, with a few additional bolls of grain for feed) would not appear very difficult to be got over : If the clergyman is young and vigorous at his admiffion, he might for a time difpenfe with a riding horfe, performing his journies on foot.

As fuch an arrangement may not readily take place, it may be proper to confider,

II, *The beft mode of managing glebes, as they are at prefent conftituted.*——In this view of the fubject it may be proper, for the fake of method, to confider the ftate of glebes, First in towns, or where population is frequent ; Second in country parifhes, where population is thin.

First, in towns, or where population is numerous and labour properly fubdivided, and where every convenience and accommodation can be procured for hire ; it would undoubtedly be moft advantageous for the clergyman to contract his eftablifhment of fervants to what is indifpenfably neceffary for mere menial fervice, i. e. to one houfemaid, or a houfemaid and a little girl as affiftant, if his family is numerous : To let his glebe for rent to fome contiguous farmer who could labour it without additional expence of hands or horfes : To buy his milk, cheefe, butter, and meal, if he

has

has no meal in his ftipend; and to hire his riding, and the carriage of his fuel, &c.

As, however, a clergyman can grant no fecurity of tenure beyond his own incumbency, and of courfe the tackfman can have no fecurity of continuance of intereft, to induce him to launch out in improvements of diftant return; as by confequence fuch lands muft neceffarily be doomed to remain in a ftate of comparative fterility: it might therefore, in the view of public utility, be ftill more expedient that the land in fuch fituations fhould be entirely taken away from the clergyman (excepting, no doubt, what fuffices for garden, fhrubbery, poultry-yard, and fuch like) and that a compenfation fhould be given him in an annual payment. That the intereft of the clergyman may however at all times be confulted, let there be no alienation of the glebe, unlefs upon application of the incumbent clergyman to that effect, or of the Prefbytery in cafe of a vacancy: And further, to prevent any fuch meafure from being applied for collufively, let no fuch application on the part of the incumbent be valid, without the confent of his Prefbytery. When an application comes forward to the ordinary Judge of the bounds in this proper fhape, let it be provided for properly by law, that the glebe fhall be fold to the beft advantage, by roup or by Jury; let the price then be divided amongft the heritors *pro rata* of their valued rent; and let an addition to the ftipend, equivalent to the legal intereft of the purchafe money, be allocated *in grain* upon the lands in the fame ratio.

SECOND, In country parifhes where population is unfrequent, where labour is not fubdivided, and where of courfe conveniences cannot be had for hire; it may be indifpenfably neceffary for the clergyman, in point of accommodation to poffefs land.

If,

If, in such situations, he can obtain possession of no more land than *a mere legal glebe*, it is evident, from what has been already stated, at what disadvantage he must farm it; how dear his accommodation must stand to the clergyman; how dear to the public, from the idle expence of labour in effecting nothing, which if properly applied might have been highly productive.

If the glebe is properly inclosed and subdivided, I should apprehend that the most profitable mode of occupancy, would be *to lay out the whole in grass*; and, alternately, to pasture the different fields for a season; and to close them up for hay after having all the winter's dung spread upon them as a top dressing in spring. The cattle kept would be merely one horse, which would perform no work but the carrying out of the dung to the field to be allotted for hay; and to carry in the hay; the other cattle would be milk cows. The only expence of servants would be an house-maid and assistant girl. The fuel must be hired in. Probably it might be necessary to buy in yearly a quantity of fodder, and certainly some straw for litter to the cattle—if any part of the glebe could be converted into water meadow, it would greatly add to the winter provision of fodder, allowing all the dung to be laid upon a different field for hay. This scheme however necessarily implies, that the carriage of fuel can be procured for hire.

A still better resource (where attainable) would be to rent a small quantity of land lying contiguous; which, in conjunction with the glebe, might constitute the requisite size of farm taken notice of   It is however, evident, that no *legal* arrangement can possibly be formed to secure clergymen, in such situations, in the requisite size of farm. Neither does there exist any stable motive of interest to secure such *voluntary* arrangement on the part of any of the

conterminous

conterminous heritors. For the farm of the size required, is too small to constitute a farm by itself, for the occupancy of a practical farmer ; it would be necessary for that purpose too, that it should have accommodation of separate houses, which cannot be erected but at an expence disproportionate to its value : Either therefore, it must have separate houses, which (in paying rent for the original outlay and in upholding) must cost disproportionately dear to the clergyman : Or the heritor must lye at the mercy of each successive incumbent, who may refuse to rent the farm unless at an inadequate price. As no arrangement can possibly be formed to ensure such accommodation, the clergy in country parishes must continue to farm their glebes in the disproportionately expensive and embarrassing modes already stated.

I must, however, still revert to the scheme suggested, (p. 400-1) as the most preferable mode of accommodation, viz. *the augmentation of the glebe to the proper size of a farm ; with a proportional reduction of the stipend.* Yet from the unproductive state in which the lands of the clergy must necessarily remain, from the insecurity of their tenure, it would certainly be expedient to render them alienable, according to the plan suggested (page 402) so soon as the state of population and subdivision of employment, rendered it no longer necessary for the accommodation of the clergyman to possess land——a state to which the majority of country parishes cannot be expected to arrive in the course of centuries to come, if at all.——What is suggested, just now, naturally leads to the inquiry,

III, *What is the best mode of supplying such inducement to the Clergy, as shall lead them to the permanent improvement of their glebes ?*——In regard to *want of inducement*, the glebes of the clergy stand in even a worse situation, as to chance of improvement, than lands vested in corporate bodies. Even
where

where lands are poffeffed by corporations, and occupied by the whole of the members in undivided commonty (a mode of occupation infallibly condemning them to a ftate of comparative non-production, fo long as it continues) it is ftill *poffible*, though I own, *not very probable*, that the members may have the good fenfe, and may alfo fortunately agree to let the whole to a fingle farmer upon fuch fecurity of tenure as fhall communicate to him an intereft leading at leaft to all the neceffary outlay of mere foil-improvements——though no doubt the fyftem of univerfal fuffrage, however it may be admired in theory, is generally found good for nothing, when the queftion is to conduct bufinefs upon a rational plan. The clergyman has, however, no farther intereft in his glebe than his own uncertain life, or ftill more uncertain incumbency ; and can communicate no more permanent fecurity to the tackfman. Without doubt, in the courfe of their profeffional education, moft of the clergy receive a tincture of the liberal arts (a mode of education, by the way, which the decifions of the laft General Affembly have moft decidedly enforced) and *in point of tafte*, may be fuppofed ready to execute many improvements to which they can have no fufficient inducement, *in point of intereft :* The general improvement of the lands muft, however, reft upon more efficient principles than *mere tafte*, elfe it will make but flow progrefs.

Several fchemes have been fubmitted to the General Affembly to create in the clergy a certain intereft in the improvement of their glebes, particularly in thofe of diftant return, and moft important confequence fuch as draining, planting and inclofing ; though all attempts at an arrangement to this effect, have as yet, been unfuccefful. The general idea of the plans laft fubmitted to the General Affembly (fo far as I recollect) feemed equitable : viz. *that the Church fhould apply for an Act of Parliament, vefting in the Incumbent*

cumbent and his heirs a recourse against his successor in office for his outlay in improvements.

Many difficulties, however, present themselves as to the general arrangement and practical execution of such a scheme.

1*mo*, The improvements taken under the comprehension of a statute of this nature, must be such as cannot be supposed to indemnify the improving incumbent, during the ordinary period of an incumbency; otherwise an unnecessary bribe is thrown out to induce improvements which would take place of course : They must also be of a nature readily defined, and whose expence can be readily ascertained. Under such limitations, perhaps a general statute could only properly apply to *inclosure, and trees left standing*; in regard to the last too it would seem hard to oblige the successor to pay for them at their value, unless he were to be at liberty to cut and sell them—if the value the glebe would give in rent is to be ascertained at the time an incumbent begins to improve, and the value to be also ascertained upon his incumbency ceasing, and the purchase money of the difference of value, is to be charged against his successor ; in that case the Jury would need to be able to judge betwixt the *mere nominal difference* in respect of the difference of the value of money, (which may take place to a considerable extent during an incumbency) and *the real difference* arising from the increase of the powers of production.

2*do*, Is the expence of improvement, once ascertained, to be entailed as a perpetual debt against every successor in office ; or is the first immediate successor to be made the *scape goat* and to pay the ransom for the whole ? If it is to be a perpetual debt, must there be a fresh valuation upon each succession ; or is no allowance to be made for deterioration ?

3*tio*, At whose direction are the inclosures or the plantations to be conducted ? Every one knows that either may be

so injudiciously planned, as to deteriorate instead of improving the value of the subject: or executed in such an overproportioned expensive mode, as all the effected improvement cannot possibly repay. Is the direction and the execution then to be left to the good sense or the whim (as it may happen) of the incumbent; or must he, in order to have the benefit of the recourse, previously submit his design to the Presbytery or ordinary civil judge, and obtain their approbation; and afterwards have the expence regularly ascertained at their sight? If he is reduced to this necessity of subjecting himself to the opinion of other people; is there no danger of his relinquishing his design, rather than be thwarted in his opinion?

4*to*, It is almost unnecessary to mention that in this, as in all laws, where exact specification is attempted, care must be taken to prevent attempts at mere literal compliance with the evasion of the spirit of the law.

Upon the whole it would appear; 1*mo*, That though more improvement in point of taste, and without permanent interest may be probably expected from the clergy, than from any other class in equal circumstances: Yet in consideration of the want of permanent interest, it might be still more expedient, in the view of public utility, that the clergy should possess no land at all, beyond a garden or shrubbery; excepting in such cases where land is indispensably necessary to their accommodation.

2*do* That in all cases where the accommodation, intended to be furnished by the possession of land, can be obtained for money or hire; an option should be allowed of alienating the glebe from the church, upon the plan suggested

3*tio*, That where the occupancy of land is indispensibly necessary to accommodation; the glebe should in all cases be enlarged

enlarged to the proper fize of a farm, keeping labouring fervants and horfes to accomplifh every neceffary work by its own internal ftrength without neceffity of co-operation; as fuggefted : With option, when circumftances change, of alienating the glebe, (as fuggefted ̗ .)

4to, That meantime (to conftitute an intereft in improvement) a ftatute fhould be obtained, contrived in the beft manner devifeable, vefting a legal recourfe in the improving incumbent and his heirs againft his fucceffors in office for his outlay.

The fchoolmafter has a falary from the heritors of 8l. 6s. 8d. as alfo a falary out of the Poors' money as clerk to the kirk feffion, of 13s. 4d. making in all 9l. He has alfo provided and kept in repair by the heritors, a dwelling houfe, confifting of one apartment upon the ground, like the dwelling of a day labourer; and a fchool for teaching; together with a few falls of ground for planting kale. The wages for teaching are, per quarter, for Englifh alone, 1s. 6d.; for Englifh with writing, 2s.; for Englifh with writing and arithmetic, 2s. 6d. The heritors in augmenting the wages eight years fince to their prefent rate, which is 6d per quarter on each branch, made no regulation in regard to the learned languages: Thefe indeed are growing lefs in requeft——a fheep farmer, by far the moft extenfive farmer in this parifh, after having his oldeft fon properly inftructed in Englifh, writing, arithmetic, with book-keeping and a little of menfuration, hired him as one of his fhepherds, as the proper apprenticefhip to his profeffion.

The fcholars pay only for the precife time of their attendance, and there is a vacation generally of fix weeks during the harveft: Moreover, the children of day labourers are often occafionally taken from the fchool, when their fervices are needed;

needed; and from the age of ten they are generally employed in herding cattle thro' ſummer, attending the ſchool only in winter. The kirk ſeſſion pay for the children of the poor, from the Poors' funds, in teaching them to read. The ſchoolmaſter, when there is a demand for it, teaches a night ſchool by candle light, during the quarter when the day is at ſhorteſt; where thoſe who had received leſs education in their youth attend for writing and arithmetic, paying for it out of their firſt earnings of wages.

Taking the whole at an average, we may reckon 20 ſcholars at 2s. per quarter, for four quarters of the year, hence wages for teaching, - - L. 8 0 0

The other perquiſites of office are for proclamation of banns of marriage, 1s. 8d.——for regiſtration of a birth, 8d.——for an extract from the regiſter of births, 6d.——for atteſtation of moral character from the kirk ſeſſion, upon removal to another pariſh, for an individual 4d. for a family 8d. The whole

above perquiſites may average yearly, -	3	0 0
Salary before-mentioned from heritors, -	8	6 8
Ditto, from the kirk ſeſſion, - -	0	13 4

Total, L. 20 0 0

This with the dwelling houſe and the kale yard conſtitute the whole emoluments——by far too ſmall a recompence for ſuch a laborious profeſſion.

No man decently qualified for the office could poſſibly be found willing to accept of it as his *ultimatum:* and in fact, Scots ſchools are generally filled by young men proſecuting their ſtudies for the clerical profeſſion, who are willing to accept of the office in the meantime till ſomething better caſts up.

It ſometimes happens that a wealthy farmer in the neighbourhood

bourhood is willing to take the young man who is fchoolmafter into his family ; and to afford him bed, board, and
wafhing for fuch attendance as he can beftow upon his
younger children who are unable to go the diftance to fchool,
before and after the ordinary hours of teaching the public
fchool ; which, in fact, doubles the income.   Being able to
hold out an inducement of this kind, two competitors appeared for the fchool of Newlands, which was to be fettled
by election of the heritors upon comparative trial, fince my
incumbency ; both of whom, befides the ordinary branches,
were qualified to teach both Latin, and Greek.   The fuccefsful candidate, about two years afterwards, ftood trial for
a better fchool, which was advertifed to be fettled in the
fame manner ; and, without either perfonal acquaintance of
the electors, or any weight of recommendation, farther than
his own merit, carried the election over ten other candidates who had prefented themfelves.

Augmentation of the Emoluments of Schoolmafters, would feem
to be a meafure both equitable and expedient.

As one mode of augmentation, might it not be proper to
throw fuch things in the Schoolmafter's way, as might afford
him fome little emolument, without taking him too much
from his proper employment ?——Such as clerking to Truftees
upon the public roads ; to juftices ; to heritors, at parochial
meetings ? Might not the fchoolmafter keep the fidepoft-
offices, where only a runner is requifite ; the opportunity of
the fcholars would be very ufeful in fending intimation of
letters lying at the office to people that don't regularly fend
to the office for letters ; &c.

Where the number of fcholars is fo few, and the wages of
teaching are fo low, there might be ground to apprehend, if the
falary is very much augmented, that all the difference of emolu-

                                                        men

ment arifing from affiduous, in place of remifs teaching, would
conftitute too inconfiderable a motive to excite diligence.
In this view, might it not be expedient, that *part* only of
the augmentation fhould be given as falary; that the remaining part fhould not be fixed, but ambulatory, and dependent upon fuccefs in teaching, to be judged of by the number of fcholars attending the fchool? To this end, might
not a fund be created, under management of the heritors,
out of which the fchoolmafter is to receive quarterly a certain *premium* upon each fcholar attendant upon the fchool;
the number to be afcertained by atteftation of the parifh minifter? Let the premium be fixed at a certain rate per fcholar, upon a number not falling fhort of what may be readily
fuppofed to attend, upon decent diligence in the teacher;
the rate of premium for each to rife progreffively, in proportion to the excefs of the actual number above that fixed
upon as the teft.

The Poor have no ftated penfions; to the end *that no certain dependence may be created, deftructive of induftry and exertion.*
There are no poors rates. The poor are fupplied occafionally and difcretionally, as need is, by the minifter, who is treafurer; who has no rule but his own knowledge of diftrefs as
it occurs to his own obfervation, or is communicated to him
by the neighbours of the objects in diftrefs, together with
his own rough computation of what the funds may afford.
The only capital ftock is 80l. fecured upon bond of the
truftees for the turnpike roads. For thefe fixteen years by-
paft there has been no addition made to the capital; the
annual income being equalled by the expenditure.

The

The following ftatements will give an idea of the expence, of the fupply, and of the mode of adminiftration.

TABLE I. ANNUAL AVERAGE EXPENCE.

	Stock at intereft.	Annual expence of fupply.		
		L.	s.	d.
From July 1773, till July 1782,	No Stock	12	2	4⅘
	£.			
From Do. 1782, till Do. 1790.	80	21	1	11½
From Do. 1790, till Do. 1795,	80	31	15	

N. B. At my admiffion in 1790, being lefs acquainted with the people, and wifhing always to err rather in excefs, than defect, as to the poors fupply, the average comes to be higher than it might have been.

| From July 1795, till July 1798, | 80 | 24 | 15 | 3¾ |

The average as appears, has been upon the increafe; owing in part, to the difference of the value of money, and probably in part to greater liberality and wealth; at prefent the average may probably be taken at 25l.

II. TABLE

TABLE II. POORS FUNDS.

	Average of yearly Poors Funds.		
	L.	s.	d.
By dues for mortcloth, at 5s. for the best, and 2s. 6d. for the inferior one—upon an average of five years.	1	8	$4\frac{4}{5}$
By dues for proclamation of banns of marriage, at 1s. 2d. each, including some *extra* payments—upon an average of five years,	0	12	8
By annual interest of the capital of 80l.	4	0	0
By balance to be made up by annual voluntary collection that the annual income may equal the annual expenditure,	18	18	$11\frac{1}{5}$

N. B. Fines for cattle trespasses are frequently sent to the Poors treasurer; I have sometimes received 30s. in a season.

Total, equal to expenditure, L. 25 0 0

III. TABLE

TABLE III. MODE OF ADMINISTRATION.

THE YEAR.	Total number receiving and besupplied, and receiving 5s. yearly.	Number receiving above 5s. and below not exceeding 10 shillings yearly.	Number receiving above 10s. and not exceed 1l. yearly.	Number receiving above 1l. The sum marked here is the highest given, excepting next column. No receiving above 1l.				Extraordinary cases where more than usual has been given.
				No.	L.	s.	d.	
From 1st Jan. 1773, till ditto 1774.	21 and one orphan.	10	6	4	1	1	1	0	1 orphan at 3l. 6s.
From 1st Jan, 1774, till ditto 1775.	18 and one orphan.	8	3	5	2	1	5	6	1 orphan at 3l. 16s.
From 1st Jan. 1775, till ditto 1776.	18	8	3	4	3	1	5	6	
From 1st July 1782, till ditto 1783.	30 and one orphan.	15	6	4	5	2	8	6	1 orphan at 4l. 3s. 6s.
From 1st July 1783, till ditto 1784.	27 and one orphan.	10	7	7	3	2	1		Expence of 1o1 son meal fold at low price 6l. 11s.
From 1st July 1794, till ditto 1795.	39 and one orphan.	15	8	6	10	2	6	0	1 orphan 1l. 10. Expence of finding a father to a foundling 3l. 9s.
From 1st July 1795, till ditto 1796. N.B. The expence now with 6 children this year was 39l. 4s.	53 and a widow with 6 children.	22	10	8	13	2	6	8	A widow with six young children 3l. 0s. 10d.

In the laſt year included in Table III. there was an extraordinary collection for the poor, which amounted to about 30l. one half of which was given by the heritors; the reſt from farmers and ſubſtantial tradeſmen.

In regard to Table III. it muſt be obſerved that the numbers ſupplied are taken from the treaſurer's books; in which, when a family is relieved, the name of the head of the family only is marked; ſo that the number of individuals relieved may be taken at leaſt at double of what is ſtated in the table.

Beſides ſupplying the poor, the ſalary of the kirkſeſſion clerk and the kirk officer or bellman, together with that of the Preſbytery and Synod, are all paid out of the poors funds; amounting to about 30 ſhillings yearly; *and this conſtitutes the whole expence of management.*

Some time ago an heritor in a country pariſh brought an action before the Court of Seſſion, in regard to the above *miſapplication* of the poors funds; and the Court, upon ſtrict legal principles, found *that it was a miſapplication*; the funds being, in intention, deſtined for other purpoſes. The reſult was, that the clergyman and kirk ſeſſion abandoned the management of the poors funds, which of courſe devolved upon the heritors. The conſequence of which was the neceſſity of appointing an heritors clerk, at the expence probably of 5l. yearly ſalary; with the eſtabliſhment of a poors rate, which had no place before, and which in all likelihood has doubled the expence. It is probable, therefore, that the above miſapplication will continue to go on; upon the authority of cuſtom, notwithſtanding of the deciſion; and it will not raſhly be challenged by the heritors.

There are 11 heritors, 6 of whom conſtantly or generally reſide. Landed eſtates within the pariſh, (excluſive of mine-

rals) run from about 120l. to 600l. *per annum.*—The rents from coal and lime may be worth better than 400l.

Nothing further worth communicating hath occurred, since the date of the original Report, in regard to omissions, to additional information, or to general observations.

STATISTICAL ACCOUNT

OF

SCOTLAND.

PARISH OF PEEBLES.

(COUNTY OF PEEBLES, SYNOD OF LOTHIAN AND TWEEDDALE, PRESBYTERY OF PEEBLES.)

By the Rev. WILLIAM DALGLIESH, D. D.

Name and Situation of the Town and Parish.

PEEBLES, the name of the burgh and parish, in the oldest writings *Peblis*, seems plainly to have been taken from the pebbles with which the soil abounds, particularly where the town was first built. Being the county town, and the seat of a presbytery, Peebles gives name to both. The town stands on the N. side of the river Tweed, where Peebles' Water falls into it; the old town on the W., and the new on the E. side of that water, joined by two bridges carried over it,

and

and communicating with the country on the S., by an ancient and well built bridge of 5 arches over the Tweed. The landward part of the pariſh · is from E. to W. 5½ miles, and from N. to S. 10 miles, and contains 18,210 acres. The river Tweed, running through it from W. to E., divides it into nearly equal parts. Peebles, called alſo Eddleſtone water, ſubdivides the N. part of it. The royal burgh of Peebles ſtands in the centre, and in a ſituation remarkably pleaſant. It is built in a beautiful and healthy opening in a hilly country. It has the Caſtle of Horſburgh, ſituated on a gentle eminence on the E. ; the Caſtle of Needpath, emboſomed in an amphitheatre of wood, on the W. ; the rich ſtrath of Eddleſtone water, adorned with gentlemen's ſeats, on the N. ; and a variety of thriving plantations on the S. Like as in the Tempe of Theſſaly, the river, in clear ſtreams, and beautiful windings, flows through the middle of the vale, which, on both ſides of the river, is adorned with rich meadows, and fields of corn. Verdant hills, covered with flocks and herds, riſe gently all around ; and higher mountains, emitting ſprings more ſalubrious than Oſſa or Olympus, rear their lofty ſummits behind, and terminate the proſpect. The ſituation of Peebles is as healthy as it is pleaſant. The ſoil is dry, and the air well ventilated and pure. The Tweed runs through a track of 80 miles, taking the ſtraight, and 100 miles, following the ſerpentine line of its courſe, and falls 1500 feet : But though it has finiſhed one-third only of its courſe, it has fallen two-thirds of its deſcent at Peebles, which is only 500 feet above the level of the ſea. Situated in a centrical part of the country, Peebles has the rains from all quarters, in a very moderate degree : ſo that the average quantity yearly is only 25 inches. And guarded on the N. E. by the higheſt part of that long range of mountains which runs from Lammermuir to the head of Eddleſtone water, Peebles commonly is not viſited by the eaſtern fog one day in the year.

Soil,

Soil, Culture, and Rent of Lands.—The foil on the level of the Tweed, and Eddleftone water, is clay mixed with fand, and fit for corn or grafs. The lands rifing a little higher are generally loam on a gravelly bottom, and produce excellent barley, oats, and all green crops. The foil on the fkirts and fides of the hills, is an eafy and rich earth, and thefe grounds, where not inclofed, are kept alternately in natural grafs and in corn. Improvements in agriculture have of late years made a rapid progrefs in the parifh of Peebles ; 1500 acres are already enclofed. There are 700 acres more of infield ground, a great part of which will be enclofed in a fhort time. Of outfield ground, which is fometimes in tillage, but more commonly in natural grafs, for pafturing cows and horfes, there are 800 acres. The other lands, being hilly, afford excellent pafture for fheep, and are employed for this purpofe. The lands nigh the town are let at from 40 s. to 50 s. the acre. Within thefe 20 years, the rental of the parifh is become double ; and in 110 years, feptuple ; for the valuation in 1681 was 5036 l. Scots. The prefent rental is now above 3000 l. Sterling, paid to 16 heritors, of which two only, and the burgeffes, who are many of them proprietors of lands, refide in the parifh. The Peebles grey pea has long been in high eftimation all over the country for feed ; as alfo are the oats, which, raifed from a warm foil, make excellent feed for lands that are higher and colder. With regard to potatoes, firft imported into Britain by Sir Walter Raleigh, and the moft ufeful root that ever was imported into this, or any other country, they are nowhere cultivated with more care, and raifed in greater excellence and increafe than at Peebles. Ground is parceled out for planting from 1 to 6 pecks, at 1 s. 6 d. the peck ; 110 or 120 fquare yards are ufually allowed to the peck. The proprietor or poffeffor of the ground ploughs it till it is clean, drives out the dung, and plants the

potatoes

potatoes with the plough; and besides having his ground cleaned and manured, has a reasonable rent for his lands, and price for his labour. The little tenants furnish the dung and feed, assist in cleaning the ground, and planting the potatoes, hoe and dig them after their hours of working, which contributes to their health, and have their potatoes for half of the price at which they could otherwise purchase them, and which, to many families, furnish a third part of their subsistence at a very cheap rate.

Animals.—The Tweed abounds not only with trout, but salmon, which visit the higher parts of it for spawning, towards the end of the year. Accordingly the Peebles Arms are 3 salmon. In the parish there are 200 horses, and 500 cows, both much better than in former times. The number of sheep is about 8000. The ancient kind is still generally retained; but by their being kept fewer in number, and being better fed, they are much improved in quality. As the grounds in this part of the country are generally dry and healthy, the sheep are not so liable to disease as in many other places. Of these, what is called the *sickness*, is generally the most common and the most fatal. It is an inflammation in the bowels, brought on by the full habit of the animal, by sudden heats and colds, by eating wet and frosted grass, or by lying on wet grounds; and might, in most cases, be prevented by bleeding, by gentle treatment, and by change of pasture. It is a pity that the most harmless, and the most useful of all animals should, in this respect, have so long been the most neglected. By a better knowledge of the diseases of the sheep, their natural causes, and the means of preventing or curing them, many thousands of them might be annually saved to their proprietor, and to the country.

Population,

Population, &c.—According to Dr. Webſter's report, the number of ſouls then was 1896. The inhabitants in this pariſh, of all denominations, in 1791, are 1920, diſtinguiſhed as follows:

In the Old Town, - - - -	350
In the New Town, - - -	1130
In the landward part of the pariſh, - -	440

Under 5 years of age,	263	From 50 to 60	158
From 5 to 10 - -	284	—— 60 to 70 - -	164
—— 10 to 20 - -	365	—— 70 to 80 - -	50
—— 20 to 30 - -	258	—— 80 to 90 - -	8
—— 30 to 40 - -	192	—— 90 to 100 - -	2
—— 40 to 50 - -	176		

1920

Seceders and Cameronians, 61	Average of marriages	
Miniſter of the eſtabliſhed	yearly for the laſt 12	
church, - - 1	years, - -	12
Miniſter of the ſeceſſion, 1	Births for ditto,	56
	* Burials, - -	52

Inoculation has been practiſed for many years in this county by able ſurgeons, with great ſucceſs, and becomes more and more general. Above a thouſand have been inoculated, without one dying. Nay, ſome parents have even inoculated their children themſelves, and have perfectly ſucceeded. The inhabitants of the pariſh, in town and country, are generally healthy, and live many of them to very advanced

---

* From the number of communicants in each pariſh, entered laſt century on the records of the preſbytery, as the rule by which the money then given to their burſar was levied from the ſeveral pariſhes, it is evident that the population of this pariſh, and of this county in general, has, ſince that time, decreaſed more than one-fourth part. This is owing to the annexation of farms, and throwing down of cottages, by which the great tenants are enriched, but the ſmall ones, and the cottagers, are almoſt wholly extinguiſhed; and manufactures not having been eſtabliſhed in towns and villages, the people muſt go elſewhere, as neceſſity impels, or inclination leads them.

ced age. Lately there were 6 men living at the ſame time, within fifty yards of one another, in the old town of Peebles, whoſe ages together amounted to 518 years, and who, ſeveral of them, died near 100 years old. The people are regular in their attendance on the inſtitutions of religion, ſober, peaceable, and virtuous; ſo that, in the memory of the oldeſt perſon living, no native of Peebles has either been baniſhed, or ſuffered capital puniſhment. In the way in which holidays of human inſtitution are now obſerved in Europe, it is of advantage to induſtry, to virtue, and to religion itſelf, that we have ſo few of them in Scotland. In every age and country, the Sabbath has been, and ever muſt be, the great ſupport of religion and of virtue among mankind. Nothing has ſo much hurt the devout ſanctification of that holy day in other countries, as men's being accuſtomed to employ one part of a holiday in devotion, and the other in diverſion: And nothing has tended more to preſerve a due obſervance of the Sabbath, a reverence of God, and veneration for religion and its ordinances in Scotland, than this, that our holidays are moſtly obſerved with the ſame religious ſanctity as the Sabbath.

Stipend, Poor, Schools, &c.—The church, which is elegant and ſubſtantial, ornamental to the town, and commodious for the pariſh, was finiſhed in 1783. And the manſe was built in 1770. The ſtipend is 1200 l. Scots, and 50 l. Scots for communion elements. The glebe contains 6 acres. The Duke of Queenſberry, as Earl of March, is patron. The poor have no regular ſupport but from the intereſt of between 400 l. and 500 l. Sterling in the management of the kirk ſeſſion, the collections at the church doors on Sabbath, and the ſmall ſums ariſing from the uſe of the pall and hearſe, amounting to about 60 l. Sterling yearly: Beſides what the magiſtrates give to indigent perſons from the revenues of the town, and

and which they justly vary as the exigencies of the times require. As the burgh is the greatest part of the parish, the magistrates and council have always appointed schoolmasters for the use of the whole parish ; one for teaching the Grammar, another the English school, and have provided them with proper houses and salaries. Private schools also have always existed, and of late have become rivals for fame of education with the public ones. All the masters are able, and all of them are emulous, which to make the best scholars. At these schools no fewer than 250 children are at present educated, many of them from different parts of the kingdom, and who, for boarding and clothing, bring into the town annually above 1000 l. Sterling. Poor children are educated by the kirk-session from the poor's funds, and no part of them is more properly applied. The institution of parochial schools is to the honour, as well as the utility of Scotland. It shows the wisdom and patriotism of our ancestors in a high degree. At these necessary and useful little seminaries of literary and religious knowledge, established by law in every parish, many have received the first principles of literature, who have become ornaments to their country, and blessings to mankind. What a pity is it, that in a country of increased, and of yearly increasing opulence and expense, the salaries of so useful a class of men are not increased in proportion !

Modern Improvements in Trade and Manufacture, &c.— Formerly Peebles was supported chiefly by the houses and burgh acres belonging to the burgesses, by their merchandise and their trade, and by the many valuable commonties granted by the kings of Scotland to the burgh for its loyalty and good services. Now, improvements begin to be carried on upon a larger scale. Of late years, about fifty houses have been built or thoroughly repaired. Woollen, linen, and
cotton

cotton weavers are making greater exertions, and larger houses are built for them. The magistrates have long provided the community with excellent flour, barley, corn, and fulling mills. Dr. James Hay of Haystown, besides improving his valuable estate, and setting an example of general improvement, has built a lint-mill for the accommodation of the country. Mr. William Ker of Kerfield, has erected one of the completest breweries and distilleries, and made a new and useful improvement in the art of brewing : Perceiving a part of the fine effluvia of the hop to fly off during the boiling of the worts, he contrived a most ingenious and effectual method of preserving it. He covers his copper with a close, but moveable top of the same metal, having a pipe descending from it, and carried through cold water, like the worm of a still, by which means the steam is condensed and conducted into a common receiver, where the oil of the hop floating on the surface of the watery part, is skimmed off, and returned into the worts when the boiling is finished. By this means a third of the hop is saved, and the most aromatic part of it is preserved, so as to give the beer a finer flavour, and keeps it from souring till it is brought to a greater age and excellence. He has formed a design of erecting a woollen manufacture according to the most approved plan, which will also be of general utility.——By the great increase of trade and opulence, the price of labour of all kinds has increased one third part within these twenty years. Men servants have 6 l. or 7 l., and maid servants 3 l. Sterling of yearly wages, besides their victuals. Common labourers have 1 s. a-day, without victuals, and masons and carpenters 1 s. 6 d. All classes are better educated, better lodged, better clothed and fed than in former times. It is also happy for those in the lower classes, that though Peebles is the thoroughfare for oatmeal, carried from the richer corn country on the east, to the mining and manufacturing

facturing country on the weft, yet the average price of this meal for twenty years paft, has not exceeded 9 d., or at moft 10 d. the peck; and it is a received maxim, that while a labourer can earn a peck of oatmeal in a day, he will, in common cafes, be able to fupport his family.

Antiquities and Curiofities.—The Celtæ, a numerous and powerful people, who fpread over a great part of the north and weft of Europe, and who, as Julius Cæfar informs us, were, in the neighbouring country, called alfo Galli, were the firft inhabitants of Britain, and the Celtic or Gaelic was its firft and univerfal language. About the beginning of the Chriftian æra, the Romans fubdued and provinciated what of the ifland lies fouth of the Forth and the Clyde, and introduced in many places the Latin. The Saxons in the 5th, and the Danes in the 9th and 11th centuries, made invafions and fettlements in Britain, and introduced their language. By thefe means, and by the great numbers of the Englifh, who, upon the Norman conqueft, came into the fouth of Scotland, and had lands given them, the Celtic language gradually gave way in this part of the country, to the Roman and the Saxon, of which our prefent Englifh language is compofed. Of thefe things veftiges ftill remain in this parifh and in the neighbourhood. At Lyne, four miles weft from Peebles, is a diftinct Roman Caftra Stativa, 500 feet fquare, with two ditches and three ramparts, containing between fix and feven acres. Three miles fouth from this camp, and on the other fide of the Tweed, is a hill called Cademuir, anciently Cadhmore, fignifying in Gaelic, " the great fight;" on the top of which are four Britifh camps, one of them much ftronger than the reft, furrounded with ftone walls, without cement, in fome places double, and where fingle, no lefs than five yards in thicknefs; without which, and out of the ruins of which, have been erected

erected near 200 monumental ſtones, many of them ſtill ſtanding, and others fallen down,—indications that in very early
times, when the Gaelic was the common language of the
country, and when the Romans had as yet been the only invaders of it, a great battle had been fought on that hill, and
that at the ſtrong camp on the top of it, numbers had been
killed, and were buried. On the extremity of the pariſh toward the N. W., is a high hill called Melden, properly Mel-
tein, " the Hill of Fire," from the fires kindled on the top of
it, anciently in worſhip of the Sun, or afterward to give ſignal
to the ſurrounding country, when enemies appeared in the
Frith of Forth ; and round the top of it a large incloſure or
camp is viſible. Toward the eaſt part of the pariſh is a hill
called Frineti, or properly Daneti or Danes'-brae, with two
circular camps, of which the higheſt has been ſurrounded
with a ditch above ten feet in depth. Many other camps are
to be ſeen on eminences and on the tops of hills, all over the
country, veſtiges of ancient invaſion and danger. In later ages,
when the ancient ſmaller kingdoms in the iſland were formed,
into the two larger ones of Scotland and England, as the Cheviot hills were a natural barrier between them in the middle
of the country, invaſion and war were made by the mouth of
the Tweed on the E. and of the Solway on the W.; yet
ſmall parties of the army often penetrated for plunder into
the interior parts. The predatory diſpoſition, but too much
exemplified by the nations, was practiſed all over the country, and particularly toward the borders, where troops of
freebooters made incurſions into this part of the country every
ſummer, for carrying off, under night, horſes, black cattle,
and ſheep. In defence againſt theſe various depredations,
ſtrong caſtles were built, by the kings of Scotland, on the
lower parts of the Tweed, and were continued by the landholders along the higher parts of it, and on the waters which

on each fide fall into it. They were built of ftone and lime
prepared in the beft manner, and where larger, or fituated
nigh the caftra of former times, they were called caftles, or
when fmaller, were called towers. They confifted commonly of three ftories, the lower one on the ground floor vaulted,
into which the horfes and cows were brought in times of danger; the great hall, in which the family lived; and the higheft,
in which were the bed chambers, defigned for public as well
as for private fafety. They were, by general confent, built alternately on both fides the river, and in a continued view one
of another. A fire kindled on the top of thefe towers was
the known fign of an incurfion of the enemy. The fmoke
gave the fignal by day, and the flame in the night; and over
a track of country of 70 miles long, from Berwick to the Bield,
and 50 miles broad, intelligence was, in this manner, conveyed in a very few hours. As thefe buildings are not only antiquities, but evidences of the ancient fituation of the country,
and are now moft of them in ruins, it will not be improper to
mention thofe along the Tweed for ten miles below Peebles,
and as many above it. Thus, Elibank tower looks to one at
Hollowlee, this to one at Scrogbank, this to one at Caberr-
tone, this to one at Bold, this to one at Purvis hill, this to
thefe at Innerleithan, Traquair, and Grieftone, this laft to
one at Ormiftone, this to one at Cardrona, this to one at
Nether Horfburgh, this to Horfburgh caftle, this to thefe at
Hayftone, Caftlehill of Peebles and Needpath, this laft to one
at Caverhill, this to one at Barns, and to another at Lyne,
this to thefe at Eafter Happrew, Eafter Dawic, Hillhoufe and
Wefter Dawic, now New Poffo, this laft to one at Dreva,
and this to one at Tinnis, or Thanes caftle near Drummelzier.
Of thefe the caftle of Needpath, not far from the old town
of Peebles; and in the line of its principal ftreet, is the ftrongeft one in the beft prefervation. Its walls are 11 feet in
thicknefs,

thickneſs, and cemented with lime almoſt as hard as the ſtrong whin ſtone of which they are built. It was anciently the property and chief reſidence of the powerful family of the Fraſers, firſt proprietors of Oliver caſtle, and afterward of a great part of the lands from that to Peebles, and ſheriffs of the county; and from whom ſpring the families of Lovat and Saltoun, in the N. The laſt of that family, in the male line, in Tweeddale, was the brave Sir Simon Fraſer, who in 1303, along with Sir John Cummin, with only 10,000 men, repulſed and defeated 30,000 Engliſh in three battles fought on one day on Roſlin moor. He left two daughters co-heireſſes to his great eſtate; one of whom was married to the anceſtor of the Marquis of Tweeddale, and the other to the anceſtor of the Earl of Wigton, which families, therefore, quartered the arms of the Fraſers with their own. And the caſtle and large barony of Needpath continuing the property of the Tweeddale family, and the town of Peebles much under its patronage, the Fraſers arms are to be ſeen on the croſs to this day. There is good evidence, that Peebles and the neighbouring country, have been confiderably populous for above a thouſand years, and that they have been enlightened with the goſpel from a ſtill more ancient period; and that in after ages they received from the kings of Scotland, many expreſſions of royal regard and munificence. The firſt teachers of Chriſtianity in Britain, were called, in the original Gaelic language, Kule Dia or Culdees, that is, ſervants of God, in diſtinction to the former teachers of heatheniſm, the Druids, and taught the religion of the true God and our Saviour in much purity and ſimplicity for ſome centuries. When the ambitious biſhops of Rome, in ſucceſſion to the emperors, formed their deſign of univerſal empire, various religious orders were inſtituted, and various religious houſes were built and endowed, in this, as in the other nations in Europe, to increaſe the votaries,

riches,

riches, and power of the Romish hierarchy. The high church of Peebles, dedicated to St. Mary, which, from the remains of it in the church yard, was large enough to accommodate the parish at this time, is reckoned to have been built, or rather rebuilt, in the 11th century, when the churches were generally rebuilt in a better manner, as from some very old freestone rebuilt in its walls, it is evident that it only succeeded to one that was greatly more ancient. To the chaplains of St. Mary in Peebles, K. David granted the corn and waukmills of Innerleithan, with the adjacent lands and very extensive multures.

On the discovery of the remains of a human body that had been cut in pieces, and buried in a shrine of stone, and of a cross deposited near it, bearing the name of St. Nicolaus, it was believed, that St. Nicolaus of the order of the Culdees, and who was reckoned to have suffered martyrdom about the end of the 3d century, when the persecution of the Christians under Dioclesian and Maximian raged in Britain, had been buried in that place. About the year 1260, Alexander III. at the request of William then bishop of Glasgow, to which diocese Peebles belonged, erected on that spot a large conventual church, dedicated to God and the holy cross, and called the *Cross Kirk of Peebles*, as an account of its erection obtained in 1627, from records in St. John's college, Cambridge, and in possession of the magistrates of Peebles, more fully bears. It was built in the form of a square, with a court in the middle, 124 feet by 110 over all. The church formed the south side of the square, and was 104 by 26 feet within walls. The front wall was built with a small arch over the spot where the cross and the remains of the Saint were deposited; so that the religious, whether within or without the church, might perform their devotions at the sacred shrine. The side walls were 22 feet in height, and the front

adorned

adorned with 5 large Gothic windows. The other three fides of the fquare formed the convent, of which the fide walls were 14 feet high, and 16 feet diftant from each other, and the ground floor vaulted. It was of the order of churches called Miniftries, and contained 70 red or Trinity friars, an order inftituted in honour of the Holy Trinity, and for the redemption of Chriftians who were made flaves by the Turks, to which a third part of their yearly income was to be applied. Befides other endowments, its royal founder gave to the Crofs Kirk, about 50 acres of excellent land lying all around it. Friar Thomas its minifter, was chaplain to K. Robert IV. who gave to it the lands called the *King's Meadow, juxta Villam de Peblis*, which defcription makes it probable that Peebles was not as yet erected into a burgh royal, though the charters granted to it afterward, fhow that it received this honour foon after, either from that prince, or from James I.

A mile and an half below Peebles ftood the hofpital of St. Leonards, called afterward by corruption, Chappel yards, founded for infirm and indigent perfons. In 1427, James I. gave this hofpital to his confeffor David Rat, of the order of the preachers ; a probable evidence that James lived frequently at Peebles, and wrote there his poem, entitled, *Peebles to the Play*, in which he reprefents a great annual feftival of mufic, diverfions, and feafting, that had long been in ufe to be held at Peebles, attended by multitudes from the Forth and the Foreft, in their beft apparel. The time of this feftival was at Beltein, which, in the Gaelic language, fignifies the fire of Bell or Baal, becaufe on the firft day of May, our heathen anceftors, by kindling fires and offering facrifices on eminences or tops of mountains, held their great anniverfary feftival in honour of the fun, whofe benign influences on all nature begun to be ftrongly felt at this time, and men wifhed

more

more and more to feel as the summer advanced. The name
Beltein-day, continued and gave designation to theBeltein fair
of Peebles, long after the religion of the country, and the
festivals of the season, werechanged. Peebles is only 20 miles
south from Edinburgh, situated itself in a fine sporting country, and on the straight road to the King's Forest of Etterick.
The kings of Scotland made Peebles their usual summer retreat, for rural diversion or the administration of justice.
Many of the nobility accompanied them, whose houses in
Peebles still bear their names. Extensive lands all around, afterward granted by royal charter in property or commonty
to the burgh. Cadmuir, Hornidoun, Venlaw, and Glentorie,
were the king's property and hunting grounds. The bridge
over the Tweed seems to have been built at different times,
and the whole structure to carry evidences of similar antiquity, as the Cross Kirk, and most probably was erected by
king and subjects, as being most necessary and convenient for
both. On the S. E. of Peebles, and other side of the river, is
the gallows hill, where criminals were hanged. On the King's
moor, between that and Peebles, were the ancient tourna-
ments exhibited. There the county militia, amounting commonly to 300 horsemen, muster every year at their weapon-
shawing in June and October. Their horse races continued to
be held at Beltein, till the middle of the present century ; and
last year, when a part of that moor was converted from its
original to a more improved state, in a cairn of stones, was
found a Roman urn inverted, containing the blade of his
dagger, and the ashes of some ancient hero who had been
buried there. The town of Peebles originally extended from
Eddlestone water westward to *the meadow well strand*, the cross
standing opposite to the Ludgate. It was several times plun-
dered and burnt by the English ; so that nothing was left un-
destroyed but the churches, the manse, and the cross, which
being

being held sacred, were commonly spared. This induced the principal inhabitants to build a new town on the E. side of that water, as being a situation more easily fortified, and to surround it with strong walls and gates, which continued till the two kingdoms were united. In consideration of these great losses, and that the town of Peebles had always been distinguished for loyalty, fidelity, and good services, not only the usual privileges of royal burghs, but the extensive lands already mentioned, and a toll on the bridge of Tweed, were, by royal charters, granted to it at the reformation of religion in Scotland in the 1560, when the needless multiplicity of churches was abolished, and convents were dissolved. The high church in the old town was demolished, and the cross church, as being nearer to the new town, was converted into the parochial one, and employed in the offices of reformed religion till January 1784, when the new church having been built within the town, was opened for religious worship by the present incumbent. The cloister was converted into houses for the schoolmasters, and public schools, and was used for these purposes to the beginning of this century, when it became ruinous. In the year 1621, James VI. renewed and confirmed all the rights, privileges, and lands granted to the burgh by his royal predecessors: and whereas a number of churches, chapels, and altars had, in times of Popery, been erected and endowed by pious persons, in honour of angels and saints, for the purpose of saying mass for the souls of their own friends deceased, all these, with their revenues, his Majesty granted, in all time thereafter, to the magistrates, council and community of Peebles, on condition of a small annuity to be paid into the Exchequer, and their offering their daily convent prayers to Almighty God for his Majesty and his successors. In times of Episcopacy, the minister of Peebles was Archdean of Glasgow, parson of Peebles and Mannor, and had the parsonage-

tithes

tithes of both parishes, then worth 6000 merks yearly. The
vicar in Peebles had the glebe of 80 acres, still called the Kirklands, though at the Reformation very little of these lands
were left to the church, together with the vicarage-tithes,
part of which is given by the patron of the parish to the master of the grammar-school. At the Reformation, and afterward, when the lands and revenues of the church were dif-
posed of to other purposes, it would have been wiser to have
reserved a proper portion of these lands for the constant support of the parochial clergy, a smaller part of it to be occupied by themselves, and the rest to be let by them for their
use. This would have been a better provision for the established clergy, than either the *ipsa corpora* tithes, which are
often a check to agricultural improvements, and a bone of
contention between the pastor and people, or stipends modified
out of these tithes, which decrease in value as the expense of
living increases. The small legal glebe of 4 acres of arable
land, when ploughed by the parishioners, as was formerly the
case, might be some advantage to the minister. Now, when
he must keep two horses and a servant to cultivate it, it is a
loss, in place of a gain. Whereas, if every minister in the
Church of Scotland, having a country parish, had been provided in a glebe of 20 or 30 acres, he would, without either
loss to himself, or avocation from the sacred duties of his office, have directed the proper culture of it, and generally
would have set an example of improvement in every parish,
which would have been followed, and proved of great and general advantage to the country.

PARISH OF SKIRLING.

(County of Peebles.)

By the Rev. Mr WILLIAM HOWE.

Situation, Extent, Surface.

THIS parish lies in the county of Tweeddale, or Peebles. The western boundaries of the parish are also the boundaries of the shire. It is in the presbytery of Biggar, and synod of Lothian and Tweeddale. It is two miles and a half long, and nearly the same in breadth. The general appearance of the surface is uneven. We have no mountains; but there are three small green hills in the parish. On part of two farms there is some short heather. The soil is fertile, though generally light. Being much above the level of the sea, the air is pure and wholesome. Owing to our high situation, the crops are often damaged by frosts, which sometimes set in about the middle of August. The house of Skirling appears, by the vestiges of the walls, to have been large. It was surrounded by a morass or bog, except a small space on the south-west side, and that was defended by turrets. The entry to the house was by a bridge of stone over this bog.

Fairs —We have four annual fairs here; the first on the Tuesday before the 12th of May; the second on the 3d

Tuesday

Tuesday after the 11th of May; the third on the first Wednesday after the 11th of June, and the last on the 15th of September. At those fairs are sold horses, cows, shoes, saddlery ware, coopers articles, sickles, and pedlars goods.

Population.—From a survey of the parish, there are at present in it, under 10 - - - 49

from 10 to 20 - -	56
from 20 to 50 - -	105
from 50 to 70 - -	18
from 70 to 85 (the age of the oldest person)	6

Total 234

Males - - - 120
Females - - - 114

234

In Dr Webster's report, the number is 335.

Productions.—Natural grass is found here on the hills and plains. White clover grows spontaneously in some fields. We have pot-herbs of all sorts, and various kinds of ash, elm, beech, plane, and fir trees. A great part of the parish has lately been sown with grass-feeds for pasture. There are between 70 and 80 horses in the parish. The chief crop here is oats, with which between 300 and 400 acres are an-nually sown. Each acre, at an average, will produce between 5 and 6 bolls. Between 30 and 40 bolls of pease are the ut-most that are sown in one year; this crop being most readily damaged by frost. Potatoes and turnips thrive in this soil. An acre of potatoes planted in the drill way, with the plough, will produce about 20 bolls Linlithgow measure,

and

and fell for between 4 s. and 5 s. a boll; cows and horfes feed well on them. Every farmer here fows five or fix lippies of flax feed; cottagers and thofe who have fmall poffeffions, two or three lippies. Each lippie produces between 12 lib. and a ftone of fcutched flax. The wafte ground in this parifh ferves for fheep walks; and there may be of fuch ground between 70 and 80 acres.

Church.—The living here is L. 38 : 17 : 8; one chalder of bear, 17½ bolls of meal; a manfe and a glebe, containing 7 acres, 3 roods, and 19 falls. John Carmichael of Skirling, fucceffor to the late Lord Hyndford, is patron. The church here was probably firft built as a chapel of eafe for the proprietor and his tenants. It appears to have been rebuilt in 1720. The manfe was built in 1636; and rebuilt in 1725.

Poor.—The perfons receiving charity here, at prefent, are one family of five children, another of two, and two fingle perfons. None of thefe receive weekly or monthly penfions, except one perfon. They only receive, occafionally, fuch fupplies as we are able to afford, from the collections in the church, the hire of the mort-cloths, and for proclamation of banns. The whole of thefe may amount to between L. 4 and L. 5 *per annum.* We have no ftock, but a few pounds to anfwer any extraordinary demand.

Fuel.—The fuel here is moftly coal, which is brought from the diftance of 15 miles. There is only one mofs in the parifh, which is nearly exhaufted.

Mifcellaneous Obfervations.—In this parifh there are 10 farmers. One of thefe poffeffes five farms. Other two poffefs two farms each. Each of thefe 10 farms contain, at an

average,

average near 200 acres. The rent, at an average, is 4s. *per* acre. Besides these ten farms, there are ten smaller possessions about this village, which are inclosed with hedges and ditches, and with belts of planting. They are rented at 20s. and 25s. *per* acre. There is a map of the parish in the hands of Cornelius Elliot, Esq; writer to the signet. I suppose there are between 2000 and 3000 acres in it. The roads in this parish, are, at present, in bad repair, owing to a great part of the lead, from Leadhills and Wenlockhead, passing from one end of it to the other. The statute labour is exacted in kind, and is found to be inadequate to the keeping of the roads in proper repair.

PARISH OF STOBO.

(County of Tweeddale.)

By the Rev. Mr ALEXANDER KER.

Situation, Surface, &c.

THE pariſh of Stobo is ſituated in the county of Tweed-dale, in the preſbytery of Peebles, and ſynod of Lothian and Tweeddale. It is about ſix miles long, and between three and four miles broad. One part of the pariſh is mountainous, and fit only for ſheep paſture; another part of it is arable, and capable of cultivation. Some of the hills are green, but moſt of them are covered with heath.

Soil.—The ſoil of the arable land is various; ſome parts are a wet clay, interſperſed with ſtones; when drained and limed, they give good returns. There is another part, lying on the ſide of the river Tweed, which is a mixture of earth, clay, and ſand. This land yields very good crops, although it does not, in general, receive from the farmer that juſtice, in point of improvement, which its quality deſerves, owing to the inundations of the river Tweed, to which it is in many places expoſed, and by which, in ſome parts, it is over-run with a conſiderable current. This land is peculiarly adapted for paſture. It produces a thick ſtool of natural graſs, which is well adapted, either for fattening cattle, or for milk

cows,

cows, whofe butter, in refpect of colour and richnefs, may be diftinguifhed from the milk of any other cows, which pafture upon the higher grounds. The greater part of the land is a light, but fertile foil, lying upon a bed of gravel. This foil, when properly cultivated, never fails, when the feafon is fhowry, to produce excellent crops ; but, in a hot or dry year, it is very much parched, and, of courfe, the labour of the moft fkilful and induftrious farmer is defeated. It may be obferved, that the land is in general ftoney ; and, what is remarkable, in the hollows, where the ftones moft abound, (in fuch quantities, that a plough, when at the beam, does not reach the bottom of them), there the heavieft part of the crop upon the field is produced. It may be accounted for in this way, that the ftones, by fheltering or keeping warm any fmall quantity of foil, which is amongft them, in the cold feafons, and by protecting it from the fcorching heat of the fun, in the hot feafons, always occafion a good crop.

Ploughs, &c.—The Scotch plough is chiefly ufed in the parifh, as it is beft adapted to the nature of the ground. The practice of ploughing with oxen was for feveral years almoft totally given up, till of late, that fome of the farmers have begun to revive that antient practice. In ftrong ftoney land, which is frequently to be met with in this parifh, oxen are preferable to horfes. The oxen move at a flow, but perfevering pace, and take the draught along with them ; whereas the metal of the horfe is foon raifed by refiftance and the whip ; of courfe he becomes reftive and unmanageable. The oxen have alfo the advantage of the horfes in point of economy, being maintained at much lefs expence. The chief objection againft oxen ploughs is the flownefs of their movement ; but, when the fuperior execution of their work is confidered, where the ground is crofs

and

and ftoney, and that they can continue in the yoke two hours longer than the horfes without any injury, the objection has little or no weight.

Climate and Difeafes.—The fituation of Stobo is dry, and the air pure. The ftate of health, which the inhabitants in general enjoy, is the beft proof of the wholefomenefs of the climate, few or none of them being affected with any peculiar difeafe.

Rivers.—The river Tweed, which runs through this parifh, and divides the north part of it from the fouth, has its fource in the parifh of Tweedfmuir, at a fountain called *Tweeds Well*, about 18 miles diftant from Stobo, and 7 from Moffat.

Antiquities.—The Sheriff Muir is the chief place which difcovers fome remains of antiquity. It is a flat uncultivated heath, with fome ftones upon it, which have the appearance of being monuments; from which circumftance fome have concluded that it muft have been once the fcene of battle. But there is no record or hiftorical evidence of the fact. There are two erect ftones of confiderable fize, about fix feet diftant, which are probably the fite of a grave, by fome fuppofed to have been a Druidical temple. From the center of the grave, there are a number of ftones about a foot high, erected at regular diftances, and extending eaftward in a curved direction. Two cairns are likewife raifed upon this muir, the one confiderably larger than the other; both of them, it may be prefumed, to perpetuate the memory of perfons of diftinction. Not far diftant from the two erect ftones already mentioned, is a large round cavity, in the form of a bafon, called *Pinkie's Hole*; it is about 90 paces in cir-

cumference,

cumference, and, at the centre, is between 6 and 7 feet below the level of the adjacent plain ; whether it is the effect of nature or of art, it is difficult to determine. There is another cavity near the largest cairn, which is much larger than Pinkie's Hole, being about 140 paces in circumference ; but it is neither so deep, nor so regular in the formation, having a small ridge in the middle of it. There are also, upon the muir, a few small circular appearances, which are evidently the effect of art. The Sheriff Muir is the place where the Tweeddale militia met. It was thought expedient, whilst the unfortunate animosity subsisted between the sister kingdoms, that each county should embody a militia, who were summoned to appear before the sheriff-depute on a certain day, and at an appointed time and place. This muir being both centrical for the county, and well adapted for mustering the militia, was the place appointed by the sheriff for that purpose ; hence it was called the *Sheriff Muir*, and still retains the name.

Slates.——There are two seams of slate in one hill, nearly of equal quality, which must have been wrought for many ages past, as the oldest houses in the district of country, to which they have been carried, are covered with them. The slates are of a dark blue colour, split to a proper thickness, and, for durability, and strength in proportion to their thickness, are believed to be inferior to no slate whatsoever, as no decay is observed in the slates of the oldest houses covered with them. The seams of slate having been long let, with a large farm in which they are situated, little attention was given by the tenant to the working of them, and the country was ill served with them ; but the quarries are now wrought, to a great extent, by the present proprietor, and his lessees, and the slates are said to be much improved in size.

Inclosures.

Incloſures, &c.—Part of the eſtate of Stobo, contiguous to the houſe, was incloſed early in this century, to which the preſent proprietor has added largely. The incloſures eaſt from the manſe extend about a mile, and to the weſt about two miles, and in depth, from north to ſouth, from half a mile to a mile. The river Tweed is the ſouth boundary. The fences are quickſet hedges, or dry ſtone walls. Incloſures are begun in other parts of the pariſh, but hitherto they have made no conſiderable progreſs. There are few full grown trees in the pariſh, except in the old incloſures of Stobo, where there are a good many; and in the new incloſures, conſiderable young plantations have been made of all kinds of trees uſually planted in Scotland. The farmers are in general ſenſible of the advantages of incloſures. One farmer, upon a three-nineteen years leaſe, has begun to incloſe part of his farm at his own expence; and others, upon ſhorter leaſes, ſolicit the aid of their landlords, (who are not averſe to encourage them), to aſſiſt them in making ſmall incloſures.

Productions.—Oats, bear, and peaſe are the ſtaple crops in the pariſh. Wheat is ſown, but in ſmall quantities. Turnip is ſown by thoſe who have incloſures; and potatoes are found to be ſo generally uſeful, and the ſoil ſo well ſuited to the growth of them, that they are raiſed by every perſon. Clover and rye-graſs are alſo ſown, and ſome ſow as much flax or lint-ſeed as is neceſſary for family uſes. There is more grain produced in the pariſh than is neceſſary for the maintainance of its inhabitants.

Population.—The number of inhabitants, of which this pariſh conſiſted, preceding the year 1734, is not aſcertained. From the remains of old houſes and old towers, which are now much defaced, but are ſtill in the remembrance of old people,

people, it appears that the population is confiderably diminifhed. The greateft part of the depopulation took place
previous to the year 1734. If there is any decreafe fince
that period, it is very trifling, as appears from the examination roll of the parifh at that time, compared with the examination roll of this year. Since the year 1734 it has undergone fome changes in regard to numbers. In that year
there were only 200 examinable perfons in the parifh, perfons from eight years of age and upwards. In this ftate it
continued till the year 1741 or 1742, when it had an increafe
of numbers, from having the half of the parifh of Dawick
annexed to it; in confequence of this circumftance, the
numbers were increafed from 200, to between 240 and 250.
Of late years, however, the numbers have decreafed. There
are at prefent in the parifh only 221 examinable perfons,
and 97 that are not examinable, or under eight years of age;
total, 318 fouls. Among this number there are 15 Seceders.
The number of males, from eight years of age and upwards,
is 119; the females, 102. There are 60 houfes in the parifh, and 5 inhabitants, upon an average, to each houfe. In
Dr Webfter's report, the number is 313. The births, for
thefe eight years paft, are, at an average, about 9 *per annum*;
during the fame period there have been 36 burials at the
church, but then 13 of thefe perfons did not refide in the
parifh at the time of their death; fo that 23 only have died
for thefe 8 years paft, being, at an average, about 3 *per annum*.
There have been only 10 marriages during the laft 8 years.

Church, &c.—The church of Stobo is Gothic, and appears
from hiftory to be between 4 and 500 years old. The remains of a font, an oven, and other apparatus peculiar to
the Popifh church, are ftill to be feen. It was called in ancient times the *Parfonage of Stobo*. It appears from the original

ginal rights of Lord Wigton, once patron of this pariſh, that it was a parſonage, having four churches belonging to it, which were called the *Pendicles of Stobo*, viz. the church of Dawick, upper and lower Drummelzier, Broughton, and Glenholm. Dawick is now annexed to Stobo and Drummelzier, and what was called, in the original rights of Lord Wigton, *Upper Drummelzier*, is now a diſtinct pariſh, and is called *Tweedſmuir Pariſh*. The ſtipend is 49 l. 8 s. 10⅔ d. Sterling money, 60 bolls of victual, part of which is meal, and part bear. Beſides the ſtipend, the miniſter of Stobo receives from Sir James Naſmyth 10 bolls of meal, which is converted at the Mid-Lothian Fiars, being the rent of one half of the glebe and graſs of Dawick annexed to Stobo. There is a manſe, and a glebe of 21 Engliſh acres, which is all incloſed, and ſubdivided with ſtone walls and quickſet hedges. The preſent incumbent incloſed the moſt part of the glebe at his own expence.

Poor.—There are very few perſons at preſent upon the poor's liſt; any ſupport which they receive ariſes from the weekly collections, and from the intereſt of ſome money which belongs to the kirk-ſeſſion.

School.—There is but one ſchool in the pariſh, which is taught by the eſtabliſhed ſchool-maſter. His yearly ſalary is 5 l. 11 s. 1⅓ d. There are about 24 ſcholars; from thoſe that are beginners, or confined to the reading of Engliſh, he receives one ſhilling *per* quarter; and from thoſe that are taught writing and arithmetic, one ſhilling and ſixpence. He has a comfortable houſe, which was built about 15 years ago.

Fuel.

Fuel.—There is no particular inconvenience which the inhabitants of this parish labour under from its local situation, but a difficulty of procuring fuel. There is no peat which can pay the labour of manufacturing. And as to the turf it affords, though generally used, it is of a very inferior quality. There is no good coal nearer than Lothian, which is 18 English miles distant.

Miscellaneous Observations.—The valued rent of the parish is 2874 l. 9 s. 8 d. Scotch, the real rent about 1143 l. Sterling. There are three proprietors, none of whom reside in the parish. The number of tenants is 11, their ploughs 14. There is an excellent breed of sheep in the parish, they are remarkably sound and healthy, of a middle size, and in number about 5000. There are 81 horses, and 190 black cattle in the parish. There are also a good number of black cattle, mostly of the Highland kind, which are bought either early in the summer, for the purpose of feeding, or in the autumn, in order to eat up the foggage or after-grass. The high road which runs through this parish, and which is commonly called *Stobo Hedges*, from its being bounded on each side by a hedge for some miles, was completely made some years ago. The roads which join it, on the west and east, have also been made of late years. The statute labour is commuted. There is no turnpike in the parish. There are two bridges over the Water of Lyne, which is the boundary, on the east, between this parish, and those of Newlands, Lyne, and Peebles. One of them was built by contribution within these few years; the other, though an old bridge, is very sufficient, and makes the access between this and Peebles very easy. The bridge which was lately built over the Water of Lyne, was in consequence of a road being made along the side of Lyne Water, which joins the

Peebles

Peebles road upon the eaſt, and the Kirkcurd road upon the weſt. This road is completely finiſhed, and is of great advantage to travellers coming from the weſt country by the way of Peebles. There is alſo a bridge over Biggar Water, which is the boundary on the weſt between this pariſh and Glenholm. This bridge opens up a free communication between this pariſh and the road leading to Moffat.

PARISH of TRAQUAIR.

(COUNTY OF PEEBLES, SYNOD OF LOTHIAN AND TWEED-
DALE, PRESBYTERY OF PEEBLES.)

By the Rev. MR. JOHN WALKER.

Name.

THE parish of Traquair consists of the old parish of St.
Bryde, and the greatest part of the parish of Kailzie,
which was suppressed as far back as the year 1674, and partly joined to this parish, and Innerleithen. The water of
Quair, which has its rise, and its whole course in the parish,
has given origin to the name, which, until the annexed part
of Kailzie was added, lay upon the slopping sides of the hills
which supply its current: and as the valley of a stream is
called its strath in Scotland, it is easy from Strathquair to de-
duce Traquair. In a charter granted by Robert, Duke of
Albany, in favours of William Watson, son to William Watson

fon of Cranſton, containing a grant of the lands of Traquair, &c. dated at Edinburgh, anno 1409, it is ſpelt Traquar.

Extent, Situation, Surface, &c.—The greateſt length of the pariſh is along the ſouthern bank of the Tweed, which lies in the direction from E. to W. between 8 and 9 miles. From the Tweed to the ſource of Quair is from 4 to 5 miles, which is its greateſt breadth in the direction from N. E. to S. W. It contains, according to Armſtrong, who made a ſurvey of the county about 16 years ago, 17,290 acres, about 4000 of which are arable. The figure is very irregular, being frequently interſected by the pariſh of Yarrow. It is bounded on the N. by the Tweed. The general appearance of the pariſh is hilly, rocky, and mountainous. Minchmoor, over which the old road to Selkirk paſſes, is more than 2000 feet above the ſea, and Gumſcleugh, and ſome other heights in the pariſh are at leaſt 200 feet above Minchmoor. The hills, in general, afford excellent paſture for ſheep. The ſoil on the low grounds, though in general ſhallow and ſtony, is fertile; and on Tweed haughs there is a conſiderable depth of loam depoſited by the river in the courſe of ages. The ſouth ſides of the hills are generally green, while their northern expoſure is heathy, and of a darker complexion. There are no volcanic appearances in any part of the pariſh, though many of the neighbouring mountains, according to ſome theories, may be thought to ſupport ſuch an opinion, as they are piked or conical. The common whin rock, a finer kind approaching to the baſaltes, a coarſe ſort of granite, and a conſiderable quantity of ſlate are the only kind of ſtones found in the pariſh. The ſlate was formerly wrought in conſiderable quantity, but they have of late rather dug at the top, than opened the quarry properly, and on that account the ſlates are found not to bear expoſure to the air without ſhivering. The noble family of

Traquair

Traquair have made feveral attempts to difcover lead mines, and have found quantities of the ore of that metal, though not adequate to indemnify the expenfe of working, and have therefore given up the attempt. Not long fince, a fpecimen of the Galena ore was found in one of the ftreams which falls into Quair water.

Climate, Difeafes.—The air is dry and healthy, though there are no well authenticated inftances of longevity. The lower part of the parifh enjoys a mild and temperate air, though the tops of the hills are covered with fnow, and the attraction of the mountains often deluges the upper part with rain, when almoft none of it is felt in the vallies. The clouds are often feen floating in the air, attracted from mountain to mountain, when there is funfhine below. The inhabitants generally enjoy good health, and are fubject to no epidemical difeafes. Rheumatifm more generally prevails than any other diforder, which is generally denominated the pains; the caufes of which, perhaps, are the poor manner of living, the badnefs and dampnefs of the houfes, the fcarcity and dearth of fuel, and an attachment to fifhing at night with lights, which is principally practifed early in the fpring, and late in the autumn feafons, after the Tweed is flooded with rain. In fummer 1789, the fmall-pox, which, for feveral years, had not vifited the parifh, prevailed very much, and cut off feveral children; but though there was a great prejudice in the minds of the inhabitants againft inoculation, many of them were prevailed upon to inoculate their children, and all of them did well, the experience of which has gone far to remove their former prejudices.

Fifh, Birds, &c.—The river Tweed, which runs along the whole N. fide of the parifh, formerly produced a great
quantity

quantity of falmon, which are now but feldom caught, excepting after the river has been flooded : it is probable, therefore, that the methods employed to prevent the fifh from getting up the river, are the caufes of their decreafe. Confiderable quantities of trout are caught in Tweed and Quair water. What is called the fea-trout is more frequently found
in the Quair ; both the fea and burn-trout are of an excellent
quality. They are principally diftinguifhed by the whitenefs
and rednefs of the fifh. The trout are caught from the beginning of April to the end of September ; they are chiefly
taken by the net, which deftroys angling. The king's fifher
has been frequently feen on the banks of the Tweed. Large
flights of wild geefe are frequently feen paffing from the S. to
the N. in the harveft feafon. The plover, fieldfare, woodcock,
dotterel and cuckoo, are frequently feen in their feafon. The
largeft kind of raven, and the true hunting hawk, annually
hatch their young in Glendean's banks. The fox is alfo a
conftant inhabitant of them.

Population.—According to Dr. Webfter's report, the number of fouls in 1755 was 651. From the beft information,
there is reafon to believe that the parifh, about 40 years ago,
was double in population to what it is at prefent. There were
then 2 confiderable villages in it : the one is entirely gone ; and
a few ftraggling houfes are all that remain of the other. Farms
now poffeffed by one, were then in the hands of 2, 4, and e-
ven 6 farmers, and the number of cottagers, befides the inhabitants of thefe villages, greater. The number of perfons
from 20 years old, and upward, might then amount to 400,
when, at prefent, there are not above 239 ; of thefe 129 are
females, and 110 males. The whole fouls in the parifh at
prefent are 446 : Under 10,—118 ; Under 20,—88 ; 48 of
whom are males, and 40 females ; under 50,—181 ; under 70,

—39 ;

—39; under 100,—19: of thefe laft, the oldeft is 89, who enjoys fuch health as fometimes to walk to church, though diftant from him above three miles, and to return home again without being greatly fatigued.

Sheep, Horfes and Cattle. The ftaple commodity of the parifh is fheep, of which there are fuppofed to be about 10,000. Large diftricts are occupied by one farmer, feveral of whom have part of their fheep-walks in the parifh of Yarrow, though their houfes are all in the parifh of Traquair. There are 98 horfes, and about 200 head of black cattle. The value of wool has greatly increafed within thefe few years, though they, in general, have their farms ftocked with Scottifh black faced fheep, they being reckoned better adapted than any o-ther for the lands in the parifh.

Agriculture, Heritors, Tenants, &c.—The whole of the ploughs employed by the farmers, are the old Scottifh ploughs, excepting two, which are of an improved conftruction : but plough is fuppofed to anfwer beft ; they are fome-times drawn by 4 horfes, generally by 2. When 2 horfes are employed, they are directed by the man who holds, when there are 4, they are conducted by a boy. It is impoffible to afcertain the number of acres employed annually in tillage. The principal crops in the parifh are oats and barley. There is a fmall quantity of ground fown in wheat, but nothing e-qual to the confumption. The parifh exports confiderable quan-tities both of oats and barley. It is believed from good au-thority, that there are annually exported of the laft mention-ed grain 500 bolls. A fmall quantity of turnips is annually raifed, which anfwers very well ; and almoft every individual in the parifh has his crop of potatoes. Either turnips, po-

tatoes,

tatoes, or peafe (of which a confiderable quantity) are fown
as a preparation for a fucceeding barley crop *.

The fheep lands, and the ground employed in tillage, are,
in general, occupied by the fame perfons. One who has no
fheep, but employs the ground he rents folely in tillage, pays
for fome of it 25 s. the acre; but, in general, the arable
ground is not the half of that price, nor worth it. There are
5 heritors in the parifh. By far the greateft proportion of the
lands belong to the Earl of Traquair, who formerly refided in
it at Traquair Houfe; but the whole family, for feveral years,
have been on the Continent. There is only one refident heritor at prefent. The greateft part of the parifh is poffeffed
by 10 farmers, one of whom pays above 300 l. a-year, 3 a-
bove 200 l., 5 above 100 l. There is a number of fmaller
tenants. The whole inhabitants of the parifh are employed
in agriculture, except the few following: 6 weavers, 5 joiners,
1 blackfmith and an apprentice, 2 mafons, 1 fkinner, and an
apprentice, 1 fhoemaker; the whole of whom are employed
by the inhabitants, except the fkinners, who export their dreffed fkins to Edinburgh. There are, befides, 5 tailors, who
are likewife employed by the inhabitants †. There are 12
Seeders,

---

* Oats are fown from the beginning of march Old Style, to the end of April:
Barley from the middle of April to the end of May: Peafe from the 20th of
March till the middle of April: Wheat from the middle of September to the
middle of October. The crops are generally cut down early in the feafon, the
reflexion from the hills caufing them to ripen quicker than might be expected.

† The number of fervants in the different branches of hufbandry vary according to the feafon of the year. Female fervants are more numerous in fummer than in winter, being engaged for ewe-milking and harveft work in general, at 3 l. and from 1 l. to 1 l. 10 s. in winter. A male fervant at 6 l. Out-
herds are paid by the free grafs to a certain quantity of fheep, or the ufual wages, 52 ftones of meal and a cow's grafs. The married fervants, of which there
are a great many, have, in general, 5 l. 10 s., their provifions in their mafter's
family, a free houfe and a garden, with as much land as they can manure, to
plant

Seceders, moftly of the Antiburgher congregation, and 3 Roman Catholics. The proportion of the annual births to the
whole population, is as 1 to 27 ; the annual deaths as 1 to
38, and a fmall fraction. Each marriage, at an average, produces from 5 to 6 children. There are from 3 to 4 marriages annually. The union of farms is to be confidered as the
great caufe of depopulation in this parifh. And the abfence
of the noble family who formerly conftantly refided in it, and
muft have given employment to a variety of labourers, muft
likewife have greatly contributed.

Stipend, Church, Manfe, Poor, &c.—The value of the
living, including the glebe, is about 78l. Sterling. The mo-
nied ftipend is 54l. 16s. 11d., and 16 bolls of oatmeal, and
8 bolls of bear. The glebe contains about 11 Scots acres,
which, together, make the fum above fpecified. The King,
in right of the Archbifhop of Glafgow, is patron of the old
parifh of St. Bryde. The Earl of Traquair was patron of
the fupprefled parifh of Kailzie; but that family being Catholic, could claim no right in the fettlement of Traquair.
The church was rebuilt about 9 years ago. The heritors, in
fpring 1790, very liberally contributed for rebuilding the
manfe for the prefent incumbent, which is not as yet finifhed,
and they are likewife to rebuild part of the offices, which,
when completed, will render the minifter's accommodation
very comfortable.—There are, at prefent, 10 perfons receiving alms, who are all, excepting one, who, it is faid, has
been bedfaft upwards of 23 years, able to do a good deal towards their own maintenance. Thefe 10 perfons are upon
the feffion's roll, and the annual amount of money for their
relief,

plant potatoes, or fow barley upon. The male fervants are more numerons in
winter than in fummer. The married fervants, befides their former emolument?,
have their fuel brought home by their mafters.

relief, is 23 l., arifing from mortified money, a voluntary affeffment of themfelves by the heritors of 6 l., and the collections at the church. The beginning of the mortified money
belonging to the poor of the parifh, was a donation of 1500
merks left by a Mr. Gerome M'Call, minifter or parfon of
the parifh before the Revolution, to which 300 merks by Mr.
Alexander Veitch of Glen, one of the heritors of the parifh;
and 100 l. Scots by Mr. Thomas Moffat merchant in Peebles,
were foon after added. The money now belonging to the
poor, amounts to 207 l., laid out at 4 per cent. intereft. Befides this fum, Alexander Brodie, Efq. who was born in the
parifh, now living in Carey Street, London, has fince 1782,
fent, at different times, the fum of 65 l. 16 s. to be diftributed
among, both fuch as are upon the feffion's roll, and to poor
houfeholders. This gentleman's liberality, both does honour
to himfelf, to the place of his nativity, and to human nature: and are the beft evidences to mankind that he merits
that affluence which his genius and induftry have acquired.
Mr. Brodie's liberality, added to the fum above mentioned,
makes the fituation of the poor very comfortable.

Morals.——Within lefs than 30 years, the people of the
parifh have changed their character very much to the better.
They were then much addicted to drinking to excefs. There
were at that time more than 6 alehoufes; at prefent there is
only one public houfe, which is feldom, if at all frequented,
but by thofe who are tranfacting bufinefs, or by travellers,
and is on thefe accounts neceffary. They are now fober, and
induftrious, and are generous, and humane, when called to
the exertion of thefe qualities, as was evidenced both in the
dearth of 1782, and fince, to a poor widow, who was left
with 6 children. They enjoy, in a confiderable degree, the
comforts and advantages of civilized life. Even the pooreft

in

in the parish, are, by the generosity of Mr. Brodie, formerly mentioned, furnished with the means of having their children properly educated, who has, for a considerable time past,
sent annually to the schoolmaster 5 l. 5 s. for educating the
poor children in the parish ; which, as it furnishes the means
of instruction to such as might either be deprived of it, or
who might enjoy it in a more sparing manner, is a very considerable advantage, and must redound to the honour of the
liberal contributor.   No instances are known of any being
banished from the parish, nor of any who have left it for misconduct of any kind.   There is not one of them but what is
a native of Scotland.

School.—At an average, there are 30 scholars who may be
taught english, writing, arithmetic, and book-keeping. The
teacher can also teach mensuration.   The greatest number of
his scholars, are such as are learning english.   For a country
schoolmaster, he has an exceeding good hand of writing,
and teaches both arithmetic and book-keeping very well ;
though few of his scholars are able to attend so long as to
feel much benefit by his accomplishments.   The emoluments
of his office are very scanty, and no way adequate to his usefulness, which, though no partial evil to that race of men,
renders it the more to be regretted. He receives 6 l. from the
heritors, 5 l. 5 s. from Mr. Brodie ; the fees arising from the
office of session-clerk, annually may amount to 1 l. 10 s.
He has likewise a free house and garden. As a considerable
number of his scholars are upon the charity, the school-
wages are no great matter, being but a perfect trifle a-quarter. As a precentor, he is very well qualified for his office.
His whole emoluments can hardly exceed 20 l., and with that,
by great economy, he supports decently, a wife and 5 small
children.

Antiquities

Antiquities and Natural Curioſities.—The buſh *aboon* Traquair, which in former times might be a conſiderable thicket of birch-trees, the indigenes of the ſoil, is now reduced to 5 lonely trees, which ſolitarily point out the ſpot, where love, and its attendant poetry, once probably had their origin. Part of the houſe of Traquair is of very remote antiquity, was built on the bank of the Tweed, eaſily defenſible from that ſide, and might poſſibly, in the days of hoſtility, be properly guarded on the other. It was in the form of a tower. There have been ſeveral other tower houſes in the pariſh, one of which is ſtill almoſt entire at Cardrona. The tradition of the country is, that there was a continued chain of theſe houſes ſo ſituated on both ſides of the Tweed, as by lights placed in them, intimation might be given from one to another of the approach of any foe. There are ſeveral places denominated Cheſters, where there are evident marks ſtill remaining of lines of circumvallation, moſtly circular in their form, which ſeem rather places intended for a ſecurity to their cattle againſt ſudden incurſions, than regular encampments. Tradition dignifies them by the denomination of Roman camps. They are all conſtructed upon the top of eminences not eaſily aſſailable, and every particular diſtrict has its own. Their frequency is perhaps the beſt indication of their uſe. Glendean's banks are remarkable for their extent and precipitous elevation. They are more than half a mile in length, and from 200 to 300 feet in height, and are truly a tremendous chaſm, as denominated by a certain author.

Names of Places.—Kailie, Cardrona, Glen, Fethen, Glenlude, Fingland, Teniel, Bold, and Quair, are probably derived from a Celtic origin. Grieſton, Know, and Scrogbank, &c. are not of ſo remote derivation. Grieſton abounds with ſlates, and has given origin to the name, expreſſive of the

colour

colour of that ftone. Know is borrowed from its fituation, being on a fmall elevation above the courfe of Quair; and the name of Scrogbank is borrowed from the farms, being partly covered with juniper bufhes, and other brufh-wood, which, in the old dialect of the country, received the general denomination of fcrogs. Though many of the places ftill retain their Celtic names, the language has been for many hundred years, perhaps, loft. The inhabitants, in general, fpeak the old Scottifh dialect.

State of the Poor in 1782 *and* 1783.—During this period of public calamity, the poor of the parifh were liberally af-fifted. Such as were upon the poor's roll, received their ufual monthly allowance; befides which, according to their neceffity, they were ferved with a proportionable quantity of meal, partly at the expenfe of the heritors, tenants, and kirk-feffion, and partly at the reduced price of 22 d. the ftone *.

Advantages and Difadvantages.—The diftance from coals, is a difadvantage under which the whole of the inhabitants labour, and the ill repair in which the public roads are kept, makes the difadvantage the greater. The parifh is equally diftant from lime; fo that both comfortable accommodation in the inclemency of winter, and the improvements of agricul-ture, would be greatly benefited by a proper attention being paid to them. It is believed, that the ftatute-work not ex-acted in kind, as was formerly the cafe, but demanded in money, would be fufficient to make proper roads through the parifh,

* The money laid out in the parifh for relief to the poor in that period of fcarcity, befides the ordinary contributions, was upwards of 40 l. The parifh adopted their plan of procedure at that time, from the method ufed during the fcarcity of the year 1740. Since the years 1782 and 1783, the feffion's contri-butions are more than doubled.

pariſh, though a toll-bar has been erected without any viſible advantage within the pariſh *.

* It is ſaid, that the road between Edinburgh and Carliſle, would be ſhortened about 27 miles, was it to paſs through the pariſh; and report likewiſe adds, that a public ſpirited gentleman has offered to contribute one half towards building a bridge over the Tweed, which, if it were carried into execution, would be a conſiderable advantage to the whole pariſh and neighbourhood, as, in place of going more than 20 miles for coal and lime, it would bring theſe neceſſary articles within leſs than 14 miles of the pariſh, and beſides opening the intercourſe between England and Scotland, produce many other ſalutary advantages. The road, ſo far as the line of direction is known to me, is perfectly practicable.

PARISH OF TWEEDSMUIR.

(County of Tweeddale—Presbytery of Peebles—Synod of Lothian and Tweeddale.)

By the Rev. Mr THOMAS MUSCHET.

Erection, Extent, Soil, Hills, Rivers, &c.

THIS district, formed anciently a part of the parish of Drummelzier, but was erected into a distinct parish in 1643. It is about 9 miles in length, and in many places as much in breadth. It is a hilly country, with some flats and morasses. A number of the hills are very beautiful, being covered with grass to the very tops; others have a mixture of heath; some are of a great height, particularly Hartfield and Broadlaw, which are about 2800 feet above the level of the sea. The river Tweed has its source at the south-west extremity of the parish, and runs through it in a north east direction. It is joined by the waters of Core, Fruid, and Talla, besides several smaller burns or rivulets, all of which abound with trouts.

Cultivation and Produce.—The arable parts of the parish produce oats, barley, &c. upon a light loam, with gravel and sand at the bottom; but, owing to the great rains, and early frosts, the crops are very precarious; indeed the whole of the parish is by nature principally adapted for pasture. The mutton fed upon the heathy hills and flats, is remarkable for delicacy

delicacy of taste and flavour; although small, and seldom weighing more than 10 or 12 lbs. per quarter, it is far superior (for the table) to the large mutton fed upon a low and rich pasture.

Sheep and Wool.——The whole of the parish contains 15 farms, which feed about 15,000 sheep, besides a necessary number of horses and black cattle. The graziers in the north of England, are particularly fond of the Tweedsmuir breed of sheep; they buy them of all ages, and drive them to their farms, where they are much esteemed, being healthy and good thrivers. A number of the young sheep are sold at the Linton markets, in the month of June, to be driven to the Ochil and Alva hills, and other places in the Highlands of Scotland; a number of lambs, yeld sheep, and draught ewes, are sold to the butcher, and help to supply the markets of Edinburgh, Glasgow, &c. The sheep farmers, commonly called storemasters, begin to smear their sheep about the middle of October, with a mixture of tar and butter, which, after separating the wool, is laid close to the skin in regular layers all over the body, to destroy the vermin that breed on sheep, and protect the animal against the inclemency of the weather. This operation, no doubt, lessens the value of the wool, but it is found to be absolutely necessary. The fleeces thus impregnated with tar and butter, are shorn about the middle of summer, and lately sold at 6s. and 6s. 6d. per stone; a great part of them is sent to the manufacturing towns in Yorkshire; some to the north of Scotland; a small part is manufactured into coarse cloth for family use, and some is spun into yarn, and sold in that state. Several attempts have been made to improve the staple of wool in this parish, by introducing an English breed of sheep, from those belonging to Mr. Bakewell; but they were found not to answer, as they were very

unhealthy

unhealthy, and never arrived to the size or fatness of the native sheep. Mr. Tweedie of Oliver, however, a respectable heritor in this parish, has found the Cheviot breed as hardy as the native.

Population.——The population of this parish has decreased considerably. About 70 years ago, the lands were occupied by 26 tenants, but the farms have since that period been gradually enlarged in extent, and of course diminished in number; even of the 15 to which they are now reduced, so many are engrossed in the hands of the same persons, and these often settled in other parishes, that there are only 3 farmers at present resident in the whole parish. The whole number of dwelling houses is only 51, and of these 3 are inns, situated at the Crook, Beild, and Tweedshaws, upon the high-way from Edinburgh to Moffat, Dumfries, &c. which passes through this parish along the banks of the Tweed, and is often, (especially in that part of its extent which lies within this parish), in a very bad state, but will now meet with a thorough repair. The whole number of souls, at present in the parish, is only 227; the return to Dr. Webster, in 1755, was 397, so that there is a decrease of 170. Before the practice of inoculation was introduced, the small pox frequently carried off great numbers of the children. The inhabitants of Tweedsmuir are in general stout and healthy, and many live to an advanced age. During the last 10 years, there have been 77 baptisms, 33 marriages, and 56 burials.

Church, School, and Poor.——The church was built in 1648. The stipend was paid some years ago, partly in grain, and partly in money; but an equitable conversion having been agreed upon, at the rate of 12 s. 6 d. a boll for the grain, the whole stipend is now paid in money, and amounts to 75 l. Sterling
a-year.

a-year. The Duke of Queenſberry is patron ; the lands in the
pariſh belong to 7 different heritors, of whom only 1 reſides. The poor are aſſiſted by the weekly collections at
church ; a ſchool was lately inſtituted, and a ſchool houſe
built ; the heritors fixed the ſalary at 100 merks Scotch, but
the ſcholars are few in number.

Antiquities.—Some remains of antiquity are to be ſeen in
this pariſh, near the highway ; and a few miles above the
Beild there are ſeveral cairns, which have probably been raiſed over ſome ancient graves* : Veſtiges of ancient caſtles ſtill
remain at Oliver ; at Fruid, where a family of the name of
Fraſer formerly reſided ; and at Hackſhaw, the ſeat of the ancient family of the Porteouſes.

* Near Nether Menzion, on the banks of the river Fruid, is the grave of Ma-
rion Chiſholm, who is ſaid to have come hither from Edinburgh, while the
plague was raging there, and to have communicated the peſtilential infection to
the inhabitants of three different farms in the pariſh, viz. Nether Menzion, Glen-
cothe, and Fruid, by means of a bundle of clothes, which ſhe brought with her ;
in conſequence of which, a number of perſons died, and were buried in the ruins
of their houſes, which their neighbours pulled down upon their dead bodies.

INDEX

Act of Parliament, 333—334

Agricultural improvement, 8, 9, 22, 25—26, 31, 36, 40, 42—50, 60—61, 84, 94, 100—104, 110, 124—126, 143, 147, 152, 158, 166, 168, 177, 179, 183, 190, 191, 198—200, 206, 216, 217, 223, 231, 241—242, 244, 246, 254, 263, 264, 265—266, 269, 271, 288, 292, 301, 302, 307, 321, 327, 330—331, 345, 370—371, 425, 428—429, 443, 447, 493, 503—504, 527, 530, 532, 539, 540, 549—550, 561, 563, 583, 587, 604, 605, 626, 629, 638—639, 642, 647, 650, 653, 656, 700, 712, 714, 742, 764, 776, 781—782, 784—785, 786, 800—802, 806, 825, 826, 831, 839, 871, 876, 889, 894, 896

Agriculture—crops, 1—2, 3, 7—8, 20, 25, 26, 27, 46—47, 84, 86, 100—102, 106, 117, 124—125, 130, 133—134, 147, 151—152, 153, 168—169, 177—178, 183, 191, 195, 198, 201—202, 212, 217, 222, 230—231, 241—243, 245, 250, 255, 264, 266, 268—269, 280, 285, 289—290, 292, 293, 301, 302, 313, 318, 326, 332, 369, 371, 386, 387, 409, 418, 426—428, 429, 442, 447, 448—449, 461, 462, 480—481, 492—494, 503—504, 526, 527, 532—533, 540, 554, 556—557, 562, 580—582, 602—603, 605—606, 614—615, 642—643, 646, 647, 650, 653—654, 655—656, 666, 677, 680—683, 700, 701, 727, 739, 743, 746, 755, 756—757, 779, 783, 791—794, 803—804, 813, 814, 825, 846—847, 871—872, 887, 890—891, 894, 903—904, 911

—implements, 228, 243, 373, 450, 580, 606

Alcohol, drunkenness, 15, 74, 99, 105, 117, 138—139, 499, 515, 524, 527, 699, 906

Alehouses, inns, spirit shops, 121, 138—139, 149, 172, 229, 295, 478, 543, 594, 652, 696, 741, 748, 760, 785, 837, 841, 906, 913

Almshouses, 602

Antiquities, 4, 14—15, 30—31, 61—68, 76—77, 92, 96—97, 107—109, 127—128, 140—141, 150—151, 159, 161, 169, 181, 186, 192, 206, 227—228, 235—236, 248, 252, 259, 274—275, 322, 335, 337, 377—379, 382, 400, 401—404, 404—407, 412, 422—423, 436—439, 440, 445, 458—459, 468, 480, 505—509, 511, 545—546, 557—559, 571—574, 575—576, 585, 594, 607—609, 613, 630—634, 638, 643—644, 657—658, 705, 709, 720, 731, 740, 753, 759—760, 772—773, 788, 789, 810—811, 820, 829, 870, 877—884, 892—893, 908, 914

Barracks, 223

Bleachfields, dye-workings, 11, 135, 332, 444, 516, 565—566

Breweries, distilleries, 11, 71, 87, 444, 515—516, 876

Buildings, improvement, construction, 6, 11, 38, 54, 87, 98, 132, 135, 213, 299, 375, 395, 443, 687, 733, 779, 782, 786, 875

Index

Index

Cotton manufacture, 566, 807, 839, 876

Craft guilds, 451, 511

Customs, duties, taxes, 11, 29, 98, 99, 105, 106, 167, 172—173, 203, 342—343, 370, 395, 433, 511, 519, 567, 587, 835—837, 844—845

Dairying, 46, 278, 372, 385—386, 588, 603, 784, 797, 803, 826, 832—833, 848, 890—891

Dearth, famine, 27, 234, 473, 610, 626, 643, 661, 718—719, 786—787, 901

Diet, 152, 167, 173, 295, 426, 520—521, 604, 654, 807, 809, 876

Dress, 105, 167, 228, 249, 297, 408, 479, 514, 547, 649, 662, 732, 807, 876

Education—moral and religious, 355—356, 620, 624, 821

Educational improvements, 142, 194, 233, 313, 523, 620, 627, 662, 772, 876

Emigration, migration, 475, 490—491, 635, 639, 807

Eminent persons, 19, 25—26, 78, 79, 80—81, 141—142, 145, 148, 165, 168, 400, 411—412, 435—436, 443, 445, 457—458, 462, 517, 577, 628, 630, 641, 720, 726, 744, 768—769, 771, 772, 788, 832, 835

Exports, 72, 106, 134, 147, 171, 247, 264—265, 289, 371, 444, 490, 677—678, 728, 739, 746, 757, 799, 903

Fertilisers—dung, lime, marl, seaweed, 2, 3, 8, 17, 20, 29, 37—38, 42, 43—44, 85—86, 91, 96, 101—102, 124—126, 134, 143, 145, 149, 151, 174, 181, 183, 193, 198, 199, 205, 206, 223, 235, 242, 250, 254, 264, 278, 290, 302, 321, 327, 330, 332, 364, 370, 371, 374, 417, 429—430, 442, 447, 503, 527, 532, 540, 554, 557, 561—562, 580, 583, 604, 656, 658, 659, 680, 695, 698, 700, 739, 755, 783, 789

Ferries, 652

Feudal services, 133, 181, 224, 244, 247, 286—287, 373, 759, 785, 789, 821, 835

Fiars' prices, 208 (facing)

Fish, 2, 10, 29, 89—90, 95—96, 113, 123, 131—132, 145, 166, 176, 188, 197, 210—211, 219, 240, 269, 270, 286, 318, 326, 365, 383, 395—396, 419, 435, 478, 486—487, 518, 538, 539, 553, 556, 587, 597, 625, 630, 648, 666, 676, 697—698, 719, 722, 742, 745, 765, 781, 791, 814, 872, 902

Fishing industry, 89 – 90, 95 – 96, 113, 155, 172, 211, 258, 272, 901

Floods, 18, 211, 457, 627, 651

Friendly societies, 392 – 393, 456, 523 – 524, 787

Index

Index

Lamm	8	0	0	6	0	0	4	0	0	4	1?	0	3	16	0
Merse	7	4	0	6	17	0	4	0	0	3	12	0	4	4	0
Lamm	6	6	0	6	5	0	3	16	0	3	6	0	3	18	0
Pease,	10	14	0	6	8	0	4	4	0	4	16	0	4	10	0
Meal,	8	8	0	7	4	0	4	8	0	4	0	0	4	14	0

Str	1768.			1769.			1770.			1771.			1772.		
Wheat	L.9	0	0	L.8	16	0	L.8	12	0	L.11	4	0	L.11	6	0
Merse	5	2	0	6	8	0	6	18	0	8	0	0	9	0	0
Merse	4	10	0	5	14	0	6	10	0	7	0	0	8	8	0
Lamm	4	10	0	5	2	0	6	2	0	6	10	0	8	0	0
Merse	4	14	0	5	11	0	6	3	0	7	4	0	7	1	0
Lamm	4	4	0	4	16	0	5	8	0	6	0	0	6	0	0
Pease,	7	16	0	5	8	0	6	8	0	5	12	0	7	8	0
Meal,	5	14	0	6	3	0	6	18	0	7	16	0	8	0	0

Str	1780.			1781.			1782.			1783.			1784.		
Wheat	L.10	16	0	L.9	16	0	L.12	16	0	L.11	0	0	L.11	8	0
Merse	6	6	0	6	0	0	12	0	0	9	9	0	9	0	0
Merse	5	14	0	5	14	0	10	16	0	8	14	0	8	14	0
Lamm	5	14	0	5	2	0	10	0	0	8	8	0	8	8	0
Merse	6	3	0	4	19	0	9	0	0	7	7	0	7	10	0
Lamm	5	16	0	4	13	0	7	9	0	7	0	0	7	0	0
Pease,	5	0	0	5	2	0	11	8	0	6	16	0	8	8	0
Meal,	6	9	0	5	17	0	11	8	0	8	8	0	7	16	0

Str	1790.			1791.			1792.		
Wheat	L.12	8	0	L.11	4	0	L.11	8	0
Merse	8	14	0	10	0	0	11	0	0
Merse	7	16	0	9	0	0	10	4	0
Lamm	7	4	0	8	8	0	9	18	0
Merse	7	4	0	7	4	0	7	10	0
Lamm	6	12	0	6	3	0	6	12	0
Pease,	8	0	0	6	16	0	7	12	0
Meal,	7	16	0	7	10	0	8	8	0

PARISH of HUTTON,

(COUNTY OF BERWICK.)

By the Rev. Mr ADAM LANDELS.

Situation, Surface, Soil, Rivers, &c.

THIS parish is situated in the county of Berwick, the presbytery of Chirnside, and Synod of Merse and Tiviotdale. Its form is very irregular. It extends from E. to W. full 4 miles; from N. to S. 3. On the S. it is bounded by the river Tweed; on the S. W. by the parishes of Ladykirk and Whitsome; on the W. by Edrom; on the N. W. by Chirnside; on the N. by Foulden; and on the N. E. by Mordington. The general appearance of the country is flat. On the banks of the Whittader, there are some rocks, but of no great height. The soil on the banks of the Tweed and Whittader, is deep and loamy; but towards the middle of the parish, it is thin, on a strong clay. The air is sometimes moist, but generally dry, and the people remarkably healthy. They were formerly much afflicted with the ague, but are now much more subject to consumptions. The Whittader, a small river that bounds the parish on the N. produces a few salmon, and great plenty, as well as great variety, of trout. The Tweed

produces

produces a great quantity of falmon, gilfes, and whitling trout, the laft of which are carried to London alive, in wells in the Berwick fmacks, and weigh generally about 3 lb. Ten boats or cobles are the higheft number allowed to be kept on this fide the river, in the parifh. The falmon are of the greateft value in the months of January and February. One falmon, from the fifhing of New-water, in January 1791, not 2 ftone weight, fold for L. 3 : 0 : 2, at Berwick, for the London market. The rent of the fifhing waters is upwards of L. 200 a year, and about 12 men are employed. The tide flows to Norham caftle, which is 10 miles from Berwick. A boat of 30 tons can come up the river to New-water Ford, which is 6 miles from Berwick.—There is great plenty of moorftone and freeftone on the banks of the Tweed and Whittader, moft excellent for building, and of a fine white colour. The haugh-lands on the Tweed and Whittader, are fometimes flooded, when there is any remarkable fall of rain or fnow.

Animals, Agriculture, &c.—The cattle are of the Tees-water breed, large and handfome ; and when properly fed, will weigh upwards of 100 ftone Englifh. The fheep are alfo of a large kind. Wedders are often fold, when 2 years old, for L. 1, 15 s. the head, when fhorn ; and their fleece is worth 5 s. 6 d. or 6 s. One proprietor has juft now fold 50 wedders at L. 105, after they were fhorn, their fleece, for the 2 years, worth 12 s. Wool is fold at 15 s. and 16 s. the ftone, 24 lb. to the ftone. Ewes are fold for breeding at L. 2 a head, and great prices are given for the hire of rams of the Leiceſterfhire breed, for the feafon. Hog-fheep, before they are fhorn, are fold at L. 1, L. 1, 4 s. and L. 1, 7 s. the head, for the Yorkfhire markets. There are about 170 horfes, befides young ones. About 3000 fheep at the Martinmas, 2000 more of lambs

at

at the Whitfunday; and upwards of 450 cattle.—There are about 5200 acres of land in the parifh. The one half of it in corn and turnips, the other half in hay, pafture, and wood. About 200 acres of wood. The annual rent of the parifh, land, mills, fifhings, &c. is L. 4000 Sterling. The rent of the beft arable ground is L. 2, 2 s. the acre. Confiderable farms are let at L. 1; inferior lands, at 10 s. and 15 s. Many of the farms are of that fize, as to let at L. 300 and L. 400 yearly. One reckoned worth L. 500 a-year, was rented, lefs than 40 years ago, at L. 50 or L. 60 a-year. There are 50 ploughs, all of them the chain plough, drawn by 2 horfes. The land in the parifh is all inclofed.

Population.—According to Dr Webfter, the number of fouls was 751. The prefent ftate of population is as follows :—

From 10 years and under,	-	234
From 10 to 20,	- -	172
From 20 to 30,	- -	138
From 30 to 40,	- -	141
From 40 to 50,	- -	83
From 50 to 60,	- -	61
From 60 to 70,	-	44
From 70 to 80,	- -	40
From 80 to 90,	- -	7

In all, 920

Of whom are males, 417. Females, 503. In the village of Paxton, 271. In the village of Hutton, 210. In 1770, there were, according to the regifter, 30 baptifms; deaths, 12. In 1780, 32 baptifms; deaths, 14. In 1790, 28 baptifms; deaths, 20. The heritors having confiderable property, are 8; befides a number of fmall proprietors.

proprietors. There are about 12 farmers, befides feveral carters, who occupy fmall portions of land, and who are employed in driving lime and coal. There are about 20 handicraftfmen, 8 or 10 apprentices.—There is no other kind of emigration but that which takes place at the Whitfunday, when there is a removal of many hinds, herds, and cottagers, into neighbouring parifhes ; whofe places are, at the fame time, filled up by others of the fame defcription, who are actuated by an unaccountable defire to change their habitations, though they feldom ameliorate their fituations. Nothing but the expectation of better pafture for their cow, can be affigned as a reafon ; for their gains, as they are called, which are, fo many bolls of corn, potatoes planted, and lintfeed fowed, &c. are the fame every where in this corner of the country.

Stipend, Poor, &c.—The value of the living, including the glebe, is about L. 115 Sterling. The King is patron. The church was rebuilt in 1765, has lately been ceiled, plaftered, and flagged, and is now a very handfome country place of worfhip. The manfe is new built, and, for the credit of the heritors, a very good one.—There are only 9 perfons on the poors roll ; 2 or 3 more receive occafional charity. The weekly collections don't exceed L. 10 a year. The half of which is appropriated to the fupport of the poor. That, with 3 months cefs, amounting on the whole to about L. 25, is equal to all the demands of the poor at prefent. There is befides the intereft of a mortification of L. 100 Scots.

Prices, Wages, &c.—The price of beef and mutton, is from 3½ d. to 4½ d. the pound, 16 ounces to the pound ; veal, from 4 d. to 6 d. ; lamb, 5 d. ; pork, which is bought, falted, and fent to London by the coopers at Berwick, generally

nerally at 3 s. 6 d. and 4 s. 2 d. the ſtone, 14 lb. to the
ſtone; geeſe, from 2 s. 6 d. to 2 s. 9 d. each; ducks and
hens, 10 d. each; rabbits, 1 s. the couple; butter, 8 d.
the pound; cheeſe, 7 s. the ſtone; wheat, L. 1, 13 s. the
Berwick boll; barley, 18 s.; oats, 15 s.; and peas, L. 1,
4 s. All the above articles, 30 years ago, ſold at leſs
than half the price. The wages of day-labourers are generally 1 s. a-day in ſummer, 1 s. 6 d. in hay and corn
harveſt, 8 d. and 9 d. in winter; carpenters and maſons,
1 s. 6 d. The wages of ſingle men ſervants, L. 6, 10 s. to
L. 7 the year; women, L. 3, 3 s. to L. 3, 10 s. The only
fuel is coal, brought from Northumberland, between 8 and
9 miles diſtant, at 2 s. 6 d. and 3 s. the load; the hire,
2 s. 6 d. in ſummer, and 3 s. in winter.

Miſcellaneous Obſervations.—The ſtyle of living among
the poor people here, is very different from that in England; and the earnings of the women, added to thoſe of
the men, make a more conſiderable ſum than that ſtated
in the account of the poor in England; and hence the in-
duſtrous and œconomical among them, bring up their families, when in health, very decently, without any aſſiſtance from the pariſh funds. The people are all of the ordinary ſize, except the pariſh ſchoolmaſter, who is computed to be 7 feet 4 inches high; his trunk is very large,
his legs long, but not well made; there appears a weakneſs in them, and in his knee joints, ſo that he walks
badly. He is very unwieldy, looks unhealthy, and is only
25 years of age. He is very gentle in his manners, good
humoured, and obliging. He teaches Latin, mathematics,
arithmetic, writing, and Engliſh, very well; has a very
numerous ſchool, above 60 ſcholars, and gives very general ſatisfaction.—The people are in general very ſober, in-
duſtrous, and œconomical. There is a moſt material change
to

to the better, both. in living and drefs, within thefe 20 years. There is no remembrance of a murder or a fuicide having been committed.—The roads are tolerably good. One, which leads to Berwick from the weft part of the country, is excellent. The crofs roads will foon be good, as the funds are confiderable, there being above L. 80 Sterling collected annually for ftatute-labour. The produce of one toll already in the parifh, and another foon 'to be erected, will be above L. 300 Sterling a-year.—In the year 1782, meal was fold to the poor people at reduced prices, for which the opulent chearfully contributed.—Mr Philip Redpath, the late minifter, was a man of great worth and learning, and well known for his tranflation of Boethius.

PARISH OF LADYKIRK.

(County of Berwick—Presbytery of Chirnside—Synod of Merse and Tiviotdale.)

By the Rev. Mr. Thomas Mill.

Name, Situation, Extent, and Soil.

THE ancient name of this parish was *Upfettingtoun,* which James IV. changed to Ladykirk, after having built a handfome church in it, which he dedicated to the Virgin Mary. It was within this church, that the fupplemental treaty, to that of *Chateau Cambrefis,* was concluded between the Englifh and Scots Commiffioners, and the duplicates were exchanged the fame day at Norham. On Holywell haugh, oppofite to Norham Caftle, Edward I. and feveral of the Scottifh nobility met, to fettle the difpute betwixt Bruce and Baliol, relative to the fucceffion to the Crown of Scotland. This parifh lies along the banks of the Tweed, is 2¼ miles long and one broad, and contains about 3500 Englifh ftatute acres. The country is flat, and interfperfed with a few rifing grounds. The foil in general is very good, and confifts of a deep loam. in fome places gravelly, and in others on a clay bottom. It is all capable of bearing good crops, with judicious cultivation: fome of the outfields were formerly infefted with whins and fome heath, both of which have long ago been totally eradicated.

Agriculture.

Agriculture.—The husbandry on both sides of the Tweed, is, in general, conducted with judgment and spirit: To give a particular detail of the practice would much exceed the bounds of this report, but as the tenants in a great measure depend on their live stock, and of course on the condition in which it is kept, they pay very particular attention to their grass lands, and the manner in which they are laid down, as it is found that the grass of land, in high condition, will not only keep a much heavier stock, but will fatten it much sooner, than the grass which we too frequently see growing on good lands, in many parts of the kingdom, under bad management *.

Sheep.—The sheep, in general, are very good, and are of that kind commonly known by the name of the new Leicestershire breed, which were first introduced into Leicestershire by Mr. Bakewell; they are found, in point of profit, far to excel any other kind of sheep in this country. The wedders after having been twice shorn, at 26 months old, or so, weigh from 20 to 28 lb. per quarter; and the ewes, when fattened, from 19 to 26 lb. Three fleeces and a half commonly make a stone

* The grass seeds are sowed with the first crop, after turnips or fallow, instead of the fourth or fifth crop, which was the practice about 30 or 40 years ago; and the succeeding corn crops are taken after the grass is plowed up. By these means there are no corn crops lost; and the grass has the benefit of the fallow and the manure, and throws up great crops, when compared with exhausted lands, which are commonly full of *couch* and other noxious weeds. Harvest generally begins about the 20th of August, and ends in September. The grass lands remain in pasturage from 2 to 5 years, when they are broken up for oats.—The English plough, with the feathered sock, is the only one used here. It is drawn by a pair of horses, and managed by one man. Oxen were formerly more used; but from their inability to drive manure and coals from any distance, and the slowness of their step, they have fallen into disrepute, excepting for home work, which they are exceedingly well calculated to answer.

ftone of wool, which fells from 15 s. to 18 s. per ftone, and goes into Yorkſhire to be manufactured, excepting a fmall quantity which is fent to Aberdeenſhire. This breed of ſheep are uncommonly good feeders, but often do not carry fo much tallow as many other kinds do, in proportion to their weight. Mr. Culley has undoubtedly the merit of having firſt introduced this breed of ſheep into the country, about 20 years ago or more; and at prefent there are 8 or 9 people in the diſtrict of country betwixt the Cheviot and Lammermuir-hills, whofe ſheep ſtock are very highly improved. The ſheep of the low part of the country are all of this kind, and are found the more profitable the oftener that they have been croffed by the beſt breeds. The number of them, as well as of the horfes and black cattle, depends fo much upon the ſtate of the lands in different years, whether in corn or in paſturage, that it is almoſt impoſſible to give an exact account of them: In general, there may be from 1500 to 2500 ſheep in the pa-riſh. The ſheep formerly in this country, called *Muggs*, were a tender, ſlow feeding animal, with wool over moſt of their faces, from whence the name of Muggs. There is hardly an individual of this fpecies now to be met with in the neigh-bourhood. Mr. Culley's kind of ſheep, on the other hand, have open countenances, without any wool on the face from the ears forward, and are as kindly feeders as the others are ſlow ones. They are neither long bodied, nor long legged, but well made, handfome ſheep, deep in their cheſt, broad at their ſhoulders, loins, and crops, which laſt are thrown well back; and they are deep and broad of their breaſts, which are well feen before; and ſtand on well proportioned, clean, fmall boned legs. Mr. Culley's ſtock is almoſt entirely fprung from Mr. Bakewell's, as he wifely perceived that Mr. Bakewell was in the right tract of breeding, long before moſt people would allow it.

Black

Black Cattle and Horses.—The black cattle here are of the
short-horned breed, and from the attention now paid to them,
it is probable, that they will be brought to a great degree of
perfection. The steers of the best kind of this breed, when
3 years old, and fat, will weigh from 60 to 75 stone (of 14lb.
to the stone), and if kept to a proper age, will weigh from 85
to 110 stone ; some individuals may even weigh a great deal
more. It may, perhaps, be proper to mention, that it is not
large sheep and cattle, that the farmers here wish to breed ; it is
the small, well shaped, kindly sort, that will raise most money
in a given time, from a given quantity of grass, turnips, or
other food. The cows give from 16 to 24 English quarts of
milk in the day ; some cows may give a great deal more, but
such are only exceptions from the major part. When properly fatted, the cows will weigh from 50 to 80 stone. There
are, in general, from 250 to 300 black cattle, and from 70
to 90 horses in the parish.

Fish and Birds, &c.—The river Tweed abounds with salmon, trouts, eels, &c. The salmon fisheries let here from
50l. to 100l. a year ; nearer Berwick they increase very much
in value. The salmon are all sent to the London market,
where they bring great prices. There is plenty of game, as
partridges, hares, &c. ; and in the winter, woodcocks, and
sometimes woodpeckers appear. In the spring, wild geese
frequent the country. Goosanders, wigeons, and cormorants,
resort to the Tweed in severe winters, and sometimes grebes,
and speckled divers ; and in the lakes there are numbers of
mallards and teals.

Population.—The inhabitants have increased considerably
within these 40 years. The return to Dr. Webster in 1755
was only 386. There are now from 580 to 600. Two years
ago

ago the number amounted to 534, and it has increafed confiderably fince that period: The people are moftly employed
in hufbandry, in raifing grain to fupply lefs fertile countries,
and in feeding live ftock, which are fent commonly to Newcaftle, Shields, and Sunderland.

Stipend, Rent, Wages, and Prices of Provifions.—The minifter's ftipend is 800 l. Scotch, or 66 l. 13 s. 4 d. Sterling.
The rents of this parifh are from 14 s. to 30 s. the Englifh
acre. The farms let at from 300 l. to 600 l. a-year, and the
tenants are for the moft part rich and profperous. A hind's
wages are from 14 l. to 16 l. per annum. The price of beef
and mutton in this country, after midfummer, is about 3 d.
in winter 3½ d. and in the fpring from 4 d. to 5 d. per lb. but
the prices are moftly regulated by the demands from the
Morpeth markets.

PARISH OF LANGTON.

(COUNTY OF BERWICK, SYNOD OF MERSE AND TIVIOT-DALE, PRESBYTERY OF DUNSE.)

By the Rev. Mr. ALEXANDER GIRVAN.

Name, Situation, Extent, Soil, Air.

LANGTON is fituated in that diftrict of Berwick-fhire called the Merfe. Its name, perhaps, was taken from the long ftraggling town of Langton, which extended from near the boundary towards Dunfe to with-in a few paces of the houfe of Langton, and the prefent parifh church. The town was of long ftanding, and, like other border towns, fuffered at different times from the incurfions of the Englifh, having been burnt in 1558, by Sir Henry Percy and Sir George Bowes ; and at other times pillaged by marauding parties from Berwick and the other fide of the Tweed. Mr. Gavin, the late proprietor, finding a town fo near his houfe a hinderance to his im-provements, offered to its inhabitants to feu, on eafy terms, a pleafant and healthful fpot of ground about half a mile diftant. His offer was accepted ; and in a fhort time, not

one

one ftone was left upon another of the old town of Lang‑
ton. The new village is named Gavintown, in honour of its
founder, and contains at prefent 159 perfons. The parifh
is in figure triangular. The mean length may be about 4½
miles, the mean breadth 2¼. It contains about 7200 Eng‑
lifh acres. From the E. to the N. W. limit, the afcent
is gradual; from S. to N., the afcent is the fame as far
as the foot of the high grounds, known by the name of
Langton Edge. On this edge, all the enclofed and culti‑
vated part of the parifh is prefented to the eye, as well
as the whole breadth of the Merfe, and of Northumber‑
land as far as Wooler. And here the reflecting traveller,
after recollecting with regret, how often the flat below him
has been rendered, by direful war, a defolate and enfan‑
guined plain, is pleafed with the variety and abundance
with which peace and well directed induftry, in modern
times, have clothed it. The foil of the parifh is various.
In the lower and cultivated part of it, the foil is generally
a loam of a reddifh colour, well adapted to turnip huf‑
bandry, and to the raifing of oats and barley, and fown
graffes. There are fome fields of a very deep and rich
loam, which make good returns when fown with wheat.
All the fields are enclofed either with a ftone fence, or
with a ditch or hawthorn hedge; and here fome of the
hedges, with the hedge-row trees, are found to thrive as
well as in any part of the kingdom. The higher part of
the parifh, which confifts of 5 fheep-farms, is covered with
fine green pafture, and is accounted as dry and found
fheep ground as is to be met with in the S. of Scotland.
The air, as we have no ftanding water near us, and are
placed in the upper part of the Merfe, is reckoned as
pure and healthful as in any quarter of the county.

Agriculture,

Agriculture, Cattle, Rent, &c.—Little was done for the improvement of the land here before 1758. Langton-burn, a ftrong and clear ftream which runs through the parifh from N. W. to E., had its banks planted with foreft trees to a confiderable extent, about 80 years ago. The trees throve well, and have been long, and are ftill a fhelter and ornament to the houfe and enclofures of Langton, as well as a beauty in the face of the country. Several fields too had been enclofed with fences of different kinds a fhort time after the Reftoration, and had been for many years let from year to year for grafs to troop horfes. The foldiers, who were accommodated in barracks on the eftate, and in the town of Langton, fpoke of the pafture as the beft their horfes came to in the kingdom, and were particularly pleafed with the pure water which is to be had in plenty in every grafs field. In 1758, Mr. Gavin purchafed the eftate, lying in the parifhes of Langton, Dunfe, and Longformacus. From that period till the time of his death in 1773, he was employed in the improvement of it. The plans he laid down were judicious, and the profecution of them unremitted. The grounds were cleared of furze, and broom, and ftones, and of every thing that could impede the operations of the plough. The rock marl, with which the eftate abounds, and lime from the Northumberland hills, at the diftance of 16 miles, were laid on as the foil required; the fields were divided with fkill, and enclofed in the moft fubftantial manner. In a fhort time, Langton affumed a moft cultivated appearance, rewarded the attention, and repaid the expenfe the proprietor had beftowed upon it. The rent in 1758 was 1100l.; in 1773 it was let at upwards of 3000l. There are in the parifh 30 ploughs, all of them according to Mr. Small's conftruction. The number of horfes is

about

about 70, exclusive of young ones; the number of black
cattle (December 1793) 380; a number less than usual,
on account of the apprehended scarcity of fodder: The
breed, a mixture of the Merse and Lammermuir kinds.
The sheep amount to upwards of 3500, and are of the Northumberland, Tweeddale, and Lammermuir breeds.—The
highest yearly rent for land within the parish, paid by one
farmer, is 900l; the lowest, 35l. There are several small
possessions, which bring from 15l. to 35l. of rent; but
the tenants of them are employed chiefly in driving lime
to the greater farmers, coals to tradesmen and others who
have not horses of their own, and stones and gravel to the
highways. All the enclosed grounds of the parish are let
from 2l. 2s. to 15s. the English acre. The leases are
usually for 19 years. The rent is all in money; no kain
or services are asked by the proprietors. There are 2 corn
mills in the parish, to which the tenants are thirled; but
this restriction has not, in my time, been considered as
any hardship. The valued rent of the parish in the cess-
books is 3092l. 14s. 2d. Scotch. The present rent is
nearly 2660l. Sterling, of which 2600l. belong to the
estate of Langton; the remainder to two gentlemen who
hold of the proprietor of that estate. Of the three heritors, two reside in the immediate neighbourhood, and the
principal heritor resides in the parish occasionally.

Population, &c.—According to Dr. Webster's report,
the population in 1755 was 290. The number of souls in
the parish, according to a correct list taken in the month
of July 1793, is 435. Of these 211 are males, and 224
females. In the same month, there were 65 married
couples, 8 widowers, and 20 widows. All the widowers
have

have children, and all the widows, except two. The ages
stood nearly as follows :

Under 10,	120	Between 50 and 60,	40
Between 10 and 20,	76	60 and 70,	22
20 and 30,	66	70 and 80,	17
30 and 40,	47	80 and 90,	1 *
40 and 50,	46		

The number of inhabited houfes is 87 ; a few are at
prefent uninhabited. There are 12 farmers, befides thofe
who occupy fmall poffeffions, 9 mafons, 7 houfe carpenters and plough-wrights, 8 weavers, 3 fhoemakers, 2
blackfmiths, 2 tailors, 2 thatchers, 1 cooper, 3 hedgers,
apprentices included, and 4 day labourers. The reft of
the men are in general hinds, ploughmen, barnmen, and
fhepherds. The unmarried women, who are not hired
from year to year, are employed in fpinning to manufacturers and others throughout the winter, and in the fummer and harveft are occupied in hoeing potatoes and turnips, hay-making, reaping corn, &c. The great bulk of
the people are hearers of the Eftablifhed Church, but a
confiderable number are attached to the Relief, Burghers,
Antiburghers, and Cameronians, and go to Dunfe and
Chirnfide to hear fermon †.

Stipend,

* The regifter of baptifms, marriages, and burials, has never been
kept with any degree of exactnefs ; and I wifh not to have any thing inferted in this account, for the truth of which I cannot anfwer.

† A fchoolmafter, who officiated as precentor in the parifh, about 30
years ago, is faid to have been (very innocently, in my judgment) the
occafion of much feceffion here. Anxious to improve the church pfalmo-
dy, one Sunday afternoon, without confulting the minifter, he, with a
few vocal friends who were acquainted with his intention, made a trial
of finging the pfalm without reading the line. This innovation fo fhocked
many of the hearers, that they never afterwards could be reconciled to
the Eftablifhed Church.

Stipend, Church, School, Poor, &c.—The ftipend is 50 bolls of oats, 32 bolls 2 firlots 2 pecks of barley, and 28 l. 17 s. 8 d. money. The corn glebe was formerly about 5 acres of the beft land in the parifh, to which was added the pafturage of 2 horfes and 2 cows, fummer and winter, over an extenfive range of rich grafs; but, near 30 years ago, the manfe being removed to the village of Gavintown, 10 acres of very indifferent outfield land, lying contiguous, and 4 l. 2 s. of money, were accepted in lieu of the old glebe and pafturage. The patronage belongs to the Countefs of Breadalbane. The church was built in 1736, and is at this time in a ruinous ftate. The manfe, built in 1766, was, at that time, among the beft, if not the very beft manfe in the county. It is ftill in tolerable repair. The fchoolmafter has a fmall houfe in Gavintown to teach in. His falary is 100 merks, and 10 s. of fee for acting as precentor and feffion-clerk. His fcholars may be reckoned, on an average, 20 in number, whom he inftructs in reading, writing, and arithmetick. The eftablifhed fees of the fchoolmafter are 1 s. 2 d. a-quarter for reading and writing, and 2 s. 6 d. a-quarter for arithmetick. With this fmall income, being himfelf a virtuous man, and having an induftrious wife, he has brought up a family, and been always refpectable. The poor on the roll are ufually 9; 2 or 3 more receive an occafional fupply. The yearly collection in the church amounts to about 5 l., the one half of which is referved for fuch perfons as decline being put on the roll; the other half is added to the parochial affeffment. The affeffment, on an average of 5 years, is 28 l. 14 s.; the one half paid by the heritors, the other half by the tenants. The poor have at all times been well fatisfied with the provifion made for them. When, on a particular occafion, any thing extraordinary

has

has been wanted for them, it muſt be told, to the honour of the proprietors of Langton, that the requeſt of the kirk-ſeſſion was never refuſed *.

Antiquities.—On the farm of Raecleugh-head in the pa- riſh, there have been, in ancient times, two military ſta- tions. The extent of both can be eaſily aſcertained, as the ditches are diſcernible at a diſtance to this day. Theſe ſtations, it is thought, were occupied during the wars carried on between the two kingdoms. In the reign of King Williṃ III., there was a conſiderable encampment of both horſe and foot oṅ the farm of Langhope-birks. The troops, it is ſaid, were encamped there at the deſire of Patrick Earl of Marchmont, a nobleman who very de- ſervedly poſſeſſed much of the confidence of his ſovereign. The

---

* *Price of Proviſions and Wages* —The price of proviſions in this pa- riſh, leſs than 40 years ago, did not amount to one half of the preſent coſt. Our fleſh-market is in Dunſe, and, in that market, the advance upon the different articles ſold, has, within theſe few years, been very great. Beef and mutton are from 3 d. to 4½ d., pork from 3 d. to 4 d., veal from 3 d. to 5 d. the lib. Amſterdam weight. Lamb is never below 3 d. ; hens are ſold at 10 d. and 1 s. each ; eggs from 3 d. to 7 d. the do- zen, according to the demand for them at Berwick for the London market ; butter from 8 d. to 10 d. the lib. of 23 ounces. Hinds, or farmers men ſervants, with families, hired by the year, have from 16 l. to 18 l. of gains or wages ; an urmarried man ſervant, victualled in his maſter's houſe, has from 6 l. to 8 l. ; a maid ſervant for houſe-work has from 3 l. to 3 l. 5 s. yearly, but when hired for out-work, ſuch as hoe- ing turnips and potatoes, milking ewes, &c. 4 l., and ſometimes more : labouring men have, by the day, from 1 s. to 1 s. 2 d. in ſummer, and 10 d. in winter : women employed by the day in hoeing turnips, hoeing and digging potatoes, have from 6 d. to 8 d. : in harveſt the men have from 1 s. 3 d. to 1 s. 6 d. ; the women from 10 d. to 1 s., with victuals. A maſon's wages are from 1 s. 6 d. to 2 s. ; a carpenter's from 1 s. 2 d. to 1 s. 8 d. a-day, without victuals ; a tailor's from 6 d. to 8 d., with victuals.

The state of the kingdom at that time might render the collection of forces in different parts of the kingdom a measure of great prudence. In 1792, on clearing the ground of a heap of stones which had been collected upon the top of the Crimson, or Cramestone Hill, on the N. side of the village of Gavintown, several earthen urns, of different sizes, were dug up. The urns contained human bones, but had no inscription upon them. In the lands of Middlefield and Crease, there are several coffins of stone, containing human bones. On measuring one of them, it was found to be 3½ feet long, 2 deep, and 2¼ broad. In the neighbourhood of the places where the coffins are found, there is a field which still retains the name of Battlemoor.

Miscellaneous Observations.—The people are in general above the middle stature, and dress, perhaps, better than their circumstances can well afford. Three brothers in the village of Gavintown, without any stock to begin with, and without friends, have, by the making of shoes, in less than 20 years, acquired upwards of 800l. I wish I could record, that all the workmen of the parish have been equally economical, industrious, and successful. Mr. Alexander Low in Wood-end, who rents of the estate of Langton to the amount of 900l. a-year, hath, by experiment and observation, acquired much knowledge of rural economy. He hath greatly improved several of the implements of husbandry, and is the inventor of a steelyard for weighing hay, &c., which it does with exactness, and is easily removed from field to field. The steelyard is made by James Allan wright in Gavinton, near Dunse, and sold by him at 6l. 6s. There are different quarries in the parish of the best free-stone. Peat and turf may be had in the

the vicinity of the parifh, and at a moderate price, but coal from Northumberland, though, on account of the diftance, and the badnefs of the roads, it coft about 8 s. 6 d. for a two horfe cart, is the fuel moft ufed.

There is one publick houfe in the village. If it be in any degree a nuifance, we have ourfelves to blame, as the fheriffs of the county will grant it no licenfe, without a certificate fubfcribed by one or two perfons in the parifh, of refpectable character.

PARISH OF LAUDER.

By the Rev. Dr JAMES FORD.

Name, Situation, and Surface.

THE name of Lauder seems to be of Celtic original, derived from the word *lade*, which signifies the passage, or course, and sometimes the mouth of a river; and it is literally applicable to the situation. It is situated in the highest part of the Merse, or Berwickshire. It extends about eight miles from north to south; but the bulk of the parish is contained in four miles, upon the strath of Lauder water. It is bounded by the parishes of Channelkirk, Stow, Melrose, Earlston, Legerwood, and Westruther. The soil is rather light and sandy. It is in general fertile; and, of late, has been highly cultivated. The ground rises gradually from the river, on each side, to hills of a moderate height, and mostly green. They are covered with a mixture of heath and juniper, which makes excellent sheep pasture.

Cultivation, Produce, Farms, &c.—There may be about nine square miles in corn and hay grass. Sown grass, for pasture and for hay, is much cultivated. The hay sells from 4d. to 7d. per stone, according to the demand. Good crops of wheat have been produced: but this grain is thought to be

too

too exhausting for the soil. Excellent oats and barley are raised, and exported weekly to Dalkieth and Edinburgh, especially oats and oatmeal. The soil produces flax in great perfection; but, at present, it is only cultivated for the use of the inhabitants. Turnip and potatoes are reared to a great extent; and sheep and oxen fed here with much advantage. The average rent of farms is from L. 50 to L. 150 *per annum.* In the neighbourhood of Lauder, the land lets from 20 to 40 shillings per acre; but the average rent of arable land is from 5 to 10 shillings per acre. Since the late improvements in husbandry commenced, some farms have been divided into two or three, and some smaller ones have been united, according to the skill or ability of the tenant. There is little land inclosed, except in the neighbourhood of Lord Lauderdale's house. All are convinced of the advantages of this practice; and it will probably advance with considerable rapidity. There was formerly abundance of natural wood, especially on the low grounds, and by the side of the river. It was long ago wed out; but the proprietors are beginning to plant again.

Minerals, &c.—There are some copper mines, but, it is supposed, not sufficiently rich to defray the expence of working. Moor-stone is every where to be met with. It is used for inclosing, and is very proper for the purpose, being large and flat. The slate found here is of an inferior quality. Adder-stones, arrow points of flint, commonly called *elf* or *fairy stones*, are to be seen here; and, in the neighbourhood, stones of fanciful shapes, as of snails, worms, and other animals. They are found after heavy rains, by which they are washed out of their beds.

Sheep.—The number of sheep produced and fed in this parish,

riſh, is ſuppoſed to amount to 10,000. The breed is, of late,
conſiderably improved. Taking the produce of this, and of
the neighbouring pariſhes, into conſideration, the town of Lauder ſeems to be one of the beſt ſituated places in Scotland for
the eſtabliſhment of a woolen manufacture. Turnips are
much cultivated for feeding ſheep; but, ſince the late game
act, the hares have become ſo numerous as greatly to injure
the crops of that valuable article.

Population.—There are at preſent about 2000 ſouls in the
pariſh. Its population has been increaſing, particularly ſince
an eaſy communication was opened between different parts of
the country by means of turnpike roads. 1500 of the inhabitants are above 10 years of age. About 1000 of theſe reſide in the country part of the pariſh, and the remainder in
the borough of Lauder. The annual average of marriages is
about 8 or 10; that of births and deaths about 30. Each
marriage, at an average, produces 5 children. The people,
in general, live long. Many have ſurvived 90, and ſome even
100, during the incumbency of the preſent miniſter. Some
are below middle ſtature, many above it; and the ſize of not
a few is upwards of ſix feet. The people are, generally, ſtrong
and healthy. There are about 40 farmers in the pariſh, and
a conſiderable number of artiſts in the borough and country.
There is in this pariſh a ſeceding miniſter; though the number of ſeceders is but ſmall. There are two writers, and two
ſurgeons. As this pariſh, when Dr Webſter made his inquiry, contained only 1714 ſouls, it has increaſed, within 40
years, about 300 in population.

Church, and Stipend—The church of Lauder was originally a chapel of eaſe to Channel-kirk, or Childrens Kirk, being
dedicated to the holy Innocents. At the Reformation, Lauder

der was made a parochial charge. At first, the church stood on the north side of the town, fronting Lauder fort; and it was in this old church that the Scotch nobility were assembled, when they determined to make a prisoner of James III.; and the house in which he was seized is still standing. The stipend, including the glebe, is between L. 90 and L. 100 *per annum;* half money, half victual.

Poor.—The number of poor in this parish is about 30. Their maintenance amounts to about L. 80 *per annum;* arising from affessments, Sunday's collections, and dues for lending the pall, called in Scotland the *mort-cloth.*

Wages.—The wages of a country servant is from 5 to 7 pounds *per annum;* of labourers from 9 d. to 1 s. a-day; of carpenters, masons, and gardeners, about 1 s. 3 d. The price of every kind of labour is greatly increased; reapers wages are almost doubled. The wages of women servants have advanced from 20 to 40 shillings *per annum;* and of such as work at turnips, and milk ewes, to L. 3 per half year.

Miscellaneous Observations.—The air is pure and healthy; and this place has been often called the Scotch *Montpelier.* The land rent of the parish may be about L. 6000 Sterling. There are six heritors of rank, only one of whom resides in the parish. The number of feuers, or smaller possessors of land, is considerable. There are about 100 ploughs, and many of them of modern construction.

For 30 years past, much improvement in education, manners, and the mode of living, as well as in several other particulars, has been introduced into this part of the country. In a course of about 10 miles, between Lauder and Tweed, the
river

river turns between 20 and 30 miles, some of which have been lately erected for the purpose of grinding barley and wheat. There are now turnpike, parochial roads, and bridges made, and kept in good repair, by the toll-bar money, and statute labour commuted into money, according to the number of servants and horses. The turnpike roads have been the cause of many other improvements. Coal, lime, and the establishment of a woolen manufacture, are wanting. The people are generally active and spirited, and have always been ready to engage in labour of any kind : Many of them are, at present, both in the army and navy. The poor in general consider themselves able to bring up a family with an income of about L. 12 Sterling.

In 1782, and 1783, the situation of the inhabitants was truly deplorable. It was the end of December before the harvest was finished, after a great part of the crop was destroyed by frost and snow. None of the farmers could pay their rent ; some of them lost from L. 200 to L. 500 Sterling. The country, however, was greatly relieved by the importation of white pease from America. Many found great advantage in feeding their cattle with furze or whins, beat into a mash. The poor were relieved by the expenditure of the public funds, which supplied them with grain at a moderate price. There were likewise several liberal contributions for this purpose. But the situation of this part of the country, and it is believed, of all the south of Scotland, was still worse in 1766 : In consequence of a parching drought during the whole summer, two-thirds of the cattle were slaughtered at Martinmas, and sold at 3 farthings a pound. Many of those that remained died at the stall in the subsequent spring, after having consumed all the straw that could be provided for them. Bear straw sold at 1s. 6d. per threave.

Prior

Prior to that period, not above four or five small beeves were killed in Lauder market at Martinmas. Since that time, in consequence of the cultivation of turnip and grass, there has been plenty of the best beef and mutton through the whole year.

Peat and turf were formerly used here for fuel ; but, since the turnpike roads were made, coal, though transported from the distance of 15 miles, is used for that purpose both in town and country. The farmers find it most for their advantage to bring home lime in the summer season, and coal when returning from Edinburgh or Dalkeith markets. These two, with Kelso and Haddington, are the markets nearest this parish.

Antiquities.—A considerable quantity of Spanish, Scotch, and English coins, have been dug up. The antiquity of the first extends no farther than the age of Elizabeth. The Scotch and English belong to the age of Edward Longshanks, and Alexander I. of Scotland ; and some of them are of a later date. The minister of Lauder is in possession of some of these coins, and also of several Roman coins, whose inscriptions are, *Lucius Flaminius, Julius Cæsar, &c.* There are many Pictish and Scotch incampments in this parish and the neighbourhood. All of them are of a round or oval figure, and are called *rings* by the common people. The Roman encampments were square or rectangular ; but none of them are to be seen in this part of the country. The largest Scotch or Pictish encampment in the parish is on Tollis-hill, or Tullius-hill. It is on the road between Lauder and Haddington, and is supposed to have got its name from a Roman army passing through this country, and commanded by a Tullius. Many tumuli are to be seen in Lauder moor, on
the

the old road to Melrose, where it is probable some battles have been fought, as fragments of swords, bows, and arrows, are found there ; but no record or tradition is known concerning them. The arrows were pointed with flint-stone, tapering from the juncture, about an inch long.

Lauder Fort.—Towards the north of the tower of Lauder, by the river side, stands Lauder fort. This fabric is near 500 years old. It was built by Edward Longshanks, who had over-run Scotland. It was rebuilt, and converted into a dwelling-house, by the Duke of Lauderdale, in the end of the last century. There are some noble apartments in it, and rich stucco work, according to the taste of that age. One of the old apartments is preserved as a curiosity.

PARISH OF LEGERWOOD.

(COUNTY OF BERWICK, SYNOD OF MERSE AND TEVIOT-
DALE, AND PRESBYTERY OF LAUDER),

From Materials communicated by Meſſrs MURRAY *and*
MIRTLE *of this Pariſh.*

Situation, Extent, &c.

THE pariſh of Legerwood lies in the ſhire of Berwick,
in the preſbytery of Lauder, in the Synod of Merſe
and Teviotdale. It is nearly on the confine between Lauderdale and the Lammermuir-hills. Immediately around
it are the pariſhes of Gordon, Earlſton, (or Elreſlington),
Melroſe, Lauder, Weſtruther.—It is an area of about three
miles in length by two and a half in breadth, or of nearly
eight ſquare miles. It conſiſts of an aſſemblage of hills,
gently riſing to a conſiderable height from the eaſtern bank
of the Leader. Anciently, as we have reaſon to believe,
theſe hills, and the intermediate glens, and all the circum-
jacent

jacent country, were covered thick with wood. The Britons, the Romans, the Anglo-Saxons, the Picts, the Scots, succeffively poffeffors of thefe regions, confumed by degrees the greater part of the woods, in the ravages of war, in opening paffages through the country, in fuel and domeftic ufes, in clearing the ground for cultivation. The marfhes and the ftrata of peat-earth likewife evince, that much of the ftanding timber was anciently fuffered to grow to decay, to fall down, and to moulder away on the ground where it had been produced. Here, as in almoft every other part of Scotland, the deftruction of the native woods appears to have been fucceeded on the hilly grounds by the growth of heath, on the lower and flat tracts by the ftagnation of water, and by moffes and water-plants. Such was the general afpect of the lands of this parifh, except on fome narrow fields around the farm-fteads, till it was happily changed by the cultivation of thefe laft 30 or 40 years.

Soil.—On the lower declivities of the hills, and in the narrow vales dividing them, the foil is commonly a deep ftratum of blackifh mould, compofed of fand from comminuted fragments of the adjacent rocks, of the exuviæ and remains of decayed vegetables, and of oils and falts from the atmofphere and from manures. On the cultivated uplands the ftratum of the foil is more fhallow, and is of a reddifh colour, as containing a larger fhare of ftony matter from the rocks, and a fmaller proportion of vegetable mould. The marfhes prefent deep ftrata of peat-earth, of which the appearance and qualities are fufficiently known. Its compofition is evidently, where it is the moft perfect, from the remains of decayed ligneous vegetables, with the occafional intermixture of a portion of the remains of gramineous vegetables, and fometimes of a little fand. Sometimes,

times, by the efficacy of its several ingredients, vegetables of all forts, and even other fubftances, are long preferved from decay in fuch beds of peat-earth. Hence are the trunks, not only of oaks, but alfo of other trees, often found, unconfumed and frefh amidft ftrata of this earth; and hence the graffes, which often appear in a ftate of good prefervation, in peats of a light, fpungy confiftency. The chemical conftituents of pure peat-earth, are plainly, carbone or pure coal, oils of different forts, the refinous extract of vegetables, and fimple earth. On the dry heathy heights in this parifh, the foil is commonly a thin layer of gravel, of peat-earth, or of both together.

Climate.—As to climate, the fnows and frofts of winter act here fometimes perhaps a little longer, and with fomewhat more feverity, than in the more fouthern, lower lying, and more richly cultivated lands of the Merfe; by the relative highnefs of its fituation, too, this parifh is not a little expofed to the winds and rains of fpring and autumn; and where the foil is thin and dry, its vegetation is liable to be parched by the droughts of fummer. In the end of April 1795, the progrefs of the labours of fpring was nearly eight days later here than on the low grounds of Mid-Lothian.

Difeafes.—The difeafes with which the inhabitants of this parifh are liable to be afflicted are, the epidemical difeafes common through the whole kingdom, fmall-pox, meafles, &c. and thofe other diftempers which are ufually thought to be produced by exceffive toil, and by unfeafonable expofure to a cold and humid atmofphere, fever, cough, catarrh, rheumatifm, confumption, &c. They are mentioned in this place, becaufe there is believed to be always

an

an intimate connection between the diseases prevalent in any district, and the nature of its climate.

Wild Animals.—The wild animals of this parish are not now numerous. The fox sometimes infests the sheep-pastures. Hares are plentiful. Those little mischievous quadrupeds, which prey upon poultry, have not yet been wholly exterminated. The houses, barns, and barn-yards are not free from mice and rats. Adders, although rare, are sometimes seen basking among the heath, in the warm days of summer. The rivulets afford trouts. The tracts covered with heath, are frequented by muirfowls, and the corn-fields are haunted by partridges. During the long continued and intense severities of the winter 1794-5, many of these wild animals perished by cold and hunger, and many, in the extreme weakness to which they were reduced, became an easy prey to whoever chose to pursue them. One gentleman had a number of hares taken alive, which he confined in an apartment, and fed plentifully with corn till the snow began to disappear, then generously set them at liberty.

Number of Inhabitants.—The number of the inhabitants of this parish has increased, in proportion as its cultivation has been extended and improved. In the year 1755, the population of Legerwood was stated to Dr Webster to amount to 398 souls. It is inhabited at present by 422 persons in all, of both sexes, and of every age and condition.

Heritors.—Among these ordinary inhabitants, is only one of the hereditary proprietors of the lands, Major Shillinglaw of Birkhillside. The other heritors, six in number,

the

the Marquis of Tweeddale, —— Kerr, Eſq; of Morayſton, G. Innes, Eſq; of Stow, John Spottiſwood, Eſq; of Spottiſwood, Captain Orde of Eaſt Morayſton, are non-reſident.

Farmers.—The whole lands of the pariſh are divided into 17 farms, large or ſmall, which are occupied by as many different farmers. Theſe farmers, and the hinds, labourers and ſhepherds in their ſervice, with their reſpective families, compoſe almoſt the whole population.

Huſbandry.—Huſbandry is, then, almoſt the only mode of induſtry purſued here. Until within theſe laſt 50 years, the farmers of Legerwood were almoſt excluſively graziers and ſhepherds. What little tillage they carried on, for the purpoſe of raiſing bread-corn for the immediate ſupply of their own families, was upon a plan of agriculture which has ſince appeared to have been extremely unſkilful. The ground was broken up with a fallow; three ſucceſſive crops of oats were then raiſed upon it; after this, it was left for eight or nine years unploughed, that it might, in this period of ceſſation, recruit its exhauſted fertility.

At length, as a more enlightened and induſtrious agriculture began to advance, with its improvements from the ſouthern diſtricts of Berwickſhire, northwards, through the reſt of Scotland; the farmers of Legerwood were by degrees convinced, that even as graziers they ſhould be greatly gainers by a more extenſive, and a more ſkilfully conducted tillage. They adopted, one after another, that rotation of crops which ſtill prevails in the pariſh. The fallow is diſuſed; ley is for the two firſt years after it has been broken up, ſown with oats; on the third year it is manured with dung, and ſown with turnip-ſeed, or with peaſe, if dung be wanting for manure; yet a fourth year, the ſame field is ploughed.

ploughed, and the feed is now oats or barley, with grafs-
feeds. Where the foil is light and thin, only three fucceffive crops are raifed upon it; the fecond of the crops of
oats above mentioned being here omitted. After this rotation of crops, the field remains unploughed, till the graffes,
of which the feeds were mixed with the laft feed of barley
or oats, begin to be exterminated from the fward, and the
native heath and bog-graffes to be unfeafonably renewed.

The manures employed in thefe proceffes of agriculture
are folely dung, as is above mentioned, and lime, imported
from Mid-Lothian. The dung from the ftalls of the cattle
is carefully accumulated in the farm-yard, and is, in the
proper feafon, conveyed thence to be fpread upon the fields
under tillage; or the cattle are at times folded in the fields,
fo as to manure the ground of the fold as they drop their
dung, without farther care on the part of the owners, than
that of removing the fold occafionally from one fituation
to another. The diftance of the lime kilns of Mid-Lothian
would render lime an enormoufly expenfive article of manure to the farmers of Legerwood and its neighbourhood,
were it not that grain and other things are ufually carried
to Dalkeith market, in the carts which return loaded with
lime. Fields covered deep with ftrata of peat-earth are
often quickened by the manure of lime to amazing fertility. Where the foil is of fufficient depth, dung often produces an exceffive luxuriancy of crop, in which the vegetation is wafted in ftraw and empty ears.

The foil of many parts of thefe lands does not want
ftrength fufficient for the production of wheat; but a previous fallow would generally be neceffary, in confequence
of which there would be but one crop obtained in the courfe
of two years; and no one crop of wheat would be equal in
value to two crops of oats, barley, or turnips.

Potatoes

Potatoes are cultivated in conſiderable quantities in this pariſh, as over the reſt of Scotland; but do not enter invariably into the rotation, and are not in any peculiar degree a favourite article of crop.

Various ſorts of ſeed-oats have been tried here. Blainſley oats and red oats are the two ſpecies the moſt generally ſown. Red oats are found to ſucceed peculiarly well on the ſoil and in the climate of Legerwood; yielding, at an average, eight bolls in the hundred of larger increaſe than any other ſort of ſeed oats; thickening ſurpriſingly on the field as they grow up, from a thin ſowing; enduring the autumnal winds with comparatively little ſhaking of the ears; affording the beſt ſtraw; and giving, in meal, half a ſtone more from the boll of rough corn, than the Blainſley oats yield.

But turnips are, above all others, the favourite article of crop. They are precious, as green food, equally to ſheep and black cattle during winter; the manure and culture neceſſary to produce a crop of turnips, ſerve admirably to prepare the field for the cultivation and produce of the enſuing year; the waſte of the turnips that remains unconſumed by the cattle, forms alſo a rich manure to the ground on which they are ſcattered.

Horſes are the only beaſts of draught or burden employed in this pariſh. All the implements of huſbandry, carts, ploughs, harrows, &c. are of the moſt advantageous conſtruction known in the county. A double plough for turnips, the invention of Mr Paterſon, and formed to be drawn by one or two horſes, is alſo in uſe here, and is found to afford a very convenient abridgment of labour. Two threſhing-machines have been already erected in this pariſh, and there is a third about to be ſet up in the preſent ſummer (1795), at the firſt coſt of from L. 60 to L. 100 Sterling. But this expence is quickly repaid by the ſaving of labour, which is obtained from the uſe of the threſhing-machine.

machine. Here are two corn-mills, which are in part supported by the reftrictions of thirlage upon the lands of the
parifh. Happily, modes of mutual accommodation have
been generally adopted between the farmers, the millers,
and the landholders, which prevent thefe reftrictions from
being felt as intolerably grievous. The ploughmen in this
parifh are eminently dexterous and fkilful. Three fmiths
and two joiners perform that work in wood and iron, which
is requifite to repair, from time to time, the implements of
farm-labour, &c.

Yet, however fkilful and induftrious the agriculture of
Legerwood, even a ftranger might judge, at a firft afpect,
that the feeding and fattening of fheep and black cattle are
the primary objects of the induftry of the farmers of this
parifh.

Inclofures, Roads, &c.—No inconfiderable portions of
the lands ftill lie here and there in undrained marfhes, or
are bleakly covered with their native barren heath. Here
is a general want of inclofures; and thofe which appear
are chiefly turf-dikes; for indeed the climate, and the nib-
bling of the fheep, are unfavourable to the thriving of
hedges; and ftones, for ftone walls of any kind, are extremely fcarce. Except in two or three inftances, the parifh bye-roads are in a very indifferent ftate. The uplands
and flopes are bare of wood, as in thofe wild fcenes into
which the improvements and decorations of cultivation
have not yet been admitted.

Animal Stock.—The horfes and other animals maintained
on thefe farms are numerous. An hundred and fix horfes,
old and young, are kept for the faddle or the draught, and
to fupply the gradual wafte. The fheep are no fewer than
3769. The black cattle are at prefent 559; and here are
59 fwine.

The

The sheep are of a breed from Northumberland, valuable alike for mutton and for wool. They are annually smeared with butter and tar, mingled in the proportion of four pounds of butter to one pint of tar. They, equally with the black cattle, feed in winter on hay and turnips; and in summer find their food on the open pastures.

Gross yearly Produce.—Upon these lands, with this stock, and by these modes of management and cultivation, the farmers of Legerwood furnish a gross annual produce of

6000 bolls of corn, worth		L.	4500	0 0
Wool, to the value of	-		400	0 0
Sheep sold,	-	-	1300	0 0
Black cattle,	-	-	1070	0 0
In their total value,	-	L.	7270	0 0

Yearly Consumption and Expence.—Out of this gross value rents are to be paid to the amount of

amount of - -	L.	1430	0 0
The poor are sustained by an assessment of		30	0 0
The parish roads are repaired and extended by an assessment of - -		25	0 0
The expences of labour, of feed and manure, of the renewal of the animal stock, and of the maintenance of the families of the farmers, cost annually - -		3785	0 0
	L.	5270	0 0
		2000	0 0
	L.	7270	0 0

Surplus of the yearly Produce.—Thus, of the gross produce of the lands, there remains, after the deduction of these various *items* of annual expenditure, only the sum of L. 2000 as a compensation for the toil and skilful management of the farmers; as interest upon the value of their unperishing

unperifhing ftock ; as a gradual repayment of that part of
their ftock which is funk in improvements upon the lands ;
and as clear profits upon the various bargains of fale and
purchafe which they tranfaft in the courfe of the year *.

This would appear no very confiderable return, if we
fhould compare it with the value of the ftock and labour
by which it is produced ; and again, with the profits which
the fame quantity of ftock and labour would afford in feveral departments of trade and manufactures. Yet it exhibits, in no unpleafing light, the advantages which attend
the profecution of agriculture, where the hufbandman is
encouraged by a leafe fufficiently long, and reafonable in
its terms, to lay out his fortune freely in the cultivation of
his farm, and to exert upon it all his induftry and ingenuity. For moft of the lands in this parifh are poffeffed
by the tenants upon long and eafy leafes, which have given
great encouragement to bold and expenfive agricultural
improvements. By this management, the landholders are
perhaps ftill more highly gainers than their tenants; becaufe, in the *firft* place, rents that are eafily made out of
the lands, are punctually paid, without deficiency or litigation; and, in the *fecond* place, becaufe the value of lands
is much more rapidly augmented in thefe circumftances,
than in the cafe of fhort leafes and racked rents.

Hinds.—The circumftances of the country, and the generofity of the farmers, are fuch as to reward the toil of
the hinds, or labourers, in this parifh, with a very liberal
fhare of the produce of the lands. Married are almoft always preferred to unmarried male-fervants, fhepherds, or
ploughmen. They are fettled in fnug cottages on the farms
to which they for the time refpectively belong. In grain,
money,

* It is even probable, that many other fums of unafcertained expence
muft be deduced from this fum of L. 2000 before the clear profit only
fhould remain.

money, and other articles for their ſupport or accommodation, they receive an yearly wage, varying with circumſtances from L. 15 to L. 20 Sterling. Beſides, each hind,
poſſeſſing a cottage, is, at the ſame time, obliged to furniſh
to his landlord and employer, a female-labourer, his wife,
daughter, or ſervant, to work occaſionally throughout the
year for the hire of 8 d. a-day.

Markets for Exports.—Of the grain, peaſe, wool, oxen
and ſheep annually produced in this pariſh, the owners, after reſerving thoſe portions which are neceſſary for the various uſes of domeſtic conſumption, ſell the reſt to dealers,
who reſort hither to purchaſe them, or export them for ſale
to the markets of Dalkeith and Kelſo. The wool is commonly purchaſed by or for woollen-manufacturers from
England, Galaſhiels, or Peterhead. Some ſheep of that
age at which they are termed *hogs*, and a few black cattle,
are occaſionally ſold into England. But, for grain of all
ſorts, for oxen, cows, and ſheep, Dalkeith is the ordinary
and principal market. Formerly here, and in the neighbourhood, were ſeveral dealers in meal, who purchaſing
the corn from the farmers, manufactured it into meal for
the markets of Kelſo, Lauder, and Dalkeith. At preſent,
the two millers of the pariſh ſtill continue very properly
to deal as meal-mongers; but moſt of the grain is exported
unground.

Imports.—As to the requiſite imports of coals, lime, gro-
cer's goods, draper's goods, hardware, ſtationer's goods, &c.
theſe are all obtained from Kelſo, Lauder, Dalkeith, and
Edinburgh. Kelſo affords the beſt and moſt convenient
market for butchers meat. Lauder is the neareſt poſt-
town, but too ſmall a place to ſerve to any conſiderable extent as a market. An attempt which is now made to find
coals

coals on the Earl of Lauderdale's estate, near Blackshiells, if successful, will furnish a considerably nearer market for this article of fuel, than those coal-works immediately around Dalkeith and Edinburgh, from which it is at present procured.

Houses.—Here are, at Corsbie, at Westmorayston, and at Whitslade, three ancient towers, monuments of that state of the arts and manners of our ancestors; in which, saving ecclesiastical edifices, there were no buildings in this country, but the fortress and the cottage; and in which, all the accommodation that was sought in a house, was barely shelter and security. The present dwelling-houses are dispersed over the farms; only, on the farm of Legerwood (proper), is there such an assemblage of houses together, as composes a hamlet, or incipient village. The houses of the farmers are commonly of two stories in height, handsomely and comfortably fitted up within, with a square of office-houses and a kitchen-garden contiguous, and having flocks of poultry feeding round them. The houses of the hinds are dry, snug, and comfortable, affording to these honest labourers better domestic accommodation than the greatest noblemen enjoyed five or six centuries ago, in the strongest and most spacious of those castles, the ruins of which we still admire.

Manners, &c.—The inhabitants of this parish appear to be in general healthy, sober, virtuous, industrious, and intelligent. Except about 40 Dissenters, they are all content with the religious instruction to be received in their parish-church; the minister of which enjoys a living of about L. 90 Sterling in yearly value, with a manse and a glebe. The children of the hinds are carefully sent to the parish-school, to learn reading, writing, arithmetic, and the

first

firſt principles of religion ; the pariſh-ſchoolmaſter enjoying, befide the wages, a falary of L. 11 : 6 : 8 Sterling. The farmers are enabled to give their children all the real advantages of what is ufually called *a liberal education*. Moſt of the articles of drefs uſed here are imported, not manufactured within the pariſh. Here are two or three tailors, and one weaver.——The language of this pariſh having, for thefe laſt 1200 years, been chiefly Saxon, is at prefent, with that fpoken through all Berwickſhire and in Northumberland, more fubſtantially Saxon than the language of any other diſtrict in Great Britain. The names of places in this pariſh are all, or almoſt all, purely Saxon : As, for inſtance, *Legerwood*, fignifying precifely, *the hollow wood*, or the *hollow place in the wood*, and accurately expreſſive of the fituation of the farm which bears the name, and communicates it to the pariſh : *Corſbie*, quaſi *Caer-bee*, *the Caſtle*, a name compounded from a Britiſh and a Saxon word, having both the fame fignification, fo that there was probably a Roman ſtation here, before the Anglo-Saxons came into the iſland : *Boon*, *the Upper Farm, or Dwelling*, &c.

PARISH OF LONGFORMACUS.

By the Rev. Mr SELBY ORD.

———————

Name, Situation, and Surface.

IT is uncertain whence the name of this parish is derived. It is in the shire of Berwick, presbytery of Dunse, and synod of Kelso. It is twelve miles long and six broad ; surrounded by the parishes of Dunse, Langton, Greenlaw, Westruther, Cranshaws, and Abbey St Bethun's. It is quite hilly ; being in the midst of that ridge of hills which divides the flat and rich lands of East Lothian from the beautiful, well inclosed, and highly cultivated plains of Berwickshire. The greatest part of the surface is covered with heath, eaten by small black faced sheep, which, when removed to good pastures, may be so fattened as to weigh 10 or 12 pounds the quarter.

Cultivation and Produce.—The lands near the rivers Whitadder and Dye, have been improved by lime brought from East Lothian at the distance of 17 miles, and have been made to raise oats, barley, pease, rye-grass, red and white clover, and turnip. But the farmers are prevented from great exertions by the high rents, the great expence of manure, the badness of the roads, and the distance of markets.

markets. The increase of corn is from two, or even one, to six. The present land rent amounts to L. 1700 a year. There are 9 heritors. The patron of the parish, Mr Home, is the only residing one.

Climate and Population.—The air is dry, cold, and piercing. The only diseases are rheumatisms and cutaneous disorders, which seem to be occasioned by poor food, damp houses, and want of cleanliness. Population, owing to large farms, to the tenants residing at a distance, and to part of the lands being turned entirely into pasture for sheep, is on the decrease. The number of souls is 452 ; of families, 100 ; of persons from 16 to 60 years of age, 112. The number of births, in these last six years, is 47 ; of marriages, 21 ; of deaths, 27. Many people born in this parish being obliged to seek employment in other parishes, all who die in the parish not being buried in it, and those only registered that are buried here, the deaths bear but a small proportion to the births.

Poor and Wages.—There are 5 families, consisting of 13 persons, upon the poors roll. They receive L. 15 *per annum ;* which is raised by weekly collections at the church, and occasional cess upon the lands. A labourer's wages is 1s. a-day ; masons and joiners 1s.; tailors, 6d. and their meals. Household men servants wages are 6 or 7 pounds *per annum*, and women, 3 and 4 pounds.

Miscellaneous Observations.—The stipend of this parish is L. 100. There are about 70 horses, 500 score of sheep, and 200 head of cattle. There are favourable appearances of copper ore. Attempts were made to work it a few years ago ; but patience and perseverance were wanting. Some cart loads of ore were dug up in making a road : The present minister

minister smelted some of it, and found it very rich. There are two hills of a beautiful shape, known by the name of the *Dirrington Laws.* There is a heap of stones at a place called *Byrecleugh,* 80 yards long, 25 broad, and 6 high. They were collected, probably, by some army, to perpetuate a victory, or some other remarkable event. The mosses and moors in the parish supply the inhabitants with fuel; but some coal is brought from a distance. The people, accustomed to the pastoral life in their early years, are rather inclined to indolence and ease. Their condition might be improved by the introduction of manufactures.

PARISH OF MERTOUN.

(County of Berwick, Synod of Merse and Tiviotdale, Presbytery of Lauder.)

By the Rev. Mr. James Duncan.

Name, Extent, Surface and Soil.

THE name of this parifh has been uniformly the fame, and the etymology commonly given of it is, *The Town of the Mire.* At a period very remote, this derivation might perhaps be proper, though the general appearance at prefent by no means juftifies it. In length it is nearly 6 miles, and in breadth from 2 to 3. The weftern part ftands high, and is extremely picturefque. From Bimerfyde-hill, the property of Mr. Haig, over which one of the moft publick roads in the parifh paffes, the eye of the traveller is at once gratified with every thing beautiful and magnificent, wood, water, hills, ruins, and fertile fields. The reft of the parifh, gradually declining to the S., is alfo extremely pleafant; the profpect being agreeably diverfified with excellent enclofures, beautiful hedge-rows,

and

and thriving plantations. The foil towards the Tweed, particularly the haughs, is fharp, with a gravelly bottom; towards the N., and indeed through the reft of the parifh, with very few exceptions, it is a ftiff clay, with a till bottom.

Improvements.—While other places have been advancing in improvement, this parifh has not been neglected. About 40 years ago, the tenants were miferably lodged, the fields open and expofed to every blaft, and hardly a tree to be feen, a few about the houfes of the different proprietors excepted. Now the fcene is agreeably changed; the tenants poffefs warm and comfortable houfes, many of them large, and moft of them flated; the greater part of the arable land is enclofed, and furrounded with belts and clumps of plantation. The eftate of Mr. Scott of Harden in particular, which comprifes nearly two-thirds of the whole, exhibits a greater extent of neat thriving hedges and plantations, than perhaps is to be met with in the S. of Scotland.

Agriculture and Produce.—Previous to the year 1766, the old Scotch plough only was ufed, and no manure thought of but what the farms produced. Since that period, immenfe quantities of lime have been annually driven from Lothian and England, at the great diftance of 26 miles. It anfwers extremely well; and though each cart, of 5 bolls, all expences included, cofts 10s. 6d., the farmer finds his account in ufing it. Two horfe ploughs are generally ufed, and the moft approved methods of hufbandry keenly followed. The quantity of grain annually fown, and the average return of each boll, is nearly as follows:

Bolls

Bolls Sown.			*Average Return of each Boll.*
Oats from 700 to 750,	-	-	5
Barley from 160 to 180,	-	-	6
Wheat from 100 to 130,	-	-	7
Peafe from 100 to 130,	-	-	5

Befides the above, there are generally from 180 to 200 acres in red clover for hay, and from 100 to 120 acres in turnip. The total number of acres in pafture and tillage, may be about 5550.

Black cattle, young and old, from 540 to 560.

Sheep, from 1400 to 1500.

Horfes, young and old, from 120 to 130.

The cattle are moftly of the Balmerfhire breed, and the greater part of them reared in the parifh. The fheep are of different kinds, and moft of them brought from different quarters. Mr. Scott of Harden made feveral attempts to improve them; for an account of which, fee Prefent State of Hufbandry in Scotland, Vol. II. The horfes in general are ftrong, and many of them, when taken to market, bring high prices *.

Population.—The population, according to the moft exact information that can be procured, is confiderably diminifhed. About 60 years ago, there were 4 populous villages, 2 of which are now extinct, and the remaining

2 gra-

* *Price of Labour.*—Ploughmen from 8 l. to 10 l. a-year, befides board and lodging; barnmen the fame, or if paid in kind, 1 boll for every 24 he threfhes; a hind, 8 firlots of oats, 8 firlots of barley, 4 firlots of peafe, 1 peck lint-feed fown, 1 firlot potatoes planted, 1 guinea for fheep, and a cow kept fummer and winter; women, 1 l. 5 s. and a pair of fhoes, during the winter, and from 1 l. 10 s. to 3 l. during the fummer; wrights 1 s. with meat; mafons 1 s. 8 d. without meat; day-labourers 1 s. 2 d. in fummer, 1 s. 6 d. in harveft, and 1 s. in winter; women, when employed at hay or turnip, 8 d., and 1 s. 4 d. in harveft.

2 gradually difappearing. With refpect to the abolition of the firft, the numbers cannot be greatly leffened, as it chiefly confifted of 6 farmers, their cottagers, and 2 or 3 mechanicks, who are now fettled more conveniently in the centre of their refpective farms. The non-exiftence of the fecond muft have made no fmall diminution, as there are people yet alive who remember to have feen 50 houfes all inhabited ; and fome of thefe fay, that they have heard their fathers mention double that number ; and indeed this tradition feems to be well founded, as the ruins of feveral houfes are ftill vifible. The third, which was nearly equal to the fecond, is fo mutilated, that fcarcely a tenth part remains. The fourth hath not fuffered fo effentially, though the blank is too perfpicuous not to be obferved. At the fame time, it is certain, that the return to Dr. Webfter in 1755 is ftated only at 502 fouls, confequently there is a difference of 55 in favour of the population at prefent.

The numbers and ages, as taken in 1791, are :

Under 12,	145	Of the above,	
From 12 to 15,	19	Batchelors who keep houfe,	4
15 to 20,	34	Widowers, -	4
20 to 30,	81	Widows, -	7
30 to 40,	133	Farmers, -	16
40 to 60,	90	Pendiclers, -	10
60 to 70,	37	Smiths, - -	4
70 to 80,	14	Wrights, - -	4
80 to 90,	4	Weavers, - -	4
	———	Clothier, - -	1
Total,	557	Egglers, - -	2
		Families, - -	104

Abstract

ABSTRACT *of* BIRTHS, MARRIAGES, *and* DEATHS.

Years.	Births.	Marriages.	Deaths.
1784,	13	6	5
1785,	7	4	5
1786,	10	9	3
1787,	10	7	1
1788,	9	7	8
1789,	14	3	8
1790,	13	2	6
1791,	12	5	9
1792,	17	6	5 *

Stipend, School, Poor, &c.—The church was built in the 1658, and has undergone many repairs : at preſent it is both neat and warm. The manſe was built in the 1767, and was repaired in the 1791, the year after the preſent incumbent was admitted. It is delightfully ſituated ; and if an extenſive view of the adjacent country, Mr. Scott's pleaſure-ground, and the windings of the Tweed, could compenſate for dampneſs, execrable architecture, and diſtance from the church, might be ſaid to be very comfortable. The ſtipend was augmented 10 l. in the 1776, and is at preſent 32 bolls barley, Linlithgow meaſure, 48 bolls meal, 460 l. Scotch in money, communion elements included, with a glebe of 14 Engliſh acres, and a garden half an Engliſh acre. There is a ſchool, with a ſalary of 8 l. 6 s. 8 d., beſides a dwelling-houſe and garden. The number of ſcholars,

* *Climate and Diſeaſes.*—The air is ſharp and clear, and conſequently not inimical to health. Agues, before the lands were encloſed and drained, were very prevalent ; the moſt common diſeaſes now are, conſumptions, ſlow fevers, rheumatiſm, dyſenteries, ſcrofula, &c. Meaſles, ſmall pox, and chincough, ſometimes make their appearance, but are ſeldom very fatal.

lars, throughout the year, may be from 30 to 40.—Poor's rates were eftablifhed in the 1771, and are nearly 21l. a-year; which, with the average annual collections 11l., is generally fufficient. The heritors, however, by no means reftrict themfelves to this, but cheerfully affefs themfelves to the full amount of what the minifter and feffion deem neceffary. The landlords and tenants pay in equal proportions; and though the latter are not confulted when the affeffment is made, they have never been known to grudge their fhare.

Fifheries.—There are no rivers in the parifh, but the Tweed, forming the fouthern boundary; there are 3 inconfiderable falmon fifheries, which together may amount to 20l. or 25l. a-year. They might unqueftionably be greatly improved, were the mode of fifhing altered. The proprietors, however, have never as yet beftowed any attention on this object; and confequently the fifhers follow the practice of their forefathers, angling, fetting fmall nets in cairns, when the river is in flood, and killing them with lifters, when the river is fmall and the evening ferene; and this they call burning the water, becaufe they are obliged to carry a lighted torch in the boat. Long nets, fuch as are ufed near to Berwick, and upon the Tay and Tummel in the N., might certainly be employed in many places with great fafety and advantage.

Proprietors and Rent.—There are 5 heritors, all of whom have dwelling-houfes in the parifh. The valued rent is 5675l. 10s. 6d. Scotch.: real rent about 2400l. Sterling.

Minerals.—There is an inexhauftible ftore of freeftone all along the banks of the Tweed; but one quarry only,

only, the property of Lord Buchan, has been wrought for
ſeveral years. The ſtone is of a reddiſh colour, very durable, and will admit of the fineſt poliſh.

Antiquity.—The abbey of Dryburgh, ſo much admired
by travellers, lies in the S. W. corner of this pariſh ; but
as an account of it, written by the preſent proprietor, the
Earl of Buchan, is publiſhed in Groſe's Antiquities, it is
needleſs to be very minute. The only thing which deſerves our notice is, that his Lordſhip, while he has diſplayed much taſte, and expended a great deal of money in
digging up a variety of ſtones of curious ſculpture, and
placing them in ſuch a manner as to gratify and attract
the eye of the viſitor, has certainly, in ſome reſpects, leſſened that veneration which ſo ancient an edifice is apt to
inſpire.

Character and Manners.—The inhabitants in general are
remarkably induſtrious, ſober, and contented. From time
immemorial, they have been diſtinguiſhed for their moderation, both in civil and religious matters ; and no inſtance
has been known of any being guilty of thoſe enormous
crimes which are the ſin and reproach of a nation.

Diſadvantages.—Though moſt of the neceſſaries of life
are produced in the pariſh, hardly any of them are ſold in it.
Even meal, in ſmall quantities, can only be procured from
neighbouring mills, there being none here : An inconvenience, however, which will be of ſhort duration, as a
mill is now building in the moſt centrical ſituation in the
pariſh. Butcher meat cannot be obtained without ſending to Kelſo, Jedburgh, or Melroſe, the neareſt of which
is 6 miles. There are few houſehold articles, but what
muſt

must be brought from some other quarter. The roads, for 5 months in the year, are extremely bad : An evil, however, which it is to be hoped, will be corrected. The distance from coal and lime is a hardship severely felt, both of which must be driven at the distance of 26 miles. Want of carriers is another inconvenience ; every person being obliged to send on purpose for the most trivial articles.

PARISH of MORDINGTON.

(COUNTY OF BERWICK, PRESBYTERY OF CHIRNSIDE, SYNOD OF MERSE AND TEVIOTDALE.)

By the Rev. M GEORGE DRUMMOND, *Minister.*

Situation, Form, Extent, Erection, Etymology, &c.

THIS parish is situated in the S. E. corner of the county of Berwick. Its borders are washed on the South by the river Whitadder, and on the East by the German Ocean, near which it joins the lands belonging to the town of Berwick upon Tweed, commonly called *Berwick Bounds*. Its form is irregular, much resembling the letter g.—Its length from S. to N. is between 3 and 4 miles ; its breadth towards the northern extremity is above two miles, though at one place, towards the South, it is only the breadth of the minister's glebe, which is all that separates the parish of Foulden from the Berwick bounds. Its original extent was very small, consisting only of the barony of Mordington, and the estate of Edrington, till the year 1650 ; when the lands of Lammerton, (of much greater extent than the whole of what before

that

that period conſtituted the pariſh,) were disjoined from the
pariſh of Ayton, and annexed to Mordington. Lammerton
had originally been either a ſeparate pariſh, or a chapel of
eaſe to Ayton. * The building in which public worſhip
was performed ſtill remains, and is now the burying place
of the family of Lamerton. The writer of this article has
not been able to learn the etymology of *Mordington. Lam-
merten* is probably derived from the French, *la mer,* expreſ-
five of its ſituation, being immediately on the ſea ſide,

Surface and Soil.—On the South, towards the river Whitadder, the ground is flat, and riſes by a gentle and gradual
aſcent to the North, for more than half the length of the
pariſh; when it attains a very conſiderable elevation above
the level of the ſea, to which the lands again gradually deſcend on the eaſt of this ridge. For ſome ſpace from the
Whitadder, the ſoil is a ſtiff clay, well adapted for wheat
and beans; from thence to the ſea ſide, the land is a light
loam, on a rotten rocky bottom, which renders it excellent
for raiſing turnips and ſound for grazing ſheep. The moſt
elevated part of the ridge is thin and poor, though the greateſt

* The church or chapel of LAMMERTON, is noted to have been the place
where King JAMES IV. of Scotland was married to MARGARET, daughter
of HENRY VII. of England, in the year 1503; which paved the way for the
happy Union, firſt, of the two Crowns, and afterwards of the two kingdoms.
Some alledge, that it was built on purpoſe for the celebration of that marriage. A tradition has long prevailed in this part of the country, that, on account of the ceremony of his marriage having been performed in this chapel,
the King of Scotland granted to the clergyman of this pariſh, and his ſucceſſors, in all time coming, the liberty of *marrying people without proclamation
of banns.* It does not appear, however, from any of the hiſtories of theſe
times, which the author has conſulted, that there is any foundation for this
tradition.

eſt part of it has been plowed, and it ſeems all capable of cultivation.

Climate and Seaſons.—The dryneſs of the ſoil, and its vicinity to the ſea, render the air pure and healthy, and occaſion a quick and early vegetation. There are no diſeaſes peculiar to this diſtrict. In the lower part of the pariſh, as in moſt of the flat grounds in this part of the country, the ague was formerly prevalent among the lower claſſes of the people. The cauſe of that diſtemper, which aroſe chiefly from the exhalation of the vapours from the ſtagnated water, in wet and marſhy grounds, being now in a great meaſure removed, by the mode that is ſo generally adopted through this county of draining and incloſing the fields, the diſeaſe is leſs frequent. And the ſame reaſon may perhaps be given for the decreaſe of comſumptive complaints, throughout the whole of the lower parts of Berwick-ſhire. The prejudices of the country people in this quarter, againſt inoculation for the ſmall-pox, are gradually wearing away; and conſequently that diſtemper is becoming much more mild, and leſs deſtructive than formerly. Though the inhabitants in general are healthy and robuſt, yet there have not been many remarkable inſtances of longevity in this pariſh. Some however have appeared.

Agriculture.—The ſituation of this diſtrict, as well as the ſoil of a very conſiderable of it, is peculiarly favourable to the purpoſes of agriculture; the lands, in general, being of a dry and manageable ſoil, which the ſkilful farmer can turn to the greateſt advantage; and the climate being ſo favourable, that grain of every kind, even in the lateſt and moſt backward ſeaſons, is commonly brought to full maturity. Beſides which, it has the command of two of the beſt and

moſt

moſt uſeful manures, lime and dung ; both of which are to be got in the town and neighbourhood of Berwick, which is only 4 miles diſtant. Theſe local advantages have not been unattended to, by thoſe perſons who occupy the lands. Great quantities of lime are annually bought, and are employed both in improving the waſte lands, and in manuring thoſe that are already improved. And even dung is now beginning to be brought in conſiderable quantities from Berwick, a practice which, if perſevered in, muſt in time greatly add to the fertility of the ſoil ; and, notwithſtanding the expence, with which the purchaſing and driving of it is attended, will, without doubt, ultimately turn out to the advantage both of the proprietors and tenants.

Produce and Exports.—Nor is leſs attention paid to the management than to the manuring of the lands. Unfettered by thoſe prejudices, and that obſtinate attachment to ancient cuſtoms, which are ſo great a bar to cultivation, and have ſo much retarded the progreſs of agriculture in other parts of Scotland, a ſpirit of improvement as well as of induſtry is diſcernible among the farmers in this and the neighbouring pariſhes : In conſequence of which, every ſpecies both of white and green crops are raiſed, and, in general, in the greateſt perfection ; particularly barley, oats, peaſe, turnips, and artificial graſſes. Though the ſoil is, in many places, ſuitable for wheat and beans, yet they are raiſed in ſmaller quantities than the other kinds of grain ; probably becauſe the former does not ſo readily fall in with a rotation, in which green crops are chiefly ſtudied, and becauſe there is not, in this part of the country, a ready market for the latter. Potatoes are raiſed not only for home conſumption, but great quantities from this neighbourhood are alſo annually
ſhipped

ſhipped at Berwick, and ſent to London, Newcaſtle, and different parts of York-ſhire. This pariſh alſo produces a much
greater quantity of grain, than is ſufficient for the ſubſiſtence
of its inhabitants, which is either diſpoſed of in Berwick,
where it generally meets with a ready market, or ſold to
the millers in the neighbourhood, many of whom carry on a
great trade in meal, barley, &c.

Turnip Husbandry.—The time of ſowing and reaping the
different kinds of grain, is the ſame with that of moſt of
the other pariſhes in the lower part of Berwick-ſhire, with
the advantage of being as early as any of them. Turnips
are generally ſown from the end of May to the beginning of
July. Though they are ſometimes ſown in what is called
broad-caſt, that is on ridges made up in the ſame manner as
thoſe on which barley, oats, or any other grain are commonly ſown ; yet they are more frequently raiſed on drills, from
24 to 30 inches wide. This latter method is preferred, on
account of its giving an opportunity for horſe hoeing, and
thus occaſioning leſs manual labour, and conſequently leſs
expence in thinning and cleaning them. When they are
brought to maturity, which is generally about the month of
October, they are made uſe of for feeding cattle and ſheep,
either on the grounds on which they are raiſed, or on neighbouring graſs fields, into which they are carried ; or they are
brought home for the purpoſe of feeding black cattle in
houſes or ſhades. On the light and dry ſoil, the feeding of
ſheep on the ground where the turnips grow, is reckoned a
moſt valuable improvement, as the land, looſe and friable,
both by nature and by the frequent plowing neceſſary for raiſing the turnips, attains, from the conſtant trampling of the
ſheep, a ſubſtance and ſolidity which makes it highly fit for
plowing ;

plowing ; and from the great quantity of dung left on the surface, inures a luxuriant crop of grain and hay in the following years. When the turnips are brought home for feeding cattle in the ftall, they likewife become a ufeful and a valuable crop, not only from the immediate profit which arifes from them, but alfo from the great return of manure which they afford for fucceeding crops. From the favourable nature of the foil, the turnip-husbandry is conducted on an extenfive fcale in this, and many of the neighbouring parifhes. And as great attention is paid to the cultivation, fo great improvements have of late been made in the conftruction of the utenfils for fowing and for facilitating the operations of the husbandman, in rearing this ufeful plant. The greateft enemy to the culture of turnips, is a fmall infect, which in fize and fhape very much refembles the flea. It commonly attacks the plants at a very early period, immediately after they begin to vegetate ; and in fome feafons makes fuch dreadful havock among them, as not only to injure, but frequently totally to deftroy the crop. The beft remedy againft this evil is to fow them early and very thick ; 4 lib. at leaft or 5 lib of feed to the Englifh acre. This feems a method well calculated to infure a crop of turnips. The fly feldom remains many days on the ground, and when fuch a quantity of feed is fown, though the firft growth may be deftroyed, yet as every fucceeding fhower, or even dewy night, for a confiderable time, occafions a frefh vegetation of feed that has been buried deeper in the ground ; it is next to a certainty that fome one of thefe growths will efcape the ravages of the fly, and produce a fufficiently plentiful crop. Many have been the inftances of the propriety of this theory, in this parifh, within thefe few years. In their more advanced ftate, turnips are in fome feafons attacked by a caterpillar. Though the injury which they receive from it is frequently confiderable,

ble, yet it is feldom fo great as to occafion a total failure of the crop.

Swedifh Turnip.—It may not be improper in this place to mention that the *Ruta Baga*, or the *Swedifh turnip*, has been cultivated with confiderable fuccefs by the two heritors of this parifh. In a country like this, where ftock occupies fo much attention, and renders fuch benefit to the farmer, fome root or plant feems wanting to give to the cattle, between the time that the turnips begin to fhoot, and of courfe, to ceafe to afford nourifhment, and the coming in of the grafs. The *ruta baga* feems admirably calculated for that purpofe. For befides being later of fhooting than the turnip, it lofes not its nutritive qualities after it has fhot, but retains all its juices and folidity : Whereas it is well known that a turnip, after it has put forth its flower, becomes dry, light, and reedy, and in every refpect unfit for feeding either cattle or fheep. Horfes too feem very fond of it ; and one of the gentlemen above alluded to, has this winter given them to his out-lying young horfes, who eat them with great eager-nefs. He was led to try this experiment, from obferving that when thefe young horfes broke out of the field, they conftantly fed on the *ruta baga*, though in the fame field there was a large quantity of turnips, which they never of-fered to touch. Another extraordinary quality of the *ruta baga* is, that it feems impoffible to make it rot ; though bit or trod upon by cattle or horfes, it never rots, but whatever part of the root is left, nay, if fcooped out to the fhell, it remains perfectly frefh, and in fpring puts out a new ftem. It is needlefs to obferve that the oppofite of this obtains with the turnip. The culture too of this valuable root is perfectly fimple : When firft attempted in this parifh, the gentlemen

followed

followed the rules laid down in the news-papers, viz. Raising
the plants in a hot bed, and then transplanting them into
the field. This method never answered; they rose to no size;
but on their trying them by the seed sown in the field, and
managed in every respect the same as turnips, (only sown a
month earlier) all their expectations were gratified, and
good crops followed. Both roots and leaves are also excellent for culinary purposes; and for that cause, numbers of
people in this neighbourhood now raise a few in their gardens for the pot. Before concluding this article, it is worth
mentioning, as an example of what feeding will do, when
carried on according to the above system, by a constant succession of green food: There is an ox at present in the parish,
bred by one of the heritors, which, though only 4 years old,
is allowed by all judges to be above an hundred stones
weight; *i. e.* the weight of the four quarters only. He never has been housed, and never got any thing but turnips,
grass, and a little hay. His dam, when in calf of him, was
bought for 6 l. Sterling.

Rotation of Crops —The usual rotation of crops is, first oats,
then turnips; after these, barley with grass seeds, which
makes the succeeding crops hay; and the ground, upon which
it is raised, is commonly allowed to remain in grass for pasture some years; after which it is again taken up, and managed according to the above rotation. Two crops of oats
are sometimes allowed after the land has lain long in grass:
But in no other case are two white crops allowed to succeed
each other, and the tenants are seldom permitted to have
more than the half of their lands in tillage. Wheat is generally sown on the strong clay lands after plain fallow; and on
the dry grounds it is sometimes sown after clover, ley, and some
times on the lands where the turnip crop has failed. There is
always

always, however, a great proportion of the lands in grafs ; and
as the fields are generally laid down in good order, they not only afford greater profit to the farmer in this ftate, than he
could derive from the fcanty produce of a conftant fucceffion
of corn crops, but alfo amply repay him for the reft he gives
them, by the luxuriant crops which they yield when taken up,
after having been paftured for fome years. By this mode of
management, to which the tenants are bound down in their
leafes, the lands are not only kept clean, and freed from thofe
noxious weeds, which are fo prejudicial to the grain fown, or
the plants raifed on them, but are alfo prevented from being
impoverifhed by over-cropping.

River, Fifh, and Mills.—The river Whitadder, which wafhes the fouthern boundary of this parifh abounds in trouts,
eels, &c. And at certain feafons of the year, large quantities of falmon, and falmon trouts, come up, which afford good
fport to the anglers. In fpawning time, great numbers of
falmon go up the river, even almoft to its fource, to depofit
their fpawn. Till of late years, great havock ufed to be made
among them at that feafon, by the country people ; but fince
the paffing an act of the Legiflature, for preferving the fifh in
the river Tweed and the ftreams running into it, thefe practices have been greatly checked, by the exertions of the magif-
trates and proprietors, to the great benefit of the valuable
fifhings on the Tweed. On the eftate of Edington, befides a
mill for other kinds of grain, there are two mills for grinding wheat, in which about 300 bolls are every week made
into flour.

Coaft, and Sea Fifh.—On the coaft, which, towards the Eaft
of the parifh, is very bold and rocky, there are abundance of
all

all the kinds of fiſh that are to be found in the mouth of the Frith of Forth, which are ſold at very reaſonable rates. Lobſters and crabs are in plenty, but there are no oyſters or muſcles. The lobſters are almoſt all carried to London by ſmacks that come along the coaſt for that purpoſe, at ſtated intervals.

Minerals, Game, &c.—In the rocks on the coaſt, great quantities of lime-ſtone are to be found, though not of a good quality : Coal and iron ore alſo make their appearance, and immenſe blocks of free-ſtone of the fineſt ſort. The uſual kinds of game, which are to be found in the lower parts of Berwick-ſhire, are here in great plenty. On the higher grounds in this pariſh, dotterels are ſuppoſed to appear ſooner than on any parts in the ſouth of Scotland. Woodcocks are often found in the early part of the ſeaſon, poor, weak, and exhauſted, probably from their long flight acroſs the German Ocean.

Population.—If, as is generally ſuppoſed, the monopoly of farms, and the abridgement of labour, in conſequence of the improved ſtate of agriculture, uniformly operate to the diminiſhing the number of the inhabitants, certainly the decreaſe of the population of this pariſh ought of late years to have been conſiderable ; as the whole lands, except what are in the poſſeſſion of the proprietors are, at preſent, farmed by three tenants, one of whom is not reſident, but farms to a conſiderable extent in a neighbouring pariſh. From any enquiries, however, which the incumbent has made, he does not find that the decreaſe has been ſo great as might have been expected. And he ſhould imagine, that, if a full inveſtigation were made of the matter, there would be leſs cauſe than is generally ſuppoſed, for regretting that union of farms, which

which now fo generally prevails in this and many other parts of Scotland. It would indeed be unlucky, if a mode of farming, which muſt be allowed greatly to increaſe the moſt uſeful and moſt neceſſary commodities of a country, ſhould have a tendency to diminiſh the number of its inhabitants. For there cannot be a doubt, that by the preſent ſyſtem of huſbandry, which prevails in this part of the country, the grounds produce a much greater quantity of every ſpecies of grain, and afford ſuſtenance to double the number of cattle, ſheep, and ſtock of every kind, than they did before this mode was adopted. Its being carried on by fewer hands, in conſequence of the abridgement of labour, and a greater proportion of the lands being thrown into graſs, though it muſt no doubt diminiſh the number of the people employed in the purpoſes of agriculture, and in many pariſhes, where that forms the ſole employment of the inhabitants, render ſuch pariſhes leſs populous; yet it does not follow, as a juſt inference from thence, that the number of inhabitants in the country at large is thereby diminiſhed. It has only the effect of making the ſuperfluous hands betake themſelves to other occupations, and thus become the means of increaſing the number of our manufacturers, and furniſhing labourers for other uſeful and important purpoſes; ſuch as making and repairing the public roads, incloſing and draining the fields, &c. And there cannot be a doubt, that even in this county, where the monopoly of farms is perhaps carried to a greater-length, than in any other county in Scotland, it will be found, when the extent of its whole population is aſcertained, that the number of its inhabitants is rather increaſed than diminiſhed: And that the diminution in many of the parochial diſtricts, from the cauſes above mentioned, is more than counter-balanced by the additional increaſe in the towns and villages. This reaſoning will appear the more concluſive,

five, when the fact is ſtated, that the population, whatever decreaſe it may have ſuffered within theſe 20 years, is actually nigh doubled, ſince the late eminent Dr Webſter made up his eſtimate of the whole population of Scotland:

For the number of ſouls at preſent in the pariſh is	335
Whereas the whole population, in 1755, was only	181

Hence there is a clear increaſe, of no leſs than	154
Of theſe there are males, - -	148
——————————— females, - -	187
The number of families is exactly -	62

Employments.—Like moſt of the other pariſhes in the county of Berwick, the chief employment of its inhabitants is huſbandry. 'Till of late, there were indeed two manufactures carried on within the bounds of the pariſh, though none of them on an extenſive ſcale, the one a ſtarch, and the other a ſoap manufacture. They are both, however, given up, at leaſt for the preſent. Beſides thoſe employed in the purpoſes of agriculture, there are, as in all other country pariſhes, a few who follow ſuch mechanical occupations, as are requiſite for the accommodation of the inhabitants; ſuch as joiners and ſmiths, for manufacturing the utenſils of huſbandry—tailors, weavers, &c. There is one fiſhing boat belonging to the pariſh, which gives employment to 5 fiſhermen, who are as active and induſtrious as any in this part of the coaſt.

Prices of Labour.—The wages of men ſervants who get their board in the houſe, are from 7l. to 8l. a year; of women ſervants, from 3l. to 4l. Servants who have families, and live in ſeparate houſes, are not paid in money, but receive a certain quantity of meal or grain, have a cow grazed,

their

their coals brought home, and several other perquisites, the whole of which may amount to 16l. a year. Day-labourers commonly receive 1s. 4d. per day in summer, and 1s. in winter, except in hay-time, and during harvest, when there is a considerable advance in their wages. Those who take work by the piece generally earn a considerable deal more. There has, for these some years past, been a gradual rise on the price of labour for weeding turnips, probably owing to the gradual extension of the turnip-husbandry, which requires a greater number, and consequently makes a greater demand for labourers. The wages are now 10d. per day; whereas, a few years ago, they seldom exceeded 6d. This species of labour is generally performed by women and boys, who are very expert at it.

Roads.—The great post road from Edinburgh to London, by Berwick and Newcastle, runs through the East side of this parish. The road from Dunse to Berwick passes through the South part of it. This, as well as all the other great and leading roads through Berwick shire, is made and repaired by the money which is levied at toll-bars, which have lately been erected. The institution of turnpikes has been of the greatest utility to this country. Formerly, the roads were often in such a situation, as to render impossible, either for carriages or horses to get through; whereas, there is now an open and an easy communication, at all seasons of the year, for horses and carriages of every description. The cross roads are also in a rapid state of improvement; they are made and up-held by the statute labour, which is commuted.

Heritors, Rent, &c.—There are only two heritors in this district, both of whom reside. The real rent of the parish is about 2000l. Sterling. The valued rent is 2,045l. 18s. 6d. Scotch. The monthly cess is 32l. 14s. 8d. Scotch.

Church.

Church, School, and Poor.—The church was built in the year 1757, and the manſe a conſiderable time before. The latter has lately undergone a complete and thorough repair, and is now comfortable and commodious. The ſtipend is paid partly in money, and partly in grain ; the amount of the whole, including the glebe, is, *communibus annis*, from 85l. to 90l. ALEXANDER RENTON, Eſq; of Lammerton is patron. The author of this account has been greatly indebted to this gentleman, for his obliging information and aſſiſtance in drawing it up. The ſchool-maſter's ſalary is 7l. per annum. The poor are maintained chiefly by aſſeſſments on the heritors and tenants, the collections in the church being trifling. Until within theſe 10 years, there never was a perſon on the poor's roll. Since that time they have not been numerous. At preſent there are only two that receive a weekly aliment.

Antiquities.—Monuments of antiquity are not very numerous in this pariſh : We have, however, a camp of conſiderable extent, which, from its form, is unqueſtionably Daniſh. It is ſituated on the N. W. extremity of the pariſh, and commands a beautiful proſpect over a vaſt tract of country. It ſeems to have been a well choſen ſtation for the predatory excurſions of barbarous ages, and alſo for keeping up a communication with the ſea, from which it is at no great diſtance. It is ſurrounded by two deep trenches, which are ſtill very entire ; the mounds of them ſeem once to have been faced with ſtones. Many of theſe ſtones have been carried away for different purpoſes : what is remarkable, a kind of ſtone has been found there, which is not to be ſeen in any other part of the country, except in the bed of the river Whitadder, from whence they muſt have been brought, a diſtance of near 4 miles, and all up-hill, which in thoſe days muſt have

been

been a work of much toil and labour. The hill on which
the camp ſtands is called *Hab* or *Hobcheſter*. A little to the
South-Eaſt of this camp is a hill of no great height, but riſing
abruptly, on which ſeveral unfortunate women were burnt
for witch-craft, ſo late as the beginning of this century. It
is ſtill called the *Witch's Know* §. EDINGTON CASTLE, the
ruins of which now ſhow its former ſtrength, alſo demands
our notice. It is ſituated on the banks of the Whittadder,
near the ſouthern extremity of the pariſh, on a ſteep rock,
totally inacceſſible from the Weſt ; at the foot of which the
river flows. In feudal times, it was an excellent protection
againſt the inroads and depredations of our neighbours, on
the other ſide of the Tweed. It has been a ſolid and ſubſtantial building, as what remains of the walls are compoſed
of immenſe ſtones, ſtrongly cemented together.

Advantages and Diſadvantages.—The advantages, attending
the ſituation of this pariſh, greatly overbalance any diſadvantages to which it may be liable. Situated within 4 miles
of Berwick, (to which there is an excellent road,) the inhabitants can with great eaſe procure whatever may be wanted, either for convenience or luxury. There alſo they find
a ready market for whatever they have to diſpoſe of ; the
farmer, in ſome degree, for his fat ſtock of every denomination, and always for his corn ; and the cottager for his eggs,
butter, cheeſe, or fowls. And, in like manner, they can be
ſupplied with whatever they ſtand in need of, as well and as
cheap in Berwick, as in any place in the North of England.
Whatever elſe the farmer has to diſpoſe of, he there meets
with

§ The ſpot on which the execution took place was plainly to be ſeen a-
bout 4 years ago, but is now plowed up and cropped with the reſt of the field ;
a ſort of ſuperſtitious veneration for the ſpot, where human blood had been
ſhed, ſeems to have preſerved it for many years.

with his buyers, whether it be wool, cattle or sheep; Berwick being on the straight road to Morpeth, Sunderland and Shields, the great marts of our stock; and Yorkshire, in the same way, for our wool; the jobbers in these different articles repair thither at particular seasons, and carry off whatever we have to part with. 'Tis difficult then to say, what would meliorate the situation of the inhabitants of this parish. Fuel presents itself as the readiest means of making their state more comfortable. At present they are, 'tis true, 7 miles from coals; but as it is good road, and the tenants drive so many loads to each cottager, this inconvenience is the less felt, more especially as the prime cost is very moderate. But there is a reasonable hope that even this drawback may shortly be removed; as there is no doubt, that, on the northern extremity of the parish, there is a workable coal, which, it is understood, the proprietor intends ere long to open up, and which will be of the greatest benefit to the parish, as well as to the neighbourhood.

Character.—Actuated by a sense of these advantages, the inhabitants of this parish are industrious, frugal and orderly, submissive to the laws, and attentive to the wish of their superiors. No inhabitant has been convicted of a crime before a Court of Justice, in the memory of man. And what shews the regularity of their conduct in the most conspicuous light, is, that in July 1792, when the most atrocious riots prevailed in this county, on account of the institution of turnpikes, not one inhabitant of this parish was carried before a magistrate, or even suspected of being concerned in those shameful enormities which disgraced the county: though perhaps the burden, (if there be any,) falls heaviest on them, being situated at the eastern extremity of the county, and though they, who pay toll, do not travel ten yards on the road, on their way to Berwick.

PARISH OF NENTHORN.

(PRESBYTERY OF KELSO, SYNOD OF MERSE AND
TIVIOTDALE, COUNTY OF BERWICK.)

By the Rev. MR. ABRAHAM KER.

———————————

Name, Extent, Surface, &c.

THE name is derived from some remarkable thorn trees.
The present incumbent remembers a very large one in the
parish. The length of this district, from S. to N. is about 4
miles, and the breadth from E. to W. about as much *. The
measurement is about 1900 acres. It is mostly low ground
with a moderate descent to the S. except a rising in the north
part of the parish, the north side of which falls to the N.
The soil in some parts is remarkably good, a small part of the
north end, however, is very poor muir ground upon a deep
clay. The air is good and healthy.

Rent.—The real rent of the parish is about L. 2040. The
inclosures are among the very best in Scotland for keeping cows

or

* From Armstrong's map of Berwickshire, it appears the length of this parish is only 2½ miles and the breadth little more than 1½.

or feeding cattle or sheep, and producing milk and fine butter. A cow's grass cannot be got in these inclosures under
L. 3; and they are let at more than L. 2 per acre for summer
pasture. There are 4 heritors, one of whom resides.

Population.—The relation to Dr Webster in 1755 was 497
souls; the present number of inhabitants is between 300
and 400; the diminution being owing to the setting large farms,
and casting down two villages. For 4 years preceding 1792,
the births were 44, the deaths 13, and the marriages 9. There
are 8 farmers, 2 smiths, 4 wrights, 2 weavers, and 3 masons
in the parish.

Stipend, and Poor.—The stipend is L. 600 Scotch, 2 chalders of barley, and 2 of oat meal, with a glebe of 6 acres.
The King is patron. The number of poor on the roll is 6,
and the amount of the assessment for their support for the first
half year of 1792, is L. 12 : 12.

Miscellaneous Remarks.—The stone in the parish is generally
blue whin stone, with one quarry of red free stone; on the
side of the water of Eden are two rocks commonly called the
Meikle and Little Thairn.—There is one lake called Lurgie
Loch.—Dotterels appear in a little flock on the muirs for a few
weeks in June.—Both clay and shell marle are used here for
manure.—Coal is the common fuel, brought from England,
and from Lothian. The price is about 1s. per Cwt.—There
are in the north part of the parish 2 or 3 stones with large
seams, which it is said Mr Pocock when passing that way
thought to have been cemented together : but they have been
carried from the Lurgie craig, where are plenty of such stones.
When broken, they do not break at the seams. They have
been dug up, but nothing was found under them.

PARISH OF POLWARTH.

(COUNTY OF MERSE.—PRESBYTERY OF DUNSE.—
SYNOD OF MERSE AND TIVIOTDALE).

By the Rev. Mr ROBERT HOME, *Minister.*

Form, Situation, and Extent.

THIS parish is of a triangular form, and terminates in a point in the east, where the four parishes of Polwarth, Fogo, Edrom, and Langton, all meet. It is about 3 miles long, and its utmost breadth about 2.

Soil and Cultivation.—The soil is various; the greatest part clay, and some of that on a tilly bed, which is best adapted for grass; other parts of it are gravellish, and some sandy. On the north-west there is a considerable extent of muir.— The whole of the parish is inclosed, excepting a small farm, and the muir allotted by the proprietor to the use of the village, for pasture and fuel. Above 1500 acres are in old grass, and subdivided into inclosures of from 10 to 30 acres, all of them sufficiently watered. These are let annually by public roup, and bring very high rents, for the accommodation of those farmers, who breed more flock than they can maintain at home.

Produce,

Produce, Proprietor, and Rents.—The principal crops in the parish are oats and barley, a few peafe, and fometimes a little wheat. Turnips have of late years become a more general crop, and fucceed well. There is a confiderable quantity of old timber, of good fize, befides much young planting, which are, in general, very thriving.—Great attention has been paid by the Earl of Marchmont (fole proprietor of the parifh) to the dreffing of the hedges; many of them are allowed to be the fineft in the country. The valued rent of the parifh is 1624 l. Scotch. The real rent is about 1000 l. Sterling. Grafs land lets at from 10 s. to 30 s. per acre; arable land from 17 s. to 20 s.

Population.—The village of Polwarth is the moft populous part of the parifh. The population has, on the whole, increafed within thefe 40 years, as will appear from the following table:

POPULATION TABLE OF THE PARISH OF POLWARTH.

	Families.	*Souls.*
In the village	55	184
In the country	17	104
Total in 1793	72	288
Number of fouls in the whole parifh, as returned to Dr Webfter in 1755		251
Increafe		37

PROFESSIONS IN THE VILLAGE.

Wrights	3	Tailors		2
Mafon	1	Shoemakers		5
Smith	1	Tanner		1
Weavers	2	Carters		3

Village, Climate, and Diseases.—The village of Polwarth is situated on very wet, and even swampy ground, so that almost in every house they have a hole dug to collect the under water, which requires to be often emptied in wet weather; and yet the inhabitants are very healthy, being neither subject to rheumatic nor aguish complaints. The present incumbent, who has been minister of the parish 24 years, does not remember any epidemical distemper prevailing in the village *.—The houses are very much scattered, not above 2 or 3 at most being situated close to each other. It is probably owing to this circumstance, that epidemic distempers do not spread.—In the middle of the village there are two *thorn trees*, at about 6 yards distance from each other, around which, it was formerly the custom, for every new married pair, with their company, to dance in a ring; from hence the song of *Polwarth on the Green*. But this custom has fallen much into disuse, there not having been above 2 instances of it these 20 years.

Manner of Living.—Almost every householder, along with his house, rents a small portion of land, called *an acre*, but which is often nearer *two*. With the produce thereof, together with what they can spare from their gardens, and the use of a considerable extent of muir, which they enjoy by the indulgence of the proprietor, they are enabled to keep one cow each, and most of them what is called *a follower*. As the rents of their small possessions are very moderate, they live comfortably, and seldom remove, most of the families having been in the village for several generations
back;

* In autumn 1790, an epidemic fever and sore throat, which was very prevalent in Dunse, and in every village round about, made its appearance in two different houses in Polwarth at the same time, but spread no farther.

back; and, for every houſe that becomes empty, there are always ſeveral competitors. The 3 carters above mentioned have a larger portion of land, and keep 2 horſes, with which they plough the people's acres; and bring home their turf, which is their principal fuel.

Church * —On the front of the church there is the following inſcription :—*Templum hoc Dei cultui in eccleſia de Polwarth, a fundi dominis ejuſdem prius deſignationis, dein cognominis, aedificatum et dicatum ante annum ſalutis 900, rectorioque beneficio dotatum Sed temporis curſu labefactum, a Dno.* JOHANNE *de* SANCTO CLARO† *de Herdmanſton, genero Dni. Patricii de Polwarth de eodem, circa annum* 1378, *reparatum, tandem vero vetuſtate ad ruinam vergens, ſumptibus utriuſque proſapiae haeredis, Dni.* PATRICII HUME, *Comitis de* MARCHMONT, &c. *ſummi Scotiae Chancellarii, et Dnae.* GRISSELLÆ KAR, *Comitiſſae, ejus ſponſae, ſepulchri ſacello arcuato recens conſtructum, et campanarum obeliſſco adauctum fuit. Anno Domini* 1703. The living conſiſts of 64 bolls of oats, 32 of barley, 24 l. 17 s. Sterling in money, with a manſe, and a glebe of about 14 Engliſh acres.

Poor.—The number of poor upon the roll of the pariſh amounts to twelve, and they receive in all, according to their different ſituations, 26 l. 13 s. 4 d. which is raiſed by aſſeſſment, whereof one half is paid by the proprietor, the other half by the tenants. Beſides the inrolled poor, there are ſeveral who receive from the kirk-ſeſſion interim

---

* ADAM HUME, as appears from his tomb-ſtone, was the firſt miniſter after the Reformation. The three laſt miniſters, as well as the preſent incumbent, were all HUMES.

† That is, Lord JOHN SINCLAIR.

terim fupplies ; and others, particularly the widows of fuch
as have been fervants or day-labourers to the Earl of Marchmont, are allowed, by his Lordfhip, fome a ftone, others
half a ftone of oat meal per week, which, with the produce of their own labour, enables them to live comfortably. It may alfo be obferved, that there are many old and
infirm men, to whom his Lordfhip. (who has always been
remarkable for his humanity and attention to the poor people in this parifh, as well as upon other parts of his eftates),
gives work, or rather wages for what they are *unable* to perform.

UNITED PARISHES OF SWINTON AND SIMPRIN.

(PRESBYTERY OF CHIRNSIDE, SYNOD OF MERSE AND TIVIOTDALE, COUNTY OF BERWICK.)

By the Rev. MR. GEORGE CUPPLES.

Extent, Name, &c.

THIS diſtrict extends 4 Engliſh miles from E. to W. and about 3 or 3¼ from N. to S. Swinton and Simprin became one pariſh by annexation, and by the tranſlation to Coldſtream of Mr Jolly, then miniſter of the latter, on the 24th September 1761. This tract is very irregularly indented ; Swinton, the principal village where the church and manſe ſtand, is too near the E. end, and the N. ſide, to be quite in the centre of the pariſh ; but in ſo ſmall a diſtrict no real inconvenience is felt from this circumſtance. As to the origin of Simprin or Simpron, it is uncertain what it means. There is hardly any doubt but Swinton was derived from ſwine, with which the adjacent plains abounded, and by which they were infeſted of old. Heroes, it is ſuppoſed, firſt became ſuch by clearing the earth from ſavage animals, and thereby aſſert-

ing

ing man's supremacy in the globe; such a hero became the founder of Swinton family, by refcuing thefe fields from deftructive animals, and enabling his difmayed countrymen to eat inftead of being eaten by them; he had thefe fields affigned him, and has tranfmitted them to a very long feries of defcendants. This fact does not reft merely in tradition, for it is certain that fwine make a great figure in the arms of the family; that there are feveral perfons who ftill retain the name of fwine without the additional fyllable; and that the animal itfelf, no longer an object either of terror or of fuperftition, is now become a favourite fource both of commerce and food to the inhabitants.—The appearance of the parifh is in general neither uniformly flat, nor is it mountainous or rocky; it exhibits a fet of gentle elevations in long ridges, generally from E. to W. with alternate flats betwixt them. The foil for the moft part is fertile, and to a very high degree productive of grafs, natural or artificial, and grain of all forts; except fome of the flats, a few of which are too marfhy for corn, and even rather unmanageable as to grafs, if the feafon be not uncommonly dry. The foil in general is deep; below what has been already mellowed by frequent tillage, by manure, and change of crops, a ftrong tenacious clay prevails to a very great depth. Of courfe, the roads are deep, miry, and often almoft impaffable in winter; when new made, they feldom continue good for any time; gravel is diftant and often fcarce; and the clay foon fwallows up fuch hard materials as are employed. It appears that the art of road-making ftill wants much of that perfection which it formerly had, and may perhaps attain. The fame foil, which is miry and dirty in winter, is devoid of moifture and parched in dry fummers, expofing the inhabitants at one time to all the inconveniencies of exceffive moifture, and at other times to all the hardfhips of exceffive drought. Cattle have been driven from the N. fide of the parifh to Blackadder, and

from

from the S. fide to Tweed, for water; but the ingenuity of the times has now in a great meafure fupplied this defect, by deep ponds or very deep wells; and this diftrict is now very rarely, though fometimes, diftreffed by want of water. In fpite of thefe and other inconveniences, plants, animals, and men multiply and thrive exceedingly. From fome undrained marfhy grounds, from fome low lying fpots which long retain the waters in a ftagnated ftate, the air is often moift, foggy, and feemingly unwholefome, though not fo much fo as one would conclude, the inhabitants living as long, and enjoying as much health as in other places; except that there is one difeafe very prevalent, namely the ague, the caufes of which feem to be the miry nature of the ground, the fogginefs of the air, the miferable huts the common people till of late lived in, a defect in cleanlinefs, and the fcanty portion of animal food which falls to their fhare. The virulence of this difeafe, however, feems to be a good deal abated, owing to the univerfal inclofing of the grounds, draining off the moifture, a very confpicuous improvement in the houfes, perfonal cleanlinefs, and a great alteration for the better in diet. But this difeafe fome years returns with fuch unexpected frequency and force, as often baffles all fpeculations concerning it.

The only ftream of any note in the parifh is Leet, which abounds with pike *.

Minerals, &c.—There is great plenty of free ftone, particularly one excellent ftone quarry is wrought in the farm of Swinton quarter, on which the family of Swinton retained a fervitude

* A regular fofs can be ftill traced in the church yard round the church, which was a ftrong ftone building, into which it would feem the parifhioners upon a fudden alarm retired till their countrymen, roufed by a certain fignal, came to their affiftance. Then they fallied forth, and aided by their neighbours drove off the fouthern invaders.

tude when they fold the land. It is much ufed in building; and the ftone is fo much in requeft as to be fent for from confiderable diftances. As moft human advantages or difadvantages arife from fome flight local circumftances, it is probable that to this quarry the parifh owes a fet of ingenious operative mafons, highly regarded in their line, cadets perhaps from the Swinton family, and prior to the additional fyllable which has long ago both lengthened and foftened the name. Except ordinary whin-ftone and freeftone, no other minerals are to be found here. All the coals come from Northumberland, at 8 miles diftance at leaft from Swinton.

Population Table.

Population in 1755 in		Weavers	8
Swinton	351	Handycraftsmen	28
———— in Simprin	143	Journeymen & apprentices	21
Total	494	Houfehold fervants, male	
Number of fouls in 1791	898	and female	45
Males	481	Labouring men fervants	30
Females	417	Tradefmen	35
In Swinton village	357	Shopkeepers	4
In Simprin do.	73	Farmers	2
Under 10	258	Surgeon	1
From 10 to 20	152	Dancing mafter	1
From 20 to 50	341	Fiddler	1
From 50 to 70	120	Heritor, refident	1
From 70 to 87	27	———— non-refident	2
Births in 1790	25	Burgher, Antiburgher,	
Males	17	and Relief Seceders	90
Females	8	Cameronians	2
Deaths in 1790	22	Proportion of marriages	
Confiderable farms	14	to the whole populati-	
Farmers and their families	123	tion	1 to 64
			Proportion

Proportion of births, do.	Valued rent, Scotch L. 4750	
- - - 1 to 32	Real rent, ſterling L. 4030	
———-—— of deaths do.	Engliſh acres - - 5120	
- - - 1 to 42	Average rent per acre 16s.	
Inhabited houſes - 180	Horſes - - - 168	
Average number of per-	Black-cattle - - 778	
ſons in each houſe - 5	Sheep - - - 1517	

The preſent incumbent had occaſion ſome dozen of years a-
go to take an accurate liſt of the inhabitants upon a rumour of
a Scottiſh militia, and finds they are now more numerous by
98. The increaſe is to be aſcribed entirely to Lord Swinton's
judicious attention to improve and enlarge his village of Swinton, partly by perpetual feus, and partly by leaſes of 999 years,
which laſt mode gave great offence, and made ſome of the tenants aſk what was to become of their houſeleſs poſterity at the
end of that period. The real increaſe lies upon this village, as
the other parts of the pariſh rather muſt decreaſe, for theſe reaſons; univerſal incloſing has in a great meaſure ſuperſeded
hands; two horſe-ploughs, where the ſame man holds and
drives, have made fewer boys neceſſary; and farms becoming
larger, and grazing prevailing more, fewer hands are required to cultivate them. Swinton has increaſed rapidly. About
30 years ago there were not 100 perſons in it; whereas it now
contains 351 ſouls; and it is inconceivable how many of the
neceſſaries of houſe-keeping, and how many conveniencies can
be now found here, which 25 years ago the inhabitants had
to ſend many miles for *.

Nothing

---

* It is almoſt impoſſible that any perſon in this place ſhould die for want of
the neceſſaries of life. Againſt ſo dreadful a diſaſter the ſecurities are a fertile
ſoil, a very regular poor's rate, a humane people, both gentry and others being ready to contribute liberally where any extraordinary caſe claims their attention;

Nothing that can be called emigration has happened here for many years; fome boys, girls, men and women are at the hiring markets in the neighbourhood, engaged to ferve out of, or in the parifh. In this way many in form of hynds, cotters, cot-men, &c. flit in hopes of better ufage, often from whim or caprice; and every Whitfunday exhibits them removing or returning with their whole furniture and apparatus in a cart or two. But fuch changes imply no fettled difcontent, arifing often merely from levity and a love of change, either in them or their mafters. No doubt feveral have accepted tempting offers of employment in other parifhes or in other counties, but they are generally fuch as the farmers would have been fondeft of employing at home.

There are no uninhabited houfes. The number of houfes is 180, and the average number of perfons to a houfe is almoft exactly 5.

Natural Productions, Advantages and Difadvantages.—This parifh produces in great abundance all the vegetables and and plants known in the fouth of Scotland, along with fuch trees as are encouraged and taken care of; and does a great deal more than fupply itfelf with all forts of grain; exporting a confiderable quantity of corn by means of the merchants at Berwick and Eymouth.—The feafons of fowing and reaping vary greatly, yet the eligible time of fowing wheat is from the 20th of September to the 20th of October, fpring wheat is fown any time in March.—The beft feafon for field peafe or beans is from the laft week of February to the laft week of March.

tention, along with a difcretionary power in the minifter for fudden emergencies; fo that the charity of the parifhioners is in little hazard of being either abufed or withheld. In 1782, a trifling attention, firft to the penfioned poor, and fecondly to fuch as were in temporary ftraits, removed all complaints within this parifh. Some perfons fufpected to be in want modeftly declined the proffered aid, and others refented the offer as an infult.

March. Cold feed oats are fown as early in March as the ground and weather will admit ; but hot feed oats may be fown three weeks later ; barley from the middle of April till the 8th or 10th day of May. The harvest is reckoned early, when it begins before the 20th of Auguft.—The advantages which this parifh enjoys are a very fertile and productive foil ;—the neighbourhood of the Tweed, and furnifhing, by its carters, fuch as lie to the north and weft with coals and lime, by their hired carts and horfes ; a centrical fituation with regard to the market towns of Berwick, Kelfo, Dunfe and Cold-ftream.—The difadvantages are, a ticklifh foil, eafily hurt either by drought or rain, tho' no fpot is more fertile when the feafon exactly fuits it ; moft impracticable roads, which no fkill nor attention hitherto has made effectually good ; the having no fuel but coals from Northumberland brought acrofs the Tweed at a ford precarious, and often fatal by the rafhnefs of the men and the fudden rife of the river : every feafon fome horfes are loft in it ; no peat, no fuel, no timber, except the fcanty and uncertain fupply of thorn-hedges cut and fold ; and the total want of manufactures.

Rent, Changes of Property, Agriculture.——The valued rent of the parifh is L. 4750 Scots: The real rent is about L. 4030 fterling ; the number of Englifh acres (exclufive of 14 acres of glebes) is 5120 or thereabouts, which is nearly 16s. an acre at an average ; the higheft rent yet known is 25s. per acre for a few acres, the farm of Swinton quarter gives 23s. per acre, and the loweft rent here is 8s. There is all the certainty fuch fubjects admit of that this rent, inftead of finking, will rife confiderably.

It has already been mentioned, that the founder of the Swinton family got the lands of Swinton as a reward for his valour in clearing the earth of thofe deftructive animals, wild boars.

The

The family afterwards became ftill more confpicuous, by affift-ing Malcolm Canmore to recover the throne of his anceftors; and that fovereign confirmed to them the property of the whole parifh of Swinton, by one of the firft charters granted in Scot-land, ftill preferved in the archives of Durham. During the commonwealth, the then reprefentative of the Swinton fami-ly having efpoufed the caufe of Cromwell, the eftate was for-feited at the reftoration of Charles II. but it was given back at the Revolution. However, a long exile, while their revenues were fequeftrated, had fo involved the family that it became ne-ceffary to fell the three farms of Mont Suir, to the Kerrs of Morrifton, who ftill poffefs them. And fome years afterwards, the father of the prefent Lord Swinton fold three farms for L. 5500 to Provoft Coutts, whofe heirs fold them about 1754 for L. 6500 to William Hall of Whitehall, who, after many meliorations at a great expence, fold them to Patrick Lord Elibank for more than double of his purchafe money. How-ever, after all thefe alienations, the Swinton eftate is ftill a noble and extenfive property. The whole parifh of Simprin was long the property of the antient family of Cockburn of Langton, but their affairs falling into diforder, the eftate was fequeftrated, and purchafed, about 1758, by Patrick Lord Elibank, for L. 18,000.—The moft confpicuous object in Sim-prin is the very high and fpacious barn built by the Cockburns, confifting of a threfhing floor and large and lofty granaries. Lord Elibank thinking its height expofed it to ftorms, lowered the roof confiderably, but left the gabels ftanding, fo that they ftill fhew the original altitude of the building, which is feen from almoft every part of Berwickfhire. Thefe are, exclufive of the grafs parks of Swinton and other pafture grounds extend-ing to 720 acres, about fourteen farms in the parifh; and each farm-er occupies 320 acres at an average. One farm of 414 acres is let at 23s. another of 400 acres at 14s. a third of 477 acres

at

at 15s. a fourth of 370 acres at 18s. and a fifth of about 300 acres at 12s. per acre.—The farmers are allowed by their leaſes to plough half of their farms annually, the other half being occupied by paſture or ſown graſs. The former is uſually divided into five portions, one in fallow, one in wheat, one in peaſe or ſome other green crop, one in barley, and one in oats. Were this practice ſtrictly followed, a tenth part of each farm would be in wheat; but as in ſome farms and in ſome ſeaſons this will not do, it will be nearer the truth to compute a twelfth of each farm, according to which eſtimation there will be annually 366 acres ſown with wheat in the pariſh. About 228 bolls will be required to ſow them, and the produce, reckoning 8 bolls after one, will be 1824 bolls of wheat; which at 30s. per boll will give L. 2736. From the above data it will be eaſy to compute the quantity and value of the other productions of the pariſh. The farmers are prevented from ſowing turnips to any extent by the impracticability of pulverizing their ſtrong ground to the fineneſs this ſeed requires, and the difficulty of getting the roots off without leaving dangerous impreſſions upon the ſoil. To remove them by horſes or carts is very hurtful; and when ſheep are folded on them, the holes made by their feet render the ground unfavourable for bearing the ſucceeding crop of barley. The farmers therefore prefer taking fields of turnips in the neighbouring pariſhes, at from L. 2 : 10s. to L. 5. per acre. It was formerly cuſtomary to ſow graſs ſeeds among barley after the ground had carried ſeveral crops ſince it was fallowed and limed; but the farmers now begin to ſow graſs ſeeds among the young wheat in ſpring, and this method is thought to ſucceed much better than the former.

Betwixt the two longitudinal elevations or ridges of Swinton quarter and Greenrig lies a flat low piece of ground of a very conſiderable breadth, often overflowed by the ſwellings of the Leet, which great pains have been taken to drain, and which

is

is moſt productive of graſs, and even ſometimes of corn in a
very dry ſummer. If the large and expenſive canal, made by
William Hall, Eſq; to ſecure a ſpacious bed for the Leet while
paſſing through his grounds, were continued weſtward through
Lord Swinton's lands to Swinton mill, it would contribute much
to the fertility of the ſoil and the health of the inhabitants *.

Eccleſiaſtical State.—The Crown is patron of this united pariſh.
The ſtipend conſiſts of 100 bolls of oats, Linlithgow meaſure,
106 bolls of barley; L. 12 : 12 : 8 vicarage teinds, all which,
excluſive of houſe and garden, and including the 2 glebes, a-
long with ſervitudes of 2 horſes and 2 cows, may amount to
L. 136 ſterling, *per annum* †.

The manſe was built in 1771. At the annexation it was on
good grounds believed, that the old church of Swinton would
hold all the inhabitants of both pariſhes; but the village of
Swinton increaſing very rapidly, the new comers felt themſelves crowded, and therefore applied for an enlargement of
the church. They aſked the conſent of the heritors to build an
aile for themſelves, the ſeats to deſcend with their houſes and
gardens

* The family of Swinton by their extreme antiquity conſtitutes the greateſt curioſity of the pariſh. Sir Iſaac Newton in his Chronology calculates, that
in no ſeries of Kings the average duration of each of their reigns exceeds 21
years; now it would appear that 22 barons, including the preſent proprietor, have
occupied the lands of Swinton during the long period of 731 years, which ſuppoſes that in a moſt turbulent ariſtocracy, amidſt feudal broils and foreign wars,
a ſeries of border chieftains enjoyed their eſtates at an average each more than
33 years.

† 56 bolls of the victual ſtipend are paid out of Paxton in the pariſh of
Hutton; a chalder of barley is paid out of the lands of Eymouth; and L. 26 :
5s of vicarage out of the lands of Horndean in the pariſh of Lady-kirk. Theſe
irregularities probably aroſe from the dependance of this pariſh on the abbacy
of Coldingham; the abbot drawing the beſt victual out of this diſtrict, and
paying his dependent clergy from places where the grain was worſe in quality.

gardens to their heirs, and to be inseparable from their possessions.——This the heritors most readily granted, and 28 of
these zealous heads of families, at their own expence, and in a
great measure by their own hands, did in 1782, add a very
handsome aile to the north side of the church, which was built in
1729. The old fabric was taken down on account of an apprehen-
sion that it was in a ruinous and dangerous state; whereas on
setting about pulling it down it appeared to be uncommonly
strong, and might have stood for ages. In the middle of the
church below ground is a vault very neatly built of hewn stone,
extending a considerable length, long the burying place of
the family of Swinton; but being generally full of water, it
is now no longer used for that purpose *.

Miscellaneous Remarks.——Many changes have indeed happened in the village and in the parish since the year 1754. At
that time Swinton consisted of a few miserable huts not containing 100 persons, and Simprin contained the whole inhabitants of that parish. By a division into three farms, the parish
has increased in numbers, though the village of Simprin has
declined a little; but Swinton now consists of one spacious
square,

---

* A stone figure of Allan Swinton, the 5th Baron of that family lies in an
arched open niche on the south wall on the right hand of the pulpit, with this
inscription, *Hic jacet Alanus Swintonus miles de eodem.* In his folded hands, which
rest upon his breast, he grasps a round awkward stone, and above him are very
ill shaped figures of pigs and of a brood sow. No date can be discovered; but
it is well known that he died about the year 1200. The stone he grasps in his
hand is by immemorial tradition said to allude to a large clew of yarn, by the
dexterous use of which in one hand, while he used his sword with the other,
he dispatched a great wild boar in that field in Swintonhill which, from that
event, still retains the name of Allan's Cairn; so it would appear that this
gentleman engaged in the same manly sports, the same dangerous exercises,
and was emulous of the original fame of his family, long before his time
become great and conspicuous.

square, with a green in the middle, where two fairs are held,
one in June, and the other in October.—At one corner is a
large well-built public house. A street issues from the square
east towards the kirk, hard by which stands the manse, raised
by its situation considerably above the level of 3 public roads,
which meet below it. Every house almost without exception
has its clock, and not a few of the owners have watches besides; a considerable quantity of loaf bread is brought from
Edinburgh, but especially from Berwick, Dunse, Coldstream,
and Norham. No regular butcher market is held here; but
many black cattle, swine, and sheep are killed occasionally,
and sold to the villagers from the adjacent farms, especially in
the week of the sacrament, the two weeks of the fairs, and
about Martinmass. The price of poultry begins to rise by the
new institution of an Edinburgh carrier, though still it is
not unreasonable *.

About 1754, three farms in this parish were occupied by
Northumbrian stewards of Northumbrian farmers; on the
other farms lived a set of plain unpolished farmers, scarcely dif-
tinguishable from their hynds, either in dress, information,
or mode of living. Now a most comfortable change for the
better has taken place. Of the present farmers some no doubt
still exhibit that sort formerly known by the appellation of
gude men, the toiling and struggling cultivators of small farms;
but a second sort occupy large territories, early and intimately
acquainted with the theory, the practice, and the commerce
of

* Hens sell from 7d. halfpenny to 9d. a duck at 9d. a goose at 1s. 8d. and
2s. a turkey from 3s. to 4s. The incumbent's two servant maids cost him 3 guineas; his man servant L. 6 : 13s. and his boy 1 guinea *per annum*; and these
are nearly an average of the farmers prices; it being understood that wages
are always for many reasons much higher in summer than in winter. The
average price of grain for some years might be stated at 10s. 6d. for a boll of
oats, 13s. for barley, 18s. for peas, and 30s. for wheat; all Linlithgow measure or six Winchester bushels.

of farming, ſhrewd and ſenſible, in eaſy, and ſome in affluent circumſtances, independent either of lairds or factors; they live in a neat, handſome, and hoſpitable manner, and give their children a very extenſive education.——Some of them have had a liberal education. They employ in farming the conſiderable funds acquired by their fathers in the ſame line of life; ſtill retaining however their laudable literary curioſity and taſte for the belles lettres. So that while this diſtrict yeilds to many of the neighbouring pariſhes in the ſize, neatneſs, and conveniencies of farm houſes, in the eaſy circumſtances and even opulence, in the intellectual attainments, the ſocial, and hoſpitable manners of the farmers, it has no occaſion to envy any pariſh whatever. Even the hynds and cotters derive ſome improvement from living near ſuch ſuperiors; for beholding in them the advantages of neatneſs, of cleanlineſs, and knowledge, they ſtrive as much as their circumſcribed ſphere will admit to imitate them, giving their children as much reading, writing, and figures, as they can ſpare time for, along with a little dancing. Theſe hynds and cotters ſeem to live ſnug, happy, and contented, except when ſickneſs or want of œconomy diſtreſs them.

The poor are maintained by a poor's rate laid on by the heritors, as truſtees for the poor, along with the miniſter of the pariſh, on whom no ſmall ſhare of the trouble falls. During the life of the late Lord Elibank, merely to gratify a whim of his Lordſhip, the poor's rates of the two pariſhes were kept ſeparate; but they have been ſince thrown together, after an ineffectual oppoſition from the Simprin tenants, who apprehended that the growing ſize of Swinton would aggravate their expences on this ſcore.——Theſe rates have always been the chief ſupport of the poor, the collections at the church doors being very ſcanty indeed. The number of poor at preſent, is 12; the ſum raiſed for their ſupport is L. 32 : 14s. which divided

vided among the 12, gives L. 2 : 14s. 6d. each, which may aid, but cannot fuperfede their induftry, or the kind offices of their immediate friends.——The people of this parifh are humane, clever, and ingenious, and feem to have the advantage of the Northumbrians on one fide of them, and of the Eaft Lothianers on the other. The incumbent, after a very long refidence among them, cannot find any truth in the obfervation of an ingenious, learned, and witty Lord, who faid that the natives of the Merfe were engendered in mud, brought up in mud, and that their ideas were all muddy.

Inclofing they have been long reconciled to, and it has for fome time been univerfal; the commutation of the ftatute labour into money they fubmit to with a tolerable grace.—— Turnpikes and toll-bars, with which they are now threatened, they moft heartily abhor. *

* Moft of the labourers in hufbandry are hired by the half year; the day labourers are often a fet of neat, clean, young girls, who feed in their parents houfes, and employ themfelves in that eafy and wholefome exercife, for 4d. 5d. or 6d, according to their age and fkill, without victuals from their employer; and who deck themfelves out with their purchafes in Swinton October fair by their gains. Mowers have without meat generally 18d. a day, though they often undertake it at 2s. or 2s. 6d. per acre. Stout women reapers have from 10d. to 11d. and 3 meals.—Men 1s. and fometimes 13d. and their meals. Corn is generally threfhed by weight for the 25th part of what is threfhed and dreffed, but during harveft no ftout man at his liberty will threfh upon any other terms, than being paid as a reaper. Carpenters and mafons always find their own meat, and are paid from 1s. 3d. to 2s. according to their fkill, the nature of the work, and the length of the day. Taylors, who always get their meat where they work, now exact 8d. per day. A coal cart drawn by two horfes is loaded at the coal-hill for from 2s. to 3s. according as the coal is fmall, great, or fplint; the two laft being double of the firft, and the hire of the cart and horfes to Swinton is 3s. which is encreafed every mile as carters carry them farther.

PARISH OF WESTRUTHER,

(County of Berwick.—Presbytery of Lauder.—Synod of Merse and Teviotdale.)

By the Reverend Mr WILLIAM SHIELS.

Origin of the Name.

THE village from which this parish takes its name was formerly called Wolfstruther. This name, according to tradition, originated from the number of wolves with which the neighbouring grounds abounded.

Westruther was formerly a part of the parish of Gordon. It was first erected into a separate parish about the middle of the last century. Upon the application of the heritors, who complained of the distance of the church of Gordon, a minister was appointed in the year 1647 to a chapel at Bassandean, in the south side of the present parish. About two years after, for the better accommodation of the north parts of the parish, a church was built at the village of Westruther, where it still continues. This chapel belonged to the nunnery of Coldstream. The walls of it still remain, to the height of 12 or 14 feet, and inclose the burying-ground of the Homes of Bassandean.

Extent and Situation.—This parish is about five miles long, and four miles broad. It lies on the south side of that range of

of hills called Lammermuir, by which it is ſeparated from Eaſt-Lothian. The London road by Coldſtream enters the pariſh from the north, about the 28th mile ſtone from Edinburgh, paſſes through the ſouth-weſt ſide of it for the ſpace of about four miles, and then enters the pariſh of Greenlaw.

Population in 1755,   591
———— in 1783,   685
———— in 1791,   730

Villages.—The only villages are thoſe of Weſtruther, Wedderly, and Hounſlow. Weſtruther has of late been conſiderably increaſed by a number of houſes built on feus. Each few, along with a houſe and ſmall garden, has generally two or more acres of land to ſupply the family with corn, potatoes, &c.—The village of Wetherly is much diminiſhed within theſe thirty years.—Hounſlow is entirely a new erection. It is ſituated on the London road betwixt the 30th and 31ſt mile ſtones from Edinburgh. The firſt houſe in this village was built in the year 1775. It conſiſts of feus granted by Mr Home of Baſſandean, and contains upwards of 70 ſouls.—As the land in this neighbourhood was within theſe twenty years covered with barren heath, it is perhaps unneceſſary to obſerve, that this village has very much improved the appearance of the country around, as well as raiſed the value of the adjacent grounds.—The feuers in theſe two villages of Weſtruther and Hounſlow have each a privilege of peats for fuel in the moſſes that are next them.—The climate of this pariſh is conſiderably colder than the lower parts of the country. It is, however, remarkably healthy. Perhaps this is, in part, owing to its open and elevated ſituation. There does not appear to be any diſeaſe to which the people are particularly ſubject. Inſtances of longevity are

pretty

pretty frequent. There is juſt now living a woman aged 93 ; and, within theſe few years, two men died at the age of 95 or 96. Several attain to 80 and upwards. It is worthy of remark, that three miniſters in ſucceſſion, though each above thirty years of age at his admiſſion, ſerved the cure of this pariſh from 1647 to 1782, a period of 135 years.

Soil.—The ſoil is of various qualities. Perhaps there may be one half of the lands in the pariſh not capable of being cultivated to any advantage by the plough. One part of theſe is bog-land, on which grows a kind of coarſe graſs, that is ſometimes paſtured by young cattle ; ſometimes it is cut for hay, and is reckoned excellent winter food for cattle that are not of ſufficient age to be fed on turnip. Though a great part of this land has already been drained at conſider-able expence ; yet, as this is the only ſpecies of improvement of which it is capable, certainly more ought ſtill to be done to carry off the water, which, in particular places, continues to ſtagnate.

The other part of theſe lands that are not capable of be-ing cultivated with advantage by the plough, conſiſts of ground covered with deep moſs, or which, from the height of its ſituation, even where the ſoil is tolerably good, is not adapted to the raiſing of corn, and conſequently would not pay the expence of improvement by lime, which is the only manure that has been uſed with effect to any extent for bring-ing in heath lands in this corner of the country.

The other half of the lands in the pariſh may be divided into ſuch as are already cultivated by the plough, and ſuch as are capable of being cultivated in this manner.

The ſoil of theſe lands is, in ſome places, a whitiſh cold clay, which is by no means favourable to the views of the huſbandman. In other places, particularly towards the ſouth

ſide

fide of the parifh, the foil confifts of a reddifh earth, on a free-ftone bottom. This earth, where it has been long in cultivation, and often dunged, has become a rich loam, and is excellent for every fpecies of crop that is adapted to the climate. Where this reddifh foil is not fo deep and ftrong, it is inclined to be fharp and gravelly. This alfo is very fit for cropping, and particularly is well fuited to the turnip hufbandry, and to the raifing of white and broad clover.

This and the neighbouring parifhes have been in a progreffive ftate of improvement ever fince the making of the turnpike-roads, by which there is eafier accefs to manure; and the product of the land is carried to market at lefs expence.

The benefit derived from good roads, however, muft always be partial, and much limited, while the crofs roads continue in the miferable condition in which they are to be found at prefent not only in this neighbourhood, but alfo in many other places of the country. But, as this fubject has often of late been under the confideration of the gentlemen, it is to be hoped that fome effectual method will foon be adopted for correcting an evil that has long been felt and complained of. When by this means the intercourfe between the different parifhes and the different parts of the fame parifh fhall be rendered more eafy and expeditious, new vigour will be imparted to that laudable fpirit of improvement which of late years has fo much increafed the intrinfic value of the lands in this county, and roufed the induftry of the people to exertions highly beneficial to themfelves and to the community at large.

Among the improvements in hufbandry that have been introduced into this part of the country, none have been attended with more happy and more extenfive effects than the raifing of turnips and broad clover. As the turnips, from the

froft,

frost, or from their flying up into seed, if the winter be fresh, are often rendered in a great measure useless, long before the return of the grass, some crop that would answer for food to the fatting cattle in the spring, is more wanted here than in the lower parts of the country, where the frosts are seldom so severe, and where the spring sets in at a more early period.

Early oats seem very much adapted to the climate of this parish ; that species called red oats, in particular, are found to succeed well.—Beside the dung raised in the different farms, the only manure here used is lime, which is brought from Lothian, at the distance of 17 or 18 miles.

Horses, Black Cattle, and Sheep.—There are in this parish 160 horses, 700 black cattle, and 5000 sheep. Considerable attention is now paid to the improvement of the breed of stock of every kind.—The extent of the different farms is very various. The highest may be rented at 260 l. and the lowest about 20 l. Within these 20 years, some of the farms have doubled their rents.—The price of labour through all this country is higher, in general, than in the Lothians, and not so high as in Northumberland. A man that is hired for the year gets 6 l. 10 s, 7 l. or 7 guineas, along with his victuals. A day-labourer gains 1 s. *per* day, or 8 d. with victuals. In hay time and harvest he will gain 10 d. or 1 s. with his victuals.—The price of female labour is considerably raised of late years. This is, in a great measure, owing to an additional number of hands being wanted to carry on the operations of husbandry in its modern improved state. Many of these operations are performed by the women fully as well as by the men, such as turnip hoeing, &c. A female servant who was hired a few years ago at 30 or 35 s. for the summer half year, will now, when employed in works of husbandry, gain 2 l. 5 s. 2 l. 10 s. or 2 l. 15 s. for the same period.

period. The winter wages are much the ſame as formerly. A woman, when employed by the day in turnip hoeing, gains 6 d. or 8 d. without victuals.

Church and Poor.—The ſtipend was lately augmented, and is, by the new decreet, 83 l. 6 s. 8 d. Sterling, and 2 l. 10 s. for communion elements, beſides the glebe. The miniſter is alſo entitled to ſix days caſting of turf on the lands of Mr Home of Baſſandean.

The poor are ſupported by the weekly collections, amounting to 8 l. or to 10 l. and an aſſeſſment according to the valued rent, which is paid in equal proportions by the proprietors of land and their tenants. The one half of the collections is diſpoſed of by the kirk-ſeſſion for the relief of individuals, or families that have accidentally fallen into diſtreſs, and have not had an opportunity of being received on the roll of enliſted poor, or who perhaps wiſh for nothing more than a little occaſional ſupply, till the recovery of health, or the removal of ſome preſent calamity put it again in their power to ſupport themſelves without being burdenſome to the public.

The money expended yearly in ſupport of the enliſted poor never exceeded 24 l. Sterling till this preſent year, when, from an additional number of poor, it has increaſed to 36 l. This ſum is made up by the remaining half of the collections, the intereſt of 24 l. ſunk for the benefit of the poor, and the aſſeſſment above mentioned. Beſides the 24 l. the intereſt of which goes to the aſſeſſment, there is another ſum of the ſame amount, the intereſt of which is diſpoſed of by the ſeſſion to the relief of occaſional poor.

The higheſt allowance this year to a pauper is 3 l. 7 s. 6 d. the loweſt about 1 l. It is always underſtood, that, if their neceſſities increaſe, the kirk-ſeſſion will be ready to give them
ſome

ſome additional ſupply. It is eaſy, however, from the ſmallneſs of the allowance, to ſee that it is only meant as an aſſiſtance. The truth is, the poor uſually live in their own houſes, or in the houſes of ſome of their connections, and are able, in moſt caſes, to do ſomething for themſelves.

The aſſeſſment is laid once in the year by the heritors, who meet for that purpoſe along with the miniſter and kirkſeſſion. This meeting is called by an intimation from the pulpit at leaſt ten free days before.

The heritors ſome years ago, inſtead of giving the whole allowance to the poor in money, adopted a plan of giving a conſiderable proportion of it in oat-meal, which cannot be ſo readily perverted from the charitable purpoſe for which it is beſtowed.

UNITED PARISHES

OF

WHITSOM AND HILTON,

(COUNTY OF BERWICK, SYNOD OF MERSE AND TEVIOT-
DALE, AND PRESBYTERY OF CHURNSIDE),

By the Rev. Mr GEORGE CUPPLES, *Minister of Swinton.*

Situation, &c.

THE united parishes of Whitsom and Hilton, in the
presbytery of Chirnside, Berwickshire, are conjectured to extend in length from W. to E. about 4½ miles
English ; from S to N. the breadth does not exceed 2½ miles.
They are bounded by Edrom parish on the W. and on
the N. ; by the parish of Hutton on the E ; and by Swinton and Ladykirk on the S.

Farms,

Farms, &c.—They contain the following farms; in enu-
merating and defcribing which, I begin from the weft, and
go eaftward.

1. The firft I fhall take notice of is Weft-laws, the property of Robert Hepburn of Clerkington, Efq; confifting of
about 665 acres; the rent of which is only L. 140, upon a
leafe; which, from change of times, has proved moft dif-
advantageous to the proprietor, without much enriching
the humane, but indolent tenant; as the leafe foon expires,
it will no doubt be more than tripled. Weft-laws contains
a great deal of fertile, dry, and well-expofed grounds; but
much of it marfhy and wet, and many neglected fields,
over-run with whins, &c. but very capable of being improved, when a new leafe and an enterprifing tenant fhall
fall to its fhare. The farmer's old, plain, and unadorned
manfion, office houfes, and the cottages of his hinds and dependents, form a little village on one of thefe long eminences with which this part of the country abounds, from
which elevation the farm derives its name; this fituation
commands a fine profpect, and may eafily be rendered dry
and commodious.

2. Weft Newton, the property of Charles Buchan, Efq;
confifts of 250 acres, rented at L. 130, upon a new leafe,
(for it has long been occupied by the prefent tenant and
his father), which commenced at Whitfunday 1794, the
validity of which is now difputed by the proprietor, in a
procefs before the Court of Seffion. Seventy acres of it are
bad, extremely fo, being moory and marfhy, from the watery fituation of the farm, which renders it often inacceffible from moft quarters; it is ufually called Buchan's
Ifle.

3. Eaft

3. Eaſt Newton, the property of James Dickſon of Ánton's-hill, Eſq; conſiſts of about 250 acres, much exceeding indeed in moiſture, but containing more good, dry, and fertile ground than the former. It is rented at L. 160, upon a leaſe nearly expiring; and this farm, along with 17 detached acres at the north-eaſt corner of it, rented at L. 17, and amounting, with the rent of Eaſt Newton, to L. 177, conſtitutes the property of Mr Dickſon in this pariſh at preſent.

4, Langrigg is, as its name implies, a long narrow ſtrip of land, conſiſting of 155 acres Scots meaſure, or 186 Engliſh. It is low, but well improved and ſkilfully cultivated, as it has very long been in the occupation of the proprietor, its rent cannot be preciſely aſcertained, but it is not over-rated in its preſent ſtate at L. 1 Sterling *per* acre, and of courſe gives L. 186. It is the property of Joſhua Tart, Eſq; and gives a vote for a Member of Parliament. This eſtate pays only 6 s. 8 d. to the miniſter, the ſuppoſed converſion of a boll of oats of old; the new ſtipend not yet localled.

5. Ravelaw and Eaſt-Laws, the property of Sir Alexander Don, Baronet, occupied in one farm, conſiſts of 466 acres, the rent of which is L. 372. Along with ſome wet, marſh, low lying ground, it contains no ſmall proportion of good, fertile, dry, and well expoſed ground, well improved, and ſkilfully cultivated.

6. In our progreſs, there occur certain ſmall portions of ground, too ſmall to conſtitute a farm, yet not to be omitted in this account of the pariſh. 1ſt, the 17 detached acres at the north-eaſt corner of Eaſt Newton, already mentioned as part of the property of James Dickſon, Eſq; occupied by one family; theſe few acres are exceedingly fertile.

fertile, and well improved, rented, as before ftated, at L. 17. Adjoining to which, on the eaft, lies a feu of John Bow-maker's, about 11 acres, now occupied by an ingenious cart-wheel and plough-wright and fmith, the only confide-rable mechanic in this parifh; his rent L. 14 Sterling; thefe acres are remarkably good and well cultivated; they reach to the glebe of Whitfom on the eaft, which glebe is rather incommoded by a feu of a fmall fraction of an acre, and a houfe upon it, inhabited by one old woman on the north of the manfe; and ftill more effectually has this glebe been hurt by clay huts; a fmall inclofure of 4 good acres, now rented at L. 6, on the fouth fide of the glebe, (which the minifters of this parifh had very long poffeffed at a fmall rent), being taken from them on a pique of the Laird of Wedderburn, and the refumption ratified by the Court of Seffion; it now belongs to the Earl of Wemyfs.

7. Handie's-hill, a gradually afcending ridge of a confi-derable length, leads from the manfe eaftward to the vil-lage of Whitfom. Handie's hill belongs to the Earl of Wemyfs, and is one of thefe farms afterwards to be men-tioned, as conftituting the very confiderable farm occupied by John Hogarth.

8. The village of Whitfom, the only one now in the united parifhes, is very inconfiderable, and has no trade nor manufacture of any kind; it is principally formed by the houfe and offices of the farmer of Whitfom on the weft end; the houfe and offices of a feuer at the eaft end; a fine modern houfe of a feuer on the fouth-eaft; the fchool-mafter's houfe and fchool, with a few private weavers and fhoemakers, thefe conftitute the whole village, which con-tains 143 fouls. The farm at the weft end of Whitfom belongs to —— Bofwell of Blackadder, Efq; rented at

L. 342,

L. 342, for not many more than 342 acres. The feu at the east end of Whitſom belongs to John Cunningham, who occupies alſo Aitchiſon's feu; theſe two feus contain 38 acres, well worth as many pounds. The feu on the ſouth ſide is John Herriot's, of 60 acres, which are rather under-valued at a guinea an acre, equal to L. 63. Indeed, all the lands about this village are moſt fertile excellent ſoil, and fine expoſure.

9. We ſhall next enumerate the farms occupied by an opulent and conſiderable farmer, John Hogarth, under the Earl of Wemyſs, their proprietor:

1ſt, Hurdie's-hill, already mentioned, which contains 5 families, and forms a ſort of ſuburbs on the weſt end of Whitſom.

2d, Hilton, about three-fourths of a mile to the eaſt of Whitſom. formerly a ſmall village, with a kirk and manſe, both now in ruins, in conſequence of the annexation and the different arrangements made by the farmers. The whole old pariſh, excluſive of Tandinfield, contains only 9 families, conſiſting of 50 ſouls.

3d, The Weſt Vaults, which, along with Eaſt Vaults, under another tenant, contains 28 ſouls in 7 families.

4th, Cantrigg and Deadrigg, on the ſouth ſide of the pariſh, containing 29 ſouls in ſeven families. All theſe are moſt fertile ground, eſpecially near the old village of Hilton, where the fields are not exceeded in fertility by any part of the county at a diſtance from the towns.

10. South of Hilton lies Tondinfield, the property of Anthony Foſter, Eſq; occupied by a farmer, who does not reſide upon it. It contains 270 acres, rented at L. 220: The ſoil, expoſure, and cultivation excellent, as the name ſeems to imply; containing, in 7 families, 32 ſouls.

11. On

11. On the north of Hilton, on Hilton-hill, lies Myre-
fides, well named from its low, marfhy fituation, divided
into two parts, one of them a feu of George Purves, confifting of about 20 acres, fuppofed equal to L. 15 ; and a
fmall farm of about 40 acres, part of Mr Bofwell's eftate,
which pays L. 38 of rent to the proprietor, and L. 6 to an
old farmer for quitting it to the prefent tenant.

12. Immediately north of Myrefide lies the farm of
Dykelhead, the foil much inferior to the foil of Hilton and
Tondinfield, and rented low accordingly at L. 132, part of
Mr Bofwell's eftate, as is likewife now French-Law, within
thefe few weeks purchafed by him from a Mr Scott of
Alnwick, at nearly 40 years purchafe, rather from its con-
tiguity to his other grounds, than its fertility, which is certainly, however, fuperior to Dykelhead ; it is conjectured
to have got its name from the French, either as allies or
foes, having made a neighbouring eminence their ftation
while in this part of the country ; the rent is L. 50. To
the north of it lies Moorhoufe, a very fmall detached piece
of ground belonging to the fame proprietor ; the moft
northerly, and the very worft foil in the parifh.

13. North-weft of Dykelhead and French-Law, the feu
of Leethead, belonging to Robert Chirnfide, confifts of 44
acres, moft of it good fertile ground, well worth L. 1 Sterling *per* acre.   Here rifes Leet, which, inconfiderable as it
is, is the only ftream which has obtained a name in this
parifh ; it is minutely defcribed in the account of Swinton,
where it becomes more confiderable.

14. Due eaft of Hilton-hill lies the large extenfive farm
of Wynnefield, called fo from Wynne Johnftone, Efq; its
late proprietor, and now the property of the Earl of
                                                    Wemyfs,

Wemyss. Wynnefield confists of 650 acres. The farmer's house is a little more than an English mile upon a public road, very gradually sloping from Hilton-hill, and the fertility and value of the land sensibly declines as it recedes from Hilton ; and this decrease in the goodness of the soil is most perceptible on the north side of the road.

Population.—According to Dr Webster's report, the population in 1755 was 399. At present, this parish contains in all 590 souls; of which number, 206 are men ; 246 women ; and 139 children at or about 10 years of age. One of these men is 93, and one woman 94 ; this old woman is found and healthy, and as she came in with the century, so there is good reason to believe she may see it out.

Ecclesiastical State.—The present incumbent is Mr John Waugh, in the 82d year of his age. He was ordained a dissenting minister in Alnwick in 1743, and admitted minister of Whitsom at Whitsunday 1755; he is a widower, and has 3 children ; the eldest, a daughter, married to the minister of Swinton ; the second, Robert Waugh, surgeon of the 93d regiment ; and the third, John Waugh, minister of Menmoor in Angus-shire, in the presbytery of Brechin. The stipend, by a very recent augmentation, now modified, but not localled, is in money   L. 82   0   0
And for communion-elements now given,   5   0   0
Along with two small bolls of wheat, value   2   0   0
One chalder of barley, value in money   12   0   0
One chalder oat-meal, value ditto   -   12 16   0
                                                 ─────────────
The whole being   -   -   L. 113 16   0
With two glebes, amounting together to 28
    acres, well worth L. 1, 10 s. *per* acre, or   42 16   0
                                                 ─────────────
                                      L. 155 16   0
                                                The

The annexation, which had been some years before decreed, took place in 1735, by the translation of Mr George Home from Hilton to Whittingham in East Lothian. Mr Waugh's immediate predecessor in Whitsom was a Mr Calder, brother of Cadwalleder Calder, Esq; author of a very neat account of the Five Nations of Canada. The church was, in my remembrance, a miserable thatched building, which, though now slated, is still very ill seated, narrow and incommodious. It will be acceptable to all concerned, if the Earl of Wemyss, patron and principal proprietor, resume a plan of John Stewart, Esq; his predecessor in the estate of Vaults, and in the patronage of Whitsom, (as Robert Johnston, Esq; of Hilton was in the estate and patronage of Hilton), of building a handsome church upon Handie's-hill, a most commodious situation both for the villagers and the parish at large, and not more remote from the manse than the present church, which is most inconveniently detached both from the village and from the manse. All the parishioners are staunch Presbyterians, either of the Establishment or of the Secession; the Seceders are not above 1 in 12 in proportion to the adherers to the Kirk.

Poor.—The poor have, till very lately, been supported by the ordinary collections on Sunday, and the box was rather rich; but of late a very slender tax has become necessary.

School.—The schoolmaster of the united parish has a salary of about from L. 8 to L. 9 Sterling, a house, a school, and a very small garden, with kirk-dues, and some perquisites arising from his collecting the road-money. However, by the prudent choice of schoolmasters, some able teachers have occupied this place, and have had great numbers of scholars in penmanship, languages, mathematics, and the practical

practical arts derived from them ; and some very worthy members of society in the learned professions, and in inferior lines, owe their education to Whitsom school, till they went either to the Universities, or to their apprenticeships.

Miscellaneous Observations.—The grains sown in this parish are oats, barley, wheat, pease, beans, veatches, rye very seldom ; and the roots cultivated in the fields are potatoes and turnips ; no grasses have I met with but rye-grass and clover, red or white. No animals are to be found, but horses, by which the whole tillage is performed ; black cattle, sheep, and here and there an ass for medical purposes. No curiosity occurs here, except that Deadriggs certainly derives its name from some skirmishes of the hostile borderers ; and that East and West Vaults got their names from certain Vaults, formed of old in several places of this parish, for secreting their effects, upon any alarm from the south.

It is rather extraordinary, that no one heritor or proprietor has so much as a house within the parish, except Joshua Tait, Esq; This circumstance cannot have a good effect, but must retard the civilization of the parishioners, and tend to circumscribe the religious and political views of the people ; as gentlemens seats, where the owners reside any part of the year, never fail to diffuse a degree of urbanity, politeness, and subordination, very salutary to society ; industry is rewarded, ingenuity and arts flourish. This inconvenience of the absence of the great is gradually abating by the rapid improvement in the education, manners, opulence, and mode of living of the present farmers. Some of them have a taste for books ; and not a few live in a style which their lairds 40 years ago did not exceed. One of these tenants, if he had his abstemiousness and self-denial,

would

would be truly the untutored and unlettered fage defcribed by Horace,

> " Abnormis fapiens craffaque Minerva."

> " His native energy defpifes rules;
> " Nor takes he fenfe or fcience from the fchools."

The common people are moderate, fenfible, and fober; nor have any of them for thefe 40 years been charged with a capital crime. Nor do I recollect either riot, violence, or diforder among them. Such as have had an opportunity of a better education, have imbibed it with docility and fuccefs. Nor do I know, on the other hand, any inftances of very fplendid abilities, or extraordinary exertions among them. Any thing like commerce with them confifts in the fale of corn, eggs, poultry, &c. to Berwick.

ADDENDA.

1. I have not been able to afcertain the acres nor the rents of each farm of ———— Bofwell of Blackadder; but his acres, on the whole, are nearly about 960, and his rent very exactly L. 560.

2. Neither the acres in general of the Earl of Wemyfs, nor the particular acres or rent of each of his farms, do I know; but his rent is certainly about L. 1100.

ROXBURGHSHIRE

ROXBURGHSHIRE

KEY TO PARISHES

1. Melrose
2. Lessudden
3. Maxton
4. Roxburgh
5. Makerston
6. Smallholm
7. Kelso
8. Stichill and Hume
9. Ednam
10. Sprouston
11. Part of Galashiels (Selkirkshire)
12. Part of Selkirk (Selkirkshire)

13. Bowden
14. Ashkirk
15. Lilliesleaf
16. Ancrum
17. Crailing
18. Eckford
19. Linton
20. Yetholm
21. Morebattle
22. Hownam
23. Oxnam
24. Jedburgh

25. Southdean
26. Bedrule
27. Hobkirk
28. Castleton
29. Cavers
30. Kirkton
31. Minto
32. Part of Selkirkshire
33. Wilton
34. Hawick
35. Part of Roberton (Selkirkshire)

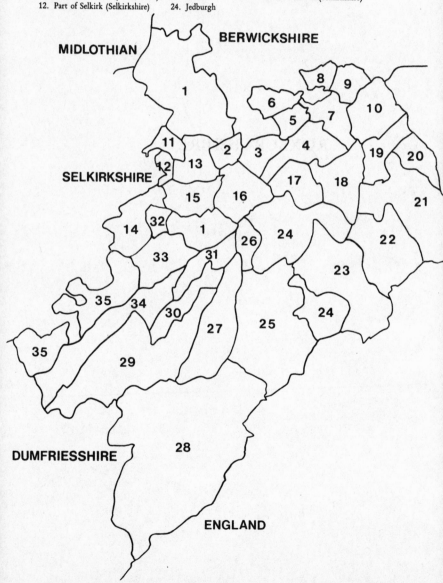

PARISH OF ANCRUM.

*(Presbytery of Jedburgh.—Synod of Merse and Ti-
viotdale.—County of Roxburgh.)*

By the Reverend THOMAS SOMERVILLE, D. D. *Minister
of Jedburgh.*

Extent and Name.

THE parish of Ancrum, situated nearly in the center of
the county of Roxburgh, stretches 5 miles in length
upon the N. side of the river Tiviot, which divides it from
the parishes of Jedburgh and Bedrule. The extreme length
of this district is not less than 6 miles, and its breadth does
not exceed 4.—The name of the village, Alncromb, as it is
written in ancient records *, signifies, as I have been informed, in the Gaelic, crook upon river; and is exactly descriptive of its situation on the south side of Ale, where the river
runs in a curve or crooked direction, and the adjacent banks,
to which the village approaches, exhibit the side of an ellip-
sis. The parish of Langnewton was annexed to that of Ancrum in the end of the last century, and forms the N. W.
and part of the N. side of the parish, as now described. The
river Ale, issuing from the loch of that name in the county
of Selkirk, takes its course through this parish from W. to
E. separating, as I conjecture, the old parish of Langnewton;
and

* See Charter of William to the Abbey of Jedburgh.

and diſcharges itſelf into Tiviot at the diſtance of half a mile below the village, and a quarter of a mile above Ancrum Bridge on the great road to Jedburgh. This river abounds with excellent trout, and affords better ſport to the fiſhers than any other in this country.

Soil, Agriculture, &c.—The ſoil, in the lower grounds of the pariſh upon the ſide of Tiviot, is rich, conſiſting of a mixture of ſand and clay, and, in ſome places, particularly near the village, of a loam. In every ſeaſon it produces good crops of wheat, barley, potatoes, turnips, and ſown graſs. On the higher ground or ridge, which pervades the pariſh from E. to W. and, on the declivities expoſed to the N. the ſurface is a heath, wet, partially ſtony, covering a bottom of cold clay; but the flat ground, on both the Ancrum and Langnewton ſide of Ale, is naturally rich, though, being of a deep and ſtiff clay, it is not ſo eaſily ploughed, nor are the returns ſo certain, as in the Tiviot haughs or holmes.

There was formerly a conſiderable extent of wood in this pariſh; but none of long ſtanding remains, except upon the banks of the Ale near the village of Ancrum, and that which is in the environs of Ancrum-houſe, on the oppoſite ſide of the river. There are ſeveral young plantations of fir and white wood belonging to Sir John Scott, Admiral Elliot, &c. and ſome, comprehending not leſs than 100 acres, upon the eſtate of Sir George Douglas, in the barony of Langnewton. Theſe are all thriving; and already begin to embelliſh the aſpect of the country, which was formerly bleak and deſolate.

The ſituation of Ancrum-houſe, where, according to tradition, the village formerly ſtood, is picture{f}que and attractive. The ſurrounding fields are beautifully diverſified both in figure and ſurface. Spots of verdant lawn, ſometimes level and ſometimes ſloping, craggy knolls, ſcattered trees, and

steep

steep banks upon the verge of the river, in some places naked and of broken surface, and in others clothed with wood, exhibit a rare assemblage of romantic objects. The trees surrounding Ancrum house deserve to be particularly distinguished in a statistical description, being, I believe, the oldest and most beautiful in this country. They consist of oaks, beech, elms, planes, and limes of a large size and bushy top. The prospect from the house down the vale of Tiviot, and bounded by the lofty mountains of Cheviot, is grand and extensive.

Ecclesiastical State, &c.—Sir John Scott is patron of the united parishes, and titular of Ancrum. The emoluments of the minister of Ancrum may be moderately stated at the value of 150 l. *per annum.* He enjoys no part of the stipend paid to the minister of Langnewton before its annexation. The church is in good repair. The heritors have voluntarily augmented the salary of the schoolmaster; and built a schoolhouse larger and more commodious than in any other country parish in this presbytery.

The poor are maintained by a quarterly assessment proportioned to the valued rent. The weekly collections in this parish are, I believe, disposed of by the kirk-session for *interim* supply ; and, as I have been informed by the late incumbent, contribute more effectually in this way to alleviate the quarterly assessments, than by paying the one half of them to the collector for the poor, as is the case in other parishes. The last quarterly assessment was at the rate of 3 s. 6 d. *per* quarter on each hundred pounds Scotch of valued rent, and the number of the poor upon the roll 24.

Population.—An enumeration of the people has been lately

ly made by the schoolmaster for the purpose of this work, and stands as follows :

Males in Ancrum parish - - - - -	337
Females in ditto - - - -	387
Children under 10 years - - -	223
Total - - - - -	947
Males in Langnewton parish - - -	69
Females in ditto - - - - -	82
Children under 10 years - - -	48
Total - - - -	199
Total in both parishes	1146

The return to Dr Webster in 1755 was 1066 souls.

From the report of the grave-digger in Ancrum, who keeps an exact list of all the funerals, it appears that, during the last eight years he has been in that office, they amount precisely to 200; but this relates only to the old parish of Ancrum. There is a church-yard in Langnewton where the inhabitants of that district are buried, and some in both the districts of Ancrum and Langnewton are buried in neighbouring parishes.—There are many Seceders adhering to the Burgher, Antiburgher, and Relief congregations, in Jedburgh; but the generality of the people continue in the establishment.

Heritors, Value of Land, Improvements, &c.—The Duke of Roxburgh, Sir John Scott, Sir George Douglas, Admiral Elliot, Mr Carre of Cavers, Major Bennet of Sandhill, Mr Ogilvie of Chesters, and Miss Stewarts, are considerable heritors. There are several small heritors, and some feuers in the village of Ancrum, who possess farms of a few acres contiguous to their own property; but the greatest part of the land in this parish is let in large farms, though not so large as in the neighbourhood. The most considerable part of the

farms

farms in this parifh is ploughed, though a few cattle and
fheep are alfo kept on them. A great proportion of the
land is inclofed, partly with dry ftone dikes, but moftly with
ditch and hedge; and fome cattle and fheep are fattened
upon turnips and grafs for the market. Some of the largeft
and beft cultivated farms in this parifh are let at 1 l. *per* acre,
and grafs inclofures, for the fummer only, have been let at
the rate of two guineas *per* acre; in the open muirland
ground, the rent cannot be eftimated at more than 4 s. or 5 s.
per acre. The valued rent of the united parifhes of Ancrum
and Langnewton amounts to 12,332 l. 2 s. Scotch, and the
real rent exceeds 4000 l. Sterling.

Minerals, &c.—There are feveral freeftone quarries in this
parifh. The ftone is eafily wrought and of a durable quality, as appears from its entire ftate in fome of the oldeft
buildings. Shell marl has been found in diff-rent mofles,
and particularly on the eftate of Belches, belonging to Mr
Carre of Cavers, where it has been ufed, and has contributed to the improvement of the neighbouring farms. There
are two bridges over the river Ale in this parifh; one at the
church, which is narrow, and feems to have been intended
principally for the convenience of the parifhioners on the
north fide of the river; the other was erected about twenty
years ago a little below the village; and has greatly contributed not only to the accommodation of the immediate
neighbourhood, but to that of the parifhes weft of Ancrum,
by rendering their communication with Jedburgh, Kelfo, and
the Merfe, at all times certain and fafe.—There is a lintmill,
built fome years ago by Sir John Scott, in the neighbourhood
of Ancrum; and, as there is not another within many miles,
it meets with good encouragement, and it is to be hoped will
promote the culture of an article which has hitherto been
lefs

lefs attended to in this country than in other parts of Scotland *.

There

* The Roman road from York to the Frith of Forth, after
paffing through the north eaft part of the parifh of Jedburgh,
cuts a fmall part of the north corner of Ancrum. Upon the
top and declivity of the hill eaftward, on the border of Maxton
parifh, veftiges of a Roman camp may ftill be traced. The
ridge in the parifh of Ancrum, over which the prefent road to
Edinburgh paffes, is at the diftance of about a quarter or half a
mile weft of the line of the Roman road. It is called Liliard's
Edge, from a lady of that name, who, upon an invafion of the
Englifh during the regency of the Earl of Arran, fought with
mafculine bravery, and fell under many wounds upon this fpot,
confecrated to her memory. As the Englifh, commanded by
Lord Rivers, were repulfed, though their numbers were fuperior, courtefy muft incline us to fuppofe, that the high fpirited
and animating example of our Scottifh Amazon chiefly contributed to the glory and triumph of the day.

The moft venerable fragment of antiquity in the parifh is the
Maltan wall or walls, upon a rifing ground at the bottom of the
village of Ancrum, clofe to the fide of the river, where it turns
its courfe towards the S. E. Thefe walls were ftrongly built
of ftone and lime in the figure of a parallelogram, and, afcending on one fide from the plain adjacent to the river, were confiderably higher than the fummit of the hill which they inclofe;
but are now levelled with its furface, and a fmall part of them
remain. Vaults or fubterraneous arches have been difcovered
in the neighbouring ground, and underneath the area inclofed
by the building. Human bones are ftill found by perfons
ploughing or digging in the plain at the fide of the river, which
is an evidence of its having been formerly occupied as burying-
ground. The name, which thefe walls ftill retain, gives the colour of authenticity to a tradition generally received in this
part of the country, that the building, and furrounding fields,
had been vefted in the Knights of Malta, or Knights Hofpi-
tallers of St. John of Jerufalem, who, upon account of their
fplendid atchievements and meritorious fervices in the holy
wars, had acquired property even in the moft remote kingdoms
of Chriftendom. On the banks of the Ale, below the Houfe of
Ancrum, there were feveral caves or recefses, and not lefs than
fifteen may be ftill pointed out. In fome of them there are alfo veftiges of chimneys or fire places, and holes for the paffage
of fmoke from the back part of the cave to the outfide of the
bank.

There were formerly many malt-kilns in the village of Ancrum. Old people fpecify the number of eighteen or twenty having been in conftant occupation in the days of their fathers; an evidence of the extent of the contraband trade carried on by the Scottifh borderers previous to the union.

Mifcellaneous Obfervations.—The people, in general, are induftrious, healthy, and robuft; and there have been inftances of extraordinary longevity in this as well as in neighbouring parifhes, though it is remarkable that no perfon now living in it exceeds the age of feventy five. Mr Cranftoun, the laft incumbent but one, attained to the age of eighty four, during fifty feven years of which period, he had been minifter of the parifh; and he and his fon were the only Prefbyterian incumbents in Ancrum from the Revolution till January 1790, a fact that probably has not a parallel in any other part of Scotland. The late Mr Cranftoun, during the firft fifty years of his miniftry, had never been rendered incapable of performing his duty by indifpofition. Though, for the laft feven years of his life, from the increafing infirmities of age, he found it convenient to accept of the occafional affiftance of his brethren: and difcontinued preaching altogether the two laft, being regularly fupplied by an affiftant at his own expence, yet his health was found, and his mental faculties entire and vigorous. A comprehenfive underftanding, and

bank. From thefe appearances, it is natural to conclude, that, though thefe caves, fo frequently found on the banks of rivers in border counties, were originally intended for places of concealment and fhelter, yet, after the happy event which put an end to interior violence and depredation, they were probably affumed by the poorer claffes for places of habitation, and improved by fuch farther accommodations as the rude or fimple tafte of the times required.

and a penetrating difcernment of characters, improved by a
wide compafs of obfervation *, great facility and force of expreffion,

* Reflecting upon the information and pleafure derived from
my intercourfe with Mr Cranftoun, I embrace this opportunity
of recommending to young perfons, who are inquifitive for
knowl dge, to reverence the hoary head, to court the company
and converfation of thofe whofe wifdom has been enriched and
dignified by the experience of multiplied years. If this advice
were more ftrictly attended to, interefting anecdotes, and valuable information, which elude the notice of general hiftory,
while they are recent and familiar, would often be conveyed by
authentic tradition; and acquiring importance from the rapid and
ftrange viciffitudes they exhibit, as well as from their contraftand
connection with modern events and manners, would, at length,
enter into record, and be refcued from the gulph of oblivion.
By accumulating a ftore of facts, our views of paft hiftory
would become more correct and enlarged; and the fpeculations
of the philofopher and politician, relative to future events, and
to meafures affecting the interefts of pofterity, would be founded upon the moft folid bafis.

The plan of this ftatiftical hiftory feems well calculated to
fupply what has hitherto been a *defideratum* in literature; and, in
the eftimation of future generations, the locality and minutenefs
of the circumftances which it contains, will conftitute not the
fmalleft part of its intereft and utility. Enlightened by fuch
inftruction, we are enabled to inveftigate the fources of prejudices and cuftoms, the elements of characters and manners, and
the caufes of events, of which, otherwife, we are utterly at a lofs
to give any explanation or account. I illuftrate this obfervation by a fact ftrictly pertinent to my prefent argument. There
are few, perhaps none in this parifh, who have heard of the perfecution of Mr Livingfton the minifter of Ancrum after the Reftoration. He was univerfally refpected in the church for his
piety and for his popular talents as a preacher, and dearly beloved by his flock. He was banifhed in his old age, becaufe he
could not, in his confcience, conform to Epifcopal government,
and keep the King's fafts. Many of his people fhared the fame
fate; and in that number fome boys, becaufe they adhered to
his principles, and were guilty of rudenefs to the curate who
was appointed his fucceffor. But, though the ftory is not remembered, the effects of it are ftill permanent and operative,
and an antipathy to every form and inftitution fuppofed to be
derived from Epifcopacy, has been inftilled with the rudiments
of

preffion, with good humour and affability, rendered his, conversation fingularly inftructive and pleafant.

of education, and fofters prejudices which we behold with candour and allowance. when acquainted with the grounds on which they were originally founded.

In a moral and religious view, the knowledge of local facts is important, for enabling us to form a proper eftimate of privileges peculiar to our own times. It is certainly more fafe and candid to compare our political condition with that of our fathers, than with refined and vifionary theories of perfection which never exifted in any preceding age. The peace and liberty which we enjoy, contrafted with the perfecution and tyranny under which they fuffered, are the moft obvious and forcible arguments for loyalty to our Sovereign, a reverence for our laws, attachment to our conftitution, and gratitude to heaven

PARISH OF ASHKIRK.

(*Counties of Roxburgh and Selkirk.*)

By the Rev. Mr SIMON HALIBURTON.

Situation, Extent, and Surface.

THIS parish lies in the counties of Roxburgh and Selkirk; the greater part of it, however, is in that of Roxburgh. It is in the presbytery of Selkirk, and synod of Merse and Teviotdale. The parish is of a square form, about seven English miles long, and three broad. This parish may be called hilly, but most of the hills are free from heath to their very tops. The soil in general is light, and in several parts spongy.

River and Lakes.—There is only one river in the parish, which runs through it from west to east; it is called *Ale*. There are four lakes within, and eight partly without the bounds of the parish, none of them above a mile in circumference, all which discharge their waters into the river Ale. This river abounds with trout. The lakes produce large trout, perch, and pike in considerable numbers.

Horses and Black Cattle.—The number of horses is about 140, and that of black cattle about 442. About 92 calves
are

are bred yearly, part of which are diſpoſed of when fat, and part retained for keeping up the ſtock.

Productions.—There was formerly, perhaps, too much grain ſown here, and the paſſion for doing ſo is ſtill great. The average increaſe is only three or four ſeeds, which plainly ſhews, that the land is very ill cultivated, or better adapted for paſture than for corn. Many of the farmers have got pretty much into the uſe of raiſing green crops, eſpecially potatoes, cabbages, and turnips, which anſwer well. Finding the great advantage of the latter, in feeding their ſheep and black cattle, it is likely that they will continue to cultivate ſuch kinds of crops. So much, indeed, has this practice prevailed of late, that there are now 107 acres employed in this way.

Land-rent and Heritors.—The land-rent is about L. 2000 Sterling. Within theſe fifteen years it has riſen about a fourth. This increaſe may be aſcribed to the melioration of the land by marl, from a moſs of great extent, which was drained about 15 years ago, as well as to the general riſe of markets. There are nine heritors, only one of whom reſides in the pariſh. Sir Gilbert Elliot, Baronet, of Minto, is patron.

Church.—In the month of April 1790, the church was begun to be rebuilt, and is now nearly finiſhed. The manſe was built in 1785. The ſtipend amounts to L. 57 : 9 : 5 in money, and 90 bolls of victual, one half oat-meal, one half barley, Teviotdale meaſure.

Population.—There are now in the pariſh of Aſhkirk 539 ſouls, of whom there are,

Under

	Males.	Females.
Under 10 years of age -	62	59
Between 10 and 20 - -	62	58
20 and 50 - -	114	109
50 and 70 - -	32	35
70 and 100 - -	1	7
	271	268
	Males	271
	Total	539

Since the year 1755, the inhabitants have decreaſed about 90 ſouls ; in Dr Webſter's report the number being 629. The people of this pariſh are induſtrious, frugal, temperate, and devout.

Fuel.—The fuel principally uſed is peat or turf, which are not abundant. The more wealthy pariſhioners bring coals, for the uſe of their families, from Lothian, or from the Engliſh borders. The places whence theſe coals are procured are about 30 miles diſtant from Aſhkirk.

Poor.—The number of poor who ſtand upon the roll of the pariſh is 10 ; they are maintained by aſſeſſments, and the weekly collections in the church. The heritors aſſeſs themſelves in a certain ſum, to be raiſed in proportion to their valued rents. The proprietor pays one half, the tenant the other, and the diſtribution is made quarterly.

PARISH OF BEDRULE.

By the Rev. WILLIAM BROWN, *Miniſter of that Pariſh.*

Situation, Extent, &c.

THE pariſh of Bedrule is ſituated in the centre of the county of Roxburgh, in the preſbytery of Jedburgh, and ſynod of Merſe and Tiviotdale; and is in length from North to South, upwards of four miles, and in breadth from Eaſt to Weſt between two and three. It is bounded by the pariſh of Jedburgh on the Eaſt, by Abbotrule (now annexed to Hobkirk and Southdean, but formerly a pendicle of Bedrule) on the South, by Hobkirk and Cavers, from which it is, for the moſt part, divided by the Rule on the Weſt; and by Minto and Ancrum on the North-Weſt and North, from which it is ſeparated by the Tiviot. It is ſomewhat of an oval figure, and conſiſts, at preſent, of nearly an equal quantity of arable, paſture, and muir-land. The ſoil is, in general, as good as is to be met with in moſt grounds of the above deſcription :

And,

and, as the foil, fo the furface and climate are unequal, which, indeed, is generally the cafe over the county, by the fudden tranfitions from hill to dale. The lands towards the Rule and the Tiviot, are, therefore, more deep, warm, and fertile. In thofe towards the hill called the Dunian *, the foil becomes more light, thin, and barren; the air keen and penetrating: yet, in regard to the foil, there happens to be a remarkable exception, for, on the fame range of hill to the weftward, oppofite the village of Bedrule, there is an uncommonly fine and deep foil; and in the above grounds, where the foil is in general remarkably deep, there is alfo found limeftone, and different ftrata of clay marle. A good deal of the land in that part of the parifh is at prefent rather *fpouty.* But, as it is a gentle declivity from the fummit of the hill to the banks of the river, it might be the more ea-fily rendered dry by judicious draining.

Proprietors and Tenants.—There are three great, and five lefs confiderable proprietors in the parifh, two of whom u-fually refide. There are nearly the fame number of tenants, who all manage their farms according to the modern practice of hufbandry; and one of them, Mr Brown, the tenant of Newton, a farm the property of Thomas Elliot Ogilvie, Efq; of Chefters, has, in the courfe of a few years, fhewn how much may be done by improvement in this parifh, both for the advantage of the tenant, and the patrimonial intereft of the proprietor. Mr Bell younger of Mainflaws, and the tenant of Rewcaftle, both in this parifh, appear to be fol-

lowing

---

* The Dunian is wholly in the parifh of Bedrule; but owing perhaps to part of it having been for fome time poffeffed by the tenant of an adjoining farm in the parifh of Jedburgh, the author of the Statiftical account thereof has been led to fuppofe, it was partly fituated in that parifh.

lowing his laudable example, and, we hope, will likewiſe
acquire, thereby, conſiderable gain to themſelves, and merit,
as all ſuch moſt deſervedly do, the grateful thanks of their
country.

Population —The return to Dr Webſter in 1755, was 297
ſouls. The number of inhabitants at preſent, (1793) is a-
bout 25⁰ ‖. Of theſe there are 127 males, and 132 females.
Under 10 years of age about 69. From 10 to 20 about 50.
From 20 to 50 about 105. From 50 to 70 about 28. From
70 to 80 ſix. From 80 to 90 one.

Weavers 6 ; taylors 3 ; wrights 2 ; gardeners 2 : blackſmiths
2 ; one of whom not only accommodates the village of Bedrule, in that line, but, notwithſtanding his local diſadvantages of diſtance from materials, and eſpecially from coal, alſo
employs conſtantly a number of hands in the manufactory
of nails, whereby this part of the country has been, for ſome
time, abundantly and well ſupplied with that uſeful article ;
and the neceſſity of importing it, as was formerly the caſe,
thereby prevented, money kept in the country, and people
employed at home, who otherwiſe would probably have been
obliged to travel to a diſtance in ſearch of their bread ; male
ſervants 44 ; female do. (including a number of women who
are chiefly employed in what is called *out-work*, as hoeing
the turnip, making the hay, reaping the harveſt, removing
the corn from the ſtack to the barn, &c.) 48 ; journeymen
                                                    nailers,

‖ It may be proper here alſo to inform the reader, that the inhabitants
of Spittal, Toner, Dykes, and Faſtcaſtle, in the pariſh of Cavers ; and Doves-
haugh, Doveſhaugh-brae head, Wells, Weſt-lees, Billerwell, and Birch-hill,
in the pariſh of Hobkirk, are much nearer the church of Bedrule, than their
own pariſh churches ; as alſo thoſe of Fodderlee, Fodderlee-bank head, and
Fodderlee-birks, (which are ſituated in the pariſh of Abbotrule, formerly a
pendicle of Bedrule,) now united to Hobkirk.

nailers, &c. 9 ; poor receiving fupply *in* the parifh 7 ; *out* of the parifh 4.

Live Stock.—There are in the parifh, of work and faddle horfes, 55 ; black cattle 200 ; of thefe, above a fcore are annually fed for the butcher, befides a number of fheep and young ftock, moft of which are brought into the parifh in the winter feafon, from the Highlands, where they are graz-ed in fummer, it having now become a general practice, for the fame tenant to occupy farms in both the high and low part of the country, with that particular view ; fheep 100 fcore, moftly of the Cheviot breed ; a flock of the common goats of this country, of above a dozen, and alfo a few of the Weft India kind, which here breed and thrive well ; fwine 40 ; carts 18 ; ploughs 18 ; 2 horfes are commonly put to one plough, and Mr Brown ploughs a good deal with oxen, 2 alfo going in one plough, and without a driver, the fame as horfes.

Crops and manure —There are fown annually in the parifh about 350 bolls oats ; 50 bolls barley ; 15 wheat ; 30 peafe ; 20 potatoes ; and of late a few acres of tares, at New-ton, which are mown green, and given to the horfes There have been ufually fown of late years, about 100 acres tur-nip ; and nearly the fame quantity in artificial graffes. There is alfo ufually about the fame quantity in what is cal-led *naked fallow.* Lime is the manure chiefly ufed here in the improvement of land, notwithftanding the diftance from which it muft be brought, and confequently the expence at-tending it.

Mills, &c.—There is a corn mill and a bleachfield in the parifh, both upon the Rule, and at a fhort diftance from the
village

village of Bedrule. There was alfo formerly a corn mill on
the Tiviot, near Newton, the fite of which, in confequence
of alterations occafioned by floods in the courfe of that river, within thefe 40 years, is now fcarcely difcernible. Two
orchards : One dovecot ; but there happens alfo to be three
very near in the neighbourhood.

Rooks.—The crops fuffer lefs from the beautiful
and ufeful bird the pigeon, than from the crow or rook,
which feems to increafe in number with improvement in
agriculture, and which, as the pigeon, not only devours vaft
quantities of grain, but alfo deftroys the potatoe and turnip,
and the moft hearty and luxuriant roots of the artificial
graffes ; all which, if not fo injured, feem to thrive well
in this part of the country. Might it not be proper, therefore, efpecially for the Board of Agriculture, *at leaft to recommend* the obfervance of an old law, paffed in the reign of
our James I. refpecting thefe very deftructive birds ? For
though, when kept in due bounds, they are believed to be,
upon the whole, rather ufeful than hurtful, by alfo devour-
ing flugs and grubs, &c. more concealed enemies of the
fruits of the earth ; yet, from their prefent aftonifhing numbers, and their feeming yearly more and more to increafe,
there certainly never were ftronger reafons, than at prefent,
in this part of the country, for the enforcement of that law,
at leaft, till their numbers be again rendered moderate. Indeed, did fuch an act not already exift, the reafons for it
have here become of late fo] ftrong and urgent, as to give
good ground for the enactment of a law to that effect. As
the act is fhort, and may not be generally known, we deem
it proper here to infert it.

James 1ft, Parliament 1ft, c. 19. " Of bigging of ruikes
in trees." " *Item,* For thy that men confidderis that ruikes
biggand

" biggand in kirks zairdes, orchardes, or trees, dois greate
" fkaith upon cornes : It is ordained, that they that fik trees
" perteinis to, lette them to big, and fuffer on na wife that
" their birdes flie away. And quhair it be tainted that they
" big, and the birdes be flowin, and the neft be funden in
" the trees at *Beltane,* the trees fal be fairfaulted to the King,
" (bot gif they be redeemed fra him, throw them that they
" firft perteined to,) and hewin downe, and five fchillings
" to the Kingis unlaw."

Rent.—The *valued rent* is 3475l. 13s. 4d. Scots. Of the
real rent, one tenant pays about 37ol. Sterling, another a-
bove 2ool. Sterling, another about 2ool. Sterling : Two
fmall farms, together with certain lands, poffeffed by tenants
whofe farms, in the parifhes of Jedburgh, Ancrum, and
Cavers, adjoin thereto, may be rated at 13ol. Sterling.
All the other lands in the parifh are in the natural poffeffion
of the proprietors.

Villages.—There were anciently four *villages* in the parifh,
which are now much decayed, and the number of houfes
greatly diminifhed, viz. Bedrule to the Weft, Newton to
the North-weft, Rewcaftle to the North-eaft, and Fulton to
the South-weft, from the centre of the parifh.

Bedrule.—The *origin of the name* of *Bedrule,* (by the people ufually pronounced *Bed de Rule*) is uncertain. What feems
moft probable is, that is fignifies the *feat* or *refting place* of *Rule,*
or *Regulus,* probably the tutelar Saint of the parifh. But
whether the Saint, or the ancient family of *Rule (de Rule),*
gave name to the river, that village and other places upon
its banks ; (for befides Bedrule there are in the neighbourhood
the town O'Rule, Hallrule, and Abbotrule) or whether the
river

river derived its name from the family of Rule, or from St Rule, is uncertain; or, perhaps, from the rapidity of the ſtream (for its ſtream is very rapid) it ſignifies *Roul, (Roll)* as in ſome old papers it is alſo written. Whether any of theſe be the true derivation is doubtful. But, it is moſt certain, that the chief of the family of *Turnbull*, a branch of the very ancient family of Rule, had his principal reſidence at Bedrule Caſtle, in ancient times, a ſtrong hold, pleaſantly ſituated behind the church, on the bank of the river; a ſituation equally remarkable for proſpect, for ſafety, and for beauty; from the ſite of which (for the caſtle itſelf was demoliſhed ſome time ago) though its elevation above the bed of the river be not very great, are ſeen diſtinctly, to the North-weſt, the moſt elevated tops of ſome of the hills by Ettrick and Yarrow, and the Eildons by Melroſe Abbey; the Reid Swyre to the South-Eaſt, the ſource of the Reid and the Jed taking different directions, the Reid mixing with the waters of Tyne, and falling into the ſea at Newcaſtle; the Jed, with thoſe of the Tiviot and Tweed, which reach the ſea at Berwick; and South-weſtward, the ſame frontier tract from whence the Liddel derives its ſource, which, after uniting with the Ewes and the Eſk, falls into the Solway Firth, a branch of the Iriſh Sea. The view is more confined towards the Eaſt and the Weſt, yet the tops of the Dunian and Ruberſlaw * hills in the neighbourhood, were ſituations moſt ſuitable in martial times, by the lighting of fires, for giving the alarm to the dependents and friends of the family, either for the purpoſe of defence or attack, on the ſudden approach of an enemy.

Newton.

---

* Height of the Dunian from the level of the ſea, - 1031 feet.
————— Ruberſlaw - - - 1419

Newton—Was anciently the property of a family of the furname of Ker, who appear to have been cadets of Ferni-hirft. There was alfo a houfe of ftrength there, now like-wife demolifhed: but the beautiful avenues of venerable trees ftill remaining, befpeak to the paffing traveller fome-thing of the confequence and tafte of its former inhabi-tants.

Rewcaftle—Situated upon a more elevated ground, than e:-ther Bedrule or Newton, is confidered by fome as a place of great antiquity. Indeed, it is faid, however unlikely from its prefent appearance, that the Courts of Juftice were ori-ginally held there, and afterwards removed to Jedburgh The origin of the name, and whether it has been derived from proprietors of the furname of Rewcaftle, or whether *it* may have given the furname to that family, is uncertain. Be that as it may, both furname and place are certainly of con-fiderable antiquity.

Fulton—Has now fcarcely any veftiges of its ancient confe-quence, except fome remains of its tower, which are ftill ftanding, and fometimes ufed by the tenant as a *bught* for his fheep. The well known furname Fulton, correfponds to the name of this place; but we do not adventure to con-jecture, whether there have been any connection between the one and the other; for we have been able, as yet, to trace lefs of its hiftory, even by tradition, than any of the former.

Encampments.—There are plain veftiges of a regular en-campment, on an elevated ground, almoft at an equal dif-tance between Bedrule and Newton. From its figure, which is ftill diftinct, it appears to have been Britifh. There

is

is another, at the diſtance of about half a mile to the eaſtward, which, from its ſquare figure, ſeems to have been
Roman. They are both but of ſmall ſize, and occupy an
area nearly of the ſame extent. The former is ſurrounded
by a mound of earth, the latter by a mound and foſſe.

Minerals.—There is great appearance of coal in the lands
of Bedrule ; and though the proprietor made lately an attempt to diſcover it, and was, for an individual, at conſiderable expence in the ſearch, and though there were certainly ſome thin ſeams found, yet, in the iſſue, he was not ſo
ſuccefsful as his laudable perſeverance moſt juſtly merited ;
not owing, as is ſtill thought, by any means to the uncer-
tainty of the ſymptoms, but to the great deepneſs of the main
ſeam.

Indeed, an attempt of that nature, eſpecially in a diſtrict
where coal has not as yet been diſcovered, certainly ought rather to be undertaken upon ſuitable conditions, by a ſociety,
than attempted by an individual, however patriotic or liberal
his ſpirit, unleſs his fortune be vaſt indeed. Nor, at any rate,
ought the experiment to be committed to the management
of obſcure or unſkilful people, or confined to a ſhort ſpace of
time, or the limits of one eſtate or pariſh ; but, after moſt
careful examination, according to the advice of ſcientific men,
of well known ability and character, the moſt likely ſpot in
a diſtrict ought to be pitched upon, and wherever the probable trial is made, moſt ſeriouſly perſevered in. Such a ſcheme
would be truly patriotic, and probably, in the iſſue, become
no leſs gainful than honourable to the undertakers, and of
unſpeakable advantage to the proprietor of the lands where
there happened to be found ſo great a treaſure, and would be
an univerſal bleſſing to this otherwiſe naturally rich and happy country.

There

There is abundance of free-ſtone in the pariſh, of different kinds, red and white, both of excellent quality. Mainſlaws quarry not only ſupplies Jedburgh and the neighbouring country, but ſtone from thence is alſo tranſported to the town of Hawick, at about ſeven miles diſtance, and ſometimes a conſiderable way beyond it.

Roads and Bridges.——A branch of the great road from London to Edinburgh paſſes through the South part of the pariſh. The great road between Berwick and Carliſle directs its courſe through the North part the whole breadth of the pariſh. This road, the whole way acroſs the iſland, is remarkable for variety and beauty, particularly where it paſſes through this pariſh and neighbourhood. Indeed, every where, it is preſenting the traveller with ſcenes, delightful, new and intereſting. One while he has an extenſive proſpect of a rich and improved country, moſt of it in as high a ſtate of cultivation as perhaps it is capable of, thereby, at the ſame time, diſplaying the ſkill and induſtry of its proſperous inhabitants; the ſecurity, wealth, and freedom of the ſubject; the happy effects of the arts of peace, under the protection of law and good government; and in that very country, in thoſe very fields, which formerly were filled, in conſequence of the jarring intereſts, diſputes, and quarrels of two high-ſpirited and warlike nations, with deſolation, carnage, and blood; by the happy union of which, particularly in this tract of country, *the ſword is beat into the ploughſhare, the ſpear into the pruning-hook.* Another while, as he proceeds onward, and the vale becomes more contracted; the hill and the dale; the rock and the ſtream, here and there preſent themſelves, and the well-laid out plantation, at a diſtance, and the near coppice of natural wood, ſkirting the banks, and hanging over the margin of the ſtream——

theſe

these, with their various inhabitants, and still more diversified by other amusing and interesting objects, form together, successive groups of the most various and pleasing of rural scenery. Nor will the reader be surprized at this description, when he is informed, that this delightful road, directing its course by the pleasant towns of Coldstream, Kelso, Hawick, Langholm, and Longtown, conducts the traveller often upon the banks, almost always in view, of the charming rivers, the Tweed, the Tiviot, the Ewes, and the Esk, whose pastoral streams, render so delightful the most beautiful part of the Arcadia of Scotland. A branch of the same road, leading by Jedburgh, was lately made through this parish, by which a mail passes three times a week. The statute labour is here commuted, and the money thereby raised usually laid out on making and repairing the roads in the parish.

There are two bridges in the parish, both across the Rule, one near the village of Spittal, on the great road before mentioned, between Berwick and Carlisle, consisting of two arches ; the other consisting of one large arch, on the road from Hawick by Bedrule to Jedburgh.

Hills.—The Dunian merits particular notice, not so much from its own height or magnitude, as from the remarkable situation upon which it stands ; and, though rather small of itself, and diminishing in its appearance, the nearer one approaches it, yet, from its peculiar situation, it is almost every where seen from beyond where the waters begin to descend to the western shores of the island, to the utmost boundary of the eastern coast. As, in ancient times, churches and crosses were usually erected in the most conspicuous and elevated situations, to reach the eye of the pious traveller, or persons in distress, so, this remarkable hill, (*Dunian*, by those acquainted with the Gaelic language, being said to signify

nify

nify *John's Hill* might, for the same reason, be dedicated to
the beloved disciple of Christ, that it might become the medium of safety and comfort to the numberless votaries of
the favourite disciple of Jesus, in jeopardy either by land or
by water, especially when their eye could not catch in its
view a sacred fane or salutary crucifix. For, notwithstanding the smallness of its size ; owing, not so much to its elevated, as strikingly obvious situation, it is plainly seen almost
every where in all directions, particularly over that vast tract
of country, comprehending what were formerly the middle
and eastern marches, or frontiers of the two kingdoms, extending from the western extremity of the Reidswyre, to
the German ocean, and overlooking, in a singularly commanding prospect, an immense extent of classical ground,
equally celebrated in poetry and song, as it is memorable in
the page of martial history. For, the prospect from this remarkable eminence, different from that from the site of Bedrule castle, is almost alike open to all quarters. Near, and
eastward below, the spectator views, as it were in a bason,
the town of Jedburgh, much distinguished by the venerable
ruins of its formerly rich and magnificent abbey, anciently
the peaceful and happy retreat of Monks of the order of St.
Augustin. At a greater distance, and to the north west,
and on the opposite side of the silver streamed Tiviot, as in
an amphitheatre, opening to the south, the eye is struck
with the plain, yet elegant modern house of Minto, which,
though remarkable for its romantic situation, is greatly more
distinguished as the birth place of eminent patriots, states-
men and legislators, guardians of their country. To the
south-east, and at still a farther distance, appears also strikingly in view, the house of Edgerston, equally distinguished
for the fidelity, prowess, and loyalty of its inhabitants, as
it is remarkable for its having continued for many ages, the

seat

ſeat of an ancient Scottiſh Baron, the neareſt to the Engliſh,
now the Britiſh capital ; and thereby, in this famous Iſle,
has at laſt become, inſtead of the utmoſt barrier of the
northern, happily the centre of the United Kingdom. Weſtward, he views, from its ſource, the beautiful windings of
the woody Rule, where it iſſues in three ſtreams from the
lofty mountains, the Not O' the Gate, Fana, and Wind
burgh, to where its rapidly rolling flood mixes with the Tiviot, oppoſite to the caſtle of Fatlips, which is moſt roman-
tically ſituated north of that river, almoſt in a line with the
courſe of the Rule, on the ſummit of the eaſternmoſt, and
moſt picturesque of the Minto craigs ; hills which, for ſituation and natural beauty, are not ſurpaſſed by any in this
country.

Poor.—The indigent here are chiefly ſupported by aſſeſſment ; a method, however well-intended, and, in the preſent
ſtate of ſociety, in many parts of the country, perhaps unavoidable, is doubtleſs, at the ſame time, often hurtful to
the deſerving poor, to humanity, and the intereſt of thoſe
on whom the burden is laid. There are 500 merks which
were mortified (ſunk) to the poor of the barony of Bedrule
1695, by William Ramſay in Bedrule mill, and Margaret
Turnbull, his wife ; of which it is ſaid, (for the writer never ſaw the deed of mortification itſelf) the family of Cavers Carre are left truſtees. Mrs Mary Ann Stevenſon, relict of the Rev. Mr James Borland, mortified (ſunk) 100l.
Scots to the poor of this pariſh, of which, in the account
thereof, in the pariſh record, the Seſſion appear to have
been appointed by her the overſeers. But, with the deed
of mortification itſelf, if ever any was executed by Mrs
Borland, the writer is not as yet acquainted. The latter
ſum, with other monies, ſavings of the Seſſion in former
times

times, are ſtocked out at intereſt, in two *cumulo* ſums, the
one of 45l. the other of 11l. Sterling.

Parochial Regiſter.—The regiſter of the names of children
born in the pariſh, ſeems to have been carefully attended to
from the commencement of the above mentioned record
1690, until the enactment of a late act of Parliament, laying
a ſmall tax thereon ; which, very different from the purpoſe
thereby intended, here operates as a prohibition. For, although the tax be ſmall, and doubtleſs trifling to many, e-
ven of the common people, in towns, where money is plenty, and wages high ; yet, not a few of the labouring poor,
eſpecially in remote parts of the country, conſider it as hard ;
and, therefore, whatever can be ſaid, as it entirely depends
on their own choice, whether they have their childrens names
recorded in the pariſh regiſter or not, do, moſt of them, in
this pariſh at leaſt, diſcontinue a practice ſo neceſſary in ſociety, and often ſo uſeful and intereſting to individuals ;
and, unfortunately, from the poverty of the people, this
ſeems to be moſt generally the caſe in the country, where,
different from populous towns, there is almoſt no other
means to ſupply that omiſſion ; and, unluckily, thoſe are
the people, who, notwithſtanding their mean circumſtances,
uſually rear, on their ſcanty earnings, the moſt numerous,
uncorrupted, and hardy offspring ; and, thereby, happily
counteract the baneful effects of idleneſs, immorality, and
diſſipation in Society. Such, therefore, in every view, are
well entitled to have their childrens births recorded, thereby,
not only to diſcover the changes, reſources, and ſtrength of
the nation, but alſo, ſo far as to themſelves or poſterity may
be intereſting or agreeable, to have the place of their birth,
their age and memory, preſerved on record. We therefore
accord

accord with the author of the Statiſtical Account of the pariſh of who ſuggeſts the propriety of grant-
ing them a ſmall premium for doing this, rather than to prevent them, by the impoſition of a very trifling, and conſequently unproductive tax ; and, were this the caſe, it would
certainly ſeem neither hard nor unreaſonable, were the Legiſlature to charge with a tax, all thoſe who, notwithſtanding ſuch indulgence and favour, neglect to acquit themſelves of a duty ſo neceſſary, both to their children and ſociety.

School.—The ſchoolmaſter has what is called a legal ſalary, which, when fixed by law, as the *minimum,* was a ſum of
conſiderable value, but now, from the aſtoniſhing change on
the value of money, is a ſorry pittance indeed. As they are
moſtly the children of poor people who attend him, the
wages are alſo low, and he has nothing now allowed him, as
he formerly had, for teaching poor ſcholars. His ſchool-
houſe* is almoſt a ruin.

Manſe.—The manſe is alſo in a bad ſtate ; but, as it has
been twice condemned, once by a jury of tradeſmen appointed by the preſbytery, according to law, 20th June 1792 ;
another time, by a ſecond jury of tradeſmen, by order of the
Court of Seſſion, mutually choſen by the heritors and preſbytery, 26th July 1793 ; it is to be re-built, and in a ſituation more dry and leſs expoſed than the preſent one, and alſo
at a ſmall diſtance from the church.

Stipend, &c.—The living of Bedrule was originally, what,
according to our law, is called a benefice. The whole teinds

in

* For a ſchoolmaſter's right to a ſchool-houſe and ſalary, *vide* Act 5.
Parl. 1. Cha. I. Act 26. Seſ. 6. Parl. 1. K. W.

in the parish, viz. both parfonage and vicarage, having per-
tained, *pleno jure,* to the kirk or parfon. And this was the
cafe, not only before, but alfo a confiderable time after the
Reformation, as well when Prefbyterian church government
prevailed, as while Epifcopacy was the eftablifhed religion of
this country. But, during the civil wars, a confiderable
change feems to have taken place, by no means favourable to
the living. Yet, notwithftanding, the minifter, till lately,
had right by a decreet of locality of ftipend, paffed 19th February 1662, to 400l. Scotch money, and 35 merks for furnifhing communion-elements, with 3 chalders, 5 bolls and
odds victual, and the whole vicarage teinds, *ipfa corpora,* of
the baronies of Bedrule, Rewcaftle, and Knowfouth, in lieu
of a fmall additional fum of money, alfo allowed for furnifhing elements, and an additional quantity of victual, contained in a decreet of modification of ftipend, dated 13th February 1650, on which faid decreet of locality was founded.
But by a late modification, the ftipend is confiderably altered,
of which the writer is, as yet, unable to give a full account.
Jofeph Hume, Efq; of Ninewells, in Berwickfhire, is patron
of the parifh.

The *glebe**, in an inftrument taken by Mr Henry Ellot,
minifter of Bedrule, as far back as 3d June 1640, in the language

* Each landward minifter, by act 118, Parliament 12. James VI. 5th June
1591, (befides his ftipend, &c.) is entitled to 4 acres Scotch, equal to 5 acres
Englifh, of the beft arable or *infield* kirk-land in the parifh, contiguous or
neareft to the church, over and above what is occupied by his manfe, offices,
garden, and ftack-yard, for which there is ufually affigned half an acre; and
by Act 7th, Parliament 18th, James VI. 9th July 1606, if there be no kirk
lands of that defcription in the parifh, near to the church, as from faid act
appears to have been the cafe in a number of parifhes in the kingdom at
that time, particularly on the borders, and in the Highlands, to have the
whole or whatever was rendered thereby deficient, made up of kirk land
outfield,

guage of thoſe times, deſigned, *the whole glebe and kirklands**
has been a good deal ameliorated by former incumbents,
though much ſtill remains to be done. The progreſs
they have made in clearing it of immenſe quantities of
granite or whin ſtones, with which, notwithſtanding all
that has been done, it ſtill abounds, is the ⸭moſt eſſential and durable improvement that has been made. For
though, in its original ſtate, it might be judged equal in
value to 4 acres Scotch, (5 acres Engliſh,) of good arable land, yet, from their improvements, and the extent of its
ſurface, which, with the bed of the river, that partly inter-
ſects it, and a ſteep bank occupied by wood, † all taken together

outfield, ſufficient to paſture four ſouwns, in lieu of each acre arable, to which
he was otherwiſe entitled, being deſigned him. From this, as well as from
other cauſes, particularly on the borders and in the Highlands, it happens
that ſome glebes are of greater extent than others, independent of graſs ſufficient to paſture one horſe and two cows being aſſigned according to act 24th,
Parliament 1ſt, Charles II. 1663, to which, notwithſtanding, by ſaid act, the
miniſters of theſe pariſhes are alſo entitled : *vide* Mackenzie's obſervations
on act 17th, Parliament 18th, James VI. And, therefore, from the difference
of the ability and pains of incumbents in improving ſuch glebes, as well as from
their ſize and the nature of their ſoil, obviouſly proceeds the difference of their
value. Hence the importance of adopting ſome reaſonable plan, as has been
often ſuggeſted, the more effectually to excite all miniſters, who are able, to
do ſo, without prejudice or loſs to thoſe who do it, their families or heirs, on
the event of their removal or death. By this means, though ſucceſſors were
bound to make a reaſonable allowance for important and durable improvements, at the ſight of arbiters choſen by the parties, the livings would be benefited, while none concerned could be any way injured.

* As " *the glebe and kirk land of the kirk of Jedburgh*," *vide* ſaid record, 25th
March ſame year; *vide* alſo chap. 62. Par. 5. James VI.; chap. 10. Par. 23.
James VI.

† Though the miniſter had been in uſe to cut the wood on his glebe, yet
the heritors of Bedrule, ſoon after the admiſſion of Mr George Dickſon,
queſtioned his right to do ſo, who, when the cauſe was tried in the Court
of Seſſion, obtained a decreet in favour of his title, paſſed 30th July 1754,

by

gether, may contain an area of near three times that quantity; it is now of greater value, and might be rendered still more so, were it compleatly cleared of earthfaft ftones, and properly drained and inclofed.

The minifter has neither his * *foums grafs*, as fome of his predeceffors appear to have had, nor any allowance for them, that he knows of.

There was formerly a large common in the parifh, on which, by ufe and wont, he had right to pafture, &c. It was

by Lord Drumore, Ordinary on the bills. In confequence of which, the minifter is in the practice, as he has always been, of difpofing of the wood on his glebe like any other crop, according as he judges proper, without any moleftation or interference whatever.

* In ancient times, when it was neceffary to unite the people as clofe as poffible by a common intereft for their common defence, and in defence of their country, it was cuftomary for the land called *infield* or arable, to be held and occupied by proprietors and tenants, in what was called *run-rig*, each, as his property was fmall or great, having been thereby able to *roum* and fodder in winter, a number of cattle in proportion to the quantity of his arable land. And, for the fame reafon, it feems probable, that the land *outfield*, in many places, was occupied in common, each proprietor or tenant, in a certain diftrict, parifh, or eftate, having been thereby entitled to *foum* or pafture on the *outfield land* in fummer, in proportion to the number and kinds of cattle he was thus able to *roum* or fodder in winter, by means of his fhare of *infield-land*.

A *foum* is faid to have confifted of about ten fheep or one cow, a horfe having been confidered as equal to two *foums*.

The minifter of every landward parifh, has, by law, Act 24. Parl. 1. Cha. II. 1663, befides what is ufually called his arable glebe, as above mentioned, alfo right to *grafs* or *grazing* for one horfe and two cows; or to have a fufficient quantity of fuitable land, near the church, laid off for that purpofe; or to have 20 l. Scots paid him annually in lieu thereof, a fum, at that time, fully equivalent thereto, or temporal land defigned: For though Act 31. Parl. 1644, refpecting an arable glebe; and Act 45. Parl. 1649, refpecting grafs, were repealed by Act refciffory; yet the above mentioned Act 24. Parl. 1. Cha. II. 1663, was certainly meant to ferve all the purpofes of faid acts, in favour of the eftablifhed clergy.

was divided 9th September 1696, without any ſhare being
laid off to the miniſter in lieu thereof. Againſt theſe dila-
pidations, the then incumbent, Mr James Borland, as miniſter of Bedrule, proteſted, in his own name, and in name
of his ſucceſſors in office, miniſters there; and this he did
on the ground, and at the time, when the heritors were occupied with their arbiters in dividing the ſame; and, there-
upon, took inſtruments in the hands of Thomas Cranſtoun,
notar public, in preſence of ſundry witneſſes, as a copy of
ſaid inſtrument, now before the writer, more fully ſhews.
But Mr Borland, having been then advanced in life, ſeems
to have done this merely to exonerate himſelf, and to preſerve, as well as he could, a right to any of his ſucceſſors,
who might think it expedient, fully to proſecute it: " For,
the law has ordained, that the miniſter or parſon, *quatenus
parſon*, never dies, but he and his ſucceſſors are viewed in
a corporate capacity. Hence, all the original rights of the
parſonage are, in the eye of the law, preſerved entire and
inviolate to the ſucceſſor. The preſent incumbent and his
predeceſſor, who lived a century or more ago, are, in law,
one and the ſame perſon; what was the right of the one, is
ſtill the right of the other." There was likewiſe a ſmall
common near the church called *Gourlay Bog*, on which the
miniſter of Bedrule was alſo in uſe to paſture, and, like the
former, was divided, but at a later period, without any part
thereof being aſſigned him, or any indemnification, as yet
made for the loſs the living thereby ſuſtained. He has
right to caſt 10 *darg* ‡ of *turf* ‖ annually, viz. 6 on the muirs
of Fulton, Corſcleugh and Bedrule; 2 on Newton Muir,
and 2 on Rewcaſtle Muir. Indeed, as coals are at a very
great

---

‡ A *darg* of turf is as many as can be caſt with one ſpade in one day.

‖ For a miniſter's right to fuel, &c. and all other privileges, according
to uſe and wont, *vide* chap. 165. Parl. 13. James 6th, 21ſt July 1593.

great diſtance; and the roads, till of late turnpikes were made, a great part of the year almoſt impaſſable; and no peat in the pariſh, it ſeems probable, that turf, which is here, in general, remarkably good, was the fuel chiefly uſed in former times But now that coals are attainable, though, owing to the great diſtance they are brought, and to toll-bars on the road, very expenſive; even the pooreſt people in the pariſh, uſe a few of them.

Church.—The antiquity of the church, we are as yet un-able to trace; but, from its figure and conſtruction, it ſeems to have been built in thoſe times, when the conſtitution of men was greatly more ſtrong than it is at preſent; for, ac-cording to the cuſtom of our hardy forefathers, it is partly below ground, and the windows, or rather ſlits, are not made to open and ſhut, by which the air is unavoidably affected, and rendered ſomewhat like that in a family vault or damp cellar. The whole fabric is much decayed, and has been, for a conſiderable time, in a ruinous ſtate.

Notwithſtanding our other improvements, we are extreme-ly ſorry we have to regret the bad ſtate of many of our pariſh churches, and that thereby ſo little encouragement is given to the people to attend public worſhip there, where it is ob-viouſly the intereſt, as well as the bounden duty of the teach-er to inſtruct them to fear God, to honour the King, to obey the good Laws, to reſpect and revere the happy Conſtitu-tion of their country, and to pray that thereby liberty and peace may not only be enjoyed by them in their days, but al-ſo conveyed full and entire to their children, and, by the ſame happy and liberal means, tranſmitted unimpaired to the lateſt poſterity. We are the more particular on this head, for the information of *ſtrangers* §, many of whom, we underſtand,

form,

§ It may be proper here alſo to inform ſtrangers, that the Eſtabliſhed
Clergy

form an unfavourable opinion of the religion, people, and clergy of this country on that account; as, with the greateſt juſtice, we are able to aſſure them, that the bad, and indeed very indecent ſtate in which they find many of the pariſh churches

Clergy of Scotland are ſupported by a ſmall part of the ancient patrimony of the national church, the remainder thereof being moſtly in the poſſeſſion of lay *titulars* or impropriators, whereby, properly ſpeaking, the public can be un-derſtood no more to contribute to the maintenance of the Eſtabliſhed Clergy, than to that of theſe lay *titulars*, or impropriators of the patrimony of the church. Therefore, by our law, when it is judged neceſſary, from the change on the value of money, or any other obvious and onerous cauſe, for the court of teinds, which was originally a committee of the Parliament of Scotland, to grant what is called an augmentation, or, more properly ſpeaking, to bring the mi-niſter's preſent ſtipend ſomewhat nearer to its original value, they can have recourſe to theſe funds only; and no landholders or others are affected either with ſtipend, or what is called augmentation of ſtipend, but only ſo far as they are proven to be poſſeſſed of them; and though the ſmall remains of the patrimony of the church, that are ſtill reſerved by the Conſtitution for theſe purpoſes, were, by law, alſo ſecularized, and either applied for the lightening of the taxes, or granted, by royal favour, as the reſt have been, to individuals, for ſervices real or ſuppoſed, this would not diminiſh, but, perhaps, rather in-creaſe the burden on thoſe on whom it preſently lies, who can pretend no right thereto, more than they can to the old church lands, or free teinds he-ritably poſſeſſed by others, or the free teinds of their own eſtates, which they, their anceſtors, or authors, have neither obtained by favour from the Crown, nor as yet purchaſed, according to law, from their lay *titulars*, or impro-priators. As the ſecularization of theſe funds, when underſtood, in point of intereſt, is little to be deſired by heritors, ſo alſo, if they view the matter properly, as little by the commonalty, not even by Diſſenters themſelves; and, we believe, is really ſeriouſly deſired by few who have a ſincere regard for the good of their country: becauſe we know of no *ſpecies* of *Chriſtianity* it would not be obviouſly the intereſt of ſociety to be the Eſta-bliſhed Religion, rather than *none*; for, however in ſpeculative points they may differ, and, in theſe, often more in words than ideas, in their regard for morals, we are ſatisfied, all the ſincere are perfectly united, and we believe that moſt, even of Diſſenters, who feel the comfort, and admit the uſefulneſs of ſocial worſhip and public inſtruction, are alſo friendly to the preſervation

of

churches in this country, neither proceeds from the genius
of Presbytery (the Established Religion) the temper of the
people of Scotland, nor the taste of the Established Clergy,
who all feel, and often express the hardship of their situation

in

of the establishment of parochial churches and schools. And that this is the
case, is evident from this, that none do more heartily accord with the common, and perhaps, in too many instances, well founded outcry against the late
frequent annexations and suppressions in different parts of the country. And,
therefore, the only difference on that head is, as is natural and supposeable, that
each would wish the clergy and schoolmasters, settled in the parish churches
and schools, established by law, of their own sect or profession. But all must
see, that in this, as in a few speculative opinions, in which sects differ from
each other, they are not only opposed to all who at present adhere to the E-
stablished Church, by far the major part of the community, but are also thereby equally in opposition to the inclinations and wishes of one another. Nay,
farther, when the matter is duly considered, the annihilation of an Established Clergy, as it is against the inclination, so, obviously, it would be contrary to
the secular interest of the people. For there is not, perhaps, a popular complaint better founded, and, in the justice of which all descriptions of men are
more agreed, than that against the modern custom of the the money raised in
the country by the non-residence of many of the landholders, different from
the practice of their fathers, being spent so much at a distance from it. Now,
by our excellent Constitution, the clergy of Scotland are all without exception bound to reside. By this means all that they receive in stipend, out of
the lands of their respective parishes, &c. is, thereby, not only kept in the
country, but, most of it, spent in the several parishes and nearest market towns
to these parishes, in which, both by the laws of the church and the state, they,
the clergy, are bound to reside. Whatever, therefore, be the wish of those
(we trust they are but few) who are equally inimical to order, to law, and to
good government, as they are to religion, we are satisfied, that few, if any,
of any description, even of Dissenters, at least in this part of the country, have
so far degenerated from the well known principles of their pious and virtuous
ancestors, as to wish national religion altogether abolished, but only, that it
were of that sect or party of which they are members. But supposing it o-
therwise, we would ask such, What they would think of a Government or
State, suppose Great Britain, that would seize upon all that has been disponed
by individuals for the support of religious worship and public instruction, it

in this reſpect, and their hearty diſapprobation thereof ; and
ſome of the people thus circumſtanced, even go the length
to give it as the reaſon for their remaining at home in bad
weather, and others, of deſerting the Eſtabliſhed Church altogether,

is no matter, if it has been tolerated by law, of what ſect or deſcription ?
Would this not cut down, at one ſtroke, the pious funds of all the Diſſenters,
together with the remaining part of the patrimony of the church, ſtill reſerved by the Legiſlature to be applied according to its original intention, for
the ſupport of national religion, *i. e. public worſhip* and *inſtruction ?* The Eſtabliſhed Clergy of Scotland, as was ſaid, being, by law, moſt ſtrictly bound to
reſide, none of them, therefore, are capable of holding pluralities, or any living, *in commendam*, by which means, independent of the ſuitableneſs of this
ſalutary regulation, the money they receive in ſtipend, &c. as was alſo mentioned, is neceſſarily circulated in the pariſhes and neareſt market towns to
where it is raiſed, by which means the people have not only immediately the
benefit of their inſtruction, advice, and friendſhip, but alſo, mediately, of the
ſtipends they receive, by their being expended amongſt them. By the law of
Scotland, alſo, the poor of every deſcription or ſect whatever, without exception, in each landward pariſh, have a legal title to call upon the eſtabliſhed
miniſter, and he is bound, if the heritors and tenants do not duly aſſeſs themſelves in what is reaſonable for their maintenance, upon proper information,
to report to the Judge Ordinary, what appears ſo to him, and aid the may
be otherwiſe altogether helpleſs, and thereby prevent what might, in ſome
caſes, perhaps, prove a fatal delay. For the miniſter is uſually unable, however diſpoſed, himſelf to ſupply them, or to find any other certain means
whereby to ſupply them, according to their often great and urgent neceſſities.
And, therefore, this benevolent and wiſe regulation, in our law, though ſeldom exerciſed, is a moſt neceſſary and proper ſecurity to the poor, eſpecially
in theſe times, different from thoſe in which landholders generally reſided in
the country, and regularly attended the church ; by which means, they not
only had an opportunity to hear and know weekly, the ſtate of the poor in
the pariſh, but, beſides contributing themſelves, of ſetting an example to their
tenants and dependants, alſo, to contribute to their relief ; whereas, it is now
too generally cuſtomary for them, not only to reſide the greateſt part of the
year, if not altogether, in the Capital, or ſome great town, but, when in the
country, rarely, if at all, to attend public worſhip. As this modern practice
has already greatly affected ſociety, ſo it is particularly hurtful to the intereſt

together, and attending divine fervice with the Diffenters,
whofe houfes of worfhip, though built by contribution, are
decent, convenient, and comfortable; and choofe rather to
do this, though accompanied with expence, than attend the
Eftablifhed Clergy in thofe churches where their health is in
danger. Strangers will naturally wifh to be informed from
whence the neglect proceeds. Candour, however painful,
obliges us plainly to ftate the anfwer. By the law and practice of Scotland, different from what obtains in fome other
countries, the burden of building and repairing the churches
eftablifhed by law, particularly in *landward* or country parifhes, is not raifed by affeffment on all poffeffors of lands and
houfes, whether tenant or proprietor, indifcriminately, nor
raifed by briefs, but is raifed from lands only; and, therefore, by the fame right, according to the Conftitution and
prefent exifting law of Scotland, by which our *heritors* or
landholders in the act called *parifhioners** poffefs their eftates,
they

reft and comfort of the modeft and deferving poor, by fo much breaking off
their connection with the wealthy, and, in moft cafes, even preventing them
being known to them; by which means, the modeft and fhamelefs, the induftrious and flothful, the deferving and worthlefs, are unavoidably placed on
the fame footing, and claffed indifcriminately on the fame common roll; which,
though in an affeffment of that nature, can fcarcely be avoided, is obvioufly
the occafion of many and great evils, befides increafing the *poor-rates.*

* *Parifhioners*, i. e. *heritors.* This expreffion is equally agreeable to the
law and practice of Scotland : " For, (in the words of a great lawyer ‡ on
that head) all who have lands in a parifh, are confidered as *parifhioners*, without refpect to their refidence, *as to all parochial burdens,* which are proportioned to the valuation of every heritor's lands in the parifh, and not to his
quality or his lands in other parifhes." Act 54. Parl. 3. Ja. 6. 1572. " And
(in the words of the fame great man) the church yard is fenced with dykes,
partly for ornament, and partly as a prefervative to the dead bodies, from

being

‡ Forbes on Teinds, pages 209 and 215.

they are bound, befides upholding manfe and fchool-houfe, to build and repair the parifh church, church-yard walls, &c. where their lands are fituated, in a reafonable and decent manner. Hence, as is obvious, fuch landholders, and they only, who neglect to do fo, *give ground* for that reflection; and the bad ftate of many of the parifh churches of this country, thereby become fo juft a caufe of complaint to the people, to the very people, who by their adherence to the eftablifhed religion of the country, certainly do fhew themfelves not the leaft friendly to our happy Conftitution, in church and in ftate; thereby, alfo, as is obvious, the laws are infringed, and the moft peaceable and religious of his Majefty's fubjects, much aggrieved. For, the law of this country is fo well and fo wifely framed, as to lay the burden of building and repairing the church and fchool-houfe, &c. upon the rich, to relieve the poor, not upon perfons, but upon property, therefore, no individual's rights or property are or can be, invaded or affected thereby; nor can any perfons or claffes of men, of whatever defcription, be any way interfered with, but as proprietors of lands, *for their lands only ;* on which exprefs condition they are conveyed and held; and, therefore, by neglecting to acquit themfelves of thefe legal engagements, to which they are bound by the fame tenure they hold their eftates, as well as to fulfill fo pious and important

being digged up and devoured by beafts. The building and repairing of churches and church-yard dykes, was once referred to the Privy Council, act 76. Parl. 9. 2d May 1693. But now the parifhioners, *i. e. heritors*, muft build and repair the church yard dykes with ftone and mortar two elns (yards) high, with fufficient ftiles and entries, and the Lords of Seffion are to direct letters of horning againft them to that effect: Act 232. Parl. 15. Ja. 6. 1597." The parifhioners (heritors) are alfo bound to provide communion cups, tables, and table cloths, &c. *vide* chap. 6. Parl. 22. Ja. 6. 1617.

portant a duty; they, at the fame time, plainly fhew a high difrefpect to the worfhip of God, and a great difregard for the Conftitution and Laws of their country, by which they are fecured and protected in the enjoyment of their rights and property.

It may be afked, Is there no *compulfitor* provided by law in hard cafes? There is. But, not to mention how averfe the people refiding in a parifh, naturally muft be to enter into a procefs at law with the very perfons of whom they farm their lands; the trouble and expence of fuch a procefs, with men fo weighty and powerful, is an objection to them for the moft part infurmountable. And it is the more hard, as there is no reafon to doubt, but that the people in the communion of the Eftablifhed Church would be equally forward, according to their abilities, to re-build and repair their churches, as the Diffenters are their houfes of worfhip, were it not, that the law has fo wifely ordered it otherwife, by laying the burden of fupporting the eftablifhed religion of the country, on lands purchafed and held on that exprefs condition, whereby all perfons of whatever defcription, except propri. tors of lands *for their lands only,* are, juftly fpeaking, exempted; and thofe alone, who are inclined to adhere to the eftablifhed church, are affected by their neglect; and thus, thereby, either made to fuffer, or involve themfelves in a procefs of law, which, for reafons above mentioned, they rarely adventure upon; or abfent themfelves from divine fervice; a cuftom, alas! become too common; or take refuge among the Diffenters, whofe houfes of worfhip are duly attended to, and where the people fit, in the fevereft weather, dry and comfortable: and, it is proper to add, what certainly ought to have much weight, that however inclined thofe adhering to the Eftablifhed Church, in moft country parifhes, may be to accommodate themfelves, if the law had not or-

dered

dered it otherwife, this is in a great meafure to them impracticable, not only by their diftance from one another, but more
efpecially their generally low circumftances, who, notwithftanding, as our happy Conftitution has fixed it, have as good
a right, by law, to enjoy the advantages of religious inftruction and education, by the wife inftitution of parochial clergy, and eftablifhed fchoolmafters, as their more wealthy
brethren in cities and in towns, to whom, by their nearnefs
to one another, their numbers and greater wealth, the want
of thefe eftablifhments, fo particularly neceffary in the country, might, however proper alfo in towns, by the inhabitants
thereof, be more eafily fupplied ; whereas, if the poor and
fcattered inhabitants in moft landward parifhes, be deprived
of the benefit of their eftablifhed churches and parochial
fchools, as appointed by law, many of them, efpecially in
remote fituations, muft unavoidably lofe the advantages of religious inftruction and education, † fo interefting, not only
to

† As mortifications and donations amongft diffenters are intended to fupport a particular church or fect, according to the will of the donors, fo the
funds in Scotland, appropriated by law for the fupport of public teachers, in
landward diftricts or parifhes, ought, in like manner, ever to be confidered as
facred depofits, wifely preferved by the legiflature in favour of the community, in order that people in the meaneft circumftances, and moft retired fituations, may always have the opportunity of being inftructed in true religion, " to do juftly, to love mercy, and to walk humbly ; to do to all
" as they would they fhould do to them, were they in their circumftances,"
and whenever the inftitution of public inftructors has a different tendency,
which, we are apt to believe, is feldom the cafe, this by no means proceeds
from the nature or principle of the inftitution itfelf, but from the perverfion
of its original intention and obvious ufe, and this the community ought, therefore, ever moft carefully to guard againft, and alfo againft any of its members
being conftrained to attend the Eftablifhed teachers, in preference to others,
or thofe who do attend them, being any way difturbed on that account.

to themselves and their children, but also to the political health and happiness of the state.

It will probably be supposed, that the minister of the parish, in particular, is thereby called upon, in duty, to insist for the fulfilment of the law ; but, not to mention what is usually the case, his utter inability, in point of circumstances, to enter the lists with a number of wealthy and powerful opponents, and that, too, without any other aid or countenance, but the goodness of his cause ; he is almost certain of being thereby involved in inexpressible difficulties ; and, in the issue, as has often been experienced, may not only have the mortification of being disappointed of success, but also, however unjustly, of being thereby held up as litigious, teasing, and troublesome.¶

It

¶ Indeed it may be proper, in this place, to observe, in general, that the people seem more dissatisfied at their inability to render the laws efficient, than at what they consider the most unequal and heavy of the taxes : that some of them chuse rather to submit to oppression and the loss of their property, than contend in a law suit with the wealthy, &c. because they are afraid, which ever way it go, of the effects thereof, while their rich opponents, from their greater wealth, &c. would be scarcely at all affected by it, and they can thereby easily, also, perplex and prolong the business, and carry it from one Court to another, where, from the greater expence, distance, &c. they, their feeble antagonists, are still more unable to contend :—And that this is sometimes effectually held out *in terrorem*, when any of them happen to be hardy enough to presume to maintain their just rights, contrary to the pleasure of their more opulent neighbours. ‡ To add to these hardships, they also complain, that they have not access for ordinary, to those by whom they are aggrieved, to plead their cause or state their case, hardships and grievances, but only through people employed by them, of whom they have usually a still more unfavourable

‡ *From the words of a certain great man,* (Dr Johnson) *it is evidently his opinion, that* " *No scheme of policy has, in any country yet, brought the rich and poor* " *on equal terms, into Courts of Judicature.*" *But he seems not altogether to despair of it ; for he adds,* " *Perhaps experience improving on experience, may in time ef-* " *fect it.*"

It is for reasons such as these, and not from a want of desire on the part of the people and minister of Bedrule, to have every thing put on a legal footing, that the church-yard wall is in great disrepair, that the gate is so broken down and neglected, as not to prevent the intrusion of swine, and thereby to alarm the people in the neighbourhood for the graves of their deceased relations ; that the church bell, which has been long rent, is now altogether useless by the want of a tongue ; that the beadle is without a salary ; that the manse has, till of late, been inhabited by the minister, notwithstanding its long very bad state ; that the *church and schoolhouse* still remain in their ruinous condition. And, we are sorry to say, that that kind of neglect is too common over the country ; and, not to mention that many, who from their rank or station,

unfavourable opinion ; and, therefore, to whom, though, for the most part, we believe, unjustly, they are apt to ascribe their hardships and difficulties. But, in order to judge how much this is the case, we need only remind our reader of the answer given by Charles II., though represented, at the same time, by the historian who relates the fact, as of a humane and feeling disposition, when informed of the hardships the people suffered, under the administration of a certain great servant of his : " I perceive, said he, that Lauderdale has been guilty of many bad things against the people of Scotland, but I cannot find, that he has acted any thing *contrary to my interest.*" And, therefore, notwithstanding, his confessed humanity, he neither called him to account, nor dismissed him his service, far less did he give him orders to repair the injuries done. When we have said thus much, we submit the weight and importance of our observations, with great deference, to the penetrating eye of an impartial public, particularly to those in the senate and judgment-seat, whom our excellent Constitution has happily rendered independent and free, And, the more plainly, because, we are satisfied, that the best support of any nation, the strongest pillars of any government, are, That the people's morals be sound, that their manners be civil, that their religion be liberal, that the laws, that *justice*, be equally easy and accessible to all.

ftation, as well as intereft in the country, ought certainly to
fet a better example, abfent themfelves from public worfhip
altogether, the difrefpect that is thus fhewn to law and religion, as well as difregard to the inclination, convenience, and
comfort of the people, is, in our opinion, equally impolitic in
them as it is illegal and profane. For, we may expect, and
we pray God it be not in fome degree the cafe already, that
the contempt that has been of late fo generally thrown on religion and its peaceful adherents, may, in time, excite the
multitude, who are but too apt to imitate the *vices* of their
fuperiors, rather than their *virtues*, to fhake off their honeft,
as well as pious principles, and at laft to become, if not as
profane, at leaft as corrupt as too many of thofe who efteem
themfelves their betters. When this event takes place, which,
if not wifely prevented, may be nearer than many of us imagine, thofe who have done the mifchief muft feverely feel the
effects of it, and will thereby, though, perhaps, too late, find
the *neceffity*, from the want of a better *principle*, of fetting the
example of a proper regard to the laws of God and their country, for their own *intereft* and in their own *defence*. For, whatever falfe and vain philofophers may pretend, a nation or people, without *religion* will alfo be without *principle*.

But the writer, when he has faid thus much, is at the fame
time happy, with great juftice and equal pleafure, to be able
to add, that by far the greater part of the heritors or landholders of Scotland are of a very different defcription. And,
therefore, from a real regard to the worfhip of God, the comfort, good will, and convenience of the people, and concern
for the credit of their native country, as well as from their
high refpect for its conftitution and laws, they have the parifh churches, where their lands are fituated, not only *decent*
and *comfortable*, but fome of them *elegant*.

Clergy. ¶

Clergy. ¶—Mr Joseph Tennent, who seems to have been one of the first of the Reformed clergy in this part of the country, is mentioned in an old record of presbytery, as minister of Bedrule, as far back as the 1606, and lived till about the 1631; who also held, for a considerable time, the living of Abbotrule, the cure of which he likewise served, even down to about the year 1621, when it was disjoined from Bedrule; and Mr James Ker, laird of the Grange, an estate in that parish, whose wife was charged with *witchcraft*, but, as appears from the above record, *most unjustly*, was ordained there; he being the first Protestant minister of Abbotrule after its disjunction from Bedrule. Mr Tennent was succeeded by Mr David Fowlis, who was admitted 30th October 1633, by the Bishop of Caithness § and presbytery of Jedburgh. Mr Fowlis was soon after translated to Oxnam, which, in those times, seems to have been considered as one of the most valuable livings in the South of Scotland; and Mr Henry Peirson succeeded him in the benefice of Bedrule. But the Covenanters †, soon after gaining the ascendency, both

¶ Here it may not be unworthy of remark, that the Scottish Church, in the rank of her Clergy, before her connexion with the See of Rome, was nearly the same as she became immediately on her Reformation from Popery : And, that *the Liturgy*, or *Book of Common Order*, received and used by the Reformed Kirk of Scotland, and commonly called *Knox's Liturgy*, for piety, simplicity, natural ease and energy of expression, is equalled by few, and surpassed by none.

§ This was Dr John Abernethy, then also minister of Jedburgh, and author of a theological work, entitled, " A Christian and Heavenly Treatise, containing Physic for the Soul." His name is mentioned in the printed acts of that period, as a Member of several Committees of the Scotch Parliament.

† The following extract, from the record of Presbytery, will enable the reader to form some idea, how indiscriminately the Covenant was administered, or rather imposed, upon many of the people, at that time, when the censures

both thefe gentlemen were removed from their churches, for their attachment to Epifcopacy. Mr Henry Ellot was the Prefbyterian

fures of the Church were followed up by civil penalties‡ " At Jedburgh the laſt day of February 1644 (*Inter alia*) The quilk day Mr Walter Makgill acquainted the brethrin by his letter, that having fummoned John Young and Thomas Young in Falscaſtle, before his Seffion, for not fubfcrying the Covenant, the faids perfons told the kirk officer, that they would *ken (know* or *acknowledge)* no feffion nor miniſter, *but follow the command of their maſter, my Lord Traquair;* and for refufal, he caufed fummon them before this prefbytery againſt this day, who not compearing, was ordeaned to be fummoned *pro 2do* with certification." Hence the danger of impofing indifcriminately the fame oath on all perfons of every defcription, as well as the pernicious confequence of multiplying oaths, and rendering an appeal to God, that laſt and moſt facred pledge of fecurity to fociety, too frequent and familiar to the people. Mr Macgill was miniſter of Cavers, and, as appears from the fame record, preached before the prefbytery of Jedburgh, which met there 30th July 1645, for the vifitation of his kirk, at the advanced age of 101. Faſtcaſtle, which was then the property of the Earl of Traquair, is a curious mound of earth, whether natural or artificial, is uncertain, on which, till of late, there were feveral houfes, and, though in the parifh of Cavers, is fituated fo near the fite of the Caſtle of Bedrule, as gives ground to fome to fuppofe it to have been raifed in ancient times, as an outwork to that fortrefs.

‡ *However, at the fame time, in juſtice to the memory of the Covenanters, we readily admit, that the baneful fpirit of intolerance cannot with truth be more juſtly afcribed to them than to moſt of the other fects in Europe at that time. For all who are acquainted with the biſtory of that period, well know, that the fpirit of intolerance, from bad policy and miſtaken zeal, was unhappily the marked characteriſtic of moſt of of the great contending parties of thofe times, according as they became poffeffed of power: Than which, as nothing is obviouſly more inimical to the peace of fociety and the fafety and happinefs of individuals, fo, in the jurifprudence of nations, nothing ought more carefully to be guarded againſt. For though we fee, by the fame melancholy biſtory, the* Catholic *and* Proteſtant, *the* Epifcopalian *and* Prefbyterian, *while feeling the cruel effects of that hateful fpirit, alike keenly inveighing againſt it, yet, we find them, when poffeffed of power, perfecuting in their turn: Alas! in this refpect, all evidently ſhewing themfelves equally forgetful of their own complaints and fufferings, as of the laws, precepts, and pattern of the meek and lowly Jefus, whom, as they united in confeffing the common Author of their Faith, they, (all the fincere) doubtlefs confidered as their only perfect example, lawgiver, and judge.*

Presbyterian minister who succeeded Mr Peirson, and was admitted by the presbytery of Jedburgh, assisted by Commissioners from the neighbouring presbyteries of Selkirk, Kelso, and Ersiltoun.* He died about the year 1653.

Mr

* As the following extract from the old sederunt book of the acts and proceedings of the presbytery of Jedburgh, gives the reader a distinct view of the *form* of *admission* and *institution* used by our ancestors, *Presbyterians*, and shews, with what attention and accuracy they conducted business, we, for the entertainment of the curious, insert it here :

" *At Bedroule,* 3d *Junii* 1640.

" The whilk day being appointed for the admission of Mr Henry Ellot
" to the function of the ministrie, at the parochin kirke of Bedroule, the bre-
" thren, with their elders, and the congregation, conveened day and place.
" forsaide, for that same effect, wherat Mr William Maxwell haiving preach-
" ed, Mr William Weir, moderator, performed the act of the forsaide admis-
" sion, conform to the practis of this church, in presence, and with consent
" and applaus of the heritors and parochiners of the forsaide parochin, where-
" in did assist and concurre with the brethren, Andrew Dunkison minister at
" Lasowden, Mr Alexander Reid, minister at Ashkirke, from the presbitrie
" of Selkirke, Mr Johne Douglas, minister at Yettam, from the presbitrie of
" Kelso, and Mr Thomas Donaldsone, minister at Smellin, from the presbi-
" trie of Ersiltoun. The saide day the moderator, in name of the brethren,
" asked Mr Henry Ellot, presently admitted, as hee hade done lykeways be-
" for his forsaide admission, if hee hade set any tacke of the teynds or vica-
" rage of the forsaide kirke of Bedroule, to any ; who ansred that he hade not
" directlie nor indirectlie, next the brethren, inhibit thee saide Mr Henry, to
" set any in tymes coming, without adveys and consent of the brethren ; the
" said Mr Henry promised faithfullie not to set any such tackes either of teynds
" or vicarage, without the forsaide advys and consent ; the which promis the
" said Mr Henry confirmed, with his solemn oath, in presence of the brethren.
" After which the saide Mr Henry required that the brethren would give
" him institution upon his presentation, collation, and admission, given bee
" themselves ; the whilk request, the brethren thought lawful, and therefore,
" the moderator did give the saide Mr Henry institution, by giving the bible
" to the saide Mr Henry, he standing in the pulpit, the which Bible, the saide
" Mr Henry gaive about to his elders, as use is, and tooke instruments there-
" upon,

To thofe, but a little acquainted with the hiftory of that period, it is known, that in 1649, patronage was repealed, by act of Parliament, and, that, foon after, certain of the clergy were diftinguifhed by the name of *Protefters,* from their protefting againft admitting thofe called *Malignants* (Cavaliers,) into offices of truft, or even into the Royal army, in oppofition to another more numerous, but, in general, lefs popular party of the clergy, called *Refolutioners,* from their refolving their admiffion on certain conditions : And, that, in confequence of the jarring of thofe parties, as well as the repeal of the law of patronage, the fettlement of many churches was rendered difficult at that time. Whether from thefe, or from other caufes, with which the writer is as yet unacquainted, the church of Bedrule, was kept vacant

for

" upon, in the hands of Robert Rutherfurd, notar publicke, befor the brethren
" and many of the elders and parochiners, whom he requyred to be witnef-
" fes in confirmation of his forfaide iuftitution. The faide day lykeways Mr
" Henry Ellot defired the brethren that they would bee pleafed to defigne ane
" mans and gleibe to him, at the faide kirke, the whilk defyre beeing found
" lawfull the brethren ordains the forfaide defignation to bee made prefentlie,
" and therefor the brethren went together to the mans, pertaining to the mi-
" nifter ferving the cure at the kirke of Bedroule, and ther the moderator, in
" their name and prefence, did give poffeffion to the faide Mr Henry *per tra.*
" *ditionem clavium,* as ufe is, of the whole mans, houfes, biggings, and yeardes,
" formerlie poffeft bee Mr Henry Peirfone, late incumbent ther ; as alfo the
" faide moderator, in name and prefence of the brethren, went and gaive pof-
" feffion to the faide Mr Henry, *per traditionem lapidis & globæ,* as ufe is, of
" the whole gleibe and kirke lands pertaining and belonging to the minif-
" ter ferving the cure, at the forfaide kirke of Bedroule, and of late poffeft
" bee the forfaide Mr Henry Peirfone, late incumbent ther ; in verification
" of the premifes, the faide Mr Henry took inftruments in prefence of the
" brethren, in the hands of Robert Rutherfurd, notar publicke, requyring
" likeways the lairds of Bedroule, elder and younger, with fundrie others of
" the parochiners, to bear witnefs thereunto."

for no ſhorter a period than the ſpace of five years. ‖ At laſt, Mr Hugh Scot was ſettled here, 17th March 1658. He did not continue long miniſter; for, on the re-eſtabliſhment of Epiſcopacy, he was removed from his church for non-conformity. Mr James Adamſon, miniſter of Carriden, was preferred to the living of Bedrule 7th September 1664, and continued miniſter here during the reigns of Charles and James, and ſeems to have died about the time of the Revolution. He was ſucceeded by Mr James Borland, in 1690, who was the firſt miniſter ſettled here after preſbytery became again the eſtabliſhed religion. Mr Borland was ſucceeded by Mr John Gilchriſt in 1714, who, in 1748, was ſucceeded by Mr George Dickſon, to whom the preſent miniſter ſucceeded in 1788. And, it is remarkable, of theſe above mentioned nine incumbents, ſince the Reformation, except Mr David Fowlis, who was tranſlated to Oxnam, that they all died miniſters of Bedrule, or were removed from their charge, not for any fault or irregularity of conduct, but for their faithful adherence to the religion they profeſſed; and, however obviouſly of different ſentiments, fidelity and ſteadineſs in the cauſe they thought beſt, were equally remarkable in the character of all.

Advantages.—

‖ Indeed, from a remarkable coincidence of circumſtances, the records and hiſtory of this country, in general, during that period, happen to be very imperfect. For, not to mention, the records and other intereſting papers, which were carried to London by order of the Protector, having been loſt by the wreck of the veſſel in which they were returning, by order of Government, after the Reſtoration, on the Lothian coaſt, near Royſton, (Caroline park,) General Aſſemblies were interdicted during the Uſurpation: a Provincial Synod was, therefore, then the higheſt Eccleſiaſtical Court in this country; and the whole records of the provincial ſynod of Merſe and Tiviotdale, preceding 1708, and, probably, containing an account of the cauſe of that very long vacancy, were unfortunately deſtroyed by accidental fire in the manſe of Morebattle.

Advantages.—This parish is situated in the centre of a prosperous though not very populous county, intersected by the great road between Berwick and Carlisle, touched on by a branch of the London road to Edinburgh, not more than two miles distant from Jedburgh, about 7 miles from Hawick, both excellent market towns. The land is in general of a dry soil, yet watered by a considerable number of springs, rivulets and brooks, in most places of easy access and at convenient distances from each other. Besides, upon the West and North it is for the most part bounded by the before mentioned pure and copious streams of the Rule and the Tiviot.

Disadvantages.—The great distance from coal, the badness of the road from Spittal bridge to the southern extremity of the parish, by which the people in this part of the country, usually pass or make a great circuit, to Reid, in Northumberland, for coal, and Windburgh, a considerable mountain on the borders of Liddysdale, for lime; and the badness of that from Bedrule to Jedburgh, the nearest market town, are disadvantages not only to this parish, but also to the neighbourhood, and which, with no great difficulty, may, and, we hope, soon will be removed, as both these roads, run, in general, on a gentle declivity and favourable bottom, and are near excellent materials.

Conclusion.—It will be observed, that the writer of the foregoing Statistical Account has avoided repeating the same things, so properly taken notice of in the accounts of the various parishes in this part of the country, already published; and, therefore, whensoever that is felt as a defect by the reader, it will be only necessary for him to suppose, that the inhabitants of the parish of Bedrule have nearly the same religious and political sentiments; predilections and prejudices§,

ces*, are nearly of the fame fize, ftrength, and vigour of body and mind, and, from fimilar caufes, are liable to the fame
difeafes, as mentioned in one or other of thefe accounts :
That the fame animals, fowls, and migratory birds, roam in
the field, and fly in the air, indifferently over this and the
neighbouring parifhes ; That the rivers abound with nearly
the fame kinds of fifh, in the fame feafons of the year, of the
fame quality, flavour, and fhape, and in general alfo nearly
of

---

* It may be proper here only to remark, in general, that the people in
this country feem not now fo ftrongly attached to their lairds or mafters as
formerly ; and that the predilection of many to their native foil, and a certain unfortunate family, is greatly diminifhed ; the former being much weakened, the latter almoft every where worn out. Indeed, they feem now, in
general, more anxious how they live, than where ; how they are governed,
than by whom ; what the laws are, than who are their makers ; and how
juft and equal foever they be, are apt to confider themfelves protected thereby, only fo far as they have it in their power to render them efficient. Thefe
changes, we believe, may be eafily accounted for. In this country, formerly, the greateft refpect was generally paid to family ; for then almoft every
perfon confidered himfelf of fome family, and was thereby led to think
he had an intereft therein. And his intereft, in this real or fuppofed
connection, was, for the moft part, not merely ideal. For, then, it was the
pride of the laird or mafter, to have his tenants, retainers, and even domeftics,
of his own furname, many of them his near relations, and he commonly
treated them as fuch. By this means, his will was ufually as law to them ;
his honour their honour ; his intereft their intereft. And, we are affured,
where this is ftill the cafe, the fame is ftill the effect. But where the caufes
are changed, it will not feem ftrange, that the confequences are alfo different.
And however this change, in the minds of the people, may affect individuals,
it is certainly, at prefent, not eafy to fay, what, in the long run, its effects
may be on fociety ; but, it is evidently much altering the ftate of mens
minds, as well as that of the country ; and we earneftly pray, it may, in the
iffue, be equally beneficial and improving to both. With regard to their religious fentiments, though the people be not lefs divided, we are happy to obferve, they feem, in general, lefs prejudiced againft one another than formerly ; which proceeds, we believe, much, if not entirely, from the liberty of
opinion, our excellent Conftitution fo happily affords to every well intentioned and reafonable man,

of the fame fize : And that, allowing for the difference of climate in the uplands, the midlands, and the lowlands, feed time and harveft, the modes of cropping, and the management of black cattle and fheep, are nearly the fame ; and where there happens to be a diftinction, that it more commonly proceeds from the fkill and induftry of individuals, than the general fyftem of conducting that kind of bufinefs in the different parifhes· And, it is worthy of remark, that, with little exception, the fame obfervation applies to the greater part of this diftrict. This, the writer trufts, will be alfo his apology for having been particular in his account of other things, which though in themfelves, perhaps, not more interefting, yet, from their fpeciality, or having been overlooked, or but flightly noticed by others, he judged entitled to his attention.

PARISH OF BOWDEN,

(County of Roxburgh, Synod of Merse and Teviotdale, and Presbytery of Selkirk),

Drawn up by a Friend to Statistical Inquiries, from Ma-
terials chiefly furnished by Mr Andrew Blaikie,
Tenant in Holydean, *who has resided* 35 *Years in that*
Parish.

Name, Boundaries, and Extent.

IN the charter granted by King David I. to the Abbey
of Selkirk, mention is made of *Bothenden*, which feems
to favour the conjecture of this parish being named after a
St Bothen or *Bodwin*, and the fcite can still be pointed out
of his tower near the village. Yet the name may be derived from a *den* or *dean* in the *bow* or curve of a fmall rivulet, which is defcriptive of the place where the church is
faid to have once ftood. It is bounded on the N. by Melrofe parifh ; on the E. moftly by St Bofwells, though
partly alfo by Langnewton annexed to Ancrum ; on the S.
by Lilliefleaf; on the W. by Selkirk ; and on the N. W.
by

by Galafhiels. Its greateft length from E. to W. is 6
miles. Its greateft breadth from S. to N. is about 4½
miles. At an average it may be about 4 by 3 miles.
The whole parifh having been meafured, either for the divifion of run-rig lands, or for being let by the acre, is
known to contain nearly 6700 acres *.

Surface, Soil, and Climate.—The furface is much varied.
One of the Eildon hills, and one half of another, are in
this parifh. From one broad and elevated bafe, three conical tops arife, which, from their fituation in a flat country, more than from their height, are feen at a great .di-
ftance. Some parts of them alfo being covered with a
kind of red ftone, without a pile of grafs, have a fingular
and ftriking appearance. Several little eminences and
ridges run from W. to E. with fmall vallies of fine meadow between them, all abounding with fprings of water,
which, when collected, run into Tweed, about two miles to
the eaftward of this parifh, except one or two ftreamlets
which fall into Ale water, its fouthern boundary. In general, the whole parifh is naturally graffy, except about
200 acres, including the higher parts of thefe ridges, which
are inclined to broom or furze, and about the fame quantity bearing a kind of ftunted heath. About 3-4ths of the
parifh have been, at one time or another, under the plough.
The other 1-4th confifts of bog, mofs, and plantations of
fir and foreft trees. Of thefe laft there are too few, efpecially as they are profitable to the proprietor, as well as to
the farmer, for fhelter, and to the people for fuel. There
is fome old wood, but of no great extent. Two-thirds of
the parifh are inclofed moftly with ditch and hedges of
                                                        thorns,

* Here, and throughout the following account, the Englifh acre is
always meant, as is alfo the Teviotdale meafure, which is precifely 1-5th
more than the Linlithgow ftandard.

thorns, which thrive well when properly taken care of. The ſoil of far the greateſt part is a white binding clay on a tilly bottom, which retains moiſture, becomes hard in drought, and can only be laboured and ſown to advantage when the ſeaſon is neither too wet nor too dry. About 1-6th of it is well adapted to wheat ; another 1-6th is ſharp, lets water eaſily ſink, is very manageable, and produces good turnips, corn, and graſs. Moſt of the pariſh is, on the whole, as well ſuited to paſturage as to tillage, and will pay as well. The expoſure in general is high and eaſterly, which, together with the clayey ſoil, renders the crops often late, precarious, and apt to ſuffer much from rainy harveſts and early froſts. In the 1782, a great deal of corn was uncut at Martinmas, and ſeveral farmers, in-ſtead of paying their rents from their crops, were obliged to purchaſe grain. Many oats yielded that year no more than 3 ſtone of meal *per* boll.

Farms, Rents, Heritors.—The farms are very unequal, paying L. 400, L. 200, L. 100, L. 70, L. 60, and even ſo low as L. 10, and L. 8 Sterling of yearly rent in money, beſides a few carriages, one half of the poors-rates, and one half of the ſchoolmaſter's ſalary. The ſoil differing greatly in value, lands, in farms, are let at from 15 s. to 5 s. *per* acre. Some ſmall fields near the villages of Middleham and Bowden are rented for conveniency for L. 1, 10 s. *per* acre, while ſome tracts of outfield high lands do not fetch above 2 s. 6 s. The whole real rent of the pariſh may at preſent amount to L. 2300 Sterling. The valued rent is L. 8030, 11 s. Scots * ; of which the largeſt half belongs to the Duke of Roxburgh, his valuation being L. 4121, 11 s. Scots.

* A new analyſis of the valuation of the whole county reduces the valuation of this pariſh to L. 7930 : 10 : 10.

Scots. There are only three other confiderable proprietors, all of whom occafionally refide, and about 50 fmall feuers in Bowden and Middleham, who pay of teind, feu, &c. to his Grace about 1-8th of the yearly value of their fub-jects *.

Cultivation, Manures, and Produce.—There were formerly 26 ploughs in the parifh, each drawn by 2 oxen, and 3, or at leaft 2 horfes; and 10 or 12 drawn by 2 horfes only. No oxen are now employed. Some attempts to work them by themfelves are not likely to fucceed; fervants being prejudiced againft them, and doing all in their power to prevent this practice from taking place. There are at prefent 44 ploughs, each drawn by 2 horfes, and both driven and held by one man. The change has not contributed much to raife better crops, or to benefit the farmer. The Englifh plough, with the broad or plate fock, is univerfally ufed; though fome are returning occafionally to the old Scots plough, which is certainly preferable in ftony or ftrong clay lands. Several moffes in the parifh and neighbourhood, abounding with fhell marl, have lately been drained. Thofe in the parifh belong to the Duke of Roxburgh, and the marl is ufed only by his tenants; but in the neighbourhood, it is fold at 6 d. *per* cart drawn by one, and at 9 d. *per* cart drawn by two horfes, and can be carried 6 or 7 miles to good advantage. Thirty of the one, or forty-five of the other, are laid on an acre of the fharp dry land. Strong clay lands require more. Lime is alfo brought from Mid Lothian, about 28 miles, at the rate of 12 s. *per* cart, containing nearly 3 bolls of fhells, and ufed in the proportion of 6 carts to 25 of marl. Both contribute

to

* Their number is daily decreafing, the richer purchafing the propertie of the poorer.

to raiſe excellent crops of corn and graſs. Lime produces better grain, but marl anſwers beſt for graſs, eſpecially for paſture. After trying many varieties of every grain, the moſt approved are now white oats, barley bear, (ſo called to diſtinguiſh it from rough bear, or big); early peaſe, here called hot ſeed; and Kentiſh, or Cleaveland wheat. Very little rye is ſown, and no flax but for family uſe. On about 1650 acres, about 1100 bolls of different grains are annually ſown; nearly as follows, *viz.* 120 of wheat, 100 of peaſe, 750 of oats, and 130 of barley; which laſt is followed by a hay crop. There are beſides 140 acres, yearly, in turnip; 50 in potatoes; and 160 in fallow. Turnips are generally ſucceeded by barley; potatoes ſometimes by barley, but more commonly by oats; fallow partly by wheat and partly by oats; and lands, ploughed out of lee or paſture, are always ſown with oats. After maintaining the inhabitants, the annual exports may be about 350 bolls of oat-meal, at L. 1, 5 s. *per* boll; 300 ditto of barley, at 18 s.; and 450 ditto of wheat, at L. 1, 2 s. amounting in all to L. 1202, 10 s. *per annum.*

Horſes, Black Cattle, Sheep, and Wool.—There are 160 horſes of different ages in the pariſh, one-fourth of which are too young for labour. The black cattle of all ages may be 540. About 90 are reared yearly, and about 50 are ſtall-fed for the butcher, which weigh at an average from 45 to 50 ſtone of 16 lb. Dutch weight *. The cows of the ſame breed, when fattened, weigh about 36 ſtone. About 80 ſwine are annually fed, moſtly by tradeſmen. They are bought in England in October or November, when 3 or 4 months old, at 10 s. or 12 s. each; and after feeding
for

* The Dutch weight is always meant, when meal, grain, or butcher meat are ſpoken of. The Scotch weight, of 24 Engliſh lb. to the ſtone, is uſed for ſelling wool, cheeſe, butter, and hay.

for 4 months on the refuse of potatoes, and a little bruifed oats or barley, they weigh 10 or 12 ftone. Being killed fo young, they are very fine food, and of great fervice to a family. The number of fheep is about 2300, moftly of the white-faced long-bodied kind, and weighing from 12 lb. to 14 lb. *per* quarter. Till of late, little attention was paid to the improvement of wool; but now the encouragement given by premiums, and the force of example, have, perhaps, carried the ftock of fheep here to as great perfeftion in that refpeft as the climate and foil will admit. The wool has fold for 18 s. *per* ftone. The common difeafes of the fheep are the rot, a kind of confumption occafioned by overftocking the paftures, and by rainy feafons, efpecially a rainy autumn; and the *fturdy*, or water in the head, which attacks them when about a year old, chiefly in the months of April, May, and June; and is of fo corrofive a nature as to perforate the fkull into holes large enough to admit a pea or fmall bean. One fheep in 40 falls by this difeafe. Such as are affefted by it become at firft giddy, afterwards ftupid, and feldom or never recover. No ewes are milked. The cheefe and butter, made from cows milk, are moftly confumed in the parifh, efpecially the latter; which is much ufed in *falving* the fheep, at the rate of from 4 lb. to 6 lb. to the Scotch pint of tar.

Population.—The population of this parifh in 1755 amounted to 672 fouls. At prefent (January 1794) the parifh contains 217 families, and 860 perfons; of whom there are,

Under 10 years of age,	-	223
Between 10 and 20,	-	189
Between 20 and 50,	-	321
Above 50,	-	127
Total,	-	860

Of

Of theſe, 10 are above 80 years ; and of theſe 10, 3 are 85, and 2 are upwards of 90.

The births, marriages, and burials, recorded in the pariſh-regiſter, for the laſt 8 years, are as follow :

Years	Births	Marriages	Deaths
1785,	14	6	15
1786,	15	9	18
1787,	19	10	15
1788,	13	5	10
1789,	14	6	10
1790,	16	5	7
1791,	11	6	7
1792,	9	4	13
Total,	115	51	95
Average yearly,	$14\frac{1}{8}$	$6\frac{1}{8}$	$11\frac{7}{8}$

Moſt of the inhabitants are either feuers, farmers, or cottagers employed by them, except the after mentioned, *viz.*

14 Wrights,	2 Shoemakers,
3 Coopers,	6 Grocers,
1 Wheelwright,	3 Blackſmiths,
13 Tailors,	1 Founder,
11 Maſons,	2 Flaxdreſſers, and only
12 Weavers,	4 Alehouſe-keepers.

About one third of the inhabitants are Burghers and Antiburghers. The latter have a meeting-houſe in the pariſh ; the congregation of which, from this and other pariſhes, pays their miniſter L. 60 *per annum*. There are 4 corn-mills, each of which draws ſome multures ; but that ſervitude is beginning to be aboliſhed. A threſhing machine is newly erected, which does a great deal of work ; but when the prime coſt, and intereſt thereon, tear and wear of every kind, the number of hands, and the extraordinary waſte of horſes, are all taken into the account, it may not be of great profit to the proprietor.

Fuel

Fuel and Labour.—There are no manufactures, owing to the dearnefs of fuel. Coals muft be chiefly depended on ; and they are brought 28 and 30 miles from Lothian, at the rate of 1 s. *per cwt.* Few or no peats are to be had ; but the people are much benefited by weedings of plantations, which are frequently fold in the neighbourhood. Small feuers and tenants, who have not ground enough to employ themfelves and horfes, drive coal, lime, and marl for hire ; the lime at 9 s. and the marl at 1 s. 4 d. *per* two-horfe cart, or at 4 s. *per* day for a man, cart, and 2 horfes. The wages of a man-fervant, who eats in the houfe, are from L. 7 to L. 8 Sterling *per annum.* Maid-fervants get L. 2, 10 s. and L. 2, 15 s. for the fummer, and L. 1, 5 s. for the winter half-year. But a married farm-fervant, who provides his own victuals, receives about the value of L. 14 or L. 15 Sterling in oats, barley, peafe, flax, potatoe, and the maintenance of a cow through the year. Upon thefe wages he may bring up his family in a decent manner, and give his children a tolerable education, if he and his wife be induftrious and frugal. In harveft, which commonly lafts about four weeks, a man gets L. 1, 6 s. and a woman L. 1, and their maintenance. At all other times, a man gets 1 s. 2 d. *per* day, and a woman 7 d. or 8 d. in fummer *, and a man 1 s. in winter, both furnifhing their own victuals. Men working by the piece do at leaft 1-4th, if not 1-3d more than on day's wages ; which makes their employers let as much work by the piece as they can. A mafon earns 1 s. 8 d. and a carpenter 1 s. 6 d. *per* day without victuals. A carpenter gets 1 s. and a tailor 8 d. with their victuals. Servants wages are doubled within thefe 40 years.

Difeafes.

---

* Summer, with men on day's wages, begins on 13th February, and lafts 8 months.

Diseases.—No difeafes are peculiar to this parifh. Fevers, at an interval of perhaps 8 or 10 years, have proved mortal ; and the natural fmall pox carry off many children. Inoculation, that falutary mean of preferving them, is far from becoming general ; the Seceders being much prejudiced againft it, though in many families it has been attended with its ufual fuccefs. Confumptions are not unfrequent ; but, on the whole, the people enjoy good health.

Ecclefiaftical State, Schools.—The church is old, long, narrow, and needs reparation. A vault adjoining to it is the burying-place of the ducal family of Roxburgh. The coffins are above ground ; and fome of them, by the dates upon them, have ftood upwards of 200 years, and are ftill entire. An excellent manfe and office-houfes are newly finifhed. The ftipend confifts of 5 chalders of victual, Lin meafure, 2-3ds of which are oat-meal, and 1-3d is barley, 400 merks in money, and 40 merks for communion-elements. The glebe is 16 Englifh acres, about 3 of which are meadow. The Duke of Roxburgh is patron. The parochial fchoolmafter at Bowden has a falary of L. 8, 6 s. 8 d. Sterling, and about 70 fcholars. Of thefe, 30 read Englifh at 1 s. *per* quarter, 25 both read and write at 1 s. 6 d. and about 15 commonly are taught arithmetic, book-keeping, and mathematics, on fuch terms as can be agreed upon. The fchoolmafter has about L. 3 for collecting poors-rates, and a dwelling-houfe and garden worth L. 2, making in all about L. 30 yearly. There is alfo a fchool and a fchool-houfe at Middleham. The mafter has a falary of L. 3, and gets his victuals, during the teaching feafon, from the different families, according to the number of children they have at the fchool, which, at an average, is about 30, fo that he cannot draw annually above L. 7 or L. 8 Sterling.

Poor

Poor.—The number of poor on the roll for the laſt ſeven years has been 20. They are all maintained in their own houſes, or boarded in other families. The annual ſum expended upon them, may amount to L. 65 Sterling, which is levied at two different times in the year from the proprietors and tenants equally. This aſſeſſment is laid on by the proprietors; but the tenants have a vote in the diſtribution of it. The collections at church on Sundays are ſmall, and do little more than pay the ſalaries of the precentor and beadle. There is only one beggar in the pariſh; but ſtrolling poor from other places come among us at all ſeaſons.

Roads.—The roads are pretty well taken care of by the Juſtices of the diſtrict. Formerly 1 s. 6 d. for each man, and 2 s. for each horſe, were levied annually for ſtatute-labour. By a late act of Parliament, it is now laid on according to the valued rents, and paid by the poſſeſſors. The management is veſted in Juſtices of Peace and Commiſſioners of Supply, and other truſtees. The utmoſt they can exact is 10 s. Sterling on the L. 100 Scots of valued rent, but they can make it as low as they pleaſe when the ſtate of the roads allow.

Birds and Beaſts.—There are plenty of partridges, ſome plovers, woodcocks, ſnipes, curlews, and other birds, both ſtationary and migratory, which are common in this part of Scotland. Little injury is done by birds of prey; but much was formerly ſuſtained from foxes, to which the furze and bruſh-wood on the lower ſkirts of Eildon, both in this and Melroſe pariſh, afford cover. Of late, however, their number has been diminiſhed by the Noblemen and Gentlemen

of

of the Caledonian Hunt, and others who keep hounds. Hares abound.

Character of the People.—The people in general are sober and industrious. Few of them engage in adventures or speculations, except in the line of farming, and even there with a prudent caution. Their divisions, in religious opinions, do not now occasion so great a want of cordial intercourse as formerly, and the prejudices of sects are daily dying away.

Antiquities.—The remains of a military road, with circular stations or camps, at the distance of two or three miles, supposed to be Roman, can be traced, running nearly N. through the centre and broadest part of the parish, about a mile to the westward of the church, from Beaulieu in the parish of Lilliesleaf to Caldshiels in the parish of Galashiels. In some places, all vestiges of it are destroyed by the plough; but in other places traces of it are still visible, in the form of a large ditch, about 20 feet wide; and in some spots, of two ditches of that width, at the distance of 50 feet. The camps or stations are all on eminences in view of each other; and different weapons, or instruments of war, have been dug up by people ploughing or ditching around them, as well as in the adjacent mosses.

There was, not long ago, a strong fortification, of its kind, at Holydean or Haliedean, once a residence of the family of Roxburgh. The court-yard, containing about ¾ of an acre, was surrounded by strong stone and lime walls, 4 feet thick, and 16 feet high, with slanting holes, between five freestones, about 30 feet from each other; from which an arrow or a musket could have been pointed in different directions. Upon an arched gateway in the front there was a strong iron gate. Within the court stood two strong

towers,

towers, the one of 3, the other of 5 stories, confisting of 8 or 10 lodgeable rooms, besides porters lodges, servants hall, vaulted cellars, bakehouses, &c. The roof and flooring, being all of the strongest oak, if kept in the state in which they then were, might have stood for a century. But during the minority of the present Duke, while he was abroad, without his knowledge, his then commissioner ordered this building to be mostly pulled down, merely for the sake of getting the freestones in them to build a large farm-house and appurtenances, at the distance of 3 miles, though the difficulty of separating these stones from the lime made them a dear purchase. Some of the vaults still remain, and are used by the tenant; and about 160 feet of the court wall are perfectly entire, which makes the demolition of the rest to be much regretted, as the whole building was stately and ornamental to the place, as well as venerable for its antiquity. One stone, preserved from the ruins, and now a lintel to the door of the farm-house at Holydean, has in the middle an unicorn's head and three stars, with this inscription on either side :

Feer God. Flee from sin mak to the lyfe		Everlasting to the end Dem Isbel Ker 1530

About 140 yards from the principal house on the top of a precipice hanging over a burn, there had been a chapel or place of worship, and a burying ground, as appears from a number of grave stones, handles of coffins, and pieces of human bones, which have been dug up from time to time. Hence probably has arisen the name *Holydean* or *Halie-dean*.

The greatest curiosity, perhaps, of its kind in Britain, is a stone dike without lime, which incloses about 500 acres of this farm, and has stood more than 300 years, yet is still a tolerable fence. It has at first been 6 or 7 feet high,

with

with capftones. In an old tack, this inclofure is called, " *The great deer park of Haliedean,*" and was once full of wood; but it has long been fubdivided, and all the trees cut down, except a few old birches.

Here, as well as in other parts of Scotland, many birch, fir, and oak trees have been found in the moffes; fome of them 3 feet in diameter, and feveral of the firs and oaks quite found. They generally lie from 3 to 8 feet below the furface. Human bones alfo, and many horns of different animals, have been dug up, quite beyond the fize of the largeft to be any where feen at this time. How the former were laid there, and how the latter acquired their enormous fize, leaves room for conjecture. Where they are found, the fubftance of the mofs is condenfed fog, to appearance as frefh and diftinct as that upon old lea ground. This too may afford matter of curious fpeculation.

The family of Carre of Cavers deferves alfo to be mentioned, as one of the moft ancient in the S. of Scotland. Their chief refidence, for many generations, has been in the parifh. George Carre, Efq; of Nifbet, a Lord of Seffion, was defcended from a branch of this family. They are fuppofed to have fprung from Kerr of Ferniherft. One of their anceftors claimed the title of Lord Jedburgh; but from the different manner in which they fpell their name, it feems probable, either that they are a diftinct family, or a very old cadet.

PARISH OF CASTLETOWN,

(County of Roxburgh, Presbytery of Langholm, Synod of Dumfries.)

By the Rev. Mr James Arkle, *Miniſter.*

Origin of the Names.

THE origin of the modern, as well as of the ancient name of this pariſh, is abundantly plain. Upon the ſummit of a precipice, about 100 feet perpendicular, on the eaſt bank of the river Liddal, and immediately above the church, there was a ſtrong fort or caſtle, the rampart and foſſee of which remain entire : near to theſe, in the place where the preſent road was formed, and in ſeveral other parts in the immediate neighbourhood, many hearth-ſtones were dug up, where a town or village had formerly ſtood. Hence the name of *Caſtle-town.* But the ancient name of this diſtrict, and indeed that by which it is ſtill moſt frequently denominated, was *Liddiſdale*, from the river Liddal, which runs through it in a direction from eaſt to ſouth. In the ancient hiſtories, and geographical accounts of Scotland, it is called the county of Liddiſdale, and in old writs it is deſigned the *Lordſhip* of that name.

Erection,

Erection, Form, and Extent.—This pariſh formerly belonged to the Preſbytery of Jedburgh; but when the five churches of Eſkdale were erected into the Preſbytery of Langholm, it was added to them in the year 1743. This was done on account of its great diſtance from the former ſeat of the preſbytery. Its form approaches nearly to that of a triangle, whoſe baſe runs from eaſt to weſt, along the head of Teviotdale, and whoſe oppoſite vertex points to Solway frith. It contains, according to the map of the county, about 52,160 acres. It is the largeſt pariſh in the ſouth of Scotland, being upwards of 18 miles in length, and 14 in breadth.

General Appearance, Woods, &c.—The general appearance of the upper part of the pariſh is mountainous; the lower part is hilly; and all of it, at a diſtance from the banks of the rivers, is bleak and wild to a high degree. But its appearance along the banks of the rivers is altogether different. Theſe are generally covered with natural woods, or young plantations in a very thriving ſtate. The barren wilds are entirely hid from the view; the windings of the river, and the fine holm land on every ſide, preſent the moſt pictureſque ſcenes, or exhibit rich proſpects to the eye. Theſe are juſtly deſcribed by our native poet, Dr Armſtrong, in his poem on Health *. The inhabited part of

* ———————— Such the ſtream,
On whoſe Arcadian banks I firſt drew air.
Liddal, till now, except in Doric lays,
Tun'd to her murmurs by her love-ſick ſwains,
Unknown in ſong; though not a purer ſtream
Through meads more flow'ry,—more romantic groves,
Rolls toward the weſtern main. Hail ſacred flood!
May ſtill thy hoſpitable ſwains be bleſt
In rural innocence; thy mountains ſtill
Teem with the fleecy race; thy tuneful woods
For ever flouriſh, and thy vales look gay,
With painted meadows, and the golden grain! Book III.

of the parifh confifts of two vallies. That along the Hermitage is about ten miles in length, from the fource of the
river to the point where it lofes its name in the Liddal.
At the head of this river the country is entirely mountainous. The mountains are very high and fteep, but are generally dry, and afford excellent fheep pafture. The
greateft part of this ftream is fringed with natural wood;
it poffeffes much rural beauty, and exhibits the paftoral
fcenes of life in great perfection. The other valley, or
ftrath, is that along the fides of the Liddal. Near the head
of the parifh on the eaft, the rivers Liddal and Tyne, which
runs by Newcaftle, take their rife, in the midft of an immenfe bog, furrounded by mountains. This place is very
properly named *Dead water*, becaufe for a confiderable
fpace neither of them can be traced as a running ftream.
The Tyne winds flowly to the eaft, between the bleak
mountains and the dreary waftes of Northumberland, by
Keelder Cafle *. The Liddal runs due weft for a few miles,
and then runs due fouth. This part of the country is
mountainous, high, cold and moift, and lies under the
thick and folitary gloom of continual fogs. For ten miles
down the river its banks are entirely naked; the hills on
each fide produce a great quantity of grafs. At the point
where it is joined by the Hermitage the banks are covered
with trees. On the north fide the thriving plantations of
the Duke of Buccleugh, and on the fouth the plantations
and woods of Mr Elliot of Whitehaugh, near the confluence
of the rivers, form a landfcape highly beautiful. Here the
valley widens confiderably, and improvements are every
where feen. From this hill you reach the confines of
Canonby; the ride is very much admired by travellers.
The new town rifing in view, and building upon an elegant

* Keelder Caftle is a hunting feat of the Duke of Northumberland.

gant plan ; the femicircular groves of trees, and the fertile fields, and windings of the river Liddal, contribute their various beauties to delight the eye.

Mountains.—The principal mountains are Tudhope, Millenwood-fell, Windhead, Greatmoor, Dun, Dod, Hermitage, Peel-fell, Roan-fell, Larifton-fell, Carby-Laws, and Tinnis hills. The laft mentioned is feen as a land mark at a great diftance out at fea. None of thefe mountains have been meafured by the barometer. But when Mr Stobie furveyed the county, he meafured thofe of the Cheviot, Cartawifp, &c. and when on the top of the higheft in this parifh, he compared them with others by the Theodolite; by this it appears Tudhope is 1830 feet above the level of the fea. Millenwood-fell and Windhead are about 2000 feet. Thefe are the higheft of them.

Rivers and Fifh.—The rivers are the Liddal, the Hermitage, the Tweeden, the Kerfhope, (which divides the two kingdoms), the Tinnis and the Blackburn; with feveral other ftreams of inferior note. All of them are plentifully ftored with trouts, and afford excellent fport to the angler.

Climate and Longevity.—The climate is very damp, owing to two caufes. From its proximity to the Atlantic Ocean, a great collection of vapour arifes, which is attracted by the mountains, and poured down in torrents of rain. The other is owing to the nature of the foil and furface of the hills themfelves. They are generally covered to the very fummit with a deep ftratum of mofs, which retains the moifture ; under the mofs lies a bed of till, through which the water cannot eafily penetrate. Notwithftanding the dampnefs of the air, thofe who are bred in the country enjoy good health, and many of them have arrived at a
great

great age. An inſtance occurs of one Mr ELLIOT of Red-heugh, who lately, at the age of 86, rode 50 miles in one day, without any inconvenience, tranſacted buſineſs at a public market, and returned to his houſe next evening, without ſleep. One man now alive, JAMES LILLICO, married his third wife at 72, is now upwards of 93, enjoys good health, and manages his ordinary buſineſs; another, at the age of 80, is in full vigour, and frequently walks to Edinburgh. A woman, named Margaret Wyllie, died a few years ago at the age of 113, in the poſſeſſion of all her faculties till the day of her death.

Diſeaſes.—The ſcrophula prevails frequently among the young, and rheumatic and ſtomach complaints among thoſe more advanced in life. Inoculation is general. Laſt ſpring a great number of children, ſome men, and women the mothers of children, were inoculated, and all of them did well. At preſent the ſmall-pox rages in the natural way, and has carried off many. Prejudices ſtill remain againſt inoculation, chiefly among the Seceders. Conſumptions are frequent. Epidemic fevers ſometimes viſit us, but are ſeldom fatal.

Sheep, Wool, &c.—The rents of the pariſh ariſe chiefly from ſheep, black cattle and horſes, and from tillage. The ſheep are of the long kind; there are no ſhort ſheep in the country. The breed of ſheep has been very much improved of late years, by ſeveral individuals, who have purchaſed rams from the eaſtern borders. The moſt intelligent obſerve, that croſſing the breed is not only the beſt method of improving the ſheep and wool, but alſo of preventing the diſeaſes to which they are liable. By continuing the ſame ram, the ſheep are weakened, and diſeaſes multiplied, or rendered more inveterate; by changing him,

it

it is found that the *ſturdy*, and other diſeaſes, are leſs frequent. The diſorders moſt prevalent are, the ſturdy, the
ſickneſs, the louping ill, the rot, and the braxy. Wedders
and draught ewes are ſold to dealers from Yorkſhire. The
wool is ſold for clothing to the manufacturing towns in
England. Laſt year it ſold at from 15 s. to 19 s. the ſtone;
this ſeaſon from 11 s. to 15 s. The decreaſe is owing no
doubt to the ſtagnation of commerce. Moſt of the farms are
ſeparated from each other by ſtone dikes; but even where
they are not, the flocks are permitted to wander at large
in their reſpective paſtures. They are never confined in
hirſels, nor in folds by night; they ſeek their food at large,
and they know beſt where it is to be found. They are all
over-laid with tar; ſome uſe palm oil in place of butter, and
approve of it. The ſheep are carefully waſhed before ſhearing.
The practice of milking the ewes is very much diſconti-
nued; where it is continued, it is only for a ſhort time.
It weakens the ſheep, and renders them leſs able to endure
the ſeverity of the winter. Every farmer provides a conſiderable quantity of hay againſt the ſtorm, and when neceſſary, feeds regularly. Before this method was adopted,
much loſs was frequently ſuſtained in ſtormy ſeaſons.

Black Cattle.—Some farmers bring a conſiderable number of black cattle from the markets of Falkirk, Crieff, and
Down. They are ſupported during the winter by the foggage and coarſe hay, and ſold in the ſpring; or fed in good
paſture through the ſummer, and ſold fat about Martinmas;
kyloes at from L. 3 to L. 5 Sterling. Thoſe bred in the
country are of the Dutch, Lancaſter, or Galloway kinds.
The large kind ſell at from L. 6 to L. 9 Sterling. Their paſture is generally coarſe, excepting what lies upon lime-ſtone,
which is very fine, but the produce is always very great.
The butter which is made, even on the coarſeſt paſture, is
not

not excelled by any in Britain. It is commonly obſerved, that the coarſer the paſture is, the butter is the better and the richer. Even the moſſy ground, though in appearance barren, is of great uſe both for black cattle and ſheep. The plant, called *the moſs*, riſes before any other in the ſpring, affords excellent nouriſhment, and is carefully ſought after by the flocks. In theſe coarſe lands, there is a conſtant and regular ſucceſſion of different ſpecies of graſs, which riſe in their reſpective ſeaſons throughout the year.

Soil, Produce, and Cultivation.—The arable land at preſent in tillage lies chiefly on the banks of the rivers. Many hundred acres, formerly in tillage, are thrown into paſture on account of the high prices of ſheep and wool. The ſoil of the holm land is excellent. It is ſometimes of a light, but moſt frequently of a very deep and fine loam, and where it is properly cultivated, it produces exceeding good crops. Wheat has been ſown, and turned out very well. The ordinary crops are barley, or rough bear, peaſe, oats, flax, potatoes. Turnips have lately been introduced, and ſucceeded very well. Laſt ſummer, travellers·from Edinburgh ſaw no turnips by the way equal to thoſe on the fields in this place. Within theſe few years, a conſiderable quantity of graſs ſeeds have been ſown, and have produced excellent crops. From the nature of the holm land, and ſituation of the country, turnips, barley, and graſs ſeeds, ſucceeded by early oats, will probably be found the beſt rotation.—The ploughs in uſe are, the Engliſh plough, and Small's chain plough. The former, drawn by 4 horſes, is ſtill uſed by ſome farmers, though, from the nature of the land, there can be no doubt that Small's chain ·plough, with two horſes, would execute the work, and anſwer the purpoſe much better. The ridges are made very narrow, and

consiſt

consist of 8 furrows *. One farmer uses a pair of oxen with Small's plough, and approves of them.

Seasons.—Though the hills are moist, yet from the reflection of the sun from each side of the valley, and its favourable exposure in the summer, the weather is very warm, and the harvests are early. As soon as vegetation commences in the spring, it shoots forth with wonderful vigour and with great rapidity, and the ordinary productions of the garden arrive at great perfection. Our harvests are much more early than in Canonby, or even part of Cumberland, though both of which countries lie to the south of Castletown. Oats and pease are sown in March and April; barley in the end of April or beginning of May, and they are all reaped in September.

Population.—The population of this parish has decreased a little within these 40 years, as appears from the following table. This decrease is easily accounted for, by several farms, formerly let to different tenants, being now possessed

* The whole of the holm land along the banks of the river appears formerly to have been covered with wood, and the sides of the hills to have been almost entirely in cultivation; the furrows and ridges are plain and evident. But at this period, to sow corn on those places, or to expect a crop, would be equally vain. What is the cause of this change? When the vallies were covered with wood to a certain height, were the sides of the hills more warm? Were the seasons themselves then more kindly, as tradition positively affirms? Or were the inhabitants obliged to cultivate the high grounds, when the lower were covered with wood? About the middle of the hills, on each side the river Liddal, a deep ditch, or a strong wall, appears to have been drawn almost the whole length of the country, beneath which lay the arable ground, where the old furrows and ridges appear, and all above was either for pasture or common. In those days every kind of fence was necessary, not only from beasts of the field, but also from the inroads of the plunderer.

ſeſſed by one, and not a few by perſons, who do not reſide in, or belong to the pariſh at all.

STATISTICAL TABLE OF THE PARISH OF CASTLETOWN.

Number of ſouls, in 1755, as returned to Dr
Webſter,   -   -   -   1507

Ditto in December 1793, { Males, 666 | In all, 1418
{ Females, 752 |

Majority of females,   86 Decreaſe, 89
Number of inhabitants in the new village, 70

	Marriages *.	Baptiſms *.
In the year 1709, - -	4	38
————1710, - -	7	50
From 1749 to 1774, - -		464
From 1763 to 1770, -	43	

AGES.

* With regard to marriages and baptiſms, the pariſh regiſter is very imperfect. Several books have been loſt, which make blanks of conſiderable periods. There is a minute inſerted in the ſeſſion records, of date 17th January 1649, which mentions, " That the Engliſh army, com- " manded by Colonels Bright and Pride, and under the conduct of Ge- " neral Cromwell, on their return to England, did lie at the kirk of " Caſtletown ſeveral nights, in which time they brake down and burnt " the communion tables, and the ſeats of the kirk ; and at their remo- " ving, carried away the miniſter's books to the value of 1000 marks " and above, and alſo the buoks of ſeſſion, with which they lighted their " tobacco pipes, the baptiſm, marriage, and examination rolls, from " October 1612 to September 1648, all which were loſt and deſtroyed." From the accuracy with which this record had been kept, the loſs of it is very much to be regretted. If we may form any judgment from the number of churches and chapels in the pariſh at that time, with the burying grounds, and alſo from the ruins of many houſes and villages, the number of the inhabitants muſt have been much greater at that pe- riod than at preſent. No account of the burials can now be given, be- cauſe there are three burying grounds ſtill uſed, and a mortcloth, the property of private individuals, and not belonging to the kirk-ſeſſion.

AGES.

No. of souls under 10 years of age, - 342

— Between 10 and 20, 280

————— 20 and 50, 516

Between 50 and 70, 234

————— 70 and 80, 31

————— 80 and 90, 14

————— 90 and 100, 1

CONDITIONS AND PROFESSIONS.

No. of Heritors, resident, 4

————— Ditto occasionally, 3

————— Ditto non-resident, 4

————— farmers, - 46

————— shop-keepers, 9

————— surgeons, - 1

————— students at the University, - 2

————— clergymen, - 2

————— school-masters, 3

————— innkeepers, 3

No. of smiths, 5

————— masons, 12

————— joiners, 14

————— weavers, 16

————— shoe-makers, 8

————— cloggers, 3

————— tailors, - 13

————— millers, 3

————— bakers, 4

————— poor on the roll, - 74

FARMS AND RENTS.

Number of led farms *, 15

Greatest rent of these about - L. 300

Valued rent in Scotch money, L. 15,860

Real do. St⁸. about L. 6000

STOCK.

No. of sheep, - 36,000

————— black cattle, 1200

No. of ploughs, 44

————— carts, about 150

Commerce, Provisions and Labour.—The only markets for butcher meat, groceries, &c. are Hawick and Langholm ;

* Farms are styled *led,* when one tenant possesses two or more, and does not reside on them.

holm; ſo that the prices of theſe articles are regulated by thoſe places, with the addition of a conſiderable expence for carriage. Butter, ſold formerly at 4 d. afterwards at 6 d. ſells now at 9 d. *per* pound; a conſiderable quantity is put up in firkins, and ſent to Newcaſtle for the London market. Dealers buy it on the ſpot, and this ſeaſon pay L. 1, 13 s. L. 1, 14 s. and L. 1, 15 s. *per* firkin, of 56 lb. Engliſh. The price, however, frequently varies, running from L. 1, 1 s. to L. 1, 10 s. Cow-milk cheeſe ſells for 4 s. 6 d. *per* ſtone, and ewe-milk for 7 s. or 7 s. 6 d. Hens and ducks ſell at 6 d. each, chickens at 3 d. and geeſe at 1 s. 6 d. and 2 s. Theſe articles have varied little in price theſe ſeveral years. The prices of labour have riſen exceedingly within theſe 40 or 50 years, as appears from the following comparative ſtatement:

	Wages in 1740.				*Wages in* 1793.			
A man ſervant * with maintenance, from L. 3 to	L. 3	10	0		from L. 8 to L. 10	0	0	
A woman ſervant with ditto, in ſummer, - -	0	16	6†			2	10	0
Ditto in winter, - -	0	5	0			1	5	0
A day labourer in winter, without maintenance	0	0	6			0	1	0
Ditto in ſummer with ditto,	0	0	6			0	1	0
A tailor in winter, -	0	0	4			0	0	8
Ditto in ſummer, -	0	0	6		with maintenance,	0	0	8
Price of a pair of ſhoes,	0	4	6			0	6	9.
Ditto of a pair of clogs,	0	2	6			0	2	6

Church.

* Only 15 years ago a man's wages were commonly L. 3, or L. 3, 10 s. and the very higheſt did not exceed L. 6.

† Of this ſum 12 s. 6 d. was paid in money, and the other 4 s. in one ſtone of wool. About the year 1730, a woman's wages were only 5 groats and a woollen jerkin.

Church, &c..—The church was built in 1777. The rain penetrates through the walls, and part of the timber is already rotten. The manſe and offices are a heap of ruins. They were built on the top of a hideous precipice, about 100 feet of perpendicular height ‡, where there is not a drop of water for the uſe of man or beaſt. The late Mr Rutherford found a ſmall ſpring about the middle of the rock, which he endeavoured to draw up at a great expence ; the well was continually filling up, and is now entirely waſhed away. It is propoſed to build a manſe and offices in a more agreeable ſituation next ſpring. The preſent incumbent is accommodated in the mean time with a houſe a little more than two miles from the church. The living is L. 83 : 6 : 8. The value of the glebe cannot be accurately aſcertained, as an exchange of land between the Duke of Buccleugh and the miniſter is juſt completed, which will be more convenient for both parties ; at preſent the whole of the land is in the moſt wretched condition. A few of the inhabitants attend a Seceding meeting houſe in the lower part of the pariſh, built about 30 years ago, and at preſent very much on the decline. All the reſt belong to the Eſtabliſhed Church.

Old Chapels.—There have been no leſs than 5 chapels or churches in the pariſh, beſides the pariſh church. The Wheel Church at the head of Liddal, Hermitage, on the river of that name, Dinlabyre, Ettleton, and Chapel-know, on the borders of Canonby. Ettleton and Hermitage are ſtill uſed

‡ Some years ago a woman going from the manſe at night, fell from the top of the precipice into the river ; her thigh bone only was broken ; ſhe is now in perfect health.

ufed as burying-grounds, and many grave-ftones appear in the others. The Wheel Church has been of excellent workmanſhip. The population of the country muſt certainly have been far greater in thoſe times. The Wheel Church has been pretty large; many grave-ftones appear in the church-yard; yet, when ſtanding on the ſpot at this time, there are only 3 farm houſes in view, taking in a circle of many miles.

Schools.—The ſchoolmaſter's ſalary is L. 8 : 6 : 8, beſides his perquiſites ariſing from his office of ſeſſion-clerk, precentor, marriages, collections, the poor's rates, and ſchool fees. The ſchool houſe is in good repair; but the ſchool is in very bad order. The number of ſcholars at preſent is very ſmall. There are two other ſchools in the pariſh, ſupported by private contributions.

Poor.—There is no place where the poor are better provided for than in this pariſh. Poor's rates were eſtabliſhed in 1774. The heritors pay one half, and the tenants the other; it is levied quarterly; the money is paid moſt punctually, and immediately applied. Thoſe upon the roll receive from 5 s. to L. 1 : 2 : 6 *per* quarter, according to their neceſſities. The preſent aſſeſſment is L. 56 *per* quarter. In the years 1782 and 1783 ſeveral perſons received temporary ſupply, and when the meal fell lower in price it was withdrawn. The weekly collections at the church, ſince the poor's rates were eſtabliſhed, are exceedingly ſmall. But from theſe, from fines paid by delinquents, and from marriages out of church, perſons not on the poor's roll, and in diſtreſſed circumſtances, are relieved. No perſon is allowed to beg. A friendly ſociety was eſtabliſhed a few years ago; the members pay 5 s. at
entering

entering, and so much *per* quarter; it promises to be very useful.

Roads.—It must appear very strange to any person acquainted with the improvements, which other parts of Scotland have received by means of roads, when it is mentioned, that, in this very extensive country, not a yard of road had ever been attempted to be formed, till within these few years. The statute labour has long been commuted. For about 16 miles along the Liddal, the road lay rather *in* the river than *upon its banks*, the only path being in what is called *the Watergate*, and the unhappy traveller must cross it at least 24 times in that extent. The same thing still takes place, with respect to the Hermitage, as far as it runs. At length, by the exertions of two of the heritors, fortunately for the country, possessed of public spirit, Mr OLIVER of Dinlabyre, and Mr ELLIOT of Whithaugh, a road was begun, and is now carrying along the side of the Liddal for several miles. Hawick being almost the only market from which we receive meal, groceries, spirits, iron, &c. &c. the want of a road to it is attended with much inconvenience and expence. But the funds, arising from the statute labour, are perhaps inadequate to keep so many miles of road in such repair as the country requires, and much less to make new ones. Unless some other method is adopted, the present road cannot be completed, and there is no reason to hope, that the road along the Hermitage can be formed in the present generation. There is much intercourse with both Hawick and Langholm, by weekly markets, fairs, &c. and the difficulty of travelling to those places is inconceivable. Every article must be carried on horseback; and through these deep and broken bogs and mosses we must *crawl*, to the great fatigue of ourselves, but the much greater injury of our horses,

without

without the hope of a more comfortable mode of travelling. As we have hitherto had no roads, it is not to be expected that we ſhould have had bridges. The two rivers, Liddal and Hermitage, divide the pariſh for about 26 miles; there never was a bridge on either of them. From a conſiderable ſum of vacant ſtipend, with the aſſiſtance of the ordinary fund, one was built over the river Hermitage in 1792; and laſt autumn another was completed over the Liddal. Theſe, together with that part of the road already made, are of the greateſt ſervice to the country, and to many travellers, who begin to paſs this way from Carliſle to the northern markets, and to Berwick-ſhire, the road being much nearer than by Langholm and Moſs-Paul.

Fuel.—The fuel chiefly uſed is peat, of which there is an inexhauſtible fund in every part of the country. There is alſo coal in the lower part of the pariſh, wrought on the eſtate of Mr Oliver. It is ſold at the pit at 3 d. *per* buſhel, or 6 d. *per* load. Carriers, who bring goods from Hawick, commonly return loaded with coal.

New Caſtletown.—As there is not a village in the pariſh, labourers and mechanics have long been very inconveniently ſituated for houſes. For their accommodation, and no doubt to encourage manufactures, the Duke of Buccleugh, has for ſome time paſt, intended to build a new town. At length a place was fixed on, and a plan made out. It is ſet down on the farm of Park, on the banks of the Liddal, in a field of upwards of 100 acres of fine land, and is named *Caſtletown*. It is to conſiſt of two principal ſtreets, bearing the names of the two rivers, *Liddal* and *Hermitage*, with ſeveral croſs ſtreets at right angles. Hermitage-ſtreet is begun, and advancing rapidly. There is a ſquare, called *Douglas Square*, in the centre, for a market place,

place, conſiſting of about two acres of ground, round which
the buildings conſiſt of two ſtories. Near each extremity
there is a ſmaller ſquare. The ſtreet is 54 feet wide; in
the principal ſquare it is 100 feet. It was begun in March
laſt; and at preſent there are 23 houſes either inhabited,
or nearly finiſhed. Each houſe coſts from L. 35 to L. 40
Sterling. They hold of the Duke, pay a ſmall ſum by
way of feu-duty, and have each a good garden. Every
feuer has graſs for a cow on the hill, for which they pay
L. 1. For each houſe they have two acres of holm land,
for 14 years, for which they pay a certain ſum. A ſituation more favourable for carrying on manufactures is
ſcarcely to be found. Its local advantages are very great.
Within 100 yards of peat, and only about 3 miles from coal,
it has water at command to drive machinery of any extent.
Wool, the ſtaple commodity of the country, grows on the
ſide of every hill. There is an excellent road lately made
by Canonby to Carliſle, the Solway frith, &c. Poſſeſſed of
theſe advantages, it ſolicits ſome perſon of enterprize and
induſtry to improve them. When we conſider what has
been done in Galaſhiels, &c. and in ſituations far leſs favourable, it is hoped the time is not far diſtant, when ſuch
advantages as theſe will attract the attention of the manufacturers either of flax, wool, or cotton; and inſtead of
ſending the wool, the raw material, to Leeds, Hudderſfield,
&c. by a long and expenſive land carriage, it will be manufactured here where it grows, enrich the country by encouraging induſtry, adding to population, and by giving
bread and employment to hundreds of all ages.

NATURAL HISTORY.

Reptiles, Fiſh, and Quadrupeds.—The reptiles produced
in the pariſh are, toads, lizards, and adders. The laſt is
not numerous.—The fiſh are, trouts, lampreys, eels, ſkelly,

or chubb, falmon, grilfe, &c. The falmon were very plentiful in former years, but fince the bay or mound was built at Netherby, few get up at any time, and none but in the time of a great flood. The wild quadrupeds are foxes, hares, wild cats, pole cats, weazels, the white weazel, often feen in winter, hedge hogs and Norway rats. Tradition affirms, that the earth of Liddifdale has a peculiar quality of banifhing the common rat from Teviotdale. It is certain, that only a few years ago, carriers on their return to that country loaded their horfes with it, and carried it away for that purpofe. But it is affirmed, with more probability, that it is only fince the Norway rat was introduced, that the common rat has been extirpated.

Birds.——Black-cocks, groufe, partridges, grey plovers, wild ducks, fnipes, wood-pigeons, buzzards, ftannels, owls, crows, ravens, herons, jackdaws, magpies, thrufhes, blackbirds, ftarlings, linnets, and gold-finches, frequent the woods. The bittern was formerly numerous, but is now feldom to be feen. The birds of paffage, that vifit us in the fpring, or beginning of fummer, are, the King's-fifher, water crow, white and yellow feed birds, the black and fand martins, the fwallow, cuckoo, rail, curlew, green plover, fand lark, ftone chatterers, with different fpecies of gulls and fhieldrakes. Teal and widgeons are feen in fpring when the waters are fwelled with rain. The birds that vifit us in autumn are, the fieldfare and the wood-cock. Eagles, or earns, are frequently feen, but have no place of refidence here *.

Minerals.

* A well authenticated inftance of the amazing ftrength of this bird occurred a few years ago upon the farm of Roughlee in this parifh. One morning, when the fhepherd was going round his flock, he faw an eagle coming over the Hermitage-hill immediately above him, with fomething bulky in his
talons

Minerals.—There is great plenty of lime-ſtone in the pariſh, of different qualities. A draw kiln was erected laſt year on the Hermitage, and burns a conſiderable quantity. Several pits of marl are found on the farms of Flight, Kerſhope, and Tweeden, to appearance of excellent quality; but this, as well as other treaſures, are locked up from uſe by the want of roads. Beſides, the coal mentioned at Lawſtown, ſome ſmall crop ſeams appear on the Tweeden, &c. From the ſtrata of metals, it is apprehended, there is coal in ſeveral places, but no trials to any great extent have been made. Free-ſtone quarries of excellent ſtone are every where found, excepting at the head of the Hermitage, where there is nothing but blue whin-ſtone.

Medicinal Springs.—There are ſeveral ſprings in this pariſh, ſtrongly impregnated with ſulphur. There is one at the head of it, in that part called *the Dead Water*, unfortunately ſituated in the middle of that vaſt moraſs where the Liddal and the Tyne take their riſe. In wet ſeaſons it is weakened by the ſurrounding water. It is much frequented by perſons afflicted with cutaneous and ſcrophulous complaints, who receive great benefit from it. They drink the water, and uſe it as a warm bath. But the patients are

---

talons. Struck with the novelty of the ſight, he kept his eye upon the bird, and ſaw him ſit down at a little diſtance. He ran to the ſpot, when the eagle had diſengaged from his talons a fine lamb, and was preparing to tear him in pieces, which the man reſcued, and carried home. At that inſtant, a medical gentleman was viſiting a patient in the ſhepherd's family. He examined the lamb, found it a fine male, the ſkin of the ſhoulder torn, but the bone had prevented the talons from injuring the vital parts; he ſewed up the wound, and it recovered and did well. On enquiry it was found, that the ſhepherd of Peel, the ſame morning, ſaw an eagle ſeize a lamb of his flock, and fly off with it, in the line of direction to the place where the lamb was found. The diſtance of the one place from the other is not leſs than five miles. JOHN ELLIOT, of Redheugh, Eſq; furniſhed the writer with this anecdote.

are expoſed to danger and incovenience from the want of
proper accommodation. The wretched hovels in the
neighbourhood being continually damp and wet. On the
farm of Dinlabyre, another ſpring of the ſame kind is
found; the collection of water is much greater, but at preſent almoſt loſt in the bog in which it is placed. A third
is on the farm of Shortbuttrees, of excellent quality; all
theſe might be highly beneficial, if the ground were properly drained and attended to. A very ſtrong mineral ſpring
is found at Lawſtown; but as its water has not been anali-
zed, it is uncertain to what claſs it belongs.

Petrifying Water.—There are ſeveral ſprings of this
kind. One is found on the Tweeden, exceedingly powerful, and containing a great quantity of water, where large
maſſes of petrified matter appear on every ſide converted
into ſolid ſtone. The progreſs of the petrifaction is diſtinct
and beautiful. The fog, which grows on the edge of the
ſpring, and is ſprinkled with the water, is about eight
inches high; the lower part is converted into ſolid ſtone;
the middle appears as if half frozen, and the top is green
and flouriſhing. The petrified matter, when burnt, is reſolved into very fine lime. The ſpring itſelf, when led
over the fields in little rills, fertilizes them exceedingly.

Caſcades.—There are ſeveral beautiful water-falls on the
river Tweeden, the little ſtreams of Dinlabyre, Harden, and Sundhope. But on the river Blackburn, ſuch
ſcenes are ſeen in all their beauty and variety. Sometimes the river ſhoots over a perpendicular rock, in one
unbroken ſheet of water, forming a beautiful caſcade; at
other times it is darted over tremendous precipices, and
rages furiouſly among the huge maſſes of the rock below.
In this wild and romantic vale, nature appears in various
                                                    forms.

forms, now beautiful, then awful, fometimes fublime, and
frequently terrible. The author of this account meafured
the principal falls. One is 27 feet perpendicular in height,
another 31½; the breadth of the rock over which it falls,
36; a third is 37½ in height, and 20 feet wide.

Natural Bridge of Stone.—One of the greateft curiofities
to be feen in this country, or perhaps in Scotland, is a natural bridge of ftone over the fame river. It ftretches
acrofs the ftream, and joins the hills on each fide. It is
55 feet long, 10 feet wide, and the thicknefs of the arch is
2 feet 4 inches of folid ftone. It is not compofed of one
entire rock, but has the appearance of many ftones about a
foot and a half fquare, fet neatly together. The bridge
flopes a little downwards, and the water rufhes under the
arch, through an opening of 31 feet.

Woods.—The natural woods confift of oak, afh, birch,
and alder. Confiderable plantations have been made of
Scots fir, fpruce, larix, oak, afh, beech and plane. They
are all in a thriving condition. There is at prefent growing on the river Blackburn, an old afh tree, the trunk of
which meafures 18 feet in circumference, one branch of it
9 feet, and another 8. The trunk is hollow within; five
perfons of ordinary fize may eafily fit in it at the fame
time. Laft year the river Liddal, in the time of a high
flood, threw up the trunk of an oak tree, oppofite to Hag-
gihaugh, the feat of Colonel Elliot of Larifton. Not only
the bark, but great part of the wood, feems wafted by age;
notwithftanding which this venerable trunk, as it now lies,
meafures 26 feet in length, and 10 feet in circumference,
and is perfectly ftraight. There is fcarcely a tree within
view of the place where it lies, excepting a few Scotch firs.

Eminent

Eminent Men.—This parish gave birth to the celebrated Dr ARMSTRONG, whose father and brother were ministers of it.

Antiquities.—There are several monuments of great antiquity in the parish, but their origin and their history are involved in much obscurity. Even tradition itself says little concerning them. There are also several old gold coins in the possession of Mr Elliot of Red-heugh*. Though this parish comprehended a great part of the middle march between the two kingdoms, yet excepting a few detached facts, there is nothing of consequence preserved or related by historians. As it lies directly along the English Border, it must have been, for a long period, the scene of action, of fierce contentions, barbarous feuds, and marauding expeditions, which took place between the two nations, when, before the union, and before law and civilization took place, inroads were constantly made by both parties upon each other, and the stronger arm carried away every thing both from the house and from the field. These exploits have been recorded in the poetry of the times, which are still sung by the aged, and listened to with eagerness by the young. They contain an account of the heroic atchievements of those days, that is to say, of the inroads made and repelled by the marauders on each side of the Border †.

Castles.

---

* They were found on the farm of Priest-heugh, in the neighbourhood of this parish. Some years ago a box was found in the side moss, containing about 120 silver coins, about the value of 3 d. each, variously inscribed. Some of them were clipped, or cut in the edges, and not coined. Some copper or brass vessels, of antique forms, were found in a moss on Shortbuttrees, and sent to the Duke of Buccleugh.

† The following extracts from the ancient records of the Courts of Justice

Caſtles.—Hermitage Caſtle ſtands upon the bank of the river of that name. It has been a very ſtrong building, near 100 feet ſquare, defended by a ſtrong rampart and ditch †. The walls are almoſt entire. The inner part is

a

Juſtice * exhibit a ſpecimen of the tranſactions of thoſe times. Several perſons mentioned in it are the heroes in the old ſongs and ballads:

" At the Treeves, or Juſticiary meeting of the Lords Wardens, to hear all complaints, 1581.—Weſt Marches againſt Liddiſdale, Sir Simon Muſgrave, Knight, with Thorn of the Todhill and his neighbours, complain upon Robin Elliot of the Park, Sim Elliot. Clemie Croſier, Gawens Jock, and their complices, for 60 kine and oxen, a horſe, and the taking of Thom Routledge priſoner."

" *June* 1582.—Matthew Taylor, and the poor widow of Martin Taylor, complain upon Old Laird of Whithaugh, Young Laird of Whithaugh, Sims Thom, and Jock of Copſhawe for 140 kie and oxen, 100 ſheep, 20 gaits, and all their inſight, L. 200 Sterling."

" *October* 1582.—Sir Simon Muſgrave, deputy of Bewcaſtle and tenants againſt Walter Scot, Laird of Buckleith, and his complices, for 200 kine and oxen, 300 gates and ſheep."

" *November* 1582.—Sir Simon Muſgrave complains on the Laird of Mangerton, Lairds Jock, Sims Thom, and their complices, for burning of his barns, wheat, rye, oats, big, and peas, worth L. 1000 Sterling."

" Weſt of England againſt Liddiſdale L. 3230."

" Liddiſdale againſt the Weſt Marches, L. 8000."

    * *Hiſtory of Cumberland.*

† It is ſaid to have been built by a Lord Soules, then Warden of the Border; but it does not appear, that there is any accurate account of its age. Smollet mentions that Alexander II. built a caſtle in Liddiſdale, which gave ſuch offence to Henry III. of England, that he made war upon the king of Scotland. 1240. This, in all probability, was the caſtle of Hermitage. Among the remarkable places in the county of Liddiſdale, Hector Boece mentions " the Caſtle of Hermitage, now demoliſhed." A great part of the ancient caſtle appears to have been thrown down, and the ancient part of he architecture is eaſily diſtinguiſhed from the more modern. Biſhop Elphinſton mentions, that Sir William Douglas, Earl

of

a heap of ruins. Within a few yards of the castle are the remains of the ancient chapel of Hermitage †, now in ruins, in the middle of the burying ground still in use. The font is in the wall of the church-yard. The castle of Clintwood, on the farm of Flight, appears to have been a very strong building; the foundation, and a little part of the

of Liddisdale, beat the English out of all Teviotdale, and took the castle of Hermitage in the year 1340. In this castle Sir Alexander Ramsay of Dalhousie was starved to death by the same Sir W. Douglas; who, fired with jealousy because Sir Alexander was made Sheriff of Teviotdale, surprised him in the church of Hawick when holding an assembly, carried him to the castle, and threw him into a dungeon with his horse's furniture. This happened in 1342 *. Some years ago, a mason employed in building a dike in the neighbourhood, had the curiosity to penetrate into a vault in the east end of the castle. Having made an opening, he descended by a ladder; and in a vault, about 8 feet square, he found several human bones, with a saddle, a bridle, and sword; he brought out the bridle and sword. The bit was of an uncommon size; the curb of it is in the possession of Walter Scott, Esq; Advocate. In the dungeon he found a great quantity of the husks of oats Report says, the granary of the castle was immediately above this vault, and that Sir Alexander subsisted for some time on what fell down into the vault. From these circumstances it is highly probable, that the bones were those of that gentleman, and that this was the vault into which he was thrown, and starved to death. This castle was also visited by the ill-fated Queen Mary, in the year 1561, on occasion of Bothwell's being wounded by John Elliot in Park. She came from, and returned to Jedburgh in the same day, not only a long journey, but over mountains, and through marshes almost impassable. In one of those marshes, a few miles from the castle, her horse stuck in the moss, which is still called *the Queen's Mire.*

    * *Mackenzie's Lives.*

    † The chapel, castle, and river derive their name from the cell of a hermit, who had retired thither. He could not have chosen a more solitary spot, nor one more fit for mortification or for contemplation. They give title to the eldest son of the family of Deloraine. Lord Henry Scot, third son of James Duke of Monmouth, by Anne Duchess of Buccleugh, was created Earl of Deloraine, Viscount Hermitage, 1706 *.

    * *Douglas's Peerage.*

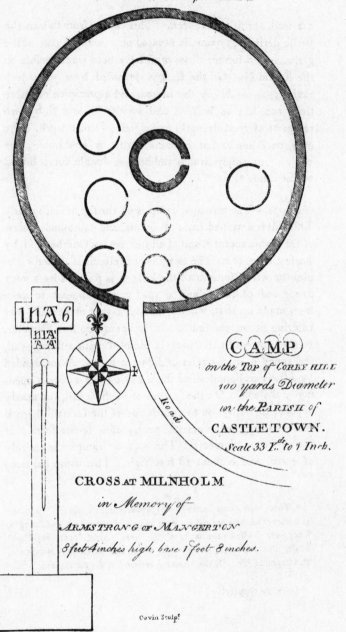

CAMP
on the Top of CORBY HILL
100 yards Diameter
in the PARISH of
CASTLETOWN.
Scale 33 Y.ds to 1 Inch.

Road

CROSS AT MILNHOLM
in Memory of
ARMSTRONG OF MANGERTON
8 feet 4 inches high, base 1 foot 8 inches.

Gavin Sculp.t

the wall, are still to be seen. This castle, from which the parish derives its name, is situated on the upper part of the glebe, and in former times must have been impregnable on the E. and N. On the E. it is defended by a very deep ravine; on the N. by the Liddal, and a precipice of more than 100 feet in height; and on the W. and S. by two ramparts of great strength, and a fosse of great depth. The only peel house that remains entire is Hudshouse; the vault is immensely strong, and has had double doors, bolted on the inside *.

Camps.—The principal camp is on the top of Carby Hill. This hill is detached from all others, and commands a view of the whole country, and of all that part of Cumberland, by Beese-Castle, &c. The camp is entirely circular, and occupies the whole summit of the hill; it is fortified by a very strong wall of stones, and a road plainly appears to have been made up to it, winding round a part of the hill, and entering it on the south. It is about 100 feet diameter. In the centre a small space is inclosed with a strong wall, and round it are 8 circles of different sizes †, all surrounded by a stone wall, and all of them having had a door or opening to the east. On the summit of the Side-hill, and nearly opposite to Carby, on the north side of the Liddal, there is another strong encampment, nearly of a square form. It is 300 feet in diameter. The wall or rampart is entirely of earth, and is about 18 feet high. This camp has none of

---

* There were many square towers formerly in this country, the place of residence of the principal families, and all of them places of strength. They were chiefly on the banks of the river Liddal, *viz.* Peel, Hudshouse, Prickinghaugh, Whithaugh, Hillhouse, Riccarton, Mangerton, Puddingburn, &c. Of these nothing remain but the foundations.

† See the copperplate.

of the interior circles of the former. On the farm of Flight, and near to the castle of Clintwood, there are two camps at a little distance from each other ; the one round, and fortified with a stone wall * about 100 feet diameter ; and the other square, about 168 feet in length, with two ramparts of earth †.

Picts Works.—There are a great many *round-abouts* in the parish, commonly called *Picts Works.* They are all circular, and strongly fortified by a wall, composed of large stones. They are frequently found, the one at a little distance from, and opposite to the other. There are two nigh Heeds-house, two on the farm of Shaws, one on Toftholm, one on Foulshiels, one on Cocklaw, one on Blackburn, and one on Shortbuttrees ‡. On the farm of Millburn there is a small circle enclosed by 9 stones, which seems to have been a Druidical temple. Tradition says Lord Soules was burnt there. The hill is called *Nine-Stone Ridge.*

Cairns.—There are many cairns ‖ in different places. The most remarkable of these is on the farm of Whisgills.

The

---

* This year (1793) the wall was carried away to build a stone dike, and at a considerable depth, among some large stones, there was found the head of some weapon, or instrument of fine brass, 4½ inches long ; the one end is fitted to receive a shaft or handle, the other is widened, and is formed and sharpened like the edge of a hatchet. The other article found has the appearance of a small sword of mixed metal, about three feet long, but was broken by the workman before the writer hereof could get them into his possession.

† A learned gentleman informs me, that a Roman legion wintered in Liddisdale, cut down wood, and drained marshes.

‡ The stones of this last were lately removed ; and on the south side there was found a place 10 feet wide, and 20 feet long, paved with flat stones, and inclosed by others on each side, set on edge, within which there seemed to be ashes and burnt sticks.

‖ On the farm of Cleugh head one was removed, and an urn found full

of

The quantity of stones is immense, and they are mostly of a very large size. Near these, there is a large stone set on end, about 5 feet high, called *the Standing Stone*. This cairn is in the middle of an extensive and deep moss. It can be approached on horse-back only on one side, and that with much difficulty. There is not a stone to be seen near it.—Upon the march between the parishes of Castletown and Canonby, and upon very high ground near to Tinnis-hill, there is a cairn of great extent, and consisting of free-stones of great size. It is 86 yards long; it is not possible to approach it on horse-back. The stones are chiefly of a square form, of immense weight, and what is very remarkable, there is not a stone to be seen, nor a place where stones could be found, within a great distance of the place. At the north end of it, there are several large stones set on their edges, forming a square, and covered over by one stone. Near to the south end there is one standing perpendicular, evidently so placed by the hand of man, 7 feet above the moss, and 13 feet in circumference. This was anciently called the standing stone, and was considered the north boundary of Canonby, or the debateable land *. On examining the ground near it, I found five other stones, nearly of an equal size with the former, all inclining to, or lying on the ground, forming a circle, the diameter of which is 45 yards. How these stones were collected, for what purpose, or what the circle has been, which is formed by stones of such immense weight and size, I leave to others to determine.

Cross.

---

of ashes, which soon fell in pieces. In this cairn were discovered a great number of stones, formerly used for *knocking* bear, or making barley. Some among them was a stone cross, about 4 feet long. Some other cairns have been opened, and ashes found inclosed by 4 stones set in a square form.

* Vid. History of Cumberland.

Croſs.—At Milnholm there is a croſs of one ſtone, 8 feet 4 inches high, ſet in a baſe 1 foot 8 inches *. This is a piece of great antiquity. A ſword 4 feet long is cut out on the S. ſide of the croſs, and immediately above ſeveral letters, as will appear from the repreſentation of it in the plate.

Diſadvantages.—The diſadvantages this country labours under, from the want of roads, are very great. Improvements to any conſiderable extent can never be carried on while theſe are wanting, and the means of improvement which the country itſelf poſſeſſes are locked up from uſe. The cottages, and moſt of the farm-houſes, are in very bad order. Another diſadvantage ariſes from the froſts in ſpring, and the early part of harveſt, to which the country is ſometimes expoſed, and which prove chiefly hurtful to the potatoes and peaſe.

Character.—The people in general enjoy, in a reaſonable degree, the comforts of ſociety, and are contented with their ſituation. They are by no means fond of a military life.

---

* The tradition concerning it is this :—One of the governors of Hermitage Caſtle, ſome ſay Lord Soules, others Lord Douglas, having entertained a paſſion for a young woman in the lower part of the pariſh, went to her houſe, and was met by her father, who, wiſhing to conceal his daughter, was inſtantly killed by the Governor. He was ſoon purſued by the people, and, in extreme danger, took refuge with Armſtrong of Mangerton, who had influence enough to prevail on the people to deſiſt from the purſuit, and by this means ſaved his life. Seemingly with a view to make a return for this favour, but ſecretly jealous of the power and influence of Armſtrong, he invited him to Hermitage Caſtle, where he was baſely murdered. He himſelf, in his turn, was killed by *Jock of the Side*, of famous memory, and brother to Armſtrong. The croſs was erected in memory of this transaction, near to Ettleton church-yard, where he was buried, and almoſt oppoſite to Mangerton.

life. The majority are of the middle fize, but many of
them confiderably above, and feveral under it. Notwithftanding the want of roads, and their great diftance from
church, (many of them being 8, and even 10 miles diftant),
they are remarkable for their general and conftant attendance on religious ordinances, and exemplary in their conduct during the time of divine fervice. They make an
excellent appearance on fuch, and on all other public occafions; they are clean and well dreffed, in coloured vefts,
and cloth of English manufacture. They are diftinguifhed
by their hofpitality and humanity, ever willing to contribute to the relief of thofe in diftrefs *. Few law-fuits have
occurred; no punifhments have been inflicted; and few or
no traces of the border or barbarous cuftoms are now to be
feen. It is impoffible to conclude this article without re-
marking the ftriking contraft between the former and the
prefent fituation of the country. The inhabitants feel the
happy change, and are fenfible of the fuperior bleffings
they enjoy. It was formerly the fcene of fierce contention, of barbarous feuds, of plunder, and of defolation,
when there was neither fecurity of property nor of life. At
prefent we can only trace the foundations of the ancient
caftles, the ftrong holds of their fierce poffeffors. Their ufelefs walls are thrown down, and converted into fheep folds,
and their fwords have become rufted in their fcabbards, or
have been almoft literally beaten into plough-fhares.
" Every one fits in peace under his own vine, and his own
" fig tree, and there is none to make him afraid."

---

* An inftance of this very lately occurred:—On a day fet apart by
the Synod, for thankfgiving for the favourable harveft, it was fuggefted
from the pulpit, to collect a fum for affifting in procuring warm clothing
to our brave countrymen in Flanders. Next Sabbath they were forward,
from the higheft to the loweft, to contribute to this humane purpofe,
and enabled their minifter to tranfmit a confiderable donation to the
Lord Provoft of Edinburgh.

PARISH OF CAVERS.

(County of Roxburgh.—Presbytery of Jedburgh.—Synod of Merse and Tiviotdale).

By the Rev. Mr Thomas Elliot, *Minister.*

Form, Extent, and Appearance.

THE parish of Cavers is irregular in its form, and of
considerable extent, being upwards of 20 miles long
from W. to E. and from 7 to 2 broad. The appearance of
the western part of the parish is hilly, and that of the eastern
flat Some of the hills are of considerable height; from one
of them, called the *Wisp*, may be seen both the east and west
seas.

Rivers, Soil, and Produce.—The soil in the lower part of
the parish from the church to the eastern boundary, at the
confluence of the two rivers, *Tiviot* and *Rule*, is rich and fertile, and produces good crops of wheat, oats, barley, and
pease. Clover, rye-grass, and turnips, are also raised in considerable quantities. The land there lets from 15 s. to 30 s.
per acre. The soil of the upper parts is perfectly adapted
to the purpose to which it is chiefly applied, viz. the breeding of sheep.

Sheep

Sheep and Wages.—The number of sheep in the parish is about 12,000; they are of the long white-faced kind, which bear the short clothing wool. The breed has been much meliorated of late, by means of rams got from the borders of the Cheviot hills, and the wool now sells at from 14 s. to 17 s. per stone. A common labourer will earn 14 d. per day in summer, and 10 d. in winter. A man-servant employed in farm work, gets from 6 l. to 7 l. *per annum*, with victuals; a maid-servant, from 3 l. 10 s. to 4 l. 10 s. A shepherd, on a farm where the master resides, instead of wages, is allowed to keep sheep; and on a *led* farm, is allowed three score and ten, and a milk cow, which may be valued at 18 l.

Proprietors, Rent, &c.—There are 11 heritors in the parish, and, except the Duke of Buccleugh, all the principal ones reside in it. The valued rent is 18,921 l. 16 s. 8 d. Scotch. The real rent is about 4700 l. Sterling.

Population.—The number of births, deaths, and marriages, cannot be precisely ascertained, as few of the Seceders enter their childrens names in the parish register. From Dr Webster's report, however, it is certain, that the population of the parish has increased considerably within these 40 years. The number of inhabitants at present (1794) is about   1300
The number of souls, in 1755, was   -   -   993
Increase   307

Church and Poor.—George Douglas, Esq; of Cavers is patron of the parish. The living consists of 83 l. 6 s. 8 d. Sterl. in money, and 2 and a half chalders of grain, half meal, half barley; together with a manse and garden, and a glebe of 11 English acres. Besides the parish church, there is a chaple of ease erected, for the convenience of the western parts

of

of this parish, and that of Hawick. The chaplain who performs
the duty, is partly paid by the Duke of Buccleugh, and the ministers of Cavers and Hawick, and partly from a subscription
by the people. The number of poor receiving weekly support
is about 40, for which the heritors assess themselves, to the
amount of 140 l. yearly. The weekly collections are given
by the kirk-session to the poor not belonging to the list of
pensioners.—There is, in the village of *Denholm*, a Cameronian meeting-house, which is attended by several of the inhabitants and neighbourhood, who are between 2 and 3 miles
distant from the kirk; few of them, however, join in communion with them.

Eminent Men.—Lord Heathfield *, so justly famed for his
military exertions, particularly his gallant defence of Gibraltar,

* GEORGE AUGUSTUS ELIOTT, Lord HEATHFIELD, the 9th
son of Sir Gilbert Eliott, Bart. of Stobs, was born at the pater-
nal estate in the year 1718. He shewed an early inclination for
a military life, and soon became an officer in the 23d regiment
of foot, the Royal Welsh Fusileers. He left this regiment, and
went into the corps of engineers at Woolwich, where he continued till the year 1740, when he became adjutant in the 2d
troop of horse guards. He served in Germany, and was wounded at the battles of Dittengen and Fontenoy. In March 1759,
he was appointed to the 15th regiment of light dragoons; and,
in the August following, headed the second line of horse under
the Marquis of Granby, at the battle of Minden. Being constituted a lieutenant general, he was, in 1762, ordered from
Germany, for the purpose of assisting, as second in command,
at the memorable reduction of the Havannah. He was appointed Commander in Chief in Ireland in 1774, but being dis-
gusted, on his arrival, he made a request to be recalled, which
was complied with; and, upon the death of Lord Cornwallis,
he was made Governor of Gibraltar in his place, which fortress
he bravely defended during the late siege, in the years 1779,
1780, 1781, and 1782 In 1783, he was granted a pension of
2000 l. *per annum*, and created a Knight of the Bath; and, in
1787, was raised to the dignity of a peer of Great Britain. The
honours

tar, in the years 1779, 1780, and 1781, is sprung from the family of Stobs, now reprefented by Sir William Eliott, Bart, one of the principal heritors of this parifh.

Antiquities —The remains of the Roman or Saxon fortification, called *Catrail*, runs through this parifh, from S W. to N. W. towards Selkirk and Galla Water. There are feveral camps to be found in the upper part of this parifh. Some of them appear to have been Roman camps, and others Saxon *.

honours which he had thus juftly acquired, he did not long enjoy, for he died in the year 1790.

* At a place called *Carlenrigg*, a number of Roman urns were dug up about 5 years ago; but when thefe camps were formed, or the urns depofited, the prefent incumbent has never been able to difcover. At Prieft-haugh, a great number of gold coins were found, fuppofed to have been depofited by fome of the attendants of Queen Mary, when fhe vifited Bothwell at the Hermitage Caftle. At a fmall wood, near Carlenrigg Chapel, the famous JOHN ARMSTRONG was taken and flain.

PARISH OF CRAILING.

(COUNTY OF ROXBURGH.)

By the Rev. MR. DAVID BROWN.

———————————

Situation, Extent, and Surface.

THIS parish is situated in the county of Roxburgh, in the presbytery of Jedburgh, and synod of Merse and Teviotdale. In the records of presbytery it is called, the united parishes of Crailing, Nisbet, and Spital. Crailing and Nisbet were distinct parishes, and Spital is said to have been an hospital, belonging to the abbey at Ancrum. The time of annexation is very antient. It is of a circular form, near 4 English miles in diameter. The river Teviot flows eastward, in beautiful windings, through its centre *, where it is joined by the Oxnam from the south, nearly at right angles.

About three fourths of the parish are arable land, very rich and fertile. The haughs, about a mile broad, in the middle of the parish, are of a deep loamy dry soil. Towards the south,

the

* The centre of the parish is 13 miles from Hawick, 7 from Kelso, and 45 from Edinburgh.

the ground rifes gradually from the valley; the foil becomes of a fharper, and more ftoney kind, and then runs out into fheep pafture. On the fouthern boundary there are confiderable plantations of wood; moftly fir, except on the banks of the Oxnam, where there is a quantity of timber, of various forts, along the borders of a fmall and romantic glen; in the bottom of which, there is a flat of rich pafture. The river winds through it, but occafionally touches high and fteep rocks, partly covered with natural wood. At the foot of this glen, are fituated, Crailing houfe on one fide of the Oxnam, and the manfe on the other. This fpot is well adapted for beautiful pleafure grounds; in the keeping up, and improving of which, the prefent proprietor is at confiderable pains and expence. The grounds, on the fouth fide of the parifh, are moftly inclofed and fubdivided with hedges, and rows of trees.

The north fide of the parifh contains little haugh land, the ground beginning to rife more immediately from the river. The foil is rich and dry, fit for any crop. On the northern boundary, there is a confiderable extent of fheep pafture, in which, there is a beautiful green hill, called *Penelheugh*, the only one in the parifh. The grounds on that fide, though interfperfed with a few clumps of fir trees, are moftly open; except towards the weft, at Spital, now called Mount-teviot, where there are large inclofures, with hedge rows and belts of planting, and a confiderable quantity of full grown timber.

This parifh is a fmall portion, but, at the fame time, the loweft, warmeft, and moft fertile, of that beautiful tract of corn country, on the banks of the Teviot, 20 miles in length, from Hawick to Kelfo, which is commonly known by the name of Teviotdale.

Climate,

Climate, &c.——The climate is dry and wholesome. No diseases are peculiar to the parish ; and the people are generally long lived. One man died a few years ago, who was said to be 106. At present there are several persons in the parish about 80, and likely still to see many years.——There is a circumstance, which may be mentioned here, as a proof of the mildness of the climate, and fineness of the soil of this parish, which took place in the late attempt, that was made to cultivate tobacco in Scotland : In one season, a tenant, in this district, drew L. 115 for tobacco plants, and afterwards raised a crop on 12 or 13 acres, which he sold upon the ground, for L. 320 ; but an act of parliament intervening, (the policy, or the justice of which, need not here be entered into,) the purchaser was unable to fulfil his bargain, and the farmer was compelled to dispose of his tobacco to Government, at only 4d. per pound ; at which rate, it brought him only L. 104. It appeared, from the trials made at that time, that tobacco would thrive well in the southern parts of Scotland.

Rent of the Parish.——The valued rent . is L. 8733 Scots. The real amounts to about L. 2500 sterling. The rent of the best land in the parish, is L. 1 : 10 per English acre. The land, in general, is let, not by the acre, but in the lump.

Number of Proprietors, Tenants, &c.—There are two great and one small proprietor, or feuer in the parish. One of these, Mr Hunter of Crailing, resides at his country seat during the summer. Mount-teviot-lodge, (a seat of the Marquis of Lothian,) has not been occupied by the family for some time past. There are four farmers, who pay L. 100 ; other four, upwards of L. 200, one L. 300 *per annum* ; besides

a

a number of smaller tenants. But there is not now in the parish, above one-third of the number, that there were 40 years ago.

Population.———The population of the country part of the parish, has, of late years, greatly diminished, owing to the monopoly of farms. But, on the whole, the increase is confiderable, when compared with the report made to Dr Webfter, in 1755, where it is stated, at only 387 fouls. The number of persons, at prefent, in the parish, by actual enumeration, are as follows :

Of the Established Church - - 280	
Their children, under 10 years of age, or there-	
by - - - - 172	
	—— 452
Seceders - - - 130	
Their children - - - 90	
	—— 220
Total in the parish	672

The proportion of Seceders has been much about the same for many years.

The following is a statement, extracted from the parish register, of the births, marriages, and deaths, for the last ten years :

Abstract

Abstract of Births, Marriages, and Deaths.

Years.	Births.	Marriages.	Deaths.
1781	10	7	10
1782	18	10	14
1783	13	5	5
1784	24	4	2
1785	15	5	4
1786	22	5	1
1787	14	7	3
1788	18	5	7
1789	16	3	2
1790	13	9	7
	163	60	55
Yearly aver. near	16	6	5

The list of deaths is not very exact, as no record has been kept, of persons belonging to this, who have been buried in other parishes.

State of Agriculture.——It is believed, that there is not, in any part of the kingdom, a better system of agriculture. No expence is spared in procuring manure. Marle is got at Eckford, one mile distant ; but lime is brought from Northumberland, about 23 miles. And one of the most considerable farmers in the parish, is this year making trial of gypsum, or plaster of Paris, which has, of late, been much recommended. The marle is sold so high, that lime is reckoned cheaper, notwithstanding the distance of carriage. The turnip, and every species of drill husbandry, is carried on here in the highest

higheſt perfection. The plowmen of this pariſh, have, at no competition, been excelled in the neatneſs of their work; and the farmers are remarkable for keeping capital horſes, and e-quipping them to the beſt advantage. No ſight can be more delightful, to one who is fond of a country life, than to ſurvey the rich haughs of Crailing, and the fields of Niſbet, in a fine morning, during the beſt ſeaſons, for the toils of agriculture.

Crops.—This pariſh produces a great proportion of wheat, beſides all the other kinds of grain of the beſt quality. The culture of turnips is much attended to, and with great ſucceſs. They are generally eaten by ſheep on the fields. The ſheep are incloſed by nets, made for the purpoſe; by means of which, 400 or 500 are confined within the bounds of 4 or 5 Engliſh acres at a time, till the turnips are all conſumed. The ground being well prepared for the turnips, and thoroughly cleaned while the crop is upon it, the neceſſity of ſummer fallowing is precluded, and is, therefore, ſeldom practiſed in this pariſh. The ſheep leave the ground richly manured, and wheat is generally ſown upon fields thus prepared, any time before Chriſtmas. There are, upon an average, about 220 acres of turnip annually conſumed in this pariſh, by ſheep from neighbouring pariſhes, and from the Engliſh border, which are thereby thoroughly fed for the market, to the number of about 2200, allowing 10 ſheep to an acre. Such turnips, as are not conſumed in this way, (which are not a few,) are given, by the farmers, to their young ſtock, both of cattle and ſheep. The turnips, that are late of being conſumed, are ſucceeded by a crop of barley, which is frequently accompanied with graſs-ſeeds. The crops of this pariſh, and of Eckford to the eaſt, are generally more early, than even thoſe of the Lothians.

Price of Labour.—The average wages of a man-servant, living in the house, are about L. 7 ; those of a woman about L. 3 : 10. The wages of men-labourers, furnishing their own meat, are 10d. a day, from Martinmas to Candlemas, and 1s. the rest of the year, except in time of harvest, when they are somewhat higher. The wages of women are, at turnip-weeding, and other farm-work, in summer, 7d. a day, and at shearing in harvest, 1s. furnishing their own victuals.

Carts and Ploughs.—There are 48 carts and 44 ploughs. The ploughs are of Small's construction ; and though all made in the parish, they are not inferior to his manufacture. They are always drawn by a pair of horses, and one man both drives and holds the plough.

Animals, Fish, &c.—There are about 140 horses and 350 black cattle in the parish. The stock of sheep is about 2400. The breed is between the best border ewes, and Bakewell's and Culley's tups. The lambs, for some years past, have sold at from 8s. to 11s. a head ; the wool is all laid, and sells at about 86s. per stone of 24 English lb. from 3 to 8 fleeces go to the stone. Such is the attention here paid to the culture of sheep, that many are bred and reared even on the best grounds.

The rivers Teviot and Oxnam, already mentioned, abound with great variety of trout. Vast numbers of sea trout come up in summer and autumn, and afford excellent sport to the angler. There are some pike of a large size in the back waters or deserted channels of the Teviot. There are a great many grilse, and some salmon in that river.

Mineral Spring.—The only thing of the kind in the parish, and that even scarcely worth mentioning, is a small spring near the manse, within a few yards of the minister's well, of which

which the common people talk very highly, as a cure for the cholic.

Villages.—There are three villages in the parish, viz. Crailing, and Upper and Nether Nisbet. But, indeed, they scarcely deserve the name of villages, being inhabited only by such labourers and tradesmen, as are necessary for the purposes of the neighbouring farmers.

Ecclesiastical State of the Parish.—The present church and manse were built about 35 years ago. The church is small, but handsome, well-finished, and in good repair. It stands remote from all other buildings, on a small eminence near the south bank of the Teviot, where that river is joined by the Oxnam, which is about the centre of the parish. When this church was built, the church of Nisbet was thrown down, and not a vestige of it now remains. The hospital and chapel at Spital were long ago demolished, and even the burying-ground there has been totally abandoned for many years. Nothing but a few tomb stones now mark the place, and these are almost grown over with trees and weeds. But the burying-ground at Nisbet is still used, by all the Nisbet and Spital side of the parish.—There are no remains of the old church of Crailing, which stood within a few yards of Crailing house; but the parishioners on Crailing side, and some also, who have left the parish, still insist upon using the old burying-ground, although the proprietor of Crailing has, in lieu of it, given them an ample space around the new church; and although their late minister set them an example, by erecting there a tomb for himself some years before he died.—The manse stands upon the old site of Crailing manse, nearly about half a mile south from the present church. The king is patron. The living consists of 85 bolls of meal, and a little more than 75 bolls of barley, Linlith-

gow

gow measure. The minister is titular of the vicarage tithes, consisting of lambs, wool, lint, hemp, hay, &c. which he lets at present for L. 30 : 10 sterling. It is believed they may be rented considerably higher. There is likewise a glebe of 9 acres and 17 poles English, and a manse, &c. all which are in value according to the rate of the times.

There is no dissenting meeting-house in the parish. The Seceders here are accommodated at Jedburgh, which is about 3 miles distant.

State of the Schools—There are two established schools in the parish, viz. one at Crailing, and one at Nisbet. The schoolmaster of Crailing has L. 5 : 11 1⅓, as salary, and about L. 3, as being parish and session clerk. He has also the interest of money, left by bonds for his use, to the amount of L. 3 : 15 *per annum*. The schoolmaster of Nisbet has L. 2 : 15 : 6⅔, as salary, and 10s. for collecting the poor's rates of the barony of Nisbet. The school-fees are very small, being, for English, 1s. per quarter, for English and writing, 1s. 6d. and for English, writing, and arithmetic, 2s. 6d. The annual average number of scholars, for the last 6 years, has been 48 at Crailing school, and 36 at Nisbet.

State of the Poor.—They are supported by poor's rates. It is found, by written records, that, between 30 and 40 years ago, the poor in this parish, in number about 8 persons, were supported, or relieved in their own houses, for about L. 14 sterling *per annum*. Of late years, about 14 persons, at an average, have been maintained in the same way, for L. 27 *per annum*.

Roads, Bridges, and Boats.—The turnpike road on the south banks of the Teviot, betwixt Hawick and Kelso, passes through this

this parifh. The other roads are kept in repair by ftatute money. There is a bridge over the Oxnam, near the manfe,
which is the only one in the parifh. It was built about 20
years ago, by fubfcription, and is ftill in good repair; it will
no doubt be upheld by the turnpike funds.——The neareft
bridge over the Teviot, is that at Ancrum, a fhort way a-
bove. But, for the conveniency of the parifh, the heritors up-
hold a boat, and pay a boatman. To this they are bound, on
account of the annexation of Nifbet and Spital to the church
of Crailing; and on Sundays no fare is exacted, from perfons
attending the parifh church.

Antiquities.——A Roman road or caufeway paffed through
the weft part of this parifh, the traces of which are ftill to be
feen. There are alfo veftiges of two encampments on the top
of Penelheugh; and that they belonged to the Romans, we
are led to conjecture, from their vicinity to that road. One of
them feems to have been ftrongly fortified, and though now
totally demolifhed, it ftill retains the name of the Caftle.——
The fite of it is very high, and commands a moft extenfive
profpect; taking in at once all the windings of the Teviot from
Hawick to Kelfo, and part of the feveral beautiful ftreams
which join it in that courfe. The whole county of Berwick is
alfo feen from it, and a part of the German ocean. The view
is bounded on the fouth by the lofty mountains of Cheviot,
and, on the north, by the Lammermuir hills.

Nifbet is noted, by tradition, for being a ftrong-hold of
fome of the antient marauders of the border. Many perfons
are yet living, who remember the ruins of two ftrong towers
at the village of Nether Nifbet, and ftones of excellent work-
manfhip are ftill dug up from time to time. It alfo deferves
to be mentioned, on account of its antiquity, and the fingu-
larity of its tenure; that the proprietor of the barony of Crailing

ling is bound to furnish, a guard of his own vassals, for the circuit Court of Justiciary, when it meets at Jedburgh. On this account, there is annexed, to that barony, the property of some acres of land at Lanton, in the parish of Jedburgh, which is called the Crowner's lands.

Disadvantages.—It is a disadvantage, to which the lowest haughs of the parish are liable, that the rivers sometimes swell to such a height, as to carry off either the corns when cut, or the manure, when lying on the surface, and thus to destroy the labours of the farmer. What renders these floods more destructive is, that they are often unexpected, and sudden, by great rains falling in the distant mountains, when no symptoms are perceived by the inhabitants of this, and of the neighbouring vallies.

But the chief and general disadvantage of this parish, is the distance from coal, and the great expence of land carriage, on that and all other commodities. Although a considerable quantity of fire-wood is annually sold at Crailing plantations, yet it is generally thought, that coals are the cheapest fuel. They are brought from Etal in Glendale, and from Rychester on Reid water, a branch of the Tyne, both in Northumberland, and both distant about 23 miles. But still it is some comfort to observe, that these coals are of a very excellent quality.

Means of Improvement.—The improvements of this parish, and of the neighbouring districts in general, have been very rapid for some years, owing to the establishment of turnpike roads, and to the great success in the culture of turnip ; and it is hoped, that there will soon be an easy communication with the German ocean, by means of the proposed canal. If that should take place, it will necessarily lead to the establishment of manufactures, and thereby increase the population, extend the improvements, and double the value of estates in this part of the kingdom.

PARISH OF ECKFORD.

(County of Roxburgh or Tiviotdale—Presbytery of Jedburgh—Synod of Merse and Tiviotdale.)

By the Rev. WILLIAM PATON, A. M.

Name, Situation, and Extent.

THE ancient name of this parish, as appears from a passage in Sir Richard Baker's Chronicle, was *Ackforth* *, or *Aikeforthe*. In all modern writings it is styled Eckfoord and Eckford, the original derivation being from the Gaelic or Celtic,

* " In the 13th year of King Henry the VIII. and of James V. of Scotland, " Anno Domini 1522, when the Duke of Albany was established governor of " Scotland, he approached the southern borders with an army of 8000 men, " probably to observe the motion of the English upon the confines of Scotland, " but made no invasion into England; while the Marquis of Dorset, warden of " the east and middle marches, entered *Tiviotdale* with a number of English " forces, burnt all the towns and villages on every side as he marched north- " ward, and amongst others *Ackforth*, Grimslay, *Sessforthe* manor, &c.; and " upon Good Friday following withdrew back into England with his plunder, " amongst which were 4000 head of cattle."

Baker's *Chronicle*, page 259. Ridpath's *Border History*, page 515 *in the note.*

Lord Dacres was next year appointed warden general of the borders of England opposite to Scotland. From the above quotation it would appear, that Ackforth, now styled Eckford, was at that period a place of some consequence; but no other account can be found of its original state.

Celtic, the ancient language of the whole ifland. The original names of many places in Scotland are ftill retained, with
occafional alterations, probably introduced by the Dano-Saxon
dialect. It is faid to fignify in the Gaelic the *Horfe Ford.* A
ford is commonly known to be a fhallow part of a river proper for paffage; accordingly, at no great diftance from the
manfe, there is a very fafe ford acrofs the river Tiviot from
S. to N.

The extent of the parifh from N. to S. is fix miles and 3¾
furlongs in length, and from E. to W. 4½ miles in breadth.
It lies in the latitude of 55° 32′, and longitude of 10° 6′ weft
of London, according to Mr. Stobie's map of the county,
publifhed in 1770; (69¼ ftatute miles to a degree). The form
is triangular, or nearly approaching to it. It is feparated by
Tiviot, oppofite to the church, from the barony of Ormifton.
The water *Kail* runs through it from S. to N. and is emptied
into Tiviot, a little to the eaft of the church. It is nearly at
an equal diftance of 4½ miles from Jedburgh and Kelfo.

Soil, Surface, Climate and *Difeafes.*—Upon the banks of
the river Tiviot (which runs from weft to eaft through the
county, and empties itfelf into the Tweed at Kelfo), the foil
is generally light loam, rifing in gentle eminences fouthward.
It has been originally covered with heath, but by proper cultivation, is now rendered green and fit for pafture. There
are no remarkable hills in this diftrict, nor any wafte lands,
except Cavertoun Edge, which has been of late chiefly devoted
to the annual horfe races; although even fome part of that fpot
is in cultivation. Part of Woodend Hill has been lately
planted with firs, and within a few years will afford a beautiful landfcape. The air here is dry and falubrious. Seldom
any epidemical difeafes prevail, excepting the ague, which
visits

visits this neighbourhood in the spring, occasioned by the moist exhalations from the fens, and the easterly winds from the Cheviot Hills, at the distance of a few miles southward. The people are in general healthy; but no instances of remarkable longevity have occurred during the incumbency of the present minister.

Cultivation and *Produce.*—A considerable change in the mode of agriculture has been introduced within these few years. The English plough universally prevails, and 2 horses instead of 4 oxen and 2 horses are now adopted. Raising turnips, with the preparation for that crop, supersedes summer fallowing entirely. They succeed remarkably well in a dry and light soil through the whole country. Oats and barley are the grains most commonly sown. Wheat, however, is now more frequent than formerly, after fallow, turnips and potatoes; which last is much and justly encouraged for family use, as well as for horses, cattle and swine. Pease, by many judicious farmers, is not considered as a profitable crop, since broad clover and rye-grass have been introduced; but they are continued to be sown in smaller quantities, to mix with barley, for the bread of labouring people and cottagers of all descriptions. The raising of hemp is dropt here; but that of lint is continued, although not in such quantities as formerly, both for family use and the public market. It is sold on an average at 11 s. or 12 s. *per* stone *. An early kind of oats

was,

---

* That which grew at the Wester Moss was in the highest reputation, for the bluish cast which it acquired, from the quality of that stagnated water in which it was steeped. It sold at about 15 s. or 16 s. the stone. But since that moss was drained (for the purpose of digging a seam of marle found there) it has lost that peculiar colour which enhanced its value. Steeping lint in running water is found prejudicial to flax, destructive to fish in rivers, and otherwise a great nuisance, and accordingly is under very severe prohibitions by the justices of peace.

was, in 1776, introduced by Mr. James Church, tenant in Mofs-tower, on part of the Duke of Buccleugh's eftate in this parifh. He raifed them from 60 grains of Polifh oats, which he obtained from a friend, and planted in a corner of one of his fields about the 14th of June that year. Their produce turned out very confiderable. They have been fown on his farm every year fince without degenerating. The foil inclines to gravel or light loam ; and by experience they are found to anfwer beft on dry land in good heart. They ripen by a month earlier than common oats, although fown at the fame time and upon the fame ground. They muft be cut down fooner, and not allowed to continue growing until per∙ fectly ripe, as they are more eafily fhaken than any other grain. They commonly yield between 11 and 12 ftone of meal to the boll of oats, which in this country is 5 *fulls* or firlots for oats and barley, and 4 firlots for wheat, rye, and peafe ; fo that upon weighing a boll of thefe oats (including the weight of the fack), the whole amounted to 28 ftone by the Kelfo ftandard. The reputation of thefe oats has increafed fo rapidly, that they are now generally fown in this country, as well as through moft other parts of Scotland, feveral parts of England, and they have even found their way acrofs the Atlantic to America. The grain of every fort commonly fown here, is fufficient for the confumption of the inhabitants. Quantities are fold by fample in the weekly markets of Kelfo and Jedburgh, at the prices then current. * Horfes have of late

* Wheat is fown in September, and more frequently in October; rye much about the fame time; oats in March and beginning of April; peafe about the middle of that month ; barley from the middle of April to the middle of May ; turnips from the beginning of June to the middle of July; harveft commences, in favourable feafons, about the end of Auguft, and generally through the month of September. The prices of grain and provifions vary according to cir-cumftances and the ftate of the preceding crops; wheat, at an average, fells

at

late years advanced in price, especially such as are fit for huſbandry and carting. Black cattle are generally of a good
ſize, being bred from large Engliſh bulls. Although there are
not any ſtock farms, properly ſo denominated, in the pariſh,
particular attention has been paid to the breed of ſheep within
theſe few years. Their wool is much finer, and conſequently
is riſing in price, which is from 15 s. to 16 s. at an average
per ſtone. There are 16 lb. of 24 oz. to the pound in the
ſtone. The ſale has been very quick, and the demand ſtill continues. The incloſing of land with hedge and ditch is now
prevalent, and meets the inclination of the farmer, who finds
his profit and convenience thereby. They allow their land-

lords

at 30 s. the boll uſed in this country; barley from 15 s. to 18 s.; oats 15 s.;
peaſe and rye at 16 s. The demand from other places frequently makes a conſiderable alteration in the market. Oatmeal is always ſold by the ſtone weight,
the ſame as butcher meat, the medium price about 1 s. 6 d. 16 ſtones to a boll;
beef uſually 3½ d. the pound; veal, mutton, and lamb, at 3 d.; pork 4 d.; geeſe
1 s. 6 d. ſtript of their feathers and ready for uſe; ducks and hens 8 d; turkeys 2 s.
6 d.; all at an average. The wages paid to domeſtic ſervants have increaſed much
ſince the improvements in agriculture took place; a man receives annually 7 l.
and a woman 50 s. with maintenance; day labourers 8 d.; women 6 d.; wrights,
10 d.; maſons 1 s. in ſummer, and 10 d. in winter; taylors 8 d.; turnip hoers and
hay makers, 8 d.; a man for harveſt work 1 s., and a woman 9 d., with their
diet. Hinds, who provide their own diet, are allowed a free houſe, graſs for
their cow in ſummer, and fodder during winter and ſpring, 8 bolls of oats for
meal, 2 bolls of barley, 1 boll of peaſe for family bread, and 1 firlot of potatoes
planted. Every cottager pays the rent of the houſe by harveſt labour, has a
ſmall ſpot of ground adjoining to the habitation, for furniſhing cabbage and
pot-herbs, ſome potatoes planted in the field, lint ſown, and ſometimes potatoes
or barley, as far as their dung covers the ſurface. Theſe cottagers, with their
families, are eagerly deſired by the farmers, ready at a call upon every emergency, employment being given to their children from the age of 8 or 10 years
and upwards, according to their reſpective abilities. Since the cultivation of
turnips became ſo univerſal, theſe cottages are valued at one guinea rent through
the year: The family are provided with turf brought home by their maſter.
Theſe houſes are never left unoccupied, although reared at the expence of the
farmer.

lords interest for such sums of money as may be necessary for inclosing. Every farm has several upon it, generally in a thriving condition. The rent is from 10 s. to 20 s. *per* acre. The numbers of tenants has of late years diminished by the union of several small possessions into one. But to carry on the business in these large farms, a greater number of servants is required; so that this has not had so much influence in depopulating the parish as might have been expected. According to the report of the most judicious farmers, one half of their land is laid out in tillage, one four h in turnips, and the rest in pasture. Such fields as are sown with red or broad clover, and rye-grass, for hay, continue in that state for one year, and then are plowed for other crops.

Manure.—Two seams of marl, deeply impregnated with shells, were opened, about the year 1777, at Eckford Welter Moss, upon the Duke of Buccleugh's estate, the upper one of about 8 feet thick, covered with 9 feet of moss; the seam below it 7 feet at an average, separated from the other with a stratum of clay of 4 feet, without any other intermixture. The marl is found to suit a light soil, when well spread on the surface, in proportion of 60 or 70 bolls to the English acre: a strong loam requires a larger quantity. All green crops, such as pease, grass, clover, &c. receive benefit from it; and when spread on pasture ground, in the beginning of winter, and allowed to mellow by frost, it proves of very great advantage to the ensuing crop. The measure for the boll is a cube, containing 8 cubic feet: it is sold to the Duke's tenants for 3 d., and to others for 4 d.; at the distance of 3 miles for 2½ d.; at 5 miles, and all above that, for 2 d. the boll. Its excellent quality increases the demand; for it fully gratifies the most sanguine expectations of the farmer and improver of land. Lime is also much used, and with great advantage, although transported from Northumberland,

at

at the diftance of upwards of 20 miles. A quarry of lime-
ftone has lately been wrought at about half that diftance.
The experiment has not as yet been fo extenfive as fully to
afcertain its excellence for the purpofe of hufbandry. The
proprietor (by its demand) has been encouraged to erect a
draw kiln; and as it feems to increafe, another kiln is propofed to be built next feafon.

Proprietors and Rent.—Property has not undergone any
confiderable change of late in this diftrict, excepting Marlefield, purchafed by the Marquis of Tweeddale from William
Nifbet of Dirleton, Efq. along with the eftate of Grubbet.
There are 8 heritors in all: Only one refides conftantly, and
another occafionally during part of the fummer feafon. The
valued rent of the diftrict by the commiffioners of fupply,
anno 1742, is 11130 l. 13 s. 4 d. Scotch. The prefent real
rent is 3699 l. 4 s. 1 d. Sterling.

Church.—The prefent church was built about the year
1662. It was completely repaired and new feated in 1774
and 1775, and is now rendered exceedingly convenient. The
manfe was rebuilt in 1775, and is equally commodious. The
offices have been lately repaired. The glebe is rather fmall,
even including the pafture ground. Water for the family
ufe is tranfported from the river Tiviot in a water carriage,
there being no fpring in the immediate neighbourhood of the
houfe. Of late, pump wells have been dug in the villages of
Eckford, Wefter Mofs, and Mofs Tower, and fome other
places, which fupply the inhabitants plentifully with that neceffary article. The living confifts of 35 bolls 3 firlots 1
peck and 2 lippies of barley (of the meafure commonly ufed
in this county, viz. 5 firlots to the boll); 23 bolls and 4 ftones
of oatmeal (16 ftones to the boll); 32 l. 18 s. 7$\frac{2}{12}$ d. Sterling,
in money; 5 l. for communion elements; 42 lb. of cheefe,

from

from a farm in the parish, of vicarage tithes, paid regularly every year, not having been commuted; with a piece of muirland for the exclusive right of turf, which the minister generally occupies yearly, at the distance of above a mile. By the late additional expence of living, the present incumbent found it necessary to commence a process of augmentation of stipend before the Lords Commissioners for plantation of kirks and valuation of teinds. Having met with no opposition therein from his heritors, a decreet of modification was pronounced; but as the process is not quite finished, the amount of the augmentation cannot as yet be ascertained. The King is patron. Eckford, from ancient records, seems to have been a vicarage dependent upon the Abbey of *Jedworth*, commonly called Jedburgh.

Poor.—There are no parochial funds, or mortified money for the poor. Their maintenance arises from assessments every half year, at what is called a parish meeting for that purpose; the one half upon the heritors according to their valued rent, and the other half upon their tenants according to their present rents, respectively. The sum assessed is levied by a collector appointed for that purpose, who is allowed some gratuity for making the cast, and levying the money. It is put into the hands of overseers for the poor, who distribute it to those persons admitted upon the roll of pensioners, according to the weekly allowance paid, which varies in proportion to the rise and fall of grain. Persons claiming this charity, must have resided in the parish for 3 years, without interruption, before the application is made; and they are required to subscribe a bond or deed of conveyance, bequeathing their effects to the heritors at their decease, as a check to prevent concealed property, or alienating this charity, and to hinder the interference of relations in that event. These effects are seldom exacted, and therefore turn out of small account to the parish.

The

The funerals of ſuch perſons are commonly ordered to be defrayed by the meeting. When diſeaſe or misfortune attacks any perſon, as during the high price of oatmeal in 1782, and proper application is made to the meeting for charity, what is called an interim ſupply is granted. There are no begging poor in this diſtrict. The weekly collections in the church, which are but ſmall, are alſo applied to alleviate the wants of the moſt needy as they occur. The number of paupers at laſt inrolment was 24.

School.—There is a public ſchool, and dwelling houſe for accommodating the ſchoolmaſter, kept in repair by the heritors; the ſalary was lately augmented, and is at preſent 8 l. 6 s 8 d. yearly. He has a ſmall piece of ground incloſed for a garden, contiguous to the houſe: his other emoluments are, 30 s. for collecting poor's rates yearly, ſchool-fees for Engliſh, 1 s.; 1 s. 6 d. for writing, 2 s. 6 d; for arithmetic, *per* quarter each; for regiſtration of each baptiſm, 4 d.; proclamation of a marriage, 1 s.; extract of a teſtimonial for a ſingle perſon, 4 d.; for a family, 6 d.; as clerk to the kirk ſeſſion, 10 s. yearly; beſides ſome caſual articles. The number of ſcholars is from 40 to 50 at an average; but as the ſchool is not centrical, being towards the weſtern limits of the pariſh, ſome infirm perſons are generally employed to teach young children at a diſtance (in Caverton and Cefsford) the Engliſh language, and the elementary principles of religion from the catechiſm. They are furniſhed with a houſe *gratis* from the farmers, and ſatisfied for their pains with what the parents can afford.

Fuel—The fuel commonly uſed in families is coals, which are brought from a diſtance of about 20 miles, and ſome from Northumberland. Although in ſome parts of the county there is the appearance of ſmall ſeams, none of the trials hitherto made have ſucceeded, nor is it probable they will, without conſiderable

fiderable expence and perfeverance. The common people make ufe of turf, broom and furze; but thefe two laft have become fcarce, through cultivation of the land that formerly produced them. Peats are not plentiful, there being no moffes but in places where the marl is got; and this being nearly exhaufted, the poorer inhabitants muft fuffer confiderably very foon by the want of this article: and indeed the diftance from coal is one great reafon that manufactures have not been eftablifhed in this country, though wool is in great abundance, and the neceffaries of life may be obtained for the moft part at moderate rates.

Population.—The population in 1756 was about 890 fouls above the age of 8. It has often varied according to circum-ftances. An accurate ftate of baptifms cannot be obtained, as diffenters from the eftablifhment feldom order the names of their children to be engroffed; and the regifter of births, marriages and burials is not regularly kept, as the parifh clerk has no allowance for that purpofe. The dues to govern-ment for thefe are paid on the firft of October yearly: of thefe he preferves a memorandum, and afterwards enters them on the records, according to which the annexed abftract * will furnifh fome idea of the population for ten years paft.

Statif-

* *Abftract of Baptifms, Marriages and Deaths, during the laft ten years.*

Years.	BAPTISMS.			MAR.	BURIALS.		
	Males.	Fem.	Total.		Males.	Fem.	Total.
1781	14	11	25	7	3	8	11
1782	10	10	20	4	4	1	5
1783	10	7	17	5	4	3	7
1784	5	12	17	9	2	6	8
1785	13	11	24	7	5	5	10
1786	11	5	16	5	4	2	6
1787	5	9	14	8	4	5	9
1788	10	3	13	7	10	7	17
1789	4	5	9	10	4	4	8
1790	6	8	14	7	4	5	9
Total,	88	81	169	69	44	46	90

Statiſtical Table of the Pariſh of Eckford.

Length in Engliſh miles, - - -	6
Breadth, - - - - -	4¼
Population in 1755, - - -	1083
————, *anno* 1791, - - -	952
Decreaſe, - - -	131
Average of births, for ten years preceding 1791, nearly -	17
———— of deaths, for ditto, - -	9
———— of marriages, - nearly -	7
Number of males, - - -	436
———— females, - - -	516
———— males under 16 years of age, -	71
———— females, under ditto, - -	67
———— families, - - -	219
———— houſes inhabited - -	212
———— members of the Eſtabliſhed Church, -	742
———— Seceders and Relievers, - -	210
———— proprietors reſiding, - -	2
———— ———— non-reſiding, - -	6
———— clergymen, - -	1
———— eſtabliſhed ſchoolmaſters, - -	1
———— farmers, - - - -	25
———— keepers of alehouſes, - - -	2
———— ſmiths maſons, wrights, &c. - -	34
———— millers, - - - -	5
———— ſervants, - - -	106
———— poor, - - -	24
Valued rent in Scotch money, - L. 11,130 13 4	
Real rent in Sterling, - - 3699 4 1	

Roads, Bridges, Rivers, &c.—There is a turnpike road from Carliſle to Berwick upon Tweed, Newcaſtle, &c. made at the expence of the county, through the pariſh, but kept in repair

repair by the tolls. Statute labour, by a late act of parliament, is commuted at the rate of 7 s. 6 d. Sterling, for every 100 l. Scotch of valued rent. These roads are found to be of essential service for promoting speedy communication in an inland country. There is an old bridge of one arch over Kail Water, at the Mill of Eckford; the parapet walls are gone. It is said to have been built by the money arising from vacant stipends about the Revolution. There is another over the same water, near its conflux with the river Tiviot, built at the expence of the county, on the great turnpike road. The fish in these rivers are trout and salmon. The trout in Kail are preferable to those in the Tiviot: The salmon come up the Tiviot at all seasons, but in greater numbers in the months of *September* and *October*, for the purpose of spawning. The gentlemen of the county have it in agitation to form a canal from Berwick to Ancrum Bridge, up the Tweed, and to cross the Tiviot. A subscription for defraying the expence of a survey, to be taken by Mr. Whitworth, was lately set on foot, and the survey taken accordingly from Ancrum Bridge, and eastward, in the neighbourhood of this place. The committee appointed for conducting the canal, having abridged the former plan, appointed Mr. Whitworth to survey and give in an estimate of their last plan, which was reported to the meeting of the Michaelmas Head Court on the 14th of October last, of which they approved, and appointed the same committee to circulate subscription papers, towards raising the necessary fund, for carrying the work into execution.

Eminent Men.—Sir William Bennet of Grubbet, was born and resided at Marlefield, in this parish, the greater part of his life. He was a gentleman of considerable genius and learning. It is reported that he afforded assistance to the late Allan Ramsay, in composing the pastoral comedy of the Gentle

tle Shepherd, and in some other poetical productions of those times. He was very justly respected for integrity and benevolence; and indeed the whole family are said to have been remarkable for hospitality and public spirit. Their remains lie interred in an aisle, adjoining to the church of Eckford, on the north side of it, with this inscription over the door:—
Hoc monumentum sibi et suis bene merentibus, ponendum curavit Dominus Gulielmus Bennet, Eques Auratus, Anno Salutis 1724.

Antiquities.—On the south of the present village of Cefsford, the remains of the ancient castle of that name *, are yet to be seen. No date is discernible to fix the period of its erection; but from those parts of the walls yet entire, it appears to have been a place of considerable strength, both from the thickness

---

* The first proprietor of this castle, mentioned in history, was Andrew Kerr, who obtained the title of Baron of Cefsford, and got a charter of confirmation from Archibald Earl Douglas, thereafter stiled Duke of Turenne, Douglas and Longueville. This charter is dated *anno* 1446; and in the reign of Queen Elizabeth and James VI. of Scotland, *anno* 1570, the laird of Cefsford was made warden of the Scottish middle marches *; it became afterwards one of the titles of the noble family of *Roxburgh*, which it still continues to be. Such was the situation of *Scotland* before the accession of James VI. to the throne of England, that every Baron's house was more or less fortified, according to the power and consequence of its lord, or situation of his castle. Those especially, at a distance from the seat of government, and therefore not under the awe of the law, when the predatory system prevailed, found it necessary for their habitations, and places of residence, to be better defended against the incursions of the neighbouring plunderers. Cefsford castle, therefore, being only at the distance of 4 or 5 miles from the English confines, was necessarily rendered a place of security; and according to tradition, there was a subterraneous vault for concealing both persons and goods within its walls, to which access was only got by one aperture, which was opened or shut as seemed necessary by a large stone with an iron ring in it. This stone and ring have been seen by some persons still alive; but the entrance to the *peel* or dungeon is now chocked up with rubbish.

* *Redpath's History, p.* 635.

thickness of the walls (which are 12 feet at an average) the vestiges of the battlements on the top, the embrasseurs on the sides, and the remains of a surrounding moat, which was probably furnished with water from a spring above the present farm house. The roof is entirely gone. The area within the walls, discernible, is 39 feet in length, and 20 in breadth; the entry to it was probably from the N.E. About 7 or 8 years ago, in digging for stones on the farm of Hospital-land, belonging to the Duke of Roxburgh, the labourers discovered a tumulus, in the bottom of which were found two earthen pots; the one about 3 feet deep, and 18 wide; the other rather smaller; both containing blackish dust, and small fragments of human bones: Upon exposure to the external air, these vessels tumbled down and could not be preserved *. There have also been found silver coins of Queen Mary, in good preservation, near the shepherd's house in Easter Wooden, where some faint vestiges of a tower, it is said, have been traced. Part of the walls of a strong building were to be seen several years ago at Moss Tower †, so denominated from its ancient situation

tion

* Near the site of the scaffolding erected on Caverton Edge, for viewing the annual horse races, and at a gravel pit on the road between Caverton and Kelso, there was found a copper vessel, of about 6 inches diameter, enclosing an excavated wooden ball; and in both these last mentioned places, similar parcels of black dust and fragments of bones were found. In digging for stones in Wooden Hill, in the estate of the Duke of Buccleugh, to form an inclosure for a plantation of firs, two or three vessels of earthen substance, of about a foot deep, were got, containing similar dust, and fragments, supposed to be of children by their size; and about 4 years ago, in the field called the *Dales,* near the village of Eckford, a stone coffin, (or square stones erected, and covered with another large one) was seen, containing bones of a large size.

† From a passage in the Border History, § it appears, that the Earl of Sussex, anno 1570, with an English army, burnt and razed this tower, belonging to the
Laird

§ *Redpath's History, page* 635.

tion in a marsh: these walls are since pulled down. There was a chapel in former times towards the east of the village of Caverton, but no vestige remains. A small church-yard is still occupied in sepulture by some families in the parish, (and probably by some others), whose ancestors had privilege there; and a spring in the adjacent field, north of the church-yard, bears the designation of the *Holy Well*, or *Priest's Well*. A-bout a quarter of a mile south from the family house of the late Mr. Hall of Haugh-head, situated on the banks of the Kail, there is an eminence, seemingly artificial, called *Haugh-head Kipp* (the adjacent fields being level), of a circular form. It had formerly been planted round with firs, some few of which are still remaining: Upon the top of it a plain flat stone

---

Laird of Buccleugh, and still part of his Grace's estate in this district. It is reported to have been occupied by *Hepburn* Lord *Bothwell*; but no inscription or monumental information can be traced to confirm this tradition. The incumbent has seen a medal of the Empress *Faustina*, that was taken from the heart of a peat found at Moss Tower. It was about the size of a half crown; the letters and inscription were very distinct. In Wester Moss of Eckford, nuts, roots, and pieces of large oak, and other trees, have been dug up; also some horns of the red deer, very large, and the skull of a bison.—Since writing the above, the incumbent visited and inspected a place, vulgarly called the *Black Dike*, which, by its elevation above the contiguous plowed field, cannot fail of attracting observation. It is on a rising ground, about half a mile from Kail water, and to the east thereof. This tumulus measured 27 feet over; at its western extremity, where it appeared to have been dug for a small space, from side to side 33 feet. Its whole length is 342 feet; and at the eastern extremity it is 42 feet over. It lies in a direct line E. and W. The materials of which it is composed, so far as can be observed, are fine loose mould, intermixed with large stones, covered over with heath, although there is none in its immediate vicinity. This tumulus, or barrow, is reported to have been a place of sepulture in troublesome times; but no human bones have as yet been dug up. In the year 1349, during the reign of *Edward* the III. of England, and *David Bruce* of Scotland when the Scotch invaded the English borders, 5000 of their army dropt down dead of the plague, having caught the infection, which at that time raged through the realm of England; but whether their bodies were there interred is uncertain.

ſtone of an ell ſquare, bears an inſcription, commemorative of ſome rencounter the proprietor had, with thoſe who had taken violent poſſeſſion of his eſtate, and were plowing his fields. The inſcription, ſo far as could be taken down on the ſpot, is as follows, viz.

> Here Holy Hall boldly maintain'd his right,
> 'Gainſt Reef * plain force armed with lawles might;
> For Tuenty Pleughs harnes'd in all their Gear,
> Could not his valient nobl Heart make Fear,
> But with his ſword he cut the formoſt Soam,
> In two, Hence drove both Pleughs and
> Pleugh-Men home.   1620.

This perhaps may allude to what happened in the reign of James I. of England, when uniformity of religion was projected for both kingdoms, and, the Common Prayer Book being intended to be introduced into Scotland, occaſioned no ſmall diſturbance for a conſiderable time.

Character.—The people are in general economical, ſober, induſtrious, and contented with their ſituations in life; maintain ſociety amongſt themſelves, and with their neighbours; are hoſpitable to ſtrangers who accidentally come amongſt them; and are endowed with a liberal ſpirit to relieve the diſtreſſes, and alleviate the miſeries of their fellow creatures upon every emergency, according to their abilities. The only means of meliorating their condition, is by a prudent and perſevering attention to what they can perform; and, if the projected canal, from Berwick up the river Tweed, and part of Tiviot, take place, coals and lime, with foreign commodities, will be obtained at an eaſier rate, and the produce of this country exported conveniently; which would be a fortunate circumſtance, not only to this diſtrict, but to the whole county.

Miſcellanious

* *This word is much defaced.*

Miscellaneous Observations.—At the diſtance of a few yards from Ceſsford Caſtle, and to the N. W. of the veſtige of the Moat, there ſtands a venerable aſh tree, called the *Crow Tree,* expanding its branches, and covering a conſiderable ſurface with its ſhade, which, though very old, ſeems as yet in a healthy ſtate. It meaſures at the baſe 27 feet 8 inches round the girth; at 6 feet upwards, 15 feet; and at the clift where the branches (which are thick and ſtrong) diverge and ſpread, 14 feet 6 inches; ſo that its diameter, at an average, to the clift, is 5 feet, and is ſuppoſed to contain 300 feet of wood. This tree is of great antiquity, and has been often viſited and admired by the curious.—There are 3 corn mills in the diſtrict, two of them on the Kail, the other on the Tiviot; one of theſe was lately rebuilt, and the machinery properly adapted for grinding oats, barley and wheat, and for making pot barley. —There is a ſaw mill at Marlefield, on the Kail Water, where the plantation of firs, fit for dales, paling and other purpoſes, are prepared, and meet with ready ſale. There is alſo a fulling mill on the ſame river.—In June laſt, a neſt of thoſe carnivorous birds, uſually called *hooded crows*, was diſcovered by a ſhepherd on the banks of Kail. There were two young ones in it; one of which was entirely *white.* By ſome inattention it died; and its remains (lately in the incumbent's poſſeſſion), were tranſmitted to a certain virtuoſo in Edinburgh, for preſervation in his muſæum, where it may be ſeen. There are two quarries of good free ſtone, one of them at preſent not occupied; and a ſort of grey ſlate taken from the bed of Kail, now diſuſed, being apt to ſlice, and at any rate found too heavy for roofing.

PARISH OF EDENHAM, OR EDNAM.

(County of Roxburgh—Presbytery of Kelso—Synod of Merse and Tiviotdale.)

By the Rev. Mr. DAVID DICKSON, *Minister.*

Name, Situation, and Rivers.

THIS parish derives its name from a compound of *Eden* and *Ham;* being situated on the banks of the river *Eden,* and *Ham* signifying a village. The village, where the church stands, is built on the N. bank of the river Eden, which runs for more than 3 miles through this district, and joins the Tweed at Edenmouth. The parish is placed in one of the most delightful situations in Scotland, on the banks of the river Tweed. This beautiful river, after being joined by the Tiviot at Kelso, bounds the parish of Edenham, about a mile below it, on the S. and S. E. The parish is not quite a mile and a half distant from the English border, at the burn of Carham, on the opposite side of the Tweed, formerly well known by the name of the *March Burn.*

Extent

Extent and Climate.—In extent, it is about 3 miles broad, and rather somewhat more in length. The climate of Edenham, from its situation on the two rivers, is undoubtedly salubrious; yet, since the present incumbent was settled, it has been visited by different epidemical fevers, that sometimes proved mortal.

Cultivation, Surface, Hills, Soil, &c.—Agriculture is carried on to a great extent in this parish. The industry and activity of the farmers cannot be exceeded, and they are all opulent and prosperous. The surface of the grounds consists of some beautiful flats in many places, especially on the sides of the rivers Tweed and Eden. The parish contains also several fields, lying on inclined plains. There are two rising grounds, one on the N. side of the Eden, near the village, called *Edenham Hill*, and another between the Tweed and the Eden, called *Henderside Hill*. The height of neither is great, though not ascertained; but they are both highly cultivated. The soil is of various kinds: Some part of it strong clay, some of it light sand and channel, and some of it a mixture of both. In a few places there is a thin bed of moss, covering rich stores of marl. The marl has been dug for manure, at considerable expence, and it has been attended with great success. Burned lime-stone is brought in great quantities from Northumberland, at the distance of 17 or 18 miles.

Produce and Farm Rents.—The ground produces wheat, barley, pease and beans, and oats, all of the best quality, which can scarcely be exceeded in any part of Scotland. It produces also turnips, and broad clover, in abundance; and the pasture land is of the richest kind. Land rent is consequently high in price: 3l. an acre has been given here both for

arable

arable and pasture land, and inferior prices according to the quality.

Cattle and Fuel.—The farmers consider the land as too good for breeding cattle or sheep, and therefore few are reared in the parish : The sheep and cattle are mostly all bought in, and fed for the butcher to great value. Fuel is very expensive, as there are no coals, but what are brought from Northumberland, at the distance of 16 or 18 miles.

Population.—The number of inhabitants has increased considerably within these 40 years.

The present number of souls is about - - -	600
The return to Dr. Webster, in 1755, was only - -	387
Increase, - -	213

The number of births, burials, and marriages is not easily ascertained. Seceders, though obliged by law to register the births of their children in the parish register, consider the tax on baptisms as a *profanation*, and often neglect it on that account; though afterwards it may be prejudicial to their children. And marriages are often made so irregularly, by persons not legally qualified, that those, who belong to the Secession, do not willingly submit to the discipline of the Church.

Improvements and Manufactures, &c.—The population of this parish has not, however, increased in proportion to what it once promised. When the late JAMES DICKSON, Esq. M. P. became proprietor of Edenham, being a person of public spirit, he inclosed all his lands, planned and built a neat village, the houses being all of brick, covered with *pantile*, or slates;——brought manufacturers from England, and established

blifhed woollen manufactures for cloth, particularly for Eng-lifh blankets. He alfo erected a waulk mill, to promote this ufeful undertaking ; but his death marred the progrefs of thofe public fpirited fchemes. He built alfo an extenfive brewery, which is ftill carried on with great fuccefs ; and great quantities of the ale and porter, brewed in it, are export-ed to England. We have likewife a corn mill and a good bleachfield in the parifh.

Roads.—The roads are very bad. They are repaired by a con-verfion of the ftatute labour. Laft winter, however, (1792-3), an act of parliament was obtained for making feveral roads near Kelfo, and eftablifhing toll-bars. By this act, three new roads will be made through this parifh, which will be of great fervice in this part of the country, where they have been much wanted for thefe many years paft.

Church.—The church is very fmall, was built about 34 years ago, and is very infufficient. There are fome Quakers and Epifcopals, but no Roman Catholics. The number of Seceders is not eafily afcertained, as all the denominations of them have houfes of worfhip in Kelfo, and Edenham lies fo near it, that many of the inhabitants attend thefe meetings ; but all the principal farmers attend the Eftablifhed Church. The King is undoubted patron.

Heritors and Poor.—The number of heritors are four. As none of them refide in the parifh, the collections at the church doors are but trifling ; in confequence of which the poor are obliged to be maintained by affeffments, regularly laid on for their fupport.

Eminent,

Eminent Men.—Mr. JAMES THOMSON, the celebrated author of *the Seasons*, &c. was the son of the reverend Mr. Thomas Thomson, the second minister of this parish after the Revolution, and was born at Edenham in the year 1700. It is unnecessary here to enlarge upon the merits of an author so well known, and whose genius and abilities do so much honour to his native country. A proposal was made, some years ago, to erect a monument to his memory, on Edenham Hill, within view of the manse; but the plan has not yet been accomplished. Several noblemen and gentlemen, however, with a laudable zeal for the literary fame of their country, have met annually at Edenham, for some years past, to celebrate Thomson's birth day, as well as with a view to forward the execution of that design.

Antiquities.—There is a small rising ground, W. from the village, called the *Picts Know*; out of which, some years ago, were dug three stone coffins, with an urn in one of them. The Know is since inclosed, and planted with trees*.

---

* A farm in this parish is named *Comb-flat*, which seems to be so called from its containing extensive earthen mounds, called *Comb-knows*. As, before the union of the kingdoms, this was the warlike part of the country, these tumuli seem to have been raised by art, as means of defence.

PARISH OF HAWICK.

(County of Roxburgh—Presbytery of Jedburgh—Synod of Merse and Teviotdale.)

By the Rev. Mr. ROBERT GILLAN.

Name, Extent, and Appearance.

ETYMOLOGY of names is generally matter of conjecture. Hawick may be derived from the Celtic, *ha*, a mansion, and *wic*, the crook or conflux of rivers ; or from the Saxon, *haf*, the same with our *halved*, and *wick*, a common termination for a village, supposed to be formed from the Latin *vica*. To either of these derivations its situation agrees ; as the river Teviot washes the side of it towards the north, and the smaller river, *Slitridge*, divides it nearly into two equal parts.—The parish is of considerable extent, being about 15 miles long from W. to E. and 4¼ broad. The general appearance is hilly : None of the hills, however, are of any remarkable size ; they are mostly green, and afford excellent pasture for sheep.

Soil

Soil, Manure, and Rent.—The ſoils of the pariſh are vari‑
ous. The haughs, or vallies, are compounded of loam, gravel
and ſand, in different proportions. On riſing grounds between
the vallies and hills, there is loam, with here and there a
mixture of gravel. On the hills, the ſoil varies accord‑
ing to ſituation, being in ſome places light and dry; in
others ſoft and ſpungy; and in others wet and ſtiff. In ſome
farms, there are moſs and heath, though in ſmall quantities.
The ſoil of the vallies, and of the riſing grounds contiguous
to them, though not deep, is far from being unfertile; for,
under proper culture, it produces plentiful crops of oats, bar‑
ley, turnips, potatoes, clover, and rye‑graſs: and, when laid
into graſs, in proper condition, affords excellent paſture for
ſmall cattle and ſheep. The ſoil of the hills is perfectly a‑
dapted to the breeding of ſheep.—The quantity of arable land
is inconſiderable, compared with that which is ſuitable for
paſture only.—The manure chiefly uſed is dung, collected in
the town, and at the different farms. There is alſo marle in
different parts of the pariſh, which is uſed ſuccefsfuly on land
in paſture, as well as in tillage. Its effects have not been tried,
upon land appropriated to the breeding of ſheep; ſome ima‑
gining there would, and others there would not, be danger
in uſing it upon land light and dry.—The valued rent of the
pariſh is 11,591l. 11s. Scotch; the real rent about 2800l.
Sterling.

Trees and Sheep.—This pariſh does not produce any veget‑
able or trees, but ſuch as are to be found in other parts of
Scotland. Upon the banks of rivers and rivulets, and upon
the ſides of hills, the hazel, birch, hawthorn and grey willow,
ſpring ſpontaneouſly, when defended from the ſheep; a proof
that, at a former period, the country has been more covered
with wood than at preſent. Neither does the pariſh produce
any

any animals that are uncommon. The animal of the greateſt value, and chiefly attended to, is the ſheep : By far the greateſt part of the pariſh is occupied in breeding them. The number may be about 8000. They are of the long white faced kind, which bears the ſhort clothing wool, ſomewhat inferior in ſize, as well as in fineneſs of wool, to the ſheep of the Cheviot Hills. Having been thought defective in ſhape, from the lightneſs of the fore quarter, about 20 years ago an attempt was made to improve it, by means of rams of a breed highly eſteemed in England. The experiment was repeated, until it was found, that the quality of the wool was thereby deteriorated. Judicious farmers now ſtudy to improve the ſhape of the breed, by ſelecting the beſt lambs of both ſexes for breeding, without introducing a foreign mixture ; and to enlarge the ſize and render the wool finer, by increaſing the ſhelter upon their farms, by affording their flocks plenty of food, and by rendering their paſture ſweeter and better. For this laſt purpoſe, keeping a leſs ſtock, and draining of boggy or marſhy land, are reckoned of great ſervice, and attended to by good managers. Turnips and broad clover have not been given to ſheep, in this pariſh, except for fattening them ; although this practice prevails much in other parts of the county of Roxburgh. But rye-graſs is eſteemed a good ſpring food, where the ſituation of a farm admits of its being raiſed in abundance. In ſmearing, a much greater proportion of butter is uſed than formerly ; but the total diſuſe of tar has never had a good effect.

Cultivation, Climate, Produce, &c.—The time of ſowing oats is from the beginning of March to the end of April ; that of ſowing barley, from the beginning of April to the end of May. The practice of ſowing barley by the middle of April, upon land that has been thoroughly prepared the preceeding ſummer,

summer, by fallow or a green crop, begins to gain ground. It is thought, that barley sown thus early, is not so liable to suffer from drought, as when sown in the middle or end of May ; that the crop is sooner ready, and the grain larger and better ripened. In favourable seasons, September is the harvest month. But if the weather is bad, harvest is not over till the middle or end of October. This is not altogether to be attributed to climate ; but in some measure to a practice that still prevails, of sowing great quantities of oats upon high lands, which nature seems to have intended for pasture only. There is a considerable variety of climate in the parish. In the town of Hawick, and its immediate neighbourhood, the weather is often mild, when it is cold and sharp a few miles distant. In the winter season, snow, on the high parts of the parish, is often deep, while near the town there is none. The provisions produced in the parish, are more than sufficient for the supply of the country part of it, but not equal to the consumption of the town of Hawick. On this account, there is a constant importation from the neighbouring parishes of meal, barley for malt, butcher meat, butter, cheese, poultry, &c —

The

* The wages generally given to servants are,

To a plowman and other servants employed in husbandry, with bed, board, &c. per annum, - - -	L. 7	6	0
To ditto, without bed and board, - - - -	13	0	0
To a shepherd, on a farm where the master resides, - -	14	0	0
To ditto, upon a let farm, - - - -	18	0	0
To a maid, for milking ewes from Whitsunday to Lammas, -	1	1	0
To a man, hired through the whole corn harvest, with victuals, -	1	5	0
To a woman, ditto, - - - - -	0	13	0
To a maid servant, for taking care of cows in the house, per annum,	3	3	0
To a domestic maid servant, ditto, - - -	3	3	0
To a labourer, from Martinmas till Candlemas, per day, -	0	0	10
———— through the remainder of the year, ditto, - -	0	1	0
———— in hay and corn harvests, - ditto, - -	0	1	2

To

The number of ploughs in the country part of the parish, is about 30 at present, though they have not all full employment. The Scotch plough is mostly in use; but some farmers use it with the English mould board. The number of carts is about 60, of which 50 may belong to farmers and carters, residing mostly in the town.

Winnowing Machine.—The winnowing machine, or corn fanner, from the best information, made its first appearance in Hawick. Accounts, well authenticated, state, that *Andrew Rodger*, a farmer on the estate of Cavers, having a mechanical turn, retired from his farm and gave his genius its bent; and, probably, from a description of a machine of that kind, used in Holland, in the year 1737, constructed the first machine fan employed in this kingdom. In the year 1740, he sent many of them into the northern parts of Northumberland. The principal farmers there, in the course of that year, purchased and used them; and Mr. John Greigstone alone, then farmer at Wark, got 6 for his own use. The descendants of Andrew Rodger, residing in Hawick, at present supply the whole country around, and continue to send many of them into Northumberland. They sell them from 2 to 3 guineas, and make and dispose of about 60 every year*.

The

To women for reaping,	- - -	per day,	-	L. 0	1	0
—————— for hay making,	- -	ditto,	- -	0	0	7
To masons and carpenters in winter,	-	ditto,	- -	0	1	3
—————————— in summer,	-	ditto,	- -	0	1	6

* Mr. Marshall, in his Rural Economy of Yorkshire, vol. I. page 283, says, about the year 1755, " my father made a *machine fan*, from a model shewn " him, with some improvements. This was the first, that was made in the dis- " trict, and perhaps the first that was made in England." From the above account, it appears, that, long before the period mentioned by Mr. Marshall, they were in use in the northern parts of Northumberland. The facts can be attested by ANTHONY GREIGSTONE, Esq. of Lowlin, in the county of Durham.

The Town.—Hawick is a burgh of barony, independent of
the lord of erection; and has existed free from a very early
period. But the rights and documents of the burgh being
lost and destroyed, during the inroads of the English plunderers, a charter was granted, in the year 1545, by James Douglas of Drumlanark*, confirming to them such rights and lands
as they formerly held. This charter is confirmed by another,
granted by Queen Mary in May 1545.—In consequence of these
charters, the burgesses elect their own magistrates annually.
There is a standing council; in conjunction with which, the
magistrates manage the town's affairs. The whole consists of
31; viz. 2 bailies, 15 of a standing council, who continue
for life, if not legally disqualified, and 2 called quarter masters, from each of the incorporations. The incorporations are 7,
viz. weavers, tailors, hammermen, skinners, fleshers, shoemakers,
and baxters. A treasurer and surveyor of weights, measures
and markets, are annually chosen by the council. The clerk
is elected by the burgesses at large, and generally continues in
office during life. The magistrates receive resignations and
grant infeftments in the town. The sasines are recorded in
the general or particular register for sasines, as they have not,
like royal burghs, a record for the town's sasines. They ex-
pede services, cognosce heirs, and pronounce decreets in civil
causes, to any extent on which hornings and captions pass.
Hawick possesses all the privileges of a royal burgh, except
that of sending a representative to Parliament, for which it
need

---

* In this charter, one article may be noticed. One James Blair was taxed
with " one penny of the kingdom of Scotland, upon the ground of his half *par-
ticate*, for finding and furnishing one lamp, or pot, of burning oil, before the
altar of the parish church of Hawick, in time of high Mass and vesper prayers,
all holy days of the year, in honour of our Saviour Jesus Christ, and praying
for the souls of the barons of Hawick, the founders of the lamp, and their
successors."

need not repine; as it is thereby freed from many temptations to idleneſs and diſſipation, to which the inhabitants of royal burghs, by their politics, are often ſubjected.

Revenue, Market, &c.—The common, belonging to the town, was formerly very extenſive; but ſome of the ſurrounding heritors, claiming a preſcriptive right of paſturage, 6 parts of 20 were allotted to them. The town's ſhare now amounts to about 850 acres, beſides ſome places in its immediate neighbourhood, which fell not under the diviſion. Previous to this diviſion, the cattle belonging to the burgeſſes paſtured over the whole common; and this town had no revenue, except what aroſe from the dues, or entry-money of burgeſſes, which was inconſiderable. Since the diviſion, the whole common is incloſed, and about 250 acres let in one farm, beſides other detached pieces, with ſeveral areas feued for building. The revenue, ariſing from theſe, and what is exacted for paſturing the burgeſſes cattle, now amount to 130l; and ſtill common ſufficient remains to paſture theſe cattle. No part of the town's revenue is ſpent in eating and drinking, except a trifle at the King's birth-day, and the election of the magiſtrates. The magiſtrates and council lately erected a neat council houſe, brought water into the town in leaden pipes, and paved the ſtreets anew. The Duke of Buccleugh, who draws the cuſtoms of the town, contributed 50l. towards building the council houſe, and paid half of the expence of paving the ſtreets. There is a weekly market and 4 fairs, beſides a tryſt, eſtabliſhed, within theſe few years, for black cattle, &c. in October, between Falkirk tryſt and Newcaſtle fair, which promiſes to ſucceed.

Manufactures.—Notwithſtanding the diſadvantages of diſtance from fuel, and an extenſive land carriage, manufactures

are

are carried on here with confiderable fpirit and fuccefs. Several
branches are now eftablifhed ; but the moft confiderable are
carpets, inkle, cloth, and ftockings. The *carpet manufacture*
was eftablifhed in the year 1752, and has, fince that time, been
under the management of Mr. WILLIAM ROBERTSON, now a
partner. For fome years, it was aided, by a bounty of 1s. per
ftone on all the wool manufactured, from the board of Truftees for improvements in Scotland. The prefent proprietors,
fince the year 1780, befides Scotch carpets, have manufactured
feveral other articles in the woollen line ; fuch as ferges for
carpet covers, plain cloths for table covers, ruggs, collar checks,
with other articles ufed by fadlers. The quantity of wool
manufactured laft year, was about 220 packs* of laid and white
wools. Women are employed to fpin thefe in their own
houfes, receiving from the ftorehoufe one ftone at a time. The
number of people, employed in the different branches of this
manufacture, laft year, feems to have been 362.—The *inkle
manufacture* was begun in the year 1783. The only branch
yet attempted is common linen tapes and twifts. In thefe
two articles, there are annually confumed 10 tons of linen
yarn ; of which one half is fpun at home, and, when the
price of flax is moderate, the whole of it. The number of
people employed in fpinning the flax cannot be afcertained, a
confiderable quantity being fent to diftant villages, at a time,
to a perfon appointed to give it out in fmall quantities. The
other people employed may amount to 65. This manufacture,
which is yet in its infancy, was likewife aided for a few years,
by the Board of Truftees for Improvements and Manufactures
in Scotland.—The ftocking manufacture was eftablifhed by
Mr. JOHN NIXON, in the year 1780. For 4 years he was
employed chiefly in making hofe, for people who furnifhed
their

* A pack is 12 ftones ; 24lb. of white, and 25¼lb. of laid wool, to the ftone,

their own materials, called *custom work*. Since 1785, he has manufactured, on his own account, different articles in the hosiery line, to a considerable extent. From his books, he appears to have manufactured the following quantity of hose:

Coloured and white lamb's wool hose, - -	3505 pairs.
Cotton, thread, and worsted hose, - - -	594 do.
	4099

The number of people employed, are,

Frame work knitters, - - - -	13 men.
Spinners, - - - - - - -	42 women.
Seamers, doublers, and twiners, - - -	9
A foreman, - - - - - - -	1
	65

The wool is given out to women, in small quantities, who spin it in their own houses*.—The *cloth manufacture* was begun in September 1787. The first year, this manufacture consumed only 10 packs of wool; last year, upwards of 40 were manufactured. The cloth, which is narrow, is sold from 2s. to 5s. per yard, to merchants in different sea port towns in the north of Scotland. The number of persons employed, is,

Weavers, - - - - - - -	5
Spinners, occasionally employed, - - -	12
Dyers, - - - - - - - -	4
Carders, - - - - - - -	6
Persons employed in machinery in the shop, - - -	4
	31

Nursery

* The manufacture of stockings was originally begun by Bailie John Hardie, in the year 1771. He employed 4 looms; which, at an average, produced annually about 2,400 pairs, mostly of the coarser kind. He seems to have been the first, that introduced this business into this country; and, by persons taught in his shop, it has been planted in Wooler, Kelso, Jedburgh, Langholm, Melrose, and Selkirk. From family distress he abandoned it, after carrying it on for 10 years, when it was taken up by Mr. Nixon.

Nurſery and Commerce.—In this pariſh there is a conſiderable nurſery carried on by the Meſſrs. Dickſons. This nurſery was firſt eſtabliſhed at Haſſendean Burn, in a neighbouring pariſh, in the year 1729. The ground there, fit for the purpoſe, being all occupied, in 1766 they feued land in Hawick, amounting to 36 acres, to extend their buſineſs. Theſe two nurſeries contain all kinds of fruit and foreſt trees, flower plants, and roots, and flowering ſhrubs, that are naturalized to this country; beſides a great collection of exotic plants. The demand for theſe articles of nurſery is conſiderable; for, beſides ſupplying all the adjoining country, and ſeveral other parts of Scotland, they are ſent to many places of Northumberland, Cumberland, Weſtmoreland, North Wales, Lancaſhire, Cheſhire, Yorkſhire, &c. At ſome ſeaſons, there are 50 people employed in the nurſery grounds; but, at an average, 30 are employed the whole ſeaſon.—Some people here make it their employment, to buy up eggs in the neighbouring counties, and carry them to Berwick, taking ſome weeks to the amount of 150l., and, at an average, of 50l. per week through the year. Others are entirely occupied in collecting ſheep ſkins, both white and tarred, in Dumfries-ſhire, Tweeddale and Selkirkſhire. Part of them are manufactured in Hawick, and the reſt ſold in quantities to the ſkinners in Kelſo and Galaſhiels. The perſons, who collect the ſkins, through the ſheep countries, likewiſe buy up coarſe linen yarn; which, together with what is made in Hawick and its neighbourhood, (not uſed in our manufactures), is ſent to Kendal, Glaſgow, Stirling, Leith and Aberdeen. One perſon gets about 200 packs of wool ſpun into yarn, which he ſells at theſe markets.

Church and Poor.—The Duke of Buccleugh is patron of the pariſh. The living conſiſts of 91l. 13s. 4¼d., 16 bolls meal, 20 bolls barley, the vicarage tythes of a ſmall part of
the

the parish, a manse and garden, and a glebe of 15 English acres. Besides the Established Church, there are two meeting-houses; a Burgher and an Antiburgher. The distance of many places, in this and the adjacent parish of Cavers, from the parish churches, induced the inhabitants there to erect a chapel of ease. In this place, under the direction of the ministers of Hawick and Cavers, a chaplain performs divine service; partly paid by the Duke of Buccleugh, and partly by the ministers and the people; but the assistant not being in orders, little burden is thereby taken from the ministers. he number of poor, at present receiving weekly assistance, is 110: for their support, the heritors &c. assess themselves to the amount of 370l. per annum*.

Population.——The number of souls in this parish, from an accurate survey, are,

In the town of Hawick,	2320	Married persons, - -		970
In the country, - -	608	Persons under 10 years, -		600
Males, - 1378 }		——— between 10 and 20 -		618
Females, - 1550 } - 2928		——— ——— 20 and 50, -		1214
The population, in 1755, was, {2713		——— ——— 50 and 70, -		423
———		——— ——— 70 and 100, -		73
Increase, - 215				———
———		Total, - 2928		

There is no exact register kept of marriages, baptisms, or burials.

Inundation.

* Besides this provision for the poor, a number have associated, under the title of *The Friendly Society*, to support themselves in the time of sickness, or under the infirmities of old age. The members pay a trifle at their admission, and 4s. annually; and for this, when reduced by sickness or age, they receive 3s. per week; at the death of a member, his wife receives 1l. 10s., and a member, at the death of his wife, 1l., to defray the funeral expences. Besides those who are the immediate objects of this association, the society consists of many of the respectable inhabitants of the town and neighbourhood.

Inundation.—The town of Hawick, though not subject to inundations, has every reason to be afraid of them. It stands at the conflux of the rivers Slitridge and Teviot, which, after great rains, or the dissolving of the snows on the adjacent hills, rise several feet upon the houses immediately situated on their banks. A remarkable one happened in August 1767. Slitridge then rose to an astonishing height, occasioned by a cloud bursting at its source. It began to rise at 4 o'clock in the afternoon, and continued to increase till past 6, when it was 22 feet above its usual level. It marked its progress with destruction. Part of the surface of the hill, where the cloud fell, floated into the river. Corn and cattle, with every thing on its banks, were born away by the torrent. In Hawick, its devastations were great ; 15 dwelling-houses, and a corn mill, were carried off, and the rock swept so clean, that not a bit of rubbish was left to tell where they stood. At the height of the flood, a maid servant, belonging to a merchant, recollecting that in the house, now surrounded with water, her master had 300l. in gold, boldly ventured in, and got hold of the bag with the money : In returning, however, she was carried down by the stream, but was cast ashore on a green below the town, herself and the money both safe. In this alarming event two lives were lost ; both indeed through rashness and inattention.

Eminent Men.—Hawick, as far as the present incumbent can learn, has given birth to few men of considerable eminence in literature, in the field, or in rank. Some, however, who have resided in it, have shone in their particular stations. Amongst these, we must first rank GAVIN DOUGLAS*, Bishop of

* GAVIN DOUGLAS, on his first entering the church, was installed rector of Hawick, in the year 1496. Afterwards, he was appointed provost of the collegiate

of Dunkeld, author of several poems, and the admired transſ-
lator of Virgil's Æneid. Here too ſhould be mentioned, Mr,
ALEXANDER ORROCK, the firſt miniſter of Hawick after the
Revolution. He appears to have been a man rigid in diſcip-
line, and of extenſive charity. As a proof of the former,
there is told an extraordinary inſtance. The magiſtrates, having offended againſt decency and propriety, were cited before
him, and were not allowed to act in office, nor releaſed
from the thunders of the church, until they had, on their
uncovered knees, aſked pardon of God and the kirk-ſeſſion.
This is a degree of eccleſiaſtical ſeverity now happily unknown. Eminent proofs of his charity, however, ſtill remain. He bequeathed, for the poor of Hawick, 116 merks
Scotch ; and for the ſchoolmaſter 9,000 merks : He gave ſeveral
pieces of plate for the uſe of the church ; and to the miniſter
he gave his whole library, which remains a monument of ancient theological literature.

Antiquities.—There are remains of camps in this pariſh ;
but at what period they were formed, or by whom, the preſent incumbent has never been able to diſcover. There is a
place called *Catrail**, by ſome conſidered the remains of a
Roman

legiate church of St. Giles, in Edinburgh, abbot of the convent of Aberbrothick,
and biſhop of Dunkeld. He was nominated to the archbiſhopric of St. Andrews,
but his appointment never took effect. To avoid the perſecutions raiſed againſt
his family, in the year 1513, he retired into England, and put himſelf under the
protection of Henry VIII., who kindly received him, and granted him a pen-
ſion. He died of the plague in London, and was buried in the Savoy church,
in the year 1521.

* Whitaker, in his Hiſtory of Mancheſter, ſuppoſes the Catrail to have been a
barricade thrown up by the ancient Britons. He ſays, " it runs in a N. E. di-
" rection from Carnaby on the Eſk, to Gallow Water, beyond Selkirk, lined all
" the way on the W. with forts ; and even continues itſelf, by an additional chain
" of

Roman rampart ; by others, the vestiges of a fortification by
the Saxons, or the ancient Britons. A little above the town,
towards the west, is an earthen mound, of a conical figure, called the *Mote*. Some suppose this a *tumulus* ; others, a place
raised for the principal inhabitants of the town to meet, for
the distribution of justice. This last, its name and tradition
confirm. At an early period, this was common throughout
Scotland. When the chiefs and the leading people in a district met, to promulgate laws for the government of their dependants, it was generally on a hill of some eminence ; and
many places still retain the appellation, as *North Berwick
Law*, in East Lothian ; *Largo Law*, in Fifeshire ; and *Ruber's
Law*, in this neighbourhood.

Character of the People.—Although individuals in this parish, as in other places of the same extent, are given to the
vices usual in these times, yet the inhabitants, in general, are
honest, sober, and industrious. Their industry is not the violent exertion of a moment ; but steady, calm, and persevering :
And were it not for many disadvantages and difficulties, they
have to encounter, the spirit of the inhabitants of Hawick
would raise it to the first station of manufacture, in the south
of Scotland.

" of castles, along the Gallow, to the north. It was plainly designed as a barrier
" against any enemy, that lay to the S. and E. of it." Its remains in the parish of
Cavers, and on the Gallow, are still conspicuous ; but little of it is observable
in this parish.

PARISH OF HOBKIRK.

(*County of Roxburgh.*)

By the Rev. Mr JOHN RICCALTON.

***

Name, Situation, &c.

THE ancient name was *Hobſkirk*, and the modern name is *Hobkirk*. Tradition ſays that it was built by a man of the name of *Hob*, and had taken its name from the founder. The pariſh is ſituated in the county of Roxburgh, preſbytery of Jedburgh, and ſynod of Merſe and Teviotdale. It is of an oblong form, about 12 miles in length, and about three where broadeſt. The general appearance of the country is mountainous.

Soil.—The ſoil is very different both in its nature and quality. All along the ſide of the water of Rule, it is a very fertile, deep, ſtrong clay, ſome parts of it mixed with ſmall channel, and other parts with ſand. At a diſtance from the water, it is a light ſandy ſoil, lying upon the face of a cold till, and moſt of it very barren.

Mountains, &c.—The moſt remarkable mountains are Winbrough, and Fanna. Winbrough, from its baſe to the ſummit, is an aſcent of a mile and a half, and Fanna is nearly the ſame. Windbrough is ſo high, that, from its

ſummit,

summit, you have a view of both east and west seas, though both are at the distance of 40 miles. The parish abounds with free stone. Beyond Winbrough there are very good lime stone quarries, and three lime kilns; two of them upon the lands of Sir Francis Elliot of Stobs, and another upon the lands of Mr Elliot of Harrot. A little below the last mentioned lime kiln, there is a place called *Robert's Linn*, where there are large rocks of pebbles, of which are made seals and buttons of different kinds. Most of the rock is of a light blue colour. There are other parts of it finely variegated with strokes of red and yellow; and so much are they esteemed, that great quantities are carried as far as Sheffield and Birmingham.

Population,—The parish at present contains about 700 souls. In Dr Webster's report, the number is 530. The number of males and females are nearly equal. At an average for these 20 years past, the number of births has been 20, and that of deaths about 14. The number of souls under 10 years of age is - 150

From 10 to 20	- -	150
From 20 to 50	- -	300
From 50 to 70	- -	80
From 70 to 100	- -	20

The number of farmers in the parish is 32, and that of their servants 127.

Cattle.—The parish at an average contains about 500 black cattle, 9000 sheep, and 156 horses.

Productions and Rent.—At an average there are 1000 acres in tillage. As it is an Highland place, the crop consists mostly of oats, barley, pease, turnips, and potatoes. There

are

are not perhaps above 20 acres fown with wheat. The land-rent of the parifh is L. 2830 Sterling.

Church.—The value of the living, including the glebe, is L. 115. The Crown is patron. The church was repaired in 1777. The manfe was built in 1770. There are eleven heritors in the parifh, only three of whom refide in it. There are about 30 Seceders, and one Epifcopalian.

Poor.—The number of poor receiving alms is 25. The annual amount of the contributions for their relief is L. 76 Sterling.

Eminent Men.—The immortal Elliot, Lord Heathfield, Governor of Gibraltar, who, with a fortitude, a vigilance, an incorruptible integrity, and a military fkill, fcarcely to be paralleled in hiftory, defended that fortrefs againft the unit-ed forces, naval and military, of the houfe of Bourbon, was born in this parifh.

Mifcellaneous Obfervations.—The air is rather moift, but not unhealthy. No deftructive epidemical diftempers prevail in it. The common fuel is peat, one horfe-load of which, when carried to market, is fold at 1 s.; when bought on the fpot, at 6 d. There are 46 ploughs in the parifh, moftly of the Englifh kind, though fome ftill ufe the old Scotch plough. The number of carts is 70. There are three fingle-horfe chaifes, and only one poft-chaife. There is a fpecies of Briftol ftone fometimes found in the bed of the water. The number of handicraftfmen is 27, with 6 apprentices. There is only one woollen manufacturer. None have been under the neceffity of leaving the parifh for want of employment; nor have any emigrated from it, farther than to the neigh-bouring

bouring towns or parishes. None have ever perished for want, nor have any been guilty of capital crimes, or even of those more petty offences which are punished by banishment. The people in general are of a strong robust make, and a good complexion. The greatest height of stature any of them attain, is 6 feet 2 inches. There are 147 houses in the parish, and, at an average, 5 souls in each family. The number of acres has never been exactly ascertained, but the parish is famous for the best breeding grounds, which produce sheep of an excellent quality, and distinguished for a fine staple of wool. The turnpike road from Edinburgh to Newcastle runs through this parish: It was made at the expence of the county, and is kept in repair by the tolls. The people in general are convinced of the utility of public roads. Provisions are rather high. The present price of beef is 4½ d. *per* pound. Early in the spring, veal is 5 d. and seldom under 3½ d. at any season of the year; mutton 4 d. and seldom under 3½ d.; even at the most plentiful season, good lamb is never under 1 s. 6 d. or 1 s. 8 d *per* quarter, and sometimes 2 s. Pork is commonly 4 s. or 4 s. 6 d. *per* stone; pigs of three weeks old, 3 s. and, at six weeks old, generally 7 s.; a goose never under 2 s.; a duck, 8 d.; chickens, from 3 d. to 8 d.; butter, 9 d. *per* pound; cheese, 5 d.; oats, 20 s. *per* boll; wheat, 1 l. 12 s.; barley, 1 l. 4 s.; pease, 1 l. 5 s. The prices of these commodities, thirty or forty years ago, were, best beef, 2 d. or 2½ d. *per* pound; best mutton, 1½ d. or 2 d.; lamb, 5 d. or 6 d. *per* quarter, &c. Butter, 4 d. or 5 d *per* pound; cheese, 2 s. 6 d. or 3 s. *per* stone; oats, 7 s. or 8 s. *per* boll, seldom above 10 s.; barley, 11 s. or 12 s.; wheat, 18 s. or 20 s.; pease 10 s. and seldom above 12 s. Labourers in husbandry are hired at 1 s. or 1 s. 2 d. *per* day; bricklayers, masons, carpenters, &c. 1 s. 6 d.; taylors, 8 d. including victuals.

N U M-

PARISH OF HOUNAM,

IN ROXBURGH-SHIRE.

Origin of the Name.

THE parish of Hounam does not furnish much room for statistical investigation, and the few observations which occur respecting it, may be comprehended within narrow bounds. The origin of its name cannot now be ascertained. There are many places in the neighbourhood, on the borders both of England and Scotland, ending in *am*. It is believed that *ham*, in the Saxon language, signifies a habitation or village. Perhaps it was originally pronounced Hounham, or the habitation of Houna, a name not unknown at the opposite extremity of the kingdom *.

Situation and Extent of the Parish.—The parish is situated in the county of Roxburgh, in the presbytery of Jedburgh, and in the synod of Merse and Tiviotdale. It is of a circular form, surrounded by the parishes of Morbattle, Jedburgh, and Oxnam in Scotland, and bordering on the opposite side with the county of Northumberland, where the top of the Fells, a range of the Cheviot hills, is the march. The parish, from east to west, is about nine or ten miles long; and in general is about six miles broad. It may be

---

* One of the ferries between Caithness and Orkney, is at a place called Houna.

be called a hilly or mountainous diftrict; but the hills are green, and rarely incumbered with rocks or covered with heath. The land is wet and fpungy; the foil light, and better calculated for grafs than grain. The air is healthy, and the people long lived. Three perfons who had refided in the parifh from their youth, died lately, at the advanced age of 100.

Sheep.—The principal circumftance for which this diftrict is remarkable, is the Kale-water breed of fheep, fo called from a fmall ftream running through the middle of the parifh. The fheep are of a moderate fize, and produce excellent wool. Their number ufually amounts to 12,000. Attempts have been made to improve the breed, by croffing with a larger kind, but the experiments did not fucceed. Though the fheep became larger, and the quantity of the wool was increafed, its quality was inferior. The moft approved ftock-farmers, however, have not the leaft doubt that the wool might be brought to ftill greater perfection by proper management, and by croffing with fheep nearly of the fame fize, but whofe wool is the fineft poffible. The fheep not only produce excellent wool, but, as the farmers term it, they *feed well,* come to a tolerable good fize when fat, and are exquifite mutton.

Productions.—The quantity of grain produced is very inconfiderable. Several of the farms in the higher part of the parifh have fcarcely been ploughed in the memory of man. The foil being light and fandy, excellent turnips might be raifed. Some have been produced in the parifh weighing above 26 lbs. avoirdupoife. But the farmers have not as yet fucceeded in raifing this ufeful root, though they are extremely fenfible of the great advantage that might be derived from

it,

it, particularly in the ſpring. The farmers are in general too late in ſowing them. Turnips cannot be raiſed to a great ſize in this part of the country, unleſs they are ſown about the end of May or the beginning of June ; but the farmers in the pariſh of Hounam are confiderably later.

Rent of the Pariſh.—The land-rent is L. 2720. It has riſen more than a third within theſe laſt fifteen years. The valued rent is L. 914 : 4 : 9. There are 8 heritors in the pariſh, 2 of whom are reſident. There are only 14 farms, which, at an average, are from L. 250 to L. 300 *per annum.* The number of ſheep on a farm is from 50 to 100 ſcore.

State of the Church, &c.—The walls of the church were repaired about 40 years ago; but the building is ſtill very bad, and worſe than any place of worſhip in the neighbourhood. The Duke of Roxburgh is the patron. The preſent incumbent is Mr James Rutherford, who was admitted in March 1775. He is married; has a ſon and five daughters. The manſe was built in 1776; but is placed too near the river, and confequently in a damp ſituation. The ſtipend, from the Revolution, amounted to L. 75 in money, and 21 bolls of victual. In confequence of a late proceſs of augmentation, the victual ſtipend is now fixed at 63 bolls. There is no parochial fund for the poor, excepting the weekly collections, and quarterly aſſeſſments laid on the land-holders and their tenants, which yield, at an average, about L. 30 *per annum.*

Population.—The population of the pariſh has of late confiderably diminiſhed. The return to Dr Webſter, about 40 years ago, was 632. The number of inhabitants is at preſent 365. Of theſe,

One

One hundred are below 10 years of age   -   100
Forty-nine are above 10 and under 20 years   -   49
Eighty are between 20 and 30 years - - - 80
One hundred between 30 and 50 years - - 100
Thirty-fix above 50 years - - - 36

Total number   365

The number of burials do not exceed 4 each year. The births are from 10 to 12, exclufive of the fectaries, who are indeed but few, and have a regifter of baptifms of their own. There is not even a village in the parifh; a few houfes near the church not deferving that name. The number of births, about a century ago, viz. from the year 1689 to the year 1707, feem, at an average, to have been 30 in the year. From the Union of the two kingdoms, to about the time of the laft rebellion, the average number of births feem to be 20 a year. From that time, the births have gradually decreafed to the prefent number of 10 or 12. The wages of men fervants are between L. 7 and L. 8; of women about L. 4. Fifteen or twenty years ago, the wages of men fervants were about L. 5, and of women fcarcely L. 3. The wages of the fhepherds, who conftitute one half of the parifh, confift of a certain number of cows and fheep to grafe on the farm to which they belong. The people enjoy a confiderable degree of the comforts of life. They are chearful and contented; and there are but few poor.

The great decreafe of inhabitants, within the laft 40 years, is evidently occafioned by the too general practice of letting the lands in great farms; but may be, in fome meafure, owing to the mode of agriculture almoft univerfally adopted in the parifh, (efpecially fince fheep and wool brought fo high

a

a price), of converting the arable into paſture land. The lands, 50 or 100 years ago, were parcelled out into at leaſt four times the preſent number of farms. As late as the year 1750, five tenants, with large families, occupied a farm now rented by one tenant. There were alſo, about theſe times, ſeveral ſmall, but proud, lairds in the pariſh. Their lands are now loſt in the large farms, their names extinguiſhed, and their manſions totally deſtroyed.

Antiquities.—A Roman road, or *ſtreet* as it is commonly called, which can be traced to the ſouth as far as Borough-bridge in Yorkſhire, runs through part of this pariſh; it after-wards paſſes by St Boſwell's Green, where the fair is held, and then bends its courſe towards the Lothians. The only other antiquity worth mentioning, is an encampment at the top of Hounam Law, which is the higheſt hill on the border except the Cheviot. It was of conſiderable extent, and within theſe few years a large iron gate taken down from the top of the Law, was to be ſeen at Ceſsford Caſtle belonging to the Duke of Roxburgh. There are ſmaller encampments on the tops of the other hills in the neighbourhood, either made by the Romans when they invaded this country, or formed in the courſe of the many wars in which the Borderers of England and Scotland were antiently involved.

Fuel.—The principal diſadvantage under which this pariſh labours, is the ſcarcity of fuel. The common people burn turf or peat. The reſident heritors and the better ſort of farmers bring coal from Northumberland, partly in carts, from a place called Etal, about 20 miles diſtant, and partly on horſe-back, from Birdhopecraig. The latter ſpecies is abundant, and by far the moſt valuable; and it is a fortunate circumſtance for the kingdom at large, that the beſt ſpecies of fuel ſhould be

found

found even in the interior parts of Northumberland, in such considerable quantities: It could easily be conveyed to the sea by a canal; and that best nursery of British seamen, which depends on the supplying the great market of London with coals, may be thus preserved, even though they fail in the neighbourhood of the coast.

Parish of Hounam.

Additional Observations, by the Rev. James Rutherford, Minister, by whom the former account of that district was sent, though his name was omitted to be mentioned.

Sheep and Wool.——Under the article, " Sheep and wool," *add,* Calves and young sheep, not only come sooner to their size when fed on turnip, but they rise to a far greater size than they would do if fed upon grass, at least on the natural grass of the high lands; and this no doubt is partly the reason that cattle in the low country are generally of a larger size than in hilly districts.

For two or three years preceding 1791, wool laid with tar sold here and in the neighbourhood from 14s. to 17s. per stone; white wool, or wool not laid with tar, from 17s. to 19s. Some wool very lightly laid with tar brought

17s. 6d. This laft kind is by many dealers preferred to the white. One guinea was given for the wool of Pafton, lower in the country on the Englifh fide, and the higheft price given for wool on the border; 19s. was but rarely given in 1790, when wool fold rather higher than it has ever been known to do. Of laid wool feven or eight fleeces go to the ftone; of white wool nine or ten; of the long wool near the foot of the water Kale, 4 or 5 fleeces go to the ftone, and it fells at 16s. per ftone. The farmers are under the neceffity of going from home to feek a merchant for their commodities. People of 'fubftance, moft commonly from England, travel the country at a ftated feafon, for the purpofe of buying the wool, generally at the end of June or beginning of July. The price is ufually paid when the wool is bought, or on a near day. The fame mode takes place with regard to the difpofal of the fheep at a different feafon, which is ufually the end of harveft. People from England, and the low country of Scotland, buy the ewes and wedders at this time of the year, for feeding fat on turnip through the winter. The wedder fheep fell about 5s higher each than ewes.

It is generally fuppofed by the farmers in this diftrict that a manufactory eftablifhed in this part of Scotland would be of confiderable advantage to the country. It is true there is a carpet manufactory at Hawick, but that makes ufe only of coarfe wool, and is generally fupplied with wool from the weft part of Scotland. There is alfo a manufactory at Hawick and Galafhiels for cloth; but, though flourifhing and highly creditable to the undertakers, yet they are eftablifhed on a fmall fcale, and at a diftance from this part of the country where the beft wool abounds. Kelfo, or its neighbourhood, one would imagine, fhould be a favourite fpot for that purpofe. The beft wool would be at command, and the carriage would be inconfiderable. The advantages to

the

the country would certainly be great. It is a pity but that the gentlemen of the Merse and Teviotdale would take the hint. They are by no means defective in public spirit. Unless such an undertaking be supported by the landed interest, there would be little hope of success. A private individual, fearful of the event, will not be willing to launch into such a work:——and few, if they had spirit, have the means requisite to carry it on with advantage. Such a plan, properly executed, would facilitate very sensibly the rise of the value of land in this district. It would at the same time obviate a complaint, perhaps justly made by the farmers, that though the wool brings a good price, yet they receive not its full value, because there is no competition, but what arises from different persons carrying wool to the same market, who can combine together and regulate the price. By a manufactory so near too, the farmers might easily come to acquire the art of sorting the wool properly, which might turn considerably to their emolument.

A plan of this kind will not fail, it is to be hoped, to receive assistance, should the proposed canal take place between Kelso and Berwick: a work which would also redound to the great benefit of the country, should it be only to rouse a spirit of enterprise in the nation. But other obvious advantages are not wanting. The practicability of carrying the canal up the Teviot, as far as Ancrum bridge, is not disputed, perhaps it may be carried much higher up the river. Corn, which is raised in far greater quantities than is wanted for the supply of home consumption, by these means, would easily be conveyed to Berwick, where there is often a considerable demand for it, and which cannot be sent but at great expence, the distance between Berwick and Ancrum bridge being 30 miles. Coal and lime (articles of the greatest importance of all) could be brought at a reasonable

able rate from the neighbourhood of Berwick, on the English side, where they abound, to Kelfo, Jedburgh, and even Hawick, and all this extenfive and populous country. And thus would it afford in a great meafure the means of producing thofe internal refources neceffary to compenfate the expence of fo great a work. Many and wonderful are the canals that are cut in England ; fome of them through large rocks and the higheft hills. They have always defrayed the expence laid out in making them, and have been one great fource of the riches of that kingdom.

State of the Church, and of the Poor.—With regard to the legal method of provifion for the poor in Scotland, the mode of procedure obferved in this parifh is as follows—Intimation of the meeting is made from the defk by the clerk of the kirk feffion after divine fervice. Ten free days intervene between the intimation and the meeting. On the day of meeting the heritors choofe a prefes. The clerk then reads over the minutes of the former federunt. All applications of the poor are made to the prefes. To thofe, who, through accidental misfortune or difeafe, apply for fupport, is given interim fupply ; that is, fupply for that quarter only, or fo long as the prefent occafion may require. The roll of the poor being made up, the names are read over by the clerk ; and each have a fum allotted to them according to their circumftances, as can be learned from the petitioners themfelves, the minifter, or any of the elders, or tenants prefent. The fum to each is marked oppofite to their names. The names being gone through, the amount is fummed, and ordered to be levied equally on the heritors and tenants. On the admiffion of any perfon on the roll, an inventory is taken by the clerk of his effects, which then become the property of the heritors. The money thus affeffed is levied by the clerk,

clerk, and put into the hands of two or three persons chosen annually as overseers for the poor. These persons living in different parts of the parish, the money is speedily and faithfully distributed to the poor. The minister alone, if nobody attends according to the intimation, can assess for the poor. They are not suffered to want on account of the negligence of heritors, and the deed of the minister is valid.

The weekly collections in the church are, by law, the property of the session, for behoof of the poor; and are usually given to such as are known by the minister and elders to be in necessitous circumstances, and who through modesty do not apply for the legal provision.

There are no records of the poor rates farther back than the year 1749. That year 10 names are on the roll. The highest sum given to one person per quarter is 9s : the total sum is L. 3 : 3. The list of names from that time does not much increase; some years it decreases. In the year 1756, a year of great scarcity, the names on the roll are 11, and 7 to whom interim supply is given; in all 18. The total supply is L. 9 : 1. But the heritors, at same time, uplifted money belonging to the poor, and out of that fund they bought up oat meal and bear-meal, and sold it to the poor on the roll, and to others who could produce a line from the minister of their necessitous situation, at 2d per stone below market price. In the year 1759, the price of victual was greatly fallen. Those on the roll being only 9, and for interim supply 4; the sum to the whole is L. 4 : 16. In the year 1767, the number of poor is 14; the sum assessed for L. 3 : 16. In the year 1783, a year also of scarcity, the number of poor is 19, including those for interim supply; the sum assess.d L. 12 : 10 : 3. In 1784, the number of poor is 14; the sum assessed L. 10 : 11. In 1790, the number of poor is 13; the sum assessed L. 10 : 19 : 6. The highest pension to one person is L. 1 : 19,

and

and L. 1 : 1 ; the lowest to each 10s, and 7. 6d. The average to each is nearly 17s quarterly.

From the above account, it appears that the number of
poor is rather increased, but not in proportion to the rate allowed them.

Errata.—The words " wet and spungy," page 465 ought
to have been altered into " dry and somewhat spouty on the
sides up the hills :" a very material alteration.

I also beg leave to observe, that the circumstance mentioned of the Kale water breed of sheep, not being agreeable to
fact, had better been omitted ; there is really no such specification as the Kale water breed. The information respecting
this was not given by me. I was rather surprised when I
saw it.

Causes of Depopulation.—As the number of births, from the
Union to about the time of the last rebellion, acccording to
the records of the session, was diminished, it is natural to
suppose that the number of inhabitants was diminished in the
same proportion. This diminution may easily be accounted
for, from the free and safe communication which the Union
immediately opened, between two formerly hostile and contending nations. By the union of the two crowns and the
two parliaments, an open intercourse would take place, national antipathies would cease, the effects of interest and ambition would operate, and the result would be, as was easily
foreseen, that many would emigrate from the poorer to the
richer country. This spirit of emigration might be increased
by a law in our natures, which leads men in cases where they
have been restrained in any great degree to run, where it is
in their power, to an opposite extreme.

The above is a cause no doubt assignable for the decrease
of

of inhabitants on this fide of the border at large during the period here referred to. But I believe it is not the caufe of the late great depopulation. The emigration from either fide feems to be mutual. It is fomewhat remarkable that feveral of the fhepherds, and fome of the moft fubftantial farmers in the parifh have come over to refide here from the Englifh fide. This however does not in general happen in other parifhes; and I know not in any inftance, that an individual from the Scottifh fide, has emigrated to England, (I mean in this diftrict of parifhes,) and fettled there as a refident farmer, although many rent fmall farms in England, which often fuit well for raifing young fheep, to be afterwards laid on the large farms here.

The number of deaths in the parifh is to the births as 4 to 12: there muft be an increafe therefore, at leaft, of 8 fouls every year to the parifh. This would foon occafion a confiderable furplus of inhabitants more than could be accommodated with houfes, or with the means of life: they therefore muft feparate and difperfe annually in all directions; fome to the towns and villages of the neighbourhood, fome to England, where fervants wages are rather higher than in Scotland, and fome to America and the Indies.

The great and moft obvious caufe of the decreafe of the inhabitants, within the laft thirty or forty years is owing to the (perhaps too general) practice of letting the lands in great farms, and to the mode of agriculture now almoft univerfally adopted, efpecially fince fheep and wool brought fo high a price, of laying down the whole lands in grafs. The lands formerly, from 40 to 100 years back, were parcelled out into four times, at leaft, the prefent number of farms: there was alfo much of thefe farms in tillage: and confequently a greater number of people could be maintained, and more hands would be neceffary for carrying on the

the labour of the lands. So late as the year 1756, there were no fewer than seven tenants, with large families, on the lands of Hounam, now all rented by one tenant, who employs only one shepherd. There were also several small lairds : their lands are lost in the large farms, their names extinguished, and their mansions confounded in the dust.

Though this last cause operates most strongly in depopulating the parishes where the monopoly of farms is frequent, yet it is by some made a question whether it tends to depopulate the country at large in any great measure. No doubt the towns and villages will increase as the country parishes diminish ; and therefore, in this district, the villages of Yetholm and Morbattle have of late considerably augmented in the number of inhabitants and houses : yet it does not seem to be in the same proportion as the country districts around them have diminished. In this parish, where the real rent is L.2720, were the farms four times the present number, namely 56, or the lands divided into farms of L.50 each, which would amount to much the same number, at least 54, in this case there would be fifty-four or fifty-six tenants in the parish, instead of fourteen, the present number ; and each of whom might have a large family of his own, and employ a shepherd, who might also have a family ; and the other inhabitants and cottagers might be the same in number as at present. This, surely, would make a prodigious odds in favour of the population of the parish, and afford also a sufficient extra number who would find it necessary to withdraw to the towns and villages. Country places, too, are more favourable than towns, to the rearing of young children : here they are healthier, and thrive better.——Besides, hinds and shepherds, driven from their native abodes and manner of life, will be disheartened, and discouraged from marrying : it will be with difficulty they can afterwards find the means of subsistence.——

It is obfervable, that in England, which is far more populous and richer than Scotland, the monopoly of farms is little known. In many places of Scotland, particularly the
diſtrict to which Hounam belongs, a ſingle individual has
not only united four or five farms into one, in one pariſh,
but has ſeveral farms united in this manner, in different pariſhes. Theſe circumſtances taken together ſurely make
it very evident, that the monopoly of farms, and increaſe
of paſturage, is a great injury to the population of the
country at large.

Houſes.——As the number of inhabitants has rapidly diminiſhed, of courſe there are many empty houſes in the
pariſh, and many have of late been demoliſhed. In the
year 1775, there were no fewer than nine houſes, with cottagers in them, at a place called Mainſide, all of whom I
viſited on my admiſſion. In one year after, or two at moſt,
the whole of them were thrown down, to make way for a
ſingle farmhouſe and its offices. The farmers, too, paying
more attention to their ſheep walks than formerly, will
hardly allow a ſingle houſe to ſtand on any part of their
farm, except ſuch as are neceſſary for their ſhepherd's accommodation, that the ſheep may not be diſturbed by the
paſſing of people to and from the houſes. For ſome few
years after my admiſſion, there were three corn milns and
kilns in the pariſh; and for ſome years paſt there has been
only one, and that one not very much frequented. The
houſes pulled down, and uninhabited, within the laſt ten or
fifteen years, will amount to above 30; not above 4 or 5
houſes rebuilt.

Water of Kale.——Kale takes its riſe in the pariſh of Oxnam, not far above the Hindhopes. It runs meandering, in
almoſt

almoft one plain haugh between hills, from its rife, through part of the fouth-eaft fide of Oxnam, through the middle of Hounam and of Morbattle parifhes, till it enters the parifh of Eckford, a little above Marlefield houfe : then it is more confined between rifing banks, and runs more rapidly, till it falls into the Teviot, a little below Eckford kirk. The Kale contains a fine red delicious trout, fome of them of a large fize, and in great quantities. The banks of the water are little encumbered with wood ; fo that the angler meets with no annoyance in the purfuit of his diverfion.

State of the School.——There is one public fchool in the parifh, fituated near the kirk, in the centre of the parifh. The fchoolmafter has a good dwelling houfe, and a falary of L.8 : 6 : 8. His fcholars are about 16 or 18 in number. He only teaches to read Englifh, to write, and keep accompts. Scholars for reading pay 1s. 3d. per quarter ; reading and writing, 2s. ; and when arithmetic is taught, the fchool wages are 2s. 6d. per quarter. The emoluments of the fchoolmafter as feffion clerk is about L.1 : 5——as clerk to the heritors, L.3 per annum. His houfe and fchool are kept in repair at the expence of the heritors.

Alehoufes, and State of Religion.——The number of alehoufes in the parifh are two. The effect they have is rather unfavourable to the morality of the people ; who are, however, in general pioufly difpofed, and rational in their religious fentiments : which is perhaps fomewhat the more remarkable, as Gatefhaw is bordering on this parifh, where there has been, from the beginning of the Seceffion, a meetinghoufe of the wildeft kind of Seceders, the Antiburghers, who are zealous in diffeminating their principles, not fuppofed very favourable to morals and true piety. Thefe people were

formerly

formerly numerous in the parish : they are now dwindled much away, and there are not twenty of all the different denominations of Seceders; and of that number there is but one small tenant. There is but one person, a tenant, of the episcopal persuasion : not one Catholic, though they abound on the opposite side of the Fells.

Servants.——As there is but little tillage, few cottagers are employed in agriculture. It is the opinion of the farmers, that cottagers make the best servants; and that the family of a hind, or cottager, employed to work in husbandry, is enabled to live better than the family of a hired servant. A hired servant gets his wages in money, perhaps L. 7 per annum; a hind gets what is called boll, that is, a certain number of bolls of corn, and sometimes a cow also grazed, which is very convenient where there is a family of young children. A cottager gets wages at the rate of a shilling per day, victuals included; but works more hours, and more constantly, than a hired servant in general does. The customs of the people are much the same; but their stile of living is better, and their dress far more gay, than it was 15 or 20 years ago : this is observable in no class more than among servants.

Birds and Game.——The same birds are found here that are common in other parts of Scotland. In the Spring and Summer, the ear is constantly delighted with the whistling of the blackbird in the Kirkraw and Philogar plantings. Partridges and grey game abound; the blackcock is also sometimes seen; hares are also in great plenty.

Language.——The people speak a harsh, broad language; and here, as in most places on this side of Teviot, pronounce many words ending in e like ae, as me, mae, with a long
disagreeable

disagreeable tone, and use many words improperly. The names of places are mostly of English derivation; one or two perhaps of Saxon. I am in doubt whether Philogar and Chatto are of Saxon derivation. I sometimes think Philogar is a Greek word, or partly Greek. The names of the hills are given them from their situation; as, Chatto Hill, Philogar Hill, the Steeple Hill, (this is near the kirk, and may have belonged to it as its temporality;) and Sharplaw Hill, is a hill with a sharp, pointed top.

Antiquities.—It is to be remarked, that history has not recorded, nor tradition told of, a single battle fought on any spot in this parish; nor is there the vestige of any tower or fortress, though there are the remains of several such places of strength and safety in the neighbouring parishes of Morbattle and Eckford.

Miscellaneous Observations.—There are no waste lands in the parish. Almost the whole is fit for corn or pasture, a few spots of moss ground excepted; and these are most valuable, as affording the common fuel of the parish. Every farm has also meadow grounds belonging to it, which produce as much natural grass as, when made into hay, is generally sufficient, one year with another, for supplying the sheep with food in the winter season when the lands are covered with snow. A good deal of the grass is very fine; and, when well got in, makes a well-flavoured hay, and is excellent for sheep. A coarser kind is also produced, and answers fully better for black cattle. As the lands are mostly in pasture, corn of all kinds for bread, and even oats for the feeding of horses, are brought from the low part of the country, which produces much more grain than is necessary for its own consumption. There are indeed, towards the under part of the

parish,

parish, in two or three of the smallest farms, some corn produced, oats, barley and pease. But it is supposed, that it would be more profitable were the lands to be all laid down in grass. The best method of laying down is, first to lime, and then sow with barley and grass seeds, viz. 1 bushel of rye grass to 6 lb. of red, or 3 lb. of white and 3 lb. of red, clover : and should there be a change in the price of sheep and wool, the lands, being broken up, would produce most excellent crops of corn.

Most part of the parish having been, either long ago, or recently, laid off in grass, there are consequently few ploughs in the parish, not above 7 or 8, and few more carts and horses than are necessary for carrying home the fuel and hay. The farmers have generally, each of them, one short cart and two long ones, and four or five horses.

Several houses have been deserted, and their inhabitants have left the parish, because the tenants, in some instances, refuse to drive them fuel.

The 63 bolls of victual stipend, mentioned in my last, are Teviotdale measure, and should be so marked. To the stipend mentioned, there is a manse and legal glebe.

There is no record kept in the parish of marriages and deaths, only of births.

There are no roads but what may be called natural roads. The lands being hilly, and dry, and gravelly, the roads are always good in winter and summer, except a few latches to be met with in some outskirts of the parish. The statute labour of the county is lately converted into money by act of Parliament, and laid on the tenants and occupiers of land at a rate, in every parish, determined by the justices of the peace, as trustees for the roads. In every parish the assessment varies, according to its situation, and is from 2s 6d to 7s on every L. 100 Scots of rent. There is little doubt but the

money

money thus raiſed will be properly laid out. New roads are to be made, and the old ones kept in good repair. Turn-pikes are conſidered as of great importance to the country.

The lands are in a very few caſes incloſed; the ſurface of the pariſh being mountainous, and the farms being fitted for ſheep, and extenſive, do not admit of being incloſed. Though a ſmall incloſure or two near to a farm houſe are neceſſary to confine a few ſheep or cattle occaſionally, and this conve-nience every farm has. Moſt of the farms have not been mea-ſured, though I believe ſome of the Duke of Roxburgh's have. The lands are ſeldom let at ſo much per acre. The farmers calculate the value by the number of ſheep the lands are known or ſuppoſed to keep.

The number of houſes is as follows:

On the lands belonging to	Houſes.
Boughtrig - - - -	5
Upper Chatto - - - -	6
Philogar - - - - -	6
Nether Chatto - - - -	6
Mainſide, Greenhill, the Yet - -	6
Hounam Kirk, and near it - -	11
Hounam, and Hounam mill - -	8
Southcoat, and the two Granges - -	5
Sharplaw and Bearup - - -	4
Whitton, Cheſter Houſe, and Heatherlands	9
	66

Of

Of thefe there are,   Houfes.

Farm houfes   -   -   -   -   14

Shepherds houfes   -   -   -   -   18

Three common joiners, each a houfe   -   3

Two mafons, only one houfe   -   -   1

A gardener   -   -   -   -   1

A taylor   -   -   -   -   1

A miller   -   -   -   -   1

A fmith   -   -   -   -   1

One in which the Duke of Roxburgh refides for 10
or 12 days in harveft for the fake of fhooting   1

The manfe   -   -   -   -   1

The fchool and fchoolmafter's houfe   -   1

43 inhabited by cottagers, fome of them working in
the parifh as hired fervants, others as day labourers, and fome women   -   -   -   23
                                                        ———
                                Inhabited houfes,   66

STATISTICAL ACCOUNT

OF

SCOTLAND.

PARISH OF JEDBURGH.

From Materials furnished by the Rev. Dr. THOMAS SOMER-
VILLE *Minister of Jedburgh.*

Origin of the Name.

IN a charter granted by William the Lyon of Scotland, to
the abbot and monks of Jedburgh, in the year 1165 *,
the names of Jedwarth and Jedburgh are promiscuously
used ; but in modern times the name of Jedburgh alone is
retained. The name is sometimes written with a G ; and is
said to be derived from the Gadeni, a tribe who antiently inhabited the whole tract of country that lies between Northumberland and the river Tiviot. It was perhaps the capital city belonging to the tribe, and hence obtained the name
of Gadburgh or Jedburgh.

Extent.

* A fac simile copy of this charter was published at Edinburgh by A. Bell, *anno* 1771.

Extent.—The extent of this parish is considerable, being about thirteen miles long, and in some places not less than six or seven miles broad : But the figure is irregular, being frequently intersected by the parishes of Oxnam and Southdean It is bounded by Northumberland on the south and southeast, by the parish of Oxnam on the east, by Southdean on the south and south-west, by Bedrule on the west, by Ancrum on the north and north-west, and by Crailing on the northeast.

Situation and Surface.—The parish is situated within the county of Roxburgh or Tiviotdale. It is the seat of a presbytery, (that of Jedburgh) and belongs to the synod of Merse and Tiviotdale. The soil is various. The lower part of the parish, lying upon the banks of the Tiviot, is flat, and in general consists of light loam; but some part of it is gravelish, and some deep clay. By far the greater part of the parish, however, consists of hills and sheep farms. The hills are generally green and dry; but the interjacent flats are covered with bent, and rather swampy. On the whole, not above a fifth or sixth part of the parish consists of arable ground.

Climate, Diseases, &c.—The climate also varies in different parts of the parish. It is often mild and temperate in the town of Jedburgh, environed with the high banks of the adjacent river, while it is sharp and cold at the distance of a mile or two. The town itself is peculiarly healthy, fewer epidemical distempers prevailing there than in the neighbouring towns of Hawick and Kelso. The rheumatism is the most common disorder, which, though not frequent among people of better station, who are comfortably clothed, fed, and lodged, is nevertheless very general among the poorer sort of people, particularly such as are advanced in

life,

life, who, in consequence of their miserable mode of living, and still more of the coldness and dampness of their houses, owing partly to the scarcity and high price of fuel, have too much reason to complain of what they call the *pains*, or the pains within them. The air, however, on the whole, being very salubrious, there are many instances of longevity, in the parish. An old woman, who died 15 years ago, said that she was 105; but her name was not in the parish record. There are several now living, both in the town and country part of the parish, above 80. Many have survived 90 during the incumbency of the present minister; and there are three persons in the town, now living, who are above 90. There is also a shepherd in the 94th year of his age, who attends his flock as usual. The ravages which the small-pox formerly made have been greatly mitigated, innoculation being of late very general and very successful. In order to reconcile the minds of the common people to this useful practice, the heritors of Jedburgh, about ten years ago, allowed a small sum to defray the expence of innoculating the children of the poor, at a period when the disease was peculiarly fatal. This generous design was attended with the happiest success; among a thousand patients, innoculated by Dr Lindsay in the course of above 20 years practice, only two have been lost, and there is the strongest reason to believe that these two had been previously infected in the natural way. The other physicians and surgeons of the place have also been, it is believed, equally fortunate in this important branch of their practice.

Rivers.—The river Jed, which runs through this parish, has its source in the north side of the Carter-hill, in the parish of Southdean, about the distance of fourteen miles from the town of Jedburgh *. It abounds with trouts, particularly

larly

* On the south side of the same hill, the river Tyne, which runs by Newcastle, takes its rise.

larly with a species of small red trout, of an excellent flavour. The river Tiviot also passes through this parish; the banks of which at first are steep, and its course rapid, yet afterwards it flows in beautiful curves, through wide and fertile haughs. In addition to its natural, it is to be hoped, that, in time, it will have artificial streams, as it is believed, from a late survey, that a canal might be carried from the sea to Ancrum Bridge. At present, however, there are no internal commodities to compensate for the great expence which such a work would require.

Mineral Springs.—There are two chalybeate springs near Jedburgh, and there are appearances of more in different places of the parish, which have never been yet properly investigated. One of the former, called Tud Hope Well, has been used with success in scorbutic, and, it is said, in rheumatic disorders.

Hills.—The most remarkable hill in the neighbourhood of Jedburgh, is the *Dunian*, which is situated partly in the parish of Jedburgh, and partly in that of Bedrule. Its elevation above the level of the sea is 1024 feet. The ridge of hills on the south side of the parish of Jedburgh, contiguous to the English border, is considerably higher, but arising from an elevated base, the elevation is not so striking. The tops of these hills are in general conical, and those who are attached to such ideas, are at no loss to discover a variety of circumstances favourable to the volcanic system.

Woods.—About fifty years ago the parish of Jedburgh abounded with wood. A few old oaks, elms, beeches, plains, and weeping willows still remain. The wood, which begins to rise from the old stocks upon the banks of the Jed together with a variety of new plantations, form a beautiful and romantic

mantic scene on the road from Jedburgh to Northumberland.

Caves.—Vestiges of artificial caves appear upon the banks of the river Jed, particularly two large caves dug out of the rock at Hundalee and Linthaughlee. Their dimensions cannot now be ascertained, being, from the steepness of the rock or bank, almost inaccessible; but they are described by old persons, who have formerly entered into them when the access was less difficult, as consisting of three apartments, one on each hand of the entrance, and a larger one behind, which had the appearance of a great room. They were probably used as hiding places, or strong holds to shelter the inhabitants in the neighbourhood upon any sudden incursion by English invaders.

Migratory Birds.—The wood lark, bulfinch, and king's-fisher have been frequently found on the banks of the Jed. The plover, fieldfare, and dotorel, abound in the south and hilly parts of the parish. In the winter of 1788, during a severe fall of snow, a golden crested wren made its appearance. The size of it was much smaller than the common wren; the colour of the body nearly the same; but the head was adorned with feathers of a beautiful orange colour and gold.

Number of Horses, Sheep, &c.—There are 414 horses in the parish, and it is believed above 8000 sheep. There are some black cattle and horses bred for sale, but more for private use. A great number of cattle are bought in the autumn, and fed upon the foggage or after-grass, and upon turnips. In regard to sheep it may be proper to observe, that the value of wool, in the neighbourhood of Jedburgh, has been greatly increasing for several years past. The white wool in this parish has

been

been sold at from 18s. to 20s. *per* stone for the last three years, and the wool laid with tar at 15s. 16s. and some of it at 18s. In the lower part of the country, some farmers in Beaumont-Water sold their wool last season at L. 1 : 2 : 0 *per* stone. Seven or eight fleeces generally go to a stone.

Population.—There is every reason to believe, that the population of this and of the neighbouring parishes has greatly diminished since the commencement of the present century. Some years after the Union, and even when the returns were made to Dr Webster about forty years ago, the number of inhabitants in the parish was supposed to be about 6000. There is no evidence, however, of any particular enumeration having been made. At present they do not exceed half that number. The inhabitants of the town were numbered with great accuracy about fifteen years ago, and fell short of 2000. The inhabitants of the country part of the parish do not exceed 800; and there are only two or three villages containing about 100 souls. The vestiges of uninhabited houses are to be seen both in the town and in the country. This decrease is partly to be attributed to the Union between the two kingdoms, by which the trade of Jedburgh was, in a great measure, ruined, and the population of the town diminished of consequence : and partly to the union of farms, which has depopulated the country.

Effects of the Union on the Borders.—The Union of the Parliaments of England and Scotland, has in some respects produced an effect very different from what might have been expected from it. Instead of promoting the increase, it has contributed to the diminution, of the people upon the Borders. Besides, the influence of various natural propensities, which induced men to flock to the scene where active talents
were

were conftantly employed, honour acquired, and the ftrongeft national antipathies gratified, there were obvious confiderations of intereft, which rendered the fituation of the Borders
more eligible, after violence and hoftility were repreffed, by
the union of the two Crowns, and the confequent interpofi-
tion of the legiflature of both kingdoms. The inhabitants of
the Borders, while the taxes and the commercial regulations
of the two kingdoms were different, enjoyed the opportunity
of carrying on a very advantageous contraband trade, without
danger to their perfons or fortunes. Into England they imported, falt, fkins, and malt, which, till the Union, paid no
duties in Scotland; and from England they carried back
wool, which was exported from the Frith of Forth to France,
with great profit. The veftiges of forty malt-barns and
kilns are now to be feen in the town of Jedburgh,
while at prefent there are only three in actual occupation;
and the corporation of fkinners and glovers, formerly the
moft wealthy in that town, have, fince the Union, greatly diminifhed, both in regard to opulence and number. The proprietors of eftates upon the Borders were well aware of the
detriment which their property would fuffer by the incorpo-
rating Union, and in general ftrenuoufly oppofed it; and the
commiffioners for carrying on that treaty, were fo fenfible of
the lofs they would fuftain, that they agreed to appropriate part of the equivalent money, as it was called, to their
indemnification and benefit *.

The Union has alfo been the caufe of the depopulation of
the Border country, by enlarging the fphere, and facilitating
the means of emigration. While the two countries were in

a

* See Defoe's Hiftory of the Union, minute 47. obfervation
47.

a hostile state, there was neither inducement nor opportunity to move from the one to the other. The inhabitants often made inroads upon one another; but when the incursion was over, they returned to their own homes. Their antipathy and resentments were a rampart which excluded all social intercourse, and mixture of inhabitants. In this situation, misconduct and infamy at home were the only motives to emigration, and while this was the case, the exchange of inhabitants would be nearly at a par: But after the Union of the two kingdoms, and the decline or extinction of national antipathies, the balance arising from the interchange of inhabitants would run much in favour of the more wealthy country. Artificers and labourers would naturally resort where wages were higher, and all the accommodations of life were more plentiful, especially if this could be effected without the unpleasing idea of relinquishing home. To pass from the Borders of Scotland into Northumberland, was rather like going into another parish than into another kingdom.

Union of Farms.—The monopoly of farms, or the conjoining a number of small possessions into one, has long been prevalent in this part of the kingdom. There are instances in this, and in the neighbouring parishes, of individuals renting and farming lands formerly possessed by six, eight, or ten tenants; and there are instances, particularly of sheep farmers, holding two, or three farms in distant parts of the country, each of which was formerly considered as sufficiently large and extensive for one person. On the whole, this has not perhaps contributed to make the condition of the lower ranks of people worse, nor to diminish the population of the kingdom at large, though it certainly has had the effect of reducing the number of the inhabitants in every district where such a junction has taken place.

Births

Births, Deaths, and Marriages.—The number of births within the parish of Jedburgh exceed 90 *per annum.* The burials in the parish church amount, at an average of three years, only to 49; but then, some families, in the country part of the parish, continue to bury in an old chapel ground, five miles south of Jedburgh, and several in the church-yards of Oxnam and Southdean; so that no certain conclusion can be formed upon this article. The number of marriages, at an average for the last three years, amounts only to 22; but it must be observed, that there are many irregular marriages in this parish and neighbourhood.

Rent of the Parish.—The valued rent of the parish is L 23,264 : 6 : 10 Scots; the real rent, probably, above L. 7000 Sterling. The rent of the land varies. Sheep farms let from 3 s. 6 d. to 5 s. *per* acre. Some arable farms at the rate of 10 s. 15 s. and even 20 s. Land in the immediate neighbourhood of the town of Jedburgh, at from L. 2 to L. 3. Houses in the town, from 10 s. to L. 15 *per annum.*

Number of Proprietors, Tenants, &c.—There are sixteen greater, and a considerable number (about a hundred) of smaller proprietors, called here *Portioners,* from their having a small portion of land belonging to them. Of the greater proprietors, eight, either occasionally, or constantly, reside in the parish. There are two farmers who pay above L. 300 *per annum;* three who pay above L. 200; about fourteen who rent above L. 100; and a number of smaller tenants. There are three physicians, three surgeons, and ten writers, or attorneys.

Crops.—The principal crops in the parish, are oats and barley. Of late years, a considerable quantity of wheat is
sown

sown in the ground immediately surrounding the town of Jedburgh, and some on Tiviot side; but little or none in the south part of the parish. Turnips and potatoes are a general crop all over this country. The culture of turnips, in particular, has been much studied, and is greatly extended; every farmer laying out a great portion of his land in them. The soil of this country is believed to be more suitable to the growth of turnips, than that of any other part of Scotland. Formerly they were accustomed to feed cattle, in the house, with turnips; but it is now found more profitable, and has become more frequent, to let the sheep eat them in the fields. It may be proper to observe, that, from the experience of some of the most skilful farmers, calves and sheep-hogs may be fed, with great profit and safety, upon turnips; and that young beasts fed on turnips attain the same size and value, at two years old, that they formerly did at three, when fed on grass. It was formerly a common prejudice in this country, and still prevails in other places, that turnips were noxious to young animals.

A considerable quantity of pease, a few beans, a great quantity of clover and rye-grass, are sown in this parish; but little flax or hemp, excepting some for private use. Oats are sown from the beginning of March to the end of April. Early oats have been much used of late, and are found to be a great improvement. The barley is sown from the middle of April to the end of May: The turnips from the beginning of June to the middle of July: The greater portion, I believe, in drills. Some wheat is sown in September, but more in October. The wheat is generally sown after potatoes, or fallow; the barley and grass seeds, after turnips; oats upon ley, or after fallow, or pairing and burning. A greater quantity of every species of grain, than what is necessary for the maintenance

maintenance of its inhabitants, is raised within the bounds of this parish. There may, perhaps, be some doubt with respect to wheat; but it is certain that oats, and oat-meal, are exported in confiderable quantities to Lothian and Tweedale.

Orchards.—A great quantity of pears grow in the gardens or orchards of the town of Jedburgh. The trees, though very old, are remarkably fruitful; and it is calculated that the value of the fruit amounts, at a medium, to about L. 300 *per annum.*

Ecclefiaftical State of the Parifh.—There are four clergymen in the town of Jedburgh; the minifter of the Eftablifhed Church, of the Relief congregation, of the Burgher, and the Antiburgher, feceders. Their refpective examination rolls are as follows: Eftablifhed Church 800; Relief congregation 1200; Burgher congregation 600; Antiburgher 150. Total 2750 examinable perfons; that is, perfons from fix to feven years old, and upwards. In order to account for the great proportion of diffenters, it muft be obferved, that the fect called the Relief Congregation had its origin in Jedburgh. In the year 1755, the council, and the generality of the inhabitants of the town, applied for a prefentation to Mr Bofton, minifter of Oxnam, and being difappointed in that application, built a large meeting-houfe, by contribution, and invited Mr Bofton to be their minifter; feveral of the moft fubftantial members of the congregation binding themfelves to pay him L. 120 *per annum.* He accepted of their call; and prevailed upon Mr Gillefpie, who had been depofed for difobedience to the orders of the General Affembly, to join him, under the denomination of the Prefbytery of Relief; profeffing to differ from the Eftablifhed Church upon no other point, than the right of patrons to appoint minifters againft the inclina-

tions

tions of the people.   This sect, more accommodating to the
spirit of the times, have quickly spread over Scotland, and,
probably, comprehend the greatest part of the Scotch dissenters.   Near a half of all the families in the parish of
Jedburgh, and a great proportion of the families in all the
surrounding parishes, are members of this congregation.
There are not more than five or six who profess the Episcopal religion, and there are no Catholics in the parish.

The present incumbent, Dr Thomas Somerville, was admitted minister of Jedburgh in 1773. His predecessors were
Messrs Semple, M'Kay, Ruet, Winchester, Douglas, and
M'Knight, which last he succeeded in the charge. He has been
married twenty years, and has two sons and four daughters.
The King is patron of the parish. The living consists of 169
bolls, half oat-meal and half barley, Linlithgow measure ;
L. 44 in money, a manse, and a glebe of seven English acres,
in all amounting to about L. 150 *per annum* in value. A
part of the old Abbey Church is still used as the place
of worship. The manse was built about 60 years ago, and
has often been repaired at a great expence.

State of the Poor.—The number of poor upon the country
roll of the parish amounts to 55, and of those in the town
roll to 37. They are maintained by assessments. For supporting the county poor, a tax is laid upon the different proprietors of land, in proportion to the valued rents. The
common method of proceeding in this business is as follows :
The minister intimates from the pulpit, that on such a day a
meeting of the heritors and elders is to be held, for the purpose of making a provision for the maintenance of the poor
for the ensuing quarter. These meetings generally take place
near the term of Candlemas, Whitsunday, Lammas, and
Martinmas.

Martinmas. Upon the day of meeting the heritors elect a preses, after which the minutes of the former federunt, and the roll of the poor are read by the clerk. Forming a calculation from the number already standing upon the roll, and the applications made to them, the heritors assess themselves in a certain sum to be collected from them severally, according to the proportion of their valued rents. The proprietor pays one half of the assessment, and the tenant the other. Though the tenants are not mentioned in the summons, yet such of them as chufe to attend are made welcome, and their advice and information listened to by the meeting. The sum assessed is raised by the heritors and kirk-session together, in such proportions as seem adequate to the necessities of the poor. Such persons as are reduced to the necessity of applying to the heritors for charity, from any accidental transient cause, such as *disease* or *misfortune*, receive what is called *an interim supply*, i. e. a certain sum for that quarter only : The aged and infirm, and such as are likely to continue under the same necessity of depending upon public charity, are taken upon the poors roll at a certain weekly allowance. The persons taken upon the roll are obliged to subscribe a bond or deed of conveyance, making over and bequeathing all their effects to the heritors ; and though the heritors seldom exact their effects, yet the subscription of the bond serves as a check to prevent persons, who may be possessed of concealed property, from alienating the public charity. The sum assessed is levied by a collector, appointed by the heritors, and distributed by him to the persons admitted upon the roll, according to the proportions allotted to them. This mode of providing for the parochial poor was adopted in the parish of Jedburgh *anno* 1742, when the number of the poor increasing, from the scarcity and high price of provisions, the heritors and kirk-session were obliged to have re-

course

course to the legal method of obtaining the contributions of absent proprietors. These monthly assessments have varied from two shillings to three shillings and six-pence *per* quarter, on each hundred pounds of valued rent. The assessment for the last twelve months was at the rate of three shillings *per* quarter, but did not produce the sum required, viz. L. 37 : 8 : 8 *per* quarter. The deficiency is made up from the weekly collections.

The poor belonging to the borough of Jedburgh, are provided for by a plan in some respects similar to, but in others materially different from, that above described. The magistrates hold quarterly meetings, in which they assess the borough for the maintenance of their poor, and portion the sums in the same manner as the heritors do; but the assessment is not proportioned to the value of the property of individuals within the royalty; but according to a valuation of the property of the burgesses and inhabitants, estimated by sworn assessors appointed by the magistrates. The assessors, in forming their calculation, and fixing the portion of assessment to which each individual is liable, have respect not only to ostensible property, but to the profits of trade, and other supposed advantages. It is obvious that such a vague and arbitrary mode of calculation, is extremely liable to partiality and error.

The sums appropriated for the maintenance of each individual vary, according to the circumstances of the claimant. To single persons who can do no work, a shilling, one shilling and six-pence, one shilling and eight-pence, is allowed weekly. Six-pence, eight-pence, ten-pence to those who are infirm and receive small wages. Eight, ten, twelve, and sometimes twenty shillings *per* quarter have been allowed for

interim

interim supply. There are few instances of any family receiving above two shillings, or two shillings and six-pence *per* week. These proportions refer to the poor belonging to the country part of the parish; but the allowance given to the poor of the town is more scanty and inadequate.

Besides the assessments above-mentioned, the town of Jedburgh holds the principal sum of L. 422 upon bond to the session, arising from the accumulation of various legacies, the interest of which is annually distributed according to the destination of the donors: Some of it for educating poor children, some for the relief of poor householders, some appropriated to the poor within the town, and some to the poor of the town and country equally. A great portion of these charities arises from legacies of the Lady Yester, who was the daughter of Kerr of Fairnyherst in this parish, and celebrated for her charity. A bridewell or correction-house has been lately erected in the town, at the expence of the heritors of the county at large, and has been found very useful in overawing vagrants, punishing smaller offences, and, particularly, for the accommodation of persons disordered in mind, who are maintained there at the expence of the parishes to which they belong.

Language.—The common people in the neighbourhood of Jedburgh pronounce many words, particularly such as end in a guttural sound, with a remarkable broad, and even harsh accent. They still make use of the old Scotch dialect. Many of the names of places, however, are evidently derived from the Erse, and expressive of their local situation in that language. For instance,—Dunian, *John's Hill;*—Minto, *Kid's Hill;*—Hawick, *Village on a River;*—Ancrum, anciently called Alnicromb, *a Crook in the River;* &c. &c.

Manners

Manners and Morals of the People.—There is rather a want of industry in the town of Jedburgh, owing to the destructive influence of borough politics ; but to this rule there are many exceptions ; and the common labourers in the country are remarkable for the quantity of work which they perform. In general, it may be observed, that all ranks of people live more soberly, and are less addicted to drinking, than they were some years ago ; and that persons in a better situation are charitably disposed, and were particularly liberal in their contributions for the relief of the poor, after the unfortunate season of 1782. Crimes are becoming every day more rare. Only one instance of suicide has occurred for these 17 years past ; and no inhabitant of the parish has been banished for these many years. Five have suffered capital punishments ; but not one of them for murder. It is, indeed, one of the most striking evidences of the progress of civilization, and one of the most pleasing effects of a regular government, that in a country, formerly the scene of depredating violence, fewer instances of crimes, or of punishments, have occurred during the last 50 years, than perhaps in any other district of equal extent in the kingdom.

Advantages and Disadvantages.—The principal disadvantage under which this parish labours, is its great distance from coal, which is found to be the cheapest fuel, though there are several large peat mosses in many parts of the neighbourhood. The nearest coal to Jedburgh is at Ryechester, distant about 20 miles, on the English border. Some Lothian coal is brought by the carts which carry grain to the Dalkeith market, and is sold at nearly the same price with the English. The county, in general, and the neighbourhood of Jedburgh in particular, is likely to derive great advantage from the improvement and extension of roads, which does great honour

to

to the activity and public spirit of the gentlemen who have promoted them. There is a turnpike road now carried from Jedburgh to Newcastle, which shortens the distance from thence to Edinburgh considerably; and there is at present a prospect of carrying one, in a direct line, from Jedburgh to Boroughbridge in Yorkshire, which could not fail of being frequented, as it would render the road between London and Edinburgh nearer by 38 miles than by Berwick.

Parish of Jedburgh.

A more distinct statement of the population of this parish having been received since the publication of the former account, it is here inserted.

	Men.	Women.	Children.	Total.
Edgerston Barony, - - -	79	91	69	239
Ulston, - - - -	27	27	25	79
Oldhall, - - -	2	4	14	20
Stewartfield, - - -	5	6	5	16
Chapmanside, - - -	4	2	-	6
Hundalee, - - -	10	6	1	17
Rattanraw, &c. - -	24	21	22	67
Howden, - - -	2	3	5	10
Langlee, not distinguished	-	-	-	35
Hunthill, - - -	4	7	2	13
Carried over,	157	167	143	502

	Men.	Women.	Children.	Total.
Brought over,	157	167	143	502
Linthaughlee, not diftinguifhed	-	-	-	25
Mofburnford, do. -	-	-	-	38
Kerfheugh and Fairnyhirft, do.	-	-	-	94
Thickfide, - -	5	3	3	11
Swinie, - - -	6	7	14	27
Harden-peel, not diftinguifhed,	-	-	-	12
Wells, do. -	-	-	-	17
Crailing-mill, - -	-	-	-	15
Crailing-hall, - -	-	-	-	26
Upper Crailing, - -	-	-	-	48
Craigfhiel, - -	-	-	-	13
Rennifton, - -	-	-	-	9
Semmifton Townfoot, -	-	-	-	17
Semmifton Townfoot, -	-	-	-	12
Birneyrig, - -	-	-	-	5
Fendyhall, Scraifburgh, &c. not properly diftinguifhed,	-	-	-	144
	168	177	160	
Proportion of men, women and children, in fuch parts of the foregoing lift as no diftinction is made, calculated at the fame rate as where they are diftinguifhed, -	136	144	130	
	304	321	290	915
Langton, - - -	-	-	-	106
Timpendean, - - -	-	-	-	63
Bon-Jedward, - -	41	57	66	174
Ancrum-bridge, - -	-	-	-	17
Montholy - - -	-	-	-	13
Town of Jedburgh, -	-	-	-	2000
				3288

PARISH OF KELSO.

(County of Roxburgh.—Presbytery of Kelso.—Synod of Merse and Tiviotdale.)

By Doctor CHRISTOPHER DOUGLAS, *Physician in Kelso.*

Situation and Extent.

THIS district, formerly consisting of three separate pàrishes, viz. Kelso, Maxwell, and St. James's, is situated in the lower division of Roxburghshire or Tiviotdale, in N. lat. 55°. 36'. in W. long. 1°. 20'. It is of an irregular triangular figure, extending in length, from N. to S. 4¼ miles, and in breadth, from E. to W. 4½ miles. It contains from 5000 to 6000 acres. On the E. the parish of Sprouston separates it from Northumberland. The rivers Tweed and Tiviot unite at Kelso. The former divides the parish nearly into two equal parts. St. James's lies between the two rivers; Maxwell on the S. E. and Kelso on the N. and W. of both.

Rent and Proprietors.—The valued rent is 15,300 l. Scotch. The real rent, including the land in possession of the proprietors, which is by far the greatest part of the parish, is from 7000 l. to 8000 l. Sterling. The land, in this part of the country, is all measured by the English acre. It lets at 2 l. 3 l. 4 l. and sometimes 5 l. per acre, and little or none, even in the remote part of the parish, under 15 s. The Duke of Rox-

Roxburgh, superior of the town and the greatest part of the parish, resides above half the year at Fleurs. Besides his Grace, the following heritors also reside in the parish; Sir George Douglas, Bart. Rear-Admiral William Dickson, Robert Davidson of Pinnacle-hill, Robert Walker of Wooden, John Proctor of Softlaw Tower, Esqs; Capt. Scott of Rosebank, Rev. Dr Panton, Dr Blaw, and many others of smaller property.

Soil, Agriculture, and Produce.—The soil of this parish, for a considerable tract on both sides of the river Tweed, and in that part of it which lies between the Tweed and the Tiviot, is in general composed of a deep rich loam, upon a bottom of gravel; from its favourable situation, and the culture it receives, it produces early and luxuriant crops. Towards the N. W. extremity of the parish, the soil is a wet clay; in the S. it is in general thin and wet, and the bottom is a red clay; here the crops are generally three weeks later than in the vicinity of the rivers. About 20 years ago, it was a common practice to divide the cultivated land into six equal parts, each of which, in regular succession, got a summer fallowing, and all the dung that the farm produced, lime being then seldom used in agriculture. The crop immediately after the fallow was always wheat, the second barley, the third oats, the fourth pease, and the fifth oats or wheat; after these crops it was often laid out into pasture, sometimes fallowed again. By this management the lands were always foul, so that the crops, excepting the first, and sometimes the second, were mostly poor. But lime having of late been very generally employed as a manure, and turnips, potatoes, and sown grasses introduced along with it, the following rotation is adopted with success through the whole

whole parifh. The land in tillage is divided into four equal parts, one of which is fown with turnips, or planted with potatoes; for both, the land muft be carefully cleaned and pulverifed, as well as manured. The common practice is to fow turnips on ridges 30 inches wide, and the feafon moft proper for this is, from the 10th to the end of June; when fown earlier, they are apt to fhoot in autumn; and, if later, they feldom grow to a large fize. Potatoes are planted from the middle to the end of April, in ridges 30 inches afunder. The fucceeding crop is either barley or fpring wheat, which is thought by many to anfwer as well as when fown in autumn; the third hay, and the fourth oats or wheat, unlefs the land has been laid down for pafture, in which cafe a fourth of the old grafs land is ploughed up, and fown with oats; fometimes the third crop is peafe inftead of hay, but this practice is every day lefs prevalent. By this mode of cultivation, the crops are good, the land kept clean and rich, and at an expence comparatively fmall. Upon fome fields of a clay foil, the management is a fummer fallow, with the following rotation of crops, firft wheat, fecond peafe or beans, third barley, fourth oats; and upon very poor land of this kind, when too wet for turnips, and too wet as well as too weak for wheat, after a fummer fallow the firft crop is wheat, the fecond hay, and the third, if not left for pafture, oats. A confiderable part of this parifh is kept in grafs, and paftured with fheep and black cattle; but as moft of the fields are let for a fummer pafture only, it is impof-fible to afcertain the number of fheep and cattle. that are fattened in the parifh upon grafs and turnips during the year. It is however well known, that, owing to the high price of wool, and the conftant demand for fheep and cattle, both

at

at the Edinburgh and Morpeth markets, nothing has paid better for many years paft *.

Bridges.—At Kelfo there is an elegant bridge over the Tweed, confifting of fix beautiful arches, built in the year 1756, by a fubfcription from the county at large, but particularly by the inhabitants of this parifh of every denomination, who diftinguifhed themfelves by their liberality. An act of Parliament has lately paffed, for building a bridge over the Tiviot, a little above its junction with the Tweed, which will make a free communication with the weft part of the county, much wanted, and likely to prove, in many refpects, highly advantageous to the public.

Antiquities.—A confiderable part of the ABBEY of Kelfo †, formerly an immenfe edifice, ftill remains, and exhibits a venerable monument of that tafte for magnificence, which diftin-

* The common hire of a labourer, per day, is from 1 s. to 16 d. but, in hay time and harveft, from 16 d. to 20 d. Male fervants, maintained in the houfe, receive from 6 to 8 guineas yearly; women, from 3 l. to 4 l. 10 s. Moft of the men fervants, however, are hired as hinds. Their wages, at an average, amount to 18 l. a year. A great part of the fummer work, fuch as hay-making, hoeing of turnips, potatoes, &c. is performed by young girls, who, being early accuftomed to ufe the hoe, are more expert at this work than the men. They receive from 4 d. to 8 d and country mafons and carpenters, from 16 d. to 22 d. per day, without victuals.

† The Abbey of Kelfo was built by St David, king of Scotland: He had a predilection for an order of monks called Tyronenfes, whom he firft planted at Selkirk; but not thinking it an eligible fituation for his favourites, he foon removed them to Roxburgh, (in 1126), and at laft tranflated them to Kelfo, where he, in 1128, founded for them a magnificent church, and other buildings in the Saxon ftile. This abbey was dedicated to the Virgin MARY and St. JOHN the Evangelift;

diſtinguiſhed antient times. But, while it contributes to the ornament of the ſurrounding country, and the pleaſure of ſpecta-

gelift: Its privileges were very conſiderable, and its endowments liberal The monks were exempted from toll, and leave was granted to them and the abbot, to receive the ſacraments of the church from any biſhop they pleaſed, in Scotland and Cumberland. The abbot was allowed to wear a mitre, to make uſe of other pontifical diſtinctions, and to be preſent at all general councils. It is related, that this order was particularly attentive to agriculture, and that, beſides huſbandmen, they maintained within their monaſtery all kinds of mechanics, whoſe profits were depoſited in the common ſtock, for the ſupport of the order. If this was the caſe, David ſhewed good ſenſe and reaſon, in patronizing an order of men, who promoted the improvement of the arts, as well as the intereſts of religion, in an age when ſcience and philoſophy, feebly, if at all, illuminated the kingdom. Small fragments of pillars, antique ſtones, ſtatues, &c. evidently belonging to the abbey, have been found at different times, and ſome of them are ſtill to be ſeen at a conſiderable diſtance from the fabric, affording a lively, though melancholy emblem of the all-ſubduing power of time.

The church of St. James's was ſituated between the rivers Tweed and Tiviot, near to Roxburgh Caſtle, and on the very ſpot on which the greateſt fair in this country, as well as one of the moſt antient, called St James's Fair, is now held. This church was dedicated, *anno* 1134. No part of it remains above ground, but the place where it ſtood is perfectly obvious. The Duke of Roxburgh, a few years ago, employed labourers to trace the foundation. While carrying on this work, they dug up a tomb-ſtone, which had been erected to the memory of Johanna Bullock. It was pretty entire; and, beſides ſome elegant Popiſh ſculpture, had the following inſcription in Saxon characters, *Hic jacet Johanna Bullock, quae obiit anno* 1371. *Orate pro anima ejus.* Hiſtorians mention a William Bullock, a favourite with Edward Baliol, and generally ſtiled the King's beloved Clerk. As this name is ſeldom found in Scotland, it is probable that Johanna Bullock was the daughter, or a near relation, of this eminent perſon, eſpecially as he frequently reſided at Roxburgh Caſtle. There was alſo found a conſiderable quantity of wheat and barley, in a charred ſtate, ſcattered on a tiled pavement; as were alſo ſeveral pieces of glaſs and brick, which ſhewed obvious marks of fire. All theſe circum-

fpectators, it, at the fame time, recalls the mortifying remembrance of that rudenefs and barbarity, with which neighbouring kingdoms carried on hoftilities againft each other.
The venerable appearance of this ruin is marred, by the addition of an aile built in the laft century, for the accommodation of the family of Roxburgh, when part of the building
was ufed for the parifh church. This uncouth modern addition entirely fhuts up one very large arch, and the half of
another, befides 7 of a fmaller fize above; but from the value which the Duke of Roxburgh puts upon it as a ruin;
and from his defire to preferve it in its priftine ftate, there is
much caufe to hope, that we fhall foon fee this modern building levelled with the ground, and the genuine antient remains fecured from injury by an inclofure. It has not, like
moft of the Gothic buildings, any minutenefs of ornament,
but has a tendency, by its plainnefs and magnitude, to in-
fpire the mind with the grand and the fublime, rather than
the pleafing and beautiful.

ROXBURGH CASTLE * ftands upon an eminence of confiderable

circumftances render it probable, that this church was burnt
down in fome of the border wars.

At a fmall diftance from this church, ftood a convent of
mendicants of the order of St. Francis, on the north bank
of the river Tiviot, a little above its confluence with the Tweed.
Within thefe few years, a fine arch of their church remained,
and other parts of the building, which are now almoft wholly
effaced. This monaftery was confecrated by William Bifhop of
Glafgow, in the year 1235.—In the parifh of Maxwell, fouth
of the Tiviot, and nearly oppofite to Roxburgh Caftle, ftood
Maifon Dieu, an afylum for pilgrims, the difeafed, and the indigent.
The fite of this houfe is well known; and upon the very fpot
where it ftood there ftill remains a village, bearing the antient
name. The guardian of this houfe, NICHOL DE CHAPELYN,
did homage to EDWARD I. of England *anno* 1296.

* The many ftruggles, which the two kingdoms had, for the
poffeffion

fiderable extent, and is furrounded with a deep trench, ſtill viſible, which the garriſon could fill with water at pleaſure, and over which a draw-bridge was placed. The wall which furrounded the fortreſs is in a great meaſure deſtroyed, but ſome parts of it ſtill remain pretty entire, which diſplay a-mazing ſtrength from their thickneſs and ſolidity.—Upon Mr Walker's eſtate at Wooden, there are the veſtiges of a Ro-man tumulus *. There are alſo ſeveral of the ſame kind in
different

poſſeſſion of this fortreſs, render its hiſtory of more importance than that of any near the borders. It frequently changed maſ-ters; and, in the reign of HENRY VI. was in the poſſeſſion of that monarch. JAMES II of Scotland having laid ſiege to it, his army made themſelves maſters of the Caſtle, in a great meaſure deſtroyed the works, and reduced it to ruins; but, pre-vious to the victory, the king was killed by the burſting of a piece of ordnance. A holly tree is ſaid to ſtand on the ſpot where this happened, on the north ſide of the river Tweed, and a little below Fleurs houſe. Near this tree ſtood a large village, which, from a croſs that remained within theſe few years, was ge-nerally called the *Fair Croſs*. But the probable origin of the name, as it has been handed down, though not generally known, is this : James II's Queen, having very ſoon reached the ſpot where the lifeleſs body of her huſband lay, is reported to have ex-claimed, " There lies the *fair corpſe*," whereupon it received the name of *Fair Corpſe* or *Corſe*; and, in proceſs of time, the change from corſe to *croſs* was eaſily effected. The Queen, ſoon after this fatal accident, obſerving that the army was diſ-heartened, and that the chiefs were for raiſing the ſiege, uſed every means to excite their courage, and, among other things, told them, that although their king had fallen, he was but one man, and that ſhe would ſoon give them another king, her ſon James III. who next day arrived in the camp, and was crown-ed in Kelſo in the 7th year of his age. This heroic and well timed addreſs, produced the deſired effect; the ſpirits of the whole army were rouſed; and, renewing the attack with re-doubled ardor, the garriſon ſurrendered in a few days. From this period the Caſtle has remained in ruins, although it was in ſome degree repaired, by the Lord Protector, Somerſet, in the reign of Edward VI.

* This tumulus conſiſted of a vaſt number of ſtones, piled
upon

different parts of the country, generally known by the name of *Cairns.*

Picturesque Scenery.—The variety of charming prospects, which this part of the country exhibits, renders it a difficult task to select any of them. The views, however, presented from the castle of Roxburgh and the Fleurs, deserve particular notice ; but to attempt an enumeration of their beauties, were to no purpose ; for to be in any degree conceived, they must be seen. The scene which appears from Kelso bridge, and has often called forth the powers of the painter, partakes so much of the picturesque and elegant, that it excites the admiration of every spectator. From this the town is seen, with the majestic ruins of the ancient abbey, and the handsome modern fabric of Ednam house ; at no great distance to the north-west, the lofty building of Fleurs ; between the rivers, the remains of Roxburgh castle ; near to this Springwood-park ; towards the east, Pinnacle-hill and Wooden ; at the distance of a few miles, the Eildon hills rising in perspective ; as likewise the ruins of Home Castle, the hills of Stichell, and of Mellerstain ; add to these, the winding course of the rivers, before their junction, with an island in each ; one of these, and the banks of both rivers, covered with beautiful wood ; the steep precipices of Maxwell, and Chalk-heugh, and a variety of other fine objects. All these must induce every spectator of taste, to exclaim, with enthusiastic pleasure,

Hic

upon each other, and secured by a moss ; neither the same species of stone nor moss are now to be found in this parish. Near a small rivulet on the same estate, skeletons have been discovered inclosed in stone coffins.

Hic gelidi fontes; hic mollia prata, Lycori,
Hic nemus; hic ipso tecum confumerer aevo.

Town of KELSO.—Kelso, anciently, Calchow, Kelkow,
or de Calco, is fituated on the river Tweed, in an extenfive
plain, bounded on all fides by gently rifing grounds, covered
with fine foreft trees, forming a moft beautiful amphitheatre.
Its fituation is particularly taken notice of by Patten, who
accompanied the Lord Protector, Somerfet, into Scotland,
and who calls it a pretty market town.

During the border wars, which long fpread defolation and
mifery over this country, Kelso was thrice burnt down by
the Englifh : It was alfo reduced to afhes, in the year 1686,
by an accidental fire ; and nearly fo by another, about 50
years ago. At prefent, it is a handfome town, containing
many good houfes, with a fpacious market place 300 feet in
length, and 200 in breadth ; from hence, as a centrical point,
proceed four long ftreets, and two confiderable lanes. In
the fquare ftands the town houfe, the principal houfes, and
fhops, many of which would do no difcredit to the capital
of any country.

Name.—Kelfo is probably derived from the word Calx. This
conjecture feems the more probable, from an eminence on
Tweed fide, on which part of the town ftands. This height
is called the Chalk-heugh, or Calchow, one of the ancient
names of the town, and contains a great quantity of Gyp-
fum, and other calcareous matters ; all which, in the Celtic
language, were denominated Kelk, hence Kelkon ; and the
Monks denominated the feal of the ancient monaftery, Si-
gillum Monafterii de Calco. This eminence alfo affords a
delightful profpect, which, by fome, is thought to eclipfe
that from the bridge.

Government

Government of the Town.—The Duke of Roxburgh, as lay proprietor of the lands and abbey of Kelfo, is Lord of the Manor. His Grace's anceſtor, Sir Robert Ker of Cefsford, obtained this grant from James I. of England, anno 1605, on the forfeiture of Edward Earl of Bothwell, Admiral of Scotland, when it was probably made a burgh of barony.

Kelfo is governed by a Baron Bailie, appointed by the Duke, and fifteen ſtent-maſters, of whom the Duke nominates ſeven. The other eight confiſts of the Preſes of the Merchant Company, a Deacon Convener, the Deacons of the five following Corporations, Hammermen, Skinners, Shoemakers, Taylors, Weavers, and the Deacon of the Butchers, although they are not incorporated. The ſtent-maſters, under the authority of the Baron Bailie, are entruſted with the power of impoſing a ſtent or tax upon the inhabitants, as they judge their circumſtances may afford. This is levied for the purpoſe of ſupplying the inhabitants with water, conveyed by leaden pipes, to different parts of the town, for repairing the ſtreets, keeping the town clock in order, paying part of the ſchoolmaſter's ſalaries, and for ſeveral other incidents.

Sects and Religious Houſes.—Beſides the eſtabliſhed church, and an Epiſcopal chapel, there are a number of ſects, each of which has a houſe for public worſhip, and ſome of them are even elegant. Theſe are the kirk of Relief, Burghers, Antiburghers, Cameronians, Methodiſts, and Quakers. There are three Roman Catholics, and one Jew in the pariſh. The major part of the inhabitants, particularly of the genteel claſs, attend the pariſh church, and Epiſcopal chapel. The meeting-houſes are chiefly ſupported by inhabitants of different pariſhes in the vicinity. This place, being centrical and convenient, induces them to build here. The Parochial
church

church and Episcopal chapel are both new; the former, a spacious octagon, with a handsome dome, and constructed to accomodate three thousand hearers; the latter, a small neat gothic building, and has lately been ornamented with an organ.

Population.—In the year 1749, the number of inhabitants was 2900. The return from Dr Webster, in 1755, was 2781, and the number at present amounts to 4324. The annexed table contains an exact statement of the number of houses, families, males, and females, in the town and country divisions of the parish, as drawn up from an actual survey made last year, 1792.

Houses in the town	376	Skinners - -	20
Families in ditto -	826	Weavers - -	60
Males in ditto -	1644	Optician - -	1
Females in ditto -	1913	Dyers and clothiers	3
Number of souls in ditto	3557	Tailors - -	47
Under 10 - -	933	Upholsterers - -	2
From 10 to 20 -	713	Brewers - -	2
From 20 to 50 -	1416	Plaisterers - -	6
From 50 to 70 -	393	Carpenters - -	60
From 70 to 100 -	102	Midwives - -	6
Houses in the country	126	Masons - -	40
Families in ditto -	127	Smiths - -	15
Males in ditto -	365	Copper and white iron	
Females in ditto -	402	smiths - -	6
Number of souls in ditto	767	Staymakers - -	3
Under 10 - -	193	House painters -	2
From 10 to 20 -	141	Glovers - -	4
From 20 to 50 -	334	Carriers - -	3
From 50 to 70 -	78	Carters - -	40
From 70 to 100 -	21	Labourers -	162

Cler-

Clergymen	7	Stocking weavers	7
Medical practitioners	6	Gardeners	10
Writers or attorneys	11	Nailers	7
Schoolmasters	7	Cutlers	3
Booksellers and printers	2	Watchmakers	4
Shopkeepers	30	Glaziers	2
Bakers	32	Barbers and hair-dressers	6
Butchers	24	Milliners	4
Inn and alehouse keepers	40	Mantua-makers	8
Saddlers	12	Pastry cooks	2
Shoemakers	147		

The disproportion between the average number of each family of the town and country, is owing to the number of widows and single women, who live more conveniently in the town, and get employment more readily than in the country. In 38 years, the increase of inhabitants has been 1543. This great increase may, in part, be accounted for, from the destruction of many villages in the neighbourhood, occupied by small farmers and mechanics. From the enlargement of the farms, many were obliged to follow other trades, and Kelso being the metropolis of the district, they flocked there for habitations and employment; and, in proportion as labourers and mechanics have become fewer in the country, Kelso increased in population.

Fairs, Markets, Manufactures, &c.—The weekly market day is Friday. There are twelve high markets in the year, two before and one after the term days of Whitsunday and Martinmas; the two first are for hiring male and female servants; the last is generally employed by the servants in mirth, and in laying out their wages before they enter again

into

into ſervice. On theſe days, the concourſe of people being great, and beyond what is known on the like occaſions in any part of Scotland, it is productive of immenſe profits to the ſhopkeepers, milliners, &c. among whom they lay out incredible ſums of money, principally for wearing apparel, and female ornaments. The other ſix high market days are in March and the end of autumn; the former for purchaſing horſes for ſummer work, ſuch as, driving lime, coal, &c.; which being over, they ſell the horſes again before winter ſets in, owing to the high price of fodder at this ſeaſon.

There are three fairs in the pariſh, including St. James's, which is held on the 5th of Auguſt; two in the town, one of theſe on the 10th of July, the other on the 2d of November. When theſe fairs were eſtabliſhed, they were wiſely deſigned; the firſt was for buying lean cattle, to be fed during the ſummer and autumn months, upon meadow and paſture ground; and, when fat, they were brought to market, and ſold for winter and ſpring food, called Marts, being immediately killed and ſalted. In theſe days, freſh meat was not to be got during winter; but, ſince the introduction of turnip huſbandry, the market is plentifully ſupplied with the very beſt fed cattle during the whole year. The ſummer fair being no longer of its original uſe, it would be a great advantage to the ſtockholders, to have it altered to the end of Auguſt; this would ſuit dealers in cattle to purchaſe, at a convenient time, to drive them ſouth to Woolpitt market, held in September. Fairs ought to ſucceed one another from north to ſouth, until ſtocks arrive in London, the *ne plus ultra*. The great concourſe of people, of all deſcriptions, who attend the weekly markets, is the principal ſource from whence the inhabitants derive their ſupport; but, of all other ranks in ſociety, they are moſt obliged to the farmers, who come here in great numbers to ſell immenſe quantities
of

of grain, particularly wheat, all by the sample. They are a most respectable body. Their farms, advanced to the most perfect state of cultivation, shew, that, in ingenuity and industry, they are not inferior to the farmers of any other country; and with respect to depth of information and liberality of sentiment, they ought to be esteemed what they really are, a society of independent country gentlemen.

Articles of Trade.—The shopkeepers, who are the most respectable class of traders, deal to a great extent, in all kinds of woollen drapery, haberdashery, hosiery goods, groceries. and hard wares; and have likewise a great demand for various kinds of grass seeds. These different articles amount to a great sum; but, from the difficulty of ascertaining it, I forbear giving a statement; it may, however, be curious and interesting to mention the quantities of exciseable wines, spirits, &c. consumed yearly in Kelso, and the adjacent country, exclusive of what is commissioned by people of the higher rank, from wine merchants at a distance.

	Gallons.
British spirits - - -	17690
Foreign spirits - - -	2028
Foreign wine, French - - -	220
Foreign wine, not French - -	2560
	libs.
Green tea - - - -	272
Black tea - - - -	10292
Coffee - - - -	388

The bakers make into bread 3000 Winchester quarters of wheat flour annually. The brewers make 2570 barrels of

of ftrong ale and beer, each containing 36 Englifh ale gal-
lons. The butchers have lately been accommodated, by the
Duke of Roxburgh, with a large and excellent market place.
Upon an average, they kill annually,

Black cattle - - -	700
Calves - - - -	620
Sheep and lambs - - -	8000
Swine - - - - -	600

The fkinners drefs from 70 to 80000 fheep and lamb
fkins. They alfo fend to Manchefter and other places,
the wool of 40 or 50000 *mort* fkins. Thefe are, the fkins
of lambs, either brought forth dead, or which die early.
They likewife collect and fend away above 5000 hare fkins*.
The fhoemakers, by far the moft numerous clafs, make annually 30,000 pair of fhoes, and from 3 to 400 pair of boots.
Thefe are all fold at different fairs in Northumberland, and
in Kelfo market. The high wages the journeymen receive,
and the price of leather, precludes mafters from the benefit
of exportation.

The weavers yearly make about 20,000 yards of flannel,
or what are locally called, plains; and from 9 to 10,000 of
different kinds of linen, which they call cuftom work.
Stocking weavers work annually from 3 to 400 dozen of
pairs. Dyers and clothiers are principally employed in dying, and dreffing, what they call country work, made by individuals for private ufe, in pieces from 50 to 60 yards in
length. They alfo dye home-made cotton pieces for private wearing. The copper and white-iron fmiths, fell every
article

* Of rabbit, fox, polecat, and otter fkins, from 500 to
600.

article of kitchen utenſils, tea kettles, &c. and have a great demand for them at all the markets *.

Prices of Proviſions.—Grain, by the Wincheſter quarter, has ſold for ſome years paſt, in Kelſo market, at the follow-ing average prices :

Wheat	L. 2	0	0	Peaſe	L. 1	5	0
Barley	1	0	0	Beans	1	5	0
Oats	0	15	0	Rye	1	0	0

Beef,

* It is but juſtice, due to merit, to make particular mention of JOHN GIBSON optician in Kelſo, as a man of genius, who has made ſeveral improvements in optical inſtruments. His rectifying teleſcopes ſhew objects very diſtinctly, by rendering them brighter, and more free from tremors, than any we have ſeen. This ariſes partly from the compoſition of the ſpecula, all of which he caſts himſelf, and partly from the correct figure and high poliſh he gives them. He has invented a reflecting microſ-cope, which ſhews minute objects, with much greater exactneſs, than any made upon the refracting principle. The conſtruction of it is very ſimple, and it is eaſily managed, and adapted to ſhow both opaque and tranſparent objects, which can be applied to it with much facility. He has been equally ſucceſsful in the execution and improvement of the achromatic teleſcopes. He obſerved, that, in the beſt of theſe inſtruments, ſome of the co-lours were not corrected, and found that it lay in the principle; for, on examining the nature of the crown and flint glaſs, of which they are made, he diſcovered, that the diſtance of the colours, in the oblong images, formed by priſms, made of theſe kinds of glaſs, were not ſimilar; and, therefore, that all the different coloured rays, could not be united in the ſame point. Whether, by uſing flint glaſs of a different compoſition, or by ſome other device, we know not; but he has not only over-come this error in the principle, but likewiſe that ariſing from the ſpherical figure of the compound lens. Some of his teleſ-copes, 4$\frac{1}{2}$ feet in length, with triple object glaſſes, bear, with the greateſt diſtinctneſs, a magnifying power of more than 240 times. Theſe teleſcopes he makes of four different lengths, one foot, two, three, four and a half feet, and mounts them either in ſliding tubes or on ſtands, by which they are fitted for aſtronomical purpoſes.

Beef, mutton, veal, and lamb, are from 3d. to 5d. per lib.
Dutch weight; pork is somewhat less in value : Butter
from 8d. to 10d. per lib. of 24 oz.; Cheese from 4s. to
5s. the English stone. A goose 2s.; A turkey from 2s. 6d.
to 3s. and 4. A fowl from 10d. to 1s.; and chickens 4d.
to 6d. each. Eggs from 3d. to 6d. per dozen. Coals from
9s. 6d. to 10s. 6d. per cart, containing 12 cwt. This article has of late been higher, but is again approaching to the
old price. This market is well supplied with fish of various
kinds; and, upon the whole, at a cheap rate, considering
the distance from the sea, but, as the price varies much, no
average can be fixed; salmon, early in the year, being sent
to London, even when caught at Kelso, will bring 1s. 6d.
per lib. The great salmon fisheries upon Tweed, are near
the mouth of the river; they gradually lessen in value, as
they become more distant from the sea.

Ecclesiastical State, Schools, and Poor.—The stipend is, in
money and victual, 100 guineas, per annum, exclusive of a
house and garden, and a valuable glebe, measuring between
six and seven acres. It is worthy of remark, that, during
this century, there have been but two incumbents, Mr Ramsay, and the present much esteemed and worthy pastor, Mr
Cornelius Lundie.

There are two established schools, one for Latin, and the
other for English. The tutor has a salary of 22l. per annum, a house and garden, and 5s. per quarter for each of
his pupils. He has about 50 scholars. The office of session-clerk, is generally annexed to his employment, which
is worth about 12l. a year. The English master's salary is
5l. 13s.; 2s. 6d. and 3s. 6d. per quarter from his pupils;
the first for being taught reading; the second reading and
writing; and the third arithmetic, in addition to the other

two

two. His ſcholars are from 100 to 130. There are alſo four other Engliſh ſchools, one of them taught by the clerk of the chapel, and in good reputation. Beſides theſe, there are female teachers, for inſtructing girls in ſewing. A recent inſtitution, which does credit to the founders, and which, it is hoped, will turn out to their advantage, and to that of the public in general, is *a ſchool of induſtry*, in which employment is given to poor girls, who have ſtated hours for ſewing, knitting, and tambouring, for learning to read and write, and for inculcating moral duties.

In the year 1782, there were 57 penſioners on the poor's-roll; in April 1792, their number amounted to 92, of whom 23 were men, 48 women, and 21 children. Their weekly allowance came to 5 l. 6 s. 5 d. of which the heritors paid 3 l. 14 s. 6 d. and the town 1 l. 3 s. 7 d.; the balance was made up by part of the money ariſing from charitable legacies.

Births and Deaths.—The births amount to about 200 annually, but, owing to the number of diſſenters from the eſtabliſhed church, and others who neglect to regiſter their baptiſms, it is impoſſible to aſcertain the number. Surely the ſmall tax for regiſtration, which may in future be of eſſential conſequence to the children, and of preſent information to the public, ought to be enforced.—For five years ſucceſſively, the deaths, upon an average, amounted to 134, ſo that only one out of 32 die in the year.

Climate and Diſeaſes.—Eaſterly winds, accompanied with froſt, ſleet, and moiſture, prevail here, as well as upon the whole eaſt coaſt, for three or four months in the year. They produce intermitting fevers, rheumatiſm, and other febrile affec-

affections, and never fail to aggravate the complaints of valetudinarians; yet, from the very favourable situation of the town, their baneful effects are less felt here, than in any other spot in the country. There is no situation in the north where the climate is so mild; which the author has observed when travelling south in the spring, when the foliage of the hedges and trees was more advanced about Kelso, than in any situation north of York.

It is true that the climate becomes colder in proportion as one ascends from the Tweed, so much so, that at a mile or two south or north from Kelso, a considerable change is felt in the air, and strongly marked in the progress of vegetation.

However healthy the people are in this parish, which is obvious from those proportion the advanced in life bear to the whole number, and from only 1 in 32 dying annually, yet many of the young and beautiful fall victims to consumptions, and other scrophulous affections. These diseases are frequent over all the north of England and south of Scotland. This may in part be owing to the prevailing cold east winds obstructing perspiration; to the constant vicissitude of weather, to which our insular situation subjects us; and to the inhabitants not paying due attention to their clothing, nor to their persons, in point of cleanliness. Their diet, though chiefly farinaceous, and esteemed wholesome, from the quantity which the labouring class use daily, may be one cause of laying the foundation of glandular and visceral diseases. Although the mechanics in town generally eat meat for dinner, the labourers in town and country seldom do so; but one and all of them live much upon hasty pudding, and boiled potatoes with milk; without deviation, they all breakfast or sup upon the one or the other. Most of the adults eat of this food, at a meal, from 6 to 8 English

pounds

pounds weight, including milk; children in proportion. Surely this amazing quantity of food muſt injure the tone of the ſtomach, and, from the air let looſe in digeſtion, to what an immenſe magnitude may it not be diſtended, by which the whole chylopoetic viſcera muſt be much oppreſſed. Hence flatulency and indigeſtion ariſe, which is ſoon follow-ed by bad concoĉted chyle, which gradually debilitates the ſyſtem, and is followed by glandular affeĉtions, eaſily obſerv-ed in the large bellies of children, owing to the meſenteric glands being obſtruĉted. Other ſcrophulous ſymptoms gra-dually ſucceed, and tubercles being formed in the lungs, ul-timately produce conſumptions. The ſame cauſes, which ex-cite pulmonary affeĉtions in the young, lay the foundation for viſceral obſtruĉtions in the more advanced in life. This is obvious from the ſtate of Kelſo Diſpenſary. Laſt year there were 604 medical patients admitted upon that charity, out of theſe 236 were affeĉted with one or other of theſe complaints. In 27 deaths (the number reported for the year) 18 died of theſe diſeaſes; and without doubt there were many more, whoſe deaths not being intimated to the gover-nor, could not be publiſhed in the ſtatement.

A ſcrophulous affeĉtion often remains dormant in the ſyſtem for years; and were it not for exciting cauſes which produce inflammation in the glands, many would live to old age, who now fall viĉtims to this diſeaſe; theſe are, ſevere labour, ſudden change from vegetable to animal food, the too frequent uſe of ſpirituous liquors, expoſure to cold, which ſuddenly obſtruĉts perſpiration, particularly after ſuch exerciſes as accelerate the circulation of the blood, and de-termine to the lungs, as running, leaping, dancing, &c.

Excepting diſeaſes peculiar to children, epidemics ſeldom or never prevail in Kelſo. About 4 years ago, a putrid fe-ver was introduced by a patient from the country; it ſpread, and

and proved fatal to many. The weather at the time was warm, and the air moist; but it would not probably have proved so baneful, had proper attention been paid to cleaning the gutters of the streets, and to cleanliness in general. The greatest part of the town stands upon a level, it therefore requires particular attention, to prevent water and filth of every kind from stagnating. This stigma is by no means more applicable to the inhabitants of Kelso, than to the north in general. Did they but know what a *fomes* for disease uncleanliness produces, they would instantly follow the example of their southern neighbours, who, as a late author observes, are now as remarkable for that particular attention to cleanliness, as they were two centuries ago for the contrary extreme. To the last cause, the frequent visitation of the plague has been often attributed; for ever since they became cleanly in their persons, houses, and streets, this dreadful disease has not once appeared among them.

Miscellaneous Observations.—The uncommon fertility of this country affording all the necessaries of life in abundance, and at a moderate price, its population, and the amazing number of sheep, bred upon the Cheviot and Lammermuir hills, whose wool and skins are sent to the most distant parts of the island, are circumstances so peculiarly favourable to manufactures, that one is naturally led to expect, that here they must be established and flourish; yet hitherto, unfortunately, none of any consequence has been instituted, the Kelso plains being the only one ever attempted, and even this does not increase. In general, this is supposed to be owing to the distance, and high price of coals. This opinion, however, seems not to be altogether well founded, as in many English manufacturing towns, and even in Hawick and Galashiels, the one 20, and the other only 16 miles from

Kelso,

Kelfo, coal is brought from a much greater diftance, and fold
at a higher price, than in Kelfo, yet in thefe towns they
flourifh, and are carried on to a confiderable extent ; but
although the demand were greater than it really is, if the
roads leading to the coal hills were kept in proper repair,
that neceffary article would undoubtedly be procured at a
much eafier rate. It has been obferved, that, in countries
where agriculture is carried to fuch a degree of perfection as
in this, manufactures are little if at all attended to. This
may be accounted for in part, from the thirft of mankind
after riches. Our farmers being by far the moft opulent
and profperous clafs in the community, this naturally induces
men of wealth to lay out their money in hufbandry, per-
fuaded that in this way they have the beft reafon to look for
a certain and fpeedy return. But were manufactures eftablifhed, they would foon exhibit another great fource of
wealth, and both would equally affift and derive advantage
from each other.

The higher clafs of inhabitants in this parifh are courteous
in their manners, liberal in their fentiments, and benevolent
in their difpofitions. A public library, which has exifted
upwards of forty years, and can now boaft of a collection of
the beft modern authors, being regularly fupplied with every
publication of merit ; together with a coffee-houfe fupplied
with the London, Edinburgh, and Kelfo newfpapers, have
contributed to render them not lefs intelligent than agreeable. The proprietors of the library have lately refolved to
erect a neat elegant houfe for the books, and for the accommodation of the librarian.

Many of the inhabitants have formed themfelves into three
different focieties, the members paying a certain fum weekly,
for the purpofe of maintaining any of their number who
may be fick ; in cafes of death, for defraying funeral expences,

pences, and giving a small annuity to their widows. Could societies like these be made general, they would supersede poors rates, and would afford to the indigent themselves, a much better subsistence than they can obtain from the other.

It is much to be regretted, that the elegant square in which the market is held, is not ornamented with a better townhouse. The present is old and ruinous, and, from its construction, the receptacle of filth, and the harbour of vagabonds, who here lay their plans of depredation, which are too frequent among the idle and low class of whisky companions.

There is no satisfaction which renders the possession of riches more agreeable, than the power it gives the possessors of applying part to alleviate the distresses of the indigent. This country has happily many such, among whom the Hon. Mrs Baillie of Jervifwood appears most conspicuous. About 17 years ago, upon her suggesting the utility of a Dispensary, for the relief of the diseased among the lower orders of people, of all the parishes on both sides of the borders; the opulent, with a readiness that does equal credit to their honour and feelings, heartily concurred with her in advancing a sum more than sufficient for its immediate establishment, and providing for its support by an annual subscription. They have now a handsome convenient building, where the patients receive advice and medicines, and a spacious ward, to accommodate 12 patients who may stand in need of chirurgical assistance. The subscribers have now the satisfaction to see their funds yearly increase; and also the agreeable reflection of having contributed to the comfort and relief of between 8000 and 9000 persons, no less by preventing their running in debt to apothecaries, than by the medical assistance they have received.

It

It is matter of ferious regret to every perfon of feeling
and reflection, it ftrikes ftrangers with furprife, and impreffes
no favourable opinion of the inhabitants, that the church-
yard, from being uninclofed, fhould have a number of roads
running through it; and that it fhould be covered with the
fkins of animals, which the fkinners take the liberty of drying upon it; and, owing to the fame caufe, there is nothing
to prevent even fwine from turning up the graves. The
refpect which mankind, in all ages and countries, whether
refined or barbarous, have uniformly paid to the afhes of
their anceftors, fhould of itfelf be a fufficient motive to induce the heritors and inhabitants to concur in inclofing it,
and by this means to prevent ftrangers from entertaining
fentiments and fufpicions of them, for which no other part
of their conduct can afford the leaft foundation.

PARISH OF KIRKTOUN.

(Presbytery of Jedburgh.—Synod of Merse and Tiviot-dale.—County of Roxburgh.)

By the Reverend Mr BENJAMIN DICKISON.

Extent, Appearance, &c.

THE parish of Kirktoun extends in length about 8 miles from E. to W. and in breadth betwixt 1 and 2, from N. to S. Though without any distinguished mountains, the face of the country presents a continued range of hills, separated only by small rivulets, and gradually ascending from E. to W. The soil, in general, is dry, light, and shallow, with a bottom of hard or shelly rock, and productive of nutritive grass, even to the summits of the hills. Though evidently destined by nature, and, in its present unsheltered state, fit for pasturage alone, a considerable proportion of the land is kept in tillage, and sown with oats, pease, and bear, though without any regular rotation. The produce, at an average, is less than 3 after 1, and much inferior in quality to that which was sown. Potatoes and turnips are planted to a small extent, and cultivated with success. The different kinds of clover and grass seeds have been tried ; but, in general, from want of shelter and defence against pasturage at improper seasons, have either not sprung at all, or been destroyed by the winter frosts and storms. Attempts have been made,

and

and ftill are making, to meliorate the grain, and increafe the quantity, by the modern plans of hufbandry, with lime, marl, and fallowing, the effect of which, however, in this unpropitious foil and climate, is only a greater quantity of ftraw. The reafon the farmers afcribe for this unprofitable train of culture, is the neceffity they lie under of providing winter food for their cattle. Thefe indeed, and fheep, are, and ought to be, the great object of their attention, as the principal, and, at prefent, almoft the only fource of fubfiftence and wealth.

Manners of the Inhabitants, &c.—Neither the records of the parifh, the monuments of antiquity, nor the cuftoms and morals of the inhabitants, exhibit any object particularly meriting the attention of the philofopher, the politician, or the moralift, unlefs this, which, though not a fingular, is rather an uncommon fact, that its hiftory, for ages paft, may, with the ftricteft regard to truth, be comprehended in a few words, " *One generation paffeth and another cometh.*"

There is here neither town nor village. Annexed to each farm-ftead are a few cottages, reared, in general, of turf and ftone. The inhabitants are poor and indolent, contented and frugal. The indigent, to the number of 12 or 13, are fupported by a poor's rate, levied equally upon the landlords and tenants, and the collections in church, amounting in all to about 30 l. *per annum*, which fo fully fupplies the needy, that there is not an itinerant beggar in the parifh. From the purity of the air, and the temperance of the inhabitants, fewer difeafes prevail here than in any fpot of Scotland perhaps of the fame extent. Agues, rheumatifms, and confumptions, are the moft frequent. Wine is only feen at funerals, whifky at weddings; and, in 2 or 3 houfes excepted, ale is a ftranger.

Markets,

Markets, &c.—The neareſt market town is Hawick, about 3 miles diſtant, where vivres are ſold nearly at the ſame rate as in Edinburgh. The great road from Edinburgh to New-caſtle, by Selkirk and Hawick, paſſes through the middle of this pariſh; one of the great advantages of which to this neighbourhood, is the opening up an eaſy acceſs, over the border mountains, to the coal-mines in the weſt parts of Northumberland. Theſe and the peat-moſſes, with which the country abounds, furniſh abundant, though expenſive fuel. There are veſtiges of ſome wood; but, at preſent, not a tree, and ſcarcely a buſh is to be ſeen in the pariſh.

Population.—Number of ſouls in 1755 - 330

Ditto in 1792 - 342

Males - - 172

Females - - 170

Under 10 - - 63

Between 10 and 20 - 71

Between 20 and 50 - 159

Between 50 and 70 - 38

Between 70 and 80 - 8

Between 80 and 90 - 3

Families - - 66

Married perſons - 78

Children, at an average for each marriage - 4

Average of births for 6 years paſt - - 5½

Average of deaths for ditto 3½

——— of marriages for ditto - 4

Bachelors above the age of 50 - - 4

Unmarried woman above the age of 45 - 1

Widowers - - 6

Widows - - 8

Members of the eſtabliſh-ed Church - 292

Seceders - - 50

Proprietors reſident - 0

——— non-reſident 4

Farmers under 50 l. *per annum* - - 3

Farmers above 50 l. *per annum* - - 14

Smith - - 1

Carpenters - 3

Weavers - - 6

Taylor - - 1

Miller - - 1

Wages of a man ſervant *per annum* - L. 7 0 0

Wages

Wages of a maid servant *per annum*, without

victuals -   -   -   -   - L. 3 10 0

————— taylor *per diem*   -   -   0 0 8

————— day-labourer *per diem*, without

victuals -   -   -   -   - 0 1 0

————— mason *per diem*, without victuals   0 1 6

————— carpenter *per diem*, without victuals   0 1 3

School and Ecclesiastical State.—The schoolmaster of the parish has a dwelling and school-house. His income, including salary, perquisites, and school-wages, does not exceed 12 l. *per annum.* The minister's stipend was lately augmented from 55 l. to about 80 l.; but there is now depending a process of reduction before the Court of Teinds. The Crown is patron, and titular of the teinds. The glebe contains about 5 acres. The manse was built about 30 years ago, and lately repaired. The church is an old, incommodious, pitiful edifice, not sufficient to contain a third of the inhabitants, small as their number is.

Rent and Stock.—Valued rent in Scotch money   L. 4526
Real rent, in Sterling money, somewhat more than L. 1000

Number of	Value of each at an average.	Total value.
Horses - 80	12 l.	L. 960
Black cattle 400	5 l.	L. 2000
Sheep - 4000	12 s.	L. 2400
Stones of wool annually produced	- - -	500
————— Average price, 1792, 17 s. *per* stone		L. 425

From the above statement, it is evident, that, according to the present rate of markets, the farmers may pay their rents from their folds and stalls, and have a little reversion, allowing the other productions of their lands for supporting their families,

families, and paying their ſervants wages, which they may
with ſtrict oeconomy accompliſh.

Miſcellaneous Obſervations.—Though both ſoil and climate,
in their preſent ſtate, are unpropitious to improvements,
there is no doubt that the modern plans of huſbandry might
be carried on with ſucceſs. To do this, the moſt likely method would be to plant wood, in ſuch proportions and directions as might moſt effectually break the violence of ſtorms,
and thereby prevent the roots of the young plants from being
torn up or broken, and the ripened grain from being ſhaken
out. For poor grain, and unproductive crops, are more owing to the autumnal winds, than either to poverty of ſoil, or
ſeverity of climate. This would neceſſarily lead to the making of incloſures, the advantages of which are well known
to every farmer in the more cultivated parts of the country.
Beſides the improvement and increaſe of grain, and the melioration of ſummer paſture, by the young graſs and clover
being ſaved and ſheltered in winter, abundance of better food
might be raiſed for the winter ſubſiſtence of ſheep and cattle,
and a ſuperior breed of both might be thus introduced, to
the great emolument both of landlord and tenant.

It is ſurpriſing, that the proprietors here practiſe ſo little
the elegant and permanent improvement of wood and incloſure, eſpecially as they ſeem, in other reſpects, well diſpoſed
to encourage their tenants in meliorating the grounds, and
increaſing the quantity and value of the productions, by purchaſing manure, and making of roads.

PARISH OF LESSUDDEN OR St BOSWELLS.

*(Preſbytery of Selkirk.—Synod of Merſe and Teviot-
dale.—County of Roxburgh.)*

By the Reverend Mr JOHN SCADE.

Origin of the Name.

A CONSIDERABLE village in this pariſh goes by the name
of *Leſſudden*, which it is ſuppoſed to have got from its
having been once the reſidence of one Aidan, Biſhop of Lin-
disfarne. *Lis* being a Scoto-Celtic word, ſignifying *reſidence*,
Lis-Aidan, the reſidence of Aidan, by a careleſs pronunciation, might in time become what it now is, *Leſſudden*. Aidan
was educated in the monaſtery of Icolmkill, and is mentioned
in terms of reſpect by Bede, in his eccleſiaſtical hiſtory [*].
St Boiſil was a diſciple of St Cuthbert, and for ſome time belonged to the monaſtery of Old Melroſe, in the neighbourhood of this place.

Extent, Productions, &c.—This pariſh, which is ſituated on
the banks of the Tweed, within 10 miles of Kelſo, 5 of Melroſe,

---

[*] Such as are diſpoſed to inquire farther into the life of
Biſhop Aidan, may conſult Dr Mackenzie's lives of the Scotch
writers, vol. 1. p. 359. Bede, Hay's Reliquae Sacrae, and
Spottiſwood's Church Hiſtory. But the more general name of
the pariſh, and the proper name of the church, is *St Boſwells*,
from St Boiſil a French monk, who is ſaid to have founded it
about the beginning of the ſeventh century.

roſe, and 7 of Jedburgh, is from E. to W. about 3 miles long. Towards the E. it is narrow, but becomes broader to the weſtward ; and, at the broadeſt, may be about a mile and a half, or near 2 miles wide. The ſoil, in general, is good ; that which lies on the banks of the Tweed, and in ſundry other places of the pariſh, is fine; and even the grounds which are the worſt, are capable of great improvement, by the uſe of lime or marl. Of late, much has been done, and the ſpirit of cultivation continues to operate. The expence of improving with lime is great, as the lime muſt come either from the Lothian kilns, or thoſe on the border of England. Each cart-load, drawn by 2 horſes, and conſiſting of 12 firlots, coſts from 10 s. to 12 s. Six, eight, or nine of theſe cart-loads, according to the nature of the ground, are employed upon an acre ; but this expence is many times repaid with intereſt, from the melioration of the land. Fine wheat has been raiſed on ſome pieces of land in this pariſh, which, leſs than 40 years ago, were thought incapable of producing ſuch a valuable article. Wheat is raiſed in due proportion to the extent of the farms every where in the pariſh, which, in many places, yields to none in Teviotdale in point of quality. In the whole, from 450 to 500 bolls are raiſed annually. Barley is cultivated in proportional plenty, and with ſucceſs ; and the ſame may be ſaid of oats and peaſe. On the lands . near Tweedſide, the cold ſeed peaſe are commonly ſown, and as commonly productive of fine crops. In ſundry places, turnips either are or may be ſown with advantage ; they are found to grow to a good ſize. The whole lands are remarkably well adapted for yielding fine crops of graſs.

The principal market for the wheat raiſed here is Dalkeith. Peebles furniſhes a demand for a good deal. A conſiderable quantity of the barley is diſpoſed of at Melroſe, ſome at Dalkeith and elſewhere, beſide what is ground with peaſe into
bread.

bread-meal, and fold both at home and in other places adjacent. The peafe are in requeft, and find various purchafers ; and, with refpect to the oats, the manufacture of them into meal, and the conveyance of it to the Lothian markets, is an article of trade.

Rent, &c.—As in other places, fo here, land has rifen, and is upon the rife. The valued rent is 4330 l. 18 s. 2 d. Scotch. The real rent it is not fo eafy to afcertain exactly, as feveral cultivate their own lands, but it is probably from 1600 l. to 1800 l. Sterling.

St Bofwell's Fair.—St Bofwell's fair is held on a large green of the fame name, through which paffes the turnpike road from the Lothians to Jedburgh, &c. It holds in the name of his Grace the Duke of Buccleugh, and is faid to be the greateft in the fouth of Scotland. It is held annually on the 18th of July, or on the Monday following, if the 18th fall on Sunday ;· but its happening either on the Monday or Saturday, is very juftly thought to occafion much inattention to the religious obfervance of the Sabbath. The evil has been complained of, but no remedy has yet been applied. If the day be fine, the concourfe of people is immenfe ; and, whatever it be, bufinefs brings a great multitude, of which fome come from a very confiderable diftance. Sheep are a principal article of commerce. Great flocks of fheep of all denominations are brought from all parts of the adjacent country, and generally find fo ready a market, as to be difpofed of early in the morning, at lateft in the forenoon. Black cattle are alfo numerous ; and the fhow of horfes has ufually been fo fine, that buyers come from many places both of England and Scotland. Linen cloth is another article. Great numbers of people throughout the neighbouring country employ

ploy

ploy themſelves during winter in ſpinning; they endeavour to get their webs ready againſt the fair, where they are pretty ſure of a market, though not always of a ſufficient recompence for their expences and labour; neverthelefs, upon the whole, they get ſuch prices as encourage them to be induſtrious in the ſame line. The prices, according to the quality of the cloth, are from 10 d. and 1 s. to 3 s. 6 d. 4 s. and 4 s. 6 d. *per* yard. Some provide themſelves in linen at this fair, alledging that they can furniſh themſelves cheaper and better at it, than they could do by manufacturing at home. This may poſſibly be true; for, in genteel families, the expence of maintaining the workers will be higher than the ſpinſter in a cottage, while the ſkill and care beſtowed on the work are equal. Booths, (or, as they are here called, *craims*), containing hardware and haberdaſhery goods, are erected in great numbers at the fare, and ſtored with ſuch articles as ſuit the generality. The money turned in the courſe of the day at this fair is gueſſed to be from 8000 l. to 10,000 l. Sterling. The Duke of Buccleugh receives a certain rate or toll upon ſheep, cattle, and all other commodities brought into the fair for ſale. Old ſheep pay 1 merk Scotch *per* ſcore, lambs one half of that ſum, and ſo on. This toll is ſometimes collected by people appointed for the purpoſe; but it is more commonly let to ſome individual for ſuch a ſum of money as can be agreed on. The higheſt at which it ever was let was 53 l. the loweſt 33 l. and the average is ſuppoſed to be about 38 l.

Eccleſiaſtical State.—The church, between 3 and 4 years ago, was ruinous, unpleaſant, extremely cold, and injurious to health; but, by a thorough repair, has been made one of the beſt in the country. The expence incurred was 100 l. Sterling. The manſe and offices are quite new, having been finiſhed in ſummer 1791. The church and manſe are in a
pleaſant

pleasant situation on the banks of the Tweed; but the church is not in the most centrical situation for the conveniency of the parish. The stipend consists of 54 bolls of oats, 26 bolls of bear or barley, both of the measure of Dryburgh Abbey, and 24 l. 6 s. in money. The common measure of this country is the Teviotdale boll, which contains 15 pecks; but the Abbey boll contains only 14, which reduces the victual in the stipend to 50 bolls of oats, and 24 of barley, Teviotdale measure. The money stipend, 24 l. 6 s. arises chiefly out of a conversion, by which the incumbent is a great loser. The glebe consists of about 4 Scotch acres, and the land exceedingly good. In addition to this, the incumbent has some banks, in name of a grass glebe; but the greatest part of them being dangerous for either horse or cow to feed on, no material advantage is derived from them. A process to procure some small addition to the living is in contemplation *.

School.—There is an established schoolmaster in Lessudden, where he has a good comfortable house, and teaches reading of English, writing, arithmetic, book-keeping, mensuration, &c. with the principles and the books used by beginners in the Latin tongue. Beside the school wages, he has a legal salary of 100 merks Scotch; but, upon his application, the heritors, at a meeting lately held, unanimously agreed to augment his salary to 100 l. Scotch; which addition to his living, they have given him ground to believe, will be continued

* In the bank of the grass glebe next the Tweed, there are sundry springs of water, one of which is reported to be of a chalybeate quality; but no experiments which are now remembered, have been made to ascertain its properties. It has, however, been long and still is, used in scorbutic cases, some say with great success; and it is in the recollection of many, that sundry people have thought themselves so much benefited by it, that they made a point of using it either on the spot, or of having it brought to them.

nued whilſt he continued to merit their approbation as he had done. The ſchoolmaſter is ſeſſion-clerk, clerk to the heritors in their meetings, and collector of ſuch ſums as they have occaſion to aſſeſs themſelves in, for each of which offices he has a certain allowance. Fifty ſcholars, at an average, attend the ſchool through the year *.

Population.—There is no reaſon to believe that this pariſh ever was very populous; perhaps its preſent inhabitants are as numerous as at any period of which we are well informed. The village of Leſſudden, indeed, was once more populous than it is now; but then, in ſeveral other parts of the pariſh, there was ſcarce any population at all. The return to Dr Webſter in 1755 was 309 ſouls. The whole number at preſent, incluſive of children, amount to about 500. Of theſe, about 300 reſide in Leſſudden, and about 200 in the other parts of the pariſh. The people, in general, are of a ſober and frugal turn both of mind and manners. In Leſſudden there may be from 85 to 90 children, and elſewhere in the pariſh from 50 to 55.

The births, taken at an average for the laſt 5 years, are 14 annually, the marriages 5, and the burials 10.

The poor on the pariſh-roll, at preſent, are fewer than for ſome years paſt, being only 3 in number; they receive from 1 s. to 2 s. *per* week, which is raiſed by an aſſeſſment every half year upon the proprietors of land and their tenants, and, at an average for the laſt 10 years, has amounted to about 14 l. 12 s. *per annum.* The money collected weekly at the church,

---

* The wages allowed by the records of the pariſh are, for teaching Engliſh, 1 s. *per* quarter; for Engliſh and writing, 1 s. 6 d; for Engliſh, writing, and arithmetic, 2 s.; and no particular ſum *per* quarter is condeſcended upon for Latin.

church, (which is from 5 l. to 6 l. in the year), together with what is brought in by the mort-cloth and the dues upon marriage proclamations, is employed by the kirk-ſeſſion to give occaſional aſſiſtance to the neceſſitous not on the poor's roll, and at times to add to the comfort of thoſe who receive the bounty of the heritors.

Fuel.—This neceſſary of life we are obliged to procure at an expence which with difficulty we are able to afford. There are many caſes in which a moderate competency of firing, to put over the ſeverity of the winter, takes moſt of the money which a family of decent working people, after maintaining themſelves, can be ſuppoſed to ſave. All honeſt, though humble ſhifts, are therefore made to provide and ſave fuel. Coals are the common, and indeed the cheapeſt firing. They are brought to this place either from the collieries in Lothian, which are at the diſtance of 27 or 28 miles, or from Etal in Northumberland, which is 24 or 25 miles diſtant. But the greateſt part of what is uſed here, comes from the Lothians, and is brought by the returning carts, which carried from home oat-meal or grain to Dalkeith market. A cart with 2 horſes commonly brings 14 cwt. of coals, which coſt the pur-chaſer 1 s. *per* cwt. and yet the driver is ſaid to have but poor profits. From this almoſt unſupportable expence, which is more likely to increaſe than decreaſe, perhaps nothing can deliver this part of the country, unleſs the canal which has been ſpoken of as intended to come to Ancrum bridge, ſhould be carried into effect. To this ſcarcity, and conſe-quent high price of firing, may be imputed in part the too common complaint of rheumatiſm, or what ſome of the people call the *pains*, which are often very diſtreſſing, and too often not well treated by the patients themſelves.

Miſcellaneous Obſervations.—There are in this pariſh 102 horſes, and 279 black cattle. Of the latter, 90 are milch cows. The number of ſheep cannot be exactly aſcertained, as it varies in different years, according as the proprietors and farmers find it convenient to keep them.

The Tweed, which runs cloſe by Leſſudden, in addition to the beauty and pleaſantneſs which it gives to the country, is likewiſe productive of advantages. Between this place and Berwick, is a diſtance of more than 30 miles; and yet not only here, but much higher up the water, fine and large ſalmon are caught in the ſeaſon, and ſold in the country at the moderate price of from 2 d. to 3 d. *per* lib.; but the greateſt part is bought up by people who find it their intereſt to carry them elſewhere. Salmon of 28 lib. weight have been caught; but from 6 to 18 lib. is the ordinary weight of thoſe taken hereabouts; ſo that, at the proper times, the neighbourhood is ſeldom at a loſs for a ſmall ſalmon, which proves a great conveniency to families, and contributes to the bettering of the circumſtances of thoſe concerned in the fiſhing.

PARISH OF LILLIES-LEAF.

(COUNTY OF ROXBURGH—PRESBYTERY OF SELKIRK
—SYNOD OF MERSE AND TIVIOTDALE).

By the Rev. Mr WILLIAM CAMPBELL, *Minister.*

Name, Extent, and River.

THE origin of the name is uncertain. It has been wrote *Lillies-life* and *Lillies-cliffe.*—It rises from the east, where the breadth is only half a mile, with a gradual ascent to the west, where it is a mile broad from north to south. It is broadest at the middle, being, upon a medium, 2 miles and one sixth. It is five miles and a half in length, and contains between 7000 and 8000 acres.—At the head of the parish, the river *Ale,* remarkable for the quality of its trouts, divides it for a mile, and then becomes the boundary to the north and east.

Soil, Farm Rents, Cultivation, and Produce —The soil varies, being partly clay, rich loam, and partly gravelly light sand. The crofts adjoining the village let at 35 s and 40 s. per acre.—The rents in general, for several years past, have been rising, and are still on the increase, owing, in a great measure, to the improvements and mode of management. The outfield ground is light, part dry, and part swampy. The English plough, after the model of Small of Rosline,

is

is used in general. Farmers are not so fond of sowing wheat as formerly. The culture of turnips is judged of more consequence, and keeps the land in good heart. A rotation of crops, as follows, has been adopted ; fallow, turnips, oats, pease, barley with grass seeds, hay, pasture for 2 years, oats, and then a fallow. Upon lighter ground, *1st*, crop oats ; *2dly*, Turnips, pease, or potatoes ; *3dly*, Barley ; *4thly*, Hay ; then oats, &c. as before. After this rotation, there is no need of a fallow.—The distance from lime is 25 miles. —There is a marl moss at the east end of the parish, and another at the west.—The manure in both is of an excellent quality. Its effects are more discernible on grass, than on land in tillage. There are other two mosses in the neighbourhood, at 4 miles distance, from which considerable quantities of marl are brought. The old maxim, " The " fodder is best which carries corn on its top," is entirely exploded. Sir John Buchanan Riddell, proprietor of a great part of the parish, and who proposes staying here, at least occasionally, is rapidly carrying on improvements. He has marl on his estate, yet the expence must be considerable. It is not to be doubted but they will turn out to good account, and his plantations add to the beauty of the place. Swift observes, " whoever could make two ears of corn, or two " blades of grass to grow, upon a spot of ground where only " one grew before, would deserve better of mankind, and " do more essential service to his country, than the whole " race of politicians put together *." Oxen are not used in labouring

---

* In place of *plowing matches*, which sometimes are attended with a considerable degree of confusion, and some disagreeable consequences among the servants, might it not answer better, if, for instance, the proprietors of ten ploughs were to collect 50 s.? the land to be marled before sowing, and the whole work during the season reviewed ; a premium of 1 l. 5 s. to the best upon the whole,

labouring as formerly. The muir land is kept for pasturage.

Prices of Provisions and Labour.—Provisions are high priced. Butcher meat is often sold at a dearer rate than in Edinburgh; butter at 10 d. per lib. (24 oz.) a pair of fowls at 1 s. 8 d. formerly only 1 s.; cheese 6 d. per lib. formerly 3½ d.; and other articles in proportion. The manner of living is greatly changed, being much more expensive; yet the farmers are in better circumstances, and much better lodged than they were 30 years ago. The wages of a man servant are from 6 l. to 8 l. Sterling; and those of a maid servant from 3 l. 4 s. to 3 l. 15 s. *per annum.* A day-labourer gets 10 d. with his meat, or 1 s. 4 d. without it; a taylor, 8 d. with, or 1 s. without it; a wright, 1 s. 6 d.; a mason, 1 s. 6 d.; a man for weeding potatoes or turnips, 8 d. In harvest, a man gets 1 s. 4 d. a woman, 1 s. 2 d. For 20 years past, work of every kind has risen in expence one third. It is more than probable the rise will still be higher. The school fees alone are moderate. Some farmers have their corns threshed for 4 d. per boll, with maintainance; a ditch 3 feet deep dug, with the thorns set, at 8 d. per rood, and a double ditch at 1 s. 4 d.

Roads, Fuel, Diseases, &c.—The roads are in a bad state, but will be put in good repair, as money for the statute labour is to be exacted, as far as law allows. One great inconvenience the people labours under, is the distance from coals, which is not less than 30 and 32 miles. Some peats may be procured here, but so high priced, that coals at 15 s. the 12 cwt.

whole, 15 s. to the second, and 10 s. to the third. The ploughmen would thus be attentive from first to last, and justice would be done the master.

cwt. are by far the cheapeft. In the article of firing, the inhabitants muſt be at a greater expence than any pariſh in the ſouth of Scotland. Agues, 20 years ago, were very fre- quent in the village, the road being almoſt impaſſable on ac- count of putrid ſtagnated water. This being removed, and the road formed and finiſhed, aguiſh complaints have almoſt totally diſappeared. It is unfortunate that this corner ſhould be ſo bare of trees, there being plenty of ground well adapted for large plantations, particularly of firs. The weedings would be uſeful as fuel; the body of the tree profitable, in a pariſh ſo remote from the ſea coaſt; and the ground en- riched by the leaves.

Population.—It is generally believed, that the population is greatly diminiſhed, there being veſtiges of conſiderable vil- lages, where now there ſtand only one or two houſes. Since the year 1760, 9 farms have been added to ſuch as lay adja- cent; and though the rent of each was not very conſider- able, yet the honeſt tackſman cleared with the proprietor, and brought up and educated his children, who proved uſe- ful members of ſociety. But whatever diminution may have lately taken place in the population of the pariſh, from theſe and ſimilar cauſes, it is certain, that there has been an in- creaſe upon the whole, within theſe 40 years, as appears from the following comparative ſtatement:

STATISTICAL TABLE OF THE PARISH OF LILLIES-LEAF.

Number of males in the pariſh, at Whitſunday 1793	342
Ditto of females - - - -	288
Total number of ſouls	630
Ditto in 1755, as returned to Dr Webſter	521
Increaſe	109

Families

Families in the village - - - 87
Ditto in the country - - - - 59

Total 146

AGES.

Perſons under 10 years of age - - ~ 148
————— between 10 and 20 - - - 103
————— ———— 20 and 30 - - - 135
————— ———— 30 and 60 - - - 184
————— ———— 60 and 80 * - - - 60

630

CONDITIONS, PROFESSIONS, &c.

Proprietors †	- - 17	Coopers	- -	2
Miniſter	- - 1	Tailors	- -	7
Seceders of various denomi-		Bakers	- -	2
nations	- - 35	Shop-keepers	-	3
Weavers	- - 14	Licenſed ale-houſes ‡		4
Wrights	- - 13	School-maſter	- -	1
Maſons	- - 9	Scholars in winter, about		50
Smiths	- - 3	Ditto in ſummer	-	36
Annual average of births		- - -		11
————— marriages		- - -		3
————— burials		- - - -		6

RENT, STOCK, &c.

Valued rent in Scotch money - - L. 8265
Real rent in Sterling, about - - - 3000

Horſes	- - 175	Swine	- -	29
Black cattle	- 580	Ploughs	- -	45
Sheep	- - 1394			

Manufactures.

* A few of this claſs are bordering upon 80.
† Beſides theſe heritors, there is a conſiderable number of feuers.
‡ Although this village is a thorough-fare, between the weſtern and eaſtern parts of the country, there is no occaſion for ſo many ale and ſpirit houſes.

Manufactures.—Many packs of lint, till of late, were sent from Darlington, by Newcastle, to be spun. The yarn was returned by the same conveyance. At present the spinners are employed by the manufacturers in Hawick. The quantity of cloth woven for sale is not great.

Ecclesiastical State.—This parish belonged formerly to the diocese of the Archbishop of Glasgow, who built the kirk betwixt the 9th and 10th century. There is paid to that university, the yearly sum of 5 l. 7 s. 6½ d. called the *Bishop's Coat*. The kirk was rebuilt in the year 1771, and is commodious and well seated. The Duke of Roxburgh is patron. The stipend, at the conversion of grain, is about 1000 l. Scotch, and 50 l. ditto for communion elements. The manse was built in the year 1762, very superficially and confined. An addition was made to it 15 years after, and the house is this season to get some necessary repairs. The glebe is of a tolerable good quality, measuring near 11 English acres *.

School.—The heritors, a few years ago, voluntarily raised the school-master's salary from 100 merks to 100 l. Scotch. They are contracting for a new school and school-house. His emoluments, as teacher, precentor, and session-clerk, do not exceed 17 l. *per annum.*

Poor.—The poor are supported by the interest of 105 l. Sterling sunk money, and an assessment on the land, the one half paid by the proprietor, and the other half by the tenant. The weekly collections supply such as occasionally

need

* That it might be kept entire, Sir Walter Riddell, in the year 1643, disponed half an acre of land to the then minister, and his successors in office, upon which the manse, &c. are built.

need affiftance. When a perfon is admitted a pauper, a bond is figned, conveying. a right to the heritors of what effects they have. This prevents impofition. If in value the effects exceed the expenditure, the furplus is given to the neareft relations of the deceafed.

Antiquities *.—In this parifh lies the feat of the ancient family

* Upon inclofing the grounds of Bewliehill, the workmen came to loofe earth, foft and black, and found a great number of human bones, feemingly burnt to a certain degree. The fpace was upwards of 20 feet diameter, being of a circular form, and feems to have been an outpoft of a Roman camp, the veftiges of which are to be feen in a neighbouring parifh, at 3 miles diftance. The rage of conqueft knows no bounds, but the Almighty brings good out of evil; for, by the invafion of the Romans, and the fuccefs attending their arms, Providence paved the way for publifhing and introducing Chriftianity into this ifland. Military weapons have been found, and fpears fharp on both fides; large quantities of human bones, fome with ribs adhering to the back bone; heads, in fome the teeth almoft frefh. One body was pretty entire; contiguous to it were the remains of a horfe. Frequent fkirmifhes had occurred in that corner of the parifh, with the foldiers of Charles II. A numerous party of Prefbyterians, who were marching to join their brethren at Bothwell Bridge, being attacked by fome troops of dragoons, fled to Bewlie Mofs for refuge; unable to extricate themfelves, many perifhed in the mud. When the old church of Lillies-Leaf was taken down, in 1771, there was found, below one of the feats, a coffin containing feveral human heads. We may fuppofe that they had been cut off by friends, that they might not be fixed upon the ports of any of the neighbouring boroughs, as it was not poffible to drag out the bodies without being difcovered. What a bleffed toleration do we now live under? And if the conftitution under which we live, in the courfe of time, needs repairs, tender and delicate fhould the hand be that touches it. Our fathers told us of frequent meetings in Lillies-Leaf muir, for the worfhip of God. The devout affembled at the hazard of their lives; the place they chofe was retired; and one of their number was placed on a rifing ground, to give the alarm on the appearance of danger.—ALEXANDER HOME,

family of RIDDEL, of that ilk, one of the moſt ancient, if not the very oldeſt in Scotland *.

Character and Manners.—The people in general, a very few excepted †, are ſober and attentive to buſineſs, there being plenty of work for ſuch as chuſe not to be idle, or half employed. They are regular in attending the ordinances of religion, and many have made no ſmall degree of improvement in Chriſtian knowledge. They adhere ſtrictly to the ſtandards

HOME, great-grand-father of the wife of the preſent miniſter, a man eminent for his piety, and ſimplicity of manners, came from the Merſe to join with his ſuffering brethren in Divine ſervice. Under the influence of that principle which " *think-* " *eth no evil*," he informed a gentleman, on his returning home, where he had been, who gave information to the ſervants of government, whereupon he was apprehended, condemned, and hanged at the Croſs of Edinburgh.

* Tradition ſays, this family fixed itſelf betwixt the ſeventh and eighth century. A late well informed and elegant hiſtorian was of this opinion. As poſitive proofs, Walter Riddell of Riddell married Violet Douglas in 936. About and after that period, grants of land were made by the kings of Scotland, and by ſome of the Popes, particularly by Pope Alexander II. A place of worſhip was erected near the houſe of Riddell, which had a burying ground, called *Chapel Park*. When in tillage, human bones occaſionally have been plowed up. This burying place was transferred to the preſent church-yard. Upon the outſide of Riddell ayle, there is inſcribed H. R. 1110.

† Previous to the rupture with America, a woman guilty of child-murder petitioned for baniſhment, which was granted. She denied to the father her being with child, and would not hearken to his propoſals for marriage ; yet, ſo violent was his attachment to this monſter of depravity, that he accompanied her to America, in the hope ſhe would relent, and at laſt give him her hand.—A well diſpoſed woman, upwards of 70 years of age, at times ſubject to religious melancholy, aſked of a neighbour a good book to read ; *Ambroſe's War with Devils* was put into her hands, the reading of which entirely deranged her mind, and led her to commit the fatal act of ſuicide.

ſtandards of the Church of Scotland, and are well acquainted with her doctrines. They are generally ſtrangers to the neglect of family worſhip; and wiſh to give their children a decent education. The ſchool fees, for the children of ſuch as are not in good circumſtances, are paid from the weekly collections. The Seceders of different denominations are obliging in their manners; far from a narrow contracted ſpirit, no clergyman could wiſh for better neighbours.— There are two political ſocieties a few miles diſtant, who call themſelves the *Friends of the People;* but, though they are anxious to add to their numbers, not a ſingle perſon in this pariſh has joined them.—The dreſs both of the men and the women has undergone a moſt ſurpriſing change, within theſe 40 years. Thirty-two years ago, there were only 7 *hats* in the church, but at preſent there are not as many *bonnets.*

PARISH OF LINTON.

(*County of Roxburgh.*)

By the Rev. Mr ANDREW OGILVIE.

Situation, Extent, &c.

LINTOUN or LINTON, in the prefbytery of Kelfo, and fynod of Merfe and Teviotdale, is nine miles long and three broad. The clergy, it is well known, when they had power, were not inattentive to their own intereft : There is not perhaps a more agreeable rural retreat than they have here chofen for their refidence. The air, in the oppofite extremity of the diftrict, is colder by many degrees, and the ground not above one third of the value.

Soil.—The foil varies greatly ; 300 acres are bounded on the weft by Kail water, and as they rife only a few inches above it, are much expofed to inundations. In 1781, moft of this fpacious plain was under water. This beautiful ftrath, with the furrounding hills, forms a large bafon. It reaches into two adjacent parifhes, and confifts of about 12 or 1500 acres. The 300 acres, mentioned above, confift of a deep ftrong clay. It raifes young cattle, when laid down in grafs, or great crops of grain, when the feafon permits the labour of it. The rent is about one guinea *per* acre, and all of it is inclofed. The ground rifing out of flood-mark to the eaft

for

for two miles produces more certain crops. It is a dry red ſand; one fourth of the arable land is annually allotted to the production of turnips, which, in quality, yield to none in this country.

Hills.—There is only one hill which, in the plains of Babylon, would be an Atlas, but is reduced to a hillock, by the adjacent mountains of the Cheviot. The plough has found its way almoſt to the top of it; but as the uſe of lime was not known, the increaſe, it is probable, would be both ſcanty and precarious.

Lochs.—There are two lochs in this pariſh; the one is much drained, and ſo choaked with reeds, as greatly to incommode the angler in his attempts upon the large trout it contains. The other covers a ſpace of more than 30 acres, is of an oblong form, acceſſible at the verge, and exhibits a beautiful ſheet of watér. It contains no fiſh but eels; ſome of them are of the ſilver kind. A moſs of great extent and depth, confines its water to the weſt; but the peats are of a bad quality. The fuel, therefore, is moſtly coal from Northumberland.

Agriculture—Is here conducted with great dexterity. Turnip is reckoned a good fallow; near one fourth of the arable land is laid down with this uſeful root, which has turned winter into ſummer, not only by keeping the price of meat nearly equal through the year, but alſo by clothing the fields with a beautiful green in the coldeſt ſeaſon; 500 guineas would ſcarcely purchaſe what is here raiſed annually. Stock of every deſcription is thereby greatly advanced. Wool is ſeldom ſold above 18 s *per* ſtone; perhaps the white may be reckoned a little higher. The number of ſheep is about

3000

3000. Being equi-diftant from Edinburgh and Morpeth, the fat beafts are fome years divided almoft equally between thefe markets. Some inclofe their fheep, in the fummer nights, with moveable fences, which are occafionally removed, and the place lately occupied is directly ploughed, to preferve the manure in its ftrength. Much of the fheep pafture has been ploughed, and laid down with fown grafs and lime. Thirty ploughs, with two horfes each, perform the agricultural work of this parifh.

Population.—It is often mentioned with regret that there is a confiderable decreafe of his Majefty's fubjects in this parifh ; 40 years ago it confifted of 27 farmers, the patron, and minifter ; now there are only 12, three of whom, with the patron, do not refide. Of the refiding farmers, only three are married. The number of houfes is reduced to 55, containing 283 perfons above eight years old ; and about 100 children befides, fo that the number is fuppofed to be greatly diminifhed. In Dr Webfter's report, however, the population is ftated at only 413 fouls ; the decreafe upon the whole, therefore, is not above 16. There have been four marriages, ten births, and fix burials, annually, upon an average, for thefe nine years paft. Three young men inlifted into the Train of Artillery laft year. More than one third of the people are Seceders. There are no other fectaries in the parifh.

Poor.—The following authentic extracts from the federunts of heritors meetings, for the laft 47 years, will fhow the ftate of the poor. The affeffment only of every 5th or 6th year fince the commencement in 1744 is here ftated, although the charge and number of poor at every meeting is regularly inferted in the records.

Affeffment

Aſſeſſment for the poor of Linton pariſh.

Number of Paupers.			Aſſeſſment.
4	in	1744	L. 8
4	in	1749	12
8	in	1756	13
9	in	1761	15
12	in	1766	18
9	in	1771	28
10	in	1777	29
11	in	1780	29
11	in	1784	42
14	in	1789	44
14	in	1791	46

This aſſeſſment, ſo diſproportionate to the preſent popula
tion, is partly owing to two young men of deranged intel-
lects, who are ſupported at the rate of above L. 9 *per annum.*
None of the poor are mendicants, although there are many
of this deſcription, chiefly from market towns, as far as
Edinburgh.

Church.—The glebe is nearly eight Scotch acres, two of
which, laſt ſeaſon, in wheat, ſold for L. 20. The ſtipend is
L. 80, and three chalders of victual. The manſe and office
houſes are all new-covered with blue ſlate. The patron is
John Pringle Eſq; of Clifton. More than one half of the
pariſh belongs to him. His houſe at Park, to the weſt of the
church, is pleaſantly ſituated in the centre of a plantation of
30 acres of trees.

Miſcellaneous Obſervations.—The rent of the pariſh is
L. 2113 Sterling, and the largeſt farm yields L. 400 *per
annum.* In repairing the church lately, there was found a
large

large grave containing 50 sculls, all equally decayed, some of them cut with the stroke of violence, belonging (it is suppo-sed) to persons slain in some border fight, of which there were many in this neighbourhood. Over one of the church doors, a man on horseback is cut in stone, killing, with a spear, a fierce animal; it is said to be the last that in-fested this district, when the woods were cut down. It seems to have been a deed of valour, as the memorial of it, we are told, is preserved on the crest of Lord Sommerville's arms, whose ancestors once possessed a large estate in this parish. It is proper to mention another curiosity in the centre of this district; five or six stones form a circle about the size of a cock-pit, called the *Tryst*: Here the parties that made in-cursions into Northumberland, used to meet; but when those that came first could not wait for the arrival of their com-panions, they cut with their swords upon the turf, the ini-tials of their names, the head of the letters pointing to the place whither they were going, that their friends might fol-low them.

PARISH OF MAKERSTON.

(*County of Roxburgh.*)

By the Rev. Mr JAMES RICHARDSON.

Name, Situation, &c.

THE etymology and derivation may be, the *Town* of *MacKer*, or *Ker's Son*. It lies in the county of Roxburgh, in the preſbytery of Kelſo, and ſynod of Merſe and Teviotdale. Its form is a long ſquare, ſtretching five or ſix miles along the north bank of the Tweed, from eaſt to weſt. Its breadth, from north to ſouth, is between four and five miles. The country is flat, with a gentle aſcent from the Tweed. The air is dry, and the ſoil fertile. There is no lake or river, except the Tweed, which produces fine ſalmon and trout. The former are ſold from 3 d. to 1 s. *per* pound, according to the ſeaſon ; but by far the greateſt proportion is carried to Berwick, pickled, and ſent to the London market. The Tweed is not navigable here. The paſtures are for the moſt part rich, and ſo very fine, that they feed the beſt mutton, though not the largeſt in this country ; with very good oxen, cows, and horſes, that fetch high prices. A good many ſwine are alſo fed.

Population.—The population of this pariſh muſt be greatly decreaſed, which is the caſe in all the neighbouring country
                                                          pariſhes.

parifhes. About 50 years ago, there were 16 fmall farmers in the village of Makerfton, where now there is not one. It contains only 12 old cottages. There were formerly about 24 farmers in this parifh, with their families and fervants, where we can now reckon only nine. I prefume, that the number of inhabitants muft then have exceeded 1000, where I can hardly find above one fourth of that number, viz. 250 or 255. Of thefe, there is nearly an equal number of males and females, about 60 under 10 years of age, and 10 or 12 between 10 and 20. All the reft are between 20 and 70 years. The total number of births, for thefe fix laft years, is 76. The marriages are only 18 in that fpace. In Dr Webfter's report the number of fouls is ftated at 165.

Church.—The value of the living, including the glebe, may be, as victual now fells, about L. 100; one half is paid in money.

Mifcellaneous Obfervations.—There is no map of the parifh, but it is fuppofed to contain about 3300 acres, which yield in rent about L. 1700 or L. 1800. Of thefe, perhaps 600 or 700 may be in pafture, on which above 1000 fheep are fed; and 160 or 180 black cattle are fed for the butcher, and for family ufe. There are 60 horfes for plough, cart, and faddle; befides one chaife and two waggons. The farms are laboured by 18 ploughs, and as many carts carry the corn to market, and bring home the coals; which are the only fuel ufed, except fome cuttings of wood, and a few whins. There is no mofs, and there are not five acres in the whole parifh, of moor land. Wheat, barley, oats, peafe, turnips, and potatoes, are the produce of the land. All the coals and lime, ufed here, are brought from Northumberland,

about

above 20 miles; or from Mid-Lothian, at a still greater
distance. A cart load of 1200 or 1400 weight costs 10s.
and often more. A turnpike road, which is in tolerable
good repair, runs through the parish. The statute labour
is not exacted in kind, but is commuted at a fixed rate.

PARISH OF MAXTON.

(*County of Roxburgh.*)

By the Rev. Mr STEPHEN OLIVER.

***

Situation, Soil, &c.

THE pariſh of Maxton is ſituated in the county of Roxburgh, in the preſbytery of Selkirk, and ſynod of Merſe and Teviotdale. It lies along the ſouth ſide of the river Tweed, where there are fine ſalmon and trout. It is nearly four miles in length, and three in breadth. The ſoil, in the upper part of the pariſh, is a ſtiff clay; in the lower, it is lighter and dry.

Population.—The pariſh is not ſo populous, as it was ſome years ago; owing, in ſome meaſure, to ſeveral farms being poſſeſſed by one tenant. About the year 1782, there was a pretty exact account taken of all the inhabitants of the pariſh. The number of perſons above 10 years of age, amounted to 262, and of children below 10 years, to 64, in all 326. In Dr Webſter's report, the number is 397. The marriages are ſeldom above four in one year, the births ſeldom above ten, and the deaths are about the ſame number.

Agriculture.—A good deal of attention is paid to agriculture. The land produces wheat, barley, oats, peaſe, rye, potatoes,

toes, turnips, and rye-grafs. The great diftance from coal
and lime is feverely felt. The valued rent of the whole parifh is L. 5390 : 6 : 8 Scots.

Church.—A good part of the ftipend is paid in victual,
which varies according to the price of grain ; *communibus
annis*, it is about L. 88 Sterling, with a good glebe. No
perfon remembers when the church was built ; both it and
the manfe were lately repaired at confiderable expence. The
bell is a good one, and has this infcription upon it ; " 1609.
" *Soli Deo Gloria. Joan. Burgenfis me fecit.*"

School and Poor.—A good fchool-houfe was lately built,
which coft about L. 80 Sterling ; the fchoolmafter enjoys the
legal falary. There are about feven or eight penfioners on
the poor's lift ; the rates are paid by the heritors and tenants, and amount fometimes to L. 25, fometimes to L. 30
Sterling, yearly.

Antiquities.—Upon the eftate and farm of Littledean, there
are the remains of an old tower, which formerly had been
a place of fome ftrength, and was built in the form of an
half moon. It was long the refidence of the Kers of Littledean, and ftill belongs to that antient family ; who have alfo
a vault, or burying ground, adjoining to the church of Maxton, where they ftill bury, and have done fo, for many generations. Upon Rutherford common, there are the remains of a Roman camp, on a rifing ground, not far from
the banks of Tweed, called, " the *Ringly-Hall*," from its
circular figure ; upon the oppofite fide of that river, there is
a deep hollow, called the *Scots Hole*, in which the Scots lay,
while this Roman camp was poffeffed by the Englifh. They
were fome days in this fituation, with the Tweed only between

tween them; when at laſt the Engliſh, being ſuperior in numbers, ventured to ford the Tweed, at a place where the village of Rutherford now ſtands, and the Scots met them on a riſing ground, on the oppoſite ſide, which is ſtill called the *Pleabrae*. An obſtinate battle enſued, in which the Engliſh were worſted, many of them ſlain, and interred in the burying ground at Rutherford. From this battle, the place was called *Rue-the-ford*, on account of the great loſs ſuſtained by the Engliſh, in fording the Tweed, to attack the Scots. This account is by tradition. The time of this battle cannot be aſcertained. The lands and barony of Rutherford, belong to Sir Alexander Don of Newton, Baronet, the repreſentative of a very antient family in the Merſe. Near the border, betwixt the pariſhes of Maxton and Ancrum, there is the ridge of a hill called *Lilliard Edge*, formerly *Ancrum Muir*. There, a battle was fought between the Scots and Engliſh, ſoon after the death of King James V. who died in the year 1542, when the Earl of Arran was Regent of Scotland. Sir Ralph Rivers, and Sir Bryan Laiton, came to Jedburgh with an army of 5000 Engliſh, to ſeize Merſe and Teviotdale, in name of Henry VIII, then King of England, who died not long after, in the year 1547. The Regent and the Earl of Angus came with a ſmall body of men to oppoſe them. The Earl of Angus was greatly exaſperated againſt the Engliſh, becauſe, ſome time before, they had defaced the tombs of his anceſtors at Melroſe, and had done much hurt to the abbey there. The Regent and the Earl of Angus, without waiting for the arrival of greater force, which was expected, met the Engliſh at Lilliard Edge, where the Scots obtained a great victory, conſidering the inequality of their number. A young woman, of the name of *Lilliard*, fought along with the Scots, with great courage; in memory

memory of which, a tomb ſtone was erected upon her grave, in the field of battle, with this inſcription:

‘ Fair maiden LILLIARD lies under this ſtane,
‘ Little was her ſtature, but great was her fame;
‘ On the Engliſh lads ſhe laid many thumps,
‘ And when her legs were off, ſhe fought upon her ſtumps.’

Some remains of this tomb ſtone are ſtill to be ſeen. It is near a Roman cauſeway, or road, which runs through the pariſh of Maxton, about two miles, and goes ſouthward towards the foot of Jed water, and northward toward the foot of Eildon hills, on the weſt ſide.

PARISH of MELROSE,

(COUNTY OF ROXBURGH, SYNOD OF MERSE AND TEVIOTDALE, PRESBYTERY OF SELKIRK.)

By the Rev. Mr GEORGE THOMSON.

Name, Extent, &c.

BEFORE the abolition of hereditary jurifdictions, Melrose was a burgh of regality. The name is fuppofed to be Gaelic, compounded of *Mull* and *Rofs*, ' a bare pro-
' montory,' remarkably defcriptive of a little peninfula a-
bout a mile to the eaft, formed by the windings of Tweed,
which is ftill called *Old Melrofe*, and famous for its ancient
monaftery, one of the firft feats of the religious Culdees in
this country. The parifh is in length from N. to S. about
7 miles, and in breadth towards the N. 5, towards the S.
near 7 miles.—The town of Melrofe is pleafantly fituated
on the north fide and bottom of the Eildon hills, and on the
edge of a fertile valley, upwards of a mile in length, interfected

ſected by Tweed runniug through it in a ſerpentine direction, and ſurrounded by hills of a conſiderable height. In
this valley, beſides Melroſe, are the villages of Danieltoun,
Darnick, Bridge-end, Gattonſide, and Newſtead, moſt of
the inhabitants of which hold their poſſeſſions in feu, as do
alſo the inhabitants of Eildon and Newtown, two villages
farther down the river, and of Blainſlie, a village on the
weſt ſide of Leader, at the north extremity of the pariſh.

Soil, Agriculture, and Produce.—The ſoil is various.
The ſouth end of the pariſh is moſtly a ſtrong clay, excel-
lently adapted for wheat. The banks of the Tweed are a
fine light dry ſoil, fit for all kinds of grain. On the north
ſide of the Tweed, the ſoil is of three kinds : 1*ſt*, A light
earth, mixed with ſand, upon a gravelly bottom ; 2*dly*, A
ſtrong clay upon a till, full of ſprings, and very wet ;
3*dly*, Moſs. For about 5 miles ſquare, the north part of
the pariſh is hilly, and makes excellent ſheep paſture, interſperſed with a few ſmall fields of corn. For its improvement it has been ſuggeſted, that the different proprietors
ſhould make large ſtrips of plantations, incloſed with
ſtone fences, both to ſhelter the land, and to conſume the
ſurface-ſtones which encumber it, and that the additional
rent would amply compenſate the trouble and expence.

Within theſe 30 years, the farmers have made vaſt progreſs in agriculture. Through their unremitting induſtry, a
great quantity of ground, formerly covered with heath,
broom, and furze, has been bared, and now produces excellent crops, or is converted into good paſture. The value
of land has conſequently very much increaſed. A feu of
ſeveral acres, purchaſed about 40 years ago at L. 10, was
lately ſold at the advanced price of L. 150 Sterling.—The
pariſh is ſuppoſed to produce double the quantity of grain
that it did about that time. The manure employed is,
                                                        lime,

lime, marl, and dung. The firft of thefe, though diftant 20 miles, and from fome places 25, is in general very much ufed. As the land, owing to this diftance, and to the advance in the price of cattle, wages of fervants, &c. is improved at a great expence ; the profit of the former fcarcely bears a juft proportion to the increafe of rent, and of every other article.

The Englifh plough drawn by 2 horfes, has fuperfeded the old heavy Scotch plough drawn by 4 oxen and 2 horfes. The rotation of crops upon the clay land is fallow, fucceeded by wheat; peafe, barley laid down with grafs and opened with oats. Upon the dry light land, it is fallow or turnip, barley laid down with grafs and opened with oats. The wheat is of an excellent quality ; the barley good, though inferior to that of the lower parts of Roxburghfhire and Berwickfhire; the oats in general produce, at an average, near 8 ftone the boll, Linlithgow meafure. Thofe of Blainflie have been long famed for feed. This muft be owing to fome peculiar coldnefs in the foil, and northerly or eafterly expofure of the fields, which makes thefe oats agree with any foil and expofure to which they are carried. There is a great demand for them from England and different parts of Scotland, and they commonly fetch fome fhillings the boll above the ordinary price of feed oats.

The parifh contains 280 horfes, 1006 black cattle, 13,720 fheep. The black cattle are of a middling fize, and excellent for fattening ; in general, they do not exceed 60 ftone when flaughtered. The fheep are of a breed between the long white-faced humble fheep, from the fouth of Teviotdale, and the fhort Highland kind. In fmearing, to one pint of tar was formerly ufed only 2 lb. butter, but now 3 lb. and fometimes 4 lb. by which, though lefs fmearing materials are found neceffary, the expence is greater ; but in return, the quantity of the wool is thereby increafed, and the qua-

lity

lity improven. This laſt effect is not acknowledged by
ſome of the farmers. A change of breed is the moſt effectual method of improving the wool, and it muſt be frequently done to prevent the wool from degenerating again, like
grain ſown often on the ſame ground. Some farmers al-
lege, that the wool might be improved to a great extent,
were they not prevented from making the attempt by the
nature of the climate and paſture, as fine woolled ſheep are
more tender in their conſtitutions than thoſe that are coarſe,
they are leſs able to bear the ſeverity of the winter-ſtorms,
and never thrive upon a wet paſture. From want of attention to theſe circumſtances in attempts to improve the
wool, conſiderable loſs has been ſuſtained in this pariſh.
As ſome paſtures, from their being wet or dry, expoſed
or ſheltered, are adapted to ſheep of a hardy or a delicate
conſtitution, this points out what quality of wool they can
produce. By a few experiments on a ſmall ſcale, the intelligent farmer will eaſily find out to what degree of improvement he can bring his wool, with ſafety to his flock.——
Allowing 100 fleeces to a pack, the pariſh produces in 1 year
$137\frac{1}{8}$ packs of wool, which ſells from 10s. to 15s. the
ſtone.

There are ſeveral orchards about Melroſe and the neighbourhood, and the gardeners raiſe a great many green and
cabbage plants, which are carried to Clydeſdale, and even
ſo far as Dumfries. The fruit and plants together, may,
at an average, yield annually L. 300.——The valued rent of
the pariſh is L. 19,985 : 4 : 6 Scots.

Manufactures.——Melroſe has long been famed for linens,
named *Melroſe land linens*, for which commiſſions have
been received from London and foreign countries. So far
back as the year 1668, the weavers were incorporated under what is called a *Seal of Cauſe*, from John Earl of Haddington,

dington, then " Lord of the lordſhip, and bailie principal of the regality of Melroſe." For ſeveral years paſt this trade has, from a variety of cauſes, been very much upon the decline. If ſomething does not occur to prevent it, Melroſe will in all probability ſoon loſe the name and *buſi-neſs*, (as they themſelves expreſs it), of manufacturing theſe linens. Its importance to this place, and its rapid decline, will appear from the following ſtatement taken from the ſtampmaſter's yearly abſtract: From the 1ſt November 1754 to 1ſt November 1755, there were ſtamped 33,282¼ yards, valued at L. 2575 : 10 : 11¼. In the 10 ſucceeding years there was no great riſe or fall in the quantity and value of linens. From November 1764 to November 1765, there were ſtamped 32,300⅝ yards, value L. 2495 : 14 : 9¼. From November 1773 to November 1774, 20,789¾ yards, value L. 2051 : 16 : 7¼. In the following 10 years, the quantity was ſo far down as 17,792 yards, value L. 1845 : 12 : 4 Sterling *.

A

---

* The following are the cauſes to which this decline has been aſcribed: 1ſt, The attention of the truſtees for manufactures, &c. has been principally directed, of late, to the encouragement of the woollen manufacture through Scotland. In Galaſhiels, and that part of this pariſh which is contiguous to it, they have laid out a conſiderable ſum in buildings and machinery ; and the manufacturers there have drawn annually, for ſeveral years, from L. 40 to L. 70 Sterling, in premiums. This has enabled them to give more to ſpinners, than the profits on linen can afford, and has, of courſe, diminiſhed the number of linen-ſpinners, and ſpoiled their hands for that employment. 2d, Women-ſervants get ſo high wages, and are ſo much employed in out-work, that a ſufficient number of them cannot be procured to ſpin linen-yarn, though the price of ſpinning it has been conſiderably advanced. About 10 years ago, the prices were only, for ſpinning 4 hanks yarn from 1 pound of lint, 1 s. 2 d. ; for 5 hanks, 1 s. 4 d. ; for 6 hanks, 1 s. 8 d. ; and for 7 hanks, 2 s. The preſent prices are, for 4 hanks, 1 s. 7 d. ; for 5 hanks, 1 s. 8 d. ; for 6 hanks, 2 s. ; and for 7 hanks, 2 s. 2 d. : Some ſpinners get for 7 hanks, 2 s. 4 d. 3dly, Since the American war, the price of Dutch flax has greatly riſen, and the land here is moſtly unfit for raiſing any.

A few hints have been suggested by the principal manufacturers for the recovery of this decaying trade. These
shall be given in their own words : " Were the trustees to
give encouragement to weavers by premiums and extras on
well made pieces of linen, as was done through Scotland a-
bout 40 years ago, it might have as good an effect as it had
then, the tradesmen being much better now than when
they began their prizes at the above period ; and were encouragement given also to young girls to spin properly,
much might be expected. This could be done by employing some spinning mistresses in different little towns through
the parish, and offering some prizes to the best spinners, in
order to prompt the emulation of the scholars. Finally,
were some attention paid by the proprietors to a decaying
bleachfield, these things, and what else their wisdom may
suggest, might still, through the blessing promised to the
diligent, recover a falling back state of business."

In order to encourage this manufacture, the bleachfield mentioned above was set on foot through the patriotic exertions of
the Reverend Mr James Brown, late one of the ministers of
Edinburgh, and previously minister of this parish. During
his residence at Melrose, and for several years afterward,
the bleaching business was carried on with considerable spirit and success. For some time past it has declined. In
dry seasons, there is a great scarcity of water in the field,
though abundance might be procured at no great expence.
The buildings are old and in great disrepair, and little is to
be expected from the proprietors. The property is divided
into a great many shares, so low as L. 5 ; so that the profits which might be derived from it are no ways adequate
to stimulate the exertions of the proprietors, most of whom
are in good circumstances, and independent of this business.
Besides, no dividends of profits having been made among
them for several years, they are little disposed to be at
much

much expence in repairs and improvements on what they already confider as a dead ftock. To carry on this bufi-nefs with advan age, the field fhould be let to an intelli-gent bleacher, or the property thrown into the hands of one or two proprietors who might find their account in fu-perintending it.

Of late, however, it is faid, that owing to the good ma-nagement of the prefent bleacher, the bufinefs has been up-on the increafe. From his ftatement, it appears, that in the year 1787 there were whitened 715 pieces of linen; in 1788—855; in 1789—917; in 1790—1202; in 1791—1232. This cloth does not all belong to the parifh, but is taken in from different parts of the country.

The woollen manufacture has of late been making confi-derable progrefs, efpecially in the neighbourhood of Gala-fhiels, for which fee the Statiftical Account of that parifh, Befides what is done by them, there are manufactured annually in Gattonfide and Melrofe, at an a-verage, about 282 ftone of wool, the cloth of which may yield about L. 1041. Since November 1791, feveral looms, both here and in the neighbouring parifhes, have been employed in weaving cottons. In addition to thofe employed by the manufacturers near Galafhiels, there are 80 looms in the parifh; 20 of which are employed in weaving cotton, 30 in woollen, and 30 in linen-work. Du-ring the fummer, when the demand is greateft, fome of the woollen looms are employed in weaving linen; but as cot-ton is found both more cleanly and more profitable than either woollen or linen, it is probable, that fhould the de-mand for it continue, the number of weavers employed in that line will gradually increafe.

Population, &c.—This parifh contains at prefent 2446 inhabitants. According to Dr Webfter's report, the numbers

bers then were 2322. There are of theſe Burgher-Sece-
ders 128 ; Anti-Burghers 151 ; Relief 53 ; Methodiſts 18 ;
in all 350 diſſenters. Beſides theſe ſectaries, ſome of the
different claſſes of Independents and Anabaptiſts mentioned in the Statiſtical Account of Galaſhiels, have, with their
manufactures, been imported into this pariſh. Mr Milne,
in his deſcription of this pariſh, publiſhed in 1743, makes
the number of examinable perſons 1800. If he comprehended all above 10 years of age, the population muſt have
undergone little alteration, but ſeems rather to have increaſed than diminiſhed *.

The

---

* A ſtatement might be given of births, marriages, and burials, from
our pariſh-regiſter, but it is very incomplete ; becauſe the Seceders, conſidering this as an appendage to the Eſtabliſhed Church, rather than an
inſtitution calculated to promote the civil intereſt of their poſterity, do
not in general regiſtrate the names of their children ; and, becauſe the
temptation to neglect this among the lower claſſes of people, has alſo been
increaſed by the late tax upon regiſtration. They think that the money
required out of their ſcanty funds, for this purpoſe, is better employed in
providing againſt preſent wants, than in ſecuring a very diſtant, and perhaps uncertain, good to their poſterity. Nor can the marriage-regiſter
be depended on, as there are many irregular or (as they are commonly
called here) o'er-the-march marriages It is ſuſpected that certificates to
this purpoſe, are ſometimes forged or antedated by the parties, in order
to conceal a previous blunder that may have been committed. This practice is alſo countenanced by ſome Epiſcopal Clergymen upon the border,
who, for the ſake of the beggarly fee of office, marry all who apply to
them, without even requiring any evidence of the parties being legally
entitled to this privilege. There have alſo been inſtances of Fiſcals in
Royal Burghs, and of other Courts, ſummoning parties before a Juſtice of
the Peace, who, on their acknowledging a previous marriage, (which perhaps never took place), decerns them to pay a fine, and adjudges one half
of it to the proſecutor. Certificates of regular proclamations have alſo
been produced, not only here, but in all the neighbouring pariſhes, from
the Seſſion-clerks of Edinburgh, Canongate, and Weſt Church, in favour
of people who were never two days reſident within their bounds ; and on
ſuch certificates, many marriages have been celebrated. This evil claims
the attention of the Legiſlature.

The prevailing difeafes in the parifh are confumptions and rheumatifms. The latter may be owing to the fevere cold to which the lower claffes are expofed during the winter, from the vaft expenfe of fuel, which cannot be ufed to fuch extent as is neceffary for their health and accommodation. Coal, their principal fuel, is diftant a mile farther than lime, and fells at 9d. and 10d. the hundred weight in fummer, and fometimes higher in winter. The ague formerly prevailed much, but for fome years has greatly fubfided. This may be owing to the improvement of the country by drains, and to the people's being better fed and clothed.—They are now getting above the prejudices againft inoculation. This happy difcovery for the prefervation of mankind is more, and more practifed, and with the greateft fuccefs. The writer of this account, as well as his predeceffors, has, in his intercourfe with the parifhioners, laboured to obviate their fcruples, and recommended the practice. Through fuch perfuafion, feveral children have been inoculated, whofe parents have afterward expreffed their gratitude. It is hoped, that in a fhort time, a practice will become univerfal, which has been already begun, and through the bleffing of God, will continue to be a mean of faving many infants from an early grave.

Religion, &c.—Notwithftanding the many religious fectaries which exift here, a fpirit of mutual forbearance prevails. That inveterate rancour, to which the divifions in our church gave birth about 50 years ago, is now almoft worn away through the friendly aid of time, the only cure for fuch an evil. All parties are difpofed to live in peace, and to interchange the offices of good neighbourhood with one another. In fo large a fociety, as may be expected, exceptions muft be made. In general, however, the people have always been diftinguifhed for their good fenfe,

ſobriety, and a decent and uniform attendance upon public ordinances. Thoſe who adhere to the Eſtabliſhed Church, are ſteady in their attachment to her principles and government, and are equally removed from a fiery bigotted zeal, and from a lukewarm indifference about religion.

Stipend, School, &c.—The Duke of Buccleugh is patron. The ſtipend, including L. 100 Scots for communion-elements, is 48 bolls of victual, 2-3ds oat-meal, and 1-3d bear, and L. 886 : 13 : 4 Scots. The glebe conſiſts of 4 Scots acres, of the worſt land in the neighbourhood, lies at an inconvenient diſtance from the manſe, and has always been reckoned by the different incumbents to be incapable of improvement, and ſcarcely worth the labouring. It is hoped, that the heritors will ſoon ſee the propriety of removing this inconvenience, in return for the many fertile fields thrown into their hands by the Preſbyterians at the Reformation, eſpecially as the miniſter receives only L. 20 Scots for a graſs-glebe.—The ſchoolmaſter's ſalary, and other emoluments, are about L. 20 yearly, beſides the fees of teaching in general near 80 ſcholars. He has alſo a commodious dwelling-houſe, and a tolerable garden. The ſtated ſchool-fees are, the quarter, for Engliſh 1s. 6d. ; for writing 2s.; for writing and arithmetic 2s. 6d.; and for Latin 5s. For the accommodation of the highland part of the pariſh, Mr Robert Moffat, portioner of Threepwood, mortified, in the year 1759, the ſum of 1000 merks Scots, the intereſt of which is, in terms of the deed of mortification, applied towards the maintenance of a ſchoolmaſter in that quarter.

Poor.—The poor are ſupported by a voluntary aſſeſſment of heritors, moſt of whom are feuars, and by the public collections made at the church-doors upon Sundays.

For

For this purpose, they regularly meet once every quarter, along with the kirk-session, to consider the state of the poor. At such meetings applications are made for admission to the charity-roll, and a weekly pension, or a temporary supply, is granted. No plan that has been adopted or conceived can be more just or beneficial than the one adopted here. By the lower classes of people the lands are cultivated, and their value increased. To whom, therefore, can they so naturally look for maintenance, when, through age or disease, they are unable to provide for themselves, as to those who may have reaped the fruits of their past industry, when in the vigour of their days, and favoured with health and strength? As the non-residing, as well as the residing heritors, are subject to this assessment; and as it is imposed according to the valuation of their respective properties, they are burdened only in proportion to their supposed advantages, from the past industry and expenditure of the poor. Upon the same principle, commerce might become an object of assessment, the value of which, (if not left to the capricious judgment of assuming superiors, but to an equitable jury), might, without entering into the secrets of trade, be nearly ascertained *.

In

---

* To prevent unnecessary applications, none are admitted upon the roll, without first surrendering all their little effects, of which a regular inventory is taken; and which effects are, upon the pauper's decease, but not sooner, sold for the benefit of the public. As their pride is generally interested to retain these effects as long as possible, few make application till forced by dire necessity. In cases of temporary distress, however, and where there is no appearance of a continuing burden, supply is granted without this surrender. The weekly pensions are small, and do not altogether supersede the necessity of charitable assistance from friends and neighbours. This will appear from the following statement: For the last 10 years, the average number of poor upon the roll, has been 148 persons; the annual expence of whose maintenance, has amounted to only
L. 87,

In addition to the above valuable account, tranfmitted by the Reverend Mr Thomfon, the prefent minifter, it may not be improper to fubjoin the following fhort extracts, from a " Defcription of the parifh of Melrofe," publifhed in 1743, by the Reverend Mr Milne, then paftor of that parifh.

Abbeys.—The Monaftery of Old Melrofe was probably founded about the end of the fixth century. Bede * gives us an account of its fituation on the bank of the Tweed †, and likewife of its abbots. This place was a famous nurfery for learned and religious men ; and probably continued till the other one at the prefent Melrofe was founded by King David. The convent of Old Melrofe was inclofed with a
ftone

L. 87, 5 s. Until lately, the heritors made a demand of one half of the weekly collections, and allowed the other half to be diftributed by the kirk-feffion ; but confidering that their terms of meeting are diftant, and that a great deal of diftrefs might intervene, which would require inftant relief, they have now given up the whole collections, to be diftributed by the feffion. Thefe collections are employed to meet the wants of fuch as may, through difeafe, be reduced to a temporary poverty ; to augment the penfions of thofe upon the heritors roll, if found neceffary ; and if the funds will admit, the heritors fometimes recommend fome of their petitioners for a temporary fupply, to be relieved out of them. For thefe reafons, there are no beggars in the parifh,—that nuifance to fociety, and oppreffion upon the public, particularly upon well-difpofed people in the lower ranks, who are lefs able to bear it. In no place, indeed, are the poor better attended to, or fupported at fo fmall an expence. Charity is here reduced to a regular fyftem of operation, which does not leave its objects to a precarious fubfiftence, but fecures for them a certain well-regulated relief in the day of poverty and diftrefs ; and the objects of it are as happy as their reduced circumftances will admit.

* The Venerable Bede was born A. D. 673.

† Bede's Hiftory, IV. 27

ſtone wall, reaching from the ſouth corner to the weſt corner of the Tweed, where the neck of land is narrow; and the foundations of the wall are ſtill to be ſeen. I do not think there has been any great building about it; for as Bede acquaints us, their churches then were all of oak, and covered with reeds. The ſituation of the place is moſt pleaſant and agreeable, being almoſt ſurrounded by Tweed, and having a fine proſpect towards Gladſwood.

About a mile to the weſt of this on the Tweed, ſtands the village of Newſtead, a place remarkable for another abbey on the eaſt ſide of it, called *Red Abbey-ſtced*.

About half a mile from Newſtead, on the ſame ſouth ſide of the Tweed, ſtands the preſent *Abbey of Melroſe*. It is famous for its monaſtery, which was very large and ſpacious, as appears from the ruins of it yet remaining; one of the moſt magnificent in the kingdom; and continues ſtill to be the admiration of ſtrangers, who, in reſpect of the height and embelliſhment of its columns, with all kind of ſculpture, the beauty of its ſtones, and ſymmetry of its parts, reckon it one of the beſt of the Gothic ſtructures they have ſeen. It was founded by King David in 1136; dedicated to the Virgin Mary, and endowed with large revenues and many immunities, as appears by the charters granted to the abbot and convent, by our kings. The monks were Ciſtertians, and the monaſtery of Melroſe was a mother church or nurſery for all of that order, in many various and remote regions of Scotland.

The church is built in the form of St John's croſs. The chancel, which is a very ſtately fabric, is ſtill ſtanding; its roof is very curious, and has much of the ſcripture hiſtory upon it. I have taken the meaſure of what is ſtanding of this church, although much of the weſt part is ſo entirely demoliſhed, that we cannot know how far it has reached in that direction. Its juſt length is 258 feet; breadth 137½;

circumference

circumference about 943 ; height of the ſouth window 24, breadth 16 ; height of the eaſt window 34¼, breadth 15½; height of the ſteeple 75 ; the ſpire gone. The eaſt window, at which was the great altar, is a beautiful ſtructure ; conſiſting of 4 pillars or bars. with a great deal of curious work between them; and on each ſide, a great number of niches for ſtatues. On the top, an old man with a globe in his left hand, reſting on his knee, and a young man on his right; both in a ſitting poſture, with an open crown over their heads. On the north and ſouth of this window, are two others of ſmaller dimenſions. The niches are curiouſly carved, both the pedeſtals and canopies, and on which ſeveral figures of men and animals are curiouſly cut. On the ſouth-eaſt of this church are a great many muſicians admirably cut, with much pleaſantneſs and gaiety in their countenances, accompanied with their various inſtruments. Alſo nuns with their veils; ſome of whom richly dreſſed. The ſouth window is very much admired for its height and curious workmanſhip: Niches are on each ſide and above it, where have been ſtatues of our Saviour and the apoſtles. Beſides, there are many other figures on the eaſt, or on the weſt ſide of this window : Monks curiouſly cut, with their beards, cowls and beads: A cripple on the back of a blind man : Several animals cut very nicely, as boars, greyhounds, lions, monkies and others. There are about 68 niches in whole ſtanding ; the ſtatues were only demoliſhed about the 1649.

So far, with reſpect to the outſide of the church. Within, on the north ſide of the croſs are beautiful pillars, and the ſculpture as freſh as if it had been newly cut. On the weſt ſide is a ſtatue of St Peter with a book open, his right hand on it, and two keys hanging on the left. On the ſouth ſide of this ſtatue, is that of St Paul with a ſword. In the middle of the croſs ſtood the ſteeple, a piece of noble architecture,

chitecture, a quarter of it yet standing, but the spire gone. The roof of the south side of the cross is still standing, where is a beautiful stair-case, much admired by strangers, the roof of it winding like a snail cap. There was within the church a vast number of fonts curiously carved, and where were altars dedicated to various saints. In the portion of the church where worship is at present performed, are two rows of pillars of excellent workmanship, especially that to the south-east, which for the fineness of it, looks like Flander's lace.

With regard lastly, to what was in part, or altogether, separated from the body of the church, there was a cloyster on the north side, a part of the walls of which is still remaining; and where may be observed pleasant walks and seats, with a great deal of fine flowers nicely cut as lilies, &c. also ferns, grapes, house-leeks, escalops, fir cones, &c. The door at the north entry of the church is curiously embossed, and the foliage here, and in several places of the church, very beautiful. There were also here a vast many fine buildings within the convent, for the residence and service of the abbot and monks, with gardens and other conveniencies; all this inclosed within an high wall, about a mile in circuit. Besides the high church, there has been a large fine chapel, where the manse now is, and another house adjoining to it, where the foundations of the pillars are still to be seen. On the north side of this house, there has been a curious oratory or private chapel, the foundations of which have been discovered this year. and a large cistern of one stone, with a leaden pipe conveying the water to it.

Camps, &c.—A little to the south of Melrose are the three *Eildon* hills. The base of them may be in compass

6

6 or 7 miles; the height of two of them to the north about
1½ mile. On the top of the north-east hill are plain vestiges of a Roman camp well fortified, with two fosses and
mounds of earth, more than 1½ mile in circuit, with a large
plain near the top of the hill, on which may be seen the
prætorium, or the general's quarter, surrounded with many
huts. It has all the properties of a well chosen camp, according to the rules of Vegetius. There is a large prospect
from it of all the country; it has many springs of good
water near it; the sides of the hill have been covered with
wood, and the camp is of that extent, that neither man,
beast nor baggage could be straitened for room. On the
north side of the middle hill, Mr Milne seems to place a
second camp, from which he says is a large ditch for 2
miles to the west, reaching to another camp on the top of
Caldshielhill. This camp (probably he means, that on the
north side of the middle hill) has been strongly fortified
with a double trench, and the circumvallations of it continued for a good way. This camp, with that called Castle-
steed, makes almost a triangle with the large camp on Eildon hills.

To the S. W. of these hills there has been a beautiful
military road, raised in some places high above the ground,
and of a considerable breadth, with military stations in some
places upon it. In some parts it is carried through lakes and
marshes, and has had a communication with the camp at
Caldshiels, and likewise with another camp on the north
side of the Tweed called the Rink.

On the head of the hill, on the side of which the village
of Gattonside is founded, north of the Tweed, there has
been a large camp. It has a wall around it of stone, about
half a mile in compass. About half a mile from this camp
to the east, on the top of the hill, opposite to Newstead,

there

there has been a large camp with a deep ditch. It feems to have been about 3 quarters of a mile in circumference, and is called the Chefter-know or Knoll.

Mr Milne defcribes other camps, feveral of them large, and gives an account of other antiquities and particulars referring to this parifh.

PARISH OF MINTO,

(County of Roxburgh, Synod of Mersk and Tiviot-
Dale, Presbytery of Jedburgh).

By William Burn, D. D. *Minister.*

Situation, &c.

THE parish of Minto is almost an oblong, extending
from east to west 3¼ miles; from south to north 2½
miles. It is bounded on the east by the parish of Ancrum;
on the north, by Lilliesleaf; on the west, by Wilton; on
the south, by Cavers, from which it is almost divided by
the river Tiviot.

Heritors.—There are three residing heritors: The Right
Honourable Sir Gilbert Elliot, Baronet, the patron, whose
estate lies on the east side, and comprehended the old parish
of Minto. The family of Minto, for ages past, have been
so eminent, both in the Senate and in the other departments
of the State, that any thing I can say might be considered as
                                                        mere

mere panegyric. The houfe is large and commodious, has a fouth expofure, and is fituated on the bank of a beautiful winding glen, extending almoft to the Tiviot, and well ftocked with a variety of old trees, with natural and artificial falls of water. In coming along one of the ferpentine walks on the fide of the glen, the ear is all at once furprifed with the unexpected noife of the largeft of thefe falls, the view being intercepted by a thicket; on advancing a little forward, the fall, the bridge, the large fheet of water, the furrounding banks, interfperfed with variegated trees and fhrubs, and the houfe, gradually open to the eye, excite the moft pleafing emotions, and form one of the moft beautiful landfcapes that can be figured: The reflection of this landfcape in the water adds to the grandeur of the fcene. The pleafure-ground is extenfive, and laid out with great tafte. A little to the eaft are Minto Rocks, interfperfed with clumps of planting, which form an awful and picturefque object. From the top of thefe rocks there is a beautiful and extenfive profpect of the different windings of the Tiviot, and the adjacent country, for many miles round. Here are the remains of a building, which, during the incurfions of the borderers, feems to have been a watch-tower. Behind the houfe, to the north, are two hills, which rife with a gentle afcent to a confiderable height, and are excellent fheep-pafture. At a fmall diftance from the houfe, and in the middle of a grove of trees, ftands the church, which is neat, clean, and well feated. The village is placed about half a mile to the weft, and contains 24 families, moftly labourers and mechanics. To the fouth-weft, an Englifh mile from the church, are the manfe and glebe. This was the boundary of the old parifh. Now, there are annexed the lands of Haffendeanbank, belonging to his Grace the Duke of Roxburgh, and the lands of Haffendean, the property of his Grace the Duke of Buccleugh.

On

On the weſt of Haſſendeanbank is the eſtate of Tiviotbank, lately purchaſed by David Simpſon, Eſq; another reſiding heritor, who has built a neat modern houſe on a riſing bank, in view of the river, and ornamented the place with a variety of plantations. On the weſt and north-weſt are the lands of Haſſendeanburn, Horſleyhill, and Huntlaw, belonging to Robert Dickſon, Eſq; the ſecond heritor in the pariſh, who has lately built a large convenient houſe a ſmall diſtance from the water. In this corner was the ſite of Haſſendeanburn church, ſuppoſed to be an appendage of Melroſe Abbey, (the farm next to it goes by the name of Monks Croft, where there was a tower called Monks Tower). The church, and moſt of the church-yard, are carried off by the water; yet, ſo ſtrong is the deſire " of " ſleeping with our fathers,' that they continued to bury here, though, after every flood, the haughs were covered with human bones, till laſt winter, a great ſwell of the river ſwept it all away, except one corner. Since that time, ſome of the dead have been lifted and carried to different burial grounds. This pariſh is now divided amongſt the pariſhes of Wilton, Minto, and Roberton. The original ſtipend was all annexed to Roberton. Here I muſt offer an advice to landed gentlemen, always to take care that the ſtipend be annexed together with their lands. The proprietors of this old pariſh have found the diſadvantage of not attending to this, by the different proceſſes of augmentation that have been raiſed againſt them by the ſeveral miniſters.

Nurſery.—On the lands of Haſſendeanburn was eſtabliſhed, by the late Mr Dickſon's father, one of the firſt nurſeries in the kingdom, which was carried on by the late Mr Dickſon, who alſo eſtabliſhed the nurſery at Hawick. Both theſe nurſeries are now carried on by the Meſſrs Dickſons;
and

and in point of extent, character, and circulation, are equalled by few, if any. They contain all kind of foreign and native forest trees, fruit trees, flower-roots, and plants and flowering shrubs, that are naturalised in this country; besides a great collection of exotic plants. From this nursery originated that carried on by Messrs Dickson and Company, Perth; that in Edinburgh by Messrs Dicksons and Company.

Soils.—The soils in the parish are various. Towards the river it consists of different kinds of loam, well adapted to turnips; farther north it is a strong clay, and clay loam. both on a tilly bottom.

Manure.—Some seams of marl have been discovered, but so small, that they do not depend on these, and drive lime and marl at a considerable distance and great expence. Lime laid down on the field, 2 s. the lime-bushel, which is equal to three Winchester bushels. Marl, 3 s. the double cart.

Acres.—The number of acres 5213; of these, 475 are planted with forest trees.

Implements of Husbandry.—The English plough is universally used with two horses. Thrashing machines are beginning to be used.

Cultivation.—The mode of cropping or rotation, until within these few years, for a long time back, was as follows:—The infield, divided into five breaks—1. Fallow, with the dung of the farm, wheat, pease, barley, oats, and then fallow again, &c.: The outfield, first folded with the cattle of the farm in general, then sown with oats for three

or

or four years, and even longer, if the return was a little more than two ſeeds; after that, fallow, without any kind of manure; then two crops of oats, and fallow again every third year, as long as it would produce a decent crop; then allowed to go to paſture.

The preſent mode followed in the pariſh:—The light land firſt well prepared for turnip, which are ſown in drills neatly made up, manured with the dung of the farm, and lime or ſhell marl, ſo far as they can be procured, not to loſe the ſeaſon for the turnip; part of which is eat on the ground with ſheep, and part with cattle in the houſe. When eat with ſheep, it is not uncommon to ſow wheat with graſs-ſeeds, which, in general, ſucceeds well. When the turnip is carried off, barley with graſs-ſeeds ſeldom fails of a good crop; then hay is taken, the fog, or ſecond crop, eat on the ground with various kinds of ſtock; then, in autumn, taken up for wheat, which is ſown with one furrow; after the wheat, oats, and then turnip; ſometimes they take up with oats, and then turnip; when the land is naturally very good, and in high order, wheat is taken after the oats, then turnip: After this rotation is followed twice, the graſs is allowed to lie for paſture two or three years, then taken up as before. The land that is too heavy for turnip, or the clay lands, are taken up from graſs with oats; then fallow with the dung of the farm, and a full dreſſing of ſhell marl or lime (25 double carts of marl, or 6 double carts of lime *per* Engliſh acre) ſown with wheat; then peaſe, then barley with graſs-ſeeds, then hay, and after that three years paſtured; then cropped as before.

Graſs-ſeeds.—When only one crop is taken, they ſow 12 lb. of red clover, and half a buſhel rye-graſs, to the Engliſh acre; when to lay in paſture, 6 lb. of white clover,

5 lb.

5 lb. of red clover, 2 lb. of rib-grass, half a bushel of rye-grass.

Notwithstanding the above mode of cropping, some, of late years, pasture the first crop, which they find pays well, and does more justice to the land.

Kinds of Stock.—The kinds of stock kept or bred : Sheep of the Cheviot breed on the outfield; on the infield, or improven lands, the Dishley or Beckwell breed have been tried, with advantage, for a few years. The short horned, or Teefwater cattle, prevail, and pay the breeder well. Number of sheep, 1680; black cattle, 380. Yet it may be supposed the parish is able to keep a great many more ; but the residing heritors are of use to let, from year to year, a considerable number of grass parks; and some of the farmers, who follow the turnip-husbandry, have a fluctuating stock. Number of ploughs 36. No oxen used at present. Besides the horses kept for the plough, there may be about 46 riding and young horses. The harvest in general is early. The whole parish is inclosed with boundary fences, and by far the greatest proportion of it subdivided with ditch and hedge, interspersed with strips and clumps of planting, which serve both for shelter and ornament.

Servants Wages.—Servants wages have been on the rise for some years. A married man, or hind, L. 6, 10 s. a cow kept, a stone of meal in the week, a firlot of potatoes planted, a peck or half a peck of lintseed sown, a free house, with a piece of ground for a garden, a certain quantity of fuel carried ; it is understood, at the same time, that the wife or children are to assist at carrying in stacks, &c. A man, within the house, from L. 6 to L. 9. A woman servant, within the house, from L. 3 to L. 4. Day labour-

ers,

ers, at an average, 1 s. 3 d. *per* day in summer, and 1 s. in winter. Women, who work out of doors upon the farm, 8 d. Harvest wages fluctuating. Last harvest high.

For some years, I have observed with pleasure the rapid progress of improvement within the parish; the happy change of the mode of agriculture; the quantity of foreign manure, both lime and marl, carried at such a distance and expence, and the advantages arising from it; the attention paid to roads and fences, so advantageous to the inhabitants, and agreeable to travellers.

Roads.—There are many public roads: The funds arising from the conversion of the statute-money being very small, and not adequate to making and keeping the roads in repair, still the principal roads are very good, owing to the attention of Sir Gilbert Elliot, who, for some years, has made and kept up, at his own expence, the roads leading through his lands; whereby the funds are applied to other roads within the parish.

Population.—The number of inhabitants, 513 souls. The increase and decrease of population cannot be ascertained with precision, many being accustomed to bury in Hassendeanburn, where no register has been kept. For some years back it has increased considerably. In 1755, it was 396. The Established Church is the only place of public worship within the parish; they attend regularly and decently. There are few Seceders of any denomination.

Poor.—The number of poor, for these two preceding years, has been, at a medium, 16, and annual payments L. 50, raised by a regular poor-rate, one half paid by the heritors, the other half by the tenants. There are L. 50 belonging to the kirk-session, the interest goes into the cash, or,

or, alongſt with the collections, is diſtributed by the ſeſſion
in interim ſupplies, in caſe of ſickneſs, or any other unfore-
ſeen calamity. In 1782, when oatmeal roſe very high,
the curators of the poor bought in a quantity, and ſold it at
a reduced price, both to the poor on liſt and poor houſeholders with large families. There are no begging poor
in the pariſh. The poor-rates are more than double within
theſe ten years, notwithſtanding the liberality of the family of Minto, who, when on the ſpot, gave a good deal
of private charity, and a weekly proportion of broth and
meat, which is continued in their abſence.

Manſe.—The manſe was removed to its preſent ſituation
in 1773, and is in good repair. The glebe conſiſts of 35
Engliſh acres. The ſtipend upwards of L. 90.

School.—The eſtabliſhed ſchoolmaſter is the only teacher
within the pariſh. He has a houſe, garden, and ſchool-
houſe; ſalary L. 12, including the emoluments of ſeſſion-
clerk, collecting the poor-rates, &c. The number of ſcholars, at an average, between 50 and 60. In March 1792,
above 50 ſcholars were ſeized with the meaſles in two days,
ſo rapid was the infection. The ſchoolhouſe was then
ſmall and confined, which moved the heritors to build one
in an airy ſituation, the moſt beautiful and commodious in
the ſouth of Scotland.

Fuel.—The diſtance from fuel, and other local diſadvantages, have hitherto diſcouraged manufactures, &c. notwithſtanding there are a number of mechanics. Weavers, 7;
blackſmiths, 3; tailors, 3; one nailor, who employs 5
hands; three carpenters, who employ 10 hands; one corn
and one lint mill. Coals in general are burnt, (which are
carried at the diſtance of 30 miles), and peats and wood.

Character.

Character.—The inhabitants are honest, sober, and industrious; seem contented with their situation, as no murders, suicides, or criminal prosecutions, are remembered to have happened. The farmers, in general, are respectable well informed people, pay great attention to husbandry, to the rearing and feeding of stock. The air is good; seldom visited with any epidemical diseases. There are no public-houses within the parish. I have not been able to discover any antiquities or natural curiosities but such as are common, viz. stone coffins, petrifying springs, large deers horns, &c. found in mosses.

PARISH OF MORBATTLE,

(County of Roxburgh, Synod of Merse and Teviotdale, Presbytery of Kelso).

By a Lover of uſefu Enquiries.

Situation, &c.

MANY places, on both ſides the borders of Scotland
and England, received their preſent names from warlike exploits that took place during the unhappy conteſt, reſpecting the independence of Scotland, in which the two
nations were ſo long engaged. It is probable, that the
name *Morbattle* was given to this pariſh at that period, although the particular circumſtance that gave riſe to it is
now, perhaps, unknown. The pariſh is bounded on the
N. by Linton; on the E. by Yetholm; on the S. by Hounam; and on the W. by Eckford.

Rivers.—The principal rivers or waters in the pariſh are
Bowmont and *Kale*, in both of which the ſalmon and trout

are

are to be found. The falmon in thefe, and all the other
waters in this diftrict of the county, are not now nearly fo
plenty as formerly ; owing, it is believed, to the cruives,
and other machineries placed in the Tweed, a little above
Berwick, by which the fifh, in their paffage up the river,
are intercepted and killed.

Village.—The only village in the parifh is Morbattle.
The ground upon which it is built was, not very many
years ago, feued out by the Marquis of Tweeddale, for the
terms of nineteen times nineteen years, at the rate of L. 5
per acre Englifh. The houfes, which are moftly of one
ftory high, and covered with thatch, are built and kept in
repair by the feuers. About 380 acres, adjoining to the
village, were, till of late, occupied in two farms, for which
was paid L. 64 of rent annually. Thefe farms, at the expiration of the leafes, were parcelled out into fmall portions, as might beft fuit the conveniency of the feuers in the
village. They are now fubdivided into about 26 fmall
pendicles or paffles, for which is paid of yearly rent L. 230.
The greateft fubdivifion pays only L. 22, 10 s. Sterling.
The rife of the rent of this land, which was almoft altogether *outfield* and hilly, is, perhaps, more than that of any
other part of the parifh. The ground, inftead of being
rendered worfe by the fmall occupiers, is much improved.
It receives a confiderable quantity of manure, and care is
taken to cultivate every inch of it, in the beft manner poffible. Being thus improved, it is extremely ferviceable in
helping to fupport many induftrious families. This village,
when the accumulation of fmall into large farms took place
in the neighbourhood, feafonably afforded a comfortable a-
fylum to feveral farmers and cottagers, who were forced
to abandon the abodes of their forefathers. The inhabitants, who amount to about 200 fouls, are active and induftrious.

duſtrious. Some of them find employment in working their horſes and carts, in agricultural operations; frequently in carrying lime and coals to the farmers in the vicinity; and alſo in cultivating the ſmall pieces of land they have in leaſe, without which they could not ſupport their horſes and cows. Some of the villagers are day-labourers, whilſt others are occupied at their ſeveral trades and handicrafts, in the cuſtomary work of the country. The leiſure hours of theſe tradeſmen are laudably filled up in managing their ſmall paſſles, and kail-yards, in which exerciſes they find a more profitable and healthful amuſement, than they could poſſibly do in frequenting alehouſes or barbarous diverſions, a practice which too much prevails with many mechanics in ſome of the great manufacturing diſtricts of Britain. The women are employed chiefly in ſpinning linen-yarn, and managing their ſmall dairies, principally in making butter and cheeſe, ſome little of which is uſually carried to market.

The inhabitants, by theſe means, are happily removed from the direful ſtate of abſolute ſervitude, and from totally depending on the caprice of others. They have a ſpur to activity and induſtry, from a view of rendering better their circumſtances in life. This excitement, which is one of the ſtrongeſt principles of human action and felicity, would be ſtill ſtronger, had they an opportunity of getting in leaſe more land added to what they already poſſeſs, in proportion as they were able to ſtock and manage it, or were ſmall farms to be got in the neighbourhood. Miſerable, indeed, muſt that claſs of men be, who are deprived of theſe, or ſimilar excitements to action. The ſtate and manners of ſociety ſhould every where be ſo formed, that people in the loweſt ſtations of life may have a foundation on which to build their hopes of advancing their circumſtances by frugality and induſtry. Such a view of their condition has a
great

great tendency to call forth every active power of the human nature ; to make them combat, with firmnefs, every oppofition that may occur, and, with refolution to overcome the difficulties that lie in the way. Animated with fuch a profpect, they will early acquire habits of induftry : A manly fpirit will ftimulate the whole of their conduct, and naturally lead them to abhor every unworthy purfuit : Succefs, in a greater or lefs degree, will crown their laudable endeavours. A conduct and a refult quite the reverfe muft infallibly characterize thofe unhappy creatures, whofe lot in fociety precludes them the hopes of ever raifing their condition above that of mean fervitude. The depreffion of all that is manly in the foul ; a rooted envy at the profperity of others, which they can never attain ; a chilling profpect of nothing but infignificancy, obfcurity and poverty to themfelves and their offspring ; and a long train of other evils, are the natural confequences of fuch a forlorn fituation. Perfons thus depreffed are unavoidably capable, and frequently willing to engage in the moft iniquitous, bafe, and cruel defigns. To prevent any clafs of men from falling into fo deplorable a condition, every precaution fhould be taken by the community. This ought efpecially to be done with refpect to the department of agriculture. Encouragement fhould be given to the meaneft fervant of rifing in the line of his bufinefs till he become a mafter. And are there not many knowing and wealthy farmers in Britain, who can remember the time when they were employed in the loweft fervice of hufbandry ? This encouragement is indeed held out to mechanics, and to thofe engaged in moft other purfuits of life ; but this can hardly be faid to be, at prefent, the cafe with refpect to farming, in thofe diftricts, where large farms are univerfally adopted. It is not in the nature of things, efpecially now when the neceffaries of life have rifen to fo high a

price,

price, that a common ſervant can, by his whole income of
about L. 15 a-year, maintain his family, and at the ſame
time acquire as much money as is requiſite to ſtock a large
farm. He and his offspring, if they do not change their
profeſſion, muſt remain for ever in a ſtate of ſervitude,
poor, helpleſs, and deſpiſed. It is happily otherwiſe in thoſe
places, where there is a proper mixture of great and ſmall
farms. It frequently happens that a ſervant, by a few
years induſtry and economy, with a little aſſiſtance from a
friend, accumulates a ſum that enables him to commence
farmer on a ſmall ſcale. In this new, but more advanced
ſituation, he exerts himſelf by every lawful means in his
power ; he is ſpurred on by a laudable emulation ; and, at
the expiration of his leaſe, is generally able to quit the
ſmall and enter on a larger farm. Taught by this gradual
progreſs through the various ſtages of his profeſſion, he directs with ſkill, he rules with moderation, and he manages
with economy. Were the inhabitants, in ſome places of
the iſland, favoured with ſuch opportunities of riſing in the
line of their buſineſs, it is highly probable that the landed
intereſt would find their profit in diminiſhing the extent of
ſome of their farms. That it was not alone the accumulation of ſmall into great farms that bettered the condition of
ſome diſtricts, but in a great meaſure the happy change
that took place in the mode of huſbandry and farming, is
a conjecture that may ſafely be ventured. The time is,
perhaps, at no great diſtance, when proprietors of eſtates
will find it as much their intereſt to diminiſh, at leaſt, ſome
of their farms, as they formerly imagined they did by enlarging them.

Heritors.—The landed property of Morbattle is ſubdivided amongſt twelve heritors ; but his Grace the Duke

of Roxburgh has by far the largeſt portion. None of the heritors but one reſide on their property in this place.

Population.—As the increaſe of the village is ſuppoſed to be equal to the depopulation of the country part of the pariſh, when ſmall farms were annihilated, the preſent number of inhabitants is ſuppoſed to be nearly the ſame as in the return made to Dr Webſter in 1755, which was then 789.

Agriculture.—Little more than one fourth part of the pariſh is at preſent under culture. It is certain, however, from the traces of the plough which yet remain on the higher grounds, that much more of this and the adjacent country was anciently under tillage than at preſent. It is generally believed, that, during the long and cruel conteſt between the two kingdoms, a great portion of the lands on the borders were kept under white crops, as it was not ſo eaſy for the plundering parties, in theſe unhappy times, to carry off crops of grain, as it was, had the land been in paſture, to drive away the cattle. The drill turnip huſbandry is carried on here with great ſpirit, and is conſidered as one of the chief improvements of agriculture in this country. Large fields of turnips are purchaſed by the graziers for feeding off with ſheep. The very ſmall quantity of lint that is produced in the pariſh is moſtly dreſſed or ſcutched by the hand at the owner's houſes.

Manufactures.—Artiſans and tradeſmen are far from being numerous in the pariſh, there being no more than are neceſſary to ſupply the inhabitants in cuſtomary work, in which are employed 4 weavers, 6 wrights and joiners, 2 ſmiths, 3 maſons, 5 tailors, 1 ſhoemaker. Tailors continue the practice of working in their employers houſes,

and

and receive 8 d. a-day, and their victuals. Wrights have
1 s. a-day and victuals, or 1 s. 6 d. without them. A small
quantity of linen-yarn is spun, some of it on the double-
handed wheel. This instrument was introduced from Fifeshire into this parish and neighbourhood, about 15 years
ago, by Mrs Morrison, wife of the Reverend David Morrison, minister in the Seceding meeting-house at Morbattle.
But little more yarn is spun than what is necessary for private use. The women in this part of the country being
accustomed to work much in the agricultural operations of
the field, are little disposed for sedentary employments, and
therefore, in general, sit down to the spinning wheel with
great reluctance. From the present disposition and habits,
both of males and females in this place, the introduction of
manufactures among them would not, it is probable, meet
with great success.

Church.—The present church was built in 1757, and
is a commodious place of worship. The stipend, including
the manse and glebe, is worth about L. 160. The Duke
of Roxburgh is patron. The Reverend James Richardson
fills at present the charge. A meeting-house, adhering to
the Antiburgher Seceders, was, a considerable number of
years ago, erected in the village of Morbattle; where a
clergyman of that persuasion regularly officiates, to a pretty numerous congregation collected from all the neighbourhood.

School.—The salary annexed to the parochial school is
100 merks Scots, with a free house and kail-yard. The
school-wages are 1 s. 6 d. for teaching the English language;
2 s. for writing, and 2 s. 6 d. for arithmetic and Latin.
The number of scholars is, at an average, about 25. His
perquisites for the session-clerkship are 4 d. for every baptism

tifm that he enrols in the parochial records, and 2 s. 6 d. for every proclamation of marriage, with a trifle for writing teftimonials, or certificates for character. His income receives an addition of L. 3 or L. 4 a-year, for collecting the poor-rates in the parifh. But this and the feffion-clerk-fhip do not belong to him as fchoolmafter; they are given him at the option of the heritors, minifter, and feffion. The whole income, however, is too fmall for enabling a teacher of youth to live in a manner fuitable to the ftation of fo public a character. The feffion-records of this parifh commence in 1697. No regifter of burials is kept.

Poor.—About 16 indigent perfons are commonly on the feffion-roll. Their principal fource of fupport is L. 1600, 3 s. 8 d. Sterling, that was, a good many years ago, bequeathed to this parifh by Mr John More, a native of Morbattle, who made his fortune in the Eaft Indies, where he died. The money was left to the management of the heritors and kirk-feffion of Morbattle, and bequeathed principally for the fupport of orphans and infirm old people. It is lent out for intereft on landed fecurity. Partly owing to this fund, the number of poor is probably greater than otherwife it would be, as people from the neighbouring parifhes refort here, from a motive of being fupported in old age, A fmall affeffment on the parifh is fometimes found to be neceffary. The collections at the kirk, amounting to a very fmall fum, is commonly diftributed by the feffion to occafional poor.

Difeafes.—This part of the country is not remarkable for any uncommon or peculiar difeafe. The inhabitants are generally healthy and ftrong, and many of them live to a good old age. The fmall-pox makes fometimes great havock among the children; and inoculation, the beft remedy

yet

yet known for that loathſome diſeaſe, is not much practiſed.

Antiquities.—The remains of ſeveral encampments, and
rows of ſtones, called *tryſt ſtanes*, are antiquities, probably
of the moſt ancient date in the pariſh. The tryſt ſtanes are
commonly on high ground. They are placed perpendicu-
larly in rows, not unfrequently in a circular direction. It
is ſaid, as alſo the name imports, that, in times of hoſtilities,
they marked the places of reſort for the borderers, when
they were aſſembling for any expedition of importance.
The ruins of Whitton-caſtle and Corbet-houſe are the only
remains of large buildings or places of ſtrength in the pariſh.

Miſcellaneous Obſervations.—The roads in the pariſh, of
which none are turnpike, are very far from being good,
and are often almoſt impaſſable. Two public houſes (ſmall
ones) in the village ſerve the inhabitants and paſſengers
with refreſhment. Formerly there were four mills in the
pariſh ; now two are found to be ſufficient to grind all the
corn that is needed by the inhabitants. About 20 acres
may contain all the growing wood in the pariſh, and theſe
were but lately planted. The chief dependence for fuel is
on coal brought from the Engliſh border, and which ſells
at a high price. There are a few peat-moſſes in the pariſh,
but the people, in general, are ſo much occupied in the field,
during ſummer, that the caſting and preparing of peats are
greatly neglected.

PARISH OF OXNAM.

(County of Roxburgh—Presbytery of Jedburgh—Synod of Merse and Tiviotdale.)

By the Rev. Mr. JOHN HUNTER, *Minister.*

[WITH A MAP OF THE PARISH.]

Origin of the Name, &c.

IN all ancient writings, the name of this parish is spelled OXENHAM, whereof the present mode of spelling it is an abbreviation. Several names in the parish are evidently taken from animals, and most probably from those, for which the various places have been most eminent: As *Hindhope*, from hind, where there had been a forest; *Swinside*, from swine, one of these having been kept in many places by every cottager; *Stotfield*, from stot, a young bullock; *Oxenham*, from oxen and ham, which, in the Saxon language, signifies a hamlet or village. The names of many other places describe and express their local situations, and other concomitant circumstances. Thus, *Millheugh*, the heugh by the mill; *Moss-burnford*, through which the burn from Scraesburgh Moss

runs,

runs, and where paſſengers croſs the water of *Jed; Bloody-laws*, a riſing ground, where much blood was ſhed by the licentious Borderers ; *Pearſlaws*, another riſing ground, where perhaps there had been an orchard ; &c. *Plenderleith, Riccalton*, and *Dolphiſton*, are moſt probably the names of their original proprietors.

Form, Extent, and General Appearance.—The figure of the pariſh bears a ſtriking reſemblance to that of Scotland. The greateſt length, from the head of Coquet water, on the Engliſh border, in a line by Swinſide, to Capehope, a farm ſtead on the N. point of the pariſh, in a direction N. W. ¼ N., is 9⅝ Engliſh miles ; the greateſt breadth, in a perpendicular direction, from Kaimburnfoot, on the W., in a line by Swinſide, to Conzierton march on the E,, is 4⅞ Engliſh miles ; on the N. it runs nearly to a point ; and about 2½ miles from the S. end, it is only 2 miles broad. The general complexion is rather bleak, interſperſed with beautiful green hills, fertile fields, and dark heath ; and almoſt unincloſed. But though it is hilly, yet there are no hills of very conſiderable magnitude.

Climate, Soil, and Diſeaſes.—The country is damp, and the air often moiſt, by rains from all directions, and in particular from the E. The rains ariſing out of Solway Frith, on the S., are conducted, as it were, along the vale of Liddiſdale, and frequently fall in great quantities on the adjoining fells, whilſt they ſcarcely touch this pariſh. The ſoil is various, admitting both the amuſements of paſturage, and the labours of agriculture. At the ſame time, the agreeable interchange of hill, dale, and ſtreams of water, gives a vibration to the air which renders it healthy, and free from agues. Certain it is, however, that rheumatiſms, conſumptions, and nervous fevers are pretty frequent.

Rivers

Rivers and Fish.—The river Jed runs along the W. boundary 2 miles. Oxnam water has its source about 2 miles from the S. end of the parish, runs N. by Oxnam, and, after a course of 11¾ miles, wherein there are many beautiful serpentine windings, falls into Tiviot below Crailing. Both the Coquet and the Kail, arise in that lofty ridge of mountains, lying in a direction betwixt N. and E., which separates Scotland and England from each other. The Coquet bounds the parish for a mile on the S., the only point in which it touches Scotland; and, after receiving a vast number of smaller streams, precipitating themselves from the mountains, quickly swells into a considerable river, which takes an easterly direction through Northumberland, and discharges itself into the British Ocean, betwixt Alnwick and Coquet Isle. The Kail, after running the breadth of the parish in a N. E. direction, takes its course, of 16½ miles, by Hownam, Morebattle, and Marlefield, and joins the Tiviot a little below Eckford kirk. These all abound in trout of an excellent quality, though, in point of quantity, the Coquet is the most distinguished. Besides, it affords a salmon fishery, many of which spawn about 4 or 5 miles from its head.

Minerals and Mineral Springs.—Attempts have been made to find coal in this parish, as well as in the neighbourhood, but without success. Limestone was found on the W. side of the parish, by Jed; but, being under a deep cover, and at a great distance from coal, the advantage of burning it is very doubtful. There is a chalybeate spring near Fairloans, on the S. end of the parish, to which qualities similar to Gillsland water are ascribed; but little of it has ever been used.

Perennial and Migratory Birds.—Game abounds here; amongst which may be reckoned the beautiful black-cock and grouse.

groufe. The woodcock, and fieldfare appear in the beginning of October, and remain during winter. The curlew, the green and the grey plover, come in March, breed in the moors, and go in the latter end of harvest. The cuckoo, fwallow, dottrel, and land and water rail, appear in May, hatch their young, and then difappear.

Population.—The population of Oxnam has decreafed within thefe 40 years †.

The return to Dr. Webfter, in the year 1755, was -	760
The prefent number of inhabitants (April 1793), is -	690
Decreafe, - - -	70

POPULATION TABLE of the Parifh of OXNAM.

AGES.	N°. Tot.	EMPLOYMENTS, &c.	Tot.
Under 10 years of age, -	175	Refident heritors, -	2
From 10 to 20, -	124	Minifter of the parifh, -	1
—— 20 to 30, -	103	Students in divinity, -	3
—— 30 to 40, -	77	Carpenters, - -	3
—— 40 to 50, -	74	Mafon, - -	1
—— 50 to 60, -	44	Smiths, - -	3
—— 60 to 70, -	52	Weavers, - -	5
—— 70 to 80, -	31	Taylor, - -	1
—— 80 to 90, -	9	Apprentices, - -	5
—— 90 to 100, -	1	Day labourers, - -	12
—— 690		Male labouring fervants, -	53
SEXES.		Female ditto, - -	33
Males, - -	298	Tenants, - -	25
Females, - -	392	In their families, -	109
—— 690		Herds, - -	13
CONDITIONS.		In their families, -	44
Widowers and widows, -	47	Wives, children and friends	
Married, -	183	of tradefmen, cottagers,	
Bachelors, -	17	&c. - - -	377
Unmarried, -	443	—— 690	
—— 690			

Average

† This decreafe of the population has been chiefly occafioned by the monopoly
of

Average of births*, for the laſt 10 years, - - -	15
————— marriages, - - - - - -	5
————— produce of each †, - - - -	7
————— of deaths ‡, - - - - -	6

Villages.—OXNAM was once large and populous; but, at preſent, there are hardly cottagers in it ſufficient for the proper culture of the land, and only 4 tradeſmen. *Newbigging* has been poſſeſſed by portioners, who hold of the Marquis of Lothian, ſince 1611. The ſole property of it, however, falls to his Lordſhip at Martinmas 1815, according to the deciſion of Lord Juſtice Clerk, to whom it was referred by both parties. *Swinſide, Dolphiſton,* and *Moſsburnford,* are inconſiderable villages.

Church, &c.—The church was built in 1738, has undergone conſiderable alterations, and is in pretty good repair §. The manſe

of farms. Not to multiply inſtances, in the village of Oxnam, between 60 and 70 years ago, there were 22 tenants, who kept about 16 ploughs, drawn by 2 oxen and 2 horſes, driven by a boy; whereas now, 3 perſons occupy the whole, and have only 7 ploughs, drawn by 2 horſes.

* The pariſh regiſter was accurately kept, from 1700 to 1710, during which, the births amounted to 398, annual average 40 nearly. Since that period, the regiſter has not been ſo accurate; occaſioned, chiefly, by the neglect of parents to ſave a very trifling expence. Within the laſt 10 years, the annual average of births has been about 15, of which only 10 are regiſtered.

† There is an inſtance of one marriage producing 22 births, and of 2 marriages out of theſe, producing each 15.

‡ During the above period, the mortcloth has been uſed 107 times, 90 of which were for interments in this church-yard. There is a ſtone in the church-yard, bearing the ages of a father and mother, 2 ſons, a daughter-in-law, and 3 grandchildren, amounting to 618, average 77 years; the oldeſt of whom was 98, and the youngeſt 70.

§ There is a remarkably diſtinct echo from the church to a ſmall eminence, 170 yards directly E. of it, in the level of the gallery.

manſe was built much about the ſame time, and has often been repaired at a great expence. The Crown and the Marquis of Lothian both gave preſentations to each of the 4 laſt mini-ſters. The living conſiſts of 30 bolls of barley, 21 bolls 1 firlot 1¼ ſtone of oatmeal, Tiviotdale meaſure †, and 30l. 2s. 2₁⁴₁d. Sterling in money *. The glebe, meaſuring 12 Engliſh acres, is worth about 14l. There are 2 church-yards, one at the kirk, and one at Plenderleith, about 4 miles S. of it; where, in all probability, there has been a reſiding vicar. The mini-ſter has alſo the privilege of turf, alternately, from 3 ſtock farms belonging to the Marquis of Lothian. A conſiderable proportion of the inhabitants of this pariſh are connected with the diſſenting meetings in Jedburgh.

School.—The ſcholmaſter's ſalary is 5l. 11s. 1⅜d., and he has 4l. 3s. 4d., intereſt of money mortified by Lady Yeſter, for teaching poor children; 4l. 15s. for collecting poor's rates; and, being clerk to the ſeſſion and heritors, 4d. for every re-giſtration and extract, and 1s. 6d. for each proclamation. The ſchool is in general well attended. The wages are, 1s. per quarter for Engliſh, 1s. 6d. for Engliſh and writing, and 2s. 6d. for arithmetic. The higher branches are taught by agree-ment. The above is the minimum legal ſalary of Scotland, and the ſchool wages are ſtill the original appointment. As the value of money is now ſo much ſunk, and as the wages of all the other claſſes are greatly increaſed, an augmentation of the
                                                                                    ſchoolmaſters

---

* The Tiviotdale boll of barley is 5 firlots, and of meal 16 ſtone.

† Beſides the above ſtipend, the former miniſters let in leaſe to the Duke of Roxburgh, during their reſpective incumbencies, the vicarage tithes of three ſtock farms, now let at 1000l., for a graſſum of 1000l. Scotch, and an yearly feu-duty of 100l. Scotch. His Grace, wiſhing to convert the graſſum and rent into an yearly ſtipend, took no leaſe from the preſent incumbent; and, it being a point of law, it is now depending before the Court of Seſſion.

fchoolmafters falaries, and fchool fees, feems to be indif-
penfibly neceffary.

Poor.—In confequence of a legal intimation of 10 free
days, the heritors, tenants, and kirk-feffion hold meetings
about the terms of Candlemas, Whitfunday, Lammas and
Martinmas. Upon the day of meeting they choofe a prefes ;
after which their clerk reads the minutes of laft federunt,
when they proceed to the roll of the poor, confider their circumftances individually, and appoint them correfponding ali-
ments. The inrolled poor amount to 24 ; and the quarterly affeffment for their relief is, at prefent, about 19l., being of late
greatly increafed, by the high prices of provifions, as well as
by the advanced age, and growing infirmities of moft of them.
The higheft yearly allowance for a fingle perfon is 4 guineas,
and for a frail old couple 6l. 9s. But when any perfon is fo
circumftanced as to require a nurfe, the heritors provide one.
In order to their enrolment they muft give inventories of their
effects, which become the legal property of the heritors, and
are expofed to fale at their death. The heritors, fteadily and
uniformly, infift upon having thefe inventories, both for en-
livening their own induftry, and for ftimulating their children
and near relations to give them aid. It is much to be regret-
ed, that a tafte for finery, inconfiftent with their ftation, prevents many from relieving their aged and indigent parents,
and other near relations, and expofes them to want, upon the
approach of ficknefs or old age ; while, at the fame time, it
deprives them of a luxury, far fuperior to that of fuperfluous
ornament, the GODLIKE PLEASURE of difpelling grief, and
COMMUNICATING HAPPINESS. The affeffment is divided a-
mongft the heritors, according to their valued rents ; and the
proportion which falls to each is paid, one half by the proprietor

prietor himſelf, and the other by his tenants, in proportion to their real rents*.

Heritors and Rents.—There are 7 heritors; but only 2 reſide. The valued rent of the pariſh is 14,101L. 10s. 8d. Scotch, and the real rent about 3,670l. Sterling. The yearly rent of the arable land is from 10s. to upwards of 20s. per acre, and of ſtock land from 3s. to 3s. 6d. per acre. Farms are rented from 40l. to about 600l. per annum. Two conſiderable ſtock farms are poſſeſſed by tenants, who do not reſide.

Produce, Cattle, Proviſions, &c.—The pariſh contains fully 20,500 Engliſh acres†, which are laid out, nearly, in the following manner:

STATE OF AGRICULTURE IN SPRING 1793.

	Eng. Acres.		Eng. Acres.
In wheat,	‡ 56	Brought forward,	1,685
— oats,	820	In paſture,	18,815
— barley,	220		
— peaſe,	140	Total,	20,500
— turnips,	140		
— potatoes,	35	**NUMBER OF CATTLE.**	
— flax,	14	Horſes,	161
— ſown graſs,	140	Cows, &c.	449
— firs,	120	Sheep, about	15,000
Carry forward,	1,685		

PRICES

* Dame Margaret Kerr, Lady Yeſter, by her letters of mortification, dated 4th November 1630 and 14th March 1638, cauſed to be built a ſchool, and a ſchoolmaſter's houſe, at Oxnam bridge end, and little dwelling houſes, for accommodating 4 poor people, commonly called *alms houſes*, at Oxnam Rawfoot; and likewiſe mortified 1000l. Scotch, the annual rent of which being 4l. 3s. 4d., toge.her with the weekly collections, is diſtributed, in ſmall proportions, amongſt ſuch indigent poor as are not on the roll.

† There is no map of the pariſh, diſtinct from Mr. Stobie's of the county; but all the heritors, except one, have accurate plans of their eſtates.

‡ The above calculations were made from the quantity of ſeeds ſown, in the
following

PRICES OF GRAIN AND CATTLE.

	In 1763.			In 1792.		
	l.	s.	d.	l.	s	d.
Wheat, per boll, of 4 firlots, - - - -	1	0	0	1	10	0
Oats, per ditto, of 5 ditto, ⁊ - - -	0	13	0	0	15	0
Barley, per ditto, of 5 ditto, - - - -	0	13	4	1	0	0
Pease, per ditto, of 4 ditto, - - - -	0	16	0	1	4	0
Turnips, per English acre, - - -				3	0	0
Potatoes, per boll, of 5 firlots, - - -				0	7	6
Flax, per stone, of 24 lb., - - -				0	11	6
Calves, unfed, - - - - -				0	5	6
Ditto, sometimes fed to - - - -				2	10	0
Black cattle, year-olds, - - - -				1	18	0
Ditto, two-year-olds, - - - -				2	18	0
Ditto, three-year-olds, - - - -				5	10	0
Wedders ditto, - - - - - -	0	10	9	1	0	0
Ditto, two-year-olds, - - - - -				0	16	0
Draught ewes, ⎰ from - - -	0	7	6	0	12	0
⎱ to - - -	0	10	0	0	15	0

PRICES OF WOOL, CHEESE, &c.

White wool, per stone, of 24 lb. Troy, - -	0	11	0	*1	1	0
Laid ditto, per ditto, - - -	0	5	6	*0	19	0
Ewe cheese, per ditto, - - -	0	4	6	0	7	9
Cow ditto, - - - - - - -				0	5	0
Butter, in firkins, per ditto, - - - -	0	7	0	0	12	0
Fresh butter, per stone, of 24 oz. per lb., - -	0	6	0	0	10	0

Cultivation.

following manner: It was supposed, that 4 firlots of oats were sown on each English acre: The wheat and pease were proportioned as 6 of oats to 4; and the barley as 10 of oats to 7: 8½ firlots of potatoes plant an acre; and 19 lippies of lintseed may be sown on the same quantity of ground.

* * To prevent confusion in the table, the highest prices of wool are here stated. White wool sometimes sold at 20s. in 1792, and laid wool sometimes so low as 16s.—Wool is supposed to drop considerably this *clip*, 1793.

Cultivation.—The upper part of the parish, towards the English Border, is found healthy stock land, but very stormy; the hills being high, and the valleys deep and narrow. The hills are mostly green and fertile, with an intermixture of heath, moss, bent, ling, sprat, &c.; partly dry, and partly wet and marshy. The arable land, in this part of the parish, is almost wholly laid into grafs. Towards the middle of the parish they raise rather more corn; but their principal dependence is upon stock. The land is inferior in quality, but not so stormy, as the Border hills. On the lower end of the parish, they depend more upon their crops than upon their flocks. Three small farms in this part of the parish keep no sheep at present.

Improvements.—The stock land has been much improved of late, by draining the wet and marshy grounds; by planting clumps of firs, for *stells* to shelter the flocks in storms; and by inclosing some part of the lands contiguous to the farm houses, for hay to the sheep in severe winters and springs. For a number of years, excellent crops of turnips have been raised on the lower end of the parish, to which the soil, which is dry and gravelly, is well adapted. The lime used for these, and for wheat, is brought, both from Tillside on the E., and from Redwater on the S. A cart load, of 5 bolls, costs 12s.; and 5 loads are commonly spread upon an English acre. The general practice is to allow the sheep to eat them upon the field. Throughout the whole parish, potatoes are raised in such quantities, as to become the principal food of the lower ranks of life for 8 months in the year. They are also used in feeding swine, horses, poultry, &c. and some are sold to the people on the fells.

Sheep,

Sheep &c.—On the upper end of this, and of the neighbouring parishes bordering on Northumberland, the sheep have been greatly improved of late, in shape, in weight, and in quality of wool. This has been effected, partly, by purchasing tups from Northumberland, and other counties in England, or by purchasing from, and exchanging them with each other ; and partly, by adopting a different mode of breeding their tups. The farmers of the last generation took their tups out of the whole flock, when they cut their lambs ; whereas now, they select a few of their best ewes, and such as have the finest fleece, which they keep apart from the rest of the flock, during the tupping season, with a good fine woolled tup, procured as above; and out of the lambs bred from these, they choose their tup lambs.—There is a good breed of horses in the parish, and many prefer them, with a little blood, for long carriages.

Commerce.—The produce of the lands far exceeds the consumption of the inhabitants. Part of the redundancy is sold at Jedburgh, and part is manufactured at the mills of Swinside and Oxnam, and carried over the fells to the stockfmen and their herds. A great quantity of cheese, of butter, and of veal is sold at Jedburgh ; the eggs are carried weekly to Berwick, and the poultry, both there and to Edinburgh, by persons who return loaded with salt, groceries, and other commodities, for supplying the inhabitants, and merchants in Jedburgh.

Seed-Time and Harvest.—Wheat is sown from the middle to the close of October ; oats, pease, and flax, from the 10th of March to the middle of April; barley, rye-grass and clover, from the middle of April to that of May ; potatoes are put into the ground during the same period; and turnips are drilled during the course of June and to the middle of July. The
harvest

harveſt begins, for the moſt part, with September; the corn is all cut in 20 or 21 working days; and, in 5 or 6 after, it is generally ſecured in the barns, and barn-yards, except when the ſeaſons prove cold and wet.

Implements of Huſbandry.—There are 42 ploughs and 52 carts in the pariſh. The old Scotch plough is entirely laid aſide, and the new conſtruction, with metal mould boards, uni-verſally adopted. Two ſtout horſes, driven by the plough-man, are quite ſufficient, except in a few inſtances, where 3 horſes are uſed, and a driver. Carts, of a light make, on wheels 4 feet 8 inches high, commonly ſtayed with iron at each corner, are uſed for coal and lime; and the long cart with rung and ſheth, for corn, peat and turf *.

Wages.—Tradeſmen are paid as follows :

		£		
Joiners receive per day, without victuals,	-	L. 0	1	6
Maſons,	-	0	1	10
Tailors,	-	0	1	2
Labourers, in ſummer,	-	0	1	4
———— in winter,	-	0	1	2
A man, in harveſt, receives, till the crop be cut, with victuals,	-	1	7	0
And a woman, during the ſame period,	-	1	1	0
Male ſervants, per annum, with board, - { from	-	6	10	0
{ to	-	8	0	0
Female ditto, ditto, - - - { from	-	3	10	0
{ to	-	4	10	0

Cottagers are taken bound to weed turnips, and make hay 12 days, at 3d. per day, with their maintenance, and

to

---

* Before the introduction of carts, a clumſy unweildy carriage, upon 2 wheels, drawn by 2 oxen, and 2, or ſometimes 4, horſes, called *a wain*, was uſed merely for dragging dung to the fields, and bringing home corn, hay and wood.

to reap in harveſt without receiving any thing but their board ; for which they poſſeſs a houſe and yard, have one or two *dargs* of turf or peat, which their maſters bring home, and give them as much ground as the aſhes will cover for ſowing barley. They have likewiſe two lippies of lint-ſeed ſown, and half a firlot of potatoes planted. Their crop, when it is good, conſtitutes a great part of their living throughout the year; and, in that caſe, their houſes coſt them little. Hinds receive 8 bolls of oats, 2 bolls of barley, 1 boll of peaſe, a cow's graſs, and 1l. 5s. for ſheep, as the wages of their own labour ; and are bound to the ſame ſervitude with a cottager for their houſes, lint, potatoes, &c. The wages of herds are conſiderably higher than thoſe of hinds, and differ according to the extent of their charge. They are paid with ſheep, and cows, which require a ſtock at beginning, and ſubject them to frequent loſſes.

Antiquities.—The only remains of antiquity are, a chapel at Plenderleith, 3 old forts, and a Roman cauſeway. The chief fortification is a tower at Dolphiſton, ſaid to have been built by one DOLPHUS, from whom it took its name. The walls are from 8 to 10 feet thick, built of hewn ſtone, and ſo cloſely cemented with lime, that it is found more difficult to obtain ſtones for building from it, than from a quarry. It has been extenſive, and divided into ſmall apartments by ſtone partitions. Several vaulted apertures are in the middle of the walls, large enough for a ſmall bed, and ſome of them ſo long, as to be uſed by the tenants for holding their ladders. On a riſing ground, a little to the S. there is an area of a chain ſquare, which is ſaid to have been a watch tower or light houſe, and ſhows that Dolphiſton Tower had been uſed as a fort, or place of refuge. The tower on Moſsburnford ground, N. from Dolphiſton, which is nearly entire, is built and
divided

divided in the fame manner, but far inferior in ftrength*. The
Roman road, or caufeway, is the eaftern boundary of the parifh,
and runs the whole length of it†. This ftreet has been traced

to

---

* The CRAG TOWER was built on a rock of fome eminence, on the E. fide
of Oxnam water, about 500 yards W. of the church. Within thefe 20 years,
it was a place of the fame conftruction with thofe already mentioned, but much
ftronger from its natural fituation, being furrounded with water on three fides.
In the memory of many now living, there was a pit in the middle of it, which
is faid to have been a road cut through the rock to the water, by which it was
fupplied when befieged. It is alfo faid to have been furrounded on the acceffible
fide, with a ftrong wall, within which the inhabitants of the neighbourhood
ufed to fhut up their cattle, to prevent the plunderers from carrying them off in
the night. Anciently, the oppofite bank of Oxnam water, on the W., was covered with wood, denominated *benwood*, and is faid to have been the rendezvous
of the inhabitants, to oppofe the Englifh freebooters, when the watch word was,
a *benwoody*. A quarter of a mile to the W., on Millheugh-farm, there is a hillock, called GALLALA-KNOW, which is faid to have been ufed in the Border
wars as a place of execution. Many buildings, fimilar to thofe defcribed, are
fcattered over the country, efpecially on the Border, which were called *peels*.——
There is a tradition, that, during the animofities between the two kingdoms, one
of the principal bells, now upon the cathedral of Durham, was carried from this
parifh. Certain it is, that OXNAM is infcribed upon it; but whether it be the
name of this parifh, or of the founder, is not determined. Some are of opinion, that as Oxnam was fubject to the abbacy of Jedburgh, the Crag Tower
might be a religious houfe, and the bell is faid to have been hung upon it.
Before the union of England and Scotland, which feem deftined, by their fituation to conftitute a mighty monarchy, among the military and turbulent Borderers, fo little acquainted with the arts of peace, and fo averfe to induftry and
labour, juftice was feebly, irregularly, and partially adminiftered; and great oppreffion and violence prevailed, when rapine was the only trade, and bloodfhed
often led the way to the fuccefsful profecution of it. By the interpofal of the
authority of both houfes of parliament, the reign of good laws is eftablifhed,
tending, in an eminent degree, to form habits of order, induftry, and virtue, to
increafe the happinefs of individuals, to promote national profperity, and to introduce a tafte for general improvement, throughout this, as well as other parts
of the kingdom.

† A number of years ago, in a field belonging to Cap-hope, on the N. point

of

to Boroughbridge in Yorkſhire, and has its direction to the Lothians by Boſwel's Green, where one of the largeſt fairs in Scotland is annually held, on the 18th of July.

Roads.—Formerly, the ſtatute labour, for county roads, from 20 to 22 feet broad, was levied from the number of men and horſes, of late at 1s. for a man, and 1s. 6d. for a horſe. In conſequence of an application from the gentlemen of this county, a few years ago, an act of parliament was granted to collect it from the tenants according to their valued rents, but not to exceed 10s. Sterling upon the 100l. Scotch. The county is divided into four diſtricts, *Jedburgh, Kelſo, Hawick,* and *Melroſe,* and each of them has a conſtable for inſpecting the roads, and for ſeizing vagrants. Though theſe do not all collect to the full amount ſpecified in the act, yet it is found neceſſary to do ſo in this diſtrict of Jedburgh, on account of its being interſected by fewer public roads. A road is now making, from *Wooden-burn Bridge,* in the pariſh of Crailing, and Kaimburnfoot in this pariſh, connecting the great turn-pike roads from Kelſo to Hawick, and from Edinburgh, by Jedburgh, to Newcaſtle. In order to complete it ſpeedily, ſome public ſpirited gentlemen have taken out a caſh account, to be paid off every half year with the ſtatute money. Attention has alſo been paid to other roads in the pariſh, whereby communication

of the pariſh, contiguous to the road, a head piece of plate iron, ſuppoſed to be Roman, was turned up by the plough, and is in the poſſeſſion of the preſent tenant. It weighs 1½ lb. avoirdupoiſe; and, although a little waſted, could never weigh 2 lb. Its brim is an oval of 7.9 inches by 6.9, without any edges, only bent forward about half an inch, before and on the ſides like the brim of a pot. It is 5.9 inches deep, and the top is a very flat Gothic arch, 10.2 inches long, jutted out before and behind. It is evidently hammered, but has not the ſmalleſt appearance of any joining. In autumn 1791, a ſhilling of Robert Bruce was found at a garden in Newbigging, and was ſold to George Currie, Eſq. advocate.

communication is greatly facilitated. Not long ago, small coal was brought from Ryechester, and great coal from Ital, on horseback, but they are now brought in carts. which have been universally adopted since the bettering of the roads.

Disadvantages.—One of the chief disadvantages, the greatest part of this parish labours under, is its distance from coal, which is still, notwithstanding, the cheapest fuel to those who have horses, but which poor people cannot afford to purchase. A two-horse cart-load of coal, from Ryechester, costs 12s. 6d., and one from Ital costs about 14s. 6d. Though this parish abounds in excellent peats and turf, yet the most populous parts have no claim to them, and are but scantily supplied with turf, of far inferior quality, from a moor, once common, and which still goes by that name. Another growing disadvantage is, the depopulation of the parish, by suffering the cottage houses to fall into decay; whereby the country is deprived of many useful members of society, and the tenant of aid for carrying on his labours, especially in harvest, when he is overtaken by storms, particularly of wind, which often do great and irreparable damage to the valuable productions of the year.

General Character.—The people are industrious, sober, and economical, and seem to have no inclination either for a military or a seafaring life. They are friendly to one another, and hospitable to strangers. The labouring part support their families in a very decent manner, and give their children a tolerable education. Even in 1783, when the pensions of the poor were doubled by the failure of crop 1782, no family in the parish solicited relief from the heritors, nor were supplied with provisions, at reduced prices, as was the case in many other parishes.

PARISH OF ROXBURGH,

(COUNTY OF ROXBURGH, SYNOD OF MERSE AND TWEED-
DALE, PRESBYTERY OF KELSO.)

By the Rev. Mr ANDREW BELL, *Miniſter of the Pariſh.*

PREVIOUS to the Union of the Scotch and Engliſh Parliaments, this corner of the land was often the ſeat of
war, and the unhappy ſcene of broils and feuds, which
uſually ſtigmatize the border inhabitants of two hoſtile
kingdoms in a barbarous age. Roxburgh was the reſidence
and rendezvous of ſome of the greateſt military, political,
clerical and Royal charaƈters Europe has to boaſt of, and
the place where ſtate councils were held with a ſplendour
                                                      and

and magnificence becoming the dignity of assemblies, in whose decisions many nations felt themselves highly interested and concerned. Hence this parish affords great room for investigation, and opens a field, whereon the historic genius might range with peculiar gratification. The following remarks, however, being intended to make part of a work, whose object is *statistical* rather than *historical* enquiry, they are chiefly limited to local and existing circumstances.

Name.—Like all etymological interpretations of the names of places, the meaning of this is extremely vague and uncertain. Camden calls the castle of Roxburgh *Marchidun*, or the hill on the marches, alluding, not to the altitude or size, but to the strength and importance of that fortress. Some nomenclators say, that Roxburgh is a contraction for Rogue's Burgh, referring to the character of its ancient inhabitants, when marauding was the trade of all the borderers. Others affirm, that Roxburgh is the proper name, and derived from a Saxon word, *Rox*, signifying strength: And others insist, that Roseburgh (as it is vulgarly designed) is the proper appellation of this place, being most expressive of its beautiful situation.

Situation.—The old city of Roxburgh stood over against Kelso, on a rising ground at the west end of a fertile plain, peninsulated by the confluence of the rivers Tweed and Teviot. These song-renowned rivers flow here in all their glory; but the Teviot has decidedly the preference, when imagination calls up to view the grand assemblage of objects that formerly lined her banks in this place. On the south angle of a beautiful peninsulated tract of land, formed by the curvitures of the two rivers, is a rich spot,

spot of ground, where David I. built a magnificent friary for some Ciftertian monks, whom he removed from Selkirk to Roxburgh ; on the middle ftood the town, both under cover from the Caftle, which was fituated on a large oblong knoll to the weft, and feparated from the city by a narrow neck of land, formed by the proximity of the rivers. " The fouth walls of the Caftle impended over the " Teviot, a part of whofe waters were directed by a dam " thrown obliquely acrofs the ftream at the weft end of the " Caftle into a deep foffe, which defended the fortrefs on " the weft and north, emptying itfelf into the river, at the " eaft end thereof *." Over this moat, at the gateway from the town, was thrown a draw-bridge, the remains of which were but lately removed. About two miles weft from the Caftle ftands the prefent village of Roxburgh, pleafantly fituated near the banks of the Teviot, on a declivity of fouthern expofure. It is divided by a fmall rivulet into the " Upper and Nether Towns," which had formerly been of confiderable extent, though they now contain only about 200 inhabitants. This village is the feat of the parochial church ; is nearly centrical to the whole parifh ; lies in the county which bears its name, and within the bounds of the Prefbytery of Kelfo, and Synod of Merfe and Teviotdale.

Extent, Surface, and Soil.—The parifh extends about 8 miles in length, and 4 in breadth at the extremities, including an area of 7000 acres of land. Its figure is irregular, and may be reprefented by a fpread eagle, with his head towards the north, his wings fhadowing eaftward and weftward. The general appearance of the country is flat and floping. The foil is moftly a rich loam, well calculated for bearing turnips or wheat : The lands are therefore very valuable,

* Pennant.

valuable, but rather unpleasant to labour, being *banky* in some places. The skirts of the parish on the west and south are moorish. A great part of that tract of land which lies between the rivers, especially about the village, is so stony, that tradition reports it to have been once all covered with houses. In very few places, however, have the stones any appearance of having ever been used in building. The grounds on the east end of the parish, and those on the south side of the Teviot, are inclosed with ditch and hedge. The fences, being in general grown up, and ornamented with hedge-rows of trees; besides, various woods, and little thickets, or clumps of wood, reared upon unarable knolls and rocky hillocks in several parts, make the country look rich and beautiful. The parish is bounded by Maxton, Ancrum, and Crailing, on the west; by Crailing and Eckford, on the south; by Kelso, on the east; by a part of Kelso and Makerston, on the north.

Agriculture.—The greatest part of this parish is in a very high state of cultivation, and yields an ample reward to the occupiers for their toil and expence in labour. Whether lying in pasture or in tillage, the fields every where around display the remarkable activity, agricultural spirit, and skill of the farmers. Equal in all kinds of husbandry within their sphere to any in the kingdom, the landholders and farmers here are particularly attentive to the cultivation of potatoes, and, being favoured by the nature of the soil, have carried it to a very high degree of perfection. Three hundred fir-lots *per* acre is a frequent produce. They are planted in drills, the distance between each plant sometimes about three feet, and are completely cleaned of weeds by frequent hoeing; the first and second time very deep, with a sharp pointed hoe, afterwards not so deep, lest the root should be injured. About the time of their blooming, the earth is laid

up,

up, sometimes in the form of a molehill, about each stalk, which is a great improvement. In this way of management the ground is well cleaned, and afterwards yields a good crop of wheat or oats. The potatoes are planted on light dry land, either naturally rich, or made so with dung. Lime is found hurtful, by making them grow *scabbed*. In order to prevent their degeneracy, the seed is carefully picked, and such as grow curled leaves are kept out if possible. Though a rotation of crops is generally observed here, by raising one green and two white, yet some of the farmers, distinguished for skill in and attention to business, are often directed by the seasons, and the various soil of their lands.

Hence the number of acres occupied by distinct species of crops can ardly be ascertained. It is supposed that one half of the whole parish is generally in pasture; the other half in tillage; and one-third of that laid down annually with grass-seeds, the ground being always first properly cleaned and prepared for them. The parish rears a great deal more grain of all kinds than the inhabitants use, and the cattle bred or fattened within its bounds are not half, scarcely the third part, consumed there. Upwards of 50 ploughs are employed in the parish, and drawn generally with two horses. Oxen are also used, and found to answer the purposes of husbandry, both in the cart and plough.

Population.—Vestiges of villages, malt steeps, cottages, and other memorials of inhabitation in various parts of the parish, indicate the population to have been formerly very considerable; but no exact list of old date having fallen into my hands, the number cannot be ascertained far back. Agreeably to a practice recommended and generally observed in the Church of Scotland, the writer, upon his induction to this cure, visited every family within its bounds,

and

and found the number of fouls in the parifh to be upwards of 1050.

A very accurate lift was again made out at the defire of the Sheriff of the county, in 1782, to affift in providing againft a fcarcity, with which this country was then threatened, and the number of fouls was found to be 1100. They do not at prefent exceed 900 *, and may be diftributed thus :

Of the Eftablifhed Church,		480
Burghers, Antiburghers, and Relief Seceders, - -		170
Cameronians and Quakers, -		9
Children, - -		241

		Males,	360
900 {		Females,	540

Families, or houfeholders,		191
Cotters, - -		121
Hinds and herds, -		23
Handicraftfmen, -		43
Apprentices to thefe, -		7
Servants, - -	115 { Males,	60
	Females,	46
Farmers, - -		22
Heritors, - -		10

The great difproportion between the males and females feems to arife from a number of cot-houfes being poffeffed by women, whofe hufbands or fons are employed elfewhere.

According

* Since this lift was taken in 1791, the population has decreafed upwards of 60.

According to the parish-register *, there has been, within the time included between the 1st of October 1783 and the 1st of October 1793,

Marriages,	-	-	76

Births,	-	-	155	Males,	77
				Females,	78

Burials,	-	114	Males,	64
			Females,	50

The exact number of births and burials cannot be easily ascertained. For various reasons many childrens names are not registered; and the people in general all over this country having an idea of property in their family burying place, carry their dead there; and by neglecting to do so, they seem to feel themselves guilty, not only of violating a natural propensity in men to sleep with their fathers, but also of infringing a sacred obligation, as they say, sanctioned by the example of patriarchs, at the cave in the field of Macpelah. In articles of population, an account of the ages of different classes of persons have been thought expedient and useful. This the writer has been obliged to omit, except with regard to children, who neither fear nor blush to tell their age; and those who glory in " prattling " o'er the tales of other years." The children mentioned above are under 10 years of age; of the other venerable class, there are 15 upwards of 70, nine upwards of 80, three above 90, and one near 100 years old. During the late incumbent's ministry here, a woman died at Fairnington about the age of 120.

State of the Poor.—At present there are 24 upon the poors roll; the monthly assessment for supporting these, including

* This reaches as far back as 1618; is remarkably regular, and has often been a proof of the utility of such records.

including collector and clerk's fees, is L. 6 : 4 : 4, levied, one half from the heritors, and the other half from the tenants, according to their real and valued rents respectively. Meetings for conducting the affairs of the poor here are held twice a-year; the tenants are always invited by the minister from the pulpit to attend on these occasions for assisting the heritors and kirk-session * in that work; and the allowance of each pauper is generally fixed according to the report of the kirk-session, or tenant under whom he lives, as to his circumstances. By this means improper applications for public charity are checked; the truly indigent furnished with a good mode of obtaining relief; and to the generous, a plan is opened for giving alms without danger of imposition. It is painful, indeed, to see parents, worn out with the toil and care of rearing a family, sometimes applying for public aid; while the very children they have nourished and brought up, will not give a mite to relieve their distress. The public, say they, is obliged to do it. This is the apology many make for neglecting to obey one of the first laws of nature, while they frequently lavish away a considerable part of their earnings upon the vanities of life. On this account some have thought there should be no law to force public charity, unless to oblige such as are in ability to support their indigent relations, especially children their parents. Alas! if filial or brotherly affection cannot melt the heart, a rod of iron, it is to be feared, would be used in vain to break it. In order to keep the number of poor on the list from increasing beyond proper bounds, and to prevent the modest and well-deserving from suffering want, the collections

made

* Heritors, or landholders, and the kirk-session in a parish, are the *legal* members of these meetings. In assessing for the poor, however, the aid of the farmers is highly proper.

made in the kirk are diſtributed among needy perſons, not on the poors roll; and in caſes of incidental poverty, an *interim* ſupply is given. The heritors ſometimes lodge money in the hands of the ſeſſion, to diſtribute as they ſee proper. This is attended with great advantages; evils often occurring that cannot be provided againſt by the general meeting, and the collections in the church being ſcarcely adequate to the claims uſually made upon them, ſuch as the ſchool wages of poor ſcholars, &c.

State of the Church and School.—Five miniſters have been ordained here ſince the Revolution, *viz.* Meſſrs Dalglieſh, Brown, Pollock, Hogg, and the preſent incumbent. The firſt of theſe was excluded from his charge at the Revolution, and returned to it afterwards; but the benefice being too ſmall to ſupport his numerous family, he was obliged to betake himſelf to ſome other employment, and leave this cure, much regretted by the people. Mr Brown was removed from his kirk in the year 1715; and had it not been for the compaſſion and humanity of a Noble Counteſs, he had felt all the diſtreſs naturally befalling ſuch as are driven from a particular line of life, to which alone they have been educated. Though a man of no ſhining abilities, and greatly deficient in that diſcernment and prudence neceſſary to ſteer the helm of conduct in a politic age, yet we feel for Mr Brown, retiring, in exile, to a remote valley, where he lived for years in a cottage on the ſide of a rivulet, (by Ceſsford), tending his milk-cow, or delving his garden—his only livelihood, and the gift of charity. The ground of proceſs againſt Mr Brown is ſaid to have been a charge of diſloyalty, which aroſe chiefly from his drinking the Pretender's health at Kelſo, in company with the rebel army. This, it is ſaid, he did with no ill intention, but ſimply thinking thereby to pleaſe Mackintoſh, the rebel commander, and thus recover a horſe the rebels had

had ftolen from him. Mr Pollock lived not long to profe-
cute the remarkable fuccefs with which his miniftry was
attended in this parifh. Defigned by Providence to in-
ftruct a rude race of men, he was endowed with many qualifications requifite for that important tafk. A robuft conftitution, and a bold impetuous temper; unwearied attention to the care of his paftoral office; and a rigid execution of difcipline; a competent fhare of various erudition,
and very confiderable powers of addrefs, procured him the
lafting memorial of having turned many from darknefs to
light. Scarcely above one in a family, before his days,
having been taught to read here, under his tuition the
youths not only obtained the elements of ufeful knowledge
at fchool, but were obliged to commit the principles of religion and morality, as recommended by the conftitution
of this kingdom, carefully to memory, and repeat them
publicly at church, which gave early and falutary ideas of
civil and facred virtues that the lapfe of time has not entirely wiped away. His few furviving difciples talk of
thefe things with delight; and difcover the mingled fenfa-
tions of joy and trembling, while they fpeak of the great
oaken ftick wherewith Mr Pollock always walked, overawing the infolent; or the engaging means by which he
encouraged the timid and deferving. Mr Hogg was a native of the parifh, and wore out his days in ferving this
cure with much efteem, refpect, and ufefulnefs. He died
on the 3d day of February 1781, in the 46th year of his
miniftry, and was fucceeded by the prefent incumbent in
the month of November following. The church was built
in the year 1752; was the firft modern houfe of that kind
in this corner of the country; is in good repair, neat and
commodioufly fitted up for holding the people. Though
plain and fimple in its conftruction, the prefent church
forms a ftriking contraft to the old one here, and fhows how
differently

differently men in ancient and modern times think of places fitteft for devotional exercifes. Agreeably, as it would
feem, to the old idea, that the fpirit of devotion likes beft
to dwell in gloomy retreats, the kirk at Roxburgh was almoft wholly under ground, roofed with a ftrong arch, and
totally overgrown with grafs. The people entered to the
place of public worfhip through an aifle * of the fame conftruction, and defcended by fix or feven fteps into the body
of the church, (perhaps the particular conftruction of that
edifice had been intended as a kind of fecurity to the wor-
fhippers in times of perfecution and danger). The manfe
has been rebuilt during the prefent minifter's incumbency,
and might be deemed a good one, did not the very damp
fituation render it both particularly uncomfortable and un-
healthful to live in. The heritors have already been at
confiderable expence in repairing it, by renewing the
ground floor, throwing drains round the houfe, &c. but all
feems, as yet, an ineffectual remedy of an evil that might
eafily have been prevented at firft. It is furely the intereft
as well as the duty of all who are bound by law to furnifh
accommodations to perfons in public characters, not only
to contract with tradefmen, but alfo to fee the work done
in a place and form that may render it moft durably comfortable. The Duke of Roxburgh is the undoubted patron of this kirk. The ftipend is L. 73 : 3 : 4, including
communion-elements, and L. 1, 10 s. Sterling in lieu of
turf-cafting. A decreet of modification paffed the 3d day
of March 1790, augmented faid ftipend by a grant of four
chalders of oat-meal, but the locality is not yet fettled.
Practices of this kind are not only very much againft a minifter's intereft, but often prove alfo extremely hurtful to
heritors,

---

* This aifle is ftill remaining, and is the family burying-place belonging
to Sunlaws.

heritors, on whom the greateſt ſhare of ſtipends finally falls. The law indeed authoriſes a miniſter to uplift his whole modified ſtipend, until localled, from any proprietor, who has ſufficient teinds within the pariſh. This, however, though ſtrictly legal, is generally thought an ungracious ſtep, is difficult to render effectual, and is ſeldom or never followed, unleſs neceſſity urges. The glebe is of conſider-able extent, but not including a graſs-glebe, nor has the miniſter any thing in lieu thereof that he knows of, has been all incloſed and much improven at the preſent incum-bent's ſole expence. But being naturally of a wet, cold bottom, and interſected by a very deſtructive rivulet, it will require conſtant attention to keep the fences in re-pair, and the land in any tolerable ſtate of culture or fruit-fulneſs. The miniſter's garden is now very good, and his office-houſes are ſuitable, had their ſituation been dry.—The number of ſcholars attending the parochial ſchool is gene-rally about 30 in ſummer, and 40 in winter. The ſchool-maſter's ſalary is L. 100 Scotch, and a *darg* of turf caſt on Roxburgh moor, according to uſe and wont. Beſides his legal ſalary, he has ſeveral little perquiſites, ſuch as 10 s. *per annum* as precentor and ſeſſion-clerk ; 20 s. *per annum* as heritors clerk ; for each proclamation of banns, 1 s. ; for every regiſtration of baptiſm, 6 d. ; and 4¼ d. for each te-ſtimonial of moral character ; theſe are here given by the authority of the kirk-ſeſſion. The ſchool-wages are 1 s. *per* quarter for reading ; 1 s. 6 d. for writing ; and 2 s. for arithmetic. Beſides the parochial, there are two ſchools in this pariſh, which accommodate children who live at a di-ſtance from the village. The ſalary of the maſters of theſe two ſchools is given by their employers. It is much to be wiſhed that country ſchoolmaſters had more liberal appoint-ments. The Duke of Roxburgh, whoſe attention to all ſuch public inſtitutions deſerves the higheſt praiſe, has aug-

mented

mented to the legal *ultimum, viz.* L. 100 Scotch, the school-master's salary here, and I believe of all the schoolmasters where he has any concern. They are still but a poor inducement for men of genius or learning, in this enterprising age, to undergo the drudgery of that most useful office. At these humble seminaries, the *million* in this country receive the rudiments of civil and moral character; and the principles children imbibe there, often direct the whole tenor of their future life. Unless the depravity of the world has rubbed off the virtuous feelings a boy was inspired with at school, we frequently find him in mature age pushed on to excellence in laudable pursuits by the same nerves which led him foremost in the youthful sport, and made him aspire at personal honour, or his master's applause, by rising *Dux* in the class through merit and industry. It might, therefore, be of great advantage to church and state, in a land where the road to eminence is open to all who will strive to attain it, were a man of a liberal and polished mind placed at the head of each of these nurseries of youth, qualified not only to teach children the alphabet, but to implant in their minds the seeds of virtue, and of that noble ambition which leads to preferment in the world, as at school, by personal worth and due submission to superiors. But this can hardly be expected, while the appointments of that office continue so extremely narrow, as to make every well-educated and virtuous man shrink back from it as a place of hopeless penury, or follow some other employment besides his school, in order to gain a decent livelihood for his family. It is hoped, however, that such arrangements will be made as may enable presbyteries (whom the wisdom of our ancestors has constituted guardians of parochial schools) to recommend men every way fit for conducting that singular system of education from whence the Scottish people have derived such consequence, and on the

proper

proper management of which the welfare of society so greatly depends. Over the parochial school of this parish a man of great integrity has presided upwards of 40 years, and many have reaped the good fruits of his labours.

Heritors.—There are ten heritors, or proprietors of land, in the parish, five great and five small. The Duke of Roxburgh is proprietor of one half of the lands in the whole parish, and bears consequently one half of all parochial burdens, except the minister's stipend, of which by law he can greatly relieve himself, being titular of all the teinds. The only great heritor who resides for any length of time is the Hon. Baron Rutherford of Fairnington. Of this gentleman's character, so universally and so justly esteemed, a small part only falls within the limits of a Statistical account. The whole estate is cultivated by the proprietor himself, and his extensive improvements have afforded bread to artists and labourers in this part of the country for many years. Besides their receiving the stated price of labour, the most humane and particular attention is paid to the comfort and health of the inhabitants; in so much, that every thing being found them, (even medical assistance when necessary), they have no need to apply to the public funds of the parish for charity. In a small village on this estate, in which there are upwards of 100 souls, the proprietor has established a school with a considerable salary to a teacher properly qualified. The schoolmaster has an additional allowance for keeping a Sunday school, where all who wish to attend are instructed in the principles of religion and morality, and proper books on these subjects put into their hands.—Inoculation of the small-pox has often been successfully practised in the bounds of his estate; and this also being afforded *gratis,* has induced the parents to comply with that salutary measure. Thus both the spiritual

ritual and temporal interests of the people are carefully attended to by the Hon. Baron *.

Of the 22 farmers who occupy the lands in this parish,
eight farm pretty extensively, the rest are small tenants.
Eleven or twelve in the village of Roxburgh are called
cotlanders, possessing from his Grace the Duke of Roxburgh
about two acres of land each, together with a house, yard,
and liberty of pasturing their cows in an adjacent *loaning*.
This, along with their own industry in some trade, enables
them to bring up their families pretty comfortably. They
have no lease of their lands, but their rents are seldom raised, and they are almost never turned away, unless they be-
have ill, or prove troublesome neighbours. All of them
have families, which being, in general, trained up in the
path of virtue and industry, promise to be useful members
of society.

Animals.—This parish contains about 160 work, 9 or
10 riding horses, and several young ones to preserve the
stock, 600 black cattle, and 4000 sheep, all good of their
kind, though not distinguished in the neighbourhood either
for size or value. Birds of all kinds, usually met with in
this country, appear here in their proper seasons.—The
Tweed and Teviot are the only rivers in the parish, and
abound with various kinds of fish, especially salmon, whose
prices are generally regulated by the Berwick market. A
small purple-coloured trout prevails much here, very delicious to eat, and is said to be peculiar to Teviot. Such
quadrupeds as generally frequent the southern parts of
Scotland, appear in various corners of this parish, and afford the sportsmen plenty of game in the season.

Advantages

* Since the above was written, this worthy Nobleman is dead, much and
most sincerely regretted.

Advantages and Disadvantages.—Though this parish is not much distinguished from those around by any particular local advantages, yet its vicinity to a good market at Kelso, its inhabitants being liable to no peculiar disease, and its very healthful climate, are properties of high estimation. Spring agues were troublesome in two or three places, which lie low and damp; but since the ground about these was made dry in the course of farming improvement, by drains and inclosing, the inhabitants have not been exposed to that complaint in any remarkable degree. Several old people complain much of what they call *the pains*, or rheumatism, owing probably to the extreme cold they are exposed to from their damp houses, and great scarcity of firing. Among the principal disadvantages under which this place and all the neighbourhood labour, is the great distance from coal, and a total want of every other species of fuel. This is a real calamity to the poor; and most heavily felt by them since they were, some years ago, all prohibited from casting turf on the moors. Every cottar used to have liberty from his master to cast a darg or two of turf.—The fine road from Berwick to Carlisle, (so beautifully described in the Statistical Account of Bedrule), passes through the south part of this parish, and is of extensive *substantial* benefit, as is that likewise which runs along the north side of the parish from Kelso to Melrose. But the high road passing through the village of Roxburgh is yet in a natural state, and on account of its extreme ruggedness is almost impassable. In consequence, however, of a bridge now building over Teviot, near Kelso, we hope this road will soon be put into a state of complete repair, being the direct line therefrom up through a rich populous country, whose comforts and improvement are much impeded by the want of it. The bridge above mentioned is remarkably handsome, and will be of vast utility to all that

populous

populous diſtrict between Tweed and Teviot; eſpecially
to the tenants on the eaſt end of this pariſh, whom the accidental magnitude of theſe rivers often interrupted in the
courſe of buſineſs. Another inconvenience ariſes to this
pariſh from its interſection by the Teviot. The lands adjacent to the river are not indeed expoſed to much damage
thereby, and a boat is kept at Roxburgh, both for ſerving
the country, and accommodating the people with acceſs to
the church ; yet the flooding of the river often prevents a
populous diſtrict of the pariſh from attending public worſhip, and *totally* deprives the children there of the benefit of
the parochial ſchool. As many landward pariſhes labour
under ſimilar inconveniencies with regard to parochial
ſchools, it is hoped that in theſe arrangements underſtood
to be going on through Scotland for better encouraging the
education of youth, ſome plan will be adopted for providing ſtated ſchoolmaſters in ſuch places as have not acceſs
to the pariſh-ſchool.

Views.—In almoſt every corner of this pariſh the eye is
preſented with objects that nature and art ſeem vying how
beſt to adorn. The beauties of the ſcenery which ſur-
rounds the ſeat of the ancient city of Roxburgh exceeds all
deſcription. A little to the weſt of this, the public road
lies along the top of a precipice lined with trees, through
which a traveller perceives the Tweed rolling " dark,
" drumbly and deep," far below him ; at a little diſtance,
on the other hand, he ſees the Teviot meandring round a
large plain, and bounded by a rocky wooded bank. While,
contemplating theſe rivers, truly beautiful when in low
water, and grand when in flood, the ſpectator ſuddenly
loſes fight of *them,* and every thing elſe but the wood that
overſhadows him in a hollow of the way. In this gloomy
path he goes only a few paces, until a moſt enchanting
ſcene

scene opens upon him all at once, the prominent features whereof are, the Duke of Roxburgh's seat at Fleurs; Sir George Douglas's at Springwoodpark; the Teviot on the right and Tweed on the left hand, two beautiful bridges over these, and Kelso, in all its glory, full in the traveller's eye, as he passes eastward. From a particular spot in the village of Roxburgh there is a very magnificent view. Looking eastward, the spectator sees nothing wild or uncultivated, and stretches the line of vision along a valley, apparently covered with trees, to the distance of 8 or 10 miles. A corn or grass field, a house here and there, and the smoke of various cots and villages curling up from amidst the forest, diversify and heighten the scene. A house on the top of a high hill, with a row of trees on each side of it, makes a fine termination to the whole. From the same spot the spectator is amused with a very different prospect westward, double the length, and bounded by the lofty mountain Carter, and its adjacent hills. From a rising ground on the south side of the parish, the curious are gratified with a romantic view of the Teviot. After being concealed by the particular arrangement of its banks, the river appears tumbling *cascade-like* from the mouth of Sunlaws caves, and instantly disappears again. The cave-mouths, and the river apparently flowing from them, produce a most singular effect. A prospect of the Teviot from Sunlaws hill, winding through an extensive dale, enriched in the highest degree both by nature and art, well deserves notice as peculiarly pleasing and grand. The widest and most abundant range of view which this parish affords, is from a rising ground or hill called *Duns-Law*, on the west angle of Fairnington estate. Agreeably to the import of its name, this eminence is said to have formerly been a station of authority and strength. An observatory, or summer-house, built on the top of it by the Hon. Baron Rutherford, commands

a

a profpect too vaft, and crowded with objects, for particular or critical remark. From this advantageous fpot of obfervation, the various powers of tafte which adorn the mind of man are called forth, and pleafantly engaged in contemplating lofty mountains, verdant hills, fruitful plains, beautiful rivers, populous towns, great woods, three renowned caftles, and a peep of the German Ocean. Under the fpectator's eye from this place the parifh of Roxburgh lies *fully* difplayed, and forms an excellent landfcape, the Tweed wafhing its border on the north, and Teviot partly on the fouth. A rich angle, all inclofed *, lying on the fouth-eaft fide of Teviot, adds much to the beauty of the whole.

Curiofities.—Among the curiofities in this parifh, two well-fprings, on the banks of the Tweed, of a petrifying quality, are remarkable. One of thefe is but a feeble fpring, and being in the midft of marfhy ground, is not very perceptible. The mofs around it, however, is all incrufted confiderably. More plentiful in its fource, the other fpring produces a more powerful effect. It feems to drip through a folid rock; but upon near infpection, that rock appears plainly to be a petrified fubftance. The powers of the water are fo ftrong, as to cruft a bit of mofs, or any capillary fubftance, within the fpace of three months, and render it hard as folid ice in the courfe of half a year. A little below this a ftratum of rock (by miners called a dike) runs acrofs the river, and forms a great natural curiofity. The rock is divided into four flits, which contain the Tweed when not in flood. Two of thefe are about 34 feet deep, and fo narrow that one may eafily ftep acrofs them. In fummer, people a-foot ufed often to pafs the river here; but

---

* This is faid to have been the firft inclofed ground in all this country.

but Sir Henry Hay Macdougal, some time ago, caused the middle rock to be blown up; and thus humanely stopped that curious, but *dangerous* passage. As the water runs through these gullets with great velocity, perpetually hurling down small stones, it emits a loud grumbling noise at *all* times; but at the break of an ice storm, it sends forth a tremendous roar like the raging sea, and is heard a great way off. In the time of frost the different shapes and hoary appearance of the ice form a grand scene; in summer, or when the river is low, a distant view excites pleasant emotions; a near inspection of the deep impetuous stream raiseth a very different feeling. These rocks are frequented by great numbers of salmon, and highly valued by fishers as a fit place for setting their nets. Three or four cart-load of fish are sometimes catched there in a morning. Such fish as lodge among these rocks a few days, it is said, turn quite black, owing, perhaps, to the effect of copper ore which appears on both sides of the river here in considerable quantity. Some of the small stones which halt on these rocks being kept in a constant eddy by the current, grind out deep round holes very *soon*, which make a curious beautiful appearance.

Antiquities.—Such as are given to that species of investigation might find many memorials of antiquity in this parish. The seat and gardens of the Franciscan monks, who settled at Roxburgh; various monuments of ghostly customs observed by those religionists; medals, coins, sundry machinery instruments; causeway paved streets and subterraneous vaults; pieces of spears, guns, and other military accoutrements; an immense quantity of iron nails, &c. found in cultivating the fields where the ancient city of Roxburgh formerly stood; spurs, and other articles of harness, got about the skirts of the castle; the castle itself,

ſelf, whereof there remains now only as much ſhattered
wall as ſuggeſts the former prodigious ſtrength and ſingular magnificence of that fortreſs ; a variety of aged *ſtately*
trees, particularly an elm, called the *tryſting-tree*, about
thirty feet round the trunk, and clothed with ramifications
remarkably grand and venerable; thoſe objects furniſh
great entertainment for the antiquarian : but the reader is
referred for a farther account of them to the Statiſtical Report of Kelſo, whoſe author has taken notice of them, and
whoſe talents, beſides ſuperior means of information, are
better fitted to do juſtice to ſuch rare monuments of antiquity *. But there are other objects in this pariſh worthy
of the antiquarian's notice. Among theſe may be reckoned a hawthorn-tree in the miniſter's garden, remarkable for
ſize and beauty, meaſuring about ſeven feet round the
trunk, and ſhading an area of upwards of thirty feet diameter. There are few objects of greater beauty to be ſeen
than this tree when in bloſſom.—The remains of a ſtrong
tower, ſituated near this village, on the top of a bank
gently ſloping down to the Teviot, are worthy of notice.
This venerable fabric has once been of great extent and
magnificence. Old people here remember its having various apartments inhabited, the windows and doors ſecured
by iron bars and gates, and the lintles and door-poſts, eſpecially thoſe of the great porch, highly ornamented by grand
Gothic ſculpture. They ſpeak with rapture alſo of the
fine gardens, the fruit-trees, and various works of decora-
tion,

---

* That theſe places belong to Roxburgh pariſh appears, from the local
memory of the oldeſt inhabitants here ; from the expreſs terms of the leaſes,
whereby the tenants of theſe lands have always held that farm ; from the
Bailie of Roxburgh barony holding his court at Friars ; from the poſitive
teſtimony of the late author of the county ceſs-books ; and from the ſtatute-
labour of Roxburgh pariſh being applied for making and repairing roads
about Friars as within this bounds.

tion, whereby they have feen this manfion furrounded. Thefe things, fo expreffive of the tafte and dignity of the former inhabitants of this place, are now quite effaced; and there remains of the tower itfelf only two apartments on the ground-floor, lighted by a few rays tranfmitted through fome flits in the wall, apparently defigned for air, or for fhooting arrows from in different directions. The apartments are ftrongly arched above; the walls are upwards of fix feet thick, and built with fmall ftones, cemented firm as the folid rock. The roof is overgrown with grafs, interfperfed by brufh-wood, fprung, feemingly, from feed blown thither from a neighbouring afh-tree. Thefe bufhes contribute much to the beautifully grotefque figure of this ruin. From this tower was carried to the late Lady Chatto's (whofe property it was) a ftrong iron gate, two fpears, a fteel cap, and a coat of mail very entire. The fpears were of fuch fize that a *rugg* faw was made out of each, and ftill to be feen here: the coat of mail was fo heavy, that a ftout young man in this village, who tried it on and effayed to walk, was not able to move with it. This ruin is called Merlin's Cave, in memory of an ancient inhabitant of that name, they fay. It bears alfo the name of Wallace's Tower; but whether it obtained that defignation, like fome other places in Scotland, merely in honour of fuch an illuftrious champion of his country; or whether, as blind Harry fays, Wallace was actually in this place, and built the tower at Roxburgh, the writer has not been able fully to afcertain. A young woman, about 70 or 80 years ago, fell from the ftair-head, where fhe was fitting fpinning one day, and foon after that the place was totally deferted. From a fuperftitious averfion probably, that ftill prevails

in

* The fteel cap is in poffeffion ftill of Mr George Cranfton at Plowland.

in this country, to any place where wilful or accidental
death has happened, the people imagining that such places
are haunted by the ghoſts of the deceaſed; that gloomy
fancy was heightened in this inſtance by the conſideration
of the poor unfortunate's being a *bride* the day ſhe died.
A little to the weſtward of this, on the oppoſite ſide of the
river, appear ſeveral caves cut out of ſolid rock, in the
middle of a high precipice, whoſe bottom is waſhed by the
Teviot, which flows here broad and deep in a ſerpentine
form. Three of theſe caves have been of large dimenſions.
One of them was uſed as a hiding place for horſes in 1745,
when the Pretender to the Crown of Britain went through
this pariſh with his army, and from that circumſtance, as
well as from its having been uſed for a ſtable afterwards,
it is called the Horſe Cave. Another, whoſe mouth is almoſt quite filled up, and inacceſſible now, reaches ſo far
back into the ground, that old people who have been in it
ſay they never got to the fartheſt end of it, and ſuppoſe this
cave had been a ſubterraneous paſſage to Sunlaws manſion-
houſe in times of danger. A third is called the *Dove Cave*,
from its having been uſed by Lady Chatto as a pigeon-
houſe. The ſides of it are full of ſquare holes cut out of
the ſolid rock, and ſaid to have been the pigeon neſts;
but ſome imagine from this circumſtance, that it had been
originally a concealed cellar, or hiding place for ſtores. It
is probable theſe caves had *all* been ſheltering holds during
the border incurſions, which expoſed the miſerable inhabitants of this country to perpetual danger and depredation.
At the mouth of one of theſe caves, in a fine ſummer evening, when the ſun has gone " *halflings* down the weſt," the
eye is preſented with a view of nature diſplayed in ſuch
glory and variety, as ſhe ſeldom aſſumes. Many veſtiges
of camps and trenches appear in this pariſh; but the moſt
remarkable encampment in it is that on the north-weſt ſide,

fo well defcribed in the Statiftical Report of Maxton, but from the local memory of the people not in Maxton pa-rifh. " The exploratory mount belonging to this camp " ftands a little eaftward on the banks of Tweed * ;" is planted on the top with trees, as a vifta from Mackerfton-houfe, and makes a very picturefque appearance, the fcene-ry round its bafe being highly romantic. A well of fe-veral ftreams iffues out of it, which, from the name †, the peculiar falubrity of the water, and the remains of nice building, had likely been once of great repute. The great Roman road (Watling-ftreet) by Borrowbridge, runs through the weft corner of this parifh; and that being thought the neareft yet found between England and Scot-land, great quantities of cattle purchafed at the Scotch markets are carried fouth this way.

Mifcellanies.—The wages of houfehold-fervants are not higher here than in the neighbourhood; thofe of day-la-bourers are often regulated by the abilities of the worker, or his employer's neceffity. Wages in general are under-ftood to be more than quadrupled within the laft forty years, and leave little ground of complaint, did not plenty create luxury, and luxury wants, which nature unadulterated fel-dom feels. The people here complain not fo much of the price, as of the mode of obtaining labour in fome inftances. Cottars are bound to be at their mafter's call through the whole year, at 8 d. *per* day generally. Confidering this *bondage*, as they call it, a hardfhip, the people ftrive to get lodgings in places where no fuch obligations are required, or where they may have victuals as part of wages, a thing feldom now granted to day-labourers here. Owing either to this, *or the monopoly of farms,* or the demolition of cot-houfes,

---

* Pennant.   † St John's Well.

houses, or, perhaps, the combination of all these, the population of this parish has decreased upwards of 200 souls within the space of ten years! a serious circumstance, were it universal through country parishes; principles of effeminacy and corruption naturally prevailing most in towns, for reasons mentioned above, the people generally emigrating from the country to towns. In an age of general prosperity, indeed, these baneful principles make rapid progress every where. An unexampled flow of prosperity has, of late years, wonderfully altered the condition, sentiments, and manners of men in this corner of the country; but the writer is happy to find the people here retain, in general, their wonted character of sobriety, kindness, liberality, and respect for the ordinances of divine worship. Indeed, the inhabitants of *Roxburgh* parish lie under peculiar obligations to virtue both civil and religious. Dwelling in peace, happiness, and safety on that very spot where their fathers knew not where to lay their heads, the sensible and reflecting feel thankful to Heaven for spreading its influence so benignly over us.

Memorials of death and slaughter appear in many parts of this parish, from human bones, sometimes scattered in the open field uncoffined; sometimes huddled together head to foot, in a hole of the earth, and covered with rugged stones; and sometimes found in cells of mouldering towers, with instruments of murder in their bowels. These sad memorials make minds of sensibility bewail the wretchedness of mankind in a rude, ungoverned state, and inspire veneration for that *excellent* constitution, under whose auspices Britons enjoy their religion, families, and home; each one sitting under his own vine and under his own fig-tree, and none to make him afraid.

Surveying the plains where armies a hundred thousand strong had marched, empurpling the earth with blood, now

abundantly

abundantly yielding food for man and beaſt, men graſp in joyful expectation that halcyon era, when the ſpears of every land ſhall, as here, be beat into plough-ſhares, and the " ſtill voice" charm the warriors confuſed noiſe into perpetual ſilence. Muſing over the razed foundations of Roxburgh, once the fourth burgh of diſtinction in Scotland ; the traces of thoſe halls, which rung twice ſeven days in honour of Royal births and nuptials ; and the rubbiſh of domes, where Princes and Nobles were wont to ſit in ſtate, the heart feels for the tranſient nature of ſublunary joy or greatneſs, and the Chriſtian's ſoul aſpires after manſions above, where moth and ruſt corrupt not *.

* Such as wiſh for a full account of this place, may conſult the Hiſtory ꞏf Scotland, Redpath's Border Hiſtory, Pennant's Tour, and particularly, a manuſcript Hiſtory of Roxburgh, formerly in the Advocate's Library, Edinburgh, and the writer ſuppoſes may ſtill be ſeen there.

PARISH OF SMALLHOLM.

(*Counties of Roxburgh and Selkirk.*)

By the Rev. Dr ALEXANDER DUNCAN.

Name, Situation, Surface, Extent, &c.

SMALLHOLM is the name of the parish. Whether it is derived from *small-ham*, a village, *holm* a wood, or *Home*, from the town of Home, two miles distant, which was formerly a garrison and a castle, is uncertain. It lies in the county of Roxburgh, in the presbytery of Lauder, and synod of Merse and Teviotdale. It is in extent somewhat more than three miles, from the north a little beyond the 34th mile stone, on the high road from Edinburgh to Kelso, to the 37th on the south. The form is irregular; it is near four miles from west to east, but at the east draws to a tongue, or small point. The turnpike road runs through the village, in the middle of which the church stands. Statute labour, when exacted, never came to any account; it is now commuted. The country is a mixture of flat and rising grounds. The soil is in different places very various, but generally a mixture of clay; though, upon the whole, when not too much of it is ploughed, or too often, it is thought to produce very good crops of oats, barley, pease, and some wheat. The air is healthy, neither is

the

the place liable to any topical or epidemical difeafe. The village, and two other parts of the parifh, have rock for their bottom, and materials of that fort are got very near the public roads, to repair them. Of the difeafes, that prevail among labouring people, four fixths are fevers; a phyfician who practifed a good many years in this country, faid that thefe difeafes abounded moft in years of plenty.

Antiquities.—On the fouth weft corner of the parifh, ftands a large fquare tower, belonging to Mr Scott of Harden. It is a beacon or land-mark at fea, to direct fhips to Berwick; it is called *Sandy-know*, or *Smallholm-tower*. The hills or rifing grounds are covered with grafs for fheep pafture. This neighbourhood, on both fides of Tweed, was formerly the warlike part of the country, and expofed to the inroads of the Englifh; the lands, therefore, all lay run-rig, that when the enemies came, all the neighbourhood being equally concerned, might run to oppofe them. After the Union of the Crowns, this contention ceafed, and property became fafe. The ravages in former times were fo frequent, that there was no bifhopric in Scotland, fouth of the Forth, until Charles I. erected the bifhopric of Edinburgh. In England, none were erected further north than Chefter in the ftreet, and Lindiffern in Holy Ifland; though on both fides of the border there were many abbacies. The reafon was, abbacies were reckoned holy houfes, and the people never touched them. But the bifhop, his palace, and furniture, were reckoned fecular; and therefore, on any inroad, the people, like the populace of Rome, on the *fede vacante*, accounted all his property lawful plunder. By this run-rig difpofition of lands in Scotland, the poffeffions were formerly very fmall; but the people of fuch villages were more numerous. Now almoft all thefe run-rig lands are divided. In the former fhape they were incapable of improvement. In this parifh, in the

years

years 1739 and 1740, 1800 acres of lands in run-rig were divided, and let into large farms. The villages and houses formerly possessed by the small farmers, have fallen down, and the lands are let to one sixth part of the former number of tenants. This is one certain cause of the decrease of the numbers of people in many places. Another is, young men going to the army and navy, many of whom never return. It was computed, that, during the two last wars, 70,000 men were recruited or raised in Scotland. It is also reckoned, besides those who have gone to North America, and to the East or West Indies, that 10,000 journeymen wrights, carpenters, bakers, gardeners, and taylors, &c. go yearly from Scotland to London. Many of them emigrate from this part of the country, sailing from Berwick and Newcastle, where the passage is short and frequent, and the freight easy.

Population.—In 1700, the number of inhabitants was 600; in 1743, the examination roll was 457; in 1790 it decreased more than 100. In Dr Webster's report the number of souls is stated at 551. One effect of the diminution of the numbers, is, in many places, to raise the price of labour. In 1744, day-labourers here had 5 d. or 6 d. a day without victuals; now they have 6 d. or 8 d. and victuals, and 10 d. or 1 s. without them. The number of examinable persons, who are inrolled after they are seven or eight years old, is 335; of these 150 are males, and 185 females.

Miscellaneous Observations.—The public roads from south to north, through the middle of the parish, were made by act of parliament, and are supported by the tolls. A good part of the parish is inclosed, and is let at 10 s. the English acre. Since 1744, the wages of ordinary or household servants are doubled, and are now from L. 6 to L. 8 a man servant in the year, and L. 3 or L. 4 a woman servant.

PARISH of SOUTHDEAN.

(COUNTY OF ROXBURGH, SYNOD OF MERSE AND TIVIOTDALE, PRESBYTERY OF JEDBURGH.)

By the Rev. Mr. WILLIAM SCOTT.

Name, Extent, Surface, Climate.

SOUTHDEAN, the name of the parish, is evidently defcriptive of its local fituation, and the former ftate of the furrounding country, as it is probable that all the neighbouring parifhes were anciently one continued foreft. The extent of the parifh is about 12 miles long, and 7 broad; this proportion continues about 9 miles, and gradually diminifhes into a narrow fpace. There are different kinds of foil; gravel, a light black earth, and a ftrong clay, in the lower parts; along the Jed, it is gravel, inclining to heath; from thence, to the afcent of the hills, it is light earth, and upon their declivity, it is ftrong clay. The prefent arable ground is very inconfiderable, as great part of the parifh is

more

more adapted to sheep pasture. The few hills are green and dry. The air is moist and chilly; greatly changes in different parts of the parish: all kinds of farm work can be carried on in the lower grounds, when it rains, or even a fall of snow appears in the heights. It is, however, a healthy parish. There are at present inhabitants above 80 years of age. The diseases most common, are rheumatisms, pains in the stomach and bowels, owing, likely, to the low and damp situation of their houses. In former times, the small-pox frequently prevailed, and in some seasons almost depopulated the country. About 12 years ago, this fatal disease raged in the lower parts of Tiviotdale, which determined Lord Douglas to hold out the advantages of inoculation to the poorer sort in this parish. The physician, employed by his Lordship, was successful. Inoculation is now become almost universally the practice.

Population.——According to Dr. Webster's report, the number of souls then, was 480. From tradition, as well as innumerable vestiges and ruins of houses, population must have been considerable about a century ago, and from general opinion, it is greatly diminished. In a late measurement of the Forest estate in this parish, the arable land is computed at 4865 acres, the evident traces of former times; the present arable ground is limited to a few hundred acres. It is said, the examination-roll in 1724, amounted to upwards of 1600. An accurate list of the inhabitants was taken about 17 years ago, and fell short of 900. This decrease became rapid, from the junction of farms. There are at present 714 souls in the parish: above 10 years of age 569. The number of deaths cannot be so well ascertained, and the marriages still less. The annual number of births is 10.

Sheep,

Sheep, Horses, &c.—It has long been the farmers greatest study to introduce the best kinds of sheep. Individuals have much improved their flocks, both from acquired knowledge and information, and with more certain advantages, by their own experience, observation, and daily practice. Most farmers keep a part of their sheep white. Smearing, however, is still generally in practice in this parish. It is said to increase the quantity of wool. It preserves the sheep also from the influence of rains, from scab, and vermin of every sort. There are 130 horses in the parish, 428 black cattle, and it is believed about 17,000 sheep. The laid wool in this parish, sold last year from 18s. to 20s. the stone, and the white wool at 1l. 4s. the stone. Seven or eight fleeces go to a stone.

Stipend, School, Poor, &c.—The King is patron of the old parish of Abbotrule, and Lord Douglas of Southdean. The stipend is 102 l. 1 s. Sterling, a manse and a glebe; in all amounting to 117 l. Sterling yearly. The church was built in 1690, and the manse in 1736, both in extremely bad order. The schoolmaster is accommodated with a house and garden. The salary is 8 l. 14 s. 8 d. Sterling. This, with the school wages, and various emoluments, makes a living of 20 l. Sterling. The number of poor is about 22. Their maintenance amounts to 56 l. a-year, arising from assessments, Sundays collections, and the mortcloth dues.

Crops.—The chief crops in this parish are oats and barley. Potatoes are common. The culture of turnip has been attempted with good success. Part of the annexed lands of Abbotrule is well adapted to turnip-husbandry. Grounds covered with broom, heath, from this beneficial practice, produces a-

bundant

bundant crops of clover and rye-grafs. Valued rent is 6387 l.
5 s. Scots ; real rent may be ftated at 3500 l. Sterling *.

Proprietors, Tenants, &c.—There are 4 proprietors, 2 conftantly refide. There are 22 greater, and 19 fmaller tenants ;
56 fhepherds, 4 mafons, 7 wrights, 2 blackfmiths, 5 tailors, 8
weavers.

Fuel.—The fuel made ufe of is of various kinds. Peat,
from different moffes, conftituted formerly the principal fuel,
and turf from the moors ; the whole fummer was fpent in
collecting fuel. Peat and turf are now ufed in fmall quantities. Coal at 4 d. the load, chiefly from Ryechefter in Northumberland. A double cart carries 6 loads : the diftance is
about 15 miles. The carriage cofts 8 s. befides the purchafe-
money.

Quarries.—There are many quarries of free-ftone, and inexhauftible quarries of lime-ftone, in the higher parts of the
parifh. There is alfo an excellent quarry of white hard ftone,
which is ufed for chimney-grates, as it endures the greateft
heats, and will laft for many years.

Antiquities.—Many tumuli, commonly called cairns, are to
be feen in different parts of the parifh. Stones have been led
away

* *Scarcity* 1782 *and* 1783.—The crop was very deficient, and the poor were
reduced to great diftrefs. Every method was taken by the attention of the heritors, to increafe the poor's funds. This could only reach to fuch as were upon
the roll, and found inadequate to their neceffities. Many labourers fuffered the
utmoft hardfhips ; and what added to the general calamity, the frofted oats and
barley gave a noxious quality to the meal. In thefe deplorable circumftances,
Lord Douglas humanely directed his agent in the country to buy good wholefome food. The bounty was continued, both to the poor upon the lift, and all
indigent houfeholders in the parifh.

away to the turnpike roads. In the centre of the heap, square stones were placed, so as to form a kind of chest, and human bones were discovered. There is also one place, where it is said a chapel stood before the Reformation, 3 miles from the old church, but almost no vestige of its walls now appears. There are ruins of many old towers, in most parts of the parish. None of them appear to have been large. In some places they stand nearly entire. At the village of Chesters, and many other places, on the adjacent heights, there are likewise to be seen the ruins of strong fortifications or camps. The form is round, and, in general, quite distinct. None of the camps are large, may comprehend above an acre of ground, and are surrounded with a double wall of earth. There is no appearance of any stone-work about them, except in the middle, which seems paved with freestone. Each camp is apparently stationed within view of Southdean-law, as tradition says, a place of observation, on which fires were kindled at the approach of an enemy.

Advantages and Disadvantages.—This parish long laboured under the greatest oppression; the numerous droves of black cattle and sheep passing into England, infested and overspread the best pasture ground. Every returning season opened a new scene of dispute, teasing, anxiety and distress to the tenant. Many regulations were framed. Boundaries fixed. Lawless trespass maintained its usual inroads. It does great honour to the gentlemen in this part of the country, that they have, with spirited and determined exertion, designed and extended roads of public advantage, and of parochial utility. The road from Newcastle at the Carter-toll, branches into this parish in two directions: the one line leads to Jedburgh, and the other to Hawick, which at once restores the farmer to the free and peaceable possession of his lands, gives an easy access

cefs to coal and lime at Ryechefter, and perpetuates a communication with the neighbouring kingdom, without moleftation
or injury. The principal difadvantage is want of fhelter, defence from the fcorching fun in fummer, and protection in
winter from the piercing winds, frequent and violent rains,
and deftroying blafts of fnow. The arable land in this parifh,
under the moft cautious and prudent management, fpeedily
returns to its native barren foil. From the fame caufe, the
beft breed of fheep may degenerate into the moft unprofitable
animal; whilft growing fhelter furnifhes certain experience,
and eftablifhes the means of recovering high and expofed fituations into a found and healthy ftate, and of improving and
preferving the quality of the flock.

PARISH OF SPROUSTON

By the Rev. Mr ROBERT TURNBULL.

Situation and Surface.

THIS parish is situated in the county of Tiviotdale, presbytery of Kelso, and synod of Merse and Tiviotdale.
It is about six English miles long, and four broad; being
bounded by the parish of Carham, in England, and by Yetholm, Linton, Kelso, Ednam, and Eccles, in Scotland. That
part of it which lies by the side of the Tweed is flat, and
liable to be overflowed; and the corn is frequently swept
off the ground. The southern part of the parish is higher
ground, though not hilly. The soil, by the side of the
Tweed, is excellent, and very fertile: No part of the parish, however, is barren.

Cultivation, Produce, and Rent.—Corn of all kinds, clover,
ye-grass, flax, turnip, cabbage, and most sorts of garden
vegetables, are raised in this parish. Oxen and sheep are fed
on turnip with considerable profit. The magnitude of farms,
which of late have been increasing, is reputed a grievance. A
farm was lately let at L. 1 : 7 : 0 per acre. The valued rent
of the parish is L. 13,263 : 6 : 8 Scots; the real rent is about
L. 4350 Sterling. There are four possessors of landed pro-

perty;

pery ; but none of them reside here. Agriculture is greatly improved. More corn is raised, and more cattle and sheep are fed for the market than formerly.

Church and Stipend.—The church and manse were built about ten years ago. The stipend, including the glebe, may be valued at L. 120. The Duke of Roxburgh is patron.

Population.—The population, as is thought, has not varied for these forty years past. There are many persons between 70 and 100 years of age. The number of souls in the parish is supposed to be about 1000. It is probable that the population has diminished considerably since the year 1714; and the union of farms is perhaps the cause of this diminution. The annual average of births, from 1714 to 1750, is 37; from 1750 to 1790, is 30. The most numerous class of artificers are weavers; there are 30 in the village of Sprouston; 8 masons and 4 carpenters. There are about 60 seceders in the parish.

Poor.—The annual average of the poor, from 1737 to 1758, is 33; and from 1758 to 1790, is 18. The average of the monthly distributions to them, during the first of these periods, (from 1737 to 1758) is L. 3 : 18 : 10 ; and the average during the last is L. 3 : 19 : 1. The oldest records that could be found of the poors rates, begin in the year 1737. The mode of providing for the poor in the shire of Tiviotdale, and the only legal mode, though not universally observed in Scotland, is this : The heritors, with the minister and elders, have the power of making up a list of the poor, and assessing for their monthly maintenance. The assessment continues six months ; the heritors paying the one-half, and the tenants the other, according to their respective

valued

valued rents. Persons who become objects of charity from
sickness, or other causes, are relieved by the session out of
the weekly collections. The poor live in their own houses.
The effects of all the poor enrolled are inventoried, and
sold at their decease, which is a check against impositions.

Price of Provisions and Labour.—The price of all kinds
of provisions, especially of oatmeal, has greatly increased ;
and, if potatoes had not been introduced, the price of oat-
meal must have been still higher. There is a considerable
advance in the wages of all servants. Men, during harvest,
receive L. 1 : 4 : 0, and women L. 1, with diet; a man hired
for a day 1s.; and a woman 10d. Forty years ago, a man's
wages in harvest was only 8d. and a woman's 6d. a-day. A
cottage must give the farmer one reaper. A labourer gets
1s. a-day in summer, and 10d. in winter. His wages are
sufficient to enable him to bring up a family. Tailors
wages are lately advanced from 4d. to 6d and 8d. a day.

Fish.—The Tweed, which runs along the north side of
this parish, abounds with salmon. They sell high in the
spring, the greatest part of them being sent by Berwick, to
London ; but the prices vary considerably ; and, in summer, they are tolerably cheap. There is a project for carrying a canal along the Tweed, from Berwick to Kelso, or
even higher.

Miscellaneous Observations.—Sea fowls appear here in
great numbers in the spring, about seed time ; they follow
the plough, and are thence called *seed-birds.* Coal, the only
fuel used here, is brought from England. The roads are
bad, owing probably to the statute labour being commuted.
It is the general opinion that turnpikes have improved the
country

country. Only one suicide has been committed in the course of more than forty years. The people, in general, are contented and industrious ; their condition, however, would be meliorated, if they had better houses: Their manners and customs remain the same as formerly ; but dress, and the mode of living, are much improved.

Parish of Sprouston.

Additional communications in 1791, from the Rev. Robert Turnbull.

There are, on the Duke of Roxburgh's estate, in this parish, six tenants whose rents have very lately been greatly raised ; one of them pays L.1 : 7 per acre : and there are seventeen small tenants who live in Sprouston, who have 100 acres divided among them, who pay at a medium above 30s. per acre. This took place about ten years ago. They have no lease. This shows how much landlords might gain by letting small farms, and encouraging the population of industrious tradesmen : for all of them, except three, who are employed in ploughing for the rest and driving coals for hire, are weavers, masons and wrights. There are on the
Duke

Duke of Buccleugh's estate ten tenants; on the laird of Hadden's four; on Sir George Douglas's estate two. The introtroduction of turnips, which takes place in every farm in a greater or less degree according to the dryness of the soil, has contributed greatly to improve the soil, and to bring great profit to the farmer; producing, when fed off by sheep, at a mean price, L.3 per acre, and afterwards fine crops of barley, oats, and spring wheat. It is not above twenty years since this improvement has taken place.

There is a very large common in England, called Wark Common, to which the farmer at Bedan, belonging to the Duke of Roxburgh, all the tenants of Hadden, and all the tenants of the Duke of Buccleugh, have a right to pasture sheep and young cattle. About sixty years ago, this right was disputed by the tenants of the Earl of Tankerville and Sir Henry Grey of Howick; they drove away to Wark the beasts belonging to the Scotch farmers, who maintained their right by force, going in a body with their servants armed with clubs, and, after broken heads on both sides, recovered their cattle, and sent them to the common, where they have pastured unmolested to this day. I have conversed with farmers who acted as principals in this fray. This common is very large, and comprehends in it several miles. There are plain vestiges of its having been cultivated with the plough; and very fit it is for that purpose.

There is at Lempetlaw, belonging to the Duke of Buccleugh, the ruins of a place of worship, and a present burial ground. It is said that the religious of the abbey of Holyroodhouse had the direction of this chapel, and that the Duke's property in the parish once belonged to the town of Edinburgh; certain it is that the Duke pays yearly L. 34 sterling to the town of Edinburgh, by whom I am paid one hundred pound Scots of stipend.

The

The village of Sprouston, that at prefent contains about 300 perfons, had, about fixty-five years ago, a common called Haddenrig, to which certain indwellers, diftinguifhed at prefent by the name of the Duke of Roxburgh's cottars, (much more numerous formerly, and who ftill pay a fmall rent yearly for their houfes, had by immemorial ufage a right to pafture fheep and cows. But the Duke's grandfather deprived them of this right, and converted the common into farms, for which the prefent Duke draws a very confiderable rent. Many of thefe cottars have been deprived of their houfes, and fome of the houfes are in ruins; and thofe that ftill remain pay a higher rent than they did when they had the right of the common.

I believe it is certain that the minifter received money from thefe inhabitants for the tythe of lamb and wool. But the then incumbent, Mr Baxter, being aged, and having it in view to obtain the fettlement for his fon, my predeceffor, in which he prevailed, gave no oppofition. This leads me to mention one of my predeceffors, Mr Ninian Hume, who was depofed foon after the rebellion in 1715 for fuppofed Jacobitifm. He had a wonderful talent for acquiring wealth; having left at his death L. 30,000 in landed property. When minifter here, he farmed land, and in particular a field contiguous to my glebe, a very valuable tract, which was inundated by the Tweed in the year 1708. On this field refted vaft quantities of corn, brought down the river from remote places, which none claiming, he fold to the value of L. 50 fterling. This field, as well as a good part of my glebe, I have feen all covered with water. The laft great flood has rendered perfectly ufelefs a part of the minifter's grafs ground; for which he has not been able, as yet, to obtain any compenfation.

There

There is an eſtabliſhed ſchoolmaſter in Sprouſton. Of late, the heritors have augmented his ſalary from 100 merks to 100 pounds Scots. He has, at a medium, forty ſcholars, inſtructed in reading, writing, arithmetic, book-keeping, and menſuration. His wages are very low ; a ſhilling a quarter for reading, and eighteen pence for writing and arithmetic. There is a ſchoolmaſter at Hadden, paid only the intereſt of 1000 pounds Scots, ariſing from 1000 merks, mortified by Lady Yeſter, and afterwards augmented by Sir Gilbert Elliot of Stobs, then proprietor of Hadden.

The tenants of Lempetlaw contribute to obtain a teacher of their children, being too remote from the pariſh ſchool.

There are three alehouſes in the pariſh ; one at the ferry-boat, one at a toll bar, another lately in Sprouſton ; yet little frequented by the inhabitants, who are of a ſober induſtrious character, yet complained of as a haunt for vagrants. Within theſe twenty years, the Duke of Roxburgh has built eight farmers houſes, with office-houſes for them, and many cottages ; the Duke of Buccleugh ſix farm houſes ; the laird of Hadden three ; Sir G. Douglas two.

There has been no perſon in the pariſh confined to jail or corporally puniſhed during my incumbency, except a few women, who reſcued a young man unjuſtly preſſed, during the war carried on in defence of our colonies.

Farmers now prefer generally carrying on their huſbandry by cottagers, who are obliged to furniſh a female ſhearer to hoe turnips and to work during hay time, to hired ſervants, who are dieted in their houſes. There are ſeveral ruinous houſes in the village of Sprouſton, chiefly the Duke's cottars. There is an excellent freeſtone quarry on the Duke of Roxburgh's eſtate, about half a mile from Sprouſton, of great utility to the gentry in the neighbourhood, and to the town of Kelſo. The cart-load of wall ſtones has been raiſed from 4d.

to

to 8d. The inhabitants of the parish are very healthy; agues are less frequent than formerly, owing, I suppose, to their eating more animal food.

There is a dispensary at Kelso, to which the poor are recommended by the minister, the session paying to it one guinea yearly.

The schoolmaster's income, including all his perquisites, does not exceed 20l. sterling yearly.

There is a great store of lime stone on the Duke of Roxburgh's estate, and that of Hadden. The laird of Hadden has last year built a draw kiln for burning limestone, which will be very profitable, worth, it is supposed, 300l. or 400l. yearly. Two of the Duke of Roxburgh's tenants burn limestone for their own use. During the Duke's minority, a draw-kiln was built in the village of Sprouston; but, to the great comfort of the inhabitants, the limestone soon run out, and it continues useless, though the stones when sold would produce a considerable sum.

When I was settled here, there was not a cart belonging to a tenant. The corn was carried to the place of sale on the back of horses; the dung led to the field, and the corn to the barn-yard, in wains drawn by oxen. Now every farmer has carts. I believe my cart was the first used in the parish. For several years past I have had none, but have every part of husbandry, and the leading of coals from England, done by hire; as I could get no land to cultivate, and the keeping of two horses and a mare cost more money than the profit arising from the glebe. The raising of potatoes in the fields, which has taken place since my settlement here, and which is now very general, has been a great blessing to the inhabitants. Every farmer almost allows his cottagers to set potatoes; and many of them let some acres for that purpose at a very high rent. I let every year a part of my glebe to the inhabitants

of

of the village, and others, with that view; and always have a good crop of wheat in ſucceſſion. I reckon that above 200 bolls of this root are conſumed by the inhabitants of this village, in their diet, and in the feeding of ſwine, which they kill for their own uſe. Mr. Stevenſon, then of Mongrenan, in the ſhire of Air, who about 15 years ago reſided at Marlefield, to manage Mr Niſbet of Dirleton's affairs, brought from that county a ſpecies of potatoes of an excellent quality, and pleaſant to eat, and very wholeſome, which is now preferred to every other kind for human uſe: it is not very large, but very productive, and lies near the ſurface in a round form. Without this valuable root, many families of induſtrious labourers, even at the advanced price of their wages, a ſhilling a day, from the ſpring time, and eightpence or tenpence when the days ſhorten, muſt have been in pinched circumſtances, when corn, butter and cheeſe ſell ſo dear.

UNITED PARISHES of STITCHEL and HUME.

(*Counties of Roxburgh and Berwick.*)

By the Rev. Mr ANDREW SCOTT.

Situation, Name, &c.

THE united pariſhes of Stitchel and Hume, lie in the preſbytery of Kelſo, and ſynod of Merſe and Teviotdale. The former is in the county of Roxburgh, and the latter in that of the Merſe or Berwickſhire. The pariſh of Stitchel is ſituated on the north eaſt corner of Roxburghſhire, and ten-twelfths of it are ſurrounded by Berwickſhire. It is ſaid that the name *Stitchel* ſignifies in Gaelic a declivity; and this name will be reckoned very proper by thoſe who have ſeen the ſituation of the houſe and village of Stitchel. Moſt part of the pariſh is 600 feet above the level of the river Tweed at Kelſo, which is only four miles diſtant. The united pariſhes will be between five and ſix miles from ſouth to north, and between three and four from eaſt to weſt. The figure is irregular, being frequently intercepted by the pariſhes ſurrounding it.

Rent and Soil.—The valued rent of the united pariſhes is L. 7623 : 18 : 4 Scots. The real rent is, at preſent, upwards of L. 3000 Sterling. A good part of the land is of a ſtrong ſoil, and bears good crops, both of graſs and grain of all kinds.

kinds. There is a good deal of clay in the foil, and in fome places the land is wet and cold, which makes it lefs fit to receive the benefit of lime. It is, however, certain, that the tenants have improved their lands in a high degree, by the ufe of lime and other attentions to agriculture. The lands are almoft all inclofed, and moftly in tillage.

Cattle.—The cattle in the parifh of Stitchel are of a larger fize than the common run of cattle, north of the Tweed, owing to the late Sir Robert Pringle, having, for feveral years, had a fupply of Dutch bulls. It is now the practice to feed cattle on turnip in the field, as well as in the houfe. Turnip is alfo given to the fheep through the winter. The fheep are chiefly of the Englifh breed, and the wool is of the fame quality, which they ufually produce.

Population.—The number of inhabitants, young and old, is nearly 1000. Of thefe there are between 3 and 400 Seceders. In Dr Webfter's report, the number is 959.

Poor.—Each barony, viz. that of Stitchel and Hume, maintains its own poor, which is done by affeffments on the proprietors and tenants, as circumftances require. There is a deed of mortification of L. 100 Sterling, by a Captain Robert Home of the regiment of foot, formerly commanded by Colonel Roger Handyfide, the one half of the intereft of which is annually diftributed at Chriftmas, to poor houfeholders in the village of Hume; and the other half to the fchoolmafter of Hume, for teaching poor fcholars born in the village.—There are eight perfons on the poor's roll in the parifh of Hume, and feveral families who receive occafional fupplies from the feffion. At prefent, there are no poor on the roll, in the parifh of Stitchel,

owing

owing chiefly to the uncommon care and attention of the family of Stitchel to the inhabitants.

Church.—The King is patron of the pariſh. The living conſiſts of 600 merks of money, and ſix chalders of victual, one half of which is bear, and the other infield oats, Linlithgow meaſure. The allowance for communion elements is L. 40 Scots, of which the one half is paid by the Earl of Marchmont, and the other by Sir James Pringle, Baronet, of Stitchel. The glebe of Stitchel conſiſts of about five Scots acres, and the glebe of Hume betwixt three and four acres Engliſh.

Antiquities, &c.—The caſtle of Hume, which ſtands in the pariſh, was for ages a noted defence to its neighbourhood, during the contentions and wars on the borders. The Earls of Home reſided in it. Our ſouthern neighbours often beſieged it. It was ſurrendered to the Duke of Somerſet in the year 1547, and retaken in the 1549. It is ſaid, that Oliver Cromwell, when at Haddington, ſent a ſummons to the governor, ordering him to ſurrender the caſtle, but that the then governor returned for anſwer; That ' *He Willie Waſtle,* ' ſtood firm in his caſtle, and that all the dogs of his town, ' ſhould not drive Willie Waſtle down.' And that this is the origin of that play, with which the children here often exerciſe themſelves. Oliver Cromwell, however, after conſiderable difficulties, made himſelf maſter of it, and in a great meaſure demoliſhed it. There is a tradition generally believed in the country, that when King James II, went to beſiege the caſtle of Roxburgh, he left his Queen in Hume Caſtle; that one day, when ſhe was upon the road to viſit her royal huſband, ſhe was met about half a mile eaſt of Stitchel Houſe, by a meſſenger, with the melancholy account of his Majeſty's being killed by the burſting of a cannon. This ſad

news

news brought on her labour pains, and she was immediately delivered of a child, upon a hill, ever since called *Queen's-cairn*. In one of the farms belonging to Sir James Pringle, in the parish of Hume, called *Hardie's Mill Place*, is a loch of about 30 acres, in which peats have formerly been got, but, in a dry summer, cattle can feed all over it ; to the north of the loch, about 200 yards distant, is a rising ground, called *Lurgie Craigs*, which consists of regular ranges of whin stones, similar, but not near so large, to those in Arthur's seat, on the foot path to Duddingston from Edinburgh. They are regular polygons of about five and six feet high, and 16 or 17 inches over ; they stand erect and close, but not adhering to each other, so that a man with a crow can easily separate them. They have all the appearance of being the same with those of the Giants Causeway in Ireland, or in some of the Western Islands of Scotland. In another of these farms, belonging to Sir James Pringle, viz. Hume-Byres, is a hill, called *Hume Pallat*, about a mile from the castle, and nearly on a level with it ; upon the west end of the hill, are the distinct remains of a fort with a fosse ; whether formerly an appendage of Hume Castle, or not, cannot now be known.

Miscellaneous Observations.—The water of Eden separates the parish of Stitchel from that of Nenthorn, for about a mile and an half. In this course it falls over a rock, nearly perpendicular, of about 40 feet high. In a flood, or in a hard frost, it is a most beautiful object. This rock is at a small distance from Newton-Don House. There are no manufacturers in the parish. Lime and coals are brought from the English side, and are exceedingly dear. The procuring fuel is one of the greatest hardships that the parish lies under. Coals are carried near 20 miles, and any peats that are used, are driven about seven. The poorer people, therefore, have but a very scanty supply of fuel.

PARISH OF WILTON.

(SHIRE OF ROXBURGH.)

Situation, Soil, &c.

THE parish of Wilton does not furnish much room for statistical investigation. It is situated in the presbytery of Jedburgh, and synod of Merse and Teviotdale.——The soil, more especially along the banks of the Teviot, is fruitful and well cultivated.——There are several marle pits in the neighbourhood; some of which have been drained, and, are of great benefit to the farmers. Lime, also, is made use of as a manure.

Population.——The population, in 1755, as returned to Dr Webster, amounted to 936 souls. The number, at present, is nearly the same, being rather above 900. The average of marriages, for the last 3 years, is 13, of baptisms, 20, and of deaths, 8; but these numbers cannot be accounted precisely accurate, as all are not recorded.

Poor.——There is an assessment for the poor, amounting to L. 100 *per annum.* The heritors and kirk-session meet

quarterly

quarterly to lay it on. The tenants are not mentioned in the ftatute, but their attendance is defired, as they pay one half of any fum that is impofed, and are beft acquainted with the ftate of the poor, in their own neighbourhood. The bufinefs is tranfacted without expence, excepting the fees of the clerk, and of the collector. The number of penfioners is between 30 and 40. The price of a ftone of meal per week, is ufually given to a boarder. To an old perfon, who can work a little, the price of half a ftone. To a widow's children, at the fame rate, per week, for each. For nurfing a child, 2s 6d weekly. The penfioners fign an affignation to the parifh, of all their effects, which are rouped at their death. It is, at prefent, in contemplation, to aliment the poor with a weekly allowance of meal, inftead of money, which may more effectually enfure a fubfiftence, and prevent an improper ufe of the public bounty. Some faving may be made, alfo, by purchafing the meal when it is cheap. School-wages for the children of the poor, medical aid, and incidental expences, are paid by the collections at the church doors, and mortcloth money, which amount to about L. 15 a year. It would be an important object of inquiry, to afcertain, how far the levying of thefe affeffments, or, poors-rates, has anfwered any ufeful purpofe, or whether the poor are comparatively in a much worfe fituation, where they are not levied.

Mifcellaneous Obfervations.——The valuation of the parifh is L. 7545 : 16 : 8 Scots. —— The Duke of Buccleugh is patron, and principal heritor.——Lord Napier, and feveral feuers, or fmaller proprietors, refide in it.—— The ftipend is fmall; but the glebe is large and valuable. ——The parifh fchool-mafter has the legal falary of 100 merks, a dwelling houfe, and fchool-houfe. There are alfo two village fchools.

schools.————The Seceders are numerous; and there are a few of the Episcopal and Relief persuasions.————A carpet manufactory employs 14, and an inkle 19 looms.————The people are, in general, industrious, sober-minded, compassionate, and devout.————Work is not difficult to be had; and provisions are reasonable.   The dearth of fuel is the greatest hardship, which the poor experiences, in this part of the country.

Additional Notes to the Account of the Parish of
WILTON,

PRESBYTERY OF JEDBURGH,

BY DR CHARTERS.

THE following numeration was made laſt ſeaſon: Males 565 ;
females 650; under 20, 546 ; from 20 to 60, 576 ; above 60, 81;
above 80, 12 ; widowers, 26 ; widows, 61. The heritors have lately elected an able ſchoolmaſter, raiſed his ſalary from 100 merks,
to 10l. and built a commodious ſchool-houſe. There are upwards
of 100 ſcholars. Lending books to the pariſhioners, I have found
uſeful, and think that pariſh libraries, conſiſting not only of religious books, but of ſuch as the Statiſtical Hiſtory, might be a
public good. The tendency to expenſive dreſs among young
women, is the ſame here as in other parts. A tax on ſilk, a-
mounting to a prohibition of it among maid ſervants, would be
an advantage to them. The poor-rate is at preſent 50l. a quarter. Some objections have been made to poor-rates, the validity of which ſhould be tried by facts. 1ſt, It is alledged that
poor-rates weaken parental and filial affection, " the holieſt af-
" fections of humanity." Let the fact be fairly enquired into,
and it will be found, that many children labour hard to prevent
their parents from receiving an aliment ; and that children in
good circumſtances who ſuffer their parents to receive it are infamous:

famous :—A proof that the cafe is rare.—During twenty two years miniftry in a pretty numerous parifh, where the poor are maintained by taxation, I have known only one inftance of children refufing to affift their parents; they forfeited the efteem of their neighbours, and banifhed themfelves to America. Affection, both parental and filial, is chilled by want : *the hind calveth, and forfaketh her calf, becaufe there is no grafs* : Under the preffure of poverty, a mother may forget her fucking child ; the child that is forfaken, or fent out to beg and to wander, or forced to labour prematurely, retains no affection for a deftitute parent : Whereas, among a widow and her children, who are kept together by an aliment, mutual affection grows. When the aged receive an aliment, their poor children are no longer depreffed with the view of mifery, which they were unable to remove, and which tempted them to turn away from their father's houfe : Filial affection returns ; they think with gratitude on a law which gives the neceffaries of life to their parents, and by adding fome cordials and comforts. they teftify and cherifh filial love. The minifter of a populous parifh, where there is no poors-rate, is diftreffed with the view of indigence which he cannot relieve, and may be tempted to turn away his eye from beholding it : But under the benign influence of poor laws, he can enter the abodes of the wretched, as the meffenger of good tidings. The law which provides for the poor, inftead of diffolving, tends to ftrengthen paftoral, and parental, and filial love. 2d, It is alledged, that the poor rate prevents the common people from laying up againft the time of need. The defire of laying up is fo ftrong, that the poor-rate has not yet, and probably never will extinguifh it. A fpirit of independence pervades the people ; they feel the humiliation of receiving alms ; they difcern the difference betwixt having of their own, and trufting to what is given. The poor law is an infurance againft unforefeen misfortune, and removes that anxious folicitude about what they fhall eat and drink and put on, which the gofpel has
forbidden.

forbidden. If a legal provision for the poor shall somewhat a-
bate the general and strong desire to lay up treasures on earth,
the effect is happy. View the poor man in his future destination, and whatever alleviates mortal cares, smooths his way to
immortality. 3*d*, It is asked, with some degree of alarm, what
will be the final consequence of alimenting the poor,—for,
wherever this tax is imposed, it increases gradually ? This gradual increase, where it takes place, may be owing to two causes ;
First, that some are induced through false shame to suffer extreme
want, rather than accept of an aliment. *Second*, that those who
appoint the aliment are at first too sparing ; the more frequently
and attentively they consider the case of the poor, they are dif-
posed to give the more. Let false shame be combated, and the
miserable instructed in their rights. Let those who have the
management of the poor, proceed till every indigent person be
fonnd out, and their real wants supplied. When all that need
have been persuaded to ask, and when those who give, have
learned to give enough, the rate will become stationary ; till
then it ought to rise. The law which gives a maintenance to
the poor, is one of the bulwarks of the British government, by
which it is defended from the rage of want and despair. Heritors and Kirk Sessions, to whom the execution of this law is
committed, will give a substantial and seasonable proof of their
attachment to our happy Constitution, by making the poor of the
land to participate its blessings. Were those who lately assumed
to themselves the amiable name, *Friends of the People*, to new-
model our Constitution, it is much to be feared, that a law in
favour of the indigent would not be found in their code ; and
if such a law were found in their code, it is still much to be feared, that the new possessors of unrighteous mammon, would not
be forward to execute the law of mercy.

N. B. The carpet and inkle factories, mentioned in the history of Hawick, are the same that were formerly mentioned in
the history of Wilton, where they actually are.

PARISH OF YETHOLM,

(COUNTY OF ROXBURGH, SYNOD OF MERSE AND TEVIOT-
DALE, PRESBYTERY OF KELSO.)

Collected from Materials communicated by the Rev.
WILLIAM BLACKIE.

Extent.

THE parish of Yetholm, or Zetholm, has never had any
other name, as far as is known, nor does it appear that
a part of any other parish has been annexed to it. Where
longest, which is nearly from north-west to south-east, its
extent is between four miles and four and a half; the
breadth generally about two miles; and the Bowmont water divides it into two parts, not quite equal, the largest being towards the north-west. On the south, and south-west,
and west, it is bounded by the parish of Morbottle; on the
north-west by the parish of Linton; and on all the other

quarters

quarters by the English border. It is hilly, but the hills are green. The Bowmont water has some pretty large haughs; and from the minister's manse to the north-west there is a piece of flat land along with these haughs, for the extent of about 1¼ mile.—About straight west, where this parish marches with that of Morbottle, there is a loch of more than a mile in circumference, in which are both pike and perch, the flat land already spoken of reaching round Yetholm Law till you come quite to the loch.

Agriculture.—About 1170 English acres are actually under tillage, and though there be some wheat sown, yet the greatest part is laid out in raising barley and oats, and turnips. Even the small tenants, who have from 1 and 2 to 10 and 15 acres, from Mr Wauchope and the Marquis of Tweeddale, have their turnip quarter, for which, on account of their vicinity to Northumberland, they find a ready market, getting, when a good crop, some years L. 3, others L. 5, to be eaten upon the ground with sheep. Much more land could be made arable.

The sheep maintained in summer (not reckoning the lambs, which are about 2500, and of which 1160 are sold off whilst lambs) are about 4800. They are generally the largest of the Cheviot breed, and if a period of 10 years is taken, it will be found upon an average, that the best prices in this country have been got for wool growing in this parish. Last summer most of it was sold for L. 1, 11 s. *per* stone. It is the short clothing-wool, and they prefer the New England tar, mixed with butter, for salve. In making the salve for smearing, they take 40 pounds of butter, 24 ounces in the pound, to 6 Scots pints of tar, with which they smear 140 sheep. A good many years ago, a trial was made in a neighbouring parish, farther up the Bowmont water, of crossing with the Bakewell breed; but it

was

was found fo far from being an improvement, that they fold them off as fpeedily as poffible.

The number of black cattle, except cows for milk, are comparatively fmall. The number of farmers horfes, both for work and riding, is 39; and of farmers and hinds or herds cows, is 50. For fome time paft only 12 oxen have been reared; 40 Highland cattle have been bought in and fed off. Among the fmall tenants, and inhabitants who have no land at all, are kept 76 horfes. The number of their milk cows may be about 64, befides fome of them bringing up young ones.

Common.—There is a common in this parifh of about 200 acres in extent, of which 40 or 50 are thought improveable. There is very little wood, and the gentlemen feem not difpofed to plant any, although there is abundance of land fit for no other ufe.

Population.—This parifh has, I fuppofe, more than doubled its population in the courfe of this century, becaufe many villages in the neighbouring parifhes of Hounam, Morbottle, and Linton, have been totally razed fince the memory of people now living, and many of the inhabitants have withdrawn into the towns of Yetholm and Kirk-Yetholm, two villages in which the greateft number of this parifh dwell; the former belonging to Mr Wauchope, and fituated upon the north-weft fide of the Bowmont water; the other belonging to the Marquis of Tweeddale, and on the fouth-eaft fide of faid water.

When the prefent incumbent was ordained in the year 1786, he, in the courfe of his parochial vifitation, found the number of fouls to be in Town-Yetholm 539, in Kirk-Yetholm 323, and in the reft of the parifh 208, making in all 1070 fouls. There were 491 males, and 579 females.

Upon

Upon taking a new ſurvey of the number of inhabitants, reckoning none but thoſe who reſide at preſent (January 1797) in the pariſh, I found in Town-Yetholm 490 ſouls, in Kirk-Yetholm 305, and in the reſt of the pariſh 181; in all 976. The population in 1755, by the return ſent to Dr Webſter, was 699.

The reaſon why the number of females exceeds that of the males muſt be, that for about 30 or 40 years paſt the country about being greatly depopulated, ſingle women unfit for farmers ſervice, or an old widow with a daughter or two, moſt of them equally unfit, took refuge in theſe villages, and earned their livelihood by ſpinning, perhaps ſome one of the family by hoeing turnips by the day, and hiring themſelves in harveſt; whilſt the males hired themſelves for herds, hinds, and farmers ſervants, and were in other pariſhes. This is not mere conjecture, for a great part of the paupers upon the liſt conſiſt of ſuch women, and I know of many more who ſtill ſubſiſt by their own labour. Beſides, ſome ſingle women, or widows, after obtaining a ſettlement in other pariſhes, come to reſide in theſe villages; becauſe ſtout women, fit to be employed the whole ſeaſon in every kind of out-work, are ſo ſcarce in proportion to the demand, that no farmer will let a cottage, but upon the condition of being furniſhed with a worker, for whom, even in the turnip-ſeaſon, they pay 8 d. or 9 d. *per* day, without victuals. Thoſe who were hired by the day in ſummer 1795 got 1 s. a-day; and men before harveſt got 1 s. and 6 d. a-day, without victuals. During harveſt many farmers in this pariſh gave for men 1 s. and 6 d. with victuals, and none gave below 1 s. and 4 d. For women 1 s. and 4 d. and none below 1 s. and 2 d. Some years ago 6 d. was reckoned equal to victuals for a day: 8 d. is now thought by ſome the proper allowance. Labourers prefer getting their victuals to an allowance in money.

In

In order to afcertain whether, in the natural courfe, the number of males be greater than the number of females, I picked out all thofe families which confifted moftly of children, and found the males more numerous than the females.

Occupations of the Inhabitants.

Tinkers and gypfies, all in Kirk-Yetholm, including women and children, - -	50
Weavers, - - -	35
Smiths, - - -	9
Wrights, - - -	15
Shoemakers, - - -	5
Coopers, one of them alfo a whlee-wright, -	3
Day-labourers, - -	49
Ploughmen and hinds, - -	25
Shepherds, - -	16
Schoolmafters, - -	4
Millers, - - -	10
Skinner, - - -	1
Retailers of merchandife, - -	6
Tailors, - -	9
Mafons, - - -	9
Waukers and dyers, - -	4
Thatchers, - - -	3
Gatherers of eggs, having no other occupation,	2
Bakers, - - -	7
Gardeners, - - -	7
Carriers, one a ftated weekly carrier to Kelfo,	9
Surgeons, one given over bufinefs, -	2
Butchers, - - -	2
Coblers, - - -	3
Pedlar, - - -	1
Fidler, - - -	1

Saddler,

Saddler,   -   -   -   1

Malſter,   -   -   -   1

Cow dealer,   -   -   -   1

Rent.—The valued rent of the pariſh is L. 7049 : 13 : 4 Scots. The real rent is about L. 2104 Sterling. It may with propriety be ſaid to be three times more than it was during the remembrance of ſome old people yet living.

Stipend.—Till lately the ſtipend was no more than 13½ bolls oat-meal, 14¼ bolls barley, 5 bolls wheat, all in Teviotdale meaſure, and L. 38 : 17 : 9$\frac{4}{12}$ in money, beſides L. 1 : 13 : 4 for communion-elements. An augmentation was lately granted of 2 chalders of oat-meal, Linlithgow meaſure, and L. 2 : 6 : 8 for communion-elements. But after all, if one conſiders, on the one hand, the great and rapid advances of rents, and on the other, the abundance of free teind in the pariſh, and that the ſtipend was never augmented before, he may be juſtified in pronouncing it too ſmall. Andrew Wauchope, Eſq; of Niddrie is patron.

School.—The ſalary belonging to the parochial ſchool is 100 merks Scots. The maſter is furniſhed with a good ſchool-houſe and dwelling-houſe. There are two or three private ſchools, for the accommodation of the inhabitants. The number of ſcholars may be about 80.

Poor—The number of poor upon the roll is uſually about 30, who receive from 2 s. 6 d. to 8 d. *per* week each, as their neceſſities may require. Beſides the ſtated poor, ſome needy families receive occaſional ſupply. The funds for anſwering theſe purpoſes ariſe chiefly from aſſeſſments. They amounted from Whitſunday to Martinmas, in the year 1795, to the ſum of L. 52, 19 s. Sterling. The collections

lections in the church, amounting to about L. 8 annually, are, at the defire of the heritors, moftly given to indigent perfons not upon the roll, with a view to prevent them from becoming a burden on the public fo foon as otherwife would be the cafe.

SELKIRKSHIRE

SELKIRKSHIRE

KEY TO PARISHES

1. Part of Innerleithen (Peeblesshire)
2. Part of Stow (Midlothian)
3. Galashiels
4. Yarrow
5. Selkirk
6. Part of Ashkirk (Roxburghshire)
7. Ettrick
8. Roberton

MIDLOTHIAN

PEEBLESSHIRE

ROXBURGHSH

DUMFRIESSHIRE

PARISH OF ETTERICK.

(County of Selkirk.)

By the Rev. Mr ROBERT RUSSELL.

Name, Situation, and Extent.

THE ancient and modern name of the pariſh is *Etterick*; but from whence it received this appellation, there is not even a tradition extant. It is ſituated in the county of Selkirk, in the preſbytery of the ſame name, and in the ſynod of Merſe and Teviotdale. It extends about ten miles every way.

Surface and Soil.—The general appearance of the country is hilly and mountainous. The ſoil in the haughs is exceedingly deep and fertile. This is occaſioned, in a great meaſure, by the inundations from the hills. As they bring down with them a great many rich particles of earth, ſo when they retire, they leave theſe behind them, which deepen and fertilize the ſoil. Very few good crops are, however, raiſed. This is owing to the great height of the country, and the frequency of the rains, which prevent the crops from coming to maturity. In a remarkably dry and hot year, the caſe is otherwiſe. Then, not only a great quantity of ſtraw, but of grain, is produced. This, however, ſeldom happens. Upon the hills, the ſoil is in many places moſſy, and fit for

nothing

nothing but fuel and pasturage. In other places, it is pretty deep and hard, but, on account of the immense height and steepness, it is susceptible of no cultivation. The air is in general moist. This is occasioned by the height of the hills, which continually attract the clouds, and the vapour that is constantly exhaled by the sun from the mossy grounds. It does not appear, however, to be unfavourable to health, as the people live as long here as those in dryer countries.

Lakes and Rivers.——There are two lochs adjoining to one another, partly in this parish, and partly in Yarrow. The one is called the *Loch of the Lows*, and the other *St Mary's Loch*. The extent of the former is inconsiderable; the latter is about three miles long, and one broad in some places. The fish, with which they chiefly abound, are pike and perch. No person, however, pays any attention to them. The Etterick is the only river in this parish. It is a small one, but abounds with excellent trout. After a course of 30 miles to the eastward, (wherein it passes through the parishes of Etterick, Yarrow, and Selkirk), it is absorbed in the Tweed, some miles above Melrose.

Mountains and Hills.——The mountains in general are high. The most remarkable are those called the *Ward Law*, and *Etterick Penn*. The former rises 1900 feet above the level of the sea; the latter 2200. The hills, for the most part, are covered with a fine green pasture. Some heath is interspersed.

Sheep.——This parish produces no remarkable species of animals, except sheep, which are allowed by all to be delicious food, and to thrive well, either when removed to the English pastures, or the Highland hills. Nothing, however, can

be

be faid for their wool. It is of the coarfeft kind, and little adapted for manufacture. A ftone of it does not bring more than 6 s. The number of fheep is about 30,000, and there are about 230 head of black cattle, and 40 horfes.

Population.—The ancient ftate of the population of this parifh cannot be exactly afcertained. It feems, however, to have been confiderably greater in former times than at prefent. In one place, about 50 years ago, there were 32 houfes; but at prefent, there are only three. From this circumftance, it would appear, that the population hath decreafed. The prefent number of inhabitants, however, amounts to 470; of thefe 222 are males, and 248 are females. In Dr Webfter's report, the number is only 397.

Productions.—Nothing but the common vegetables and plants are produced.—The Scots fir is almoft the only fpecies of wood to be feen here, and that in very fmall quantities. Indeed, there is not fo much as to anfwer neceffary purpofes. In former times, this country abounded with wood; hence it received the name, which it ftill retains, of *Etterick Foreft*. Not a veftige, however, of the ancient wood now remains. As great quantities of oak are ftill dug up in the moffes, this feems to have been the prevalent fpecies. The number of acres employed in raifing corn, roots, &c. is not exactly known. But it may eafily be conceived, that they are very few, when, in a fquare of 10 miles, there is not fo much arable ground, as to maintain 400 people with its produce. Barley, oats, and potatoes, are the only crops raifed. Wheat, rye, turnip, and cabbage, are never attempted. The parifh both exports and imports articles of provifions. It exports mutton in great quantities, and imports

meal

meal of various kinds to a confiderable extent. Cheefe alfo is another great article of exportation.

Mifcellaneous Obfervations.—This parifh poffeffes no advantage. The nearest market town is 15 miles diftant. The roads to all of them are almoft impaffable. The only road that looks like a turnpike is to Selkirk ; but even it in many places is fo deep, as greatly to obftruct travelling. The diftance is about 16 miles, and it requires four hours to ride it. The fnow alfo, at times, is a great inconvenience ; often for many months, we can have no intercourfe with mankind. It often alfo obliges the farmers to fly with their flocks to Annandale for provifion. Another great difadvantage is the want of bridges. For many hours the traveller is obftructed on his journey, when the waters are fwelled. The land rent of the parifh is between L. 2000 and L. 3000 Sterling, *per annum.* The value of the living, including the glebe, is L. 100 *per annum.* Lord Napier is patron. There are 10 proprietors of land in this parifh : none of them refide in it. The number of perfons, receiving alms, at this time, is 15. The affeffments upon the heritors for their fupport, amount to L. 37 Sterling, *per annum.* The fuel ufed here is peat. Coal is diftant 30 miles. In this parifh there are 12 ploughs, and 20 carts, but no carriages or waggons.

PARISH OF GALASHIELS.

(COUNTIES OF ROXBURGH AND SELKIRK.)

By the Rev. Mr. Douglas.

Extent, Situation, &c.

THE parish of Galashiels, in the presbytery of Selkirk, and synod of Merse and Teviotdale, lies partly in the shire of Roxburgh, and partly in that of Selkirk. The Tweed, which is here an inconsiderable river, divides it into two parts. The southern part belongs to the former, the northern to the latter county. It is of an irregular triangular form; but, at an average, may be about $5\frac{1}{4}$ miles in breadth.

Surface, &c.——The country is hilly, and may even be called mountainous; Meagle, or, perhaps, Meg-hill, or Maygilt, being 1480 feet above the level of the sea. The hills are mostly green, though some of them have a little heath. They are remarkably dry, and furnish excellent sheep pasture. In some places, spots of rock appear, either a kind of rotten slate, or rotten granite; the latter, a few feet below the surface, is hard, and useful for building; and stones, of considerable size, of both kinds, are not unfrequently found upon the

surface,

furface, remarkably hard and durable. One or two of the hills are conical; but are fo completely covered with grafs, or turf, that nothing like lava can be feen. Nor are there any figured ftones, coal, minerals, marble, freeftone, or petri-factions in the parifh.

Soil and Agriculture.—The foil is various; and the ftriking difference, between the foil on the fouth, and that on the north of the Tweed, deferves particular attention. In the former, it is, in general, deep, heavy, cold, and wet, on a bottom of clay or of rock. It is, in fome parts, perfectly red, and iron ftones are found amongft it. In other places, it is very po-rous; but though light, is not fandy, or lying on gravel.—— There are feveral fmall lakes, and moffes, which yield excel-lent peats; and, when drained, fome of them are full of fhell marle, of a good quality.—Oats, a fmall quantity of barley, and a few peafe, were the only crops raifed, till within thefe few years, that marle began to be ufed. Turnips, red and white clover, are now introduced, and the annual quantity of peafe and barley, is confiderably increafed. Of 500 acres, which, for the laft five years, have been annually ploughed, not above four-fifths, have, at an average, been fown with oats; whereas, formerly, that grain was fown upon, at leaft, nine-tenths of the ploughed ground, The other fifth is employed in turnips, clover, peafe, barley, and a few potatoes; and, fometimes, in low grounds, there are fmall fpots of wheat.— They fow as early as the feafon will permit, which is never before March; yet they reap late, feldom before September, and fometimes have corn in the fields in November.

Though only 500 acres, or thereabouts, are, at an average, in corn every year, yet, of the 2700, of which this part of the parifh confifts, at leaft 1500 acres have, in a kind of rota-tion, been torn up, partly for the fake of enriching the foil with

marle,

marle, but chiefly, becauſe unſkilful farmers, after having o-
vercropped one part, by raiſing oats for many years ſucceſſively, are forced to give it reſt, and to break up what has long lain
in paſture.   Notwithſtanding the wetneſs of the ſoil, and climate, the ſheep walks are ſufficiently dry, owing to the natural declivity of the ground, and, in ſome places, to draining.

On the north of Tweed, the ſoil, in general, is dry and
ſhallow, lying partly on gravel, a good deal on till, and ſome
on rock.   It is remarkably full of ſmall ſtones, which almoſt
every where cover the furface.   It has been found, however,
by experience, dangerous to remove them, unleſs the ſhallow
ſoil, is, at the ſame time, deepened and enriched.   They are
ſaid both to reflect heat, and to retain moiſture ; and to them
is to be attributed, in ſome degree, the luxuriance and excellent quality of the crops, in this part of the diſtrict ; which,
conſidering the ſmall depth of the ſoil, are truly aſtoniſhing.
Even here, there is a conſiderable portion inclining towards
clay ; ſome of it is ſtiff and deep, though, on the whole, not
difficult to work.   In ſome hollows, there are ſwamps, and a
kind of moſs, yielding very bad peat ; and all the ſpots,
where moſs appears, if laid together, would ſcarcely exceed
10 acres.——No marle can be found, by all the trials which
have been made ; and, though it may appear incredible, and
cannot eaſily be accounted for, it is nevertheleſs confidently
aſſerted, by ſome, who have made the ſearch, that there is no
marle in the whole range of country, from Tweed to the vicinity of Edinburgh, except in ſome places of the Merſe.

On the clay ſoil, and high grounds, both oats and peaſe are
ſown as early, and reaped as late, as on the ſouth of Tweed.
But on the dry ſoil, which, though ſhallow, produces the ſu-
reſt and beſt crops, oats are never ſown, excepting in a very
tempting ſeaſon, till the very end of March, or beginning of
April.

April. When the feed time of oats is over, potatoes are planted, and the land, defigned for barley, receives a fecond furrow.—From the 28th of April, to the 12th, or even the 15th of May, peafe are fown; and from that time, barley, till the beginning of June. This late fowing, fupplies, in fome meafure, the defect of foil; generally fecures a fufficient growth of ftraw, and never endangers the lofs of a crop, from the latenefs of reaping. In every feafon, the lateft fown grain, on dry gravelly fand, ripens before the earlieft fown on clay land; and grain of every kind, fown on dry foil, earlier than the above periods, feldom turns well out, except when the ground is very full of manure.——Though harveft has been known to commence early in Auguft, and to be moftly over in September, yet it more commonly begins with September, and ends about the middle of October.

This dry land may confift of 500 acres, of which 300 are annually in oats, and the remaining 200 in barley, peafe, clover, potatoes, and turnips, nearly in equal proportions. But as the three laft are produced in great perfection, it may be expected, that the increafe of thefe green crops, will diminifh the quantity of oats, ftill annually fown, and help to check the ruinous fyftem of impoverifhing land, by a fucceffion of white crops. A few acres here, as well as in the fouthern diftrict, are fometimes dedicated to wheat. The reft of the land in tillage, on the north of Tweed, which is either inclining towards clay, or lying in a high expofed fituation, confifting moftly of irregular fpots on the fides of hills, cannot be fo accurately afcertained, but may be fafely computed at 200 acres; on which hardly any other grain is fown, except oats, the fmall quantities of barley and peafe being fcarcely worthy of notice.

Superficial Contents and Produce.—— On the whole, the number

ber of acres in the parish, are calculated at 8000. Of these, upwards of 1200 are annually in tillage, of which above 900 are in oats, and about 300 in barley, pease, clover, potatoes, and turnips. The difference in the quality of grain, should also be remarked. In the worst season, oats, on some dry grounds, will yield at least at the rate of 8 stone of meal per boll, Linlithgow measure; while, in the same season, they will not, on wet lands, yield, 5 stone. Barley will also weigh, on dry grounds, 18¼ stones, (the Linlithgow boll,) and on marled ground, scarcely 12 stones; and, in general, all grains are heavier on a sharp soil.——There can be no doubt, but that more grain is raised, than consumed in the parish. But as a great deal of wheat, flour, and bread, is bought for consumption here, and, on the other hand, as large quantities of every sort of grain, wheat excepted, are exported to Edinburgh, Dalkeith, and Peebles, the surplus of grain produced, more than what is used, cannot be calculated with any degree of certainty.

Ploughs and Cattle.——There are 37 ploughs in the parish, mostly made after Small's model, some with moulds of cast metal, and some in the old Scottish form; which many, after trying the other, think most suitable to a stony soil. They are, in general, drawn by two horses, though four are sometimes seen in a plough, or two horses and two oxen. There are 109 horses in the parish; of which 92 are employed in draught, including ploughs, carts, and huckstering. The rest are young, occasionally, perhaps, yoked in the harrows, or employed as saddle horses. Single horse carts are mostly used, and their number may be 64; all, except 5, carrying, solely, coal, manure, grain, and wood.——The black cattle, may amount, at least, to 300, mostly young or milch cows, besides

ſides thoſe fed on turnips, the number of which cannot be aſcertained.

Sheep--Horſes and black cattle are here objects of inferior conſideration to ſheep, for which all parts of the pariſh are well adapted. According to the beſt information, their number muſt be nearly 5000 ; ſome farmers thinking it greater, and ſome leſs. This number, which cannot be far from the truth, is maintained on little more than 6000 acres ; from which circumſtance, ſome idea may be formed of the value of the paſture. They are, in general, of the long bodied kind ; rather ſmall, feeding only to 8¼ lb. rarely to 10 lb. per quarter, on the hill, but improving to 12¼ lb. and even to 15 lb. per quarter, in ſheltered incloſures. The dryneſs of the paſture, and ſmall ſize of the ſheep, give them a juice remarkably rich, and a flavour remarkably delicate. Their wool is not fine, yielding only about 12 s. per ſtone of 24 lb. Engliſh, and taking 8 or 9 fleeces to a ſtone. The value of it is leſſened by the quantity of tar, with which, it is the univerſal practice, to ſalve the ſheep, being fully equal to that of oil or butter ; but, in this neighbourhood, farmers now begin to uſe, 2 and even 3 pints of oil, or melted butter, to one pint of tar, and think their wool is improved by this change. Judges aſſert, that ſmearing is, in general, unſkillfully performed in this corner, the ſeaſon being too far advanced, and the ingredients being both improperly proportioned, and careleſsly laid on. Without entering into points, which muſt be determined ſolely by the experience of ſtore farmers, it is natural to think, that this operation ſhould take place early in the ſeaſon, before the days ſhorten ; becauſe quantities of rain and ſnow, are then apt to fall ; and when the ſheep are once thoroughly drenched, they do not readily become dry enough to receive the ſalve to advantage. Beſides, the firſt attacks of cold and wet

are

are always moſt to be dreaded and guarded againſt. Perhaps alſo, when done early, the wool will be more eaſily laid aſide, ſo as to let the ſalve reach the ſkin, which alone, and not the wool, it is intended to protect *.—In juſtification, however, of the farmers of this pariſh, let it be remembered, that about one fourth part of their profit ariſes from raiſing corn ; that their harveſt is late, and that, without neglecting their crops, they cannot well attend, earlier than they do, to ſmearing their ſheep. Let it alſo be obſerved, that, as their chief dependance is on their flocks, it is natural for them to be timorous in venturing on innovations, which may be attended with riſk; and they can only be expected to adopt, by ſlow degrees, any alteration on the mode of treating their ſheep, however promiſing it may be, until it is fully ſanctioned by experience.

Commons, Woods, &c.——There is no land in common, or lying waſte; but upwards of 60 acres are occupied by houſes, gardens, orchards, ſtack-yards, and dunghills. About 200 acres are in wood, moſtly planted, though part is natural. Lakes, moſſes, and the beds of Tweed, Gala, and Ettrick, by all of which the pariſh is either interſected or bounded, will occupy, at leaſt, 100 acres.——The produce of the orchards is trifling, conſiſting only of a few common apples, pears, and plumbs. But the woods are valuable. Oaks, aſhes, and elms, grow to a large ſize, and are of an excellent quality:

* It ſeems farther probable, that good oil, being known to defend againſt water, to meliorate wool, and deſtroy vermin, if ſubſtituted for butter, and uſed in a larger proportion to the tar, might both increaſe the weight and the quality of the fleeces. The farmers, however, in general, prefer butter to oil.

ty: Scots firs, planes, and birches, are in great abundance, and equally thriving: And the larix, the beech, the mountain-aſh, and ſeveral kinds of willow, though leſs frequent, are in great perfe&tion.——The woods are frequented by the birds and quadrupeds, which are common through Scotland: Snipes, woodcocks, ſwallows, ſea-gulls, and wild geeſe, are annual viſitants. Wild ducks remain through the year.—Little damage has ever been done by wind, thunder-ſtorms, or inundations. In ſpring, 1782, both Tweed and Gala were ſwelled higher, than they had been for 30 years before, yet did no miſchief worthy of being mentioned.

Population.——From traditional accounts, as well as from the veſtiges and ruins of houſes, the population, both of the pariſh and of the village, muſt have been conſiderable about a century ago ; and the general opinion is, that it has diminiſhed. According to the return made to Dr Webſter, in 1755, the number of ſouls then amounted to 998. Since 1770, when the preſent incumbent was admitted, the population has been on the increaſe. By a liſt, taken at that time, the inhabitants were between 870 and 880. A ſecond liſt, taken in January, 1789, made their number 901 ; of whom, 412 were males, and 489 females ; 352 were under 14 years of age, and 20 were above 70. By an accurate liſt, taken in January 1791, their number was as follows :

Males	-	- 426	Below 10 years	-	253
Females	-	- 488	Between 10 and 20		181
		——	Between 20 and 50		344
	Total	914	Between 40 and 70		115
			Above 70	-	21
Married	-	- 280			——
In widowhood	-	53			914

In

In the village of Galaſhiels, 581;—in Lindean, 51;—in the country, 282. There are 209 families; of whom, 18 are farmers, 28 are cottars, whoſe reſidence depends on their remaining in the ſame ſervice; and all the reſt are leaſeholders for a longer or ſhorter time.

The number of deaths, marriages, and births cannot be aſcertained, becauſe many bury at Lindean, and ſome in other pariſhes; and many, from neighbouring pariſhes, bury at Galaſhiels. Many of different ſectaries alſo are not married by eſtabliſhed clergymen; and a ſtill greater number neglect to regiſter the births of their children. Yet the rapid increaſe of population, and thriving ſtate of the pariſh, are plainly evinced by this circumſtance, that, on the eſtate of Mr Scot of Gala alone, there have been built, within theſe 20 years, ſix farm houſes, with complete office-houſes, and 32 good dwelling houſes, in the village; beſides 39 dwelling houſes, (on a part of the pariſh of Melroſe, which lies immediately contiguous to it,) containing 201 inhabitants, not included in the above ſtatement; all of whom, except 4 families, removed from Galaſhiels, for the ſake of getting feus, in a ſpot more convenient for carrying on their buſineſs. This ſuburb, to which hitherto no reference has been made, muſt neceſſarily be included in the following information, relative to the diſeaſes, employment, character, and religious opinions of the inhabitants.

Air, Diſeaſes, &c.——From the nature of the ſoil, the air muſt be dry and healthy. There never was, in the memory of man, any deſtructive epidemical diſtemper in the pariſh. Even the ſmall-pox, meaſles, and chincough are not fatal, nor very infectious. Though each of theſe has repeatedly viſited the village, during the laſt 20 years, yet none of them, at any time, became general or violent among the children. One

half

half of them, at leaſt, eſcaped the infection, and very few of the other half died. Inoculation is gradually gaining ground. Perhaps the mildneſs of the natural ſmall-pox, makes its progreſs ſlower, than it otherwiſe might be. Agues, and ſlow fevers are the moſt prevalent diſeaſes; rheumatiſms and piles are not unfrequent. Fluxes and dyſenteries ſometimes make their appearance. But the far greater number of deaths is occaſioned unqueſtionably by ſevere labour, and want of proper attention to cleanlineſs, diet, and health.

Manufacture of Woollen Cloth.—The manufacture of coarſe woollen cloth is here carried on to great extent. It has rapidly increaſed within theſe few years, and is now brought to great perfection. From Midſummer 1774, to Midſummer 1775, only 722 ſtones of wool were manufactured into cloth by the clothiers, and ſcarcely as much more could be made by private perſons; whereas, in the current ſeaſon (1790) 243 packs of wool, (each pack containing 12 ſt. of 24 lib. Engliſh) have been purchaſed by the manufacturers; beſides which, they receive from different quarters, wool, yarn, and weaved cloth, to a conſiderable amount, to be dyed and dreſſed for private uſe, or for ſale. The higheſt price given, per ſtone, for wool, this ſeaſon, is 19s, and the loweſt 7s 9d; but in general, the quantity purchaſed is of that fineneſs, as to raiſe the average price to 15s per ſtone. The wool, being bought in fleeces, as it comes from the ſheep, muſt be aſſorted, ſcoured, and freed from refuſe, in which proceſs, it loſes at leaſt one-fourth of its weight. A ſtone of the fineſt of it, weighed after being thus prepared, will yield 32 ſlips of yarn, each containing 12 cuts, and each cut being 120 rounds of the legal reel. Of this yarn, 1300 threads is the greateſt number put into the breadth or warp of any web, which, when finiſhed, exceeds ſeven-eights of a yard in breadth, and fetches, in

read y

ready money, at leaſt 5s per yard wholeſale from a dealer,
or about 6s, when ſold in retail. The coarſeſt cloths are made
of wool, which yields only, when ſcoured, 8 ſlips per ſtone.
They are wove with no more than 600 threads of warp in the
loom, are about ſix-eights of a yard in breadth, when finiſhed,
and are ſold, in wholeſale to dealers, at ɩs 4d per yard.——
From theſe facts, it ſeems fair to conclude, that the average
produce of wool muſt be 20 ſlips of yarn per ſtone, and that
the average price of cloth ſhould be 3s 2d per yard wholeſale.
Yet, in fact, notwithſtanding the high average price of wool,
and its conſequent fineneſs, the average quantity of yarn produced does not exceed 16 ſlips per ſtone, and the average
price of cloth wholeſale, is ſcarcely 2s 6d per yard;—a ſtriking proof of its excellence. For all manufacturers know, that
wool, ſpun beyond its fineneſs, makes unthrifty cloth; whereas a thread, coarſer than the wool will admit, is both more
eaſily drawn; and more equal; and conſequently makes the
fineſt and moſt durable cloth. In ſpinning wool, 241 women
are conſtantly employed, beſides occaſional ſpinſters. Such
of them, as have no avocations, will make 12 cuts in a day,
for which they are paid 6d. But as family concerns, field and
harveſt work, and ſuch other bye-jobs, take up a great part of
their time, let 100 days in a year be allowed for theſe avocations, and ſtill, in the remaining days of the year, they would
ſpin, at the above rate, more yarn, than can be produced from
the 243 packs of wool, purchaſed for the current ſeaſon. Yet
not only are they always furniſhed with as much wool as they
can ſpin, but three machines alſo, with 30 and 36 ſpindles
each, which, at an average, ſpin at leaſt 24 ſlips in a day a-
mong them, are employed always two, and often three days
every week. In like manner, there are 43 looms in the village and ſuburbs, 9 of which are only occaſionally uſed by the
aged and infirm, and by young boys. Suppoſing theſe 9, to
be

be equal to 2 looms conftantly occupied throughout the year; and fuppofing the 36 looms, thus made up, to weave only, at an average 7 yards raw cloth, which is equal to 4⅓ yards, drefsed cloth, each day, for 300 days in the year, they would thus weave feveral thoufand yards of more cloth, than can be made out of the above number of packs. Now, as many weavers are known not to be a week idle throughout the year, and fome of them, for a courfe of weeks in temperate weather, work 12 and even 15 yards per day, the above computation is abundantly moderate. Again, every flip of yarn is allowed, by the manufacturers, to make, at an average, a yard of cloth, confequently, from the 243 packs, containing 2916 ftone, and each ftone yielding 16 flips of yarn, there fhould be produced 46,656 yards of cloth; yet, from the moft accurate enquiry, the actual number cannot be found to exceed 43,740 yards. To reconcile thefe feemingly inconfiftent circumftances, let the following obfervations be attended to: 1ft, Many neighbouring farmers referve fome part of their wool, and many families in the village purchafe fmall quantities, which are fpun at home during winter, or given out to be fpun at the ordinary rate. The yarn is fent to the weaver, the web to the dyer, or perhaps the wool, from the beginning, is committed to a clothier, to be manufactured into cloth. A great part of the cloth, thus made, is intended for the market, though moft of it is generally for private ufe. Nor is it unufual, for the manufacturers themfelves, to buy woollen yarn, and webs from the loom, to bring forward into cloth for fale. In this manner, about 30 packs of wool may annually be fpun and woven, befides the quantity purchafed by the manufacturers. 2dly, The manufacturers do not employ all their wool in making cloth. A confiderable quantity of blankets, flannels, and worfted ftuffs for womens gowns, and childrens frocks, are made both by them and private families. And

fome

some of the coarsest of their wool is sold, and carried off for other purposes. And thirdly, The weavers, are occasionally employed in working linens, cottons, and other stuffs, from mixtures made of linen, cotton, and worsted. As the actual number of yards woven annually by them, cannot be collected from their memories, or such accounts as they keep, it must be calculated, by taking the whole 43 looms, at the low rate of 4 yards each of dressed cloth per day, and reckoning 300 days in the year, which will make them amount nearly to 52,000 yards of cloth of all kinds, ready for the market.

The price of weaving, including winding and preparing the yarn, &c. is from 2d. to $3\frac{1}{2}$ per yard. Taking the average at $2\frac{1}{4}$, a weaver earns about 1s 7d. each day; and the 43 looms will draw about L. 1000 a year. A journeyman clothier gains 4s per week, besides board; and being in constant employment through the year, without the expence of providing implements, for carrying on his work, his wages may be considered, as nearly equal to those of the weaver.

Of those who purchase wool, and superintend the whole process of making it into cloth, there are 13 masters, who employ, at present, 50 journeymen and apprentices, in assorting, scouring, and scribbling the wool, before it is given out to spin; and in scouring, milling, dying, cropping, pressing, and finishing off the cloth. The unwearied attention, which they bestow on all the various departments of their complicated employment, and the proficiency, which they have attained, have obtained for them, many years successively, almost all the premiums advertised by the Trustees for cloth of 5, 4, 3, and 2s. value per yard. It is, however, on the whole, reckoned a disadvantage, that so many different objects must occupy their attention. In England, there are *wool-sorters*, who buy, and prepare the wool for spinning; *spinsters*, who buy it, and sell the yarn to *weavers*; who again sell the webs af-

ter

ter they are wrought and ſcoured. In ſome places they are purchaſed by *dyers*, and after being milled and dyed, are ſold again to *thoſe*, whoſe province it is to fit and poliſh them for the market. In other places the perſons both dye and dreſs them.——From the materials thus becoming the actual property of thoſe, through whoſe hands they paſs, in the different ſtages of the work, it may be preſumed, that the ſeveral parts of it will be more expeditiouſly and better done, to inſure its ſelling quickly, and to good advantage. As ſpinſters will learn to examine the wool, weavers the yarn, and dyers the web, before making a purchaſe, all of them are thereby ſtimulated to take the greater care, to avoid all faults and blemiſhes, which would hurt the ſale, or leſſen the profits of their labour. Beſides, it ſeems probable, that the fewer employments any man follows, the greater will be his proficiency in them. They, who conſtantly and excluſively are kept ſcribbling wool, will work more, and to better purpoſe, than others, who are accuſtomed equally to perform every branch of the manufacturing line. In like manner, the fineſt dye will always be given by him, whoſe ſole buſineſs it is, to mix and prepare the colours, and fix them on the cloth. And the ſweeteſt poliſh will come from the hand, which is only put forth to the ſhears, the teaſle, and the preſs.——In oppoſition, however, to this reaſoning, ſpecious and concluſive as it may appear, ſome intelligent manufacturers here prefer their own method, of conducting the whole proceſs from firſt to laſt; aſſerting, that, from univerſal experience, the yarn and webs, which they purchaſe, are greatly inferior to thoſe which are made under their own eye; and aſſigning, as the reaſon of this inferiority, that, having the abſolute direction both of ſpinning and weaving, and a perfect knowledge of the reſpective abilities of ſuch as they employ, in theſe departments, they muſt eaſily perceive, and can keep out of their

webs,

webs, all faulty yarn; they muſt be acquainted with all defects in weaving; and, if they are of a nature not to be corrected, or concealed by the ſubſequent operations, which the
cloth undergoes, they can make both ſpinſters and weavers ac-
countable for their ſeveral miſtakes, which cannot thus be
amended. And the excellence of all cloth depending, in a
great meaſure, on the equality of the yarn, both as to fineneſs
and twiſting, they have the advantage of knowing and employing the hands, which come neareſt to each other in theſe reſpects, and the weavers, who excel in working finer or coarſer
yarn.

Spinning machines poſſeſs one eminent advantage over common wheels. The yarn on 30, or 36 ſpindles, is all equally
twiſted, and drawn to the ſame fineneſs. And from the nature of the motion, the twiſt cannot be hard, nor the thread
fine, which renders the cloth ſoft, firm and durable. The
moſt dexterous ſpinſter cannot twiſt ſo equally, and ſo gently,
twenty ſlips of yarn, from wool of the ſame quality, as a machine can do twenty thouſand. And it is now univerſally a-
greed, that both warp and woof, twiſted as gently as the loom
can admit, is moſt ſuſceptible of being driven cloſe by the
mill, of receiving the ſtrongeſt dye, and of acquiring the
ſmootheſt ſurface.

Artizans.——Beſides the manufacture of woollen cloth,
which is no doubt the ſtaple of the pariſh, other branches are
carried to a conſiderable extent. Ten perſons are employed,
as ſkinners and tanners, who pay, for the white and tanned
leather, which they make, from L. 66 to L. 98, of exciſe to
Government, at an average, yearly. Seventeen are wrights,
who, beſides jobbing as cabinet-makers, and houſe carpenters, and wheel and mill wrights, and making all the common implements of huſbandry, drive a very conſiderable trade,

by

by purchafing growing timber, blocking it into ploughs, carts, hay-rakes, &c. annually, all which are fold to plough and cart-wrights, and farmers, at a confiderable diftance. There are 3 black-fmiths, 3 bakers, 5 fhoemakers, and 9 taylors. The number of merchants and fhop-keepers cannot eafily be afcertained, as almoft every body buys and fells or barters.

Church, Living, and School.——The parifh church was originally fituated at Lindean, to the fouth of Tweed, but was removed, in the courfe of the laft century, to Galafhiels.—— The living, which is in the gift of Mr Scot of Gala, was, in 1775, augmented from L. 800, to L. 1000 Scots, with L. 4:3:4 fterling, for communion elements; and the glebe, (including 9 bolls, 3 firlots of barley, Linlithgow meafure, which the minifter receives annually, for a part of it lying in Lindean,) will rent about L. 15 fterling.——The fchoolmafter has L. 6:7:2 of falary, and from 80 to 120 fcholars; a tolerable houfe, but no garden. There is alfo a fchool at Lindean, with a fmall falary, faid to be a part of the parifh falary, granted when that village was confiderable for the number of its inhabitants.

Heritors, Rent, &c.——There are only 6 heritors; 4 of whom have dwelling houfes in the parifh, and two of thefe four are refident. Their *cumulo* valued rent, is L. 8225:13:4 Scots: And their real rent may amount to L. 1600 fterling, over and above all public burdens.

Poor.——The poor, at prefent, upon the roll, amount to 14, (13 of whom are females,) and that number may be taken as the average for 15 years paft. Several others receive occafional aid. The fum levied and contributed, for their fupport,

annually, is about L. 30, but it is gradually increasing. As most of them can work, their allowance is but small, in general, not above 9 d. per week, except in times of scarcity.

Disadvantages.—The greatest disadvantage, which the parish and suburbs labour under, is no doubt their distance from lime and coals; both of which they bring from Middleton, 21 miles from Galashiels, and upwards of 24 miles from several places in the parish. Notwithstanding this great distance, lime is found to be cheaper manure, and coals cheaper fuel, than the marle and peats in the southern district, though both are excellent of their kinds.——— Want of a post, is another material disadvantage, to which the village is subjected. Offices are established at Stagehall, Selkirk, and Melrose. The first, a single house, though farthest distant, is most convenient, being on the road to lime and coals; but, notwithstanding the obliging care of the postmaster there, the arrival of letters, 7 miles from a post-office, must always be tedious and uncertain. There is a certainty that the revenue, which is drawn there, would be at left trebled, were the office removed to Galashiels.—A third great inconvenience, which the manufacturers suffer, is want of a stock to carry on their work to a sufficient extent; of consequence, they are obliged to purchase on credit, and at a high rate, every necessary article of manufacture, and to sell the produce instantly, at whatever ready money it will fetch. Whereas, were they able to pay at once for all they purchase, they would both have more profit, and they could continue to manufacture their goods, without being reduced to the necessity of disposing of them, till a proper price could be obtained..

Character of the People.—In the parish and suburbs of the village,

village, there are no leſs than 15 houſes, where ale or ſpirits are retailed. Yet the people, in general, are ſober and
induſtrious in the extreme. Not one is addicted to dram-
drinking or tippling; and very rarely is a tradeſman, eſpecially a manufacturer, ſeen in liquor. A reſpectable number
attend public worſhip in the eſtabliſhed church, and about 200
receive the ſacrament of our Lord's ſupper annually. At the
ſame time, there are many, who adhere both to the Burgher and
Antiburgher principles, and a few belong to the Church of
Relief. There are alſo ſome claſſes of Independents, and
Baptiſts; beſides ſeveral who diſclaim all attachment to any
ſect whatſoever, and ſeem to have no fixed principles of religion. Concerning the numbers, and the peculiar tenets, of
theſe various ſeparatiſts from the eſtabliſhment, the preſent
incumbent has never been led to make any particular inquiry,
from an opinion, that while they are peaceable and good
members of ſociety, and " live ſoberly, righteouſly, and godly,"
the ſpeculative points, on which they may differ, are of very
little importance. And it gives him much pleaſure, to find a
ſpirit of forbearance and toleration univerſally prevailing, a-
mong all ranks and denominations in the pariſh *.

---

* For an anſwer to the queries relating to Roman and other antiquities, vid. Pennant's Tour, printed in 1772.